■ PHOTO-SYNTHESIS

■ PROFILE IN EDUCATION

■ YOU BE THE JUDGE

YOUR KEY TO *TEACHERS, SCHOOLS, AND SOCIETY, 7/E*

REFLECTION: highlights reflection questions.

OLC indicates that you should go to the Online
Learning Center for more information or to
do an activity.

www.mhhe.com/
sadker7e indicates that you should go to the
Sadker.com Website to access material.

TEACHERS, SCHOOLS, AND SOCIETY

ANNOTATED INSTRUCTOR'S EDITION

TEACHERS, SCHOOLS, AND SOCIETY

SEVENTH EDITION

MYRA POLLACK SADKER

Late Professor, American University

DAVID MILLER SADKER

American University

McGraw Hill

Boston   Burr Ridge, IL   Dubuque, IA   Madison, WI   New York   San Francisco   St. Louis
Bangkok   Bogotá   Caracas   Kuala Lumpur   Lisbon   London   Madrid   Mexico City
Milan   Montreal   New Delhi   Santiago   Seoul   Singapore   Sydney   Taipei   Toronto

CONTENTS

Each edition of *Teachers, Schools, and Society* has broken new ground by creating new features, introducing new topics, and adding new supplements. This edition adds to that rich tradition by creating an even more interactive book for students. Yet the basic premise for the text has not changed: to write a book students *want* to read, not *have* to read. While we continue to work hard to provide content coverage that is both current and concise, we work even harder to create an engaging book, one that will turn students on to the possibilities of a career in the classroom. Humor, involving scenarios, current news clips, controversial topics, and motivating stories of the famous (and not so famous) have always been part of *Teachers, Schools, and Society* and continue in this edition.

The chapters—always lauded for their student-friendly readability—encourage student engagement and reflection. The text's Web resources, located at www.mhhe.com/sadker7e, are extensions of the text and reflect our commitment to an interactive format.

Interactive Elements

The Interactive Elements are highlighted by the following icons:

REFLECTION: How you believe that p   alerts readers to a question worth considering.

 indicates that students should go to the Online Learning Center, accessible from www.mhhe.com/sadker7e, for more information or to do an activity.

 indicates that students should go to the Sadker.com Website, accessible from www.mhhe.com/sadker7e, to link to material.

The Text Content and Features Are Highly Interactive

Class Acts   Each of the four parts of this text begins with a *Class Act* written by future teachers, current teachers, and teacher educators about their involvement in education. And the *Class Acts* feature is alive, for it has taken root on the Internet. The Sadker.com Website houses *Class Act* submissions made by students using the text. Students are invited to read these and to submit their own.

Reflective Activities and Your Portfolio (*RAP*)   Following at the end of each of the four parts of this book, you will find a *RAPs* section keyed to INTASC standards. The *RAPs* provide an excellent introduction to portfolio development, and can facilitate the use of portfolios as part of your course evaluation. The *RAP* activities also offer students the opportunity to more carefully consider the ideas found in the text and to implement some of these ideas in the real world. You will discover that these activities have a reflective component as well.

What Do You Think?   This feature taps into a student's curiosity and prepares them for the chapter that follows. It links students to the Online Learning Center where they take a quick survey or self-inventory that registers their responses on issues ranging from why they want to become a teacher to how much they already know about the history of education. Responses are submitted to a national poll so students can immediately (and confidentially) see where they stand in comparison to their colleagues.

Interactive Activities   This feature, highlighted in the margin, links the student to the Online Learning Center to do a content-related activity, such as seeing how much of today's teen slang they can understand, taking a personal learning styles assessment, or responding to a multicultural literacy quiz.

You Be the Judge   This feature, which offers the reader two sides of an argument, sparks student consideration of multiple perspectives. The reflection question that follows each *You Be the Judge* can be answered on the Online Learning Center and then e-mailed to you and/or saved for the student's portfolio.

Profile in Education   This feature focuses on an educational figure whose contributions are worth noting. Those profiled range from educators and researchers, like Jaime Escalante and Jonathan Kozol, to social activists like Morris Dees and Marion Wright Edelman. Students can go to the Sadker.com Website to learn more about the profiled individual.

Photo-synthesis   Each *Photo-synthesis* includes one or more photos offering students a visual insight into an educational topic or controversy—from official and unofficial school uniforms to the different ways classrooms reflect (or deflect) computer technology. Naturally, we pose one or more reflection questions for students to ponder.

In the News   *In the News* provides short summaries of interesting education-related news items. We selected these items because we found them poignant, particularly relevant to the chapter content, or sometimes just because they were funny. The *In the News* items also provide a sense of currency to the issues and topics discussed in the text. Students are also linked to the Online Learning Center where they can read additional *In the News* summaries and submit their own.

Frame of Reference   These boxes provide a closer, more in-depth look at important topics and issues. Sometimes they offer practical classroom suggestions; other times they provide additional relevant research findings or an historical insight. And of course, to spark and focus the student's thought, we include a reflection question for each *Frame of Reference*.

Discussion Questions and Activities   This feature includes suggestions for in-class or at-home assignments, as well as questions to help the student study the chapter. Web-*tivities*, Internet-base activities, that are housed on the Online Learning Center are listed as well.

Links to Practice and Extending Materials   At the end of each chapter, students are reminded of the practice and extending materials available to them through the text's Online Learning enter and *Resources for Exploring Education* CD-ROM.

- **Chapter Review:** Students are reminded to go to the Online Learning Center to take quizzes, practice with key terms, and review key ideas from the chapter.
- **Current News from PowerWeb:** Students are reminded to go to the Online Learning Center to access current articles and news about education.
- **Extended Learning:** Students are reminded to go to their *Resources for Exploring Education* CD-ROM to access related articles, case studies, and media (video and audio clips) observations.

Reel to Real Teaching   We admit it—seeing an education-related popular movie is one of our hobbies and we agree that students can even learn from media other than this textbook. This feature located at the end of each chapter takes a look at movies that are available on videotape or DVD for student use—or even for your use in class. Included are summaries of the movie, as well as reflection questions and challenging follow-up activities that tie the movie into the course content. The Sadker.com Website has an area where students can rate the movies and see how others rated them.

For a student-oriented walkthrough of the text's features, go to page xix.

The following supplements package* of the seventh edition of *Teachers, Schools, and Society* was developed to provide you with a wealth of resources to promote interactivity in your classroom.

Annotated Instructor's Edition (AIE)

This textbook has an Annotated Instructor's Edition, available on request. The AIE is replete with marginal notes and information added to guide you through the many instructional resources and supplements accompanying *Teachers, Schools, and Society*. See page IE–12 for a full description of the AIE's features.

Instructor's Manual and Test Bank

The Instructor's Manual continues to include practical and creative classroom teaching ideas that make it one of the best instructor's resources available. For example, "grabbers" offer creative ideas for teaching a course based on this book, while videos and supplemental readings offer additional sources of information and approaches for instruction. The teaching ideas and resources offer new instructors great ideas for teaching and suggest new and different classroom activities for experienced teachers.

A test bank, with questions keyed by level of difficulty, is also available. In addition, we have included authentic assessment questions. Testing of school children is being expanded and revised in some school districts to better model what we know about learning and evaluation. We have created an authentic assessment tool, designed to use actual teaching skills with chapter content. We suspect you may want to explore our range of appraisal elements and select what works best with your program philosophy and student community. There are also some questions that teachers might encounter when they apply for state licensure. These questions may be related to the Praxis, or individual state-administered exams.

The Instructor's Resource CD-ROM

The Instructor's Resource CD-ROM includes electronic versions of the Instructor's Manual and Test Bank, a

* Please contact your local sales representative for more information.

computerized test bank, and PowerPoint slides created from the Overhead Transparencies.

Two Video Programs Accompany This Edition:

1. ***Expanded*** The *Teachers, Schools, and Society* **Video Companion** The *Teachers, Schools, and Society* Video Companion has been revised and expanded to provide multiple video segments for each chapter. In addition, relevant segments from the <u>Only a Teacher</u> series (see description below) have been integrated for easy use. This videotape was developed especially for *Teachers, Schools, and Society*. The Instructor's Manual allows you to really integrate the tape's content with your instruction. There we first describe the segment and then suggest critical questions to consider. Thus, the taped segment becomes an interactive resource for your students rather than a disconnected element. For a fuller description of this supplement, see the Instructor's Manual. The video clips are keyed in the AIE.

2. **The <u>Only a Teacher</u> Video Series** *Teachers, Schools, and Society* is also accompanied by a video series, one produced and directed by Claudia Levin and shown on PBS. The <u>Only a Teacher</u> video series is the first documentary to explore the diverse faces and many roles of the American teacher from the 1820s through the present. The series contains three one-hour segments. While it might be improbable for you to show the entire program in one sitting (unless you get a long snowy day during class time), we have integrated segments into the *Teachers, Schools, and Society Video Companion*.

Two Sets of Transparencies Accompany This Edition:

1. **The *Teachers, Schools, and Society* Overhead Transparencies** The full-color overhead transparency set of over 160 transparencies has been revised to include new figures and tables from the text. The overheads are conveniently keyed in the AIE and are directly related to the content in the text.

2. McGraw-Hill Introduction to Education Overhead Transparencies and PowerPoint Slides The McGraw-Hill Introduction to Education Overhead Transparencies include 200 full-color generic acetates related to teaching issues. These are also available on a PowerPoint CD-ROM.

Instructor's Online Learning Center

The password-protected instructor's section of the Online Learning Center contains an electronic version of the Instructor's Manual, the PowerPoint slides, the McGraw-Hill Introduction to Education PowerPoint slides, and other teaching resources. You can e-mail the authors from this site with any questions you have regarding the text or teaching ideas.

Course Management

PageOut PageOut allows you to easily create your own custom course website. Simply plug your course information into a template, click on one of 16 designs, and you can create your own professional-looking website. Powerful features include an interactive course syllabus that allows you to post content and links, an online gradebook, lecture notes, bookmarks, and a discussion board where students can discuss course-related topics.

Blackboard A Blackboard Course Cartridge accompanies this text. Simply adopt a McGraw-Hill textbook and you will receive the Online Learning Center and test bank for use in your Blackboard course. You can then customize the content as you see fit. Our Blackboard content is free for adopting instructors.

WebCT A WebCT Course Cartridge accompanies this text. Simply adopt a McGraw-Hill textbook and you will receive the Online Learning Center and test bank for use in your WebCT course. You can then customize the content as you see fit. Our WebCT content is free for adopting instructors.

Student supplements include:

Study Resource

The Student **Online Learning Center,** accessible from www.mhhe.com/sadker7e, contains student study guide materials including quizzes. Premium content—PowerWeb articles and news feeds, and Interactive Activities—are password protected (a free password comes with new copies of the text).

Interactive Resource

The **Sadker.com Website,** accessible from www. mhhe.com/sadker7e, includes resources for students to explore current education topics.

New   Extending Resource

***Resources for Exploring Education* CD-ROM** with articles, case studies, and media observations. For a listing of the resources, go to pages xxv–xxvi. The CD-ROM is packaged for free with new copies of the text or can be purchased separately.

FolioLive

*Folio*Live is an online portfolio tool you can use to create an electronic portfolio in three easy steps: 1. Use a template to create a homepage; 2. Choose to create a custom framework, or Framework to structure your portfolio; and 3. Add the artifacts to build your portfolio by uploading existing files (from Word to Power-Point to Video), linking to artifacts posted elsewhere on the Web, or creating an artifact through *Folio*Live embedded forms. Go to **www.foliolive.com** to learn more about this product or to purchase a one-year account.

The Annotated Instructor's Edition provides additional teaching resources and ideas, and links together *Teachers, Schools, and Society* with the Supplements Program. We really do love teaching and tend to be very interactive, always looking to model diverse approaches to learning. The AIE cues engage students and connect them directly with the content. The following features occur in every chapter:

- **Chapter Focus**   Provides a brief summary of the chapter's main ideas. Imagine it as the topic sentence or objective for beginning your formal lecture.

- **Grabber**   Begin class with a motivating strategy that grabs student interest and cues them into the chapter content. *Links to the Instructor's Manual.*

- **Focus Question**   The Focus Questions listed at the start of the chapter are keyed throughout the chapter as related content is discussed. *Links to the Focus Questions.*

- **Critical Thinking Question**   A thoughtful discussion prompt or point to ponder that can be used during class or as a take-home assignment.

- **Class Activity**   This references a class activity from the Instructor's Manual. *Links to the Instructor's Manual.*

- **Related Reading**   These are nontraditional readings that will embellish your unique understanding of the text themes. We have read many of them and have the rest at the top of our "free time reading" list. They can easily be incorporated into class discussion.

- **Teaching Tip**   Each tip provides a relevant example, lecture suggestion, or quick hint to improve clarity, insight, or understanding.

- **Reflective Activities and Your Portfolio (*RAP*)**   These key the *RAP* activities directly to the chapter. These activities offer the student personal involvement in a topic, as well as an opportunity for portfolio development. *Links to the RAPs.*

- **Video Companion Segment**   Links the relevant video segment to the chapter content. These can range from multiple intelligences to technology in the classroom. *Links to the Video Companion Program.*

- **Overhead**   Overhead transparencies provide a ready organization for your instruction. Specific facts, charts, and figures from the text, or supplementing those in the text, are found on these transparencies. They can highlight key points or initiate student discussion. *Links to the Overhead Transparencies and PowerPoint Slides.*

- **Global View**   Provides an international perspective to the issues discussed. Typical items might include relevant and interesting facts, useful Web links, or teaching suggestions.

- **Multiple Intelligence Connection**   This applies MI theory with student activities (for in or out of class) that are drawn from a specific intelligence. This creates an accessible way to reflect textbook content in your own instruction.

How to Use the Reflective Activities and Your Portfolio (*RAP*)

The *RAP*s are placed after each of the book's four major sections and are designed to help the student reflect on and apply the main ideas found in the text. In addition, each *RAP* is keyed to the **INTASC Standards for Licensing Beginning Teachers.** For a listing of the Standards, see your Instructor's Manual or the text itself.

Each *RAP* includes:

- *Purpose*—explains why this activity is useful, and what it is intended to accomplish.
- *Activity*—allows you to apply your readings through observations, interviews, teaching, and action research.
- *Artifact*—challenges you to collect and manage the items you will find useful for developing your portfolio.
- *Reflection*—helps you think deeply and realistically about education and your place in it.

In Case You Were Wondering

For the *RAP*s, we tried to create unique and meaningful educational opportunities. If you want your students to be really engaged and thoughtful learners, the *RAP*s might be just the right academic and effective prescription. The *RAP*s provide

- Some tasks that are done in groups (learning cadres from two to six) and some tasks that can be done independently.
- Some activities requiring school visits, while others can be done with visits to a library, video store, Internet chat room, or neighbor.
- Chances to conduct educational interviews with candidates from school administrators to old school friends.
- Issues of student diversity, deliberately infused throughout the processes.
- Technology tasks, routinely included but adaptable to accommodate varied student backgrounds and facilities.
- When applicable, forms for the *RAP* activities are available on the Online Learning Center.

Students can print these forms to help them do, present, and retain their work.

Decisions: Sooner, Rather Than Later

How can you use these *RAP*s? There are many more activities here than your students can do. We wanted you and your students to be able to choose.

- A reasonable approach might be to have students select two to four *RAP*s from each section. They could base their selections on the INTASC principles (described in the text and the Instructor's Manual). A goal, to include an activity for each principle, would assure balance. And by the end of the text, each student could then submit ten *RAP*s, one for each INTASC principle. That's a great start for continued portfolio development.
- Subgroups of your class (learning cadres of ten students) could also divide and conquer a section of RAPs. They could meet after each section to share their experiences. Accumulated *RAP*s could serve as part of your assessment or grading.

Using the *RAP* as an Introduction to Portfolios

Today, many preservice programs require the ongoing development of a portfolio. *RAP*s help the student work through the process of creating, collecting, researching, drafting, editing, and organizing their portfolios.

Building a portfolio can be thought of as a two-part process: creating an extensive *working* portfolio and then selecting just the right items for a *presentation* portfolio. During the final *RAP*, students will analyze the content of their working portfolio so they can begin to refine what becomes part of a *presentation portfolio*—deciding what gets boxed and saved and what should possibly be tossed in the trash! In the end, they will want a portfolio that uniquely and accurately represents their growing competence.

It is of course possible to require a *course portfolio*, as determined by you and detailed in your syllabus. This format could integrate your choice of textbook elements (selected *RAP*s, tests, and other assessments and extra credit activities). A *course portfolio* can be submitted by the student at the semester's end or frame a faculty-student conversation resulting in a grade. For more on portfolios, see the Instructor's Manual.

The Reflective Activities and Your Portfolio

The following is a listing of the *RAP*s and the INTASC standards they relate to.

Part I   Teachers and Students

INTASC Principle		*RAP* (Chapters 1–3 indicated in parentheses)
1:1	Knowledge of Subject Matter	Teacher Interview in Your Subject Area (1)
1:2	Human Development and Learning	The Developmental and Psycho-Social Stages of Students (2)
1:3	Diversity in Learning	Multiple Intelligence Bingo (2)
1:4	Variety of Instructional Strategies	Memories of a Teacher (1)
1:5	Motivation and Management	Write a Letter to Yourself (1)
1:6	Communication Skills	Creating a Career Information Document (1)
1:7	Instructional Planning Skills	A Mini-Lesson with a Mini-Group (3)
1:8	Assessment	Tutor Using Effective Feedback (3)
1:9	Reflection and Responsibility	Student Feedback about Your Mini-Lesson (3)
1:10	Relationships and Partnerships	Special Education Services (2)

Part II   Schools and Curriculum

INTASC Principle		*RAP* (Chapters 4–7)
2:1	Knowledge of Subject Matter	State and National Curricular Standards (4, 6, 7)
2:2	Human Development and Learning	Scoping School Culture (5)
2:3	Diversity in Learning	Curriculum Bias Detectors (7)
2:4	Variety of Instructional Strategies	Visit a "Choice" School (4)
2:5	Motivation and Management	Rules Rituals and Routines (5)
2:6	Communication Skills	A PSA: The Purpose of School (4)
2:7	Instructional Planning Skills	Effective Schools (5)
2:8	Assessment	Memoirs of a Time-Tested Student (7)
2:9	Reflection and Responsibility	Reflections of a High School Yearbook (5)
2:10	Relationships and Partnerships	Support Staff Interview (4)

Part III Foundations

Part IV Tomorrow

The *Teachers, Schools, and Society* Video Companion

The *Teachers, Schools, and Society* Video Companion was developed to be used alongside the text. The *Teachers, Schools, and Society* video takes students into the classroom to bring content and concepts alive. You'll find in the IM descriptions of the segments and activities.

Chapter 1: Becoming a Teacher
Segment 1: The Pros and Cons of Teaching
Segment 2: The Crusade to Educate Teachers

Chapter 2: Student Diversity
Segment 3: What Are the Multiple Intelligences?
Segment 4: A Multiple Intelligences Lesson in Action
Segment 5: A Challenging Student
Segment 6: Assimilating the Alien
Segment 7: Including Students with Special Needs

Chapter 3: Teacher Effectiveness
Segment 8: Teaching: More Than the 3 R's
Segment 9: Classroom Management

Chapter 4: Schools: Choices and Challenges
Segment 10: Alternative Visions: Second-Chance Schools, Educational Remedies
Segment 11: "A Tour of a Charter School"

Chapter 5: Life in Schools
Segment 12: Teaching: It's Not All Academic
Segment 13: Immigrant Students

Chapter 6: What Students Are Taught in Schools
Segment 14: Saving Souls
Segment 15: Integrating Diversity into the High School Curriculum

Chapter 7: Standards, Testing, and Controversy over Who Controls the Curriculum
Segment 16: Explaining Standardized Test Scores to Parents: A Dramatization
Segment 17: Teachers' Opinions about High-Stakes Testing
Segment 18: Alternative Assessment: Portfolios
Segment 19: Try Teaching 5 Classes a Day, 5 Days a Week

Chapter 8: The History of American Education
Segment 20: The Common School and The Teaching Profession
Segment 21: A Missionary Mind and a Fighting Spirit
Segment 22: The Teacher's Calling

Chapter 9: Philosophy of Education
Segment 23: Essentialism in Action
Segment 24: Progressivism in Action

Chapter 10: Financing and Governing America's Schools
Segment 25: School Board Meeting

Chapter 11: School Law and Ethics
Segment 26: Cheating: A Dramatization

Chapter 12: The Struggle for Educational Opportunity
Segment 27: Native American Education
Segment 28: Fighting for What's Fair
Segment 29: Social Change: Desegregating Schools
Segment 30: Identifying Classroom Bias

Chapter 13: Technology in Education
Segment 31: A Guided Tour of Technology in Today's Classrooms
Segment 32: Integrating Technology into Teaching

Chapter 14: Your First Classroom
Segment 33: Your First Day
Segment 34: Teaching in the Education Factory
Segment 35: The Fight for Teachers' Rights

Chapter 15: *Q and A* Guide to Entering the Teaching Profession
Segment 36: Respect and Salary for Teachers

The *Only a Teacher* Video Program

The documentary series *Only a Teacher* explores the diverse faces and many roles of the American teacher from the 1830s to the present. In three one-hour episodes, *Only a Teacher* presents historical background about the profession and how it developed, while giving voice to contemporary teachers and their concerns. The series plays out as a dialogue between past and present, as teachers from different eras describe their dreams and setbacks, challenges, and achievements. Go to www.pbs.org/onlyateacher/about.html for more information about the series.

While it might be preferable (artistically and cognitively) for students to view the production in its entirety, it might not be possible. Therefore, we integrated the sixteen major segments (see the description of the *Teachers, Schools, and Society Video Companion*) with *Teachers, Schools, and Society* so that you might frame the entire production with the textbook.

TEACHERS, SCHOOLS, AND SOCIETY

TEACHERS, SCHOOLS, AND SOCIETY

SEVENTH EDITION

MYRA POLLACK SADKER

Late Professor, American University

DAVID MILLER SADKER

American University

ANNOTATED INSTRUCTOR'S EDITION

Boston   Burr Ridge, IL   Dubuque, IA   Madison, WI   New York   San Francisco   St. Louis
Bangkok   Bogotá   Caracas   Kuala Lumpur   Lisbon   London   Madrid   Mexico City
Milan   Montreal   New Delhi   Santiago   Seoul   Singapore   Sydney   Taipei   Toronto

The McGraw-Hill Companies

Mc Graw Hill **Higher Education**

TEACHERS, SCHOOLS, AND SOCIETY

Published by McGraw-Hill, a business unit of The McGraw-Hill Companies, Inc., 1221 Avenue of the Americas, New York, NY, 10020. Copyright © 2005, 2003, 2000, 1997, 1994, 1991, 1988 by The McGraw-Hill Companies, Inc. All rights reserved. No part of this publication may be reproduced or distributed in any form or by any means, or stored in a database or retrieval system, without the prior written consent of The McGraw-Hill Companies, Inc., including, but not limited to, in any network or other electronic storage or transmission, or broadcast for distance learning.

Some ancillaries, including electronic and print components, may not be available to customers outside the United States.

This book is printed on acid-free paper.

2 3 4 5 6 7 8 9 0 DOW/DOW 0 9 8 7 6 5 4

ISBN 0-07-287772-3 (student edition)
ISBN 0-07-287777-4 (instructor's edition)

Publisher: *Emily Barrosse*
Sponsoring editor: *Allison McNamara*
Senior developmental editor: *Cara Harvey*
Executive marketing manager: *Pamela S. Cooper*
Media producer: *Shannon Gattens*
Lead project manager: *Susan Trentacosti*
Production supervisor: *Janean A. Utley*
Design manager: *Laurie J. Entringer*
Lead supplement producer: *Marc Mattson*
Photo research coordinator: *Alexandra Ambrose*
Photo researchers: *David & Emily Tietz*
Permissions editor: *Marty Granahan*
Cover and interior design: *Kiera Pohl*
Cover images: *© Photodisc, Inc. All rights reserved.*
Typeface: *9/12 Stone Serif*
Compositor: *GAC Indianapolis*
Printer: *R. R. Donnelley*

Library of Congress Control Number: 2004101592 (student edition)

Library of Congress Control Number: 2004101579 (instructor's edition)

www.mhhe.com

Myra Sadker and David Sadker

The Sadkers have taught at the elementary, secondary, and college levels, and have been professors at American University (Washington, DC) for more than two decades. Myra Sadker served as Dean of the School of Education for eight years, and wrote one of the first books describing gender bias in America's schools in 1973. Working together, the Sadkers became leading advocates for equal educational opportunities and gained a national reputation for their work in confronting gender bias and sexual harassment. They co-authored six books and more than seventy-five articles in journals such as *Phi Delta Kappan, Harvard Educational Review, The Journal of Teacher Education,* and *Psychology Today.* They directed more than a dozen federal education grants. The Sadkers' work has been reported in hundreds of newspapers and magazines including *USA Today, USA Weekend, Parade Magazine, Business Week, The Washington Post, The London Times, The New York Times, Time,* and *Newsweek.* They appeared on local and national television and radio shows such as "The Today Show," "Good Morning America," "The Oprah Winfrey Show," "Phil Donahue's The Human Animal," National Public Radio's "All Things Considered," and twice on "Dateline: NBC" with Jane Pauley. The Sadkers received the American Educational Research Association's award for the best review of research published in the United States in 1991, their professional service award in 1995, the Eleanor Roosevelt Award from The American Association of University Women in 1995, and the Gender Architect Award from the American Association of Colleges of Teacher Education in 2001. The Sadkers' book, *Failing at Fairness: How Our Schools Cheat Girls,* was published by Touchstone Press in 1995.

Myra Sadker died while undergoing treatment for breast cancer in 1995. Myra was always committed to creating an introductory textbook that would be both interesting and informative to students while communicating her love for teaching. That was the motivation behind *Teachers, Schools, and Society* and that is why she remains first author. In her name, Myra Sadker Advocates was established to continue her efforts and create more equitable and effective schools. You are invited to learn more about Myra's contributions and the work of Myra Sadker Advocates by visiting her website:

www.sadker.org

BRIEF CONTENTS

CONTENTS

Chapter 7
Standards, Testing, and the Controversy over Who Controls the Curriculum 235

PART III
FOUNDATIONS

Chapter 11
School Law and Ethics 391

PART IV
TOMORROW

Chapter 12
The Struggle for Educational Opportunity 440

Chapter 13
Technology in Education *481*

Chapter 14
Your First Classroom *510*

Chapter 15
Q and *A* Guide to Entering the Teaching Profession *541*

APPENDIXES

PREFACE

When we were in school, textbooks were generally informative, but uninteresting. We want this text to be both informative and fun, and we worked hard to accomplish this goal. We wrote this book to share with you the excitement we feel about teaching.

Teachers, Schools, and Society is designed for introductory courses in teacher education variously labeled Introduction to Education; Introduction to Teaching, Schools, and Society; or Foundations of Education. Whatever the label, the primary intent of such a course is to provide a sufficiently broad yet detailed exposure to the realities of teaching. The text should help you answer those all-important questions: Do I want to become a teacher? What do I need to become the best teacher possible? What should a professional in the field of education know? To help you answer these questions, we offer a panoramic (and we hope) stimulating view of education.

An Interactive Text

Each edition of *Teachers, Schools, and Society* has broken new ground by creating new features, introducing new topics, and adding new supplements. This edition continues this rich tradition by creating an even more interactive book for students. The chapters—always lauded for their student-friendly readability—have been revised to encourage more engagement and reflection. Reflection questions accompany all figures and tables, as well as many of the boxed features. The Online Learning Center and the new Sadker.com Website (both accessible at www.mhhe.com/sadker7e) are true extensions of the text. Throughout the text, you are directed to the sites to complete interactive activities or polls, respond to questions, and to access the online student study guide. See page xix for a tour of the text's features.

Content Coverage

We elected to view the field from several vantage points. In Part I, you will see the world of teachers and students from a new perspective—the teacher's side of the desk. In Part II, your field of vision will be widened so you can examine the structure, culture, and curriculum of that complex place called school. Part III then examines the broad forces (historical, philosophical, legal, and financial) that shape the foundations of our educational system. In Part IV, you will have a chance to examine, debate, and speculate about issues and trends, and explore many of the questions students typically bring to this course, often practical and personal questions. Following each of the four parts are *RAP*s. The *RAP*s offer you the opportunity to develop crucial skills related to the teaching profession and to start your teaching portfolio. The Appendixes contain information about teacher licensing, including relevant addresses, and teacher competency exams.

Style of Presentation

The trouble with panoramic views is that the observer is often at such a distance from what is being viewed that all richness of detail is lost. Vague outlines devoid of human interaction dominate many survey type texts. We worked hard to personalize this book. At various points throughout the text we replace our wide-angle lens with a more intimate view that captures the human drama as well. For example, in many chapters, we introduce traditionally dry, abstract topics with illustrative scenarios that help personalize and dramatize the topic at hand. The *In the News* feature offers insightful, humorous, and poignant educational news items taken from newspapers, the Internet, and the popular press. *Class Acts* offer personal insights into teaching and schooling. Several "pop" quizzes probe your prior knowledge and beliefs and introduce, even personalize, governance, law, and philosophy. The *Photo-synthesis* feature offers dramatic visual contrasts of pressing educational concerns, while *You Be the Judge* invites you to evaluate different perspectives on relevant educational issues. We hope that these stylistic elements, along with a writing style that is deliberately informal rather than academic, will add spice and human interest to the text.

Reflective Activities and Your Portfolio (RAP)

The *RAP* feature, formerly *Inter-missions,* includes part-ending activities designed to help you reflect on teaching, build a portfolio, and enhance understanding of the concepts in this text. To make these more practical, the *RAPs* are based on the INTASC standards.

New in the Seventh Edition

This edition of *Teachers, Schools, and Society* is designed to improve an already comprehensive text. The entire text was updated and revised to provide the most current coverage possible. Major revision was done in the following areas.

Standards, Testing and *No Child Left Behind*

The authors take a critical look at the current emphasis on standardized tests as embodied in the *No Child Left Behind* legislation. While the text summarizes the arguments both for and against the standards and testing movement, the authors provide their insights as to why they believe the current testing craze is damaging. They argue that such tests not only create a negative school environment for students and teachers, but fail to measure many important educational goals. The authors argue for more meaningful learning, more diverse assessments, and a more positive school climate.

Other Expanded Topics

Topics receiving increased attention in this edition include finance, the growing influence of business in schools, technology, bullying, and giftedness. The finance chapter now explores why so many Americans do not believe that educational dollars make a difference, as well as the legal arguments around equalizing financial expenditures among schools. The curriculum chapter has been updated to reflect current tension points in various subject areas, and an alternative curriculum is offered as an example of more meaningful learning. The technology chapter has also been updated to reflect continuing changes in that arena.

Multicultural Focus

Multicultural and gender issues have always been a major thread of this text, and continue to be a major theme in this edition. Student diversity, which may be the single most critical issue facing our schools in the decades ahead, is a powerful focus, as is the educational history of many ethnic and racial groups. The text also provides several popular theories explaining group differences in academic performance, as well as some practical strategies for nonracist, nonsexist teaching.

Reflective Activities and Your Portfolio (RAP)

Reflective Activities and Your Portfolio (RAP) has replaced the *Inter-missions* feature of previous editions. *RAP* activities can now more easily be used as part of a student's portfolio, and are intended to help students personally connect not only with the text content, but also with the INTASC standards. The *RAPs* give students a chance to tie educational issues to their own experiences. *RAPs* are intended to help students decide if teaching is right for them. Each *RAP* activity contains a purpose, activity, artifact, and reflection.

Expanded Supplements Program

The seventh edition provides several new resources for the instructor and the student. For the instructor, the *Teacher, Schools, and Society Video Companion* has been expanded to include new segments and to integrate appropriate clips from the <u>*Only a Teacher*</u> video series. For the student, a new *Resources for Exploring Education* CD-ROM includes articles, case studies and media observations related to the text. Additionally, a new Web resource, the *Sadker.com Website* (accessible from www.mhhe.com/sadker7e), provides students a home base to explore the discipline of education. Finally, access to *Folio*Live, the McGraw-Hill online electronic portfolio-building tool, is available with the text.*

---

*Ask your local sales representative about how this program can be packaged for free or at a discount with the text.

Text Features

- **What Do You Think?** links students to the Online Learning Center where they take a quick survey or self-inventory. Responses are submitted to a national poll so students can immediately (and confidentially) see where they stand in comparison with their colleagues.

- **Interactive Activities** link the student to the Online Learning Center to do a content-related activity.

- **You Be the Judge** invites students to reflect and consider conflicting points of view of current educational controversies.

- **Profile in Education** offers brief biographies of leading educators who have made, and continue to make, a difference in the lives of children.

- **Reflection** questions are included throughout the text to engage readers in educational issues and ideas. This is one example of the interactive nature of this edition.

- **Frame of Reference** provides research updates, personal anecdotes, critical statistics, and practical advice for new teachers.

- **Chapter Summaries** are organized around focus questions.

- **Chapter Review** points readers to the study tools available on the Online Learning Center.

- **Current News from PowerWeb** lists the topics that the articles and current news feeds relate to on the Online Learning Center.

- **Extended Learning** lists the resources—articles, case studies and media observations—located on the *Resources for Exploring Education* CD-ROM.

- **Key Terms and People** have references to relevant text pages.

- **Reel to Real Teaching,** included at the end of each chapter, describes relevant films and videotapes, and offers strategies for incorporating these media to highlight chapter ideas and concepts.

- **For Further Reading** provides selected annotated bibliographies after each chapter.

A full listing of the text's features is located on pages xix–xxvi.

Acknowledgments

In March 1995, Myra died undergoing treatment for breast cancer. She worked on this textbook even while undergoing chemotherapy and she was always the major force behind providing a student-friendly introduction to teaching. She will always be the primary author of this book.

Karen Zittleman is a new and wonderfully talented recruit to both the sixth and seventh editions. She is insightful and wise beyond her years. She had the major responsibility for updating the law chapter, wrote the initial drafts of the vast majority of *Profiles in Education,* found and included the Web links, constructed the annotated bibliographies included in the *For Further Reading* sections, and read through all my first drafts with care and insight. Her editorial comments have made this a stronger book. Whenever a difficult question or a puzzling organizational problem arose, Karen's insight and logic could be relied on to see us through. But it was not *all* work! The best fun was going to the movies and video store together so we could view and evaluate Hollywood's best efforts and select which to include in the *Reel to Real* feature. When we selected the ones we liked best, it was Karen who wrote the *Reel to Real* features. I am indebted to her, and consider her not only a terrific doctoral student and talented writer, but a friend and colleague as well.

Phyllis Lerner and Dan Otter worked on the four *Reflective Activities and Your Portfolio (RAP)* sections in this text. Their decades of practical school experience are reflected on those pages. Karen, Phyllis, Chris Cozadd, and Dan also contributed ideas and test questions for the Annotated Instructor's Edition and the Instructor's Manual. Jackie Sadker, one of two extraordinary daughters, reviewed the legal arguments discussed in the *Financing and Governing America's Schools* chapter. In previous editions of this book, she has worked on the curriculum chapter, helped with the editing, and indexed the book. Previous editions were improved by many students and colleagues, who are often in my thoughts. Thanks are extended to Chris Cozadd, Jane Lonnquist, Daniel Spiro, Lynette Long, Elizabeth Ihle, Nancy Gorenberg, Elsie Lindemuth, Jen Engle, Mary Donald, June Winter, Kirstin Hill, Kate Volker, Ward Davis, Pat Silverthorn, Julia Masterson, Amy Monaghan, Shirley Pollack, and Kathryn McNerney.

Our developmental editor, Cara Harvey, was a constant source of ideas and encouragement, a partner and friend in shaping and revising this text, and a great source of suggestions of just what books we should be reading for enjoyment (if we weren't writing this one). Her energy and abilities made this venture much sweeter. She also whipped the manuscript (and us) into shape. Beth Kaufman, editor on previous editions, demonstrated her commitment to us and to this edition by her continued involvement and support. Her talent and efforts have strengthened the videotape that accompanies this text, and her friendship is much appreciated. Jane Karpacz, our publisher at McGraw-Hill, was a lion in reshaping this book and gave us all the support we needed to make it a success. I am nominating her for the Publishing Hall of Fame. Wow, were we lucky!

Our thanks to Susan Trentacosti, our project manager, for transforming manuscript into book in record-breaking fashion. We also want to thank the following reviewers of *Teachers, Schools, and Society* for generously sharing with us their experiences in teaching the book:

Sherry Black, *Western Nevada Community College*

Barbara Carlisle, *Paradise Valley Community College*

Leslie J. Davison, *St. Cloud State University*

Jennifer V. Irwin, *Anne Arundel Community College*

Philip Koger, *University of Central Florida*

Mary F. Leslie, *Louisiana State University*

Judith Meloy, *Castleton State University*

Gary N. Oakes, *Simmons College*

Ronald Padula, *Delaware County College*

Veronica P. Stephen, *Eastern Illinois University*

Jay Tieger, *Florida Atlantic University*

Carlos A. Torre, *Southern Connecticut State University*

Dorothy Trusock, *Arkansas State University*

Roger Wilson, *Grand Valley Stale University*

Finally, I would like to thank my daughters, Robin and Jackie, for their tolerance, insight, and love. When they were in elementary school (during the first edition of this book), they endured the piles of paper, research notes, and drafts that made our house literally a version of the paper chase. At the time of this seventh edition, Jackie is an attorney and Robin, now Dr. Sadker, is practicing internal medicine. The editions that preceded this one all benefited from their ideas and critiques and their growing pains. They are the two most special people in my life, and Myra and I continue to dedicate this book to them.

David M. Sadker

If you think that *Teachers, Schools, and Society* was written to introduce you to the world of teaching, you are only half right. This book also reflects our excitement about a life in the classroom and is intended to spark your own fascination about working with children. The basic premise for this text has not changed through all the previous editions: write a book students want to read, not have to read. While we continue to work hard to provide you with information that is both current and concise, we work even harder to create an engaging book—one that will give you a sense of the wonderful possibilities found in a career in the classroom.

To help you determine if teaching is right for you, and to learn more about education in general, you will find Reflection questions throughout the text. These questions will put you right into the center of these issues, a personal connection that encourages your thoughtful deliberation. While the text has been designed to engage you, we also devised an absorbing "electronic-option," the website resources. The text's Web resources are accessible through www.mhhe.com/sadker7e. Here you can choose to go into the Online Learning Center that houses the student study guide, study resources and PowerWeb or into the Sadker.com Website that includes additional Class Acts, surveys, links to educational resources and other materials that will help you explore the world of Education. Throughout the text you will see links to the activities and study resources found on the Online Learning Center and Sadker.com Website. Each link includes a brief explanation of what you will find online. Now it is time for your first reflection question: How can you discover this wonder trove of electronic treasures? Easy. We have blue "hot link" type whenever there is a website connection. Visit us in our cyber-classroom at www.mhhe.com/sadker7e.

To help you discover and use all of these new interactive opportunities, we have created a key of useful icons. Look for the following as you read this book:

 highlights reflection questions.

 indicates that you should go to the Online Learning Center for more information or to do an activity.

indicates that you should go to the Sadker.com Website to access material.

Now, join us for a tour of the special features of the text.

Class Acts

Each of the four part openers includes a *Class Act*—a story from a current or future teacher about their involvement in education. You can find additional Class Acts on the Sadker.com Website submitted by your classmates nationwide. Have you had a teacher who made a difference in your life? We want to hear about that teacher, and perhaps include your story in the next edition of the text. Please submit your own story!

Chapter Opener

The chapter opener page includes Focus Questions and a Chapter Preview to prime you for the content that will follow. At the end of the chapter, the summary will be framed by these very same focus questions. The page also includes an online *What Do You Think?* activity. One such activity might be a quiz that captures your opinion on some of the topics you will soon read about. Answer the questions and then, via the Internet, find out how your peers responded. It's an opportunity to participate in our national survey system and is only one of the activities that you will find on the Online Learning Center.

CHAPTER 12

The Struggle for Educational Opportunity

FOCUS QUESTIONS

1. How do deficit, expectation, and cultural difference theory explain disparate academic performance among various racial, ethnic, and cultural groups?
2. What major developments have marked the educational history of Native Americans, Hispanics, African Americans, Asian Americans/Pacific Islanders, and Arab Americans?
3. What educational barriers and breakthroughs have girls and women experienced?
4. What classroom strategies are appropriate for teaching culturally diverse learners?
5. What impact do changing family patterns and economic issues have on children and schools?
6. How can educators respond to social issues that place children at risk?

 What Do You Think? Estimate the social, racial, and ethnic backgrounds of today's students.

CHAPTER PREVIEW

Have you ever felt the cold slap of rejection because of race, religion, color, sex, language, national origin, social class, sexual orientation, or physical or learning disability? Have you ever denied a family history that included divorce, suicide, or abuse? Frequently, the dominant culture has little tolerance for those who are in any way "different." As most of us know from personal experience, when you happen to be the one who is outside—the one who is deprived even briefly of the privileges and status of the inside group—the feeling of being labeled "less worthy" can be more than painful.

Ideally, education should be for all children. In reality, education has repeatedly labeled, tracked, and excluded students who are in any way different. These children have met prejudicial treatment early, right at the schoolhouse

door. This chapter will review the major developments that have pried open the school door and have brought these once excluded learners into the educational mainstream.

Intersecting with racism and sexism, considerable economic and social problems engulf our children and our schools. The recent past has not been kind to children, who now make up the poorest segment of society. Their survival and educational achievements are threatened by poverty, changing family patterns, substance abuse, depression, and even suicide. We will identify strategies that help keep the school door open for these troubled students as well.

Student diversity continues to increase dramatically. Teachers, schools, and society must respond, so that both equity and excellence can be achieved and maintained.

440

YOU BE THE JUDGE
FOR-PROFIT SCHOOLS

Are a Good Idea Because . . .

COMPETITION LEADS TO BETTER SCHOOLS
For-profit schools will break down the public school monopoly by creating competition and choice. As schools compete, parents (particularly poor parents) will finally have a choice, and not be forced to place their children in the neighborhood school. Just like in business, the weak schools will lose students and declare "bankruptcy." The stronger schools will survive and prosper.

SCHOOLS WILL BE ABLE TO REWARD GOOD TEACHERS, AND REMOVE WEAK ONES
The current public school bureaucracy protects too many incompetent teachers through the tenure system, and does not recognize teaching excellence. Using sound business practices, for-profit schools will reward superior teachers through profit-sharing incentives, retain competent teachers, and terminate ineffective teachers.

BUSINESS EFFICIENCY WILL IMPROVE SCHOOL PERFORMANCE
Education needs the skills and know-how of the business community. For-profit schools will implement the most effective educational strategies in a business culture. The top-heavy management of today's schools will be replaced by only a handful of administrators, and teachers will be driven to greater productivity through the profit incentives.

FOCUSED PROGRAMS AND INVESTOR OVERSIGHT LEAD TO ACADEMIC SUCCESS
For-profit schools will do a better educational job because they provide a focused and proven instructional plan. These schools avoid the public school pitfall of trying to offer "something-for-everyone." And if they falter and profits disappear, investor pressure will put them back on track.

Are a Bad Idea Because . . .

COMPETITION LEADS TO WEAKER SCHOOLS
Transplanting businesslike competition into the education arena would be a disaster. Competition is not all that business brings: false advertising, "special" promotions, a "feel-good" education—all the hucksterism of the marketplace to mislead students and their parents. Worse yet, the local public school, which holds a community together, will be lost.

TEACHERS WILL LOSE THEIR INFLUENCE AND ACADEMIC FREEDOM
Teachers who speak out against the company, or teach a controversial or politically sensitive topic, will have a brief career. The business community is quite vocal about teachers sharing in the profits, but strangely silent about what will happen during economic hard times.

PROFITS AND EDUCATION DO NOT MIX
For-profit schools are exactly that, "for profit," and when the interests of children and investors clash, investor interests will prevail. If investors demand better returns, if the stock market drops, if the economy enters hard times, the corporate executives will sacrifice educational resources. After all, while students enjoy little leverage, stockholders can fire business executives.

FOCUSED PROGRAMS MEANS KEEPING SOME STUDENTS OUT
Their one-size-fits-all approach practiced by these schools might be good for efficiency, but it is bad for students. The more challenging students, those with special needs, non-native speakers of English, or those who need special counseling, will be left to the underfunded public schools to educate.

YOU BE THE JUDGE
Do you believe that business and schools are a good or a bad match? Explain. Do you believe that profits can be made in schooling the nation's children? As a teacher, would you want to work for a for-profit school?

Many of these schools are doing a woefully inadequate job. Little wonder that many urban parents support choice plans, and would view a new charter school as an oasis in an educational desert.[34] But we need to look more carefully, for the charter oasis may turn out to be little more than an educational mirage.

151

You Be the Judge

You Be the Judge gives two sides of an argument so you can consider different points of view, and not just ours. Then we ask you to be the judge (law school not required), by responding to the reflection questions following the arguments. You can also do this on the Online Learning Center and either e-mail your response to your instructor, or save your response for your portfolio.

Profile in Education

Teaching is all about people—it's a very human connection. The people we profile are teachers, teacher educators, social activists working for children, and educational researchers. Each was chosen for an important contribution to education. And to follow up the text descriptions, you can visit the Sadker.com Website to find out more about the profiled educator.

PROFILE IN EDUCATION — Lisa Delpit

Teaching is a Delpit family tradition. As a child in Baton Rouge, Louisiana, Lisa Delpit played school as soon as she learned something new, eager to share her latest idea or fact with friends. Lisa didn't have to look far to find educational role models: her mother was a high school teacher; her father was a restaurant owner who donated meals to local elementary schools for children who couldn't afford lunch. So it was much to Delpit's surprise that her family discouraged her from pursuing a teaching career. Impressed with her academic talent, they wanted her to forge new opportunities for young black women, opportunities beyond "just being a teacher." But Lisa Delpit felt a calling to enrich the lives of students, especially those of color.

Delpit is an ardent supporter of public schools, where she believes an appreciation of diversity should be commonplace. But it is not. Too often American education fails to include, or even see, the vision of those outside the white mainstream culture. Even in the most diverse classrooms, Delpit often witnesses a prevailing tunnel vision—the richness of a multicultural lens obscured by calls for uniform standards based on traditional Eurocentric ideas. The perspectives and needs of students of color are sidelined. Delpit shares her insights:

I have come to understand that power plays a critical role in our society and in our educational system. The worldviews of those with privileged positions are taken as the only reality . . . It is others who determine how students of color should act, how they are to be judged. When one "we" gets to determine the standards for all "wes," then some "wes" are in trouble![1]

Delpit has felt this cultural tension in her own language arts classrooms. In her teacher training, she embraced the ideas that open, progressive classrooms are the most humanizing environments, that children should be in control of their own learning, and that students will learn to read and write when they are ready. Determined to use all she had learned to benefit children of color, she accepted a teaching position in inner-city Philadelphia. She put her whole-language teaching approach into action. Little attention was given to basic writing skills, like grammar, punctuation, and paragraph structure. Students instead learned to write in meaningful contexts related to their lives and culture.

Delpit knew her students were fluent. In their stories, in jump rope chants on the playground, and in their classroom discussions, she heard their verbal creativity. But they were failing academically, fluent in a language often met with silence in schools. "Whether it is known as Ebonics, jive, or street talk, it is the language spoken by many of our African American children. It is the language through which they first encountered love, nurturance and joy and one that does not lead to success in schools or society."[2]

Lisa Delpit was in a quandary. While she believed in a whole-language approach that embraced diversity, her students were struggling, unable to grasp the language skills they needed, the keys to the language of the mainstream culture. She believes that mainstream ways of speaking and writing represent a language of power that *all* students need to master for success in the larger society. Like a captain who realized that she was sailing in the wrong direction, she charted a new instructional voyage, one that used more traditional methodology. Students diagrammed sentences, learned grammar rules, and memorized verbs. And their performance improved.

But Delpit's traditional approach does not suffer from cultural amnesia. In *Other People's Children*, she shares a vision of classrooms where teachers let the voices of all students come alive and transform the traditional canon to include the knowledge of our multicultural world. For Lisa Delpit, basic skills free students to hear how the language of their culture shapes their thinking, to understand the social realities of their lives, and to become intelligent caretakers of the future. It is a language arts curriculum for all students, including "other people's children."

[1] Lisa Delpit, *Other People's Children: Cultural Conflict in the Classroom* (1995), p. xv.
[2] Lisa Delpit, "Ebonics and Culturally Responsive Schools," *Rethinking Schools* 12 (Fall 1997).

REFLECTION: What images does the phrase "other people's children" evoke in your mind? What is the opposite of "otherness"? How has the school curriculum, both formal and hidden, shaped your definitions? How would you define Delpit's phrase "the language of power"? Other than language arts, choose a content area discussed in this chapter. What is its language of power?

www.mhhe.com/ sadker To learn more about Lisa Delpit, click on *Profiles in Education.*

220

PHOTO-SYNTHESIS The More Things Change, the More They Stay the Same

During much of the twentieth century, African American students attended legally segregated schools. Today, while legal segregation has ended, segregation has not. Examine these two photos and suggest similarities and differences between segregation then and now. During the past hundred years, what other ethnic or racial groups might be photographed in much the same way?

45

Photo-synthesis

Most of us enjoy "seeing" theoretical concepts come to life. In fact, some people are more visual than verbal and greatly benefit from photographs and illustrations. That's why we developed *Photo-synthesis*—photo collages that encourage analysis. And if you need a thoughtful boost, one or more questions help you focus your inquiry.

---

op advertisement, ShopRite agreed to pay gure that only costs. Naming ShopRite Gym of actual con-

athletic facili-ning rights of opportunity to and other cur-banners from oration simply students and Mills donates r of box-tops of of purchase. hool time to a Channel One, n school and , are exploring

d commercials usiness values y Weyerhauser n their "com-group Pacific brochures ex-vironmentally e curriculum?

IN THE NEWS

Commercializing Schools: A Hidden Curriculum

The Center for Commercial-Free Public Education is concerned about marketing products to captive student audiences. Here are some examples of their concern:

- Exxon teaches children that the *Valdez* oil spill was an example of environmental protection.
- In Colorado, Burger King and 7-Up advertise on school buses.
- A Texas school roof is painted with a Dr. Pepper logo to capture the attention of passengers flying overhead.
- McDonald's teaches about deforestation, but fails to include the negative impact of cattle ranching on the rain forest.
- Clairol distributes free shampoo to students leaving school, along with a survey asking if they had a bad hair day.
- To teach the "practical applications" of algebra, Glencoe/McGraw-Hill publishers will be using articles and graphics from *USA Today* in their leading high school mathematics textbooks. Part of the agreement is that the books prominently display the *USA Today* logo.

SOURCE: *Educational Leadership*, October 1998; *San Francisco Chronicle*, June 6, 2001; *Education Week*, May 1, 2002.

What's new in education? Click on *News Feeds*.

FRAME OF REFERENCE Bilingual Amnesia

"My grandparents picked up English like everyone else back then, in school, where children learned their lessons in English, not in Spanish or Vietnamese."

"If people want to remain immersed in their old culture and old language, they should stay in their old country."

"Bilingual education has given us illiterate youngsters who can do little more than work at Taco Bell."

Sound familiar? After all, many of our ancestors came to America with few resources or funds, but they were able to learn English, pick up American ways, get through

- *School performance for immigrants in English immersion programs was horrific. From 1880 through the 1930s, immigrants were far more likely to drop out of school than to graduate, and they dropped out at much higher percentages than today's students.*
- *Non-English-speaking students in New York early in the twentieth century were 60 percent more likely than English speakers to be labeled "retarded," including more than a third of the Ital students.*

Frame of Reference

These boxes take a closer look at important topics. They provide research updates, further information about an issue, or even suggestions for classroom use.

In the News

Throughout the chapters you will find brief summaries of education-related news items. We selected these items because we found them funny, poignant, or particularly relevant to the chapter content. The *In the News* items also provide a sense of currency to the issues and topics discussed in the text. The feature will point you to the PowerWeb resources located on the Online Learning Center. PowerWeb includes articles and a current newsfeed to keep you abreast of what is going on in Education today.

---

what is needed to transform a strong teach unique in this. When a group of Olympia takes to become a champion, none of the a champions. On the contrary, the athletes cr coaching. Accomplished musicians attribut practice, as do master chess players. So too,

All you really need to know is the subject you mastery is critical in effective teaching, resea **agogy**, the art and science of teaching, esp outperform teachers with superior subject an ful teachers do not view this as an either/or both knowledge of the subject and instructi

Teacher education students are less talented nard lives on despite very mixed evidence.

INTERACTIVE ACTIVITY
What Should Teachers Learn?
Create your own teacher education curriculum based on what you think teachers need to know.

Interactive Activities

Interactive Activities are listed in the margin and can be found on the Online Learning Center under the corresponding chapter. The activities are designed to allow you to apply what you are learning in an interactive environment.

Chapter-Ending Spread

The material at the end of the chapter is designed to structure your review of the content and help you make sure you understand key ideas. Here's what you'll find there:

- A *Chapter Review* link reminds you to go to the Online Learning Center to take a quiz, practice with key terms, and review key ideas from the chapter.

- A *Current News from PowerWeb* link tells you the PowerWeb topics related to the chapter that are accessible through the Online Learning Center.

- An *Extended Learning* link lists the related articles, case studies, and media observations located on your *Resources for Exploring Education* CD-ROM.

- The *Summary* is organized by the Focus Questions at the start of the chapter.

- *Key Terms and People* will help you identify and remember the critical terminology and influential individuals discussed in the chapter.

Page references next to each entry guide you to the place that each is discussed in the chapter.

- The *Discussion Questions and Activities* are designed to promote deeper analysis, further investigation, and even an evaluation of the controversial issues discussed in the chapter. Also included are the Internet-based *WEB-tivities* you can find on the Online Learning Center.

- *Reel to Real Teaching* summarizes a popular movie, usually available on videotape or DVD, that will add to your appreciation of the information included in this chapter. We believe that Hollywood can actually enhance your education, and movies can both deepen your understanding of the chapter and offer a richer educational context. The *Reel to Real* feature provides questions and follow-up activities that guide you through the movie and the issues described in the text. Go to the Sadker.com Website to rate the movie.

- *For Further Reading* includes an annotated list of recent and influential books related to the chapter.

Reflective Activities and Your Portfolio

Part I: Teachers and Students

1:1 Teacher Interview in Your Major or Favorite Subject

INTASC PRINCIPLE 1
Knowledge of
Subject Matter

Purpose: Teachers are expected to have knowledge of both the subject(s) they teach and the students they are teaching. Deciding what to teach and how best to teach it are constant responsibilities. This activity gives you the opportunity to learn how teachers go through these tasks and to begin thinking how you might approach curricular decisions in your major subject area.

Activity: Interview a teacher in a subject area of special interest to you. Even if you plan to teach in an elementary program, select the curricular area that you savor. Focus on how the teacher decides what content to teach and how best to teach it. Here are some curricular questions to ask, but feel free to add your own to this list:

- What factors contributed to your decision to teach this subject and at this grade level?
- What do you enjoy most about teaching this curriculum? What do you enjoy least?
- How do you go about selecting what content and skills to teach?
- Do you try to offer different perspectives (multidisciplinary, multicultural) on these topics?
- Are there areas of this subject that are controversial? How do you handle these "hot" topics?
- How do you accommodate multiple intelligences in your classroom?
- How do you track and record grades? Does your school or district require a certain format? Do you use grading software?
- When do you do your planning? The week before, the night before, impromptu?
- Do you integrate other subject areas into your program?
- How do the school district's official curriculum and the textbook shape your decisions?
- Can you make your own decisions as to what topics to teach, or are you

Reflective Activities and Your Portfolio

Reflective Activities and Your Portfolio, what we like to refer to as *RAP,* give you a chance to explore your role as an educator by carefully considering what you have just read, and tying it to your own experiences. *RAPs* are intended to help you decide if teaching is right for you. And if it is right, these very same *RAPs* will give you direction as you prepare for a career in teaching. For those of you who want to start a portfolio, RAP will be your first step.

RAPs follow and connect to each of the four sections of the textbook. Each *RAP* includes:

- *Purpose*—explains why this activity is useful, and what it is intended to accomplish.
- *Activity*—allows you to apply your readings through observations, interviews, teaching, and action research.
- *Artifact*—challenges you to collect and manage the items you will find useful for developing your portfolio.
- *Reflection*—helps you think deeply and realistically about education and your place in it.

Student Resources

Here is your tour of the study and extending resources that accompany the text.

Online Resources

Your online resources are accessible from www.mhhe.com/sadker7e.

Online Learning Center

The Online Learning Center is your study guide. It includes:

- Multiple Choice and True/False Quizzes with immediate feedback
- PowerWeb Articles and Newsfeed
- Chapter Focus Questions and Summaries
- Web Links
- Interactive Activities and *What Do You Think?* Surveys referenced in the text
- *Web-tivities* and a *You Be the Judge* response area
- *RAP* forms
- Key Terms and the Glossary
- Internet Primer, Study Skills Primer, and a Learning Styles Assessment

www.mhhe.com/sadker7e   **Sadker.com Website**

The Sadker.com Website is your home base for exploring the world of Education. It includes:

- *What Do You Think?* and Current Issue Surveys
- Commentary from David Sadker on current education-related issues
- Media of the Month
- PowerWeb Articles and Newsfeeds, *In the News* archives, and links to Education news sites.
- *Class Act* archives
- Extending information on those profiled in *Profile in Education*
- Links to resources such as state departments of education, PRAXIS resources and lesson plans
- And more!

Resources for Exploring Education CD-ROM

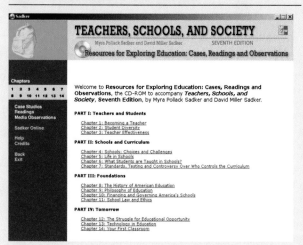

The *Resources for Exploring Education* CD-ROM is packaged with each new copy of the text. If you purchased a used text, you can buy the CD-ROM by calling McGraw-Hill Customer Service at 1-800-338-3987. The CD-ROM includes articles, cases, and media observations. For a full listing of these, go to the Student Center main page on the Online Learning Center and click on *Resources for Exploring Education CD-ROM*.

FolioLive

*Folio*Live is an online portfolio tool you can use to create an electronic portfolio in three easy steps: 1. Use a template to create a homepage; 2. Choose to create a custom framework, or Framework to structure your portfolio; and 3. Add the artifacts to build your portfolio by uploading existing files (from Word to PowerPoint to Video), linking to artifacts posted elsewhere on the Web, or creating an artifact through *FolioLive* embedded forms. Go to **www.foliolive.com** to learn more about this product or to purchase a one-year account.

TEACHERS, SCHOOLS, AND SOCIETY

PART I

Teachers and Students

CLASS ACT

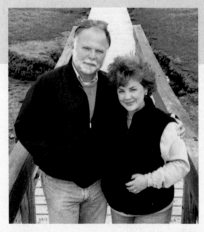

Every December I watch *It's a Wonderful Life.* I was 13 years old when I first saw George Bailey scramble down the Main Street of Bedford Falls, waving his arms and screaming at the top of his lungs, rejoicing in the beauty of life, love and friendship. As an adult who savors this film, I feel the bittersweet pang of watching a man who is reborn, glowing in the recognition that he has made a difference in the world. In the final act, as George stands in his living room surrounded by family and friends celebrating his life, I always develop that painful lump in my throat—you know the one. It stings and makes it nearly impossible to swallow. I love this film, and I always want to say that I know a George Bailey. The thing is I do—he's my dad.

My father has been teaching English and Dramatic Arts at the same high school in Massachusetts for the last thirty years. His journey has been one similar to George Bailey's—he has settled down in a small town, a teacher, committed to his family and profession, but at times frustrated. He has seen thousands of students come and go, some moving on to big and exciting things, others staying in the very same town. From time to time growing up, I'd see a glimmer in his eyes wondering, "What if . . . ? What if I'd quit teaching, what if I'd gone off traveling around the world?" These moments of wonder were not full of anger or resentment, only seconds of reflection, and perhaps a little regret for not "doing more with his life." But he always returned to teaching with a positive spirit, endless patience, and astounding energy.

Over the years my dad and I have shared lots of travels together. It was a family joke that no matter where we went, we always ran into one of my father's former students. More often than not the run-in went beyond a courteous hello and how are you. These former students, now adults with children of their own, embrace my dad, literally and figuratively. We could be standing at a light waiting to cross, sitting in a restaurant—we inevitably ran into these joyful faces who recognize the sparkling eyes, full beard and unmistakable energy of my dad. As a younger child I was somewhat bored by the endless stories recounted by these strangers. The older I got, the more I realized that these spontaneous reunions were quite special. These people were paying tribute to someone who touched their lives. It wasn't a grand parade or a front-page article or a million dollar salary bonus. They were simple yet beautifully sincere words—"You inspired me . . . You gave me the courage to try . . . You were the only one who believed in me . . . "

This may sound like a tribute to a father from an adoring daughter, and to some degree it is. But it is also recognition of something more. Just like George Bailey, my dad has a wonderful life. Through teaching he is able to reach that troubled kid who sits in the back making wisecracks and give him a reason to care about school. He has taken the shy girl who doesn't speak, put her up on the stage and helped her find her voice and confidence. He has acted as adviser and inspiration for countless young people, giving them the opportunity to learn, grow and succeed. Although I've never been a student in his class, my dad has inspired me as well. As I begin my pursuit of a Masters in Teaching, I see just how unique my father's gifts are. This year when I watched *It's a Wonderful Life,* I couldn't help but think of my father. I still got that lump in my throat—and loved it.

Amanda Helfen
American University

Read more *Class Acts* at Sadker.com

**www.mhhe.com/
sadker7e**

Becoming a Teacher

FOCUS QUESTIONS

1. What are the advantages and disadvantages of being a teacher?
2. What are the satisfactions—and complaints—of today's teachers?
3. Can we consider teaching to be a profession?
4. How has teacher preparation changed over the years?
5. Do educators and the public agree on the most effective way to prepare teachers?
6. What traits and characteristics are needed for successful teaching?
7. Is teaching a "good fit" for you?
8. What steps can you take now on the road to becoming a teacher?

 WHAT DO YOU THINK? Why Do You Want to Be a Teacher? Rate the factors influencing your decision whether to become a teacher, and see how other students have rated these factors.

CHAPTER PREVIEW

This chapter looks at classroom life through the teacher's eyes. You may be thinking: I have spent years in a classroom, watching teachers and what they do. If there is one thing I know, it is teachers and teaching! But during your years in the classroom, you have looked at teaching through "student-colored glasses," a unique but somewhat distorted view, like looking through a telescope from the lens that makes everything tiny instead of large. This chapter offers you a teacher's perspective. We give you an opportunity to consider both the pros and cons of a teaching career. Then we turn to another question: Will you and teaching be a good match?

We love teaching, but not everything about teaching is wonderful. In the past, teachers were often considered second-class citizens, pressured to conform to strict moral and social codes while being paid meager wages. Today, teaching is now center stage, a common topic in the media and in political debates. Your study of education comes at a propitious time, a period of ferment and change as teachers strive for a more professional, more influential role in U.S. society. What role might you play in tomorrow's classrooms?

The chapter is also about "us." Yes, us. We are now a team, this textbook, the authors and you. When your authors were students, we did not much like our textbooks. They were far from exciting to read. By extension, we feared that we might not like teaching. In the end, we loved teaching—but still hated our textbooks. We want this textbook to be different—to be not only informative, but also enjoyable. This first chapter offers us the opportunity to introduce the textbook, and in a sense, to introduce ourselves.

Welcome to our classroom.

CLASS ACTIVITY: A CLASS ACT
Cue students to read the first *Class Act*, and provide a follow-up question to ponder: Who is the teacher, relative, or other adult inspiring your wonderful life?

CHAPTER FOCUS
This chapter immerses students in the issues surrounding teaching as a career. Topics range from how teachers feel about their work to whether teaching should be considered a profession. The chapter lends itself to introspection—and exciting class discussions or debates. For a chapter outline, see the IM.

What Are You Doing for the Rest of Your Life?

In a "Peanuts" cartoon, Linus comments that "no problem is so big or complicated that it can't be run away from." Charles Schulz succinctly highlighted a human frailty shared by most of us—the tendency to put aside our problems or critical questions in favor of day-to-day routine. In fact, it is amazing how little care and consideration many of us give to choosing a career. It is always easier to catch a movie, surf the net, or even study for the next exam than it is to reflect on and plan for the future. This may be one reason why questions such as: "What are you going to be when you grow up?" and "What's your next career move?" make so many of us uneasy. The big question facing many readers of this text: Is teaching right for you? For some of you, teaching may become a decades-long career filled with joy and satisfaction. For others, teaching may be limited to only a few years spent in the classroom, one of several careers you explore during your working years. And, still others may reach an equally useful and important realization: Teaching is not the ideal match for your interests or skills. We'd like to help you decide whether you and teaching are a good fit.

Throughout this text, we pose a variety of questions for you to consider. We have devised a feature called *You Be the Judge,* which presents several sides of an issue, and encourages you to sort out where you stand. When the authors have a strong opinion about these or any of the issues in the text, we will not hide it from you. For example, we told you that we love teaching, but there are drawbacks, so you know pretty much where we stand. But our opinion is just our opinion, and we want you to form your own ideas. To that end, we will work hard to be fair, to present more than one side of the issue, and to help you form an independent point of view. *You Be the Judge* is one way that we hope to spark your interest and thinking on these critical issues.

In the first *You Be the Judge,* we highlight the joys and concerns of a career in the classroom. (See pp. 6–8.)

Do Teachers Like Teaching?

In this chapter, the *You Be the Judge* feature helps you focus on the pros and cons of becoming a teacher. You probably noticed that we included comments by teachers themselves revealing their perceptions and feelings about their work. A more structured attempt to assess teachers' views on their careers was carried out by the National Education Association (NEA) and the National Center for Educational Statistics (NCES), part of the U.S. Department of Education. Teachers from around the nation were asked why they decided to become teachers, and why they choose to stay in teaching.[1] Teachers elect a career in the classroom for the intrinsic rewards that make teaching pretty unique, including a desire to work with young people, the significance of education generally, and even the love of a particular subject—not a bad bunch to have as colleagues. And once in the classroom, most teachers report that they like what they are doing.

In the NEA and NCES survey, the vast majority of the teachers, about 80 percent, reported that they were satisfied with their jobs and with their working conditions. Almost 90 percent were satisfied with the intellectual challenge of their work, their job security, and their autonomy in the classroom. The teachers also gave high scores to supervisors, with solid majorities viewing their school principals as supportive and encouraging—leaders who were able to communicate their expectations and to

GRABBER: PORTRAITS AND MEMORIES OF TEACHERS
IM

RAP 1.5
Why Teach?, p. 118

TEACHING TIP
Ask students to consider their childhood memories. What careers did they contemplate for themselves? What influenced their early decision making (parents, gender, class, geography, experiences)? What is influencing them now?

VIDEO SEGMENT 1
The Pros and Cons of Teaching

FOCUS QUESTION 1
What are the advantages and disadvantages of being a teacher?

OVERHEADS 1 AND 2
Becoming a Teacher
Why Become a Teacher?

FOCUS QUESTION 2
What are the satisfactions—and complaints—of today's teachers?

The Good News . . .

YOU ARE NOT WORKING ALONE, STARING AT A COMPUTER SCREEN OR SHUFFLING PAPERS

If you enjoy being in contact with others, particularly young people, teaching could be the right job for you. Almost the entire working day is spent in human interaction. Young people are so often funny, fresh, and spontaneous. Your discussions may range from adding fractions to feeding pet snakes, from an analysis of *The Catcher in the Rye* to advice on applying to colleges. As America's students become increasingly diverse, you will find yourself learning about different cultures and different life experiences. Your life will be enriched by the varied worlds of different children— black, white, Hispanic, Asian, blended—all kinds of children. The children will make you laugh and make you cry, but always they will make you feel needed. "I still can't get used to how much my heart soars with every student's success, and how a piece of my heart is plucked away when any student slips away."[2]

THE SMELL OF THE CHALKBOARD, THE ROAR OF THE CROWD

You spend several days researching and planning your lesson on social protest literature for your eleventh-grade English class. You collect many fine poems and statements to share; you bring your favorite CDs and videos of social protest songs into the classroom; you prepare an excellent PowerPoint presentation to highlight the key labor figures and issues of the time; and you punctuate your lesson with thoughtful discussion questions and creative follow-up activities. Wow, what a lesson! The students are spellbound. They ask many questions and make plans for doing their own research on social protest. One group even decides to meet after school to create an MTV-type video of a social protest song about the destruction of the natural environment. Their animated discussion continues as the bell signals their passage to the next classroom.

When you have taught well, your students will let you know it. On special occasions, they will come up to you after class or at the end of the year to tell you "This class is awesome." At younger grade levels, they may write you notes (often anonymous), thanking you for a good class or a good year.

I'M PROUD TO BE A TEACHER

Although teacher status took a battering in public opinion in the early 1980s, the public is once again acknowledging

The Bad News . . .

STOP THE CROWD—I WANT TO GET AWAY

Right in the middle of a language arts lesson, when fifteen kids have their hands in the air, you may feel like saying, "Stop, everybody. I feel like being alone for the next fifteen minutes. I'm going to Starbucks." For the major part of each day, your job demands that you be involved with people in a fast-paced and intense way—whether you feel like it or not. Researchers report that you will be involved in as many as one thousand verbal exchanges in a single day, almost all of them with children, which could impact behavior beyond school. One kindergarten teacher warned her 40-year-old brother "to be sure and put on his galoshes. Wow! Did he give me a strange look."[3] And as America's classrooms become more multicultural, teacher interactions will become more challenging, as teachers stretch beyond their own background to connect with a diverse student population.

IS ANYBODY THERE?

After teaching your fantastic lesson on social protest literature, you want to share your elation with your colleagues, so you head for the teachers' room and begin to talk about the lesson. But it is hard to capture the magic of what went on in the classroom. You can sense that your description is falling flat. Besides, people are beginning to give you that "What kind of superstar do you think you are?" look. You decide you had better cut your description short and talk about CDF (Casual Dress Friday).

It is rare to have another adult spend even ten minutes observing you at work in your classroom. Once you have obtained tenure, classroom observation becomes incredibly infrequent. Often, the evaluation is little more than perfunctory. Some teachers feel they and their students share a "secret life," off-limits to others. Most of your colleagues will have only a general impression of your teaching competence. The word may leak out—through students, parents, or even the custodian—if you are doing a really fine job; however, on the whole, when you call out, "Hello, I'm here, I'm a teacher. How am I doing?" there will be little cheering from anyone outside your classroom.

I DON'T GET NO RESPECT

While many Americans value teaching, many others don't. One reason for this inconsistency is sexism. Occupations with

continued

The Good News . . .

the importance of teachers. Nine out of ten students give their teachers a passing grade.[4] When you become a teacher, many people will accord you respect, because they admire teachers. You will be someone whose specialized training and skills are used to benefit others. Mark Twain once wrote, "To be good is noble, but to teach others how to be good is nobler." Which would have summed up this point perfectly, except, being Mark Twain, he added: "—and less trouble."

AS A TEACHER, YOU ARE CONSTANTLY INVOLVED IN INTELLECTUAL MATTERS

You may have become very interested in a particular subject. Perhaps you love a foreign language or mathematics, or maybe you are intrigued by contemporary social issues. If you decide you want to share this excitement and stimulation with others, teaching offers a natural channel for doing so. As one teacher put it: "I want them to be exposed to what I love and what I teach. I want them to know somebody, even if they think I'm crazy, who's genuinely excited about history."[5]

Using your extended vacation times to continue your education can further advance your intellectual stimulation and growth. The Internet is a great source for finding creative teaching ideas, and staying on top of emerging developments in your field. Other helpful sources are journals, weekly educational newspapers, conferences and meetings sponsored by school districts and professional education associations. You have ready access to the intellectual community.

PORTRAIT OF THE TEACHER AS AN ARTIST

You can construct everything from original simulation games to videotapes, from multimedia programs to educational software. Even the development of a superb lesson plan is an exercise in creativity, as you strive to meet the needs of the diverse children who come into your classroom each day. Some people draw clear parallels between teachers and artists and highlight the creativity that is essential to both:

> I love to teach as a painter loves to paint, as a musician loves to play, as a singer loves to sing, as a strong man rejoices to run a race. Teaching is an art—an art so great and so difficult to master that a man [or woman] can spend a long life at it without realizing much more than his [or her] limitations and mistakes, and his [or her] distance from the ideal. But the main aim of my happy days has been to become a good teacher. Just as every architect wishes to be a good architect and every professional poet strives toward perfection.[6]

The Bad News . . .

large numbers of women generally face prestige problems, and teaching is no exception. (There may come a day when we will not have to mention this issue, but, for the time being, prejudice still exists.) Unfortunately, in our materialistic society, people's work is frequently measured by the size of the paycheck—and most teachers' wallets are modestly endowed. Despite the resurgence of support for teachers, when it comes to the game of impressing people, teachers are still not collecting a large pile of status chips.

THE SAME MATTERS YEAR AFTER YEAR AFTER YEAR

Yes, you will be continually involved in academic subject matter—but the word continually is a double-edged sword. Teaching, like most other jobs, entails a lot of repetition. You may tire of teaching the same subject matter to a new crop of students every September. If this happens, boredom and a feeling that you are getting intellectually stale may replace excitement. For some, working with students who seem unmoved by the ideas that excite you can be frustrating and disillusioning. You may turn to your colleagues for intellectual stimulation, only to find that they are more concerned about the cost of auto repair and TV shows than the latest genetic decoding breakthrough or the intricacies of current government policy.

Since you are just embarking on your teaching career, you may find it difficult to imagine yourself becoming bored with the world of education. However, as you teach class after class on the same subject, interest can wane.

THE BOG OF MINDLESS ROUTINE

Much is said about the creativity of teaching, but, under close inspection, the job breaks down into a lot of mindless routine as well. A large percentage of the day is consumed by clerical work, child control, housekeeping, announcements, and participation in ceremonies. Although there is opportunity for ingenuity and inventiveness, most of the day is spent in the three Rs of ritual, repetition, and routine. As one disgruntled sixth-grade teacher in Los Angeles said,

> Paper work, paper work. The nurse wants the health cards, so you have to stop and get them. Another teacher wants one of your report cards. The principal wants to know how many social science books you have. Somebody else wants to know if you can come to a meeting on such and such a day. Forms to fill out, those crazy forms: Would you please give a breakdown of boys and girls in the class; would you please say how many children you have in reading grade such and such. Forms, messengers—all day long.[7]

continued

The Good News . . .

TO TOUCH A LIFE, TO MAKE A DIFFERENCE

Teaching is more than helping a child master phonics or discover meaning in seemingly lifeless history facts. Each classroom is a composite of the anguish and joy of all its students. You can feel the pain of the child in the fourth seat who always knows the answer, but is too shy to speak. Then there is the rambunctious one who spills all over the classroom in a million random ways, unable to focus on any one task or project. Or that physically unattractive victim, who inspires taunts and abuse from usually well-mannered classmates. You can be the one who makes a difference in their lives:

> I am happy that I found a profession that combines my belief in social justice with my zeal for intellectual excellence. My career choice has meant much anxiety, anger, and disappointment. But it has also produced profound joy. I have spent my work life committed to a just cause: the education of Boston high school students. Welcome to our noble teaching profession and our enduring cause.[8]

BETTER SALARIES, LONGER VACATIONS

In the last two decades, the average teacher salary, adjusted for inflation, rose about 20 percent, from the $30,000 to the $40,000 bracket, though salaries vary enormously from one community to another. The average teacher in South Dakota earns only in the low $30,000 range, while California teachers average mid $50,000. Additional salary can be earned by working in the summer or accepting extra faculty responsibilities. Occupational benefits, such as health and retirement, are generally excellent. You will enjoy long vacations. A few school districts provide teachers with an opportunity to study, travel, or engage in other forms of professional improvement through an extended leave or sabbatical program. All of these considerations make for a more relaxed and varied lifestyle, one that gives you time for yourself as well as your family. Whether you use your "free time" to be with your family, to travel, or to make extra money, time flexibility is a definite plus.

The Bad News . . .

THE TARNISHED IDEALIST

We all hope to be that special teacher, the one students remember and talk about long after they graduate. But too often, idealistic goals give way to survival—simply making it through from one day to the next. New teachers find themselves judged on their ability to maintain a quiet, orderly room. Idealistic young teachers find the worship of control incompatible with their humanistic goals. Likewise, they feel betrayed if a student naively mistakes their offer of friendship as a sign of weakness or vulnerability. As a result, many learn the trade secret—"don't smile until Christmas" (or Chanukah, Kwanzaa, or Ramadan, depending on your community)—and adopt it quickly. Even veteran teachers throw up their hands in despair and too often leave teaching. Teacher-student conflict can lead to lost idealism, and worse. Some teachers are concerned with the increase in discipline problems, and a decrease in support from parents and others. How can teachers stay inspired when their classrooms lack basic supplies?[9] Trying to make a difference may result in more frustration than satisfaction.

BUT SALARIES STILL HAVE A LONG WAY TO GO

Although teachers' salaries have improved, they still lag behind what most people would call a good income. Teachers ages 22 to 28 earned an average $7,894 less per year than other college-educated adults of the same age by the late 1990s. The gap was three times greater for teachers 44 to 50, who earned approximately $25,000 less than their counterparts in other occupations.[10] A history teacher says, "It's really difficult to maintain a family . . . I'm not sure I could have done it then except for a wife who's not demanding or pushy. She's completely comfortable with the things we have, and we don't have a great deal."[11] And the following comment comes from a well-to-do suburban community: "You can always tell the difference between the teachers' and the students' parking lots. The students' lot is the one with all the new cars in it."[12] The long vacations are nice—but they are also long periods without income.

 YOU BE THE JUDGE

Which of these arguments and issues are most influential in determining if teaching is a good fit for you? Is there a particular point that is most persuasive, pro or con? What does that tell you about yourself? On a scale from 1 to 10, where 10 is "really committed" to teaching, and 1 is "I want no part of that job," what number are you? Remember that number as you read the text and go through this course—and see if you change that rating in the pages and weeks ahead.

enforce school rules. When asked about the adequacy of resources, such as textbooks, supplies, and copying machines, the majority of teachers agreed that the materials were available as needed. But not everything surveyed was rosy.

High on the teachers' "Top Ten List of Things I'd Like to Change about My Job" was salary, with 55 percent registering their dissatisfaction. Salaries, although better today than they have been historically, are still judged inadequate (Figure 1.1). But salaries are not the only concern. Incremental obstacles pile up and wear down a teacher. Teachers focus their complaints on heavy workloads and extra responsibilities, discipline issues, negative attitudes expressed by students, unresponsive school administrators, and lack of support from parents. Parental support, like most of these factors, varies dramatically from school to school. If you are interested in a teaching position with a high level of parental support and involvement, you would be well advised to begin your search in private schools and at the elementary level.

Despite the common perception that teachers are disillusioned, the majority of teachers report that they love teaching. By 2000, fewer teachers registered complaints than did teachers in the 1980s, yet the rapid turnover of teachers, as well as continuing teacher shortages, underscores the need for greater improvement in the quality of their working lives.

Professionalism at the Crossroads

What noble employment is more valuable to the state than that of the man who instructs the rising generation?

(Cicero)

Education makes a people easy to lead, but difficult to drive; easy to govern but impossible to enslave.

(Lord Brougham)

I shou'd think it as glorius [sic] employment to instruct poor children as to teach the children of the greatest monarch.

(Elizabeth Elstob)

The man who can make hard things easy is the educator.

(Ralph Waldo Emerson)

I touch the future; I teach.

(Christa McAuliffe)

Literature, philosophy, and history are replete with such flowery tributes to teaching. In many minds, in some of our greatest minds, teaching is considered the noblest of professions. But the realities of the job do not always mesh with such admirable appraisals, resulting in a painful clash between noble ideals and practical realities. In the preface to *Goodbye, Mr. Chips*, James Hilton writes that his portrait of the lovable schoolmaster is a "tribute to a great profession." But an article in the *NEA Today*, a teacher's magazine, is entitled: "Are You Treated Like a Professional? Or a Tall Child?" For many teachers, the "Tall Child" analogy is closer to the truth.

The problem is not new. Here's what Ellen Hogan Steele, a teacher who cares passionately about the privilege, responsibility, and dignity of belonging to a profession, said back in the 1970s:

> I recall a carpenter—he visited my home to discuss a renovation—talking about a school strike in a neighboring town. Unaware of my occupation he called teachers ignorant, lazy, and lucky to be employed.

GLOBAL VIEW
If you have international students in your class (or students who have been schooled abroad), ask them to discuss teacher satisfaction in other cultures. Visit the Institute for International Education (www.iie.org) for information on teacher experiences in different countries. The site also describes opportunities to teach abroad, including the Fulbright scholarship program.

OVERHEADS 3–13
Teacher Salaries

GLOBAL VIEW
Encourage students to research teacher wages internationally. How might salary impact status and lifestyle issues abroad?

TEACHING TIP
Explain the employment picture in your local school districts. Include information on hiring needs by subject area, grade level or specialization.

RAP 1.6 CAREER
Information Document, p. 119

MULTIPLE INTELLIGENCE CONNECTION
Have students imagine giant posters highlighting each of these poignant remarks. What designs or images come to mind? Might their posters hang in today's hallways or teacher's rooms?

FOCUS QUESTION 3
Can we consider teaching to be a profession?

FIGURE 1.1
Average and beginning teacher salary in 2001–2002 ranked by average salary within region.

State	Average Salary	Beginning Salary	State	Average Salary	Beginning Salary
NEW ENGLAND			**SOUTHEAST**		
Connecticut	$52,376	$34,551	Georgia	$43,933	$32,283
Rhode Island	51,619	30,272	North Carolina	42,118	29,359
Massachusetts	48,732	32,746	Virginia	41,752	31,238
New Hampshire	39,915	25,611	South Carolina	39,923	27,268
Vermont	39,771	25,229	Florida	39,275	30,096
Maine	37,300	24,054	Tennessee	38,515	28,857
			Kentucky	37,951	26,813
MID-EAST			Alabama	37,206	29,938
New York	$51,020	$34,577	West Virginia	36,775	25,633
District of Columbia	51,000	31,982	Louisiana	36,328	28,229
Pennsylvania	50,599	31,866	Arkansas	36,026	27,565
New Jersey	50,115	35,311	Mississippi	33,295	24,567
Delaware	49,011	32,868			
Maryland	48,251	31,828	**ROCKY MOUNTAINS**		
			Colorado	$40,659	$28,001
GREAT LAKES			Idaho	39,194	25,316
Michigan	$52,497	$32,649	Utah	38,153	26,806
Illinois	49,679	31,761	Wyoming	37,853	26,773
Indiana	44,609	28,440	Montana	34,379	22,344
Ohio	44,266	29,953			
Minnesota	42,175	29,998	**FAR WEST**		
Wisconsin	41,056	27,397	California	$54,348	$34,180
			Alaska	49,028	36,035
PLAINS			Oregon	46,033	31,026
Iowa	$38,230	$27,553	Nevada	44,621	28,734
Kansas	37,059	26,596	Hawaii	44,306	31,340
Nebraska	36,236	26,010	Washington	43,470	28,348
Missouri	36,053	27,554			
North Dakota	32,468	20,988	**OUTLYING AREAS**		
South Dakota	31,383	23,938	Guam	$35,038	$28,054
			Virgin Islands	34,764*	22,751*
SOUTHWEST			Puerto Rico	22,164	18,000
Texas	$39,230	$30,938			
Arizona	38,510	27,648	**U.S. Average**	**$44,367**	**$30,719**
New Mexico	36,716	27,579			
Oklahoma	32,870	27,547			

*2000–2001 salaries.

SOURCE: American Federation of Teachers, annual survey of state departments of education.

REFLECTION: How do states and regions differ in teacher salaries? What are some of the reasons for these disparities? Why do you believe that private schools can attract teachers, while generally paying less salary?

"Can you imagine thinking they should make as much as me?" he fumed.

I can imagine that. I presume my work to be as demanding and skilled as that of the carpenters I employ. . . . What do teachers want? This teacher wants to make a reasonable living, to be recognized as a person who performs an essential service, to be considered an expert in my small area of experience, to be occasionally praised when I do well and to be helped to improve when I don't. . . . In short, I want someone to know that I'm alive, and unless they do, I'll keep on kicking.

Says English teacher Carol Davis:

> We're told when to get here, when to leave, what to teach, what to want, what not to want, and how to think. . . . I'm trained in how to teach English, but I'm rarely asked for my opinion. If I were to be "promoted out of my classroom" my opinion would be more respected immediately. The irony would be that I'd no longer be teaching children.[13]

Collectively, teachers struggle to empower their profession; individually, they struggle to empower their students.

Many teachers feel that the satisfaction they realize inside the classroom is too often jeopardized by forces beyond the classroom: politicians mandating numerous standardized tests, demanding parents offering little support, and textbook publishers determining course content. Teachers desire more autonomy and control over their careers, and like all of us, want to be treated with more respect. Teachers increasingly see themselves as reflective decision makers, selecting objectives and teaching procedures to meet the needs of different learners.[14] They must know their subject matter, learning theory, research on various teaching methodologies, and techniques for curriculum development.[15] Some believe that the problems confronting teachers stem from the more pervasive issue of professional status and competence. Are teachers professionals? What does it take to be a professional, anyway? *Educating a Profession*, a publication of the American Association of Colleges for Teacher Education (AACTE), lists twelve criteria for a **profession.** We have shortened these criteria below, and ask you to consider each one and decide if you believe that teaching meets these criteria. After marking your reactions in the appropriate column, compare your reactions with those of your classmates.

Criteria for a Profession	True for Teaching	Not True for Teaching	Don't Know
1. Professions provide essential services to the individual and society.	_____	_____	_____
2. Each profession is concerned with an identified area of need or function (e.g., maintenance of physical and emotional health).	_____	_____	_____
3. The profession possesses a unique body of knowledge and skills (professional culture).	_____	_____	_____
4. Professional decisions are made in accordance with valid knowledge, principles, and theories.	_____	_____	_____
5. The profession is based on undergirding disciplines from which it builds its own applied knowledge and skills.	_____	_____	_____
6. Professional associations control the actual work and conditions of the profession (e.g., admissions, standards, licensing).	_____	_____	_____
7. There are performance standards for admission to and continuance in the profession.	_____	_____	_____

TEACHING TIP
Goodbye, Mr. Chips (1939) is a classic British film looking back on a meritorious teacher's commitment to schooling. Before Mr. Chipping's first assignment, he is warned "Our profession is not an easy one, Mr. Chipping. It calls for something more than a University degree. Our business is to mold men. It demands character and courage." So, beyond a University degree, what attributes do students suspect are necessary for today's teachers?

CRITICAL THINKING QUESTION
What remarks have students overheard about teachers? How did they respond? If they had another chance, what would they say now?

CLASS ACTIVITY: POINT-COUNTERPOINT: A PANEL DISCUSSION
IM, Activity 1:4

CLASS ACTIVITY:
BUILDING BLOCKS OF
MY IDEAL TEACHING
POSITION
IM, Activity 1:1

CLASS ACTIVITY:
STUDENT POLL
IM, Activity 1:7

INTERACTIVE ACTIVITY
Is Teaching a Profession?
Do this exercise online.
See how other students
responded to each
statement.

8. Preparation for and induction into the profession requires a protracted preparation program, usually in a college or university professional school.	_____	_____	_____
9. There is a high level of public trust and confidence in the profession and in the skills and competence of its members.	_____	_____	_____
10. Individual practitioners are characterized by a strong service motivation and lifetime commitment to competence.	_____	_____	_____
11. The profession itself determines individual competence.	_____	_____	_____
12. There is relative freedom from direct or public job supervision of the individual practitioner. The professional accepts this responsibility and is accountable through his or her profession to the society.[16]	_____	_____	_____

Do not be surprised if you find some criteria that do not apply to teaching. In fact, even the occupations that spring to mind when you hear the word *professional*—doctor, lawyer, clergy, college professor—do not completely measure up to all these criteria.

Those who developed these twelve criteria for a profession also listed another twelve criteria that would describe a **semiprofession.** Read these items carefully, and compare them with the characteristics that define a profession. Consider each item separately. Does it accurately describe teaching, or does it sell teaching short? After you have considered all the items and have marked your reactions in the appropriate column, decide whether you think teaching is actually a profession, or whether it would more accurately be termed a semiprofession.

Criteria for a Semiprofession	True for Teaching	Not True for Teaching	Don't Know
1. Lower in occupational status	_____	_____	_____
2. Shorter training periods	_____	_____	_____
3. Lack of societal acceptance that the nature of the service and/or the level of expertise justifies the autonomy that is granted to the professions	_____	_____	_____
4. A less specialized and less highly developed body of knowledge and skills	_____	_____	_____
5. Markedly less emphasis on theoretical and conceptual bases for practice	_____	_____	_____
6. A tendency for the individual to identify with the employment institution more and with the profession less	_____	_____	_____
7. More subject to administrative and supervisory surveillance and control	_____	_____	_____

8. Less autonomy in professional decision making, with accountability to superiors rather than to the profession

   _____ _____ _____

9. Management by persons who have themselves been prepared and served in that semiprofession

   _____ _____ _____

10. A preponderance of women

   _____ _____ _____

11. Absence of the right of privileged communication between client and professional

   _____ _____ _____

12. Little or no involvement in matters of life and death[17]

   _____ _____ _____

Where do you place teaching? If you had a tough time deciding, you are not alone. Many people feel that teaching falls somewhere between professional and semiprofessional in status. Perhaps we should think of it as an "emerging" profession. Or perhaps teaching is, and will remain, a "submerged" profession. Either way, teachers find themselves in a career with both potential and frustration. Yet for most new teachers, the potential outweighs the frustration. During their first five years in the classroom, 80 percent report that they would choose teaching again (see Figure 1.2).

Why does all this "profession talk" matter? You may be more concerned with *real* questions: Will I be good at teaching? Do I want to work with children? What age level is best for me? Will the salary be enough to give me the quality of life that I want for myself and my family? You may be thinking, Why should I split hairs over whether I belong to a profession? Who cares? The issue of professionalism may not matter to you now or even during your first year or two of teaching, when classroom survival and performance have top priority. But if you stay in teaching, this idea of professionalism will grow in significance, perhaps becoming one of the most important issues you face. Even now, as a student, you can become more reflective in your views of teaching and learning; you can begin to refine your own professional

CLASS ACTIVITY: TEACHING: PROFESSION OR SEMIPROFESSION? IM, Activity 1:6

TEACHING TIP This Frame of Reference presents a twist on the hourly wage of teachers— as babysitters. What is the class reaction? What other salaries frame their perspectives (music and sport stars, fast-food servers, entrepreneurs, e-traders)?

OVERHEAD 14 New Teacher Satisfaction and Willingness to Enter Teaching Again

FIGURE 1.2

New teacher satisfaction and willingness to enter teaching again.

SOURCE: Public Agenda Online, April 2000. (See also National Education Association "Status of the American Public School Teacher," 1995–1996 © 1997.)

Percent of Teachers Who Say

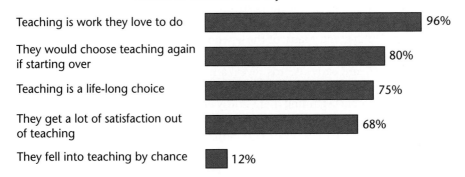

Teaching is work they love to do	96%
They would choose teaching again if starting over	80%
Teaching is a life-long choice	75%
They get a lot of satisfaction out of teaching	68%
They fell into teaching by chance	12%

REFLECTION: Why do you believe that there is a gap between the popular image of disillusioned teachers and the results of this survey? This survey data comes from those who have been teaching for five years or less. Why do you think that the past decade has been marked by an increase in the percentage of teachers who would choose a career in teaching again?

Teachers work with children only a few hours a day, and some people, not very sympathetic to the demands on teachers, believe that they should be paid pretty much as babysitters. Surprisingly, some teachers see an advantage in that system. Babysitters get about $6.00 an hour, so for a five-hour day, teachers would earn $30 per child. For a class of 25, that would be $750 a day. The school year is 187 days, so that would be $140,250. Summers, week-ends, and evenings off. Teachers as babysitters, an idea with some merit!

REFLECTION: What factors do you think should impact a teacher's pay? Class size? Subject area? Grade level?

behaviors and outlooks. Beyond your personal decisions, you will confront a difficult question faced by so many teachers through time: Is teaching a genuine profession? Or does teaching languish in semiprofessional status? The issue remains at a crossroads.

 ## From Normal Schools to Board-Certified Teachers

FOCUS QUESTION 4
How has teacher preparation changed over the years?

Basic to any discussion of professionalism is the question of how its members are prepared. As you read this brief history of teacher preparation, think about whether teachers are prepared in a way commensurate with belonging to a profession.

From colonial America into the twentieth century, teacher education scarcely existed. More often than not, teachers in colonial America received no formal preparation at all. Most elementary teachers never even attended a secondary school. Some learned their craft by serving as apprentices to master teachers, a continuation of the medieval guild system. Others were indentured servants paying for their passage to America by teaching for a fixed number of years. Many belonged to the "sink-or-swim" school of teaching, and the education of an untold number of students undoubtedly sank with them.

VIDEO SEGMENT 2
The Crusade to Educate Teachers

The smaller number of teachers working at the secondary level—in academies or Latin grammar schools and as private tutors—had usually received some college education, more often in Europe than in America. Some knowledge of the subject matter was considered desirable, but no particular aptitude for teaching or knowledge of teaching skills was considered necessary. Teaching was viewed not as a career but as temporary employment. Many of those who entered teaching, especially at the elementary level, were teenagers who taught for only a year or two. Others were of dubious character, and early records reveal a number of teachers fired for drinking or stealing.

From this humble beginning there slowly emerged a more professional program for teacher education. In 1823, the **Reverend Samuel Hall** established a **normal school** (named for its European counterpart) in Concord, Vermont. This private school provided elementary school graduates with formal training in teaching skills. Reverend Hall's modest normal school marked the beginning of teacher education in America. Sixteen years later, in 1839, **Horace Mann** was instrumental in establishing the first state-supported normal school in Lexington, Massachusetts. Normal schools typically provided a two-year teacher training program, consisting of academic subjects as well as teaching methodology. Some students came directly from elementary school; others had completed a secondary education. Into the 1900s, the normal school was the backbone of teacher education. The lack of rigorous professional training contributed to the less than professional treatment afforded teachers. The following is a teacher contract from the 1920s, a contract that offers a poignant insight into how teachers were seen . . . and treated.

CRITICAL THINKING
QUESTION
What are the unwritten
assumptions that today's
public makes about teacher
behavior? Have students
formalize their thoughts
into a *pseudo-Teaching
Contract* like the one in
the text, reflecting current
norms. As potential
teachers, extend their
wishful thinking into a
Parent Contract.

Teaching Contract

Miss _____ agrees:

1. Not to get married. This contract becomes null and void immediately if the teacher marries.

2. Not to keep company with men.

3. To be home between the hours of 8 P.M. and 6 A.M. unless in attendance at a school function.

4. Not to loiter downtown in ice-cream parlors.

5. Not to leave town at any time without the permission of the Chairman of the Trustees.

6. Not to smoke cigarettes. This contract becomes null and void immediately if the teacher is found smoking.

7. Not to drink beer, wine, or whiskey. This contract becomes null and void immediately if the teacher is found drinking beer, wine, or whiskey.

8. Not to ride in a carriage or automobile with any man except her brother or father.

9. Not to dress in bright colors.

10. Not to dye her hair.

11. Not to wear less than two petticoats.

12. Not to wear dresses shorter than two inches above the ankles.

13. To keep the schoolroom clean:

    a. To sweep the classroom floor at least once daily.

    b. To scrub the classroom floor at least once weekly with soap and hot water.

    c. To clean the blackboard at least once daily.

    d. To start the fire at 7 A.M. so that the room will be warm by 8 A.M. when the children arrive.

14. Not to wear face powder, mascara, or to paint the lips.

(Reprinted courtesy of the *Chicago Tribune*, September 28, 1975, Section 1.)

As the contract indicates, by the 1900s, teaching was becoming a female occupation. Both female workers and teaching being held in low regard, the reward for the austere dedication detailed in this contract was an unimpressive $75 a month. But as the twentieth century progressed, professional teacher training gained wider acceptance. Enrollments in elementary schools climbed and secondary education gained in popularity, and so did the demand for more and better-trained teachers. Many private colleges and universities initiated teacher education programs, and normal schools expanded to three- and four-year programs, gradually evolving into state teachers' colleges. Interestingly, as attendance grew, these teachers' colleges expanded their programs and began offering courses and career preparation in fields other than teaching. By the 1950s, many of the state teachers' colleges had evolved into state colleges. In fact, some of today's leading universities were originally chartered as normal schools.

The 1980s marked the beginning of the modern effort to reshape education. A number of education reform reports fanned the flames of controversy regarding professionalism and teacher preparation, including one written by a group of prominent education deans. The **Holmes Group,** named for former Harvard Education Dean Henry H. Holmes, debated the teacher preparation issue for several years before releasing its report, entitled ***Tomorrow's Teachers*** (1986).[18] The same year, the Carnegie Forum also issued a highly publicized report, ***A Nation Prepared***.[19] Both reports called for higher standards and increased professionalism for the nation's teachers. The Carnegie report also called for an end to the undergraduate teaching major, to be replaced by master's-level degrees in teaching. While some universities followed this recommendation and created fifth year teacher education programs (bachelor's and master's degrees required for teacher education candidates), other colleges continued their undergraduate education programs. Teacher education remains a hodgepodge of approaches. Some critics place much of the blame on universities themselves, for failing to adequately fund and support schools of education.[20]

But not all of the attention has been on initial teacher education. In the 1990s, the Carnegie Forum was influential in creating the **National Board for Professional Teaching Standards (NBPTS)**. The goal of the NBPTS is to recognize extraordinary teachers, those whose skills and knowledge indicate their high level of achievement. This is a significant departure from simply licensing new teachers who reach minimal standards. During its first years of operation, the NBPTS developed assessment procedures to identify highly competent teachers, teachers who would be designated **board-certified**. Like medicine, teaching now had not just an entry license—a standard teaching license—but advanced recognition of a higher level of skills and competencies. Thousands of educators annually compile professional portfolios (including videotaped examples of their teaching), and undergo assessment tests and interviews en route to becoming board-certified teachers. As you might imagine, the board assessment is not inexpensive. All this effort is invested in recognizing superior teachers, a concept that was not even considered a decade or two ago, and reflects the high priority the public places on education (see Figure 1.3).

As teachers aspire to board certification, states and communities are developing ways to recognize their accomplishments. Most states and a few school districts now pay for their teachers to prepare for board certification. Many teachers who become board-certified receive stipends or are placed on a higher salary scale. Others are given release time to work with new teachers.[21] Will new responsibilities be found for board-certified teachers? Are we developing a new cadre of educational leaders, "lead" or "principal" teachers? Will board certification evolve into a sort of national merit pay? Or will board certification simply become another failed attempt to transform what some view as a semi-profession into a true profession?[22] These and other pivotal questions will likely be answered during your time as a classroom teacher.

IN THE NEWS

Sweetening the Pot

How can school districts attract teachers? Offer rewards! (OK, we'll call them incentives.) Maryland is offering signing bonuses for bright college graduates going into teaching, extra pay for teachers working in high poverty areas, reduced tax rate for teachers, and a $5,000 home-buying grant.

SOURCE: "Sweetening the Pot," *2000 Editorial Projects in Education,* 19 (18), pp. 28–30, 33–34.

What's new in education? Click on *News Feeds.*

Different Paths to Teacher Education

Even as educators strive toward professional status, there is no consensus on how best to prepare teachers. The two teacher education approaches that currently

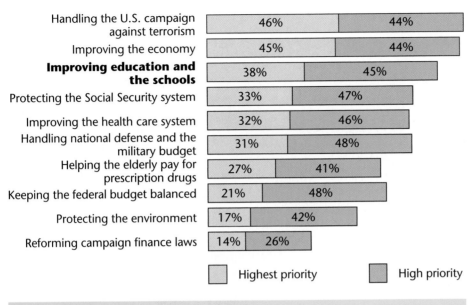

FIGURE 1.3

America's priorities.

SOURCE: Public Agenda, 2003, ABC News/*The Washington Post*, January 2002.

Handling the U.S. campaign against terrorism — 46% — 44%
Improving the economy — 45% — 44%
Improving education and the schools — 38% — 45%
Protecting the Social Security system — 33% — 47%
Improving the health care system — 32% — 46%
Handling national defense and the military budget — 31% — 48%
Helping the elderly pay for prescription drugs — 27% — 41%
Keeping the federal budget balanced — 21% — 48%
Protecting the environment — 17% — 42%
Reforming campaign finance laws — 14% — 26%

☐ Highest priority   ☐ High priority

REFLECTION: Why do you think Americans place such a high priority on improving education? Do you believe that this strong support for education helps to create a strong teacher profession? Why or why not?

FOCUS QUESTION 5

Do educators and the public agree on the most effective way to prepare teachers?

RELATED READING

One Day All Children . . . : The Unlikely Triumph of Teach for America and What I Learned along the Way by Wendy Kopp (2001).

dominate the landscape can be categorized as traditional and alternative. The traditional teacher education path is a preservice program in which students study the science of teaching and the subject matter, and then do a clinical teaching experience. These programs lead to either a B.A. or an M.A., or may simply involve a fifth year of study for those who want to obtain a teacher's license. The second, more controversial approach emphasizes on-the-job training rather than preservice preparation, and has been termed *alternative* teacher education. Students in these programs seek **alternative licensure** through a structured apprenticeship, an untraditional route to obtaining a teacher's license that is now possible in virtually all states. These alternative programs assume that beginning teachers already know their subject matter, and with some time in the classroom, can acquire and refine their teaching skills. The extent of training and support given to new teachers in alternative programs varies greatly, and this has become a point of contention. Imagine yourself in one of the nation's most challenging classrooms, and feeling less than well trained. This is the challenge facing programs like **Teach for America (TFA).** Although relatively small in size, TFA has enjoyed great success in recruiting highly motivated and talented recruits who find themselves in very distressed schools. Supporters of the program point out that many of these volunteers become excellent teachers, and that the proportion of teachers of color is higher in Teach for America than in traditional teacher education programs. Moreover, many of the challenging schools where these teachers are assigned have a difficult time finding any teachers, and eagerly welcome these new recruits. Defenders of such fast track training programs argue that "on-the-job-training" is not new, and can be quite effective.

Not very long ago, lawyers and doctors were prepared for their professions through similar apprenticeships. But many educators see such programs as the height of irresponsibility, quite the opposite of profession building.[23] Teach for America critics like

Meet Sarah, Amy and Claudia, representing a three-generation teaching family. Sarah started in 1948 when the average annual salary was under _____. Her daughter Claudia, a recently retired principal, began teaching in 1969, when the salaries had climbed to _____. When Amy entered the field in 2001, the nation's teaching wage averaged _____. Moving beyond salary, what other differences might have characterized teaching in 1948, 1969, and 2001? If you could interview these three educators, what questions might you ask?

Answers: 1948—$3,000; 1969—$8,626; 2001—$44,367.

SOURCES: American Federation of Teachers www.aft.org/; National Center for Educational Statistics
http://nces.ed.gov/pubs2001/digest/dt076.html

Linda Darling-Hammond argue that today's classroom challenges require more thorough career preparation, and that even when teachers are in short supply, professional standards must be maintained.[24] Some detractors argue that students in alternative programs learn less[25] and are more likely to leave teaching after only a few years.[26] How can teaching ever become a real profession, they ask, if we train and license teachers in such "quickie" teacher education programs?

Research is not yet conclusive on the relative effectiveness of either approach, and it would not be a stretch to conclude that strong and weak programs can be found within each model. In fact, comparing these two models may not be as productive as finding the answers to some critical questions, questions that can be asked of any teacher education program: Do the candidates have a strong background in their subject matter? Have they received effective pedagogical training? Has there been a carefully planned and implemented clinical experience?[27] As you begin your own teacher education program, whatever type it is, you may want to consider these questions and think about the specific content and skills you would find most useful. Think of yourself as a consumer of teacher education—because in a very real sense, you are. If you were to design a teacher education program, what would it look like? People hold sharply divided views on how best to prepare teachers. In 1997, Public Agenda, a nonpartisan, nonprofit organization, surveyed 900 education professors from around the nation. Public Agenda then compared their responses not only with those of the public, but also with those of practicing classroom teachers. Public Agenda's poll found dramatic differences on how people envision good teacher training. On the issues below, how do your opinions compare to those of the public, classroom teachers, and education professors?

On Discipline . . .

Are discipline problems a sign of student boredom, or an indicator that firm standards and classroom control are lacking?

The Public Agenda survey indicates that education professors believe that most students arrive at school wanting to learn and that student misbehavior is typically a sign of poor teaching.[28] Professors shy away from advocating punitive measures, and only 30 percent report that their teacher education programs stress skills such as managing a difficult classroom. Education professors stress that good teaching is an effective remedy for student misbehavior.

On the other hand, both the public and classroom teachers indicate that schools should focus more on control and discipline. Teachers indicate that even small behavior problems often lead to bigger ones, and misbehaving students can cause major educational disruptions. That is one reason why so many teachers believe that students caught with drugs or weapons should be permanently removed from school.

> **REFLECTION:** What discipline policies and rules might you create in your classroom? How do you view the relationship between good teaching and student behavior?

On Competition . . .

Should teachers create a more rigorous and competitive learning environment?

Today's schools are being pressed to meet specific standards, resulting in more testing and increased competition. Yet, many education professors have reservations about this trend. Professors report a general aversion to academic competition and external rewards, and you are unlikely to see their cars adorned with bumper stickers such as: "My kid is an honor student at Mia Hamm High School."

Parents surveyed were more supportive of a competitive learning environment, and regale listeners with vivid memories of their own school days, filled with rigorous tests, gobs of homework, and incredibly demanding teachers. (OK, maybe their memories have been colored by time, and their school days were not as challenging as they recall, and they didn't have to walk three miles uphill, in the snow, *to* AND *from* school when they were children. Nevertheless, they remember and value tougher, more demanding schools.) It's not surprising that 70 percent of the public believes that schools need to raise standards and not promote students who do poorly.

On Honesty and Dependability . . .

How much emphasis should teachers place on traditional values, such as punctuality, politeness, and even honesty?

The Public Agenda survey indicates strong support for student behavior that reflects civility and politeness, honesty and punctuality. Professors, teachers, and the public concur that these behaviors lead to more effective learning. They believe that if students were to arrive at school on time and were generally more dependable, for example, academic achievement would improve significantly. The disagreement is on how to accomplish this. Only 8 percent of the professors reported that their programs prepare teachers to handle problems such as cheating. Eighty-five percent of the professors felt that schools are already expected to deal with too many problems (see Figure 1.4).

On Urban Legends about Teaching . . .

As you can tell, the public does not lack for ideas as to what it takes to make an effective teacher. Sometimes these ideas move from the rational to the extreme: "Teachers are born, not made," or "To be a good teacher, all you really need to know is the subject you are teaching." Like the urban legend of alligators cavorting in the New York City sewer system, these teaching myths have taken on a life of their own. Let's take a brief look at some of the urban legends about teacher education.

Teachers are born, not made: It is certainly true that some students enter a teacher education program with impressive instructional skills, yet training and practice is what is needed to transform a strong teacher into a gifted one. Teaching is far from unique in this. When a group of Olympians and their coaches were asked what it takes to become a champion, none of the answers suggested that they were "born" champions. On the contrary, the athletes credited well-designed practices and good coaching. Accomplished musicians attribute their performance to hours of focused practice, as do master chess players. So too, superior teachers are trained, not born.

All you really need to know is the subject you are teaching: While it is true that subject mastery is critical in effective teaching, research reveals that teachers skilled in **pedagogy,** the art and science of teaching, especially teaching methods and strategies, outperform teachers with superior subject area knowledge. Clearly, the most successful teachers do not view this as an either/or proposition. Effective teaching requires both knowledge of the subject and instructional skills.[29]

Teacher education students are less talented than other college majors: This popular canard lives on despite very mixed evidence. On the one hand, education majors are

FIGURE 1.4

What's Worth Teaching Teachers
These are the qualities education professors believe teacher education programs should impart to their students.

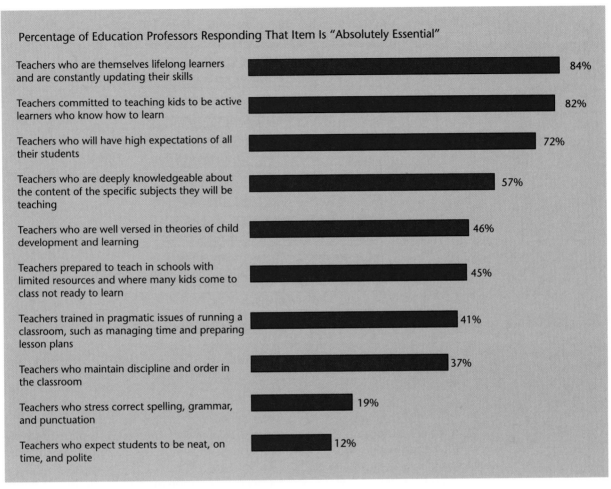

Percentage of Education Professors Responding That Item Is "Absolutely Essential"

Teachers who are themselves lifelong learners and are constantly updating their skills	84%
Teachers committed to teaching kids to be active learners who know how to learn	82%
Teachers who will have high expectations of all their students	72%
Teachers who are deeply knowledgeable about the content of the specific subjects they will be teaching	57%
Teachers who are well versed in theories of child development and learning	46%
Teachers prepared to teach in schools with limited resources and where many kids come to class not ready to learn	45%
Teachers trained in pragmatic issues of running a classroom, such as managing time and preparing lesson plans	41%
Teachers who maintain discipline and order in the classroom	37%
Teachers who stress correct spelling, grammar, and punctuation	19%
Teachers who expect students to be neat, on time, and polite	12%

SOURCE: *Different Drummers: How Teachers of Teachers View Public Education*, Public Agenda, 1997.

REFLECTION: Do you concur with the qualities rated as important—or relatively unimportant—by education professors? Are there areas of disagreement? Can you add a skill that you would like to acquire—one that is missing from this list?

less likely to score in the top 25 percent on the SATs than the general population. On the other hand, adult literacy surveys (see Figure 1.5) show that teachers attain scores similar to those of physicians, writers, engineers, and social workers.[30]

These urban legends aside, it is certainly true that teacher education programs are stronger today than they have been in years. In 1997, 64 percent of teachers gave their own teacher preparation a grade of *A* or *B*. Compare this to 1984, when only 49 percent of teachers awarded such high grades to their programs.[31] That's a remarkable—and encouraging—increase. Yet far more needs to be done. Universities typically spend less on teacher education students than those enrolled in other professional schools. Only a handful of states actually measure teacher performance

OVERHEAD 16

What Grade Would You Give Your Current Teacher Education Program?

FIGURE 1.5

Adult prose literacy scores by selected occupations.

SOURCE: David C. Berliner, "A Personal Response to Those Who Bash Teacher Education," *Journal of Teacher Education* 51, no. 5, November/December 2000.

REFLECTION: Why is there a popular perception of low teacher competence, despite their strong scores on tests like this one? Which of these occupations that score close to teaching do you find particularly surprising?

in the classroom, and as long as some alternative licensure programs place relatively untrained teachers in the classroom, teacher education will continue to be far less than it could and should be.[32]

Why the improvement? Today's teacher preparation programs typically emphasize current research as well as practical classroom skills, often working in close collaboration with local schools. Many teacher education students are studying at the graduate level, bringing more of life's experiences to the classroom than did their predecessors, all signs of positive changes in teacher preparation.

Quality professional preparation suggests not only increased professional status, but also the responsibility that goes with that training. This translates into teacher influence over school policies, procedures, schedules, and curriculum. Yet, teachers are still kept far from policy-making circles. When Andy Baumgartner, National Teacher of the Year in 2000, criticized the lack of significant teacher representation on a commission to reform education in his home state of Georgia, he quickly became *persona non grata*. The governor would not have his photo taken with him, and several politicians roundly criticized him for his audacity.[33]

In the traditional "top-down" organization of schools, teachers find themselves with little influence over education policy, and little say in how schools operate. Yet other organizations do not lack imagination in how they view or treat employees. In fact, we need only look skyward to find an innovative example of employee influence.

Southwest Airlines and Teaching

The first time we flew on Southwest Airlines, we really did not know what to expect. We knew that we paid less for the ticket than other airlines charge, and that made us nervous. We had been advised to eat before the flight, since the airline cuisine consisted of a bag of nuts. Since everything was on a first come, first served basis, we were given firm instructions: "Get to the airport early if you want a good seat." We boarded the plane, found a seat and buckled up.

As we began the takeoff, an amazing sound reverberated through the cabin. It sounded like a whistle, a railroad whistle. Dumbstruck, we wondered: what are they using to power the engines? Is there such a thing as a steam plane? Panic turned to relief as we discovered that the flight attendant was blowing into a toy train whistle. By the time we lifted off, most of the passengers were either laughing or joining the flight attendant with their own versions of train sounds. Once airborne, the flight attendants organized a contest. Each passenger willing to tell a joke on the public address system would receive a $50 voucher. The passengers, by their applause, would choose the best jokester, and that person would receive a $100 voucher (a bit higher than the price of the ticket). Someone would fly for fun *and* profit.

If you have ever flown with Southwest, perhaps you have noticed their flight attendants as they walk through an airport. They are the ones wearing shorts and polo shirts instead of traditional uniforms and suits, strolling about in sneakers instead of wingtips or heels, and smiling, if not laughing. Southwest employees look like they are going on vacation instead of going to work. Not only are they more comfortable than many passengers, they seem happier too! So what's going on at Southwest?

In a book called *Nuts!*, Kevin and Jackie Freiberg write about how Southwest Airline's founders rejected a fundamental tenet in American business, the belief that the customer is always right. At Southwest, there are things more important than the customer, even more important than making money. One of those is the happiness of employees. Yes, employees. Employee happiness creates customer happiness. Southwest prides itself on its egalitarian corporate culture, one in which the head of the company explores options and policies with *all* employees, including those with the lowest paychecks. The president visits employees during meals and at work, seeking their ideas for improvements. Meeting employee needs is a top priority. One thing they need, according to Southwest, are celebrations. Yes, celebrations. Personal and corporate accomplishments and milestones are reasons for employees to be honored and for all involved to celebrate and party. Sound strange? Southwest believes that creating a contented, even joyful workforce does more than improve employee self-esteem and create a caring corporate culture; it also sparks innovative suggestions for improved performance. Celebrations break work routines, a necessary prerequisite for viewing work in a different way, and this leads to new and creative ideas for improving performance. The company's mission is not simply to make money. The kind of motivated employees that the company wants to attract need more than a corporate profit mission to spark their commitment. Southwest's mission is somewhat egalitarian and idealistic: to open air travel to people with limited means. "It is not a job, it is a crusade," is the company motto, a crusade that keeps ticket prices incredibly low.

Have we motivated you to buy some stock? (Don't look for it to be listed under a typical three-letter code like *SWA*. The company is listed under *LUV*.) How does the stock do? Even as many airlines descend into bankruptcy or get "absorbed" in corporate takeovers, Southwest has remained independent and its stock price has soared for three decades. The company may seem iconoclastic, but the bottom line has been all

RELATED READING
Nuts! by Kevin and Jackie Freiberg (1998).

FOCUS QUESTION 6
What traits and characteristics are needed for successful teaching?

TEACHING TIP
Poll student responses to several items. Having them stand beside their seats requires them to take a clear position. It may also get some blood flowing in the midst of a long class session. Raising hands can be made more precise: a hand held high means they're *confident,* raised halfway means they're *somewhat sure,* a flip of the wrist suggests they're *only into it a bit.*

green. Its workforce is considered to be the most efficient in the industry, serving twice the usual number of passengers per employee. Southwest has few delays, and one of the best on-time records of any airline. Its safety procedures are more rigorous than the government requires, and it has been voted the safest airline in the sky. All of this comes from the cheapest airfares around.

Before you run off to buy some *LUV* stock, remember that nothing lasts forever, and despite its remarkable progress, Southwest may very well suffer some reverses in the years ahead. But the first three decades at Southwest have been amazing, and they merit a closer look. What has been the formula for the company's success? Many experts say it is the confidence that the executives placed in Southwest employees. As a result, the company attracted inspired employees and created a model workplace. But before we go any further with our airline industry story, this may be a good time to remind ourselves that we are really interested in teaching and schools (thought we forgot, right?), so let's broaden this discussion and also ask: What traits and characteristics are needed for successful teaching? How do these two sets of characteristics compare?

Here's your challenge: Sort out which of the following job attributes are listed by Southwest, and which have been drawn from the literature on effective teaching. (We did alter a few words to avoid any obvious reference to either occupation.) Put a mark in the appropriate columns to indicate which career attributes you believe are sought by Southwest, and which are drawn from teacher education sources. You certainly can check both columns, if that seems to be appropriate.

The final column is for you. Put a check in the last column if you feel that you are being described by that attribute. After you have marked your columns (but before you race off to apply for a position at either a school or an airline), we will look at the lists, and their meaning.

We are hiring for a new position, and invite you to apply. To succeed in this career, you should:[34]	Southwest Airlines	Teacher Education	Does This Describe Me?
1. Have a passion for the job (a purpose you are crazy about)	_____	_____	_____
2. Enjoy and appreciate other people	_____	_____	_____
3. Have a strong work ethic	_____	_____	_____
4. Possess a solid knowledge base	_____	_____	_____
5. Believe in continuous self-improvement	_____	_____	_____
6. Work effectively with people	_____	_____	_____
7. Be a positive member of the community	_____	_____	_____
8. Successfully respond to people's different needs	_____	_____	_____
9. Develop caring and trusting relationships with people	_____	_____	_____
10. Have a sense of humor	_____	_____	_____
11. Maintain your curiosity in life and work	_____	_____	_____
12. Not take yourself too seriously	_____	_____	_____
13. Not "hide" yourself: Be authentic	_____	_____	_____

	Southwest Airlines	Teacher Education	Does This Describe Me?
14. Dare to be different and experiment	_____	_____	_____
15. Pursue "love" and caring over "techniques"	_____	_____	_____
16. Choose service over self-interest	_____	_____	_____
17. Be committed to unleashing the human spirit, yours and others	_____	_____	_____

Have you sorted out which items come from teacher education literature, and which from Southwest Airlines? The first item, having a passion for your job, actually appears on both lists. (Did you check both columns?) In fact, the first ten items are tied to teacher effectiveness. In addition to the first statement, items 11 through 17 are from Southwest Airlines. At the core, to be effective and successful in either job requires a passion or spirit as well as strong interpersonal skills.

Why are we drawing this comparison between the attributes needed to be successful at Southwest and at teaching? We are not being paid for the plug, nor do we own stock in Southwest. We make the comparison because we believe that Southwest offers lessons for all of us. Although a stream of headlines and news stories call for improvement in the nation's schools, there is little agreement on just how to accomplish this. While some school critics demand higher standards and more testing, others believe that technology and computers hold the key to more effective schools. Still others believe that increased competition, parent choice and school vouchers will create stronger schools.

If you are not familiar with these arguments and approaches, worry not. In this text, you will learn about all of these and more. You will also learn that few if any of these education critics do what Southwest did: look to career professionals for answers. What would schools be like if teachers were more autonomous, if they were responsible for the curricular, instructional and testing decisions? How could we design schools to be happier places, where learning is a joyful experience? How can we reward teachers for going that extra mile? (These are not rhetorical questions. How do you think schools would be different if communities were committed to making teachers happy, and giving them meaningful decision-making powers?) Although the personal qualities sought by Southwest and by schools are remarkably similar, few headlines or news stories, few pundits or commentators talk about doing in schools what Southwest did in the airline industry: improving the quality of teachers' lives as a starting point to improving the education of students.

This Southwest story tells you something about us, the authors of this book: We love teaching, but want to love it more. We believe that although teaching is a wonderful career, teachers deserve more than they get, both in money and psychic rewards. We have taught in many different settings, from the military to overseas,

FOCUS QUESTION 7
Is teaching a "good fit" for you?

INTERACTIVE ACTIVITY
What Job Is This?
Match job titles to Education-related job descriptions.

IN THE NEWS

The $100,000 Teacher

Brian Crosby not only teaches at Hoover High just outside Los Angeles, he also knows how to push a button or two. That's what he did in his book, *The $100,000 Teacher*. Crosby argues that the top five percent of teachers be paid six-figure salaries, that bonuses be given for teachers in critical areas like science and math, and that weak teachers be forced to find employment elsewhere. He believes that pay should be tied to classroom performance, and urges teachers "to trade job security for professional integrity."

SOURCE: *The Baltimore Sun*, 2003.

 What's new in education? Click on *News Feeds.*

from elementary school to the university, and while each position gave us joy, we always thought of ways to make those teaching positions better. Like so many careers, teaching has both assets and liabilities, and you would do well to consider both as you look to your own future.

We Like Questions

CLASS ACTIVITY:
MEMORIES OF
MEMORABLE TEACHERS
IM, Activity 1:3

RAP 1.4
Memories of a Teacher,
p. 117

CLASS ACTIVITY:
INTERVIEW
IM, Activity 1:2

CLASS ACTIVITY:
SENTENCE COMPLETION
IM, Activity 1:5

Education is a dynamic field, rife with controversies, misperceptions, surprises, and constant change. Throughout this book, we will work hard to immerse you in that excitement, and to tweak your interest. (OK, so it's not a Stephen King *Fright Night at the School Prom* novel for that rainy day at the beach. But we do want this text to be more exciting and interesting than most, to mirror the enthusiasm that we feel about education.) Issues discussed in this text may well spark questions. A sage once said that the only dumb question is the one not asked. (While this particular sage might have been overrated, we concur with that premise.) This text is all about answering questions. In fact, at the end of the text, we list a number of questions that students typically ask: How do I get a teacher's license? Where are salaries and working conditions the best? What's on the Praxis exam? We not only ask these questions, we try our best to answer them. What if *your* question is not listed? Responding to your questions is one of the purposes of the website that accompanies this book. (Have you visited the Online Learning Center at www.mhhe.com/sadker7e yet?) In addition to attracting and answering student questions, the website is filled with useful Web links, updated news stories, study hints, sample test questions covering each of the chapters in this text, and suggested student activities. We invite you to submit your questions through the text website, and we will try to answer them. In fact, we like questions so much that we will start the questioning ourselves. The following question is a good one to ask first, because if you are interested in becoming a teacher, there is no time like the present to begin.

Q **What Steps Can I Take between Now and Graduation to Make Myself an Attractive Teaching Candidate?**

A **Become Informed about the Job Market.**

FOCUS QUESTION 8
What steps can you take
now on the road to
becoming a teacher?

Begin gathering current information about the job market and search out those particular content areas and skills that will increase your marketability. This information will help you select appropriate courses and extracurricular activities. Geography plays a role, as some local communities face critical teacher shortages, and others have an ample number. Special education and bilingual skills are often in demand, and demographics plays a big role as well. The nation's growing population of students of color is not matched by an adequate number of teachers of color, so there is a great need to attract African Americans, Hispanics, and Asian Americans into the teaching ranks. There are also too few male candidates for elementary teaching positions, and too few female teachers in physics and technology programs, so gender is yet another consideration. To find out more about the teaching job market, you can check educational associations and state departments of education, many of which are listed in the appendix of this text or found on our website. For example, you can contact the National Education Association at 1201 Sixteenth Street, N.W., Washington, DC 20036, or www.nea.org, and the American Federation of Teachers at 555 New Jersey Avenue, N.W., Washington, DC 20001, or www.aft.org.

Actor James Edwards Olmos with Jaime Escalante

For four years, Jaime Escalante had been struggling to build a strong advanced placement (AP) calculus program at Garfield, a troubled East Los Angeles school with a poor academic history. It had been difficult going, but the program finally blossomed with eighteen students, almost double the number from the year before. Every one of them passed the difficult and prestigious AP examination.

During the summer, however, an unpleasant controversy developed. The Educational Testing Service (ETS), which administers the AP exam, told fourteen of the students that a high correspondence in their answers suggested cheating. They would either have to retake the test or have their scores nullified. Escalante, the students, and others protested. There had been no cheating, they argued. It seemed to be just another example of the experts' underestimating the potential of students who are poor and Latino. But the ETS would not budge, so a retest was arranged. Even after a summer away from the theorems and formulas, all of the students passed the test again, many with higher scores than the first time.

After that, Escalante's calculus program took off, and encouraged other Garfield teachers to add and expand AP classes in history, English, biology, and other subjects. By 1987, Garfield had become known as one of the best public schools in the country.[1]

How does Escalante account for his achievements? He sums up much of his teaching as the pursuit of *ganas*, a Spanish word meaning "the will to succeed."

> Really it's not just the knowledge of math. Because to have knowledge is one thing, and to use that knowledge is another, and to know how to teach or how to motivate these kids is the combination of both. My skills are really to motivate these kids, to make them learn, to give them *ganas*—desire to do something—to make them believe they can learn.[2] Anybody, any kid can learn if he or she has the desire to do it. That's what *ganas* is about. The teacher plays an important role in education—we all remember the first teacher who really touched our lives, or gave us some encouragement, or at least appreciated our best. The teacher gives us the desire to learn, the desire to be Somebody.[3]

Escalante's own life story demonstrates *ganas*. When he immigrated to the United States from Bolivia in 1963, he had already been teaching for eleven years, ever since he was 22 years old, gaining a reputation as one of the finest teachers in La Paz. In Bolivia, he was used to teaching without textbooks or other materials, and the low salary required him to teach three sets of classes a day in order to get by. He brought his unpredictable showmanship to the United States, along with his stern father figure. While "Kimo," as he is nicknamed, can be a charming, colorful character, latecomers and those with incomplete assignments find themselves interrogated, hounded by calls to parents, and threatened with a transfer to a less effective school a very long bus ride away. Whether he has to resort to rewards, taunts, afternoon study sessions, or even mild bribery, Escalante refuses to allow students to give up.

> I use the team approach, I make them believe that we have a team which is going to prepare for the Olympics. And our Olympics is the advanced placement calculus exam. I always talk to them and tell them, "Look, we prepared two years for this competition, and you have to play strong defense. Don't let the test put you down. You're the best." And every time the kids go to take the advanced placement calculus exam, they wear the jacket with a bulldog, which is the school mascot, and the kids go to the testing room yelling "Defense! Defense! Defense!"[4]

Escalante continues:

> The teacher has to have the energy of the hottest volcano, the memory of an elephant, and the diplomacy of an ambassador. . . . Really, a teacher has to possess love and knowledge and then has to use this combined passion to be able to accomplish something.[5]

[1] Jay Mathews, *Escalante: The Best Teacher in America* (New York: Henry Holt, 1988).
[2] Quoted in Anne Meek, "On Creating Ganas: A Conversation with Jaime Escalante," *Educational Leadership* 46, no. 5 (February 1989), pp. 46–47.
[3] Ibid.
[4] Ibid.
[5] Ibid.

SOURCE: Adapted from a profile by Rafael Heller.

REFLECTION: How does Jaime Escalante's philosophy and teaching style compare to the teaching career attributes list described in this chapter? Do you think ganas can be taught (to teachers or students) in the classroom, or is it something that you are born with? How does Escalante's career mirror the positive and negative points about a teaching career discussed in *You Be the Judge* (pp. 6–8)?

www.mhhe.com/ sadker To learn more about Jaime Escalante, click on *Profiles in Education.*

For additional sources of information, check with your university's placement office. You may want to begin reading professional education journals that include information about the employment picture. Websites are often the best source of up-to-date information, so you may want to visit sites sponsored by school districts, professional associations, placement services, or your university. You can also visit real sites, such as job fairs sponsored by school districts. Knowledge about the employment picture and the kind of candidate that is in demand can give you a powerful start on your teaching career.

A Make Sure Your Coursework Is Planned Carefully.

Your first concern should be to enroll in courses that fulfill your certification and licensure requirements. We will explore certification and licensure in some depth later in the text, but for now it is worth remembering that, in addition to earning your degree, you want to leave your program licensed to teach. A second consideration is to make yourself more marketable by going beyond minimum course requirements. For example, technology and special education skills are often in demand by schools, as are elementary teachers with special competence in math or any teacher with a proficiency in a second language. Plan to develop a transcript of courses that will reflect a unique, competent, and relevant academic background. Your transcript will be an important part of your overall candidacy for a teaching position.

A Do Not Underestimate the Importance of Extracurricular Activities.

RAP 1.1
Teacher Interview in Your
Subject Area, p. 114

Employers are likely looking for candidates whose background reflects interest and experience in working with children. A day care center or summer camp job may pay less than the local car wash, bank, or restaurant, but these career-related jobs may offer bigger dividends later on. Think about offering your services to a local public school or community youth group. Try to make your volunteer situation parallel the future job you would like to have. You want to build an inventory of relevant skills and experiences as well as personal contacts.

A Begin Networking.

Through both your coursework and your extracurricular activities, you will come into contact with teachers, administrators, and other school personnel. You should be aware that these people can function as an informal **network** for information about the local employment picture, as can your professors and even your classmates. Go out of your way to let these people know of your interests, your special skills, and your commitment to teaching. This does not mean that you should become such a nuisance that people will duck behind their desks when they see you coming. It does mean that, at the right times and in the right places, you can let them know what jobs you are looking for and your skills and experiences that qualify you for those jobs.

A Begin Collecting Recommendations Now.

Studies reveal that letters of recommendation greatly influence employment decisions. Even if you find it difficult to request such letters, do not wait until you are student teaching to begin collecting them. Extracurricular activities, coursework, part-time employment, and volunteer work can all provide you with valuable recommendations. Your university placement office may be able to begin a **placement**

folder for you, maintaining these recommendations and forwarding copies to potential employers at the appropriate time.

Ask for letters of recommendation while you are in a job or course or immediately after leaving it. Professors, teachers, and past employers may move or retire, and, believe it or not, they may even forget you and just how competent and talented you are. You may be asked to help by drafting key points. Anything you can do to lighten the burden will be appreciated. Collecting letters of recommendation should be a continual process, not one that begins in the last semester of your teacher education program.

Develop a Résumé and Portfolio.

A

Traditionally, a **résumé** has been a central document considered during job applications, typically including a specific career objective and summarizing education, work experience, memberships, awards, and special skills. For example, a résumé might target a social studies teaching position in a particular area as your career objective, and it might report membership in the student NEA, an office held in school government, fluency in Spanish, experience with a student newspaper, honors you have won, and any relevant jobs, such as summer camp counselor or aid in a day care center. Many software packages have résumé templates, there are scores of books and websites devoted to résumé writing, and advisers and counselors at your school should be able to assist.

Today, many colleges and school districts are moving beyond résumés and toward **portfolios,** a more comprehensive reflection of a candidate's skills. If you would like to do something a bit more innovative than simply preparing a dynamite résumé and providing sparkling letters of recommendation, or if your teacher education program is promoting more authentic and creative assessment strategies, then you might want to consider developing a portfolio. This text will help you in that process. You will find, cleverly placed between the major sections of this book, a special feature called *Reflective Activities and your Portfolio (RAP).* The *RAP* will encourage you to reflect on your reading, undertake some interesting observations and activities, and begin collecting relevant materials for your portfolio. Even if you decide not to develop a portfolio, these *RAP* activities will be useful for developing professional materials that you can use in many different ways.

Make Good First, Second, Third, and Fourth Impressions.

A

In many education courses, you will be asked to participate in local school activities. This participation may take the form of observing or of being a teacher's aide or student teacher. (You may find the Observation Handbook in the Online Learning Center of this book particularly useful for school visits.) Recording and thinking about your impressions can be a useful step in deciding on the kind of position you want. In each case, you will be making an impression on the school faculty and administration. Good impressions can lead to future job offers. Poor impressions can result in your name being filed in the *persona non grata* drawer of people's needs.

Consider every visit to a school as an informal interview. Dress and act accordingly. Demonstrate your commitment and enthusiasm in ways that are helpful to school personnel. If you are viewed as a valuable and useful prospective member of the school community, you are a candidate with a head start for a current or future teaching position. Remember, known quantities are nearly always preferred to unknown quantities.

TEACHING TIP
Query students about their plans to undertake these first steps. Are they moving in the right direction? Are they at least moving?

SUMMARY

1. **What are the advantages and disadvantages of being a teacher?**

   You Be the Judge considers both advantages and disadvantages of teaching. Clearly teachers are underpaid, and can find themselves isolated, locked in routine, and lacking professional respect. But the job of working with children and caring colleagues, intellectual stimulation and the idea of doing important, even noble work, provide rich psychic rewards.

2. **What are the satisfactions—and complaints—of today's teachers?**

   While the majority of teachers are satisfied with their careers, a growing attrition rate reflects inadequate salaries, workload demands, and discipline problems. It is useful to recall that local conditions have a major impact on teacher satisfaction.

3. **Can we consider teaching to be a profession?**

   Critics note alternative preparation and licensure of teachers create a "semiprofession" at best, and key decisions, like curriculum, are left to others. Those who claim that teaching has earned full professional status assert that its knowledge and research base is growing, and at many universities, five years of study and training are now required. Teachers must now prove themselves through a growing number of tests for both admission to and advancement in the profession.

4. **How has teacher preparation changed over the years?**

   In colonial times, teachers were treated as meek and docile servants of the public, and teachers' conduct both in and out of school was scrutinized. In the 1800s, normal schools prepared teachers, and by the 1900s, many universities began their own teacher education programs. Several reform reports, including *Tomorrow's Teachers* and *A Nation Prepared,* urge higher standards, increased professionalism for teacher preparation, and recognition of superior performance through board certification.

5. **Do educators and the public agree on the most effective way to prepare teachers?**

   Teachers, education professors, and the general public often differ on what schools should value and emphasize. Classroom teachers and the general public are more likely than education professors to support traditional values, including punctuality, neatness, competition, and tougher promotion standards, while professors are more likely to stress the acquisition of strong teaching skills. In the final analysis, teacher candidates themselves should refine their individual strengths and weaknesses, and develop their skills by exploring resources both within and beyond their teacher education program.

6. **What traits and characteristics are needed for successful teaching?**

   Successful teachers often have a strong work ethic and intellectual curiosity, enjoy working with children and the community, and managing and motivating people. A good sense of humor can come in handy as well. Many of these interpersonal skills are also useful in other people-oriented organizations, like Southwest Airlines. Unfortunately, corporate cultures that focus on employee satisfaction and autonomy are too rarely found in schools.

7. **Is teaching a "good fit" for you?**

   A major purpose of this text is to help you assess if teaching is the right career for you. This chapter begins that process by encouraging you to rate yourself on the characteristics associated with effective teaching.

8. What steps can you take now on the road to becoming a teacher?

You are invited to use the RAP activities, further suggested readings, and online activities in this text to clarify your thoughts about teaching. We try to anticipate your questions and get you actively involved in this book, but we invite you to send additional questions to us, either through snail mail or e-mail at **www.mhhe.com/sadker7e.** If you are pretty sure that teaching is for you, we can help you reach that goal. It is wise to meet with an advisor and check the requirements *before* you choose your courses. You may also want to consider some useful steps that you can take during this time: prepare your résumé and portfolio, solicit recommendations, and stay informed about the job market. It may be early, but it is not too early.

EXTENDED LEARNING

CASE STUDIES

- Megan Brownlee: A parent is surprised to discover that her child's teacher does not encourage her to enter the teaching profession.
- Jennifer Gordon: A woman struggles during her student teaching experience.

READINGS

- Robert Holland. "How to Build a Better Teacher."
- Jonathan Kozol, Selection from *Amazing Grace: The Lives of Children and the Conscience of a Nation.*

Go to Chapter 1 on your *Resources for Exploring Education* CD-ROM to access Case Studies, Readings, and Media Observations.

KEY TERMS AND PEOPLE

alternative licensure, 17
board-certified teachers, 16
Jaime Escalante, 27
Reverend Samuel Hall, 14
Holmes Group, 16
Horace Mann, 14
A Nation Prepared, 16

National Board for
 Professional Teaching
 Standards (NBPTS), 16
networking, 28
normal school, 14
pedagogy, 20
placement folder, 28

portfolio, 28
profession, 11
résumé, 28
semiprofession, 12
Teach for America (TFA), 17
Tomorrow's Teachers, 16

DISCUSSION QUESTIONS AND ACTIVITIES

1. This chapter introduces you to the importance of well-thought-out career decision making. You can read further on this decision-making process in one of the many career books now available. For example, Richard N. Bolles' *What Color Is Your Parachute?* contains many exercises that should help you clarify your commitment to teaching. Or you may want to visit Bolles' website at www.jobhuntersbible.com/. These resources, or a visit to your career center, can help you determine what other careers present viable options for you.

2. Interview teachers and students at different grade levels to determine what they think are the positive and negative aspects of teaching. Share those interview responses with your classmates.

WEB-TIVITIES

Go to www.mhhe.com/
sadker7e to do the
following activities:

1. The Advantages and
    Disadvantages of Being
    a Teacher
2. A Closer Look at Teach
    for America
3. Why Become a Teacher?

3. Suppose you could write an open letter to students, telling them about yourself and why you want to teach. What would you want them to know? When you attempt to explain yourself to others, you often gain greater self-knowledge. You might want to share your letter with classmates and to hear what they have to say in their letters. Perhaps your instructor could also try this exercise and share his or her open letter with you.

4. Check out teacher-related websites on the Internet. Schools and school districts, professional teacher organizations, and all sorts of interest groups sponsor not only websites but also listservs, chat groups, and other Internet activities. Seek out opportunities to interview practicing classroom teachers about their own classroom experiences. (Check out our website at www.mhhe.com/sadker7e for related Web links.)

5. Imagine that you are taking part in a career fair. Someone asks why you are exploring teaching. Briefly frame your answer.

REEL TO REAL TEACHING

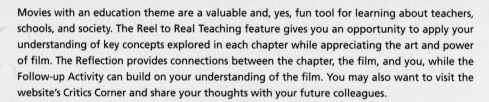

Movies with an education theme are a valuable and, yes, fun tool for learning about teachers, schools, and society. The Reel to Real Teaching feature gives you an opportunity to apply your understanding of key concepts explored in each chapter while appreciating the art and power of film. The Reflection provides connections between the chapter, the film, and you, while the Follow-up Activity can build on your understanding of the film. You may also want to visit the website's Critics Corner and share your thoughts with your future colleagues.

STAND AND DELIVER (1988)
Run Time: 105 Minutes

Synopsis: Convinced that his students have potential, mathematics teacher Jaime Escalante employs unconventional teaching methods to motivate a class of low-achieving, inner-city Hispanic students. Escalante teaches his students how to stretch beyond their limited horizons, and how to stand up when the world tries to crush their hopes.

Reflection:

1. Have your teachers ever shared with you their reasons for teaching? Did some teachers tell you through words and others through actions? What were they?

2. Most careers offer both satisfaction and sacrifice. Consider the professional and personal sacrifices made by Escalante. Would you be willing to make the same? Why or why not? You may wish to revisit the You Be the Judge feature in the chapter when contemplating the joys and sacrifices of teaching.

3. Consider how viewing *Stand and Deliver* might influence your answer to the question, "Why teach?"

Follow-up Activity: It's movie night for your campus student education association (e.g., Kappa Delta Pi, Phi Delta Kappa, Student NEA). *Stand and Deliver* is the feature flick and your task is to create a media announcement for the event. Develop a flyer, a newspaper announcement, radio advertisement, a blurb for a website, or create your own idea that really inspires your membership to attend this film.

How do you rate this film? Go to *Reel to Real Teaching* in the Critics' Corner to review this film.

www.mhhe.com/
sadker7e

FOR FURTHER READING

Amazing Grace, by Jonathan Kozol (1995). Capturing the consequences of poverty and deprivation in the lives of children in urban America, this book asks questions that are at once political and theological. What is the value of a child's life? How will schools and society help children in need?

Primary Teacher's Stress, by Geoff Troman and Peter Woods (2001). This book looks at the causes of teacher stress, asks why thousands of teachers are leaving the profession every year due to stress, and suggests ways of coping with and preventing stress.

Touching Eternity: The Enduring Outcomes of Teaching, by Tom Barone (2001). This case study of a high school art teacher and his former students explores the long-term impact teachers make on the lives of students.

What Keeps Teachers Going? by Sonia Nieto (2003). What helps great public school teachers persevere? To find out, Sonia Nieto, a renowned teacher educator, collaborates with experienced urban school teachers who effectively and enthusiastically work with students of culturally and linguistically diverse backgrounds—students who are among the most marginalized in our public schools.

What the Kids Said Today: Using Classroom Conversations to Become a Better Teacher, by Daniel Gartrell (2000). Each story includes an account of a teacher's conversation with children, as well as reflections on how each conversation can help build a stimulating and nurturing classroom.

2

Student Diversity

FOCUS QUESTIONS

1. How do cognitive, affective, and physiological factors impact learning?
2. How can teachers respond to different learning styles?
3. What are the classroom implications of Howard Gardner's theory of multiple intelligences?
4. How does emotional intelligence influence teaching and learning?
5. How can teachers meet the diverse needs of an increasingly multicultural student population?
6. What are the different levels of multicultural education?
7. What are the political and instructional issues surrounding bilingual education?
8. How are the needs of special learners met in today's classrooms?

 WHAT DO YOU THINK? Different Ways of Learning. Vote on the eight-point proposal presented on page 35 and see what the *Teachers, Schools, and Society* results are.

CHAPTER PREVIEW

CHAPTER FOCUS
This chapter reflects the great diversity of today's students, from racial and cultural differences to learning style preferences. The chronicle of bilingual education in the United States is presented in historical context. The chapter also includes an update on learners and about learning itself, such as emotional intelligence theory. For a chapter outline, see the IM.

At the dawn of the twenty-first century, basic educational concepts are being redefined, re-examined, and expanded. What does "intelligence" really mean? How many kinds of intelligences are there? What is EQ (emotional intelligence quotient), and is it a better predictor of success than IQ (intelligence quotient)? How should classrooms best be organized to meet the needs of different learning styles?

Not only are our basic concepts and assumptions changing; today's students are changing as well. An increasing number of students have their family roots not in Europe or Africa but in Asia and Latin America. As a result of an extraordinary increase in immigration to this country, the native language of well over 30 million Americans is a language other than English, creating a remarkable and

formidable challenge for the nation's schools.[1] In many schools, the terms *minority* and *majority* are gaining new meanings as student demographics change.

Another educational transformation is the increasing numbers of school children now identified as exceptional learners—learning and physically disabled, mentally retarded, and emotionally disturbed—all of whom deserve appropriate educational strategies and materials. Gifted and talented students represent another special needs population too often lost in the current educational system.

This chapter will describe the demographic and conceptual changes reshaping America's schools, as well as provide you with insights into and strategies for successful teaching in tomorrow's classrooms.

34

Different Ways of Learning

Imagine you are on a committee of teachers that has been asked to offer recommendations to the school board regarding academic climates to increase the academic performance of the district's students. It is an awesome responsibility. Here is the first draft of an eight point proposal. Take a moment and indicate your reaction to each of the points.[2]

	Strongly Agree	Agree	Disagree
1. Schools and classrooms should be quiet places to promote thinking and learning.	_____	_____	_____
2. All classrooms and libraries should be well lighted to reduce eye strain.	_____	_____	_____
3. Difficult subjects, such as math, should be offered in the morning, when students are fresh and alert.	_____	_____	_____
4. School thermostats should be set at 68 to 72 degrees Fahrenheit to establish a comfortable learning environment.	_____	_____	_____
5. Eating and drinking in classrooms should be prohibited.	_____	_____	_____
6. Classroom periods should run between forty-five and fifty-five minutes to ensure adequate time to investigate significant issues and practice important skills.	_____	_____	_____
7. Students must be provided with adequate work areas, including chairs and desks, where they can sit quietly for the major part of their learning and study.	_____	_____	_____
8. Emphasis should be placed on reading textbooks and listening to lectures, for this is how students learn best.	_____	_____	_____

You might find that these points seem to make a lot of sense. And, for many students, these eight recommendations may lead to higher academic achievement—for many, but not all. Ironically, for a significant number of students, these recommendations can lead to poorer performance, even academic failure. The reason is that students have different **learning styles**—diverse ways of learning, comprehending, knowing.

Did you notice these different learning styles in your own elementary and secondary school experience? Perhaps you see them now in college or graduate school. Some students do their best work late at night, while others set an early alarm because they are most alert in the morning. Many students seek a quiet place in the library to prepare for finals; others learn best in a crowd of people with a radio blaring; still others study most effectively in a state of perpetual motion, constantly walking in circles to help their concentration. Some students seem unable to study without eating and drinking, simultaneously imbibing calories and knowledge, they all but move into the refrigerator when preparing for tests. (These differences really strike home if you and your roommate clash because of conflicting learning styles.)

We are a population of incredibly diverse learners. Intriguing new research focusing on the ways students learn suggests that learning styles may be as unique as

GRABBERS
The Newest Intelligence
IM
Undercover
IM

FOCUS QUESTION 1
How do cognitive, affective, and physiological factors impact learning?

TEACHING TIP
Poll your students for their opinions. How might their convictions change if they assessed their current study environment *outside* the classroom?

CLASS ACTIVITY: LEARNING STYLES
IM, Activity 2:1

OVERHEAD 17
Factors Contributing to Learning Styles

FIGURE 2.1

Factors contributing to learning styles.

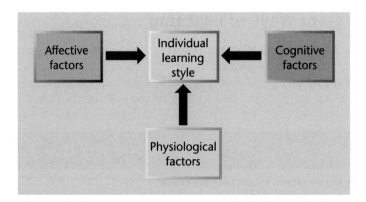

REFLECTION: Describe your own learning style by identifying at least one factor under the affective, physiological and cognitive domains.

handwriting. The challenge for educators is to diagnose these styles and to shape instruction to meet individual student needs.

At least three types of factors—as diagrammed in Figure 2.1—contribute to each student's individual learning style:

1. *Cognitive (information processing).* Individuals have different ways of perceiving, organizing, and retaining information, all components of the **cognitive domain.** Some students prefer to learn by reading and looking at material, while others need to listen and hear information spoken aloud. Still others learn best kinesthetically, by whole body movement and participation. Some learners focus attention narrowly and with great intensity; others pay attention to many things at once. While some learners are quick to respond, others rely on a slower approach.

2. *Affective (attitudes).* Individuals bring different levels of motivation to learning, and the intensity level of this motivation is a critical determinant of learning style. Other aspects of the **affective domain** include attitudes, values and emotions, factors that influence curiosity, the ability to tolerate and overcome frustration, and the willingness to take risks. A fascinating aspect of the affective domain is a concept termed **locus of control.** Some learners attribute success or failure to external factors ("Those problems were confusing," "The teacher didn't review the material well," or "My score was high because I made some lucky guesses"). These learners have an external locus of control. Simply stated, they do not take responsibility for their behavior. Others attribute performance to internal factors ("I didn't study enough" or "I didn't read the directions carefully"). These students have an internal locus of control because they have the sense that they control their fate, that they can improve their performance.

3. *Physiology.* Clearly, a student who is hungry and tired will not learn as effectively as a well-nourished and rested child. Other physiological factors are less obvious. Different body rhythms cause some students to learn better in the day, while others are night owls. Some students can sit still for long periods of time, while others need to get up and move around. Light, sound, and temperature are yet other factors to which students respond differently based on their physiological development.[3]

With this introduction to learning styles, you now know that the committee's eight recommendations will not create a productive learning climate for all students. The following section paraphrases the original recommendations, explodes myths, and provides research concerning diverse learning styles.[4]

FOCUS QUESTION 2
How can teachers respond to different learning styles?

**INTERACTIVE ACTIVITY
Learning Styles
Assessment**
Take a learning styles assessment to determine your own learning style.

Myth	*Fact*
Students learn best in quiet surroundings.	Many students learn best when studying to music or other background noise. Others need so much silence that only ear plugs will suffice.
Students learn best in well-lighted areas.	Some students are actually disturbed by bright light and become hyperactive and less focused in their thinking. For them, dimmer light is more effective.
Difficult subjects are best taught in the morning, when students are most alert.	Peak learning times differ. Some students are at their best in the morning, while others function most effectively in the afternoon or evening.
Room temperature should be maintained at a comfortable 68 to 72 degrees Fahrenheit to promote learning.	Room temperature preferences vary greatly from individual to individual, and no single range pleases all. What chills one learner may provide the perfect climate for another.
Eating or drinking while learning should be prohibited.	Some students learn better and score higher on tests if they are allowed to eat or drink during these times. Banning such activities may penalize these individuals unfairly.
The most appropriate length of time for a class is forty-five to fifty-five minutes.	This period of time may be too long for some and too brief for others. The comfort time zone of the student rather than a predetermined block of hours or minutes is the factor critical to effective learning.
Students should be provided with appropriate work areas, including chairs and desks, where they spend most of their classroom time.	A substantial number of students need to move about to learn. For these learners, sitting at a desk or a computer terminal for long periods of time can actually hinder academic performance.
Reading a textbook or listening to a lecture is the best way to learn.	Diverse students learn through a variety of modes, not only through reading or listening. While many students rely on these two perceptual modes, they are less effective for others. Some learn best through touch (for example, learning to read by tracing sandpaper letters), while others rely on kinesthetic movement, including creative drama, role-play, and field-based experiences.

Many educators believe that students have preferred learning styles and that teaching to these preferred styles will increase educational success. Following are three learning styles frequently mentioned in the literature. (Do you recognize yourself in any of these categories?) Since all of these students are typically in class at the same time, as a teacher you will be called on to use a variety of instructional approaches to reach all of them.

VISUAL LEARNERS

About half of the student population learns best by *seeing* information. They are termed visual learners.

Teaching Tips Textbooks, charts, course outlines, and graphs are useful instructional aids.

Ask these students to write down information, even rewriting or highlighting key points.

Ask students to preview chapters by looking at subheadings and illustrations before they read each chapter.

Seat these students up front, away from windows and doors (to avoid distractions).

Encourage them to ask for comments or directions to be repeated if they did not understand directions the first time.

Use overheads and flip charts.

KINESTHETIC LEARNERS

This is another popular learning style, which is also called *haptic* (Greek for "moving and doing") or *tactile.* These are "hands on" learners, students who learn best by doing.

Teaching Tips Try to plan for student movement in class presentation, as well as independent study time.

Movement should be planned to avoid distracting others.

Memorizing information can be enhanced if these learners are encouraged to physically move about the room.

Providing students with a colored desk blotter or a colored transparency to read a book is called "color grounding" and can help focus their attention.

Ask them to take notes and encourage them to underline key points as they read.

Encourage them to take frequent but short breaks.

Try to use skits and role-plays to help make instructional points.

AUDITORY LEARNERS

This is a style used less frequently than the previous two. These students learn best by hearing; they can remember the details of conversations and lectures and many have strong language skills.

Teaching Tips Provide the opportunity for auditory learners to recite the main points of a book or lecture.

Encourage these students to study with a friend, so they can talk through the main points.

Audiotapes of classroom activities can be helpful.

Suggest that they read class notes into a tape.

Encourage them to read the textbook out loud.

It can be helpful for these students to say out loud the meaning of the illustrations and main subject headings, and to recite any new vocabulary words.

Group work can be a useful class activity for auditory learners.

> **REFLECTION:** Choose a subject or topic that you want to teach. Describe three learning activities (visual, kinesthetic, auditory) that you can use to reach students with different learning styles. Which of these learning styles appeals to you? Why?

OVERHEAD 18
Creating a Productive Learning Climate: Myths and Facts

VIDEO SEGMENT 3
What Are the Mutiple Intelligences?

Learning style is not the only area undergoing demystification: our understanding of **intelligence** is also being reconstructed. The IQ score, developed early in the twentieth century, is supposed to be a measure of a person's innate intelligence, with a score of 100 defined as normal, or average. The higher the score, the brighter the person. Some of us grew up in communities where IQ was barely mentioned. In many cases this lack of knowledge might have been a blessing. Others of us grew up with "IQ envy," in communities where IQ scores were a big part of our culture. Since the score is considered a fixed, permanent measure of intellect, like a person's physical height, the scores engendered strong feelings. Friends who scored 150 or 160 or higher on an IQ test had a secret weapon, a mysteriously wonderful brain. We were impressed. But then our friend, the "genius," was stumped trying to unpack and plug in a toaster oven or got hopelessly lost trying to follow the simplest driving directions. How could this person have such a high IQ? We may have been equally

Some students learn best in cooperative learning situations.

puzzled when another friend, who scored horribly low on an IQ test, went on to fame and riches (and promptly forgot that we were ever their friends). What is this IQ score supposed to mean?

Multiple Intelligences and Emotional Intelligence

Also puzzled by these contradictions was Harvard professor **Howard Gardner.** Concerned about the traditional assessment of intelligence, with such a heavy emphasis on language and mathematical-logical skills, he broadened the concept to define *intelligence* as "the capacity to solve problems or to fashion products that are valued in one or more cultural settings."[5]

Gardner identified eight kinds of intelligence, not all of which are commonly recognized in school settings, yet Gardner believes that his theory of **multiple intelligences** more accurately captures the diverse nature of human capability. Consider Gardner's eight intelligences:

1. *Logical-mathematical.* Skills related to mathematical manipulations and discerning and solving logical problems (*related careers:* scientist, mathematician)
2. *Linguistic.* Sensitivity to the meanings, sounds, and rhythms of words, as well as to the function of language as a whole (*related careers:* poet, journalist, author)
3. *Bodily-kinesthetic.* Ability to excel physically and to handle objects skillfully (*related careers:* athlete, dancer, surgeon)
4. *Musical.* Ability to produce pitch and rhythm, as well as to appreciate various forms of musical expression (*related careers:* musician, composer)
5. *Spatial.* Ability to form a mental model of the spatial world and to maneuver and operate using that model (*related careers:* sculptor, navigator, engineer, painter)

INTERACTIVE ACTIVITY
Multiple Intelligences
Label descriptions of different intelligences.

FOCUS QUESTION 3
What are the classroom implications of Howard Gardner's theory of multiple intelligences?

CLASS ACTIVITY:
EIGHT (OR MORE)
INTELLIGENCES
IM, Activity 2:2

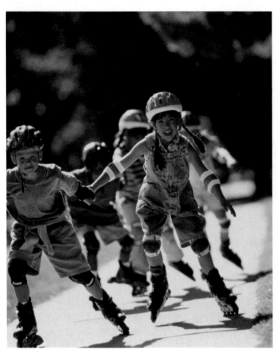

The ability to perform intricate and extended physical maneuvers is a distinct form of intelligence.

6. *Interpersonal.* Ability to analyze and respond to the motivations, moods, and desires of other people (*related careers:* psychology, sales, teaching)

7. *Intrapersonal.* Knowledge of one's feelings, needs, strengths, and weaknesses; ability to use this knowledge to guide behavior (*related benefit:* accurate self-awareness)

8. *Naturalist.* (Gardner's most recently defined intelligence) Ability to discriminate among living things, to classify plants, animals, and minerals; a sensitivity to the natural world (*related careers:* botanist, environmentalist, chef, other science- and even consumer-related careers.)[6]

Gardner and his colleagues continue to conduct research, and this list is still growing. A possible ninth intelligence being explored by Gardner concerns an *existential intelligence,* the human inclination to formulate fundamental questions about who we are, where we come from, why we die, and the like. Gardner believes that we have yet to discover many more intelligences. (Can you can think of some?)

The theory of multiple intelligences goes a long way in explaining why the quality of an individual's performance may vary greatly in different activities, rather than reflect a single standard of performance as indicated by an IQ score. Gardner also points out that what is considered *intelligence* may differ, depending on cultural values. Thus, in the Pacific Islands, intelligence is the ability to navigate among the islands. For many Muslims, the ability to memorize the Koran is a mark of intelligence. Intelligence in Balinese social life is demonstrated by physical grace.

Gardner's theory has sparked the imaginations of many educators, some of whom are redesigning their curricula to respond to differing student intelligences. Teachers are refining their approaches in response to such questions as[7]

- How can I use music to emphasize key points?
- How can I promote hand and bodily movements and experiences to enhance learning?
- How can I incorporate sharing and interpersonal interactions into my lessons?
- How can I encourage students to think more deeply about their feelings and memories?
- How can I use visual organizers and visual aids to promote understanding?
- How can I encourage students to classify and appreciate the world around them?

As instruction undergoes re-examination, so does evaluation. The old pencil-and-paper tests used to assess linguistic, math, and logical intelligences seem much less appropriate for measuring these new areas identified by Gardner.[8] The **portfolio** approach, as found in the *RAP*s in this text, is an example of a more comprehensive assessment, which includes student artifacts (papers, projects, videotapes, exhibits) that offer tangible examples of student learning. Some schools ask students to assemble portfolios that reflect progress in Gardner's various intelligences. In other cases, rather than As and Bs or 80s and 90s, schools are using descriptions to report student

RAP 1.3
Multiple Intelligences Bingo, p. 116

GLOBAL VIEW
What are signs of intelligence in varied cultural, religious, or international groups that your students represent?

CRITICAL THINKING QUESTION
Can students' imaginations be sparked to answer these questions and ask others?

VIDEO SEGMENT 4
A Multiple Intelligence Lesson in Action

Giants, Wizards, and Dwarfs was the game to play.

Being left in charge of about eighty children seven to ten years old, while their parents were off doing parent things, I mustered my troops in the church social hall and explained the game. It's a large-scale version of Rock, Paper, and Scissors, and involves some intellectual decision making. But the real purpose of the game is to make a lot of noise and run around chasing people until nobody knows which side you are on or who won.

Organizing a roomful of wired-up grade schoolers into two teams, explaining the rudiments of the game, achieving consensus on group identity—all of this is no mean accomplishment, but we did it with a right good will and were ready to go.

The excitement of the chase had reached a critical mass. I yelled out: "You have to decide *now* which you are—a GIANT, a WIZARD, or a DWARF!"

While the groups huddled in frenzied, whispered consultation, a tug came at my pants leg. A small child stands there looking up, and asks in a small concerned voice, "Where do the Mermaids stand?"

A long pause: A *very* long pause. "Where do the Mermaids stand?" says I.

"Yes. You see, I am a Mermaid."

"There are no such things as Mermaids."

"Oh, yes, I am one!"

She did not relate to being a Giant, a Wizard, or a Dwarf. She knew her category, Mermaid, and was not about to leave the game and go over and stand against the wall where a loser would stand. She intended to participate, wherever Mermaids fit into the scheme of things. Without giving up dignity or identity. She took it for granted that there was a place for Mermaids and that I would know just where.

Well, where DO the Mermaids stand? All the "Mermaids"—all those who are different, who do not fit the norm and who do not accept the available boxes and pigeonholes?

Answer that question and you can build a school, a nation, or a world on it.

What was my answer at the moment? Every once in a while I say the right thing. "The Mermaid stands right here by the King of the Sea!" (Yes, right here by the King's Fool, I thought to myself.)

So we stood there hand in hand, reviewing the troops of Wizards and Giants and Dwarfs as they rolled by in wild disarray.

It is not true, by the way, that Mermaids do not exist. I know at least one personally. I have held her hand.

SOURCE: Robert Fulghum, *All I Really Need to Know I Learned in Kindergarten* (New York: Villard Books, 1989), pp. 81–83.

REFLECTION: Was there ever a time when you did not fit neatly into a category—were you ever a mermaid? When and why? How will you make room for mermaids in your class?

---

competence. In music, for example, such descriptions might include "The student often listens to music," "She plays the piano with technical competence," "She is able to compose scores that other students and faculty enjoy," and so on. Whether the school is exploring portfolios, descriptive assessment, or another evaluation method, Gardner's multiple intelligences theory is reshaping many current assessment practices.[9]

While the theory of multiple intelligences raises fundamental questions about instruction and assessment, EQ may be even more revolutionary. **EQ,** or the **emotional intelligence quotient,** is described by **Daniel Goleman** in his book *Emotional Intelligence.* Goleman argues that when it comes to predicting success in life, EQ may be a better predictor than IQ. How does EQ work? The "marshmallow story" may help you understand:

A researcher explains to a 4-year-old that he/she needs to run off to do an errand, but there is a marshmallow for the youngster to enjoy. The youngster can choose to eat the marshmallow immediately. But, if the 4-year-old can

FOCUS QUESTION 4
How does emotional intelligence influence teaching and learning?

IN THE NEWS

Class Act

The Stuttgart, Arkansas, Junior High School varsity football team all shaved their heads so they could look more like teammate Stuart H., who lost most of his hair while undergoing chemotherapy. The coach explained: *They got together so he wouldn't feel weird, so they would all look weird together.*

SOURCE: *The American School Board Journal,* December 1997.

What's new in education? Click on *News Feeds.*

Like Daniel Goleman, Yale psychologist Peter Salovey works with emotional intelligence issues, and he identifies five elements of emotional intelligence. How would you rate yourself on each of these dimensions?

KNOWING EMOTIONS

The foundation of one's emotional intelligence is self-awareness. A person's ability to recognize a feeling as it happens is the essential first step in understanding the place and power of emotions. People who do not know when they are angry, jealous, or in love are at the mercy of their emotions.

Self-Rating on Knowing My Emotions *Always aware of my emotions__Usually aware__Sometimes aware__Out of touch, clueless.__*

MANAGING EMOTIONS

A person who can control and manage emotions can handle bad times as well as the good, shake off depression, bounce back from life's setbacks, and avoid irritability. In one study, up to half of the youngsters who at age 6 were disruptive and unable to get along with others were classified as delinquents by the time they were teenagers.

Self-Rating on Managing My Emotions *Always manage my emotions__Usually manage__Sometimes manage__ My emotions manage me.__*

MOTIVATING ONESELF

Productive individuals are able to focus energy, confidence, and concentration on achieving a goal and avoid anxiety, anger, and depression. One study of 36,000 people found that "worriers" have poorer academic performance than nonworriers. (A load off your mind, no doubt!)

Self-Rating on Motivation and Focus *Always self-motivated/focused__Usually self-motivated/ focused__ Sometimes self-motivated/focused__I can't focus on when I was last focused (and I don't care).__*

RECOGNIZING EMOTIONS IN OTHERS

This skill is the core of empathy, the ability to pick up subtle signs of what other people need or want. Such a person always seems to "get it," even before the words are spoken.

Self-Rating on Empathy *Always empathetic__Usually empathetic__Sometimes empathetic__I rarely "get it."__*

HANDLING RELATIONSHIPS

People whose EQ is high are the kind of people you want to be around. They are popular, are good leaders, and make you feel comfortable and connected. Children who lack social skills are often distracted from learning, and the dropout rate for children who are rejected by their peers can be two to eight times higher than for children who have friends.

Self-Rating on Relationships *I am rich in friendship and am often asked to lead activities and events.__I have many friends.__I have a few friends.__Actually, I'm pretty desperate for friends.__*

RATINGS

Give 4 points for each time you selected the first choice, 3 points for the "usual" or "many" second option, 2 points for the "sometimes" selection, and 1 point for the last choice.

18–20 points:	A grade—WOW! Impressive!
14–17 points:	B grade—You have considerable skills and talents.
10–13 points:	C grade—Feel free to read further on this topic.
5–9 points:	D grade—This may be a perfect subject to investigate in greater detail. Do you have a topic for your term project yet?

REFLECTION: Are you satisfied with your rating? If you earned a high rating, to what do you attribute your high EQ? If your rating was lower than you liked, how can you work on increasing your EQ?

CRITICAL THINKING QUESTION
Faced with the marshmallow experiment, what do your students think they would have done as a 4-year-old? Are their current patterns of delayed gratification similar?

wait and *not* eat the marshmallow right away, then an extra marshmallow will be given when the researcher returns. Eat one now, or hold off and get twice the reward.

What do you think you would have done as a 4-year-old? According to the social scientists who conducted the marshmallow experiment, decisions even at this age foreshadow an emotional disposition characteristic of a successful (or less successful) adult. By the time the children in the study reached high school, the now 14-year-olds were described by teachers and parents in a way that suggested their marshmallow behaviors predicted some significant differences. Students who ten years earlier were able to delay their gratification, to wait a while and garner a second marshmallow, were reported to be better adjusted, more popular, more adventurous, and more confident in adolescence than the group who ten years earlier had gobbled down their marshmallows. The children who gave in to temptation, ate the marshmallow and abandoned their chances for a second one, were more likely to be described as stubborn, easily frustrated, and lonely teenagers. In addition to the differences between the gobblers and waiters as described by parents and teachers, there was also a significant SAT scoring gap. The students who, ten years earlier, could wait for the second marshmallow scored 210 points higher than did the gobblers. Reasoning and control, "the regulation of emotion in a way that enhances living,"[10] might be new, and perhaps better, measures of what we call smart, or intelligent.

Emotional intelligence "is a type of social intelligence that involves the ability to monitor one's own and others' emotions, to discriminate among them, and to use the information to guide one's thinking and actions."[11] Goleman suggests that EQ taps into the heart, as well as the head, and introduces a new gateway for measuring intelligence, for children and adults.[12] By the way, how would you rate your EQ?

Goleman and Gardner are toppling educational traditions, stretching our understanding of what schools are about. In a sense, they are increasing the range and diversity of educational ideas. This chapter is all about diversity. The students you will teach will learn in diverse ways, and a single IQ or even EQ score is unlikely to capture the range of their abilities and skills. But these are not the only differences students bring to school. Let's turn our attention to how cultural, ethnic, and racial diversity is transforming life in the classroom.

INTERACTIVE ACTIVITY
Emotional Intelligence Quotient Quiz
Take an EQ quiz to determine your own emotional intelligence quotient.

Cultural Diversity

America has just experienced the greatest immigration surge in its history. In the past few decades, more immigrants have come to this country than at the beginning of the twentieth century, a time often thought of as the great era of immigration and Americanization. These new Americans have arrived mainly from Latin America and Asia, but also from the Caribbean, the Middle East, Africa, and Eastern Europe. Today, about one in ten Americans is foreign born.

Consider the following:

FOCUS QUESTION 5
How can teachers meet the diverse needs of an increasingly multicultural student population?

- By 2012 the west (the geographic area expected to witness the greatest changes) will become "minority majority," with no single racial or ethnic group having a majority.

- The nation has approximately 2.5 million Native Americans, a number that increases to about 4 million when including Americans claiming partial Indian heritage on the census.

- In 2000, the number of Asians, including Asian Indians, in the United States was over 10 million or 3.6 percent of the population.

- About 6 million Americans claimed multiracial heritage with 2 or more races indicated on Census 2000.

- By 2030, the number of U.S. residents who are nonwhite or Hispanic will be about 140 million or about 40 percent of the U.S. population.[13]

Demographic forecasting, the study of people and their vital statistics, provides a fascinating insight into tomorrow's schools. Demographers indicate that at the

OVERHEAD 19
Student Demographics

FIGURE 2.2

Percentage of public and elementary and secondary students by race/ethnicity.

SOURCE: U.S. Department of Education, National Center for Education Statistics, Common Core of Data (CCD), "State Nonfiscal Survey of Public Elementary/Secondary Education," 2001–02.

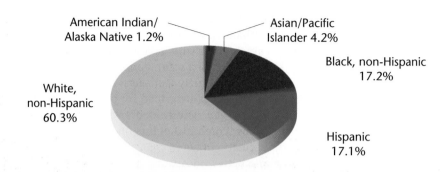

American Indian/ Alaska Native 1.2%

Asian/Pacific Islander 4.2%

Black, non-Hispanic 17.2%

White, non-Hispanic 60.3%

Hispanic 17.1%

> **REFLECTION:** Why are Hispanics found in multiple categories? What groups are also in multiple categories, yet not reflected on this chart? Why should the lines between groups be shaded? What groups are submerged within the "American Indian/Alaska Native" category?

dawn of the twenty-first century, one out of three Americans will be of color. Some forecast that by 2020 almost half the school population will be from non-European ethnic groups. Demographers draw a portrait of a new generation of students far more diverse—by race, ethnicity, culture, and language—than our country has ever known. In fact, student diversity exceeds even these demographic projections because of the way we sort and label people. Americans from Pakistan, China, and Vietnam are all counted as "Asian," despite their profound differences. And when an American whose background is African, Hispanic, and French is asked to select a single group affiliation, additional information is lost. (See Figure 2.2.) You will be teaching in a nation far more diverse than the one you grew up in.

Although the national demographics are powerful, you will not be a national teacher. You will be a local teacher, and the demographic realities you experience will be shaped by where you teach. If you teach in a large, urban school system, you will likely encounter classrooms where the majority of students are of color. In many cities today, students of color already constitute 70 to more than 90 percent of the students. If you decide to start your career in the tony suburbs outside the nation's capital, in Fairfax, Virginia, or Montgomery County, Maryland, for example, you may very well find third- and fourth-generation American children from wealthy homes attending your school, along with students recently arrived in this country—thousands of students speaking more than a hundred different languages. Of course, not every American community is experiencing dynamic population changes. You may find yourself teaching in a very stable school district, one where student demographics have remained basically unchanged for decades. But, even in these communities, changing national demographics will not go unnoticed. As the nation's population changes, so will the nation's culture, politics, and economy. To a degree, we are all part of the national fabric. The challenge for educators is how to prepare all of the nation's students for this more diverse America. (See Figure 2.2.)

 Teaching Them All

Imagine this. You have graduated from your teacher preparation program and have signed the contract for your first teaching job, and now you stand before your very first class. As you survey your sixth-grade students, you see fifteen boys and fourteen

During much of the twentieth century, African American students attended legally segregated schools. Today, while legal segregation has ended, segregation has not. Examine these two photos and suggest similarities and differences between segregation then and now. During the past hundred years, what other ethnic or racial groups might be photographed in much the same way?

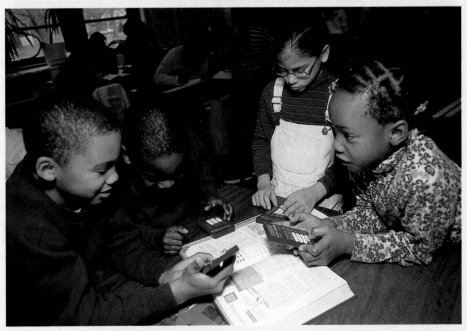

girls. As you look at your class, you realize that you will be teaching a wonderfully diverse group. Off to the right, near the windows, are half a dozen students eagerly talking in Spanish. Some African American children, comparing their schedules, look to you with curiosity. In the front of the room, several Asian American children are in their seats, looking up to you, awaiting your comments. (You do have a good opening, right?) Several white children and a few students whose backgrounds may reflect more than one racial or ethnic group are looking at the motivational posters you hung just last night. You know from reading student records that six of your students have learning disabilities, and the child in the wheelchair has muscular dystrophy. One of the children has been identified as gifted. About half of your students are from single-parent homes. A third come from middle-class backgrounds, and the remaining children are from working-class or poor families. Whew! The proverbial American melting pot looks more like a tossed salad in your class.

You know from your training, reading, and experience that each of these young lives has been shaped, in part, by geography, ethnicity, exceptionality, social class, race, and gender. You understand that these characteristics will influence how these children perceive the world—and how the world views them. You also know that each one is likely to have a learning style as unique as his or her appearance.

How will you meet the needs of these twenty-nine different learners? What strategies and approaches will you use to foster equity and excellence in your classroom?

Culture and Education 101

OVERHEAD 20
Distinctions: Stereotypes
and Generalizations

Before teaching your first class, you may be required, or you may elect, to take courses in special education, gender equity, and multicultural education. Here we offer an introduction, some suggested topics that might be found in a course designed to help you teach diverse learners. We'll call our course "Culture and Education 101." Additional information and strategies for dealing with diversity will be described later in this book.

Generalize, Don't Stereotype Although you are the teacher and your students are the "learners," be prepared to do quite a bit of learning yourself. As you assimilate information about your students, their culture, and their experiences, you will need to distinguish between stereotypes and generalizations. While the dangers of stereotyping are common knowledge these days, the usefulness of generalizations is less well known.

VIDEO SEGMENT 5
A Challenging Student

Stereotypes are absolute statements applied to all members of a group, statements that ignore individual differences. Stereotypes tend to close off discussion by providing simplistic characterizations. Generalizations offer information about groups that can help you teach more effectively. For instance, a generalization that members of a certain group avoid direct eye contact, while not applying to every group member (that would be a stereotype), is a generalization that teaches us what to expect from many if not most group members. **Generalizations** are flexible insights that provide us with clues about groups, useful information for instructional planning. Generalizations are discussion openers, recognizing that we are all members of many groups: religious, gender, geographic, class, interest, skills, and the like. Look for generalizations about your students' backgrounds that will help you plan for teaching. Avoid stereotypes.

Model Skills and Behaviors That Reflect Sensitivity Looking for the first time at ethnically diverse names on a class list, a teacher might blurt out, "I'll never be able to

Being a good teacher in the years ahead will almost surely mean dealing with a culturally diverse population.

pronounce that one!" or "That's the first time I heard that name." Such comments reflect a lack of cultural understanding and sensitivity, hardly endearing a teacher to a student. Some teachers dig a deeper hole, converting the "unusual" name to an easier to pronounce nickname or unilaterally deciding to Americanize the name, as in "Miguel, do you mind if I call you Mike?" Such names as Tomás, Twanda, Chu, Ngyuen, or Kenji may take extra effort to learn to pronounce correctly, but it is an effort that demonstrates cultural and personal respect.

Once you have learned about your students and their cultural background, you will have to take the next big step: Ensure that your knowledge is reflected in your behavior. Being responsive to cultural norms is yet another way to demonstrate cultural sensitivity. For instance, one Native American and Asian cultural norm is to shun competition. If you were their teacher, you may want to minimize the practice of publicly praising one student's work in front of others, or even providing the stage for such comparisons. You could choose to review student performance through quiet, individual conferences, rather than announcing or posting such grades. Such steps go a long way in promoting effective relationships in and beyond the classroom.

Use Classroom Strategies That Build on Student Learning Styles As was discussed earlier in this chapter, individuals, and even groups, have different, preferred learning styles. If your students are similar to the ones in the class described earlier, they are likely to bring with them an incredible assortment of educational styles and experiences. To get a sense of each student's unique approach to learning, observe each of them doing work and analyze how each approaches the curriculum. Some schools assist you in this effort by providing learning style assessments that you can administer to your students. Use this information and plan a variety of instructional options and teaching strategies that appeal to the different intelligences described by Gardner and others. Give all your students the chance to succeed.

Give Equal Instructional Attention The research on classroom interaction reflects subtle and not so subtle teacher biases. Male students tend to call out more than female

TEACHING TIP

Many students possess a story (and sometimes it's weighty) about their first, middle, family or nicknames. Some tales might be connected with religious and cultural history, gender assumptions or character traits. Open a sensitive dialogue on names and the norms surrounding them.

As I look back over a lifetime of teaching, one special student stands out. Kou was the most memorable student I've ever taught. Short, bandy-legged, and incredibly strong for a 13-year-old, he had come from a rural mountain village deep within Laos to my special-education class in the Santa Barbara suburbs. Although he was no bigger than an American nine-year-old, the hormones of puberty had thrown a dark fuzz over his lip. His voice was deep, a shock coming from that small a body. Often, he wore a bemused expression, compounded of amazement and tolerance for the Americans who were so different from his countrymen in pastoral Laos.

On the playground, Kou was king. He could throw farther, higher, and harder than any other child in school. He was unsurpassed at *hack,* a Laotian game played with the head and feet that seemed like a cross between volleyball and soccer. And in soccer, he was the best. He also carved wonderful wooden tops, which served as trade goods for the American treasures the other boys had.

In the classroom, however, Kou had a problem. The letters, numbers, and words that he painfully memorized one week seemed to vanish during the next.

Although I tried every trick in my teaching bag, nothing seemed to work. With my help, Kou attempted all sorts of experiments designed to help him learn: writing in colored chalk, making clay letters, drawing on the playground. Throughout every effort, he remained cheerful and willing. His attitude seemed to be, "Well, this is how it is in America." But his skills did not improve.

Over time, I noticed that Kou often sang to himself as he worked. "Kou, tell me about your song," I said one day. In his halting English, he told me that the song was about a woman whose man had left her all alone.

"Write it down, Mrs. Nolan," demanded La, his friend. And so our song translation project began. As the class chimed in and squabbled over the meaning of different words, Kou sang, thought, then said the words in his fractured English. I wrote the song down on a sheet of paper. When I was finished, the children all read the song aloud, then sang it with Kou. The next day, my students brought tapes of their native music to school. Suddenly, we had a full-fledged language-experience project underway! As we listened, hummed, and made illustrated booklets about the songs and read them back, the legends and stories of Laos and the Hmong people began to tumble from Kou. For the first time, he had a reason to communicate.

Brief, primitive, and loaded with mistakes, Kou's stories became the foundation for his reading, writing, and language instruction. Never a fan of basal readers, I used this experience as an opportunity to leave the textbooks behind. Kou's quickly improving skills were a source of pride for both of us. When Kou was 15, he left us for junior high. By then he could read at a third-grade level and do survival math. He still had that sweet smile and he still sang softly as he worked. He still longed for the hills of Laos and his old job of herding ducks beside a lake, but he spoke and wrote much better English.

And me? How much I had learned from Kou. Not only did he open the door into a rich and mysterious realm where ghosts walked and crocodiles roamed, but he taught me something about how to be a teacher. From him I learned about the value of starting with a student's interests—and about how powerful a learning tool sharing a culture can be.

SOURCE: Virginia Nolan, "The Song in His Heart," *Instructor* 101, no. 8 (1992), p. 94.

REFLECTION: The section on Multicultural Education lists four levels devised by James Banks. On what level would you place Mrs. Nolan's cultural approach?

students, and, even when males do not call out, teachers tend to call on them more than females. White students also garner more instructional time than students of color. The result is that white males receive more of the most precious items in the teacher's repertoire, time and attention. Even silence is not distributed equally. Teachers give males and perceived high achievers more wait time—more quiet time to respond to questions and to think about their answers. These patterns of bias are usually so subtle that teachers are not aware of them.

To avoid elusive interaction bias, you may want to ask a colleague, friend, or student to carefully and objectively tally the interactions you have with different students. Whom do you talk to the most? Who gets helped or praised the most? How is your wait time distributed?

Cooperative rather than competitive strategies can also help. Research shows that cooperative learning enhances not only achievement but relationships as well.[14] When students of diverse ethnic and racial backgrounds work cooperatively, they learn to like and respect one another, as well as focus on higher academic goals. Cooperative learning also helps mainstreamed students with disabilities gain social acceptance. But do not expect the magic of cooperative learning without your active participation: Teachers need to monitor the groups, directly teaching social skills.[15]

Similar patterns of bias exist in instructional materials, as some groups receive more attention than others. Students in your class will naturally look for themselves in the curricular materials to see how they are presented. Will they find themselves in the materials that you use or will they be invisible? Are the instructional materials free of stereotypes? Are the views and information presented solely through Eurocentric eyes or are diverse perspectives included?

Because students spend an enormous amount of time working with textbooks and related materials, curricular choices are central to classroom learning. If you were, in fact, enrolled in our fictitious course, "Culture and Education 101," you would undoubtedly invest a fair amount of time studying curriculum. One of the best-known writers in this area is James Banks, whose useful framework for incorporating multicultural concepts in the curriculum is described in the next section.

Multicultural Education

According to **James Banks,** the primary goal of **multicultural education** is to transform the school so that male and female students, exceptional students, and students from diverse cultural, social-class, racial, and ethnic groups experience an equal opportunity to learn.[16] A key assumption of multicultural education is that students are more likely to achieve when the total **classroom climate** is more consistent with their diverse cultures and learning styles.

We have already discussed individual learning styles but have yet to focus on cultural learning styles. Some educators posit that, through **enculturation,** particular groups are likely to exhibit characteristic approaches to learning. For example, based on the groundbreaking work of **Carol Gilligan,** some studies show that women are more likely than men to personalize knowledge; in general, they prefer learning through experience and first-hand observation.[17] Other research suggests that the African American culture emphasizes learning that is aural and participatory. When African American children are required to translate their participatory style onto a written test, they are likely to concentrate on the unaccustomed form of expression, to the detriment of their knowledge of the content.[18] Multicultural educators say that, if we can identify and understand cultural learning styles, we can target curriculum and instruction more appropriately. Further research in cultural and gender learning styles holds the promise of transforming tomorrow's schools.

Multicultural education also seeks to help all students develop more positive attitudes toward different racial, ethnic, cultural, and religious groups. According to a 1990s survey of more than one thousand young people between 15 and 24 conducted by People for the American Way, about half of the students described the state of race relations in the United States as generally bad. Fifty-five percent of African Americans and whites said they were "uneasy" rather than "comfortable" in dealing with members of the other racial group. However, most respondents felt their attitudes toward race relations were healthier than those of their parents.[19]

FOCUS QUESTION 6
What are the different levels of multicultural education?

RELATED READING
The Color of Water: A Black Man's Tribute to His White Mother, by James McBride (1997).

OVERHEAD 21
Banks' Approach to Multicultural Education

MULTIPLE INTELLIGENCE CONNECTION
Let students explore their interpersonal intelligence. Have them identify 4 individuals in their circle of friends or acquaintances. Where do their friends stand on issues of multiculturalism?

FIGURE 2.3

Banks' approach to multicultural education.

**Level 4:
The Social Action Approach**
Students make decisions on important social issues and take actions to help solve them.

Level 3: The Transformation Approach
The structure of the curriculum is changed to enable students to view concepts, issues, events, and themes from the perspectives of diverse ethnic and cultural groups.

Level 2: The Additive Approach
Content, concepts, themes, and perspectives are added to the curriculum without changing its structure.

Level 1: The Contributions Approach
Focuses on heroes, holidays, and discrete cultural elements.

REFLECTION: Think back to your own schooling. At which of Banks's levels would you place your own multicultural education? Provide supporting evidence. As a teacher, which of these levels do you want to reach and teach? Explain.

James Banks notes that one way to achieve more positive attitudes toward different groups is to integrate the curriculum, to make it more inclusive. He describes four approaches, described below and illustrated in Figure 2.3.[20] (Do you remember any of these approaches in your own schooling?)

1. Multicultural education often begins with the *contributions approach,* in which the study of ethnic heroes (for example, Sacajawea, Rosa Parks, or Booker T. Washington) is included in the curriculum. At this superficial contributions level, one might also find "food and festivals" being featured or such holidays as Cinco de Mayo being described or celebrated.

2. In the *additive approach,* a unit or course is incorporated, often but not always during a "special" week or month. February has become the month to study African Americans, while March has been designated "Women's History Month." Although these dedicated weeks and months offer a respite from the typical curricular material, no substantial change is made to the curriculum as a whole.

3. In the *transformation approach,* the entire Eurocentric nature of the curriculum is changed. Students are taught to view events and issues from diverse ethnic and cultural perspectives. For instance, the westward expansion of Europeans can be seen as manifest destiny through the eyes of European descendants, or as an invasion from the east, through the eyes of Native Americans.

4. The fourth level, *social action,* goes beyond the transformation approach. Students not only learn to view issues from multiple perspectives but also become directly involved in solving related problems. Rather than political passivity, the typical by-product of many curricular programs, this approach promotes decision making and social action in order to achieve multicultural goals and a more vibrant democracy. (See Chapter 7 for additional multicultural strategies and for a discussion of the debate concerning the place of multiculturalism in the curriculum.)

 ## Bilingual Education

What is going on in America? It is amazing, and disturbing, to ride on a road and see street signs that are printed not only in English but in other languages as well. What's more, even legal documents are now being written in foreign languages. How unnerving to walk down an American street and not understand what people are talking about. Maybe this isn't America. I feel like a stranger in my own land. Why don't they learn to speak English?

Sound like a stroll through today's Miami, or San Diego, or perhaps San Antonio? Good try, but you not only have the wrong city, you are also in the wrong century. Benjamin Franklin expressed this view in the 1750s.[21] He was disgruntled that Philadelphia had printed so many things, including street signs, in another language (German, in this case). Even the *Articles of Confederation* were published in German as well as English, and children were taught in Dutch, Italian, and Polish.

Bilingual education in America is hundreds of years old, hardly a "new" issue. In 1837, Pennsylvania law required that school instruction be given on an equal basis in German as well as English. In fact, that example provides us with a fairly concise definition of **bilingual education,** the use of two languages for instruction. But, almost a century later, as America was being pulled into World War I, foreign languages were seen as unpatriotic. Public pressure routed the German language from the

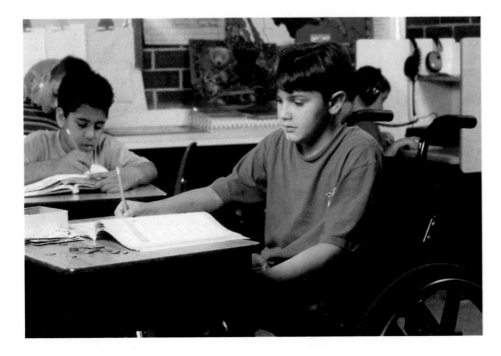

Public Law 94-142 placed students with disabilities into regular classrooms, so that they receive the "least-restrictive" education possible.

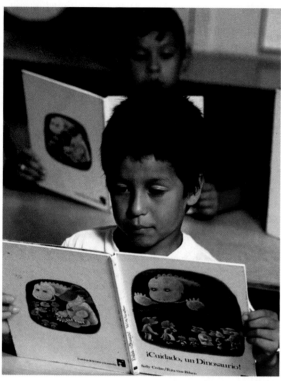

In some bilingual education programs, English is learned as a second language, while the student takes other academic work in his or her native language.

curriculum, although nearly one in four high school students was studying the language at the time. Individual states went even further. Committed to a rapid assimilation of new immigrants, and suspicious of much that was foreign, these states prohibited the teaching of *any* foreign language during the first eight years of schooling. (The Supreme Court found this policy not only xenophobic but unconstitutional as well, in *Meyer* v. *State of Nebraska,* 1923.)[22]

Despite the long history of bilingual education in this country, many school districts never really bought into the concept. In districts without bilingual education, students with a poor command of English had to sink or swim (or perhaps, more accurately, "speak or sink"). Students either learned to speak English as they sat in class—or they failed school, an approach sometimes referred to as **language submersion.** If submersion was not to their liking, they could choose to leave school. Many did.

Bilingual education had a rebirth in the 1960s, as the Civil Rights movement brought new attention to the struggles of many disenfranchised Americans, including non-English speakers trying to learn in a language they did not understand. And, unlike the 1800s, by the 1960s and 1970s education had become less an option and more a necessity, the threshold to economic success. To respond to this need, Congress passed the **Bilingual Education Act** in 1968. This act provided federal financial incentives, using what some people call "a carrot approach," to encourage schools to initiate bilingual education programs. Not all districts chased the carrot.

From the start, the Bilingual Education Act was fraught with problems. The act lacked concrete recommendations for implementation and did not specify standards. Individual school districts and, in some cases, even individual schools, experimented with different approaches. The result was a patchwork of programs of varying quality, threadbare in spots and peppered with holes where no programs existed at all. In too many cases, the act simply failed to serve the students it was meant to serve.

During the early 1970s, disillusioned parents initiated lawsuits. In 1974, the Supreme Court heard the case of *Lau v. Nichols.* This class action lawsuit centered around Kinney Lau and 1,800 other Chinese students from the San Francisco area who were failing their courses because they could not understand English. The Court unanimously affirmed that federally funded schools must "rectify the language deficiency" of these students. Teaching students in a language they did not understand was not an appropriate education. The Court's decision in *Lau* v. *Nichols* prompted Congress to pass the **Equal Educational Opportunities Act (EEOA).** Under this law, school districts must take positive steps to provide equal education for language-minority students by eliminating language barriers.

Typically in the bilingual approach, **limited English proficiency (LEP)** students learn English as a second language while taking other academic subjects in their native language. The **transitional approach** begins by using the native language as a bridge to English-language instruction. Academic subjects are first taught using the native language, but progressively the students transition to English, to their new

FOCUS QUESTION 7
What are the political and instructional issues surrounding bilingual education?

CLASS ACTIVITY: BILINGUAL EDUCATION
IM, Activity 2:3

VIDEO SEGMENT 6
Assimilating the Alien

GLOBAL VIEW
Xenophobia generally means fear and hatred of strangers or foreigners. While students may be new to the term, worldwide actions (by individuals, groups, and governments) should be familiar to them. What contemporary or historic events can they cite?

1700–1800S: THE PERMISSIVE PERIOD

Linguistic and cultural tolerance maintained the peace in the new nation. Many schools offered content-related classes in languages other than English.

1900–1960S: THE RESTRICTIVE PERIOD

The anti-German hostility during World War I linked foreign languages with alien ideologies. Most states required that all schools teach all content courses in English, and promoted the Americanization of all immigrants.

1950S TO 1980S: THE OPPORTUNIST PERIOD

The Cold War demonstrated that the lack of linguistic ability was a strategic vulnerability, and federal laws were passed to encourage foreign language instruction. The Bilingual Education Act and the *Lau* Supreme Court decisions affirmed the civil rights of language-minority speakers. Schools explored numerous approaches to bilingual education.

1980S TO THE PRESENT: THE DISMISSIVE PERIOD

With the arrival of Presidents Reagan and Bush, an era of antibilingual education re-emerged. Federal support turned into federal hostility, and political movements such as "U.S. English," "English First," and "English Only" sprung up. State actions such as Proposition 227 in California required that English replace any other instructional language used in schools.

SOURCE: Carlos Ovando, "Bilingual Education in the United States: Historical Development and Current Issues." Paper presented at the American Educational Research Association annual convention, Montreal, Canada, April 19–23, 1999.

REFLECTION: Why has teaching in English become a political issue, rather than an educational one? How does conservative political support for English-only courses conflict with conservative goals to enhance the nation's performance in the global economy? Do you believe that bilingual education is a threat to national cohesion and stability?

language. This is the most widely used approach. The **maintenance, or developmental, approach** emphasizes the importance of maintaining both languages. The goal is to create a truly bilingual student, one who acquires English while maintaining competence in the native language. Students are instructed in both languages. **English as a Second Language (ESL)** supplements either the maintenance or transitional programs by providing special ESL classes for additional instruction in reading and writing English.

Two approaches which cannot truly be considered bilingual, language submersion and immersion, remind us of the "sink or swim" mentality but are used with LEP children nonetheless. Language submersion places students in classes where only English is spoken, and the student either learns English as the academic work progresses, or doesn't. **Immersion** is somewhat less rigid than submersion, because the teacher usually understands the native language and responds in English, sometimes using a "sheltered" or simplified English vocabulary.

In schools using one or more of these approaches, problems persist. Consider the following:

> . . . last week I saw an elementary school teacher who was teaching a class of 31 children in the third grade, and the 31 children spoke six languages, *none* of which was English. The teacher had one year of Spanish in her collegiate training.[23]

As schools struggle to meet the needs of LEP students, bilingual education continues to spark political controversy. Millions of students speak hundreds of languages

TEACHING TIP

Demonstrate, by yourself or with a second language speaker, the four typical approaches to bilingual education: submersion, immersion, transitional, and maintenance. Have students distinguish the four and synthesize how language might impact learning.

OVERHEAD 22

Approaches to Teaching Bilingual Students

CRITICAL THINKING QUESTION

Have students describe their in-school bilingual experiences. How did politics outside the school impact programs?

"My grandparents picked up English like everyone else back then, in school, where children learned their lessons in English, not in Spanish or Vietnamese."

"If people want to remain immersed in their old culture and old language, they should stay in their old country."

"Bilingual education has given us illiterate youngsters who can do little more than work at Taco Bell."

Sound familiar? After all, many of our ancestors came to America with few resources or funds, but they were able to learn English, pick up American ways, get through school, and succeed against great odds, so why can't today's immigrants do the same? According to Richard Rothstein—author of *The Way We Were?*—we suffer a bad case of national amnesia, and our recollection of history differs significantly from actual events. The author believes that some bilingual programs work well, and some do not. The key is to find out which are the effective ones and to move the issue of bilingual education out of the political arena and into objective evaluation. Rothstein reminds us that

- *Bilingual education is an American tradition.* In 1837, New York City established bilingual programs for German children, and, throughout the 1800s, Maryland, Colorado, Oregon, Kentucky, Indiana, and Iowa, to name but a few, established their own bilingual programs.
- *Opinions back then were also divided.* Some believed that the programs were essential for academic success, while others thought that they slowed down mastery of English. Then as now, individuals who were being taught in bilingual classrooms—Italian, German, Polish, French, Spanish, and so on—differed as to whether or not bilingual education was a good idea.

- *School performance for immigrants in English immersion programs was horrific.* From 1880 through the 1930s, immigrants were far more likely to drop out of school than to graduate, and they dropped out at much higher percentages than today's students.
- *Non-English-speaking students in New York City early in the twentieth century were 60 percent more likely than English speakers to be labeled "retarded,"* including more than a third of the Italian students.
- *In most cases, immigrants to this country never mastered English.* In fact, *it was not until the third generation that most immigrant groups became fluent enough in English to excel in school.*
- *As World War I pulled America into the conflict, communities across the nation reacted by eliminating not only bilingual education programs but even the teaching of foreign languages,* the most popular of which was German. It was not until the Supreme Court decision in the 1970s that bilingual education re-emerged as an issue in the nation's schools. And, by then, most Americans had not only forgotten the bilingual education programs of the past, but they had also forgotten what happened to students without them.

SOURCE: Adapted from Richard Rothstein, "Bilingual Education: The Controversy," *Phi Delta Kappan* 79, no. 9 (May 1998), pp. 672–78.

REFLECTION: Why do some Americans believe bilingual education is a relatively recent phenomenon? How are political beliefs reflected in the bilingual debate?

and dialects, including not only Spanish but Hmong, Urdu, Russian, Chinese, Polish, Korean, Tagalog, and Swahili. Misunderstandings are multiplied when language barriers are accompanied by racial and ethnic differences, leading to even greater isolation and segregation for many LEP students. And, while some struggle to make bilingual education work, others believe that it never will.

Opponents of bilingual education point to studies showing that first- and second-generation Hispanic students who attended bilingual programs from the 1970s to the 1990s earned considerably less money than Hispanics who attended "English only" classes. Moreover, Hispanic students who dropped out of bilingual programs were less likely to return and complete high school than were Hispanics who attended English-only programs.[24] LEP parents despair over their children's lack of progress in learning English and graduating from school. The dropout rates for Hispanic students, the largest group of LEP students, hovers around 50 percent.[25] Many parents of students in bilingual programs now oppose these programs, an ironic turnabout, since it was parent protests in the 1960s and 1970s that forced reluctant schools and the federal

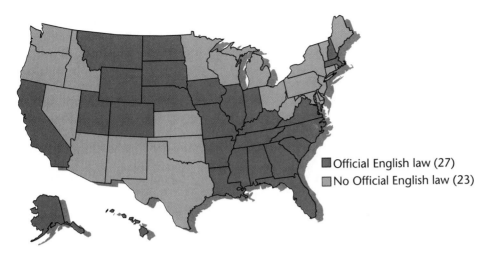

FIGURE 2.4
States with official
English language.

SOURCE: U.S. English, Inc. (2002),
Washington, DC.

■ Official English law (27)
■ No Official English law (23)

States with Official English Rule and Year Enacted

Alabama (1990)	Indiana (1984)	New Hampshire (1995)
Alaska (1998)	Iowa (2002)	North Carolina (1987)
Arkansas (1987)	Kentucky (1984)	North Dakota (1987)
California (1986)	Louisiana (1811)	South Carolina (1987)
Colorado (1988)	Massachusetts (1975)	South Dakota (1995)
Florida (1988)	Mississippi (1987)	Tennessee (1984)
Georgia (1986 & 1996)	Missouri (1998)	Utah (2000)
Hawaii* (1978)	Montana (1995)	Virginia (1981 & 1996)
Illinois (1969)	Nebraska (1920)	Wyoming (1996)

*Hawaii recognizes English and Hawaiian languages.

REFLECTION: Do you see any pattern in which states have passed this law? Does this influence your decision as to where you might want to teach? Do you believe such English Only laws have any practical impact?

government to initiate bilingual education. In 1998, more than 60 percent of the voters in California, including a sizable minority of Hispanic voters, supported an initiative to replace most bilingual maintenance programs with a fast-track transition to English. Proposition 227 required that LEP students be provided a year of English immersion instruction and then be shifted into regular classrooms where only English is spoken, unless their parents obtain a waiver. Several other states followed suit. The legality of such state laws is in the courts as of this writing.[26]

Many people worry that bilingual education threatens the status of English as the nation's primary vehicle of communication. As a result, an **English-only movement** has emerged (see Figure 2.4). Those who support this movement feel that English is a unifying national bond that preserves our common culture. They believe that English should be the only language used or spoken in public and that the purpose of bilingual education should be to quickly teach English to LEP students. In fact, they assert that bilingual education hurts LEP students, by making them dependent on their native language and discouraging them from learning English.

Bilingual education advocates argue that America is a mosaic of diverse cultures and that diversity should be honored and nurtured. One problem, they point out, is that we simply do not have enough competent bilingual teachers who can respond to the large numbers of LEP children now in our schools.[27] Bilingual advocates oppose the English-only movement, and they feel that it promotes intolerance, will turn back the clock, and may very well be unconstitutional. Education writer James Crawford points out, "It is certainly more respectable to discriminate by language than by race. . . . Most people are not sensitive to language discrimination in this nation, so it is easy to argue that you're doing someone a favor by making them speak English."[28]

In recent years, the opponents of bilingual education gained ground as Congress sharply reduced funding for bilingual education. Moreover, a score of "English-only" bills made their way through various state legislatures and Congress, although implementing these laws has proved difficult.[29] The future of bilingual education is still being defined.

What does the research say about the effectiveness of bilingual education? Unfortunately, the research is not clear. Educators are just now beginning to analyze long-term data, and they are uncovering some useful findings. In one case, the researchers found that when language-minority students spend more time learning in their native language, they are more likely to achieve at comparable and even higher levels in English.[30] Another study found that the earlier a student starts learning a new language, the more effective that language becomes in an academic setting.[31] Yet another study showed that no single approach holds a monopoly on success, and different approaches to bilingual education can each be effective, suggesting that local school systems should carefully select the programs most appropriate for their communities.[32]

One major bilingual study directed by Virginia Collier and Wayne Thomas evaluated the experiences by 42,000 students over a thirteen-year period. Early findings suggested that the students enrolled in well-implemented bilingual programs actually *outperform* the students in monolingual programs. One successful approach assumed bilingual education to be a two-way street, one in which English speakers and LEP students would learn from each other. In this model, during the Spanish part of the day, the Spanish-speaking students explained the lessons to native-English peers, while, during English instruction, the reverse took place. Collier and Thomas report that, by fourth grade, the students in these two-way classes had actually outperformed the native English speakers who attended English-only classes.[33]

More than two centuries ago, Ben Franklin expressed his fears about the multiple languages heard on America's streets. His concerns have echoed through the centuries, despite a world in which national borders seem to be blurring or even disappearing. In today's global community, Russians and Americans are working together in space, such international organizations as the United Nations and NATO are expanding their membership, and corporations are crossing national boundaries to create global mergers in an international marketplace. Moreover, technological breakthroughs, such as the Internet, have made international communications not just possible but commonplace. However, for most Americans, these international conversations are viable only if the other side speaks English. In this new international era, Americans find themselves locked in a monolingual society. How strange that, instead of viewing those who speak other languages as welcome assets to our nation, some seem eager to erase linguistic diversity (see Figure 2.5).

 Exceptional Learners

In a typical classroom, a teacher faces students with a great range of abilities, from students reading years behind grade level to students reading years ahead. Both these groups of students are described by the same broad term: **exceptional learners.**

OVERHEADS 23–24
States with Official English Laws

The Growing Number of LEP Students

CRITICAL THINKING QUESTION
With English as the most common second language in the world (and the language of international business, air travel, and technology) why do today's educators need bilingual skills?

FOCUS QUESTION 8
How are the needs of special learners met in today's classrooms?

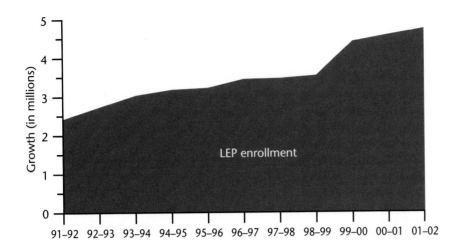

FIGURE 2.5
The growing numbers of limited English proficient students.

SOURCE: U.S. Department of Education Survey of the States, LEP students and available education programs and services, 1991–1992 through 2001–2002.

Integrating exceptional learners into the regular classroom adds further challenge to the job of teaching diverse students.

Typically, exceptional learners are categorized as follows:

- Students with mental retardation
- Students with learning disabilities
- Students with emotional disturbance or behavior disorders
- Students with hearing and language impairments
- Students with visual impairments
- Students with attention deficit hyperactivity disorder
- Students with other health and physical impairments
- Students with severe and multiple disabilities
- Gifted and talented students[34]

CLASS ACTIVITY: EXCEPTIONAL LEARNERS
IM, Activity 2:4

Today, children with disabilities constitute approximately 13 percent of the school-age population. Twice as many males as females are identified as disabled. Most students with disabilities who attend public schools are learning disabled (51 percent), another 19 percent have speech and language impairments, and 11 percent are mentally retarded.[35] (See Figure 2.6.)

We will end this chapter with a close look at issues and developments in teaching exceptional learners, from students with disabilities to gifted and talented learners. Inclusion of each of these populations stretches not only the range of diversity in the classroom but also the range of skills you will need in order to meet the needs of all your students.[36]

Exceptional Learners: An Exceptional Struggle for Educational Rights

Perhaps you have read the book *Karen*. It is the story of a child with cerebral palsy, a child who persevered despite devastating obstacles. A formidable obstacle was an educational system that had no room for children with disabilities. The book was written by Karen's mother, who, like her daughter, refused the rejection of a hostile

CLASS ACTIVITY: HISTORICAL PERSPECTIVES ON SPECIAL EDUCATION
IM, Activity 2:5

Why am I not allowed to speak Spanish at school? Why do Mexican students seem ashamed of speaking Spanish? Am I stupid for not learning English quickly so that I can do the assignments? Why are there no teachers who look like me and who share my culture and language? And why did my parents leave the warmth and comfort of Central America for the indifference and coldness of the United States?[1]

It was 1955. Carlos Julio Ovando had emigrated from Nicaragua and was anxious to show his teachers what he knew. But educationally disenfranchised by his linguistic and cultural background, he could not.

The promise of religious freedom and economic stability had motivated the Ovando family's move to Corpus Christi, Texas. In Nicaragua, the Somoza dictatorship opposed the vigorous attempts of Ovando's father, a former priest turned Protestant minister, to convert Catholics. The family was exiled. Yet, their Latin American heritage remained strong. Even after emigrating, Nicaraguan cultural traditions continued in the Ovando home and discussions of spiritual values were central to the family's daily life.

While home was a cultural touchstone for Ovando, school was foreign territory. Unable to understand the lessons in English, he felt abandoned. At age 14, Carlos was placed in the sixth grade and wondered, "Why do teachers show little interest in who I am?" In Nicaragua, the family was entrusted with home life and the school took care of the academic lessons. But school was clearly not working for Carlos.

> I do not recall my parents ever asking to see my report cards or expressing interest in visiting my school to talk to my teachers about my progress. As in the case with many other newly arrived immigrants, it may be that while tacitly interested in my academic well-being, my parents did not know how or were afraid to approach the unfamiliar American schools.[2]

Disconnected from school and doubtful of his own abilities, Ovando was experiencing education that was not so much immersion as submersion, the classic "sink or swim" approach, and Ovando was sinking, looking at America from the bottom of the pool. Ironically, a different kind of pool, a pool hall, provided to be the turning point in his life.

> The turning point in my academic career began when somebody in the church congregation saw me coming out of a pool hall and told my father. Soon after that, in the hope of saving me from sin, my father sent me to a Mennonite high school in northern Indiana.[3]

At the new school, a teacher saw Ovando in an entirely different way. Not so much English challenged, as Spanish blessed. He affirmed Ovando's Latin American roots and championed his native linguistic talent. Spurred by his teacher's encouragement, Ovando rediscovered confidence in his academic abilities. Rather than being punished for speaking Spanish, his language talents were acclaimed. He won honors, including college scholarships. Ovando now reveled in the world of ideas. He taught Spanish in a Midwest high school before going on to college teaching and writing.

His work shows how language is much more than a set of words and grammar rules: It can be a cultural link for students, one that promotes academic achievement. While critics see bilingual education as a threat to national identity, Ovando envisions a society built on the strengths of its diverse population. He challenges teachers to unlock each student's cultural touchstones: "Pedagogy that activates the student voice and embraces the local community provides a much richer environment for student understanding than pedagogy that treats students as if they were empty vessels into which knowledge is to be poured."[4]

[1]Adapted from Carlos J. Ovando and Virginia P. Collier, *Bilingual and ESL Classrooms: Teaching in Multicultural Contexts*, 2nd ed. (Boston: McGraw-Hill, 1998), p. 2.
[2]Ibid, p. 2.
[3]Ibid, p. 3.
[4]Ibid, p. 24.

REFLECTION: How is the history of bilingual education in America reflected in Ovando's story? What is the downside of promoting a monolingual society? How do you explain the popularity of the effort to make English the "official language" in the United States? Why has the maintenance approach encountered so much difficulty? If you were to teach a student like Ovando, how could you tackle these linguistic and cultural challenges?

www.mhhe.com/ sadker To learn more about Carlos Ovando, click on *Profiles in Education.*

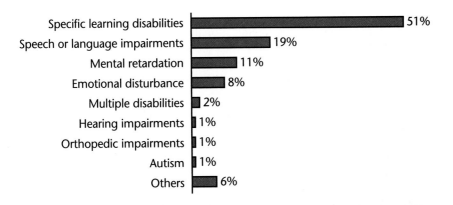

FIGURE 2.6
Distribution of students
served under IDEA.

SOURCE: U.S. Department of
Education, Office of Special
Education Programs, 23rd Annual
Report to Congress (2001),
Table 11–8.

REFLECTION: This distribution offers an insight into which special needs students teachers are most likely to have in regular classrooms. Suggest some of the accommodations a classroom teacher might consider for each of these special needs.

school and society. She wrote of her attempts to gain educational rights for her daughter and other children with disabilities:

> We constantly sought a remedy for this appalling situation which deprived so many of an education, and eventually we found a few doctors and educators who had made strides in developing valid testing methods for handicapped children. On one occasion, when I voiced a plea for the education of the handicapped, a leading state official retorted, "It would be a waste of the state's money. They'll never get jobs."
>
> We were frequently discouraged and not a little frightened as many of our "learned" men [sic] felt the same way.[37]

Such disparaging attitudes were common in our society for years and resulted in inadequate educational programs for millions of exceptional children. Today, the educational rights of these children have been mandated by courts of law and are being put into practice in classrooms across the nation.

Before the Revolutionary War, the most that was offered to exceptional children was protective care in asylums. The asylums made little effort to help these children develop their physical, intellectual, and social skills. Following the American Revolution, however, the ideals of democracy and the development of human potential swept the nation. Within this humanist social context, procedures were devised for teaching the blind and the deaf. Then, in the early 1800s, attempts were made to educate the "idiotic" and the "insane" children who today would be called "mentally retarded" or "emotionally disturbed."

For many years, the legal system mirrored society's judgment that the best policy toward the disabled was "out of sight, out of mind." The courts typically saw education as a privilege rather than a right, and they ruled that children with disabilities should be excluded from schools. The notion was that the majority of children needed to be protected from those with disabilities: from the disruptions they might precipitate, from the excessive demands they might make, and from the discomfort their presence in classrooms might cause.

The years following World War II brought renewed hope and promise. Such pioneers as Grace Fernald, Marianne Frostig, and Heinz Werner—to name but a few—conducted research, developed programs, and gave new impetus to the field of **special education.** Their work was aided by the emergence of new disciplines, such

VIDEO SEGMENT 7
Including Students with
Special Needs

as psychology, sociology, and social work. Parents also continued their struggle, individually and collectively, to obtain educational opportunities for children with disabilities. They took their cause to both the schools and the courts. Special education has broken away from the isolation and institutionalization so common in the late nineteenth century and has moved to mainstream exceptional children, as much as possible, into typical school settings.

By the 1970s, court decisions and federal law had established five critical principles of special education:

OVERHEADS 25–26
Critical Principles of
Special Education

Distribution of Students
Served under IDEA

1. **Zero reject.** The principle of zero reject asserts that no child with disabilities may be denied a free, appropriate public education. Representatives of the disabled have asserted that excluding children with disabilities from public schools violates the constitutional interpretation behind the Supreme Court's *Brown v. Board of Education* (1954) decision, which put an end to claims of "separate but equal" schooling. The courts have responded with landmark decisions in Pennsylvania (*Pennsylvania Association for Retarded Children v. Commonwealth*) and in Washington, DC (*Mill v. D.C. Board of Education*) that mandate public schools in those jurisdictions to provide a free, appropriate education to all children with disabilities. Other federal and state decisions have followed suit.

2. **Nondiscriminatory education.** The principle of nondiscriminatory education, based on the Fifth and Fourteenth Amendments of the U.S. Constitution, mandates that children with disabilities be fairly assessed, so that they can be protected from inappropriate classification and tracking. Much of the court activity in this area has centered on the disproportionate number of children of color assigned to special education classes, a situation that some claim is the result of biased testing. In one case, a court ruled that IQ tests could not be used for placing or tracking students. Other courts have forbidden the use of tests that are culturally biased, and still others have ordered that testing take place in the children's native language.

3. **Appropriate education.** While the principle of zero reject assures that children with disabilities will receive an appropriate public education, it is important to recognize that this principle goes beyond simply allowing children with disabilities to pass through the schoolhouse door. The term "appropriate education" implies that these children have the right to an education involving the accurate diagnosis of individual needs, as well as responsive programs keyed to those needs.

4. **Least-restrictive environment.** Least-restrictive environment protects children with disabilities from being inappropriately segregated from their age-group peers. Court decisions have urged that special needs students be educated with nondisabled children as much as possible. These placements can help students develop relationships and reduce their feelings of isolation. **Mainstreaming** has traditionally referred to placing special needs students in regular classroom settings for at least part of the day. The more recent term, **inclusion,** sometimes called *full inclusion,* reflects an even stronger commitment to educate each student in a least-restrictive environment to the maximum degree possible. Separate classes and schools are to be avoided unless a child's disabilities are such that education in a regular classroom, even with the aid of special materials and supportive services, cannot be achieved. When to include and when to separate is a source of constant debate.

5. **Procedural due process.** The principle of procedural due process upholds the right of the disabled to protest a school's decisions about their education. Due process entails the right of children with disabilities and their parents to be notified of school actions and decisions; to challenge those decisions before an impartial tribunal, using counsel and expert witnesses; to examine the school records on which a decision is based; and to appeal whatever decision is reached.

These five principles of special education law are encompassed in landmark federal legislation passed in 1975, **Public Law 94-142,** the Education for All Handicapped Children Act. This law offers states financial support to make a free and appropriate public education available to every child with disabilities. It was replaced and expanded in 1991 by the **Individuals with Disabilities Education Act (IDEA),** which not only provided a more sensitive description of the act's purpose but also extended the act's coverage to all disabled learners between the ages of 3 and 21, including individuals with autism or traumatic brain injuries. IDEA also provided for rehabilitation and social work services. IDEA requires that each disabled child "have access to the program best suited to that child's special needs which is as close as possible to a normal child's educational program."[38] Classroom teachers shoulder the responsibilities of monitoring the needs of each child with disabilities placed in their classrooms and of using constructive procedures to meet their needs. The law further states that an **individualized education program (IEP)** be developed to provide a written record of those needs and procedures. The law states that an IEP must be written for each child who receives special education services. The IEP must include:

RAP 1.10
Special Education Services, p. 123

A statement of the student's current performance, including long-term (annual) goals and short-term objectives

A description of the nature and duration of the instructional services designed to meet the prescribed goals

An overview of the methods of evaluation that will be used to monitor the child's progress and to determine whether the goals and objectives have been met

There is no specific IEP form that must be used, as long as goals, objectives, services, and evaluation are accurately reflected. In fact, hundreds of different IEP forms are currently in use; some run as long as twenty pages; others are only two or three pages. New teachers should learn about their school district's norms and procedures for writing IEPs when they begin teaching. Remember, it is not the format that is important but, rather, whether or not the IEP accurately describes the educational needs and the related remedial plans. While writing these IEPs will undoubtedly consume a great deal of a teacher's time and energy, it often leads to better communication among the school staff, as well as between teachers and parents. Also, the practice of preparing IEPs will likely lead to more effective individualization of instruction for all children, not just those with disabilities.

School learning environments in the future must accommodate a wide variety of individual and cultural learning styles.

IDEA has been one of the most thoroughly litigated federal laws in history. Parents whose children qualify for special education services can and do sue the school district if they believe their children's needs are not being met. Local courts agreeing with parents' views have ordered public schools to hire extra teachers or specialized personnel or to spend additional dollars to provide an appropriate education. When judges believe that a school is unable to meet the special needs of a child, even with these additional resources, they can and have ordered the public school to pay the tuition so that the student can attend a private school. The practice of judges ordering public schools to pay the private school tuition of some special needs children is currently being reviewed by the Supreme Court.[39]

There is considerable confusion in identifying learning-disabled (LD) students, in deciding who is entitled to additional resources. Educational literature reflects more than fifty terms to describe students with **learning disabilities.** By 2000, about one in every eight students was special needs, a number that has risen 30 percent between 1990 and 2000. In a few areas, like autism, growth has skyrocketed, multiplying tenfold in only two decades.[40] Meeting the needs of special needs students has strained education budgets nationwide.[41] Why the upsurge? The reasons are complex—and troubling. Some believe environmental pollutants increase children's disabilities. Others argue that special needs have always been common, but in past years went undiagnosed. Some critics wonder if today we are over-diagnosing the problem. They point to affluent communities where parents hire private psychologist to ensure that their children are identified as learning disabled. Why would they do this? In wealthy communities such labels attract additional educational resources, smaller class size, and even extended time for taking high-risk tests like the SATs.

But if special education means special privileges for the wealthy, the same diagnosis can mean fewer resources for the poor. Studies indicate that African American and Latino special education students are twice as likely to be educated in a more restrictive and separate setting than wealthier students. Poor parents struggle to make certain that the special education label is *not* attached to their children. In addition to poverty, cultural misunderstanding, low expectations, and the desire to remove "difficult" students from the classroom contribute to the high rate of African American students identified as mentally retarded or emotionally disturbed.[42] And then there is gender. While boys' behavior gets noticed, girls are quieter in class, less likely to cause discipline concerns, and more likely to turn inwardly with problems and anxieties. As a result, their special education needs often go undetected and untreated.[43] So behind the growing numbers of special education students is a disturbing imbalance as boys, students of color, and wealthy students may be over-identified, while females are under-identified.

Once identified, attention focuses on how best to educate these students.[44] Students with mild disabilities typically attend regular classrooms for part of the day, and leave for a period of time to receive special instruction in a resource room. These "pullout" programs have been criticized for stigmatizing students while failing to improve their academic performance. This concern has fueled the **regular education initiative,** which encourages schools to provide special services *within* the regular classroom and encourages close collaboration between classroom teachers and special educators. By 2000, about half of the students with disabilities spent 80 percent or more of the school day in a regular classroom.[45]

Regular classroom teachers often express concerns about their ability to handle a mainstreamed classroom:

> They want us all to be super teachers, but I've got 33 kids in my class and it's really a job to take care of them without also having to deal with special needs kids too. I'm not complaining really—I wouldn't want to do anything other than what I'm doing—but it is demanding.[46]

Although classroom teachers are expected to meet many of society's obligations, including the education of special needs students, they are not always given adequate resources for the task. Frustration is often the result. To succeed, teachers need additional planning time, appropriate curricular materials, ongoing staff development programs, and sometimes, extra classroom assistance. But even with these resources, inclusion will not succeed unless teachers genuinely support the philosophy behind this approach. They must be committed to exploding stereotypes and able to recognize the essential value of helping all children to learn together. Their talents and commitment may be put to the test in communities like San Francisco, where students unable to feed themselves, or speak, or even go to the bathroom, are mainstreamed.[47] These students are part of a first wave of severely impaired children placed in regular classrooms. Although a difficult situation for teachers, students, and parents, the belief is that they will do far better there than in a segregated and restricted environment. Inclusion is at its heart a moral issue, one that raises the timeless principles of equality, justice, and the need for all of us to learn to live and grow together—not apart.

OVERHEAD 27
Accommodations for
Special Needs

The Gifted and Talented

Precocious children are among our most neglected students. They, too, have special needs:

> In Chicago, the school system turned down the request of a 5-year-old boy who wanted to enter school early. While he waits to be allowed to enter kindergarten, the boy spends his time in the public library doing independent research in astronomy and geography. His IQ has been measured at more than 180.
>
> In Westchester County, a suburb of New York City, a 2½-year-old boy already emulates the language abilities of his parents. He speaks and reads English, French, Hebrew, Spanish, and Yiddish, and he has mastered some Danish. He is studying music theory and is conducting scientific experiments. The parents, however, are unable to find any educational facility willing and able to educate their young, gifted child. A member of their local school board told them: "It is not the responsibility or function of public schools to deal with such children." As a result, the parents considered moving to Washington state, where there was an experimental preschool program for the gifted.[48]

If you are like most Americans, you may find it difficult to consider gifted and talented children to be in any way disadvantaged. After all, **gifted learners** are the lucky ones who master subject matter with ease. They are the ones who shout out the solution before most of us have a chance to write down the problem. Others may have perfect musical pitch, are athletic superstars, become the class leaders who inspire us, or demonstrate insights that amaze and inform us. Many exhibit endless curiosity, creativity, and energy. Small wonder that there is relatively little national support for extra funds or programs targeted at these gifted students, the ones who make the rest of us feel somewhat uncomfortable, inadequate, and sometimes just plain envious.

Defining *giftedness,* like defining *learning disabilities,* invites controversy. To some, the traditional definition of *giftedness* includes those with an IQ of 130 or higher; to others, the label *giftedness* is reserved for those with an IQ score of 160 or higher. The National Association for Gifted Children defines five elements of giftedness: artistic

OVERHEAD 28
Characteristics of
Giftedness

YOU BE THE JUDGE
SPECIAL NEEDS STUDENTS

Should Be Mainstreamed Because . . .

WITHOUT INCLUSION, OUR DEMOCRATIC IDEAL IS HOLLOW

Segregating the disabled mirrors the historical segregation of African Americans and other groups, a segregation already rejected by the courts. Separate can never be equal, and all students quickly learn the stigma associated with those in "special" classrooms.

SOCIETY NEEDS THE TALENTS OF ALL ITS CITIZENS

Society needs the skills and economic productivity of all our citizens. Educating the disabled in a segregated setting decreases their opportunity for full and meaningful contributions later in life.

MAINSTREAMING IMPROVES THEIR ACADEMIC AND SOCIAL RELATIONS

Studies indicate that special needs students perform better academically when mainstreamed in regular classes. Not surprisingly, their social adjustment is also improved.

THE NONDISABLED GAIN WHEN SPECIAL NEEDS STUDENTS ARE PRESENT

In our increasingly stratified society, students can spend years in school with peers just like themselves. Inclusion provides an opportunity for children to appreciate and work with people who do not necessarily reflect their own experiences and viewpoints.

Should Not Be Mainstreamed Because . . .

MERELY SITTING IN REGULAR CLASSROOMS DOES NOT GUARANTEE A FITTING EDUCATION

A rallying cry like "democracy" sounds impressive, but we need to ensure that special needs students receive a quality education, and the best place for that is not necessarily in a mainstreamed classroom.

PULL-OUT PROGRAMS CAN OFFER SPECIAL NEEDS STUDENTS THE RESOURCES THEY NEED TO SUCCEED

Pull-out programs for special needs children can offer an adjusted curriculum, special instructional techniques, and smaller class size. Special needs students can soar in classrooms designed to meet their needs, but flounder when they are inappropriately placed in regular classes.

GIFTED AND TALENTED STUDENTS ARE AT PARTICULAR RISK

Gifted and talented students fall within the special needs category, and for them, mainstreaming is a disaster. If the gifted are not challenged, they will be turned off from school, and the gifts of our most able students will be lost to society.

WHEN SPECIAL NEEDS STUDENTS ARE MAINSTREAMED, NONDISABLED STUDENTS SUFFER

As teachers in regular classes adjust learning activities to accommodate the special needs students, other students lose out. The extra time, special curriculum, and attention given to special needs students amount to time and resources taken from others in the class.

SOURCE: Many of these arguments are found in greater detail in Jack L. Nelson, Stuart B. Palonsky, and Kenneth Carlson, *Critical Issues in Education: Dialogue and Dialectics* (New York: McGraw-Hill, 2004), pp. 441–67.

 YOU BE THE JUDGE

What training would help you meet the special needs of students mainstreamed into your classroom? Can "separate" ever be "equal"? Whose needs are of most worth, those of special needs students, or of "regular" students? Do their needs actually conflict? As a teacher, would you want special needs children mainstreamed, or pulled out? Imagine yourself the parent of a special needs child. Would you want your child mainstreamed, or pulled out?

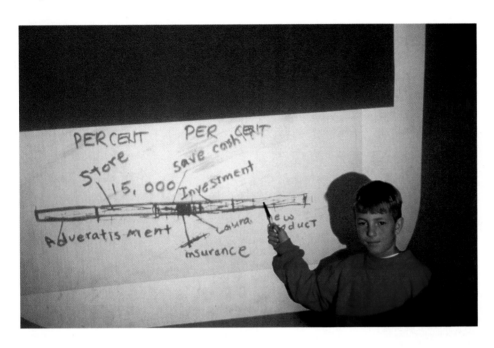

Until recently, schools did little to accommodate the special needs of the gifted and talented.

and creative talents, intellectual and academic abilities, and leadership skills. (See Figure 2.7) Noted psychologist Robert Sternberg has suggested that a new area be included: wisdom. After years of researching what it means to be gifted, Sternberg now believes that giftedness is not just about how analytical and insightful you are, but how you use such skills. A clever business executive who uses his intelligence to earn a fortune, only to leave the company and stockholders in bankruptcy, may have been quite bright, but Sternberg argues that he should not be considered gifted. "The world is getting too dangerous. We have to train kids not just to be smart but to be wise."[49] Sternberg looks to Gandhi and Martin Luther King, Jr. as examples of wisdom too often ignored in current definitions.

While definitions of *giftedness* vary, only a small percentage of our population possesses this high degree of ability, creativity, motivation, pragmatic talent, or wisdom making for a very exclusive club. Exclusivity can invite hostility. Since most people are, by definition, excluded from this highly select group, few believe that the gifted merit any special educational attention. To many Americans, it seems downright undemocratic to provide special services to children who already enjoy an advantage. While many parents of gifted children are strong advocates for their children, some parents of the gifted have shown reluctance to request additional educational programs for their children.

Many gifted students do not make it on their own. Highly talented young people suffer boredom and negative peer pressure when kept in regular classroom settings.[50] Instead of thriving in school, they drop out. The result is that many of our nation's brightest and most competent students are lost to neglect and apathy, and some of our most talented youth have not always succeeded at school.

Even in school districts that recognize the special needs of gifted children, opposition to providing special programs and educational opportunities continues. In some cases, funds are lacking; in others, little interest and commitment to the gifted may be the problem. Some object to special programs for the gifted because they see it as a form of tracking, an undemocratic strategy that separates the gifted from the rest of the population.

CRITICAL THINKING QUESTION

Exclusivity can invite hostility. Do students have any experience of this from their schooling? How might teachers overcome negative student tags for bright students (nerd, geek, oreo)?

FIGURE 2.7
Characteristics of giftedness.

Specific Academic Ability
Enjoys academic success in a
    particular area
Widely read in special area
Acquires basic skills quickly
    and can memorize well
Pursues subject with
    enthusiasm

Creative Thinking
Improvises, creates, invents
Exhibits original thinking
Offers multiple answers to
    questions
Exhibits a sense of humor

Leadership
Assumes responsibility
Holds high expectations for all
Clear expression and well
    organized
Well liked
Demonstrates good judgment
    and likes structure

GIFTEDNESS

Specific Academic Ability
General Intellectual Ability
Can perform abstract thinking
    and create new insights
Inquisitive and excited about
    new ideas
Quick learner and uses large
    vocabulary
Observant and a self starter

Visual and Performing Arts
Skilled self-expression through
    art, dance, drama, music,
    creative expression
Skilled at spatial perception
    and coordination

REFLECTION: Would you include Sternberg's concept of wisdom in this definition? How do these areas relate to Gardner's multiple intelligences?

Research shows that a significant number of gifted students contemplate suicide. Gifted students may be haunted by a sense of isolation and loneliness, pressure to achieve, and fear of failure.[51] Talent, giftedness, and creativity set adolescents apart at a time when the push is for conformity, for being "normal" and "like everybody else." Gifted students most often talk about their feelings of isolation:

I feel as though I'll never fit in any place, no matter how hard I try.

Basically, the challenge in my schooling has not been academic, but having to conform—to be just like everyone else in order to be accepted.

I hate it when people use you. For example, if you have an incredible vocabulary and someone wants your help writing a speech, and then later they tell you to get lost.[52]

The picture is especially dismal for females and children of color who are identified as gifted, and once identified, are more likely to drop out than gifted white males. Many experts urge the use of multiple criteria for identifying and retaining gifted students, including teacher recommendations and assessments of special talents, so that such programs could be more equitable and inclusive.

Once identified, there is no guarantee that gifted students will find high-quality programs. The regular classroom remains a major instructional resource for gifted

RELATED READING
And Still We Rise: The Trials and Triumphs of Twelve Gifted Inner-City High School Students by Miles Corwin (2001).

OVERHEAD 29
Approaches to Teaching Gifted Students

A FEW OF THE PEOPLE IDENTIFIED WITH PHYSICAL, LEARNING AND SPEECH DISABILITIES:

Moses, Demosthenes, Aesop, Cotton Mather, Benjamin Franklin, Clara Barton, Harriet Tubman, Charles Darwin, Jane Addams, Franklin Delano Roosevelt, Congresswoman Carolyn McCarthy, Edward James Olmos, Cher, and James Earl Jones.

THE FOLLOWING INDIVIDUALS WERE ASKED TO LEAVE SCHOOL, DROPPED OUT OR FOUND ALTERNATIVES TO THE ADOLESCENT SCHOOL SCENE:

Salvador Dali, Whoopi Goldberg, Beryl Markham, Edgar Allan Poe, George Bernard Shaw, Percy Bysshe Shelley, James Whistler, and Frank Lloyd Wright.

REFLECTION: Do you know accomplished individuals who did not do well in school? How could education respond to the unique needs of these individuals? (You may want to research the learning issues of these well-known people.)

students. For instance, a gifted student might spend most of the day in a regular class and be pulled out for a part of the day, perhaps an hour or so, to receive special instruction. Another approach is to set up resource centers within the regular classroom, where gifted students are offered individualized tutoring.[53] At the secondary level, comprehensive high schools have augmented their offerings with challenging courses of study, such as the International Baccalaureate (IB) program, an internationally recognized degree program that includes rigorous science, math, and foreign language requirements. Special high schools, such as the Bronx High School of Science and the North Carolina School for Mathematics and Science, have long and distinguished histories of providing educational opportunities for intellectually gifted students. Other special schools have focused on programs in acting, music, and dance. Yet many believe that we need to do a better job of "gifted inclusion," by designing regular class activities that are more responsive to the needs of the gifted.[54]

Some school districts go beyond their own resources in order to meet the needs of gifted students. For instance, one such program connects gifted high school students with the local college or community college. These students spend part of their day enrolled in college-level courses, being intellectually challenged and receiving college credit while still enrolled in high school. Still other gifted students receive additional instruction through summer camps or even special year-long programs that augment their regular courses. Johns Hopkins University, for example, has been sponsoring the Center for Talented Youth (CTY) in different parts of the nation for several decades.

Many of these college programs are termed **accelerated programs,** for they allow gifted students to skip grades or receive college credit early. **Advanced placement** courses and exams (the APs), provide similar acceleration opportunities, permitting students to graduate before their chronological peers. While many Americans accept the notion of enrichment for the gifted, acceleration runs into stronger opposition. The common belief that the negative social consequences of acceleration outweigh the intellectual benefits represents an obstacle to implementing such programs for the gifted.

Whereas social maladjustment due to acceleration may indeed be a problem for some gifted children, others claim they feel just as comfortable, both academically and socially, with their intellectual peers as they do with their chronological peers.

Yet, not accelerating gifted children may lead to boredom, apathy, frustration, and even ridicule. Several studies confirm the value of acceleration, from early admission to elementary school to early admission to college. Grade-accelerated students surpass their classmates in academic achievement and complete higher levels of education. While research suggests that grade acceleration does not cause problems in social and emotional adjustment, cases of students who found acceleration to be a disaster are also plentiful.[55] No single program is likely to meet the needs of all gifted students.

Recognition of the special needs of the gifted has been slow in coming. It is estimated that most school systems provide special gifted services to between 7 and 12 percent of their students. However, with the current trend away from ability grouping, tracking, and special programs, it is possible that fewer resources will be available for the gifted in the years ahead.[56]

The qualities of effective gifted programs include a mastery dimension that allows students to move through the curriculum at their own pace; in-depth and independent learning; field study; and an interdisciplinary dimension that allows for the exploration of theories and issues across the curriculum. Moreover, an important but often overlooked advantage of these programs is the sense of community they offer, the opportunity for gifted students to connect with others like themselves. This is an important step in reducing student anxiety and alienation. When gifted students are placed in appropriate programs, they are often empowered to realize their full potential. One student was relieved to find that "there are lots of people like me and I'm not a weirdo after all." As one 12-year-old girl said,

> My heart is full of gratitude for my teacher who first wanted to have me tested for the gifted program. I'm not trying to brag, but I'm really glad there's a class for people like me. We may seem peculiar or odd, but at least we have fun and we respect each other's talents.[57]

MULTIPLE INTELLIGENCE CONNECTION
Student Diversity covers considerable territory. To deepen understanding (and explore spatial intelligence) have students design a graphic organizer for this chapter.) The organizers may yield solid evidence that everyone learns in diverse ways.

In the final analysis, it is not only the gifted who have suffered from our national neglect and apathy; it is all of us. How many works of art will never be enjoyed? How many medical breakthroughs and how many inventions have been lost because of our insensitivity to the gifted?

These questions of opportunities lost can be broadened to include many of the different student populations discussed in this chapter. How many of these students—because of their race, language, or special needs—have slipped through the educational cracks? How many cultural breakthroughs, intellectual insights, and economic advances have been lost because of inadequate school programs or unresponsive teachers? We will never know the final cost of our neglect, but we can rededicate ourselves to uncovering and nurturing the talents in all our students.

SUMMARY

CHAPTER REVIEW
Go to the Online Learning Center to take a chapter self-quiz, practice with key terms, and review concepts from the chapter.

1. How do cognitive, affective, and physiological factors impact learning?

   Individuals exhibit diverse styles of learning that are affected by attitudes (such as motivation), reasoning (organization and retention of information), and physical needs (preferences ranging from food and sleep needs to comfort levels for room sound or lighting). Because students exhibit a wide range of individual differences, there is no single optimal educational climate.

2. How can teachers respond to different learning styles?

   Teachers may need to adjust room temperature, lighting, and noise level, and plan a variety of activities to accommodate individual student needs. Teachers can work to complement various learning styles, such as visual, kinesthetic, or auditory.

3. What are the classroom implications of Howard Gardner's theory of multiple intelligences?

   Just as some educators challenge the concept of a single appropriate learning style, others challenge the notion of a single type of intelligence. Gardner's theory of multiple intelligences suggests that teachers plan their lessons to incorporate and develop these different intelligences (e.g., ask students to re-enact historical events through dance).

4. How does emotional intelligence influence teaching and learning?

   Daniel Goleman advocates that teachers develop students' emotional (EQ) as well as intellectual (IQ) gifts by helping students understand their emotions, "read" the emotions of others, and learn how to manage relationships.

5. How can teachers meet the diverse needs of an increasingly multicultural student population?

   Today, approximately one-third of the student population is of color, both enriching and challenging our schools. Knowledge about different racial and ethnic groups is critical, yet destructive stereotypes persist. Teachers should work to ensure equitable attention, nurture different learning styles, and include a curriculum that reflects the contributions and experiences of all groups.

6. What are the different levels of multicultural education?

   James Banks identifies four levels of multicultural education: contributions, additive, transformation, and social action. The contributions and additive levels are fairly superficial, while the transformation and social action approaches offer more profound opportunities to learn about the nation's and the world's rich diversity.

7. What are the political and instructional issues surrounding bilingual education?

   In *Lau* v. *Nichols* (1974), the Supreme Court ruled that schools were deficient in their treatment of students with limited English proficiency. Congress subsequently passed the Bilingual Educational Act, and many districts have robust bilingual programs. Some programs teach students in their native language until they learn English (the transitional approach), others teach in both languages (the maintenance approach), and some use English as a Second Language (ESL). Studies suggest that many bilingual programs often fall short of their goals, and some critics advocate fast-paced immersion (also termed "submersion"), an effort supported by those who want English to be declared the "official" American language. The future direction of bilingual education may be as much a political determination as an instructional one.

8. How are the needs of special learners met in today's classrooms?

   The Individuals with Disabilities Education Act (IDEA) guarantees students with disabilities access to public education, and requires that individualized education programs document school efforts and student progress. Despite this law, there are no easy answers to identifying or educating special needs children, and there is much debate around the wisdom of inclusion or mainstreaming. Included in the special education category are gifted and talented students, who are often neglected. School programs for these students usually focus on either enrichment or acceleration.

CURRENT NEWS FROM POWERWEB

To access PowerWeb, go to Chapter 2 on the Online Learning Center to read current articles and to access news feeds about:

- Bilingual Education
- Children
- Children at Risk
- Cultural Diversity in Education
- Intelligence
- Cultural Diversity in Schools
- Racial Integration of Schools
- Social Contexts of Multicultural Education

Go to Chapter 2 on your *Resources for Exploring Education* CD-ROM to access Case Studies, Readings, and Media Observations.

EXTENDED LEARNING

CASE STUDIES

- Carol Brown: A teacher sees her efforts of integrating a diverse class threatened when a child's pencil case disappears and is thought to have been stolen.
- Frances Byrne: A high school resource room teacher places a seemingly unmotivated student with learning disabilities into a high-level history seminar course. Soon after the course begins, the history teacher drops the student from the course.
- Kathryn Carlson: A resource room teacher has been unsuccessful with a student whose classification may not be warranted and whose social behaviors threaten the success of a mainstreaming program.
- Eleanor Collison: The mother of a third-grade included child expresses her frustration with the system when her son's occupational therapist is prevented from providing services to the child in his classroom.
- Carolyn Davis: An experienced first-grade teacher, who has been an inclusion teacher for three years, expresses her frustration with the inclusion process.
- Joan Martin: A classroom teacher, a special education teacher, and a principal hold different views about mainstreaming a boy with poor reading skills.

READINGS

- Nancy Gallavan. "I, Too, Am an American: Preservice Teachers Reflect Upon National Identity."
- Alejandro Portes. "Immigration's Aftermath."
- James Taylor and Richard Baker, Jr. "Discipline and the Special Education Student."
- Cornell West. From *Race Matters.*

KEY TERMS AND PEOPLE

accelerated programs, 67

advanced placement, 67

affective domain, 36

appropriate education, 60

James Banks, 49

bilingual education, 51

Bilingual Education Act, 52

classroom climate, 49

cognitive domain, 36

demographic forecasting, 43

emotional intelligence quotient (EQ), 41

enculturation, 49

English as a Second Language (ESL), 53

English-only movement, 55

Equal Educational Opportunities Act (EEOA), 52

exceptional learners, 56

Howard Gardner, 39

generalizations, 46

gifted learners, 63

Carol Gilligan, 49

Daniel Goleman, 41

immersion, 53

inclusion, 60

individualized education program (IEP), 61

Individuals with Disabilities Education Act (IDEA), 61

intelligence, 38

language submersion, 52

Lau v. *Nichols,* 52

learning disabilities, 62

learning styles, 35

least-restrictive environment, 60

limited English proficiency (LEP), 52

locus of control, 36

mainstreaming (inclusion), 60

maintenance (developmental) approach, 53

multicultural education, 49

DISCUSSION QUESTIONS AND ACTIVITIES

1. How would you characterize your own learning style? Interview other students in your class to determine how they characterize their learning styles. Based on these interviews, what recommendations could you offer your course instructor about how to meet the needs of different students in your class?

2. Can you develop additional intelligences beyond the ones Gardner identifies? (This is often best accomplished in groups.)

3. Given demographic trends, pick a region of the country and a particular community. Develop a scenario of a classroom in that community in the year 2020. Describe the students' characteristics and the teacher's role. Is that classroom likely to be impacted by changing demographics? How will learning styles and the new insights on intelligence be manifested in the way the teacher organizes and instructs the class?

4. Choose a school curriculum and suggest how it can be changed to reflect one of the four approaches to multicultural education described by Banks. Why did you choose the approach you did?

5. Investigate a special education program in a local school. Describe its strengths. What suggestions do you have for improving it?

 WEB-*TIVITIES*
Go to www.mhhe.com/
sadker7e to do the
following activities:
1. Multiple Intelligences
2. Multicultural Education
3. Bilingual Education
4. Exceptional Learners

REEL TO REAL TEACHING

CHILDREN OF A LESSER GOD (1986)
Run Time: 119 minutes

Synopsis: Special education instructor Jim Leeds brings his enthusiasm and innovative instruction to a school for deaf students.

Reflection:

1. How does this film redefine traditional notions of intelligence and the idea of one best learning style? Describe scenes in which Jim Leeds integrated the concepts of diverse learning styles, multiple intelligences, and EQ into his teaching.

2. Both Sarah and Jim ask, "If you want to speak to me, learn my language." Connect this statement with issues explored in the chapter for bilingual education. Brainstorm some linguistic and cultural parallels between bilingual and deaf education.

3. Many believe that the Deaf community has developed not only a system of communication (sign language), but also a unique and valuable culture, one that hearing people should learn more about. Using James Banks' four categories of multicultural education, how might you teach hearing students about Deaf culture?

4. Respond to the principal's remark, "No one is trying to change the world around here. We are only trying to help a few deaf kids get along a little better." What biases underlie this view? As a teacher, how might you fully develop the talents of all students in a diverse classroom, including those with special needs?

Follow-up Activities:

1. So, you wanna make a movie? Tap into your linguistic, spatial, and musical intelligences to create a sequel to *Children of a Lesser God.* Tell us about the lives of Sarah and Jim in twenty years. Has technology changed how they communicate with each other? What career choices did they make? Do they have a family?

2. A critical element in the original film was the dynamic between Jim's voice and Sarah's verbal silence. Some critics thought by telling the whole story from a hearing perspective, deafness was earmarked as a weakness to be overcome by Sarah. In *your* sequel, tell the story from Sarah's perspective. Or strike a balance between verbal and nonverbal communication styles.

How do you rate this film? Go to *Reel to Real Teaching* in the Critics' Corner to review this film.

www.mhhe.com/
sadker7e

FOR FURTHER READING

The Children Are Watching, by Carlos E. Cortés (2000). This book analyzes both entertainment and news media, grappling with issues such as how media frame diversity themes, transmit values concerning diversity, and influence thinking about topics such as race, ethnicity, gender, religion, and sexual orientation.

Crossing Over to Canaan: The Journey of New Teachers in Diverse Classrooms, by Gloria Ladson-Billings (2001). Detailing the struggles and triumphs of eight novice teachers, this book shows how good teachers can use innovation and "teachable moments" to turn cultural differences into academic assets.

Culturally Responsive Teaching: Theory, Research, and Practice, by Geneva Gay (2000). The author discusses the role of teacher expectations and attitudes, formal and informal multicultural curricula, and diverse learning styles in the effort to improve the performance of underachieving students of color.

Latino Students in American Schools, by Guadalupe Valdes (2001). Focusing on the lives and experiences of four Mexican children in an American middle school, Valdes examines the policy and instructional dilemmas surrounding the English language education of immigrant children. Samples of the children's oral and written language as well as an analysis of their classrooms, school, and community are provided.

The Power of the Arts: Creative Strategies for Teaching Exceptional Learners, by Sally Smith (2001). Illustrates how to use the arts to teach academic subjects to children with learning disabilities. Includes step-by-step instructions for arts-based projects that teach science, math, and vocabulary.

Teacher Effectiveness

FOCUS QUESTIONS

1. Are teachers born, or made?
2. How is class time organized and what is academic learning time?
3. What classroom management skills foster academic achievement?
4. What are the roles of teachers and students in the pedagogical cycle?
5. How can teachers set a stage for learning?
6. What questioning strategies increase student achievement?
7. How can teachers best tap into the variety of student learning styles?
8. What are the prevailing models of instruction?
9. What are the future directions of effective teaching research?

 WHAT DO YOU THINK? Qualities of a Good Teacher. Rate the qualities of a good teacher, and see how other students rated these qualities.

CHAPTER PREVIEW

Albert Einstein believed that they awakened the "joy in creative expression and knowledge." Elbert Hubbard saw them as those who could make "two ideas grow where only one grew before." Gail Godwin surmised that they are "one-fourth preparation and three-fourths theater." Ralph Waldo Emerson believed that they could "make hard things easy." About whom are these talented geniuses talking? You guessed it: teachers. Although these intellectual leaders shared an insight into the importance of teaching, even these artists and scientists could not decide if teaching was an art or a science, a gift or a learned skill. Perhaps it is both.

Some individuals seem to take to teaching quite naturally. With little or no preparation, they come to school with a talent to teach and touch the lives of students. Others bring fewer natural talents to the classroom yet, with preparation and practice, become master teachers, models others try to emulate. Most of us fall in the middle, bringing some skills to teaching but also ready to benefit and grow from teacher preparation and practice teaching.

In this chapter, we present recent research findings on effective instruction, focusing on a core set of skills that comprise good teaching. We also detail the prevailing models of instruction, such as cooperative learning and problem-based learning, classroom approaches that have become particularly popular in recent years. You may draw on these skills and models in your own classroom, selecting those that best fit your subject, students, and purpose.

CHAPTER FOCUS
This chapter presents relevant research and practices that support effective teaching and classroom management. Several approaches to instruction will alert readers to the skills associated with successful learning. For a chapter outline, see the IM.

GRABBER: SAMPLE THE
SAMPLER
IM

FOCUS QUESTION 1
Are teachers born, or
made?

TEACHING TIP
Ask students to recall the
best teacher they ever had.
Jot down 1–2 sentences
about that favorite teacher.
Gather several responses to
add to these comments.

CRITICAL THINKING
QUESTION
Are teachers born, or
made? Can students
support their opinions with
evidence? (Check back after
reading the chapter to
determine whether the
evidence is drawn from
effective teaching
behaviors.)

CLASS ACTIVITY
Simulated Teaching
IM, Activity 3:1

 # Are Teachers Born, or Made?

Think about the best teacher you ever had: Try to evoke a clear mental image of what this teacher was like. Here is what some of today's teachers say about their favorite teachers from the past:

> The teacher I remember was charismatic. Going to his class was like attending a Broadway show. But it wasn't just entertainment. He made me understand things. We went step-by-step in such a clear way that I never seemed to get confused—even when we discussed the most difficult subject matter.

> I never watched the clock in my English teacher's class. I never counted how many times she said uh-huh or okay or paused—as I did in some other classes. She made literature come alive—I was always surprised—and sorry—when the bell rang.

> When I had a problem, I felt like I could talk about it with Mrs. Garcia. She was my fifth-grade teacher, and she never made me feel dumb or stupid—even when I had so much trouble with math. After I finished talking to her, I felt as if I could do anything.

> For most of my life, I hated history—endlessly memorizing those facts, figures, dates. I forgot them as soon as the test was over. One year I even threw my history book in the river. But Mr. Cohen taught history in such a way that I could understand the big picture. He asked such interesting, provocative questions—about our past and the lessons it gave for our future.

The debate has been raging for decades: Are teachers born, or made? What do you think?

If you think it is a combination of both, you are in agreement with most people who have seriously considered this question. Some individuals—a rare few—are naturally gifted teachers. Their classrooms are dazzlingly alive. Students are motivated and excited, and their enthusiasm translates into academic achievement. For these truly talented educators, teaching seems to be pure art or magic.

But, behind even the most brilliant teaching performance, there is usually well-practiced skill at work. Look again at those brief descriptions of favorite teachers: Each of them used proven skills—structure, motivation, clarity, high expectations, and effective questioning.

> "We went step-by-step in such a clear way that I never seemed to get confused—even when we discussed the most difficult subject matter." *(structure and clarity)*

> "She made literature come alive." *(motivation)*

> "After I finished talking to her, I felt as if I could do anything." *(high expectations)*

> "He asked such interesting, provocative questions—about our past and the lessons it gave for our future." *(questioning)*

Although there is ample room for natural talent, most teaching is based on "tried and true" skills and models. See Figure 3.1 for a student view of teaching effectiveness. This chapter will introduce you to the research that you can put to work in your classroom.

FIGURE 3.1
Effective teaching through the eyes of students.

REFLECTION: So when you were a kid, how would you have described an effective teacher? Begin to answer the question in the empty writing space.

 ## The Mysterious Case of Teacher Effectiveness

In this chapter, we describe what research tells us about teaching skills and models of instruction that raise student achievement. Some of these research findings may seem like common sense, part of the folk wisdom about teaching. In other cases, the research findings will seem surprisingly counterintuitive, exactly what you thought was not true. Research helps us distinguish between what we "think" will work and

CLASS ACTIVITIES
Individual Statements
IM, Activity 3:3
Portrait of a Good Teacher
IM, Activity 3:7

VIDEO SEGMENT 8
Teaching: More Than
the 3 R's?

FOCUS QUESTION 2
How is class time organized
and what is academic
learning time?

**MULTIPLE INTELLIGENCE
CONNECTION**
To enhance understanding,
have students create a
visual representation and
then label allocated time,
engaged time and learning
time. Compare and contrast
their drawings with
Overhead 31 Time on Task.

OVERHEADS 30–32
Time on Task
High Success Rate

what really works. If you decide to teach, it will be your responsibility to keep up with the burgeoning and sometimes shifting **teacher effectiveness** research through conferences, course work, and education journals.[1] For now, let's introduce you to the research on teacher effectiveness.

 Academic Learning Time

Research shows that students who spend more time pursuing academic content achieve more. That's the commonsense part, and it's hardly surprising. What is startling is how differently teachers use their classroom time. For example, the classic Beginning Teacher Evaluation Study[2] showed that one teacher in the Los Angeles school system spent 68 minutes a day on reading, whereas another spent 137 minutes; one elementary school teacher spent only 16 minutes per day on mathematics, whereas another spent more than three times that amount. Similarly, **John Goodlad**'s comprehensive research study, *A Place Called School,* found that some schools devote approximately 65 percent of their time to instruction, whereas others devote almost 90 percent.[3] The variation is enormous.

Although allocating adequate time to academic content is obviously important, making time on the schedule is not enough. How this allocated time is used in the classroom is the real key to student achievement. To analyze the use of classroom time, researchers have developed the following terms: allocated time, engaged time, and academic learning time.

Allocated time is the time a teacher schedules for a subject—for example, thirty minutes a day for math. The more time allocated for a subject, the higher student achievement in that subject is likely to be.

Engaged time is that part of allocated time in which students are actively involved with academic subject matter (intently listening to a lecture, participating in a class discussion, writing an essay, solving math problems). When students daydream, doodle, write notes to each other, talk with their peers about nonacademic topics, or simply wait for instructions, they are not involved in engaged time. When there is more engaged time within allocated time, student achievement increases.[4] As with allocated time, the amount of time students are engaged with the subject matter varies enormously from teacher to teacher and school to school. In some classes, engaged time is 50 percent; in others, it is more than 90 percent.

Academic learning time is engaged time with a high success rate. Many researchers suggest that students should get 70 to 80 percent of the answers right when working with a teacher. When working independently, and without a teacher available to make corrections, the success rate should be even higher if students are to learn effectively. Some teachers are skeptical when they hear these percentages; they think that experiencing difficulty "stretches" students and helps them achieve. However, studies indicate that a high success rate is positively related to student achievement. How effectively teachers provide for and manage academic learning time in their classrooms is an important key in determining student achievement.[5] (See Figure 3.2.)

In the following sections, you will learn about research-based teaching skills that you can use to

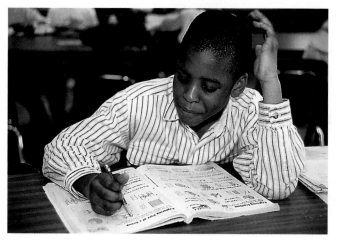

Academic learning time is engaged learning time in which students have a high success rate. When working independently, as here, the success rate should be particularly high.

FIGURE 3.2

Estimated time available for academic learning.

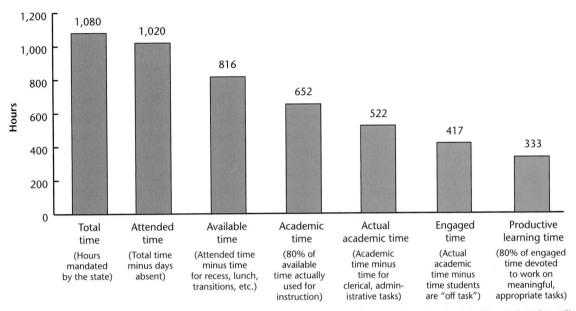

SOURCE: Carol Simon Weinstein and Andrew Migano, Jr., *Elementary Classroom Management: Lessons from Research and Practice*, 3rd ed. New York: McGraw-Hill, 2003.

REFLECTION: Only half of school time is available for instruction, and only half of that is used effectively. Identify three classroom practices that you can implement to recapture productive learning time available to your students.

increase academic learning time and student achievement. Since much time can be frittered away on organizational details and minor student disruptions, we will look first at effective strategies for classroom management. Then we will consider the instructional skills that seem consistently to produce higher academic achievement in students.

 ## Classroom Management

As 10-year-old Lynette approached the room, she could hear the noise of her class-mates. So this was going to be her fourth-grade class. Students were running everywhere. Some were drawing on the board; others were playing tag behind the library shelves. A fight seemed to be breaking out in the coat room. "Where is the teacher?" Lynette wondered. School was supposed to have started five minutes ago.

• • •

As Alicia headed to her fourth-grade classroom, she could see a smiling woman with glasses standing in the doorway and greeting students. "Hello, I'm Mrs. Michaelson," she said. "And you are?"

"Alicia Garza."

"I'm so glad you'll be in our class this year. Your seat is in the second row. Go to your desk right now and you'll find a paper you will need to fill out. It's a special interview form—everyone in the class has one—and it will give us a chance to get to

FOCUS QUESTION 3
What classroom management skills foster academic achievement?

know each other better. Be sure to look at the classroom rules posted on the board as you go in. These are very important for all of us, and I want us to discuss these rules this morning."

As Alicia entered the room, she stopped a minute to read the classroom rules:

RAP 1.2
Understanding the
Developmental and
Psycho-Social Stages,
p. 115

1. Respect other people's rights and feelings. Avoid teasing and making fun of others.
2. Raise your hand to talk. Also, raise your hand if you need help. Share your time and efforts with others. Listening is as important as speaking.
3. Respect other people's property and places. Move around the room safely, and do not disturb others.
4. If you think of a rule that will help us all live and work together more effectively, please share it with us at any time.

Walking to her desk, Alicia noticed that many students, some unknown and some familiar, were already filling out their forms, and many were quietly giggling as they did so.

"I wonder what's on that form," thought Alicia as she slipped into her seat.

These are two different classrooms on the first day of school—in those first five minutes, it becomes obvious that the students will have two very different educational experiences.

VIDEO SEGMENT 9
Classroom Management

Research shows that effective classroom managers are nearly always good planners.[6] They do not enter a room late, after noise and disruption have had a chance to build. They are waiting at the door when the children come in. Starting from the very first day of school, they teach standards or norms of appropriate student behavior, actively and directly. Often they model procedures for getting assistance, leaving the room, going to the pencil sharpener, and the like. The more important rules of classroom behavior are posted, as are the consequences of not following them.[7]

Following are three basic principles for setting expectations, in order to develop a classroom community: (1) rules should be few in number, (2) they should seem fair and reasonable to students, and (3) rules should fit the growth and maturation of the students. Not too long ago (perhaps when you were in school), rules meant obeying the teacher, being quiet, and not misbehaving. As schools have moved away from autocratic teaching styles, student responsibility and ownership of rules (or as one teacher calls them "Habits of Goodness") have become more central.

Student participation in rule formation can be handled in several ways. Some teachers like to develop the list of rules together with their students; other teachers prefer to present a list of established practices and ask students to give specific examples or to provide reasons for having such rules. When rules are easily understood and convey a sense of moral fairness, most students will comply.

Good managers also carefully arrange their classrooms to minimize disturbances, provide students with a sense of confidence and security, and make sure that instruction can proceed efficiently. They set up their rooms according to the following principles:

- *Teachers should be able to see all students at all times.* Student desks should be arranged so the teacher can see everybody from any instructional area. With all students in a direct line of sight, a teacher's nonverbal cues can often short-circuit off-task student behaviors.

- *Teaching materials and supplies should be readily available.* Arranging a "self-help" area so that students have direct access to supplies encourages individual responsibility while freeing up the teacher to focus on instructional activities.

- *High-traffic areas should be free of congestion.* Place student desks away from supply cabinets, pencil sharpeners, and so on. Minor disturbances ripple out, distracting other students from their tasks.

- *Students should be able to see instructional presentations.* Research shows that students who are seated far away from the teacher or the instructional activity are less likely to be involved in class discussions. Good teachers see the entire classroom as their stage, and they intentionally teach from different areas of the class. Placing instructional materials (video monitor, overhead projector, demonstration activity, flip chart, lab station, and the like) in various parts of the room gives each student "the best seat in the house" for at least part of the teaching day.

- *Procedures and routines should be actively taught in the same way that academic content is taught.* Initial planning and organization reduce time wasted on discipline problems and more quickly establish classroom routines and procedures.[8] For students who come from chaotic home environments, these routines offer a sense of stability. Once established, they allow teachers and students more time for academic learning.

The observer walked to the back of the room and sat down. It seemed to him that the classroom was a beehive of activity. A reading group was in progress in the front of the room, while the other children were working with partners on math examples. The classroom was filled with a hum of children working together, and in several languages—but the activity and the noise were organized and not chaotic.

The observer had been in enough schools over the past twenty years to know that this well-managed classroom did not result from magic but that carefully established and maintained procedures were at work. The observer scrutinized the classroom, searching for the procedures that allowed twenty-six students and one teacher to work together so industriously, harmoniously, and effectively.

First he examined the reading group, where the teacher was leading a discussion about the meaning of a story. "Why was Tony worried about the trip he was going to take?" the teacher asked (a few seconds' pause, all the children with eyes on the teacher, several hands raised). "Sean?"

As Sean began his response, the observer's eyes wandered around the rest of the room, where most of the children were busy at work. Two girls, however, were passing notes surreptitiously in the corner of the room.

During a quick sweep of the room, the teacher spotted the misbehavior. The two girls watched the teacher frown and put her finger over her lips. They quickly returned to their work. The exchange had been so rapid and so quiet that the reading group was not interrupted for even a second.

Another student in the math group had his hand raised. The teacher motioned Omar to come to her side.

"Look for the paragraph in your story that tells how Tony felt after his visit to his grandmother," the teacher instructed the reading group. "When you have found it, raise your hands."

While the reading group looked for the appropriate passage, the teacher quietly assisted Omar. In less than a minute, Omar was back at his seat, and the teacher was once again discussing the story with her reading group.

At 10:15, the teacher sent the reading group back to their seats and quietly counted down from ten to one. As she approached one, the room became quiet and the students' attention was focused on her. "It is now time for social studies. Before you do anything, listen carefully to *all* my instructions. When I tap the bell on my

RELATED READING

Beyond Discipline: From Compliance to Community by Alfie Kohn (1997).

CLASS ACTIVITY: OBSERVATIONS
IM, Activity 3:4

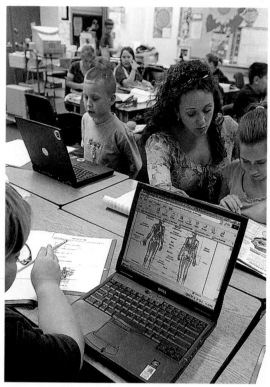

Modern classrooms are complex environments that require carefully planned rules and routines.

desk, those working on math should put their papers in their cubbies for now. You may have a chance to finish them later. Then all students should take out their social studies books and turn to page 67. When you hear the sound of the bell, I want you to follow those instructions." After a second's pause, the teacher tapped the bell, and the class was once again a sea of motion, but it was motion that the teacher had organized while the students were now taking responsibility for their own learning.

The observer made some notes on his forms. There was nothing particularly flashy or dramatic about what he had seen. It was not the type of theatrical performance that teachers sometimes put on to dazzle him. But he was satisfied, because he knew he had been witnessing a well-managed classroom.

• • •

Can you remember from your childhood those activity books in which you had to find the five things wrong in a picture? Let us reverse the game: Try rereading this classroom vignette and look for all the things that are *right* with the picture. What could the observer have noted about the teacher's behavior and her procedures that enabled her students to focus on academic content so effectively? Underline four or five examples of what the teacher did well.

In well-managed classes where teachers keep the momentum going, students are more likely to be on task. The teacher in this vignette used several strategies to avoid interruptions and to keep instruction proceeding smoothly.[9] Did you notice that

CRITICAL THINKING QUESTION

Even before you review the 5 strategies, are students able to use the vignette to predict routines of a well-managed classroom?

1. The teacher used a questioning technique known as **group alerting** to keep the reading group involved. By asking questions first and then naming the student to respond, she kept all the students awake and on their toes. If she had said, "Sean, why did Tony feel concerned about his trip?" the other students in the group would have been less concerned about paying attention and answering the question. Instead, she asked her question first and then called on a student to respond.

2. The teacher seemed to have "eyes in the back of her head." Termed **withitness** by researcher Jacob Kounin, this quality characterizes teachers who are aware of student behavior in all parts of the room at all times. While the teacher was conducting the reading group, she was aware of the students passing notes and the one who needed assistance.

3. The teacher was able to attend to interruptions or behavior problems while continuing the lesson. Kounin calls the ability to do several things at once **overlapping**. The teacher reprimanded the students passing notes and helped another child with a math problem without interrupting the flow of her reading lesson.

4. The teacher managed routine misbehavior using the principle of **least intervention.** Since research shows the time spent disciplining students is negatively related to achievement, teachers should use the simplest intervention

Good classroom management requires constant monitoring of student behavior.

that will work. In this case, the teacher did not make a mountain out of a molehill. She intervened quietly and quickly to stop students from passing notes. Her nonverbal cue was all that was necessary, and did not disrupt the students working on math and reading. The teacher might also have used some other effective strategies. She could have praised the students who were attending to their math ("I'm glad to see so many partners working well on their math assignments"). If it had been necessary to say more to the girls passing notes, she should have alerted them to what they *should* be doing, rather than emphasize their misbehavior ("Deanne and U-Mei, please attend to your own work," *not* "Deanne and U-Mei, stop passing notes").

5. The teacher managed the transition from one lesson to the next smoothly and effectively, avoiding a bumpy transition, which Kounin termed **fragmentation.** When students must move from one activity to another, a gap is created in the fabric of instruction. Chaos can result when transitions are not handled competently by the instructor. Did you notice that the teacher gave a clear transition signal, either the countdown or the bell; gave thorough instructions so her students would know exactly what to do next; and made the transition all at once for the entire class? These may seem simple, commonsense behaviors, but countless classes have come apart at the seams because transitions were not handled effectively.

This vignette illustrated routine classroom management and the handling of minor rule infractions. Sometimes teachers, of course, face more serious misbehavior, especially but not exclusively with older students. When students do not obey a simple reminder, the teacher should repeat the warning, clearly stating the appropriate behavior. If this fails, the teacher will need to apply stronger consequences, such as sending the student to the school office or calling the parents. When teachers must apply such consequences, these should immediately follow the inappropriate behavior, should be mildly but not severely unpleasant, and should be as brief as possible.[10] These episodes should communicate the message "I care about you, but I will not tolerate inappropriate behavior."

TEACHING TIP
"I care about you, but I will
not tolerate inappropriate
behavior." Can students
recall examples of a
teacher's actions that
mirrored this point of view?

A child's rage can result from abuse, powerlessness, trauma, and even normal living, events beyond the teacher's power to alter. Nonetheless, teachers must understand and manage student anger and aggression. Several classroom strategies can help:

- *Choice.* Constantly taking away privileges and threatening punishment can cause students to feel intimidated and victimized. Teachers can provide appropriate options to give a student a sense of some control and freedom. Encouraging a student to select a lunch mate or to choose a project topic offers a reasonable decision-making opportunity and can help avoid aggression and rage.

- *Responsibility.* Rechanneling student energy and interest into constructive activities and responsibilities can reduce misbehavior. When instruction is meaningful and worthwhile, boredom and fooling around are less likely to occur.[11] When students are empowered, they are less likely to vent rage.

- *Voice.* Listening to young people is one of the most respectful skills a teacher can model. Students who feel they are not heard feel disrespected. Hearing and honoring students' words (and feelings) reduce the likelihood of misbehavior.[12]

RELATED READING
Fires in the Bathroom by
Kathleen Cushman, (2003).

Listening to students was exactly what Kathleen Cushman did when she wrote *Fires in the Bathroom.* The title comes from one teenager's story of a first-year high school teacher who tried too hard to be friendly, only to have her efforts go up in flames (literally). Kindness without boundaries and rules can push even well-intentioned teachers into an abyss of chaos. Cushman's brief book offers guidelines to encourage teachers to interview their own students, to help us all remember how schools look through the eyes of students. Adolescents from around the nation were asked to tell teachers what they would like to see in their classrooms. Students advised teachers to: share your plans with me and tell me how I will be evaluated, be excited about what you teach, be firm when rules are broken, treat me fairly but remember I am an individual, give me feedback and encouragement, don't say "please" too much, and don't push yourself into my personal life.[13]

Student misbehavior challenges most new teachers even more than leading instructional lessons.[14] You will have students who will test your patience and others whose stories will tear at your heart. Being observant of student behaviors that might signal a problem is always a good idea. As newspaper stories too frequently remind us, student problems can sometimes explode into tragic violence.

OVERHEAD 33
Jacob Kounin's Patterns
to Avoid During Times
of Transition

While we can't always detect the signs of danger, we can be on the lookout and can create management plans to handle small distractions as well as major incidents. As researcher David Berliner says, "In short, from the opening bell to the end of the day, the better classroom managers are thinking ahead. While maintaining a pleasant classroom atmosphere, these teachers keep planning how to organize, manage, and control activities to facilitate instruction."[15] Berliner makes an important connection between management and instruction. Effective teachers, in addition to being good classroom managers, must also be good organizers of academic content and instruction.

The Pedagogical Cycle

FOCUS QUESTION 4
What are the roles of
teachers and students in
the pedagogical cycle?

How does one organize classroom life? Researcher **Arno Bellack** analyzed verbal exchanges between teachers and students and offers a fascinating insight into classroom organization, likening these interactions to a pedagogical game.[16] The game is so

Teachers must manage more than thirty major **transitions** every day, from one content area to another, through different instructional activities and through a myriad of routines, including having students line up, collecting papers, distributing texts, and the like. During these transitions, discipline problems occur twice as often as in regular classroom instruction. Classroom management expert **Jacob Kounin** identified five common patterns that can derail classroom management during times of transition:

- **Flip-flops.** In this negative pattern, the teacher terminates one activity, begins a new one, and then flops back to the original activity. For example, in making a transition from math to spelling, the teacher says, "Please open your spelling books to page 29. By the way, how many of you got all the math problems right?"
- **Overdwelling.** This bad habit includes preaching, nagging, and spending more time than necessary to correct an infraction of classroom rules. "Anna, I told you to stop talking. If I've told you once, I've told you 100 times. I told you yesterday and the day before that. The way things are going, I'll be telling it to you all year, and, believe me, I'm getting pretty tired of it. And another thing, young lady . . . "
- **Fragmentation.** In this bumpy transition, the teacher breaks directions into several choppy steps instead of accomplishing the instructions in one fluid unit—for example, "Put away your reading books. You shouldn't have any spelling books on your desk, either. All notes should be off your desk," instead of the simpler and more effective "Clear your desk of all books and papers."
- **Thrusts.** Classroom momentum is interrupted by *non sequitors* and random thoughts that just seem to pop into the teacher's head—for example, the class is busily engaged in independent reading, when their quiet concentration is broken by the teacher, who says, "Where's Roberto? Wasn't he here earlier this morning?"
- **Dangles.** Similar to the thrust, this move involves starting something, only to leave it hanging or dangling—for example, "Richard, would you please read the first paragraph on page 94. Oh, class, did I tell you about the guest speaker we're having today? How could I have forgotten about that?"

SOURCE: Jacob Kounin, *Discipline and Group Management in Classrooms* (New York: Holt, Rinehart & Winston, 1970).

REFLECTION: Since each of the above patterns represents a problem, can you reword the dialogue to produce a more effective transition?

cyclical and occurs so frequently that many teachers and students do not even know that they are playing. There are four moves:

1. *Structure.* The teacher provides information, provides direction, and introduces the topics.
2. *Question.* The teacher asks a question.
3. *Respond.* The student answers the question, or tries to.
4. *React.* The teacher reacts to the student's answer and provides feedback.

These four steps make up a **pedagogical cycle,** diagrammed in Figure 3.3. Teachers initiate about 85 percent of the cycles, which are used over and over again in classroom interaction. When teachers learn to consciously enhance and refine each of the cycle's moves, student achievement is increased.[17]

TEACHING TIP
Ask two students to dramatize the teacher-student interactions of the pedagogical cycle while you narrate the roles—the teacher provides the structure, then questions, the student responds and the teacher reacts.

Clarity and Academic Structure

Have you ever been to a class where the teacher is bombarded with questions? "What are we supposed to do?" "Can you explain it again?" "What do you mean?" When such questions are constant, it is a sure sign that the teacher is not setting the stage for instruction. Students need a clear understanding of what they are expected to learn, and they need motivation to learn it.[18] Effective **academic structure** sets the stage for learning and occurs mainly at the beginning of the lesson. Although the

FOCUS QUESTION 5
How can teachers set a stage for learning?

FIGURE 3.3
Pedagogical cycle and sample classroom dialogue.

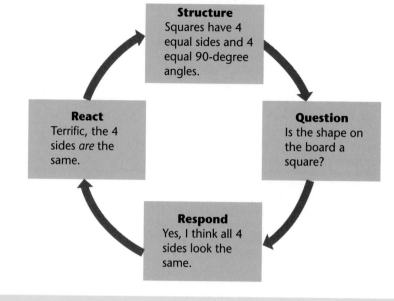

REFLECTION: Continue the classroom dialogue around the cycle again. What might the teacher and the student(s) say?

specific structure will vary depending on the students' backgrounds and the difficulty of the subject matter, an effective academic structure usually consists of

- *Objectives.* Let the students know the objectives (or purpose) of each lesson. Students, like the teacher, need a road map of where they are going and why.

- *Review.* Help students review prior learning before presenting new information. If there is confusion, reteach.

- *Motivation.* Create an "anticipatory set" that motivates students to attend to the lesson. Consider throwing out an intriguing question, an anecdote, a joke, or a challenging riddle.

- *Transition.* Provide connections to help students integrate old and new information.

- *Clarification.* Break down a large body of information. (This is sometimes called "chunking.") Do not inundate students with too much too fast. This is particularly true for young children and slower learners, although it also applies to older and faster learners.

- *Scaffolding.* Step-by-step practice and well-crafted questions support and encourage student understanding.[19]

- *Examples.* Give several examples and illustrations to explain main points and ideas.

- *Directions.* Give directions distinctly and slowly. If students are confused about what they are supposed to do, repeat or break information into small segments.

- *Enthusiasm.* Demonstrate personal enthusiasm for the academic content. Make it clear why the information is interesting and important.

A time-out area, a visit to the principal, or an hour of detention are typical disciplinary practices in elementary, middle, and high school. What school-based discipline programs can you recall from your K–12 years? Are your recollections influenced by any first-hand experiences?

- *Closure.* Close the lesson with a brief review or summary. If students are able to provide the summary, so much the better, for it shows that they have really understood the lesson.

The major activity in academic structuring takes place at the beginning of the lesson, but there may be several points throughout the lesson where substructuring or brief presentations of information are also necessary. Substructures initiate new pedagogical cycles and allow the discussion to continue. A clear summary or review is also important at the close of the lesson.

When teachers generate motivation and provide a clear introduction, all aspects of the lesson will proceed more smoothly.[20] Through effective and clear structure, the stage is set for the remaining steps of the pedagogical cycle.

Questioning

FOCUS QUESTION 6
What questioning strategies increase student achievement?

Good questioning is at the very core of good teaching. As John Dewey said,

> To question well is to teach well. In the skillful use of the question more than anything else lies the fine art of teaching; for in it we have the guide to clear and vivid ideas, and the quick spur to imagination, the stimulus to thought, the incentive to action.[21]

Since questioning is key in guiding learning, all students should have equal access to classroom questions and academic interaction. Yet sitting in the same classroom taught by the same teacher, students experience significant differences in the number of questions they are asked. Research shows that male students are asked more questions than female students, and white students are asked more questions than non-white students. One of the reasons boys get to answer questions as well as to talk more is that they are assertive in grabbing teacher attention. Boys are more likely than girls to call out the answers to the questions. In addition, when boys call out the answers to questions, teachers are likely to accept their responses. When girls call out the answers, teachers often remind them to raise their hands. Teacher expectations also play a role and are frequently cited as one of the reasons white students (perceived as higher achievers) receive more questions and more active teacher attention than students who are members of other racial and ethnic groups.[22]

If you want all students, not just the quickest and most assertive, to answer questions, establish a protocol for participation. For example, make a rule that students must raise their hands and be called on before they may talk. Too many classes offer variations of the following scene:

TEACHER: How much is 60 + 4 + 12? (*Many students raise their hands—both girls and boys.*)

TONY: (*Shouts out*) 76!

TEACHER: Okay. How much is 50 + 9 + 8?

This scene, repeated again and again in classes across the country, is a typical example of the squeaky wheel—not necessarily the most needy or most deserving—getting the educational oil. Once you make the rule that students should raise their hands before participating, *hold to that rule.*

TEACHING TIP
Demontrate the *think-pair-share* strategy with your class. Ask pairs to distinguish several lower- and higher-order questions. Or, ask them to describe the benefits of active involvement over one-at-a-time question and response patterns.

Many teachers are well-intentioned about having students raise their hands, but, in the rapid pace of classroom interaction, they sometimes forget their own rule. If you hold to that "wait to be recognized" rule, you can make professional decisions about who should answer which questions and why. If you give away this key to classroom participation, you are abandoning an important part of your professional decision making in the classroom.

There is more to managing classroom questions than taking the role of a traffic cop. For instance, you might assign pairs of students to work together (sometimes called "Think-Pair-Share") to develop and record answers and then present them to the class as a whole. Or perhaps teams of four or five students can be established to tackle academic questions on a regular basis. When students are actively involved in either of these approaches, the teacher can move around the room as a facilitator, answering questions, motivating student groups, and assessing how the groups are doing. More important, the students take ownership of the questions, asking sincere questions reflecting their genuine interests.

INTERACTIVE ACTIVITY
Questioning Levels
Match questions to the different questioning levels.

While the distribution and ownership of questions are important, the type of question asked is also meaningful. This section provides more information about the different levels of classroom questions, as well as strategies for using them fairly and effectively.

Many educators differentiate between factual, lower-order questions and thought-provoking, higher-order questions. Perhaps the most widely used system for determining the intellectual level of questions is Benjamin **Bloom's taxonomy,** which proceeds from the lowest level of questions, knowledge, to the highest level, evaluation.[23]

A **lower-order question** can be answered through memory and recall. For example, "What is the name of the largest Native American nation?" is a lower-order question. Without consulting outside references, one could respond with the correct answer only by remembering previously learned information. (Cherokee for those who do not recall.) Students either know the answer or they don't. Research indicates that 70 to 95 percent of a teacher's questions are lower-order.

A **higher-order question** demands more thought and usually more time before students reach a response. These questions may ask for evaluations, comparisons, causal relationships, problem solving, or divergent, open-ended thinking. Following are examples of higher-order questions:

1. Do you think that William Clinton was an effective president? Why or why not?

2. What similarities in theme emerge in the three Coen movies: *Oh Brother, Where Art Thou, Raising Arizona,* and *Fargo*?

3. Considering changes that have taken place in the past decade, describe the impact of computer technology on campus life.

4. Considering what you have learned in this child care course, if an infant is persistently crying, what are three things you might try to calm the child?

5. What could happen if our shadows came to life?

Although higher-order questions have been shown to produce increased student achievement, most teachers ask very few of them.[24]

Many educators think that different questioning levels stimulate different levels of thought. If you ask a fifth-grade student to define an adjective, you are working on lower-level basic skills. If you ask a fifth-grade student to write a short story, making effective use of adjectives, you are working on a higher level of student achievement. Both lower-order and higher-order questions are important and should be matched to appropriate instructional goals:

Ask lower-order questions when students are

- Being introduced to new information
- Working on drill and practice
- Reviewing previously learned information

Ask higher-order questions when students are

- Working on problem-solving skills
- Involved in a creative or affective discussion
- Asked to make judgments about quality, aesthetics, or ethics
- Challenged to manipulate already established information in more sophisticated ways

INTERACTIVE ACTIVITY
The Question
Master Game
Test your knowledge of
Bloom's Taxonomy.

LEVEL I: KNOWLEDGE

Requires student to recall or recognize information. Student must rely on memory or senses to provide the answer.

Sample Questions What does "quixotic" mean?

List the first ten presidents of the United States.

LEVEL II: COMPREHENSION

Requires student to go beyond simple recall and demonstrate the ability to mentally arrange and organize information. Student must use previously learned information by putting it in his or her own words and rephrasing it.

Sample Question In our story, the author discusses why the family left Oklahoma. Can you summarize why in your own words?

LEVEL III: APPLICATION

Requires student to apply previously learned information to answer a problem. At this level the student uses a rule, a definition, a classification system, or directions in solving a problem with specific correct answer.

Sample Questions Applying the law of supply and demand, solve the following problem. *(applying a rule)*

Identify the proper noun in the following sentences. *(applying a definition)*

Solve the quadratic equation. *(applying a rule)*

LEVEL IV: ANALYSIS

Requires student to use three kinds of cognitive processes: (1) To identify causes, reasons, or motives (when these have not been provided to the student previously), (2) To analyze information to reach a generalization or conclusion, (3) To find evidence to support a specific opinion, event, or situation.

Sample Questions Why do you think King Lear misjudged his daughter? *(identifying motives)*

What generalizations can you make about the climate of Egypt near the Nile River basin? *(analyze information to reach a conclusion)*

Many historians think that Abraham Lincoln was our finest president. What evidence can you find to support this statement? *(find evidence to support a specific opinion)*

LEVEL V: SYNTHESIS

Requires student to use original and creative thinking: (1) To develop original communications, (2) To make predictions, and (3) To solve problems for which there is no single right answer.

Sample Questions Write a short story about life on another planet. *(developing an original communication)*

What do you think life would be like if Germany had won World War II? *(making predictions)*

How can our class raise money for the dance festival? *(solving problems for which there is no single right solution)*

LEVEL VI: EVALUATION

Requires student to judge the merits of an aesthetic work, an idea, or the solution to a problem.

Sample Questions Which U.S. senator do you think is most effective? Support your selection.

Do you think that schools are too hard or not hard enough? Explain your answer.

REFLECTION: Starting with your own sample question at Level I (Knowledge) can you expand your questioning to Level VI (Evaluation)? Or, using Bloom's taxonomy as the content, create a question at each level about this classification system (e.g., Level I; List the six levels of Bloom's Taxonomy).

OVERHEADS 35–36
Bloom's Taxonomy Applied to Questioning Levels
Bloom's Taxonomy (Student Generated Responses)

Student Response

If you were to spend a few minutes in a high school English class, you might hear a classroom discussion go something like this:

TEACHER: Who wrote the poem "Stopping by Woods on a Snowy Evening"? Tomàs?

TOMÀS: Robert Frost.

TEACHER: Good. What action takes place in the poem? Kenisha?

KENISHA: A man stops his sleigh to watch the woods get filled with snow.

TEACHER: Yes. Denise, what thoughts go through the man's mind?

DENISE: He thinks how beautiful the woods are. *(Pauses for a second)*

TEACHER: What else does he think about? Russell?

RUSSELL: He thinks how he would like to stay and watch. *(Pauses for a second)*

TEACHER: Yes—and what else? Rita? *(Waits half a second)* Come on, Rita, you can answer this. *(Waits half a second)* Well, why does he feel he can't stay there indefinitely and watch the woods and the snow?

RITA: He knows he's too busy. He's got too many things to do to stay there for so long.

TEACHER: Good. In the poem's last line, the man says that he has miles to go before he sleeps. What might sleep be a symbol for? Krista?

KRISTA: Well, I think it might be . . . *(Pauses for a second)*

TEACHER: Think, Krista. *(Waits for half a second)* All right then—Eugene? *(Waits again for half a second)* James? *(Waits half a second)* What's the matter with everyone today? Didn't you do the reading?[25]

The teacher is using several instructional skills effectively. His is a well-managed classroom. The students are on task and engaged in a discussion appropriate to the academic content. By asking a series of lower-order questions ("Who wrote the poem?" "What action takes place in the poem?"), the teacher works with the students to establish an information base. Then the teacher builds to higher-order questions about the poem's theme and meaning.

If you were to give this teacher suggestions on how to improve his questioning techniques, you might point out the difficulty students have in answering the more complex questions. You might also note the lightning pace at which this lesson proceeds. The teacher fires questions so rapidly that the students barely have time to think. This is not so troublesome when they are answering factual questions that require a brief memorized response. However, students begin to flounder when they are required to answer more complex questions with equal speed.

Although it is important to keep classroom discussion moving at a brisk pace, sometimes teachers push forward too rapidly. Slowing down at two key places during classroom discussion can usually improve the effectiveness and equity of classroom responses. In the research on classroom interaction, this slowing down is called **wait time.**[26]

Mary Budd Rowe's research on wait time shows that, after asking a question, teachers typically wait only one second or less for a student response (wait time 1). If the response is not forthcoming in that time, teachers rephrase the question, ask another student to answer it, or answer it themselves. If teachers can learn to increase their wait time from one second to three to five seconds, significant improvements in the quantity and quality of student response usually will take place.

There is another point in classroom discussion when wait time can be increased. After students complete an answer, teachers often begin their reaction or their next question before a second has passed (wait time 2). Once again, it is important for teachers to increase their wait time from one second to three to five seconds. Based on her research, Mary Budd Rowe has determined that increasing the pause after a student gives an answer is equally as important as increasing wait time 1, the pause after the teacher asks a question. When wait time 1 and wait time 2 are increased, classroom interaction is changed in several positive ways.

Teacher questioning patterns have much to do with the learning climate in classrooms.

OVERHEADS 37–38

Wait Time: Changes in Student Behavior

Wait Time: Changes in Teacher Behavior

Changes in Student Behavior

- More students participate in discussion.
- Fewer discipline problems disrupt the class.
- The length of student response increases dramatically.
- Students are more likely to support their statements with evidence.
- Speculative thinking increases.
- There are more student questions and fewer failures to respond.
- Student achievement increases on written tests that measure more complex levels of thinking.

Changes in Teacher Behavior

- Teacher comments are less disjointed and more fluent. Classroom discussion becomes more logical, thoughtful, and coherent.
- Teachers ask more sophisticated, higher-order questions.
- Teachers begin to hold higher expectations for all students.

Research indicates that teachers give more wait time to students for whom they hold higher expectations. A high-achieving student is more likely to get time to think than is a low-achieving student. If we do not expect much from our students, we will not get much. High expectations and longer wait times are positively related to achievement. Researchers suggest that white male students, particularly high achievers, are more likely to be given adequate wait time than are females and students of color. Students who are quiet and reserved or who think more slowly may obtain special benefit from increased wait time. In fact, a key benefit of extended wait time is an increase in the quality of student participation, even from students who were previously silent.

Usually when teachers learn that they are giving students less than a second to think, they are surprised and have every intention of waiting longer, but that is easier said than done! In the hectic arena of the classroom, it is all too easy to slip into split-second question-and-answer patterns.

Sometimes teachers fall into a pattern of quickly repeating every answer that students give. Occasionally this repetition can be helpful—if some students may not have heard it or if an answer merits repetition for emphasis. In most cases, however, this "teacher echo" is counterproductive. Students learn they do not need to listen to one another, because the teacher will repeat the answer anyway. The teacher echo also reduces valuable wait time and cuts down on the pause that allows students to think. Teachers who have worked on increasing wait time offer some useful tips.

Some teachers adopt self-monitoring cues to slow themselves down at the two key wait-time points. For example, one teacher says that he puts his hand behind his back and counts on his fingers for three seconds to slow himself down. Another teacher says that she covers her mouth with her hand (in a thoughtful pose) to keep herself from talking and thereby destroying "the pause that lets them think."

As mentioned previously, wait time is more important in some cases than in others. If you are asking students to repeat previously memorized math facts and you are interested in developing speed, a three- to five-second wait time may be counterproductive. However, if you have asked a higher-order question that calls for a complicated answer, be sure that wait times 1 and 2 are ample. Simply put, students, like the rest of us, need time to think, and some students may need more wait time than others. For example, when a student speaks English as a newly acquired language, additional wait time could help that student accurately translate and respond to the question. And many of us could profit by less impulsive, more thoughtful responses, the kind that can be engendered by a five-second wait time.

When teachers allow more wait time, the results can be surprising. Not only do more students answer questions, there is also an increase in **student-initiated questions.** While many educators believe that questioning is at the heart of learning, students ask remarkably few content-related questions. (Students in the upper grades ask fewer than 15 percent of classroom questions.)[27] Teachers can nourish genuine inquiry and tap student curiosity by encouraging student-initiated questions. As one teacher said, "I never thought Andrea had anything to say. She just used to sit there like a bump on a log. Then I tried calling on her and giving her time to answer. What a difference! Not only does she answer, she asks questions that no one else has thought of."

Reaction or Productive Feedback

"Today," the student teacher said, "we are going to hear the story of *The Three Billy Goats Gruff*." A murmur of anticipation rippled through the kindergarten children comfortably seated on the carpet around the flannel board. This student teacher was a favorite, and the children were particularly happy when she told them flannel-board stories.

"Before we begin the story, I want to make sure we know what all the words mean. Who can tell me what a troll is?"

A 5-year-old nicknamed B.J. raised his hand. "A troll is someone who walks you home from school."

"Okay," the teacher responded, a slightly puzzled look flickering over her face. "Who else can tell me what a troll is?"

GLOBAL VIEW

Some linguists suggest that fast-paced communication with very little wait time is typical of American classrooms. Have international students speculate about their experiences: Do students sit silently until called upon? Would interruptions or calling out be infrequent? Is asking the teacher a question inappropriate?

RAP 1.8
Tutor Using Effective Feedback p. 121

Another student chimed in, "A troll is someone with white hair sticking out of his head."

"Okay," the teacher said.

Another student volunteered, "It hides under bridges and waits for you and scares you."

"Uh-huh," said the teacher.

Warming to the topic, another student gleefully recounted, "I saw a green troll named Shrek who lives in the woods."

"Okay," the teacher said.

Wide-eyed, B.J. raised his hand again, "I'm sure glad we had this talk about trolls," he said. "I'm not going home with them from school anymore."

"Okay," the teacher said.

This is a classroom in which several good teaching strategies are in operation. The teacher uses effective academic structure, and the students are on task, interested, and involved in the learning activity. The teacher is asking lower-order questions appropriately, to make sure the students know key vocabulary words before the flannel-board story is told. The problem with this classroom lies in the fourth stage of the pedagogical cycle: This teacher does not provide specific reactions and adequate feedback. Did you notice that the teacher reacted with "uh-huh" or "OK," no matter what kind of answer the students gave? Because of this vague feedback and "OK" teaching style, B.J. was left confused about the difference between a troll and a patrol. This real-life incident may seem amusing, but there was nothing funny to B.J., who was genuinely afraid to leave school with the patrol.

Recently, attention has been directed not only at how teachers ask questions but also at how they respond to student answers. When we analyzed classroom interaction in more than 100 classrooms in five states, we found that teachers generally use four types of reactions:

OVERHEAD 39
Teacher Reactions

1. **Praise.** Positive comments about student work, such as "Excellent, good job."

2. **Acceptance.** Comments such as "Uh-huh" and "OK," which acknowledge that student answers are acceptable. These are not as strong as praise.

3. **Remediation.** Comments that encourage a more accurate student response or encourage students to think more clearly, creatively, or logically. Sample remediation comments include "Try again," "Sharpen your answer," and "Check your addition."

4. **Criticism.** A clear statement that an answer is inaccurate or a behavior is inappropriate. This category includes harsh criticism ("This is a terrible paper"), as well as milder comments that simply indicate an answer is not correct ("Your answer to the third question is wrong.")[28]

Which of these reactions do you think teachers use most frequently? Did you notice that the kindergarten teacher relied heavily on the acceptance, or "okay," reaction? So do most teachers from grade school through graduate school. Our study found that acceptance was the most frequent response, accounting for more than half of all teacher reactions. The second most frequent teacher response was remediation, accounting for one-third of teacher reactions. Used infrequently, praise comprised only 11 percent of reactions. The rarest response was criticism. In two-thirds of the classrooms observed, teachers never told a student that an answer was incorrect. In the classrooms where criticism did occur, it accounted for only 5 percent of interaction. (See Figure 3.4.)

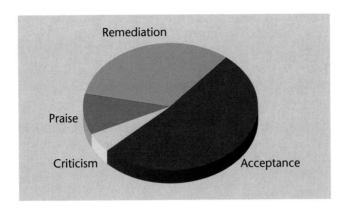

FIGURE 3.4
Teacher reactions.

REFLECTION: Most teacher reactions fall in the acceptance category. Suggest three reasons why this might occur.

In *A Place Called School,* John Goodlad writes that "learning is enhanced when students understand what is expected of them, get recognition for their work, learn about their errors, and receive guidance in improving their performances."[29] But many students claim that they are not informed or corrected when they make mistakes. Perhaps this is caused by overreliance on the acceptance response, which is the vaguest kind of feedback that teachers can offer. Since there is more acceptance than praise, criticism, and remediation combined, some educators are beginning to wonder: "Is the 'OK' classroom OK?"

Although the acceptance response is legitimate and often appropriate, it is overused. Since achievement is likely to increase when students get clear, specific **productive feedback** about their answers, it is important for teachers to reduce the "OK" reaction and to be more varied and specific in the feedback they provide. Researcher **Jere Brophy** has done an analysis of praise and student achievement. He found that praise may be particularly important for low-achieving students and those from low socioeconomic backgrounds. Brophy found that it is best when

OVERHEAD 40
Effective Use of Praise

1. *Praise is contingent upon student performance.* Praise should closely follow student behavior the teacher wants to recognize.
2. *Praise is specific.* When teachers praise, they should clearly indicate what aspect of the student behavior is noteworthy (for instance, creative problem solving or good use of evidence to support an argument).
3. *Praise is sincere.* Praise should reflect the experiences, growth, and development of the individual student. Otherwise, it may be dismissed as being disingenuous.
4. *Praise lets students know about their competence and the importance of their accomplishments*—for instance, "The well-documented review of studies on your website and the connection you made between the two tobacco filters may eventually impact the industry."
5. *Praise attributes success to ability or effort*—for example, "Your analysis of the paintings of the Impressionists is excellent. I'll bet you spent a long time studying their work in the museum" *(attribution to effort).* Or "This story is fantastic. You've got a real flair for creative writing" *(attribution to ability).* When

praise is attributed to abilities or effort, students know that successful performance is under their own control.

6. *Praise uses past performance as a context for describing present performance*—for example, "Last week you were really having trouble with your breast stroke kick. Now you've got it together—you've learned to push the water behind you and increase your speed."[30]

Just as students need to know when they are performing well, they need to know when their efforts are inadequate or incorrect. If students do not have information about their weak areas, they will find it difficult to improve.

OVERHEAD 41
Effective Use of Feedback

1. *Corrective feedback is specific and contingent on student performance.* The teacher's comments should closely follow the student behavior the teacher wants to improve.

2. *Critical comments focus on student performance and are not of a personal nature.* All of us find it easier to accept constructive criticism when it is detached from our worth as a person, when it is not personal, hostile, or sarcastic.

3. *Feedback provides a clear blueprint for improvement.* If you merely tell a student that an answer is wrong and nothing more, the student has clear feedback on level of performance but no strategies for improvement. Effective feedback suggests an approach for attaining success, such as "Check your addition," "Use the bold headings as a reading guide when you study for the exams," or "Let's conjugate this verb in both French and English, to see where the error is."

4. *An environment is established that lets the student know it is acceptable to make mistakes.* "We learn from our errors. Hardly any inventions are perfected on the first try."

5. *Corrective feedback relates eventual success to effort.* "Now you have demonstrated the correct sequence in class. Give yourself a solid half-hour tonight working on this, and I bet that you will get most of it correct. I'll check with you tomorrow."

6. *Corrective feedback recognizes when students have made improvements in their performance.* "Last week you were having trouble identifying which of Newton's Laws are applicable in each of these time motion studies. Now you've mastered the skill. You've done a good job."

An "okay classroom" allows student error and misunderstanding to go uncorrected; it lets B.J. think that the patrol will eat him up after school. In classrooms where there is appropriate use of remediation and constructive criticism, students know not only when they have made mistakes but also how to correct them. They also recognize that this process leads to growth and achievement.

 ## Variety in Process and Content

FOCUS QUESTION 7
How can teachers best tap into the variety of student learning styles?

Variety is the spice of life, the saying goes—the spice of lessons also, because variety can enhance both teaching effectiveness and student achievement.[31] Have you ever listened to a lecture for an hour and found your initial interest lapsing into daydreams? Have you ever watched a class begin a seatwork assignment with active concentration and found, after thirty minutes, that involvement had turned into passing notes and throwing paper airplanes? When the teacher fails to provide sufficient variety, lessons become monotonous and students get off task.

Effective teachers provide **variety** in both content and process. In elementary school, variety in content can involve moving from one subject area to another. In secondary instruction, the move might be in the same subject area, such as the switch from memorizing vocabulary to analyzing symbols in a short story.

As any savvy teacher knows, student interest can be maintained by moving from one activity to another during a single lesson. For example, a 60-minute lesson on the American Revolution might begin with a 10-minute overview providing the structure for the class, then move into a 15-minute question-and-answer session, then change to a 25-minute video, and conclude with a 10-minute discussion and closure. Another motivation to vary content and process in teaching is to accommodate different student

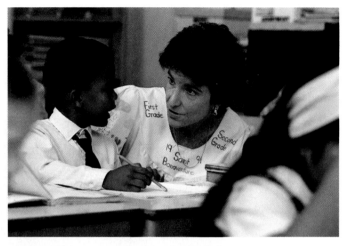

A positive classroom atmosphere that includes precise, encouraging feedback helps motivate and guide student effort.

learning styles. Some students might miss what is said in a lecture (not being auditory learners), but easily get it when the teacher shows pictures (because the visual connection is clear). Gardner's growing inventory of intelligences offers another strong argument for instructional variety. Following is a sampler of activities teachers can use to maintain student interest by varying the pattern of the lesson.

discussions	guided practice	learning centers
lectures	student presentations	music activities
films, videos, DVDs, PowerPoint	tests	art activities
	visits to websites	tutoring
role plays	silent reading	spot quizzes
simulations	games	panel discussions
small-group activities	contests	brainstorming sessions
software for individuals and groups	creative writing	students tutoring one another
	theater and drama	cooperative learning activities
guest speakers	field trips	
independent seatwork	boardwork	debates

RELATED READING
Educating Esmé: Diary of a Teacher's First Year by Esmé Raji Codell (1999). Interactive website www.algonquin.com/esme/

Many of the activities listed above can be described as "hands-on" or active learning and can be captivating for students, especially kinesthetic learners, but more is needed. Variety alone will not produce achievement: Connections must be made, or variety will be reduced to mere activity. Teachers must consider individual students and tailor activities based on their interests, learning styles, and abilities. This is no easy task, as Figure 3.5 indicates. Clear connections between the content and the activity must also be drawn, or learning can be lost. Consider an elementary student happily pasting animal pictures on charts, yet unable to explain what (if anything) he is learning about animal families. Students in a middle school may be dressing up for an evening on the Titanic, and from the lower to the upper decks, their clothing and

CRITICAL THINKING QUESTION
Some of your students' fondest memories of good teaching might be wrapped up in wonderful activities. In addition to recalling what they *did,* can they also identify what they *learned?*

FIGURE 3.5
Most important aspects of teaching and their ratings.

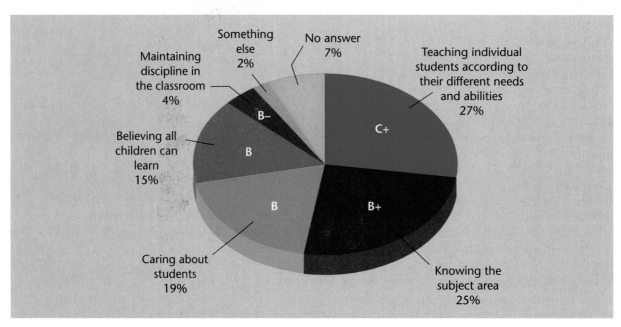

SOURCE: *The MetLife Survey of the American Teacher 2001: Key Elements of Quality Schools* (New York: Harris Interactive, Inc., 2001).

REFLECTION: The above pie chart reflects student responses to two questions: (1) Which of the following aspects of teaching do you think is most important? and (2) How would you grade your teacher on each of them? Why do you think that the most important area according to students is also the one with the lowest student rating? Can you identify two strategies that you can use to individualize your teaching?

accents reflect different social classes. Yet, if students have not connected their dress with social class and deck classifications, then they may miss learning about the relationship between social class and survival rate. Challenging students with engaging activities is admirable, but the effort must clearly connect the activity to both the content and the student.[32]

 ## Models for Effective Instruction

FOCUS QUESTION 8
What are the prevailing models of instruction?

Part of the challenge for teachers is knowing which model of instruction to choose for particular educational purposes. The following four models differ dramatically from one another, yet each may find a productive use in your classroom.

Direct Teaching

RAP 1.7
A Mini-Lesson with a Mini-Group, p. 120

Also called *systematic, active,* or *explicit teaching,* the **direct teaching** model emphasizes the importance of a structured lesson in which presentation of new information is followed by student practice and teacher feedback. In this model, which has emerged from extensive research, the role of the teacher is that of a strong leader, one who structures the classroom and sequences subject matter to reflect a clear academic focus.

With direct teaching, teachers carefully explain what students must do to accomplish a task, then present a carefully structured lesson that is usually broken down into small, manageable steps.

Researchers put forward six principles of direct teaching. They say that effective teachers use these principles consistently and systematically:

1. *Daily review.* At the beginning of the lesson, teachers review prior learning. Frequently, teachers focus on assigned homework, clarify points of confusion, and provide extra practice for facts and skills that need more attention.

2. *New material.* Teachers begin by letting students know the objectives to be attained. New information is broken down into smaller bits and is covered at a brisk pace. Teachers illustrate main points with concrete examples. Teachers ask questions frequently to check for student understanding and to make sure that students are ready for independent work using new skills and knowledge.

3. *Guided practice.* Students use new skills and knowledge under direct teacher supervision. During guided practice, teachers ask many content questions ("What is the definition of a paragraph?") and many process questions ("How do you locate the topic sentence in a paragraph?"). Teachers check student responses for understanding, offering prompts and providing corrective feedback. Guided practice continues until students answer with approximately 70 to 80 percent accuracy.

4. *Specific feedback.* Correct answers to questions are acknowledged clearly, so that students will understand when their work is accurate. When student answers are hesitant, the teacher provides process feedback ("Yes, Juanita, that's correct because . . . "). Teachers correct inaccurate responses immediately, before errors become habitual. Frequent errors are a sign that students are not ready for independent work, and guided practice should continue.

5. *Independent practice.* Similar to guided practice, except that students work by themselves at their seats or at home. Independent practice continues until responses are assured, quick, and at a level of approximately 95 percent accuracy. Cooperative learning (see the next section) and student tutoring of one another are effective strategies during independent practice.

6. *Weekly and monthly reviews.* Regular reviews offer students the opportunity for more practice, a strategy related to high achievement. Barak Rosenshine, a pioneering researcher in developing the principles of direct teaching, recommends a weekly review every Monday, with a monthly review every fourth Monday.[33]

Direct teaching works well when you are teaching skill subjects, such as grammar or mathematics, or helping students master factual material. The direct teaching model is particularly helpful during the first stages of learning new and complex information, but it is less helpful when imaginative responses and student creativity is called for.

Cooperative Learning

OVERHEAD 42
Cooperative Learning

In a classroom using **cooperative learning,** students work on activities in small, heterogeneous groups, and they often receive rewards or recognition based on the overall group performance. Although cooperative learning can be traced back to the 1920s, it seems startling or new because the typical classroom environment is frequently competitive. For example, when grading is done on a curve, one student's success is often detrimental to others. This competitive structure produces clear winners and losers, and only a limited number of *As* are possible. Sometimes classrooms are set up to be less competitive, incorporating independent study or learning contracts. In these cases, students work by themselves to reach individual learning goals. But a cooperative learning structure differs from even these less competitive practices, because students depend on one another and work together to reach shared goals.

According to researchers, cooperative learning groups work best when they meet the following criteria.[34] Groups should be *heterogeneous* and, at least at the beginning, should be *small,* perhaps limited to two to six members. Since face-to-face interaction is important, the groups should be *circular* to permit easy conversation. Positive *interdependence* among group members can be fostered by a *shared group goal, shared division of labor,* and *shared materials,* all contributing to a sense that the group sinks or swims together.

Robert Slavin, a pioneer in cooperative learning techniques, developed student team learning methods in which a team's work is not completed until all students on the team understand the material being studied.[35] Rewards are earned only when the entire team achieves the goals set by the teacher. Students tutor one another, so that everyone can succeed on individual quizzes, and each member of the group is accountable for learning. Since students contribute to their teams by improving prior scores, it does not matter whether the student is a high, average, or low achiever. Increased achievement by an individual student at any level contributes to the overall performance of the group, resulting in equal opportunity for success.

Research shows that cooperative learning promotes both intellectual and emotional growth:

In cooperative learning situations, students' individual goals and rewards are tied into group accomplishments.

- Students make higher achievement gains; this is especially true for math in the elementary grades.

- Students have higher levels of self-esteem and greater motivation to learn.

- Students have a stronger sense that classmates have positive regard for one another.

• Understanding and cooperation among students from different racial and ethnic backgrounds are enhanced.[36]

OVERHEAD 43
Cooperative Learning's
Effect on Students

Yet the practical realities of cooperative learning are not all commendable. Some students, accustomed to starring roles in full class instruction, continue to dominate the small groups. Accurate grading requires an analysis of both the individual and group performance. And, even the most committed practitioners acknowledge that cooperative learning may take more time than direct teaching. Still, as ability grouping becomes more controversial, educators are growing increasingly interested in cooperative learning as a strategy for working successfully with mixed-ability groups and diverse classroom populations.

Mastery Learning

Based on Benjamin Bloom's Learning for Mastery model developed in 1968, **mastery learning** programs are committed to the credo that, given the right tools, all children can learn. Stemming from an individualized reward structure, these programs are in use from early childhood to graduate school.

Mastery learning programs require specific and carefully sequenced learning objectives. The first step is to identify a **behavioral objective,** a specific skill or academic task to be mastered. Students are taught the skill or material in the objective; then they are tested to determine if the objective has been reached. Students who complete the test successfully go on for acceleration or enrichment, while the students who fail to demonstrate mastery of the objective receive corrective instruction and are retested. The success of mastery learning rests on the *instructional alignment,* which is a close match between what is taught and what is tested.[37]

In mastery learning, students typically work at their own pace, perhaps at a computer terminal or with individualized written materials. The teacher provides assistance and facilitates student efforts, but mastery still remains a student responsibility. Since studies have shown that many students, particularly younger ones, find it hard to take charge of their own instruction, mastery learning programs highlight the role of the teacher as instructional leader, motivator, and guide. Mastery learning is often geared for large groups, and it can benefit from technology, since computers and appropriate software can be particularly effective in self-paced mastery of skills and knowledge.

Studies suggest that mastery learning can be beneficial, particularly for students at the elementary and middle school level, and especially in language arts and social studies classes. In mastery learning:

• Teachers have more positive attitudes toward teaching and higher expectations for their students.

• In general, students have more positive attitudes about learning and their ability to learn.

• Students achieve more and remember what they have learned longer.[38]

Problem-Based Learning

Problem-based learning (PBL) has been more successful in going beyond traditional subject area boundaries. Focusing on authentic or real-life problems is at the heart of PBL, and, as you might imagine, real problems are not bound by a single

A veteran of the classroom for nearly five decades, Larry Cuban has examined America's schools from varying perspectives. He has been a professor at Stanford University and a teacher in an inner-city social studies classroom. But it was when Cuban was appointed superintendent in Arlington, Virginia, that Sharon Steindam first met him, and discovered some remarkable traits. Steindam, now Assistant Director of the National Study of School Evaluation, was a newly appointed school principal, and quite nervous about being evaluated by the new superintendent. But as she remembers, "He was the only superintendent that I worked for who truly used a variety of information about the school to help him determine how I was doing. He wanted to know why I felt certain students were doing well and others were not. And he was the most human superintendent I ever worked with. He would greet you in the grocery store and ask about your family. Cuban was a true leader, holding high expectations, providing meaningful feedback, and personally engaging."[1]

Cuban has witnessed many exciting efforts to reform and change America's schools. And yet, after sorting out nearly a century of change, he came to a fascinating insight: Teaching remains strikingly similar year in and year out. Despite the efforts of educational reformers to reshape the traditional teacher-centered classrooms of the past, most classrooms function much as they did when he was a child. In *How Teachers Taught: Constancy and Change in American Classrooms, 1890–1980,* Cuban explores why.

Historically, schools have been built around teachers, not students. Not just philosophically, but physically

as well. Classrooms featured desks all facing front, bolted to the floor, physically reinforcing the notion that the teacher is the center of instruction. As if the nuts and bolts were not strong enough, the curriculum proved the clincher. To survive instructing very large classes in eight or ten subjects, teachers became dependent on reading and dictating assignments directly from the text. Uniformity and standardization were emphasized, and top-down management was the rule. Principals told teachers what to do, and teachers told students what to do. The organizational climate did not nurture new teaching techniques.

As if all these in-school barriers were not enough to defeat change, teacher training all but guaranteed that the status quo would be maintained. New teachers were brought into the profession through a modeling or an apprenticeship program, doing their student teaching under the tutelage of veteran, often conventional, older teachers. It was a system geared to the passing down of traditional approaches and conservative attitudes from one generation of teachers to the next.

Cuban also believes that the suppression of student-based instruction was no accident. Schools were designed to mold a compliant workforce; student-centered instruction was viewed as rebellious, dangerous, and threatening to educational and economic stability. "Basically, schools reflect the cultural, political, social, and economics status quo in the larger society. The school is not an institution apart—if anything, schools tend not to be at the forefront of change in society."[2]

Since the 1984 publication of *How Teachers Taught,* technology has been hailed for its promise to revolutionize teaching. To Cuban, it is another phony revolution. In studying effective classrooms, he notes that teachers are very concerned with choosing electronic tools that are effi-

cient. Teachers ask: How much time and energy do I have to invest in learning to use the technology versus the return it will have for my students? When students use the technology, will there be disruption? Will it bolster or compromise my authority to maintain order and cultivate learning? Even teachers eager to make use of new technologies face a serious stumbling block, given the pressures to design curriculum around standardized tests. And comprehensive teacher training to use technology effectively is still lacking. Only a small fraction of teachers find the new technologies efficient. The result: "Computers become merely souped-up typewriters and classrooms continue to run much as they did a generation ago."[3]

While Cuban recognizes that classrooms have undergone a few minor reforms—experimenting with online learning, greater informality between teacher and student, and even movable chairs—he concludes that instruction at the dawn of the twenty-first century looks strikingly similar to classroom instruction nearly 100 years ago.

[1] Sharon Steindam, personal communication (June 26, 2001).
[2] Larry Cuban, *How Teachers Taught: Constancy and Change in American Classrooms, 1890–1980* (White Plains, NY: Longman, 1984).
[3] Larry Cuban, *Oversold and Underused: Computers in Classrooms 1980–2000* (Cambridge: Harvard University Press, 2001).

REFLECTION: Do you agree with Cuban? Think of a few teaching reforms that are currently taking place in a school, district, or state. Which reforms do you think will stick? Why? Which instructional practices have remained constant? What factors contribute to their persistence?

www.mhhe.com/sadker To learn more about Larry Cuban, click on *Profiles in Education.*

subject field or even by the school building. This emphasis is apparent in the other terms used to describe PBL: *experience-based education, project-based instruction,* and *anchored instruction* (because it is "anchored" in the real world). In this instructional model, a crucial aspect of the teacher's role is to identify activities that fuel students' interest, such as

- Design a plan for protecting a specific endangered species.
- Formulate solutions that might have kept the United States from plunging into a Civil War.
- How can we stop bullying and harassment in this school?
- How can pollution in a local river or bay or the ocean be checked, or even reversed?
- Develop a set of urban policies to halt the deterioration of a central city.
- How can the racism and sexism in this community be eliminated?

Finding scintillating questions and projects to excite and motivate students is critical, but it is only one aspect of PBL. Other characteristics include

- *Learner cooperation.* Similar to cooperative learning, PBL depends on small groups or pairs of students collaborating as they explore and investigate various issues. This approach de-emphasizes competition. For teachers, the goal is to guide and challenge a dozen such small groups simultaneously.
- *Higher-order thinking.* Exploring real and complex issues requires students to analyze, synthesize, and evaluate material.
- *Cross-disciplinary work.* PBL encourages students to investigate how different academic subjects shed light on each other. In exploring ecological issues, for example, students touch not only on biology and chemistry but also on economics, history, sociology, and political science.
- *Artifacts and exhibits.* Students involved in PBL demonstrate what they learn in a very tangible way. Students may produce a traditional report, or may create a video, a physical model, a computer program, a portfolio of artifacts, or even a presentation, such as a play or a debate. Teachers might organize a class or schoolwide exhibit to share the progress made by PBL students.
- *Authentic learning.* Students pursue an actual unresolved issue. They are expected to define the problem, develop a hypothesis, collect information, analyze that information, and suggest a conclusion, one that might work in the real world. The learning is authentic, not academic, artificial, or hypothetical.

While features of PBL have been around for a long time, in its current form it is both a comprehensive and demanding approach that develops real intellectual skills in students. Moreover, students function as adults in that they explore authentic contemporary issues. Working together, they attempt to solve these problems—in effect, getting a jump on the adult world, even before they are adults.[39]

 Effective and Reflective Teaching

"Less is more," is an aphorism attributed to education reformer Ted Sizer. According to Sizer, today's schools are misguided in their emphasis on "covering" material. The goal seems to be teaching and learning a vast body of information, in order to have a

OVERHEADS 44–46
Four Models of Instruction: Teaching That Works

TEACHING TIP
Use overheads to summarize the numerous attributes of good teachers. Or, have students brainstorm their own list first, then compare and contrast.

FOCUS QUESTION 9
What are the future directions of effective teaching research?

OVERHEAD 47
Directions in Teaching

sense of accomplishment, or to score well on the ever-growing number of standardized tests. But international tests in science, for example, show that, although U.S. students have studied more science topics than have students in other countries, they have not studied them in depth, and their lower test scores reflect this superficiality. In Sizer's vision of effective instruction, good teachers limit the amount of content they introduce but develop it sufficiently for students to gain in-depth understanding.

This direction for teaching and schooling marks a radical departure from the current emphasis on uniform standards, test performance, and competition. In marked contrast to the superficial nature of such test-centered curriculum, Sizer advocates deep teaching. In **deep teaching,** teachers work to organize their content around a limited set of key principles and powerful ideas and then engage students in discussing these concepts. The emphasis is on problem solving and critical thinking, rather than on memorizing.[40]

Deeper teaching of the subject also suggests a deeper understanding of students. **Differentiated instruction** swims against the tide of standardization by organizing instructional activities not around content standards, but in response to individual differences. Teachers are asked to carefully consider each student's needs, learning style, life experience, and readiness to learn. Teachers are trained to develop learning activities that recognize these differences, because students learn best when they make connections between the curriculum and their interests and life experiences.[41]

This vision of deep teaching and differentiated instruction highlights the social nature of learning and of the classroom. As the builder of a classroom **learning community,** the teacher is called on to be a guide or facilitator, skillful in conducting

The idea of the classroom as a "learning community" conceives of the teacher as someone who helps students activate their prior knowledge of some subject and become intellectually engaged with one another.

The National Board for Professional Teaching Standards has described effective teachers with five core propositions.

1. TEACHERS ARE COMMITTED TO STUDENTS AND THEIR LEARNING

Accomplished teachers are dedicated to making knowledge accessible to all students. They act on the belief that all students can learn. They treat students equitably, recognizing the individual differences that distinguish one student from another and take account of these differences in their practice. They adjust their practice based on observation and knowledge of their students' interests, abilities, skills, knowledge, family circumstances, and peer relationships. Equally important, they foster students' self-esteem, motivation, character, civic responsibility, and their respect for individual, cultural, religious, and racial differences.

2. TEACHERS KNOW THE SUBJECTS THEY TEACH AND HOW TO TEACH THOSE SUBJECTS TO STUDENTS

Accomplished teachers have a rich understanding of the subject(s) they teach and appreciate how knowledge in their subject is created, organized, linked to other disciplines and applied to real-world settings. Their instructional repertoire allows them to create multiple paths to the subjects they teach, and they are adept at teaching students how to pose and solve their own problems.

3. TEACHERS ARE RESPONSIBLE FOR MANAGING AND MONITORING STUDENT LEARNING

Accomplished teachers create, enrich, maintain, and alter instructional settings to capture and sustain the interest of their students and to make the most effective use of time. They are as aware of ineffectual or damaging practice as they are devoted to elegant practice. They know how to engage groups of students to ensure a disciplined learning environment, and how to organize instruction to allow the schools' goals for students to be met. They are adept at setting norms for social interaction among students and between students and teachers. Accomplished teachers can assess the progress of individual students as well as that of the class as a whole.

4. TEACHERS THINK SYSTEMATICALLY ABOUT THEIR PRACTICE AND LEARN FROM EXPERIENCE

Accomplished teachers are models of educated persons, exemplifying the virtues they seek to inspire in students— curiosity, tolerance, honesty, fairness, respect for diversity, and appreciation of cultural differences. They draw on their knowledge of human development, subject matter and instruction, and their understanding of their students to make principled judgments about sound practice. Their decisions are grounded not only in the literature, but also in their experience.

5. TEACHERS ARE MEMBERS OF LEARNING COMMUNITIES

Accomplished teachers contribute to the effectiveness of the school by working collaboratively with other professionals on instructional policy, curriculum development, and staff development. They can evaluate school progress and the allocation of school resources in light of their understanding of state and local educational objectives. Accomplished teachers find ways to work collaboratively and creatively with parents, engaging them productively in the work of the school.

SOURCE: www.nbpts.org/standards/five_core.html. Adapted from © 2001, National Board for Professional Teaching Standards.

REFLECTION: Can you demonstrate your understanding of each proposition with a classroom example from your past? If your schooling offers little to brag about (or your memories are faded) let your imagination give credence to the task. Envision an example from the five areas to confirm you comprehend each concept.

discussions, group work, debates, and dialogues. In this way, the teacher empowers the students to talk with one another and to rehearse the terminology and concepts involved in each discipline. Learning becomes a community effort, not an individual competition.[42]

It is not surprising, therefore, that educators are reconceptualizing schools to create more nurturing learning communities. When learning communities work well, students and teachers get to know each other well and they can develop shared academic goals. Learning communities can be encouraged through several strategies, including looping and block scheduling. In **looping,** schools "promote" teachers along with their students, a process that allows the teacher an extra year or more to get to know students in depth, to diagnose and meet their learning needs, and to

CLASS ACTIVITY:
Fishbowl Debate
IM, Activity 3:5

University Training Because It . . .

CREATES AND PROVIDES SOPHISTICATED KNOWLEDGE

Scholarship is an essential component for producing professionals. If teaching is ever to be seen as a thoughtful and reflective profession, it will be through systematic scholarship available only on university campuses.

PREPARES LEADERS, NOT FOLLOWERS

If teachers are to be more than technicians who carry out the instructions of others, they must be knowledgeable and informed about recent research and current theories. University study provides teachers with this knowledge, so that they understand not only *how* things are done, but *why* they are done as well.

EDUCATES TEACHERS TO EXAMINE CURRENT PRACTICES

Practitioners in the field are interested in staffing schools, not challenging current practices. An emphasis on vocational training and placement creates a climate where teachers are more likely to repeat past errors than explore new approaches.

ATTRACTS TALENTED PEOPLE

If bright and gifted people are to be drawn to this career, teaching must be seen as more than a vocation controlled by others. By producing intellectually active professionals, universities make teaching a more attractive career.

Field-Based Training Because It . . .

IS DESIGNED TO PRODUCE COMPETENT PROFESSIONALS

Producing skilled professionals requires a practical program not found in the university. Only real students with real needs can train real teachers. University courses cannot match real-world preparation.

PROVIDES SKILLED PRACTITIONERS, NOT THEORISTS

The best setting for learning a skill is the place where that skill is used. The best person to teach that skill is a talented artisan. Field-based training matches future teachers with the most appropriate settings and the most competent instructors.

STATE GOVERNMENTS ARE BEST SUITED FOR ORGANIZING TEACHER EDUCATION

Universities often ignore market realities, and so shortages in one teaching field develop, just as there is an oversupply in another. State-run programs could do a better job of matching training programs with job market needs.

PROVIDES SHARPER FOCUS AND FEWER DISTRACTIONS

Teaching, like other careers, takes careful and focused practice. Such focus is difficult to achieve in a university setting where other courses, abstract theories, and campus diversions intrude. Teacher education needs the intensity and focus found only in a field-based environment.

SOURCE: Many of these arguments are found in greater detail in Jack L. Nelson, Stuart B. Palonsky, and Kenneth Carlson, *Critical Issues in Education* (New York: McGraw-Hill, 1990), pp. 232–42.

 YOU BE THE JUDGE

Most teacher education programs offer a mix of university and field-based training. Is this the best of both worlds—or the worst? Consider the five core propositions identified by the National Board for Professional Teaching Standards in the Frame of Reference: What Teachers Should Know and Be Able to Do. Would university or field-based training be more effective in acquiring each of these core propositions? Support your answers.

develop more meaningful communication with their parents and families. Looping offers students an increased sense of stability and community. Similarly, **block scheduling** increases teacher-student contact by increasing the length of class periods. The longer periods allow teachers to get to know these students better, while the students benefit from an uninterrupted and in-depth academic study. If you were to teach in a school with block scheduling, you might have 75 students on any given day or in a particular semester, instead of 150.

This notion of a learning community contrasts sharply with many current practices that emphasize state- and school-mandated curriculum followed by standardized testing. It points to a more thoughtful classroom, one in which the teacher is the critical decision maker, and a reflective practitioner. Good teachers are expected to continually and intensely analyze their own practices, and to use their analysis to improve performance. "In order to tap the rich potential of our past to inform our judgment, we must move backward, reflect on our experiences, then face each new encounter with a broader repertoire of content-specific information, skills, and techniques."[43] When teachers engage in **reflective teaching,** they ask themselves such questions as

RAP 1.9
A Mini-Conference about Your Mini-Lesson, p. 122

- What teaching strategies did I use today? How effective were they? What might have been even more effective?

- Were my students engaged with the material? What seemed to motivate them the most? If I were to reteach today's class, how could I get even more students involved?

- How did I assess my students' learning today? Would there have been a better way to measure their learning? How well did the students grasp the main points of today's lesson? Do I need to reteach some of these concepts?

- Can I fine-tune tomorrow's or next week's lessons to capitalize on the gains made today?

Going far beyond the rhetorical, these questions are designed to raise consciousness, engender self-scrutiny, and result in effective teaching.[44]

SUMMARY

1. Are teachers born, or made?

   While the debate has raged for decades, most people agree that effective teaching can result from natural artistry as well as focused training.

2. How is class time organized and what is academic learning time?

   Teachers vary dramatically in the efficient use of time. How wisely a teacher distributes classroom time—defined as allocated, engaged and academic learning time—is a predictor of student achievement.

3. What classroom management skills foster academic achievement?

   Student achievement is also associated with effective classroom management. A well-managed classroom includes reasonable rules for students to follow, and teachers who can keep students on task through group alerting, smooth transitions, and similar skills.

4. What are the roles of teachers and students in the pedagogical cycle?

   The pedagogical cycle consists of four stages: (1) structure, (2) question, (3) respond, and (4) react. While the student's role is typically limited to responding, teachers usually direct classroom discourse through structure, question, and reaction.

5. How can teachers set a stage for learning?

   Most cycles of instruction begin by connecting prior learning to current objectives. Effective teachers motivate students, offer meaningful examples, give accurate directions, display enthusiasm, and present a brief closure to the lesson.

CHAPTER REVIEW

Go to the Online Learning Center to take a chapter self-quiz, practice with key terms, and review concepts from the chapter.

CURRENT NEWS FROM POWERWEB

To access PowerWeb, go to Chapter 3 on the Online Learning Center to read current articles and to access news feeds about:

- Academic Performance
- Classroom Management
- Discipline
- Excellence and Education
- Instruction
- Teacher Attitudes

6. What questioning strategies increase student achievement?

Questioning is at the very foundation of effective teaching. Although teachers rely most heavily on lower-order questions, higher-order questions are associated with higher-order thinking and should also be an important part of classroom instruction. Effective teachers use intentional strategies to allocate questions fairly among all students. One way to enhance the distribution and quality of student participation is to extend wait times 1 and 2 from less than a second to 3 to 5 seconds. Research indicates that teachers most frequently use neutral acceptance when reacting to student comments. Teacher praise, remediation, and criticism are more precise and helpful reactions.

7. How can teachers best tap into the variety of student learning styles?

Effective teachers provide variety in both content and activity. From discussions and debates to simulations and spot quizzes, teachers increase academic success by responding to the different learning styles in the class.

8. What are the prevailing models of instruction?

Four models of instruction that can lead to high student achievement include (1) direct teaching, (2) cooperative learning, (3) mastery learning, and (4) problem-based learning. Direct teaching includes teacher presentation; guided practice; teacher feedback; independent practice; and daily, weekly, and monthly reviews. In a cooperative learning classroom, students work in small groups and appraisals often reflect the entire group's performance. In mastery learning, students work at their own pace, going on to new material only when specific objectives are mastered. Problem-based learning stimulates students to explore authentic issues and investigate real-life problems.

9. What are the future directions of effective teaching research?

Differentiated instruction responds to individual student differences, unlike the popular model of standardized instruction and testing. Deep teaching promotes meaningful academic development around essential content, teaching less material in greater depth. As learning can be social, teacher expertise can steer the classroom toward a sense of community. Looping and block scheduling increase the time that students and teachers can work together. A pervasive factor for effective teaching continues to be self-analysis. The best of today's educators are reflective about their practice.

EXTENDED LEARNING

Go to Chapter 3 on your *Resources for Exploring Education* CD-ROM to access Case Studies, Readings, and Media Observations.

CASE STUDIES

- Joyce Davidson: A teacher is not making much progress with a remedial English class and is particularly concerned about an extremely shy student who is not responding to her teaching methods and style.
- Ken Kelly: A teacher having trouble with questioning and with discussion teaching visits a teacher who is holding a Socratic discussion with a fourth-grade class.
- Judith Kent: A teacher engages her students in whole-class discussion, and then the students work with partners on an assignment. She explains the planning process she went through to reteach the lesson after it had not worked with the previous class.
- Nan Miller: A teacher who is always trying new methods observes her students use a new strategy she has just presented. She is disappointed to see that some students ignore the directions and complete the assignment without using the technique.

- Dale Peters: A student teacher finds his cooperating teacher unwilling to allow him to try any innovative ideas for the students.

READINGS

- Sam Hausfather. "Where's the Content? The Role of Content in Constructivist Teacher Education."
- James Keefe and John Jenkins. "Personalized Instruction."
- Susan Warren. "Stories from the Classrooms: How Expectations and Efficacy of Diverse Teachers Affect the Academic Performance of Children."

KEY TERMS AND PEOPLE

academic learning time, 76
academic structure, 83
acceptance, 92
allocated time, 76
behavioral objective, 99
Arno Bellack, 82
block scheduling, 104
Bloom's taxonomy, 87, 88
Jere Brophy, 93
clarification, 84
cooperative learning, 98
criticism, 92
Larry Cuban, 100
dangles, 83
deep teaching, 102
differentiated instruction, 102
direct teaching, 96, 97

engaged time, 76
flip-flops, 83
fragmentation, 81, 83
John Goodlad, 76
group alerting, 80
higher-order questions, 87
Jacob Kounin, 83
learning community, 102
least intervention, 80
looping, 103
lower-order questions, 87
mastery learning, 99
motivation, 84
objective, 84
overdwelling, 83
overlapping, 80
pedagogical cycle, 83

A Place Called School, 76
praise, 92
problem-based learning, 99
productive feedback, 93
reflective teaching, 105
remediation, 92
Mary Budd Rowe, 89
scaffolding, 84
Robert Slavin, 98
student-initiated questions, 91
teacher effectiveness, 76
thrusts, 83
transition, 83, 84
variety, 95
wait time, 89
withitness, 80

DISCUSSION QUESTIONS AND ACTIVITIES

1. Do you think teachers are born, or made? Debate a classmate who holds the opposite point of view. Interview elementary and secondary teachers and ask them what they think about this question. Do some of them say that it is a combination of both? If so, why? Which part is art, which part skill?

2. Why do you think there is so much variation in how different teachers and schools use time for learning? Observe in your own college classrooms to determine how much time is wasted. For each class observed, keep a fairly detailed record of how time is lost (students six minutes late, class ends fifteen minutes early, PowerPoint presentation takes 4 minutes to set up, and so on).

3. Research suggests that, in order to achieve, students should be functioning at a very high success rate. Do you agree that this is likely to lead to higher achievement? Or do you think

that students need to cope with failure and be "stretched" in order to achieve? Defend your position.

4. Analyze teacher reactions to student answers in elementary and secondary classrooms where you are an observer and in the college classrooms where you are a student. Are most of these classrooms "okay" classrooms? Why do you think some teacher reactions are vague and diffuse? What observations can you make about the use of praise, remediation and criticism?

5. In small cooperative groups review four key terms: deep teaching, differentiated instruction, learning communities, and reflective teaching. Generate an example of each drawn from an imaginary classroom. Alter the grade level and curriculum area of your classroom. How might deep teaching, differentiated instruction, learning communities, and reflective teaching change?

OLC WEB-*TIVITIES*

Go to www.mhhe.com/ sadker7e to do the following activities:

1. Classroom Management: What Is in a Name?
2. Cooperative Learning
3. Problem-Based Learning

REEL TO REAL TEACHING

DEAD POETS SOCIETY (1989)
Run Time: 128 minutes

Synopsis: "Carpe diem! Seize the day boys, make your lives extraordinary," advises educator John Keating to his class of young men at an all boys boarding school. These words guide his unorthodox lessons that will change their young lives forever.

Reflection:

1. Do John Keating's instructional techniques mirror any of the effective teaching characteristics discussed in this chapter? What additional attributes of an effective teacher did you discover in the film that are not described in this chapter? Is Keating's teaching an art, a skill, or both? Recall scenes from the film to support your answer.

2. Questioning is not just about teachers: Students are also partners in the questioning process. Creating an environment that welcomes student-initiated questions is important to engaged learning time. How did Mr. Keating teach his students to ask questions? How did these questions deepen student understanding?

3. Consider how the character of the student body created a community. How might the storyline change in an all girls school or a historically black school?

Follow-up Activity: You've read about effective questioning and seen "on screen" effective questioning in action. Now take a turn at practicing these techniques. Compose a classroom discussion of *Dead Poet's Society*. Write out a sequence of questions, one each from the six levels of Bloom's taxonomy.

How do you rate this film? Go to *Reel to Real Teaching* in the Critics' Corner to review this film.

www.mhhe.com/ sadker7e

FOR FURTHER READING

Classroom Teaching Skills, by James Cooper (Editor) (7th edition) (2003). A self-instructional book designed to help teachers acquire basic teaching skills for classroom management, questioning, higher-order thinking, and cooperative learning.

Elementary Classroom Management: Lessons from Research and Practice, by Carol Simon Weinstein and Andrew Mignano, Jr. (3rd edition) (2003). Written in conversational style, this book combines what research has to say about effective classroom management with knowledge culled from practice. The text shows how four teachers in very different school settings create classrooms that are orderly and productive, yet humane and caring.

Looking in Classrooms, by Thomas Good and Jere Brophy (9th edition) (2003). Devoting particular attention to current issues, such as integrating traditional methods with constructivist, cooperative, and culturally diverse learning styles, this book provides teachers with the latest research and concrete skills to observe and interpret the classroom behavior of both teachers and students.

Questioning in the Secondary Classroom, by E. C. Wragg and George Brown (2nd edition) (2001). Explores a variety of questions that teachers can ask, from those requiring simple recall of information to those that stimulate complex reasoning, imagination, and speculation.

Teaching with Influence, by Peter Hook and Andy Vass (2001). Offers strategies to enhance the personal development and self-esteem of teachers as well as practical ways in which teachers can increase their effectiveness.

Young Investigators: The Project Approach in the Early Years, by Judy Harris Helm and Lilian Katz (2001). A combination of teacher interviews and accounts of classroom practice demonstrates how children of all abilities may master basic literacy skills through project-based learning.

REFLECTIVE ACTIVITIES AND YOUR PORTFOLIO

Introduction

Reflective Activities and Your Portfolio, what we like to refer to as *RAP*s, give you a chance to explore your role as an educator by carefully considering what you have just read, and tying it to your own experiences. *RAP*s are intended to help you decide if teaching is right for you. And if it is right, these very same *RAP*s will give you direction as you prepare for a career in teaching.

*RAP*s follow and connect each of the four sections of the textbook. Each *RAP* includes a:

Purpose—explains why this activity is useful, and what it is intended to accomplish.

Activity—allows you to apply your readings through observations, interviews, teaching, and action research.

Artifact—challenges you to collect and manage the items you will find useful for developing your portfolio.

Reflection—helps you think deeply and realistically about education and your place in it.

Introduction to Portfolios

The term *portfolio* has traditionally been associated with artists and investors. Most artists maintain a showcase or portfolio of their best work to woo potential clients. Usually housed in a large portable attaché case, the portfolio is a pleasing way for clients to view an artist's best body of work. Similarly, investors keep track of their financial decisions with another type of portfolio. This portfolio tracks the gains and losses and helps determine short- and long-term investment strategies.

While rooted in the world of art and investing, educators have embraced portfolios. For the teacher-in-training, portfolios can also serve as a powerful forum in which to showcase their best work, as well as demonstrate their professional growth over time.

Multiple Purposes

Portfolios serve many purposes. They are used by states for licensure and licensure renewal, by school districts for merit pay increases, and by individual schools for hiring new staff. The National Board for Professional Teaching Standards (NBPTS) requires portfolios as part of the rigorous evaluation to reward and recognize high-achieving teachers with board certification. At the classroom level, teachers are using portfolios as an alternative evaluation method. Many teachers, students, and parents have found portfolios to be an authentic way to assess achievement.

Your Portfolio

As a teacher-in-training, your portfolio will be a valuable asset in your teacher education program and in your eventual search for a teaching position. Questions to keep in mind as you assemble this showcase include:

Special thanks to Phyllis Lerner and Dan Otter for their help in creating and writing these *RAP*s.

1. What do I want my portfolio to say about me as a teacher?

2. What do I want my portfolio to say about me as a student?

3. What do I want my portfolio to say about my relationship with students?

4. How can my portfolio demonstrate my growth as an educator and learner?

5. How can my portfolio demonstrate that I will be successful as a teacher?

Consider making your portfolio:[1]

- Purposeful—based on a sound foundation, such as the INTASC Standards for Licensing Beginning Teachers

- Selective—choosing only the appropriate materials for a specific purpose or circumstance, such as a job application

- Diverse—going beyond your transcript, student teaching critiques, and letters of recommendation to represent a broad array of teaching talent

- Ongoing—relaying your growth and development over time

- Reflective—both in process and product, demonstrating your thoughtfulness

- Collaborative—resulting from conversations and interactions with others (peers, students, parents, professors, teachers, and administrators)

Getting Started on Your Portfolio—Collect, Select, and Reflect

In four places in this book, we have placed *RAPs* to help you through the process of creating, collecting, researching, drafting, editing, and organizing your portfolio. The *RAP* activities in these sections are based on the INTASC standards and provide a springboard for your own creative portfolio artifacts. Read through the INTASC Standards for Licensing Beginning Teachers included in this section (p. 112) to understand the sections your portfolio will include. Of course, you are encouraged to include other material from other sources as well.

Building your portfolio is a three-step process—*collect, select, and reflect.*

1. *Collect* items for inclusion in your portfolio by completing *RAPs* and similar activities of your choosing.

2. *Select* items for inclusion in your portfolio from this pool of artifacts. You are encouraged to select at least one item from each of the ten INTASC Standards for Licensing Beginning Teachers.

3. *Reflect* on what was learned from each activity. This self-assessment should serve as a powerful learning tool, one you will be able to return to again and again.

[1]Kenneth Wolf and Mary Dietz, "Teaching Portfolios: Purpose and Possibilities," *Teacher Education Quarterly* (Winter 1998), pp. 9–21.

INTASC Standards for Licensing Beginning Teachers

Principle 1 Knowledge of Subject Matter
The teacher understands the central concepts, tools of inquiry and structures of the discipline(s) he or she teaches and can create learning experiences that make these aspects of subject matter meaningful to students.

Principle 2 Human Development and Learning
The teacher understands how children learn and develop, and can provide learning opportunities that support their intellectual, social, and personal development.

Principle 3 Diversity in Learning
The teacher understands how students differ in their approaches to learning and creates instructional opportunities that are adapted to diverse learners.

Principle 4 Variety of Instructional Strategies
The teacher understands and uses a variety of instructional strategies to encourage students' development of critical thinking, problem solving, and performance skills.

Principle 5 Motivation and Management
The teacher uses understanding of individual and group motivation and behavior to create a learning environment that encourages positive and social interaction, active engagement in learning, and self-motivation.

Principle 6 Communication Skills
The teacher uses knowledge of effective verbal, nonverbal, and media communication techniques to foster active inquiry, collaboration, and supportive interaction in the classroom.

Principle 7 Instructional Planning Skills
The teacher plans instruction based upon knowledge of subject matter, students, the community, and curriculum goals.

Principle 8 Assessment
The teacher understands and uses formal and informal assessment strategies to evaluate and ensure continuous intellectual, social, and physical development of the learner.

Principle 9 Reflection and Responsibility
The teacher is a reflective practitioner who continually evaluates the effects of her or his choices and actions of others (students, parents, and other professionals in the learning community) and who actively seeks out opportunities to grow professionally.

Principle 10 Relationships and Partnerships
The teacher fosters relationships with school colleagues, parents, and agencies in the larger community to support students' learning and well being.

SOURCE: Adopted from *Model Standards for Beginning Teacher Licensing and Development: A Resource for State Dialogue* developed by the Interstate New Teacher Assessment and Support Consortium (INTASC). Each principle includes knowledge, dispositions, and performance expectations for beginning teachers. INTASC updates can also be accessed online at www.ccsso.org/.

Housing Your Portfolio—from Traditional Methods to the Electronic Portfolio

The choices of where and how to store your portfolio can be as diverse as the contents of the portfolio itself. As mentioned earlier, artists often use a large portable attaché case to house their portfolios. Our best advice is to store your material as you see fit. Many teachers use portable plastic filing cases or crates. Others turn their portfolios into books for easy toting. Increasingly, teachers are employing a myriad of electronic tools to reach students. These can include video, the Internet, and computer activities such as PowerPoint presentations. How can teachers best include these artifacts in their portfolios? Through something called the *Electronic Portfolio or e-Portfolio*. Many software products exist to help in this process including *Folio*Live. *Folio*Live is an electronic portfolio tool that allows you to create an electronic portfolio in three simple steps:

1. Use a template to create a homepage.
2. Create a custom framework (portfolio organization) or use a *Folio*Live framework to structure your portfolio.
3. Add artifacts to build your portfolio by uploading existing files (Word to PowerPoint to video), linking to artifacts posted elsewhere on the Web, or creating an artifact through a *Folio*Live form.

Final Thoughts

The first section of your portfolio should include an introduction to you and contact information, professional or present career objective, a brief résumé, transcripts, letters of support, and a mission or philosophy statement.

If you are new to portfolios this all may seem a little overwhelming. Don't panic. We will guide you through much of the process in the chapters, discussion questions and of course the *RAP* activities. Once you get the hang of portfolios—which won't take long—you should find them to be an extremely useful and meaningful professional tool. And like many of your colleagues, you may find yourself using portfolios to assess your own students.

REFLECTIVE ACTIVITIES AND YOUR PORTFOLIO

Part I: Teachers and Students

1:1 Teacher Interview in Your Major or Favorite Subject

INTASC PRINCIPLE 1
Knowledge of
Subject Matter

Purpose: Teachers are expected to have knowledge of both the subject(s) they teach and the students they are teaching. Deciding what to teach and how best to teach it are constant responsibilities. This activity gives you the opportunity to learn how teachers go through these tasks and to begin thinking how you might approach curricular decisions in your major subject area.

Activity: Interview a teacher in a subject area of special interest to you. Even if you plan to teach in an elementary program, select the curricular area that you savor. Focus on how the teacher decides what content to teach and how best to teach it. Here are some curricular questions to ask, but feel free to add your own to this list:

- What factors contributed to your decision to teach this subject and at this grade level?
- What do you enjoy most about teaching this curriculum? What do you enjoy least?
- How do you go about selecting what content and skills to teach?
- Do you try to offer different perspectives (multidisciplinary, multicultural) on these topics?
- Are there areas of this subject that are controversial? How do you handle these "hot" topics?
- How do you accommodate multiple intelligences in your classroom?
- How do you track and record grades? Does your school or district require a certain format? Do you use grading software?
- When do you do your planning? The week before, the night before, impromptu?
- Do you integrate other subject areas into your program?
- How do the school district's official curriculum and the textbook shape your decisions?
- Can you make your own decisions as to what topics to teach, or are you confined to the official school curriculum?
- Are selections made by you alone or with others in your department or grade-level team?
- Do professional associations influence your decisions?
- Do parents or students participate in deciding what is taught?

Artifact: "Teacher: Interview: Subject Specialty" For your portfolio, you will want to include the interview questions you ask, the teacher responses, and eventually, your reflection. Make certain that you include the place and date of the interview. You may want to re-read this artifact for some useful insights when you begin teaching. Or then again, you may want to read it in ten or twenty years, to see how much things have changed—or how much they haven't changed!

Reflection: What advice given by the teacher do you believe may influence your own decisions? How does the teacher's view of the content differ from your own? How will you decide what content to select when you become a teacher? What roles will professional associations play in your decision making? What role will parents and students play in your decision making? Why are you interested in this subject area, and how do you anticipate your interest will impact your students and teaching? What did you learn from this teacher that was surprising? Remember to attach your reflection to the artifact.

FORM:

Interview Questions for Teacher Interview in Your Major or Favorite Subject Area

1:2 Understanding the Developmental and Psychosocial Stages of Students You Wish to Teach

Purpose: Who is the average 5-year-old? 10-year-old? 15-year-old? What can they do academically? How do they behave in class? What can a teacher do to help them grow and succeed? One of the traditional ways we organize schools, by age, requires teachers to understand the progressive patterns of children's growth. An understanding of student developmental patterns will help you to develop objectives, plan activities, and assess classroom behaviors. Do you know the typical psychosocial issues of the students you plan to teach?

INTASC PRINCIPLE 2
Human Development and Learning

Activity: According to psychologist Erik H. Erikson, each individual passes through eight developmental stages during a lifetime. He calls them "psychosocial stages." Your task will be to observe evidence of these stages in the students you wish to instruct. First, gain an understanding of Erikson's work. A psychosocial or developmental psychology text is a good source of information about your students' development patterns. The Web is another great source. Type into a search engine "psychosocial" and "Erik H. Erikson."

Next, arrange to observe students in one of the following ranges Erikson identified:

- Stage 3: Early Childhood (ages 2–6)
- Stage 4: Elementary and Middle School Years (ages 6–12)
- Stage 5: Adolescence (ages 12–18)

Finally, use the chart below to document the traits and characteristics Erikson identified. Here is an example of how your chart might look:

EXAMPLE

Artifact: "Developmental and Psychosocial Stages"

Stage: 2—Early Childhood (ages 2–6)

Description: Children have newfound power at this stage as they develop motor skills and social interest with people around them. They now must learn to achieve a balance between eagerness for more adventure and more responsibility, and learning to control impulses and childish fantasies.

Evidence Observed: I observed a kindergarten class and the students would listen to the teacher's every word, but then a moment later, they would be talking to the person next to them. The students seemed keen to handle scissors and other tools of the classroom. Some of the students would hold hands with friends whenever they would venture around the room. The kids were generally very polite to each other, though one child shed tears because of a disagreement with another student.

FORM:

Developmental
and Psychosocial
Stages

Developmental and Psychosocial Stages
Stage:
Characteristics of this Stage:
Evidence Observed:

Reflection: What did you learn from this activity? Any surprises? Has this activity influenced your decision about teaching at a particular grade level? What more would you like to learn about the students? How can "average" or "typical" get in the way of your teaching?

1:3 Multiple Intelligence Bingo

INTASC PRINCIPLE 3
Diversity in
Learning

Purpose: Educators are moving beyond the traditional IQ definition of intelligence. As the text discussed, Harvard professor Howard Gardner has identified at least eight intelligences—not all of which are commonly recognized in school settings—that he believes better define the unique nature of individual human capability. An effective teacher recognizes different types of intelligences and learning styles and adapts instruction accordingly. While some teachers still tend to focus on the logical and linguistic abilities, others enthusiastically incorporate Gardner's theory into their classrooms. You may even find "MI Schools" that demonstrate MI in action. In this activity, you will be challenged to identify intelligences and to see the theory applied in lessons.

Activity: Visit two classrooms. Try to include one that your professor recommends as an MI model. Observe in each room for at least forty minutes. Use the following chart to record examples of multiple intelligences. Note both the instruction and the room displays or materials. Brainstorming with your peers before the observation will help you determine what might constitute evidence of a particular intelligence. See if your observation can fill every slot. Bingo!

FORM:

Multiple
Intelligences Bingo

Artifact: Use accompanying "Multiple Intelligence Bingo Card" to record your observations, and file the chart in your portfolio. While this initial chart will help you to detect MI in action, in future years you may wish to use it for self-analysis, a way to make sure that you are including the multiple intelligences in your own teaching.

Classroom # _____	Bingo Card	
Intelligence	**Example During Instruction**	**Display or Material Example**
Logical-mathematical		
Linguistic		
Bodily-kinesthetic		
Musical		
Spatial		
Interpersonal		
Intrapersonal		
Naturalist		
Others (your own)		

Reflection: Were any of your classrooms filled with examples of the multiple approaches to learning (any Bingo winners)? After your observations, were there any slots that remained empty? What could you do to fill those spaces? Were some classes totally geared to only one or two intelligence areas? Do you suspect that some intelligences are easy and some are always tough to use? How did particular students respond when given an opportunity to explore different intelligences? Were some confident with certain challenges and others withdrawn? How did the class respond, in general, when the lessons involved intelligences other than the logical and linguistic? What can you apply to your own classroom?

1:4 Memories of a Teacher

Purpose: Many of us choose education because of a special teacher—someone who may have inspired us to bring a special "style" to the field. This individual was probably good because he or she modeled the best of effective instruction. You may not have been consciously aware of these skills and traits when you were a student, but you knew the class was interesting, challenging, productive, and maybe even arduous. Perhaps you had friends in the class and you accomplished projects in meaningful ways. Possibly you were the star, the standout who could grasp the material and help others understand. You may have been the kid who didn't connect with others, but this teacher made your year better. Whatever the story, we suspect you have one (and hope you have many). Connecting your memories with the research on effective teaching should help you be a more purposeful, and successful, educator.

> **INTASC PRINCIPLE 4**
> Variety of Instructional Strategies

Activity: Consider one terrific educator from your past. First, brainstorm memories from that class. On the left side of a piece of paper, list each item. See what you can generate at this point without reading farther (it's tempting to peek but worth the effort to wait).

After your first and open response, use the following cues to generate even more memories. Think about the way lessons began, about the subject matter, and about the use of resources or even gimmicks.

- How was the room arranged?
- Where did the teacher "hang out"?
- Do you recall big field trips or perhaps small adventures?

- How were you engaged in academic learning?

- What management techniques or rules do you remember?

- Were transitions from one activity to another handled smoothly?

- What about questioning opportunities and teacher feedback? Did you raise your hand and were you called on? Were others?

- Can you recall anything about tests (their kind, frequency, and resultant anxiety level)?

- Were term papers, major projects, special event days, or assemblies part of the curriculum?

- What else made this teacher the one who made a difference for you?

Artifact: You may want to entitle your description "My Student Memories of a Special Teacher," or some related title. You will never be closer to these memories than right now. The longer you teach, the further from these memories you will find yourself. These memories can become a touchstone, a place to return and read and reflect on what mattered to you when you sat on the other side of the desk.

Extra Artifact: If you are still in contact with this terrific teacher, you might want to write a letter explaining the assignment and why you chose him or her as a subject. Teachers don't receive enough of this sort of recognition for their time and talent. Receiving such a letter will probably be quite meaningful. Someday you may find yourself on the receiving end of such a letter, or perhaps teaching just down the hall from that special teacher you remembered.

Reflection: Now, read your terrific teacher memories and meander back through Chapter 3, "Teacher Effectiveness." Consider each point you describe. What connections can you make between the research on instructional quality and your memorable teacher? What insights about effective instruction did you acquire? This reflection should be included with your artifact.

1:5 Write a Letter to Yourself Detailing Why You Want to Become a Teacher

INTASC PRINCIPLE 5
Motivation and
Management

Purpose: People may have already asked you why you are considering teaching. Sometimes they ask with reverent tones, other times with disbelief. (In either case, they are probably sharing something about their own perspective regarding a teaching career.) Analyze your reasons to teach, so that you can provide a good answer to the question and uncover a bit about your own thinking.

Activity: Write a letter to yourself detailing why you want to become a teacher. Draw on your experience as a student. Perhaps you want to reflect on some of the teachers you have been fortunate to have, and some of the teachers you have been unfortunate to have. Include your hopes and dreams for your students. What do you want them to gain from being in your classroom? This letter will help you better understand why you want to become a teacher, and can be a useful addition to your portfolio.

Artifact/Reflection: This "Why I Am Teaching" letter will serve as both an artifact and a reflection. Over the years, your reasons for becoming a teacher may change, or weaken, or become even stronger. You may well want to repeat this process in five or ten years, and monitor your own development. The letter will provide you with an insight and a marker of your thinking as you first considered a teaching career.

1:6 Creating a Career Information Document

Purpose: Applying for the right teaching position requires homework. You want to know where to apply, not only where the job openings are, but where you will find the "right" school for you. Visiting schools and meeting with administrators will help you learn about the school culture and offer insights into the kinds of questions you should be asking as you investigate teaching. An informational interview with a school administrator is a useful rehearsal for you and could provide timely information on the job market and hiring procedures, and a great way to begin your "Career Information" document.

INTASC PRINCIPLE 6
Communication Skills

Activity: Arrange an interview with a local school administrator (principal, personnel director). Consider going with a small group of peers (visitation team), so that your school leader is not inundated with too many requests. Review information in this text and in your community about teacher supply and demand. Develop questions as a visitation team. The following list of suggestions can also provide a framework for your conversation. Don't overstay your welcome—twenty to thirty minutes should be adequate.

- In terms of teacher openings, what grade levels, subject areas or specialties will likely be needed this year? What do you anticipate will be needed in the next few years?

- Are new schools being built? Are some being closed?

- Do teachers move in and out of the system (family leave, special grant projects)?

- What is the diversity breakdown of teachers in the district? How does this compare with the students in this school and districtwide? How do these factors affect screening and hiring?

- What is the application process for this district? Who else is involved in the hiring process? Are there individual or panel interviews? Do you require or recommend applicant portfolios?

- If you could describe a perfect candidate, what traits would that teacher possess?

- What other questions should we ask concerning the educational job market and hiring process?

- What advice would you offer beginning teachers?

- Do you have specific suggestions for the interview process?

 FORM:
Career Information Document

Artifact: Building a "Career Information" document can help you keep and build on this information, and not let it slip through the cracks. One section might be your geographic preferences including city, suburbs, or rural areas. Another might be the kind of school you prefer, such as the school's educational philosophy, types of students, colleagues and administration, testing practices, diversity of staff, diversity of student body, salary/benefit package, community support, and so on.

This might be a good place to include job-seeking strategies, such as interviewing techniques. It is your document, so you decide what works for you. The purpose is to begin a process (that will be ongoing) that places you in the school that works best for you.

Reflection: Meet with other visitation teams and compare your interviews. Are certain trends evident in your locale? How do these realities influence your own decision making? What questions remain unanswered? Is more library or Internet research needed? Is a follow-up meeting or a phone call appropriate? Consider a similar interview during a trip home or while visiting another region of the country. How does all this information affect your teaching plans? Attach your reflections to your artifact.

1:7 A Mini-Lesson with a Mini-Group

Purpose: Frankly, the best way to learn to teach is to teach. You have read information on effective instruction, and we hope you have observed many of these skills as a student. It is now your turn to put some of what you have learned into action. This activity will give you actual teaching experience, and help you to find your starting line for all the practice and teaching ahead.

Activity: Develop and teach a mini-lesson (about eight minutes to twelve minutes in length), on a familiar topic. If you play a sport or a musical instrument, have a favorite subject or hobby, you may choose a small piece of that subject to teach. Work with a small group of peers (three to five students). Use principles of direct teaching (see pp. 96–98 in Chapter 3) as your guide. Also keep in mind wait time as you ask and answer questions (see pp. 89). Your greatest challenge will be to choose a concise topic or skill. This is not the time to be overly ambitious. Any techniques you use to promote variety in process and content will be appreciated by your "students."

Dr. Madeline Hunter's research showed that effective teachers have a methodology when planning and presenting a lesson. She found that no matter what the teacher's style, grade level, subject matter, or economic background of the students, a properly taught lesson contained the following elements:

FORM:

Seven Step
Lesson Plan

Dr. Madeline Hunter's Seven-Step Lesson Plan

1. **Anticipatory Set** (focus)—Focus learners' attention on the instruction that is about to begin. This could be a teacher demonstration, video, story, puzzle or a handout prior to the actual lesson. This is also known as a "grabber" and it's a way to get your students' attention and interest.

2. **Purpose** (objective)—A clear explanation of what learners will understand and be able to do as a result of the lesson. This section should answer the question: "Why is this important to learn?"

3. **Instructional Strategy**—What content and skills need to be taught to accomplish this task? And what are the best teaching strategies needed for this instructional task (lecture, activity, video, group work, etc.)?

4. **Modeling** (show)—Provide learners with examples or demonstrations of competencies associated with the lesson.

5. **Guided Practice**—Monitor learners as they apply new information.

6. **Check for Understanding**—Evaluate whether learners have the information needed to master the objective.

7. **Independent Practice**—Assign learners to work independently, without direct teacher assistance.

For more information on Dr. Hunter visit www.foothill.net/~moorek/lessondesign.html

Artifact: Design a "Seven Step Lesson Plan" using this format. If this is your first lesson plan, you may want to title it that way. If not, come up with a title that reflects your topic or the skill you are working on.

Reflection: You did it! You taught a mini-lesson to your peers, something that many experienced faculty find frightening. Use the following rubric to assess your success. Also record your feelings. How well do you think it went? Include both your lesson plan and the rubric in your portfolio.

FORM:
Lesson Plan Rubric

	Not at all			Very well done	
	1	2	3	4	5
Anticipatory set					
Purpose					
Instructional input					
Modeling					
Guided practice					
Checking for understanding					
Independent practice					

1:8 Tutor Using Effective Feedback

Purpose: Assessment is a great deal more than testing and grading. Even the evaluative feedback you give students during one-on-one interactions is considered part of your assessment repertoire. The text covers four feedback reactions to student answers: praise, acceptance, remediation, and criticism (p. 92). Using them effectively and fairly will be one of your toughest challenges.

INTASC PRINCIPLE 8
Assessment

Activity: If your program recommends working with a K–12 student, terrific! If not, commit yourself to a tutorial opportunity with a local youngster. Although a "one-shot deal" will accomplish the goals of this activity, an ongoing relationship is an extraordinary chance for you (and a youngster) to learn. Audiotape your session (at least fifteen minutes) with the student. Remember to get permission from the student and faculty coordinator by explaining the purpose of your taping.

Artifact:
Step 1: Spend the initial five to ten minutes noting your wait time. How long do you wait for the student? How long do you wait to respond to an answer? You might find it helpful to review the section on wait time from Chapter 3 prior to your lesson.

FORM:
Tutor Using
Effective Feedback

Step 2: Use the chart below to observe teacher feedback. You may find it helpful to review the criteria for each type of feedback. Work with a partner if you are unsure about particular comments.

Average Length for Wait Time #1 _____
Average Length for Wait Time #2 _____

Feedback (Sample Entries)	Number of Responses
Praise:	
Good job!	II
Acceptance:	
Okay.	III
Remediation:	
Now read all the word parts together.	I
Criticism:	
No, that's not the way to pronounce it.	I

Reflection: What did you notice about yourself and the pattern or frequency of feedback? How did your tutorial session compare with the teacher reaction research (pp. 91–94)? What form did your acceptance comments take (okay, aha, silence)? Did your use of praise represent the attributes identified by Brophy on page 93? Was criticism clear and appropriate? Was remediation specific enough to allow the student to improve? How well did you employ wait time? How would you assess your use of these skills? What activity can you devise to help you practice and improve your feedback? Include this chart and reflection in your portfolio.

1:9 Student Feedback about Your Mini-Lesson

INTASC PRINCIPLE 9
Reflection and
Responsibility

Purpose: It's one thing for a teacher to reflect on the success or shortcomings of a lesson. It's quite another for a teacher to ask students how the class is going. University classes do this, and so do organizations like Southwest Airlines that depend on customer and employee satisfaction. Asking students about their views will help you in your own reflection and professional responsibility.

Activity: This activity can be done in conjunction with 1:7 "A Mini-Lesson with a Mini-Group," when you teach a brief lesson on a subject of your choosing. Create a student survey form to be distributed after the lesson. You can shape the survey form any way you choose, but here are a few ideas:

Artifact: Sample Student Satisfaction Survey.

Please support your comments with examples.

FORM:

Student Survey

1. Were lesson objectives clear and focused?
2. Was material presented clearly?
3. How effective was the guided practice?
4. How effective was the independent practice?
5. What did you like best about this lesson?
6. What did you learn from this lesson?
7. What could have made this lesson more effective?
8. Other comments and feedback are welcome.

Reflection: How did it feel to have others critique your teaching? Were your "students" able to support their criticism and compliments with examples? What did you learn from others that went beyond your own self-assessment? Attach your feedback to the student survey(s) and include in your portfolio.

1:10 Special Education Services

Purpose: For many preservice teachers, the laws and services for students with special needs can be complex and confusing. Gaining a professional understanding of these concerns will help anyone with career plans in education. It might even motivate you to teach children with disabilities. Begin by reviewing the information in the text that covers special education (Chapter 2, pp. 56–63).

> **INTASC PRINCIPLE 10**
> Relationships and
> Partnerships

Activity: Contact a local school district and identify the director of services for special education. Request a parent information packet that outlines the rights and responsibilities of the district regarding testing, resources, policy, practices, and all other information that would help you understand the Individuals with Disabilities Education Act (IDEA).

Highlight the key points in the literature, and take notes of what a teacher needs to do to meet the needs of special needs students.

Artifact: Create a document that will make this information more easily accessible to you when you begin teaching. Perhaps the title might be "Special Needs Reminders" or something similar. This should be an easy to read piece, perhaps even a checklist, to help you fulfill your responsibilities and create the best possible educational climate for special needs learners.

Reflection: What more did you learn about IDEA? How does it feel to look at this information from a parent's perspective? How does it feel to look at this information from a student's perspective? How does it feel to look at this information from a teacher's perspective?

II

Schools and Curriculum

CLASS ACT

As an elementary school teacher, I was particularly eager to find good multicultural books. One day, I planned to read one of the many Juan Bobo stories. Juan Bobo (Simple John) depicts a "noodlehead" who does nothing right. This character is Puerto Rico's favorite fool and simpleton and has been the mainstay for generations.

Supposedly, Juan Bobo embodies the essence of Puerto Rico—the *jibaro*—a product of three cultures: Taino Indian, African, and Spaniard. The character stands for the honest and uncorrupted life of the country folks against the pomposity and falsehood of those in the city (i.e., the aristocratic Spaniards and those imitating them). But too often Juan Bobo is instead a mockery of the *jibaros*—equated with the poor and uneducated country folks. Additionally, Juan Bobo is frequently portrayed as either a person of apparent Black and/or Indian heritage. Among Puerto Ricans, it is highly insulting to be called either *jibaro* or Juan Bobo.

As I prepared to read to them, I looked into the face of one of my students—a Latino boy of African heritage. I was transported back to my childhood and saw myself—a little girl of African heritage, also waiting for the teacher to read a story to the class. I recalled painful memories.

Growing up biracial in Puerto Rico made me aware at a very young age of the deep racism in Latino culture. Although family and friends called me *triguena* (wheat colored), I recall classmates' and even teachers' crueler taunts.

I glanced at the cover of the book I was about to read. It clearly pictured Juan Bobo as a poor country boy of African heritage. I looked back at the faces of my students—innocent faces reflecting their African and Indian heritage. What was I doing? Persons of African and Indian ancestry are the majority in most Latino countries. Yet the folklore and literature, adults' and children's alike, predominantly present characters of Spanish ancestry. Country folks and Latinos of color disappear or are presented as ignorant and superstitious, as criminals, servants, and buffoons. Those in power are White Latinos.

Over the years, I have come to an important understanding. Just because a book is "multicultural" doesn't mean it is free of bias. Juan Bobo and other culturally authentic stories have been translated into English and other languages—they can now take their biases across cultures.

I placed the book down on my lap and told the class: "Today, we are going to do something really special. Books are stories that have been written by authors so others can read and hear them. Today, I am going to tell you a story from my childhood and then, we will tell each other our stories. We are going to write our stories down and publish them so others can read them later." I proceeded: "Once I climbed a tall mountain and thought I had reached the top of the world where the Taino Indian god Yukiyu lives . . ."

Marta I. Cruz-Jansen, Ph.D.
Associate Professor
Multicultural Education
College of Education
Florida Atlantic University

SOURCE: M. I. Cruz-Jansen, (1998, Fall). "Culturally Authentic Bias." *Rethinking Schools.* Vol 13, No 1, p. 5.

Read more *Class Acts* at Sadker.com.

www.mhhe.com/ sadker7e

4

Schools: Choices and Challenges

FOCUS QUESTIONS

1. What are the various expectations Americans hold for their schools?
2. Should schools transmit the American culture or change it?
3. What school purposes are emphasized by educational reform?
4. How are magnet and charter schools, open enrollment, and vouchers reshaping our concept of the neighborhood public school?
5. Do the laws of the marketplace belong in public education?
6. Why are so many families choosing home schooling?

 WHAT DO YOU THINK? **What Do You Think Schools and Students Are Like Today?** Check off what you think and see how others respond.

CHAPTER PREVIEW

Although most of us take school for granted, the proper role of this institution continues to evoke heated debate. Are schools to prepare students for college, for a vocation, or to achieve high scores on standardized tests? Perhaps schools are really to develop good interpersonal relationships, or develop a national loyalty. Some say many school goals come down to either preparing students to adjust to society or equipping them to change and improve society. Not only do people hold widely divergent views regarding both the goals and the effectiveness of America's schools, but these views seem to vary depending on the times.

In this chapter, you will have the opportunity to examine some of the major purposes assigned to schools and some of the major criticisms that have been leveled at them. Some believe that America's schools are failing, and reform efforts have led to innovations in how schools are organized, managed, and evaluated. The recent emphasis on standards and tests once again raises the crucial question: What's a school for? The traditional link between a community and its neighborhood school is being strained, if not ruptured. In fact, the "right" to avoid the neighborhood school and choose a school is quickly becoming a major national issue. Competition among schools is being fueled by the business community, which views schools as potential profit centers. And concerned parents, in ever greater numbers, are giving up on schools entirely. The notion of parents educating their own children at home is gaining ground, and in many communities, the family room has become the classroom. Defining the place and purpose of schools has never been more challenging.

CHAPTER FOCUS
The past decade has witnessed pressure to improve school performance, but also the emergence of some penetrating questions about the very purpose of schools. The right to choose a school has become a real possibility not just a political cause. Competition among schools is being fueled in part by the business community, which views schools as potential profit centers. For a chapter outline, see the IM.

A Meeting Here Tonight

Sam Newman has been principal of Monroe High School for just under five years. Becoming principal seemed a natural step to take after teaching and coaching for eight years.

Sam's plans to improve school morale and community relations, as well as to increase faculty involvement in key decisions, pleased the school board enough to give him the principalship over two, more senior candidates. He got off to a good start. He organized rallies, proclaiming, "Monroe is tops!"; he met with parents and teachers in endless meetings; and he created teacher management teams. But all that seems long ago.

Sam now spends his time rushing from one emergency to another. He spends two nights a week trying to complete federal, state, and school district paperwork and one or two more nights attending meetings. During the day, there is an endless parade of students in trouble, teachers with complaints, outraged parents, and, of course, more meetings. Between budgets to balance and supplies to order, Sam rarely has time to think about how to significantly improve education at Monroe.

And now, to top it all off, statewide results show that Monroe students have fallen almost a year behind the norm in math and reading. He must have received a hundred calls from angry parents, complaining about higher taxes and inefficient schools, so a meeting has been called to explore solutions to the problem of declining test scores.

On his way to the meeting, Sam detours to the bathroom. As he stares into the mirror to comb his thin, graying hair, he notes sadly the almost complete disappearance of his belt beneath his belly. He once prided himself on staying in shape. Now his shape is mostly round.

But being a principal is not the same as being a coach, and a school is very different from a team. Each passing year has taught him how precious little he knows about schools. He schedules. He budgets. He writes plans. He calms parents. He disciplines

GRABBER: BUMPER STICKERS
IM

FOCUS QUESTION 1
What are the various expectations Americans hold for their schools?

TEACHING TIP
As students read, recall or play-out this scenario, ask them what each character's expectations are for schools. Do they know people like the "stars" in this episode? If they (or their parents) were attending the meeting, how would their role be written?

Today's large, comprehensive high schools reflect the diversity and the conflicting interests of the larger society.

students. But, all the while, he realizes that he has little time to shape and direct the school. He is not really leading the school—he is not even sure where to lead it; he is simply trying very hard to keep it afloat. Although he knows more about flowcharts than about philosophy, a line from his college philosophy course sticks in his mind. The line is Santayana's, and it seems to have a lot of meaning for him and for Monroe High School: Fanaticism consists of redoubling one's efforts after having forgotten one's aim.

A quick glance at his watch brings an abrupt end to philosophical speculation. He is already late. He hurries down the hallway to the meeting.

• • •

George Elbright unconsciously tugs at his tie as he mounts the long stairway to Monroe High School. He glances up at the motto, chiseled in stone. "Knowledge Is Power." He thinks back to the first time he read those words, as a 15-year-old freshman. Thirty years later, the memory still makes him perspire and pull at his tie. Funny how schools do that to you.

For George Elbright, Monroe High conjures up memories of hard work, graded homework assignments, and midterms so tough that kids sometimes broke down and cried, unable to go on. And finals! The whole year's work riding on one exam. Tests were rough then, but kids learned. Not like today. Not at all.

And that is why George is back at Monroe High. For years, he watched schools disintegrate, and complained bitterly about the lack of discipline, the growing permissiveness, courses in sex education, drug education, environmental education, and the new teaching methods that sound as if the teachers do not have to teach at all. Finally things were changing. And no wonder. The test scores were in. George Jr. failed the standardized state test. So did many of the students at Monroe. No wonder George Elbright Sr., is about to attend his first parent-teacher meeting in six years.

George reaches into his pocket and pulls out his wrinkled, handwritten list. He has to be clear and forceful. He slowly rehearses his list:

1. Teachers must reassume their responsibility. Skills development, homework, and tests should be the main activities of the classroom. Free-for-all discussion, with the teacher acting as a television talk show host instead of a teacher, has to end. Children have to learn that learning is serious.

2. Students must learn the importance of discipline and respect. Students should speak to adults with respect. We should consider a new dress code or even school uniforms. Sloppy dress and poor manners lead to lazy attitudes and poor work.

3. Kids who do not pass tests should be left back until they do pass them. Too many high school graduates can't read or write well.

4. I am tired of trying to decipher "progress reports" about my child's "social adjustment" and "satisfactory efforts." I want to see report cards with grades and without educational jargon.

5. A school is supposed to teach fundamental skills, and not sex education, human relations, or other frills and electives. It is time that schools get back to the basics.

6. And it is high time that teachers taught kids morality and ethics.

Perhaps it will work; perhaps he can get the school back on the right track. The newspapers are filled with reports that seem to support his point of view. Why, he even read a report that said schools are so weak they jeopardize America's future. At any rate, he has to try for George Jr.'s sake. All the family's hopes are pinned on him.

George Jr., would be the first Elbright to make it to college. This is no time for the school to let him down.

• • •

Shirley Weiss sits alone in her classroom, sipping lukewarm coffee from a commuter cup. The evening meeting gives her a chance to stay after school and catch up on her paperwork. She finished grading 15 minutes ago but is determined to wait until the last minute before going down to the auditorium for the meeting. Although anxious to make her position known, she is not anxious to get into one-to-one encounters with angry parents, so she waits.

She is amazed at public reaction to the poor scores on the state's standardized test. Given the teacher cuts and the large size of today's classes, it really isn't all that surprising. Everyone seems to be missing the point entirely. Teenagers today simply aren't contemporary versions of the kids who attended Monroe High ten or twenty years ago. Violence, alienation, racism, sexism, drugs, terrorism—the world is so much more complex. Kids should find out who they are and where they are going. President Jackson's 1830s fight over the National Bank does not exactly speak to them.

That is why Shirley Weiss has restructured her American history course into a contemporary social problems course. Students have to *want* to learn and grow, and that's what her course is all about. And the students do well in her course. They are genuinely interested. They study and they learn. As a matter of fact, if those test makers ever were to leave their air-conditioned, swanky offices and rejoin the real world, they would revise their tests to parallel her authentic assessments, and her kids would soar! The problem is not really with the school or the kids at all! It is with the test makers and the parents who are stuck in the past!

Shirley is good and angry as she pushes back her chair and makes her way down to the auditorium.

• • •

Phil Lambert begins to fidget as he waits for the meeting to begin. His physique and the twenty-five-year-old wooden seat are less than perfect fits.

He has not been back to Monroe since his youngest daughter graduated, almost ten years ago. And he is not overjoyed at being here now. But declining test scores represent a serious problem, not just for Phil but for the entire community.

Phil Lambert, owner of Lambert's Department Store, is also president of the chamber of commerce. Every week, he is involved with enticing professionals, even high-tech firms, and developers to relocate in Monroe. Sooner or later, the talks always turn to the quality of the school system. In a sense, the success of the schools is a barometer of the town's future growth and development. And now the barometer is falling; stormy days are ahead. Declining test scores could cost the town plenty.

But Phil is particularly upset because he has warned people about this problem for years. High school kids are getting into more and more trouble. He has recently been to court three times to deal with teenage shoplifters. And, when kids today apply for work, it is so sad it is almost funny! Wearing baggy jeans and fouling up the application form, they just come off as irresponsible and stupid. For years, Phil has been asking rhetorically, "Didn't you learn *anything* in school?" Now his question is no longer rhetorical.

The schools simply have to get down to business, literally, and begin preparing kids for the real world. Our whole nation is in economic trouble because of weak schools. More courses should be offered, stressing not only the basics but also how to get a job and the importance of the work ethic. Students have to understand that school is not a place where they can come late, dress sloppily, and goof off. Once they understand how serious the real world is, how important getting a job is, they will get serious about their schoolwork.

Lambert checks his cell phone for messages and makes a mental note that the meeting is starting sixteen minutes late. If he were to run the store the way they run the schools, he'd have been bankrupt years ago.

• • •

The late start of the meeting gives Mary Jackson a chance to unwind. She has rushed from her job to make the meeting and is beginning to feel the consequences of her long day.

As she gauges the audience, she sees that once again the "haves" outnumber the "have-nots." The middle-class, white, well-dressed parents don't look half as tired as Mary Jackson feels. But they sure do seem worried. For the first time, they are getting a small taste of the problem Mary has been fighting for years. Lower achievement scores are shaking them up. But they could never know the problem as well as Mary does. Even with the drop in scores for white kids, they are still scoring almost two years ahead of the African American students.

Mary has two daughters enrolled in Monroe High. Both are working hard, yet they cannot seem to catch up to the top students. Her kids have never had a nonwhite teacher. And her kids have never gotten into the honors track. Somehow it seems that only white students end up there.

She has tried to make the school aware of the special problems faced by students of color and females by organizing the Parents' Multicultural Task Force. Everyone at Monroe seems sympathetic, from Mr. Newman on down. But nothing has changed, and that makes her feel tired and discouraged—but not tired and discouraged enough to give up.

Mary looks around at the almost completely filled auditorium, spotting precious few black faces in the audience. But Mary would speak for those who could not come, and for those who have given up all hope of changing things. Monroe High should be their stepping-stone up, not an obstacle. Mary would tell them. The past few frustrating years have worn her patience thin.

• • •

This was the first time Karen Miller ever visited Monroe High, but it all seemed so familiar: unhappy parents gathering to complain about an underperforming school to a very tired-looking principal. This was the kind of scenario that was made-to-order for Unlimited Educational Opportunities, Inc. and their "Horizon" Schools. Karen glanced down to make certain that she had her carton filled with hundreds of multicolored brochures. She knew the plan well. She would let the parents complain, the principal would try to assuage their anxiety, and then she would announce the opening of her company's new charter school. A Horizon Charter School would promise a more focused educational program and guaranteed test score improvements by bringing business efficiency to education. No empty promise: There was a track record. She would explain that over 60 Horizon for-profit schools in other states were already compiling impressive reading and math scores. Horizon uses a Back to Basics curriculum and character education combined with extra time, extra teachers, and laptop computers to achieve its goals. But Karen would have to warn them as well: Although Horizon schools were open to all, it was likely that there would be more applicants than spaces. Karen would alert everyone to the obvious: A lottery system would have to be used to select which students will be admitted.

Karen felt good about the evening meeting, the ability of Horizon to enhance the test scores, and her own decision to leave Wall Street and use her Harvard M.B.A. to promote Unlimited Educational Opportunities. It was looking like another growth year.

• • •

Sam Newman twists the microphone stand to within a few inches of his mouth and prepares to open the meeting. He looks out at the packed auditorium and begins to assess the crowd:

> There is Pat Viola, the art teacher. What is she doing here? Art is never assessed on those tests.
>
> Oh, there's Mrs. Jackson, the chair of the Multicultural Task Force. She's not going to pull any punches about those test scores. The black students are two years behind the white students on achievement tests.
>
> And Dr. Sweig, the humanities professor from the university, is here. He's probably going to make his pitch about requiring all students to study the classics. He must have given that "cultural literacy for all" speech a dozen times.
>
> Mrs. Benoit, president of the school board, looks distressed. As long as I can find a solution that pleases everyone and doesn't increase the budget, she'll be satisfied. She needs a magician, not a principal, to run this meeting.
>
> Phil Lambert is here and Shirley Weiss. Isn't that the Elbright kid's father? Wonder what's on their minds?

Sam Newman begins to perspire. He leans forward and announces, "Okay, let's begin."

CLASS ACTIVITY: REEL TO REAL: *OCTOBER SKY*
IM, Activity 4:2

RAP 2.10
Support Staff Interview, p. 280

Good schools depend on strong community support.

The Purposes of School

FOCUS QUESTION 2
Should schools transmit the American culture or change it?

CLASS ACTIVITY: INTERVIEWS
IM, Activity 4:6

CRITICAL THINKING QUESTION
What *is* the purpose of a school? Would your response alter if you were addressing voters as an elected official, or if you were a guidance counselor trying to reach out to a potential dropout?

OVERHEADS 48–49
The Purpose of School

The Purpose and Effectiveness of Schools

Sam Newman in the vignette that opens this chapter has a dilemma on his hands. Parents and teachers are pulling him—and trying to pull Monroe High—in different directions. If it is any comfort to Sam—and it probably is not—he is confronting an old question: What is the purpose of a school?

Having spent much of your life as a student, you may find this question too basic, even obvious. Answers come quickly to mind. We go to school to learn things, to earn good grades, to qualify for better jobs, to become a better person—or to please our parents (or even ourselves). But these divergent reasons represent the view only from a student's side of the desk. There are other perspectives, broader views, and more fundamental definitions of the purposes of schools. Although brainstorming all the possible reasons for schools could lead to some creative insights, it may be more practical at this point to focus on two fundamental, yet somewhat antithetical, purposes of schools.

Purpose 1: To Transmit Society's Knowledge and Values (Passing the Cultural Baton)

Society has a vital interest in what schools do and how they do it. Schools reflect and promote society's values. There is a world of knowledge out there, more than any school can possibly hope to teach, so one of the first tasks confronting the school is to *select* what to teach. This selection creates a cultural message. Each country chooses the curriculum to match and advance its own view of history, its own values, its self-interests, and its own culture. In the United States, we learn about U.S. history, often in elementary, middle, and high school, but we learn little about the history, geography, and culture of other countries—or of America's own cultural diversity, for that matter. Even individual states and communities require schools to teach their own state or local history, to advance the dominant "culture" of Illinois or of New York City. By selecting what to teach—and what to omit—schools are making clear decisions as to what is valued, what is worth preserving and passing on.

Literature is a good example of this selection process. American children read works mainly by U.S. and British writers, and only occasionally works by Asian, Latin American, and African authors. This is not because literary genius is confined to the British and U.S. populations; it is because of a selection process, a decision by the keepers of the culture and creators of the curriculum that certain authors are to be taught, talked about, and emulated and others omitted. Similar decisions are made concerning which music should be played, which art viewed, which dances performed, and which historical figures and world events studied. As each nation makes these cultural value decisions, it is the role of the school to transmit these decisions to the next generation.

GLOBAL VIEW
Is it really plausible that the purpose of U.S. schools impacts the world? How might the despair of repressed women mold our views? Are we merely a global economy when it comes to coffee beans or gasoline?

As society transmits its culture, it also transmits a view of the world. Being American means valuing certain things and judging countries and cultures from that set of values. Democratic countries that practice religious tolerance and respect individual rights are generally viewed more positively by Americans than are societies characterized by opposing norms, standards, and actions—that is, characteristics that do not fit our "American values." Afghani women denied access to schools, hospitals, and jobs by the Taliban conflicted with our cultural and political standards and was repulsive to most Americans. Repression of religious, racial, and ethnic groups usually engenders similar negative feelings. By transmitting culture, schools breathe the breath of cultural eternity into a new generation and mold its view of the world.

But this process is limiting as well. In transmitting culture, schools are teaching students to view the world from the wrong end of a telescope, yielding a constricted view that does not allow much deviation or perspective. Cultural transmission may contribute to feelings of cultural superiority, a belief that "we are the best, number one!" Such nationalistic views may decrease tolerance and respect for other cultures and peoples.

Purpose 2: Reconstructing Society (Schools as Tools for Change)

If society were perfect, transmitting the culture from one generation to the next would be all that is required of schools. But our world, our nation, and our communities are far from ideal. Poverty, hunger, injustice, pollution, overpopulation, racism, sexism, and ethical challenges—and, of course, the dark clouds of terrorism, nuclear, chemical, and biological weapons—are societal problems on a depressingly long list. To **reconstructionists,** society is broken, it needs to be fixed, and the school is a perfect tool for making the needed repairs.

Reconstructionists hold a wide spectrum of beliefs. As you might anticipate, there are both liberal and conservative reconstructionists, each pushing schools in different directions. It is not only values that differ; strategies differ as well. At one end are those who believe that students should be made aware of the ills of society; study these critical, if controversial, areas; and equip themselves to confront these issues as they become adults.[1] Other reconstructionists are more action-oriented and believe that schools and students shouldn't wait until the students reach adulthood. They call for a **social action curriculum,** in which students actively involve themselves in eliminating social ills. For example, if a poor neighborhood lacks a day care facility for young children of working parents, the students could petition government officials and private corporations to establish a center.

This idea of students contributing to society is not unique. The Carnegie Foundation for the Advancement of Teaching recommends that every student be required to earn a **service credit,** which might include volunteer work with the poor, elderly, or homeless. The idea behind a service credit includes not only an effort to reduce social ills but also the idea of providing students with a connection to the larger community and of encouraging them to develop a sense of their personal responsibility for improving the social condition.[2] In 1992, Maryland became the first state requiring students to perform community service before they would be granted their high school diploma, and service learning became more popular nationwide throughout the 1990s.[3] In 1999, more than half of students in grades 6 through 12 had participated in service learning, although who participates, and what they do to gain service credits, is somewhat erratic. While 57 percent of girls participated, only 47 percent of boys did. Whites were more likely to participate than African Americans, and African

IN THE NEWS

Japanese View of World War II

The Japanese are quite serious about transmitting a positive image of their culture and history, but World War II is a problem. However, it is not a problem for school children. The Hiroshima memorial explains that "the situation in Pearl Harbor hurtled Japan into the Pacific war." There is no mention of Japan's surprise attack, and no explanation why Japan invaded China four years before Pearl Harbor. China and South Korea have objected to what Japan teaches the young, and have threatened trade sanctions if these inaccuracies are not corrected. They demand a meaningful account of Japan's invasion and occupation of their nations. While many Japanese teachers support such revisions, most school boards are not composed of educators, and it is questionable if any changes will be made.

SOURCE: Kwan Weng Kin, "Teachers Have No Say Over Japan Textbooks," *Straits Times Interactive,* May 21, 2001.

 What's new in education? Click on *News Feeds.*

TEACHING TIP

Invite students who completed a service credit for graduation to share their experiences. Consider making at least one class (or teacher education program) assignment that is similar to the service credit requirements in many secondary schools.

Is the business of schools just academic learning, or might the goals include fostering an awareness of the benefits of community service, such as volunteering to tutor others?

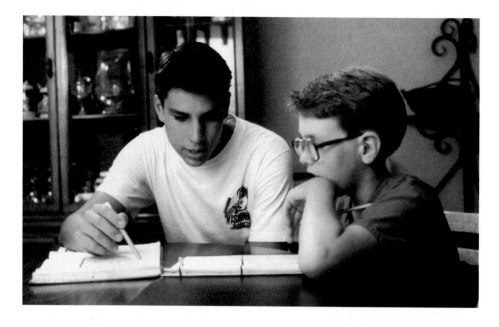

Americans more likely to participate than Hispanics. Participation increases when schools take an active role in setting up the service opportunities, and when they require it for graduation. And student participation increased with the educational level of their parents.[4]

GLOBAL VIEW
Numerous press releases continue to report international cases of child labor law violations and the sexual abuse of girls and boys. How can teachers help children to understand other children's lives?

RAP 2.6
Public Service Announcement: Purpose of Schools, p. 277

While social democratic reconstructionists are reform-minded, *economic reconstructionists* hold a darker view of society's ills and advocate more drastic, even revolutionary, action. They believe that schools generally teach the poorer classes to accept their lowly stations in life, to be subservient to authority, to unquestioningly follow rules while laboring for the economic benefit of the rich. To economic reconstructionists, schools are currently tools of oppression, not institutions of learning. They believe that students must be introduced to curricula that analyze and reform economic realities. For example, one such curriculum project targets a popular and highly visible athletic company, one that produces incredibly expensive sport shoes. This company manufactures its products in developing nations, maintaining horrid working conditions. Children in these poor countries are sold into labor bondage by their impoverished families. As young as 6, they work twelve or more hours a day, enduring cruelty and even beatings as they earn only pennies an hour. While the companies defend themselves by saying that they cannot change local conditions, economic reconstructionists believe that companies intentionally select locations because of their cheap labor costs. Economic reconstructionists point out that American children play with products made through the agonizing toil of other children. All the while, the companies profit. Educators who focus on economic reform have developed materials, websites, and social action projects that not only teach children about such exploitation but also provide them with strategies to pressure companies into creating more humane and equitable working conditions.[5]

Perhaps the most noted contemporary economic reconstructionist was **Paulo Freire,** author of ***The Pedagogy of the Oppressed,*** a book about his efforts to educate and liberate poor, illiterate peasants in Brazil.[6] In his book, Freire describes how he taught these workers to read in order to identify problems that were keeping them poor and powerless. From this new awareness, they began to analyze their problems—such as how the lack of sanitation causes illness—and what they could do to solve specific problems and liberate themselves from their oppressive conditions. Freire highlighted the distinction between schools and education. Schools often miseducate and oppress. But true education liberates. Through education, the dispossessed learned to read, to act collectively, to improve their living conditions, and to reconstruct their lives. (See *The Education Hall of Fame* in Chapter 8 for more about Freire.)

Public Demands for Schools

While preserving the status quo and promoting social change represent two fundamental directions available to schools, they are not the only possible expectations. When you think about it, the public holds our schools to a bewildering assortment of tasks and expectations.

John Goodlad, in his massive study **A Place Called School,** examined a wide range of documents that tried to define the purposes of schooling over 300 years of history. He and his colleague found four broad goals:

1. *Academic,* including a broad array of knowledge and intellectual skills.
2. *Vocational,* aimed at readiness for the world of work and economic responsibilities.
3. *Social and civic,* including skills and behavior for participating in a complex democratic society.
4. *Personal,* including the development of individual talent and self-expression.[7]

Goodlad included these four goal areas in questionnaires distributed to parents, and he asked them to rate their importance. (See Figure 4.1.) Parents gave "very important" ratings to all four. When Goodlad asked students and teachers to rate the four goal areas, they rated all of them as "very important." When pushed to select one of these four as having top priority, approximately half the teachers and parents selected the intellectual area, while students spread their preferences fairly evenly among all four categories, with high school students giving a slight edge to vocational goals. When it comes to selecting the purpose of schools, both those who are their clients and those who provide their services resist interpreting the purpose of schools narrowly.

CLASS ACTIVITY:
DETERMINING
SCHOOLS' GOALS
IM, Activity 4:5

MULTIPLE INTELLIGENCE
CONNECTION
Walk in the shoes (sandals, boots, or moccasins) of a naturalist and propose what a school's outside surroundings would *look like* to best represent educational goals.

FIGURE 4.1
Goals of schools.

OVERHEAD 50
Goals of Schools

REFLECTION: Under each goal, list specific efforts a school could make to reach the goal. How would you prioritize these goals? Explain.

What do Americans want from their schools? Evidently, they want it all! As early as 1953, Arthur Bestor wrote, "The idea that the school must undertake to meet every need that some other agency is failing to meet, regardless of the suitability of the schoolroom to the task, is a preposterous delusion that in the end can wreck the educational system."[8]

Then, in the 1980s, **Ernest Boyer** conducted a major study of secondary education and concluded,

> Since the English classical school was founded over 150 years ago, high schools have accumulated purposes like barnacles on a weathered ship. As school population expanded from a tiny urban minority to almost all youth, a coherent purpose was hard to find. The nation piled social policy upon educational policy and all of them on top of the delusion that a single institution can do it all.[9]

 ## Where Do You Stand?

CLASS ACTIVITY:
CREATING EDUCATIONAL
DREAMS
IM, Activity 4:3

Identifying school goals seems to be everyone's business—parents, teachers, all levels of government, and various professional groups. Over the years, dozens of lists have been published in different reform reports, each enumerating goals for schools. The problem arises when schools cannot fulfill all of these goals, either because there are too many goals or because the purposes actually conflict with one another. It is these smaller pieces that often dominate discussion. Should schools focus on preparing students for college? Should they try to inhibit drug use, or lessen the threat of AIDS? Perhaps schools ought to focus on the economy and train students to become members of a more efficient workforce, one that can successfully compete in the world marketplace.

Look at the following list of school goals. Drawn from a variety of sources, these goals have been advocated singly and in combination by different groups at different times and have been adopted by different schools. In each case, register your own judgment on the values and worth of each goal. When you have completed your responses, we shall discuss the significance of these goals, and you can see how your responses fit into the bigger picture.

CLASS ACTIVITY: WHERE
DO YOU STAND?
IM, Activity 4:8

Circle the number that best reflects how important you think each school goal is.

1 Very unimportant

2 Unimportant

3 Moderately important

4 Important

5 Very important

INTERACTIVE ACTIVITY
How Important Are
These School Goals?
Do this exercise online.
See how others
responded to each
statement.

	Very Unimportant				Very Important
1. To transmit the nation's cultural heritage, preserving past accomplishments and insights	1	2	3	4	5
2. To encourage students to question current practices and institutions; to promote social change	1	2	3	4	5

	Very Unimportant				Very Important
3. To prepare competent workers to compete successfully in a technological world economy	1	2	3	4	5
4. To develop healthy citizens aware of nutrition, exercise, and good health habits	1	2	3	4	5
5. To lead the world in creating a peaceful global society, stressing an understanding of other cultures and languages	1	2	3	4	5
6. To provide a challenging education for America's brightest students	1	2	3	4	5
7. To develop strong self-concept and self-esteem in students	1	2	3	4	5
8. To nurture creative students in developing art, music, and writing	1	2	3	4	5
9. To prevent unwanted pregnancy, AIDS, drugs, addiction, alcoholism	1	2	3	4	5
10. To unite citizens from diverse backgrounds (national origin, race, ethnicity) as a single nation with a unified culture	1	2	3	4	5
11. To provide support to families through after-school child care, nutritional supplements, medical treatment, and so on	1	2	3	4	5
12. To encourage loyal students committed to the United States; to instill patriotism	1	2	3	4	5
13. To teach students our nation's work ethic: punctuality, responsibility, cooperation, self-control, neatness, and so on	1	2	3	4	5
14. To demonstrate academic proficiency through high standardized test scores	1	2	3	4	5
15. To provide a dynamic vehicle for social and economic mobility, a way for the poor to reach their full potential	1	2	3	4	5
16. To prepare educated citizens who can undertake actions that spark change	1	2	3	4	5
17. To ensure the cultural richness and diversity of the United States	1	2	3	4	5
18. To eliminate racism, sexism, homophobia, anti-Semitism, and all forms of discrimination from society	1	2	3	4	5

	Very Unimportant				Very Important
19. To prepare as many students as possible for college and/or well-paid careers	1	2	3	4	5
20. To provide child care for the nation's children and to free parents to work and/or pursue their interests and activities	1	2	3	4	5

Now, think about your three most valued goals for school and write those goals below:

Three valued goals:

_____ , _____ , _____

Do your responses to these items and your three priority goal selections cast you as transmitter of culture or as change agent for restructuring society? To help you determine where your beliefs take you, record your scores on the following selected items:

PURPOSE OF SCHOOLS

Transmitting Culture		**Reconstructing Society**	
Focused Item		*Focused Item*	
1	_____	2	_____
3	_____	5	_____
10	_____	9	_____
12	_____	15	_____
13	_____	16	_____
19	_____	18	_____
Total	_____	*Total*	_____

REFLECTION: Do your responses reflect the school experiences you had, or the ones you had hoped for? Which camp are you in: transmitting culture or reconstructing society?

Let's investigate how your choices reflect your values. The current emphasis on standards, tests, and academic performance is reflected in items 1, 13, and especially 14. Are you in agreement with this contemporary educational priority? If you scored high on items 1 and 10, then you value the role schools serve in preparing Americans to adhere to a common set of principles and values. This has been a recurrent theme in schools as each new group of immigrants arrives. Some people called this the melting pot, more formally termed **acculturation,** or **Americanization** (replacing the old culture with the new American one). Others view diversity more as a tossed salad, an analogy that suggests that cultural traditions, practices and identity would be retained in America, and a high score on item 17 reflects a sensitivity to our nation's cultural diversity. Items 2, 17 and 18 suggest a commitment to civil rights and

Ever wonder how schools get their names—and which names are the most popular? The National Education Resource Center researched the most popular proper names for U.S. high schools: Washington, Lincoln, Kennedy, Jefferson, Roosevelt (both Franklin and Teddy), and Wilson. (Presidents do well.) Lee, Edison, and Madison round out the top ten names. (To date, no school has chosen Richard M. Nixon as a namesake.) But proper names are not the most common high school names. Directions dominate: Northeastern, South, and Central High School are right up there. While creativity obviously is not a criterion, politics is. Citizens fight over whether schools should be named after George Washington—who, after all, was a slave holder—and over why so few African Americans, Hispanics, and people of non-European ancestry are honored by having a school named after them. And, considering how many women are educators, it is amazing that so few schools are named to honor women—Eleanor Roosevelt, Amelia Earhart, Christa McAuliffe, and Jacqueline Kennedy are exceptions. Some schools have honored writers (Bret Harte, Walt Whitman, and Mark Twain) or reflect local leaders and culture. (In Las Vegas, you will find schools named Durango, Silverado, and Bonanza, which some complain sound more like casinos than western culture.)

REFLECTION: What choices do you think educators might make if they were responsible for school names? If students were in charge, would schools be named after sports figures or music and media stars? How do our school names reflect the power and culture in a society? What's in a name?

student empowerment, hallmarks of the 1960s and 1970s, and since history often runs in cycles, perhaps these goals will resurface in the not too distant future. Do you like the Horatio Alger folklore: hard work and a little elbow grease, and the poor become wealthy? Agree with this folklore and you probably rated items 15 and 19 pretty high. Take a little time and see where you stand on the other items. And while you look them over, consider item 20, which may seem a bit odd. After all, few people see schools as baby-sitters, but, without this "service," most parents would be overwhelmed. And consider the impact that millions of adolescents would have on the job market. Unemployment would skyrocket and wages would tumble. By minding the children, schools provide parents with time and keep our workforce down to a manageable size.

What did your ratings teach you about your values and your view of schools? Were your goals popular during particular periods of our past, or are you more future-oriented? In a later chapter, you will have the opportunity to gain insight into your philosophy of education. You may want to compare your goals for education here with your philosophical preferences as identified in Chapter 9.

CRITICAL THINKING QUESTION

The Frame of Reference discusses school names. How was your university named? Are there other school name stories that are worthy of conversation?

 ## Education Reform

Our Nation is at risk. Our once unchallenged prominence in commerce, industry, science, and technological innovation is being overtaken by competitors throughout the world. . . . If an unfriendly foreign power had attempted to impose on America the mediocre educational performance that exists today, we might well have viewed it as an act of war. As it stands, we have allowed this to happen to ourselves. We have even squandered the gains in student achievement made in the wake of the *Sputnik* challenge. Moreover, we have dismantled essential support systems which helped make those gains possible. We have, in effect, been committing an act of unthinking, unilateral educational disarmament.[10]

So began the report of the **National Commission on Excellence in Education,** *A Nation at Risk: The Imperative for Educational Reform,* released in 1983. The report cited declining test scores, the weak performance of U.S. students in comparison with

FOCUS QUESTION 3

What school purposes are emphasized by educational reform?

CLASS ACTIVITY: SCHOOL REFORM

IM, Activity 4:4

those of other industrialized nations, and the number of functionally illiterate adults. *A Nation at Risk* condemned the "cafeteria-style curriculum." The report called for a more thorough grounding in the "five new basics" of English, mathematics, science, social science, and computer science. It called for greater academic rigor, higher expectations for students, and better-qualified and better-paid teachers.

This report galvanized Americans, moving education to center stage. Remember, in 1983, we were in two wars: the Cold War with the Soviet Union and an economic war with Japan. Our national security was at stake, and poor school performance was putting the nation at risk. With the battle cry sounded, governors, state legislators, and foundations issued a wave of reports (see Appendix 3 for a summary of the salient reform reports). Within the next two years,

- Hundreds of local and state panels were formed.
- More than 40 states increased course requirements for graduation.
- Thirty-three states instituted testing for student promotion or graduation.
- Almost half the states passed legislation to increase qualification standards and pay for teachers.
- Most states increased the length of the school day and/or school year.
- Most states passed laws that required teachers and students to demonstrate computer literacy.[11]

Although state legislatures passed laws, many critics remained skeptical that such changes would truly improve education. They pointed out that these were top-down approaches, dictated from above and far removed from the real world of the classroom.[12] Teachers felt dumped on (*teacher bashing* was the phrase used to protest this), controlled, and regulated by new rules and requirements. Other critics worried that these new regulations might do more harm than good. Increasing student graduation requirements without providing for special programs could hurt racial and ethnic minorities, non-English speakers, females, special education students, and other groups not testing well. Different groups struggled to claim their place on the new list of educational priorities. To be left out of the goals for education reform could be costly, indeed.[13]

OVERHEAD 51
Waves of Reform

The reform reports—and there were many—came in three waves (see Frame of Reference). These **three waves of reform** continue to influence American education today. The first wave of reports came immediately after *A Nation at Risk* and, as previously described, viewed school reform in terms of national defense and economic competition. Corporations complained about the need to teach employees basic reading and math skills, and the military struggled to recruit technically skilled personnel for increasingly sophisticated equipment. Education critics pointed to low scores by American students on international tests, especially in math and science, as they made their case that schools were not meeting the nation's economic and technical needs. By the turn of the century, this first reform wave had trumped many educational issues and topics: It seemed as though everyone was talking about standards, the rapid growth of state tests, and the effort to identify weak performing students, teachers, and schools. While other, smaller waves followed, this first wave never ended. Politicians decried the inadequate performance of public schools, private for-profit companies sprung into existence, saying that their new schools could do a better job, and corporations lamented the fact that their new employees lacked fundamental skills.

Other critics point out that American industry has itself to blame for some of its problems, including many inefficient production practices. Educator Clinton

Wave 1—The goal of the first wave was to raise educational quality by requiring more courses and more testing of student and teacher performance. States were to assume the leadership in improving existing practices and this wave continues to be the strongest.

Wave 2—Again it was state governors who promoted improvement and accountability. Teachers were to be empowered, given more control over their schools. Some of the educational problems confronting children of color and some other students facing educational barriers were also addressed.

Wave 3—In this, the most ambitious wave, reformers called for reformulating our nation of schools. Schools should be seen as more than educational facilities. They should also provide health care, social services, and transportation. In short, the whole array of services needed to bring the child into successful adulthood should be offered at the school: one-stop shopping for educational, social, medical, and other services.

| Wave I (began 1982 to present) | Wave II (began 1986) | Wave III (began 1988) |
| "Raise the Standards" | "Restructure the School" | "Comprehensive Services" |

SOURCE: Adapted from Joseph Murphy, "The Educational Movement of the 1980s: A Comprehensive Analysis," in Joseph Murphy (ed.), *The Educational Reform Movement of the 1980s* (Berkeley: McCutchan, 1990).

REFLECTION: Which of these reform waves do you feel would be most effective? Why does the first persist? As familiar as these efforts have become, they are far from universally accepted. As Educator Larry Cuban has pointed out, "As economic productivity has gone up and down over the last twenty years, the argument has remained the same. But during the last eight years of unparalleled prosperity, nobody has given the public schools an Oscar for outstanding performance. And the reason is that there is no relationship." Researcher Gerald Bracey adds: "If you think about it, the kids who were in high school when *A Nation at Risk* was released became all the dot.com millionaires."[14]

Boutwell, author of *Shell Game: Corporate America's Agenda for Schools*, asserts that, contrary to popular belief, technical and scientific education in America's schools is stronger than ever. Boutwell believes that sinister motives might be at play. Many business leaders complaining about the lack of scientists and engineers are the same executives who fire tens of thousands of scientists and engineers as they downsize the workforce in an effort to increase profits.[15] In fact, the vast majority of new jobs are service-oriented and do not require large numbers of highly educated employees at all.

The second wave of reform, which began in the mid- and late-1980s, was led by educators such as Theodore Sizer, John Goodlad, and Ernest Boyer, rather than by politicians and business leaders. Based on research and school observations, these educators stressed the need for basic reform of school practices. Gerald Grant, for example, in his "schoolography" of Hamilton High, calls for teachers to be given more responsibility to reshape their schools, a process called **empowering teachers. Theodore Sizer** and others see the superficial nature of the curriculum as a central weakness, recommending that students cover fewer topics but study them in greater depth. The second wave of reformers are alarmed at the loss of teacher autonomy in oppressive school climates, bland teaching, and poor academic performance. They emphasize thoughtful changes: reducing bureaucracy; creating a more professionally trained, treated, and salaried corps of teachers; implementing local decision making; strengthening the role of the school principal; and studying subjects in greater depth.

RELATED READING
Waiting for a Miracle: Why Schools Can't Solve Our Problems—and How We Can by James P. Comer (1997).

The third wave of reform recognizes that struggling families are unlikely to possess the time and resources required to ensure high-quality education. Underway since the late 1980s and early 1990s, the third wave advocates **full service schools,** providing a network of social services, nutrition, health care, transportation, counseling, and parent education. School boards would be replaced by **children's boards,** made up of professionals and community members who work on the comprehensive needs of children. School policy, focused only on education, would be replaced by **children's policy,** responding to the multiple needs of children. In the late 1990s, full service schools in Florida, New York, and California were operating long hours and providing an array of community services.

> At Intermediate School 218, in the Washington Heights section of New York City, school is open by 7 a.m. for breakfast, sports activities, dance or Latin band practice, all before school "officially" opens. At the school's Family Resource Center, parents receive social services, including immigration, housing, and employment consultations. Social workers, mental health counselors, a health and dental clinic are all on site. After classes end, the building remains open until 10 p.m. for sports, computer lab, music, art, mentoring, English classes, parenting skills, and cultural classes. Intermediate School 218 is a full service school.[16]

 ## Beyond the Neighborhood Public School

At the beginning of the chapter, you listened in on the meeting held at Monroe High School. You had the opportunity to hear parents, educators, and business people express their concern, frustration, and disappointment with the test scores at Monroe High. While that meeting was fictional, it offers an insight into the strong feelings and opinions found in communities around the nation, communities disappointed

A byproduct of recent calls for educational reform has been an explosion of student (and teacher) testing to ensure that revised school goals are being met.

with their public schools. The future of the neighborhood school, for centuries the cornerstone of public education, is now in doubt. Many parents and political leaders, discouraged by the slow pace of educational change, have been experimenting with public schools beyond their neighborhoods, with open enrollments, vouchers, and charter schools, and even with business-sponsored schools designed to make money.[17] Some parents now send their children to these schools created to both educate and turn a profit. Other parents are refocusing their energies on getting their children into private schools. Other parents have given up on all schools, and have joined the growing number of Americans educating their children at home. Many parents are leaving what they consider to be a failing public school monopoly. Let's look at some of these dramatic changes, changes that may well influence where you teach. (See Figure 4.2.)

FOCUS QUESTION 4
How are magnet and charter schools, open enrollment, and vouchers reshaping our concept of the neighborhood public school?

OVERHEAD 52
Public Attitudes: Reforming or Replacing Schools

The Choice Concept

In the 1950s, economist **Milton Friedman** suggested that public schools would be more effective if they functioned as a free market, much as private schools do. Friedman believed that public schools were not working well, even back then, because there was no competition, no incentive for them to do their best. Parents were forced to send their children to the neighborhood school, and the neighborhood school had no incentive to compete with other schools or improve. It had a "trapped" clientele. But not everyone was trapped. Because they could afford private school tuition, wealthy parents were able to bail out if the public school was performing poorly. Friedman believed that everyone needed the same freedom to choose what the wealthy enjoyed.

In a 1981 study, **James Coleman** found that private schools were doing a better job of educating students than were the neighborhood public schools. Not only were

VIDEO SEGMENT 10
Alternative Visions: Second-Chance Schools, Educational Remedies

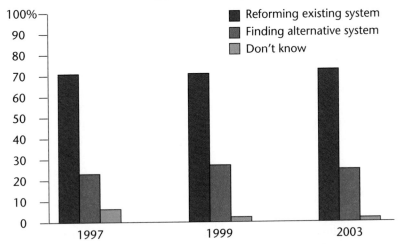

Which approach do you think is preferable—reforming the existing public school system or finding an alternative to the existing public school system?

- Reforming existing system
- Finding alternative system
- Don't know

FIGURE 4.2

Public attitudes: Reforming or replacing public schools.

SOURCE: *The 2003 Phi Delta Kappa/Gallup Poll of the Public's Attitudes Toward the Public Schools.*

REFLECTION: Why do you believe that most people prefer to reform the current system rather than find an alternative?

the students attending independent, often religiously affiliated, private schools better behaved, but they also scored higher on tests. Coleman noted that the private schools enforced more rigorous academic standards and gave teachers and administrators more autonomy. In 1993, another study found that Catholic schools not only were providing particularly effective education for inner-city students of color but also were providing this education at a lower per student cost and in less segregated classrooms than were neighboring public schools.[18] The call for **school choice** was getting louder.

Magnet Schools

CLASS ACTIVITY:
ORGANIZER FOR THE
CHOICE CONCEPT
IM, Activity 4:9

Over a quarter century ago, a number of public schools actually began a choice program, although few called it that. In the 1970s, as schools struggled to desegregate, "forced" busing became quite unpopular. But, with neighborhoods so racially segregated, desegregating schools required that students and teachers attend schools outside their local communities. **Magnet schools** were created to draw students, much like a magnet, beyond their neighborhoods. The magnet school "draw" was offering high-quality educational programs, unique programs unavailable in local schools, programs well worth the bus ride.

Today, more than a million students attend several thousand magnet schools. Magnet schools offer unique educational programs in such areas as science and technology, communication skills, career specialties, mathematics and computer science, theater, music, and art. How effective have magnet schools been? After a quarter of a century, the results are mixed. About half of these schools have helped desegregation efforts, but, in hypersegregated cities and other areas, they have had little or no impact on desegregation. In terms of educational quality, some studies suggest that students in magnet schools outperform students in other public schools and in Catholic schools. Research also indicates that those attending career magnet schools that prepare students for the world of work are less likely to be involved in fighting and drinking, and they earn more college credits than their contemporaries in public schools. Although magnet schools cost more than neighborhood public schools, these studies suggest that they may also be more effective.[19]

Open Enrollment

In 1988, Minnesota instituted **open enrollment,** which eliminated the requirement that students must attend the closest public school. Like the magnet schools, open enrollment encouraged parents to choose a school, but it greatly increased the number of schools to choose from. Any public school with available space became eligible. Arkansas, Iowa, Nebraska, and other states soon followed Minnesota's lead and introduced open enrollment legislation. However, even more radical proposals were being launched, proposals threatening to redefine, if not eliminate, the neighborhood school.

Vouchers

OVERHEAD 53
Americans View Vouchers

The approach that Milton Friedman favored was neither open enrollment nor magnet schools: Friedman proposed that **educational vouchers** be given to parents. The vouchers would function like admission tickets. Parents would "shop" for a school, make their choice, and give the voucher to the school. The school would turn over the voucher to the local or state government, and the government would pay the school a fixed sum for each voucher. Good schools would collect many vouchers and thrive, while poor schools would not attract "customers" and would go out of business. Some voucher plans would give parents the choice of selecting either a public or a private school, while other plans would limit the choice to public schools.

In 1990, Milwaukee became the site of the first publicly financed voucher program. Wisconsin lawmakers approved a plan for Milwaukee students to receive about $3,000 each to attend nonsectarian private schools, then, in 1995, amended the law to allow students to attend religious schools as well. And it is the inclusion of religious schools first in the Milwaukee voucher plan, then in a similar plan in Cleveland, that sparked a heated controversy and a round of lawsuits. The reason that religious schools are so closely involved in the voucher dispute is that they are the prime beneficiaries, receiving upwards of 90 percent of the students using such vouchers. Why is this? Two reasons: First, most private schools are religious schools, and second, most religious schools charge less than the other private schools. Most voucher plans offer modest financial support, usually under $3,000. While a $3,000 voucher covers only a fraction of the cost of a nonsectarian private school, it goes much further in covering the cost of a religious school.[20] Yet, the First Amendment of the Constitution ensures the separation of church and state, and paying for a religious education with taxpayer funds would violate the Constitution—or has all that changed?

In fact, the legal picture, once quite clear, is now somewhat cloudy. In 1971 in **Lemon v. Kurtzman** and in 1973 in the *Nyquist* case, the Supreme Court constructed clear walls limiting the use of public funds to support religious education. What became known as the *Lemon* test provided three criteria to determine the legality of government funds used in religious schools. According to Lemon, the funds (1) must have a secular purpose, (2) must not primarily advance or prohibit religion, and (3) must not result in excessive government entanglement with religion. In **Zelman v. Simmons-Harris** (2002), a narrow 5–4 Supreme Court majority ruled that publicly funded vouchers could be used to send children to Cleveland's private religious schools. Chief Justice William Rehnquist wrote that such vouchers permit a "genuine choice among options public and private, secular and religious." Justice John Paul Stevens dissented, writing, "Whenever we remove a brick from the wall that was designed to separate religion and government, we increase the risk of religious strife and weaken the foundation of our democracy."[21]

The public is also divided. A narrow majority of Americans have historically opposed vouchers, concerned that tax monies would be redirected from public to private education, particularly toward spreading religious doctrine. Yet a growing number of supporters see vouchers as expanding educational choice. Both groups may be correct.[22] (See Figure 4.3.)

Charter Schools

In 1991, Minnesota was the first state to enact charter school legislation. A decade later, nearly 3,000 charter schools in almost forty states were educating one percent of the school population. Arizona, California, Texas, and Florida have the greatest number of charter schools. So many created so quickly that some states decided to slow the process down and take a closer look at these schools. Some charters had questionable educational impact, others were drawing few students, and others raised even more serious legal and financial questions. Most charters, however, continued to enjoy public support.[23]

What are these **charter schools?** The concept is simple. The charter (or contract) represents legal permission from a local or state school board to operate the school,

TEACHING TIP
Survey the class to see what experiences they have had with state charter schools. Are there any charter school graduates or parents? Community advocates or critics? Future faculty, administrators, or developers?

FIGURE 4.3

Americans view vouchers.

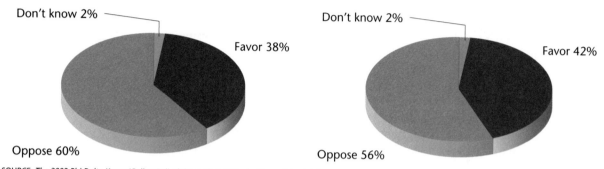

Do you favor or oppose allowing students and parents to choose private schools at public expense?

Don't know 2%

Favor 38%

Oppose 60%

Do you favor or oppose the voucher program the Supreme Court says is permissible under the U.S. Constitution?

Don't know 2%

Favor 42%

Oppose 56%

SOURCE: *The 2003 Phi Delta Kappa/Gallup Poll of the Public's Attitudes Toward the Public Schools.*

REFLECTION: The public's view on vouchers, as depicted above, is far from firm or clear. Try your own skill at polling, and ask friends and family their responses to these questions. How do their responses compare to national trends? How might you explain these similarities or differences?

CRITICAL THINKING QUESTION

Why are the numbers of charter schools growing? Do student assumptions about charters parallel the text content?

usually for a fixed period of time, perhaps five years, with the right to renew the charter if the school is successful. While charter schools must follow some of the same rules established for other publicly funded schools (for example, health and safety regulations, agreement not to discriminate), charter schools are exempt from many state and local laws and regulations. Charter schools, in effect, "swap" rules and regulations for greater freedom and the promise that they will achieve better results. A charter school typically

- Allows for the creation of a new or the conversion of an existing public school
- Prohibits admission tests
- Is nonsectarian
- Requires a demonstrable improvement in performance
- Can be closed if it does not meet expectations
- Does not need to conform to most state rules and regulations
- Receives funding based on the number of students enrolled

A charter school represents a break with the past, a new way to educate with tax dollars. A charter school might be established to improve academic performance or attendance, to explore a new organizational approach or teaching strategy, or to extend the hours of the school day or the length of the school year. Some charter schools are associated with national programs, such as the International Baccalaureate Degree, while others are independent, meeting local needs. In St. Paul, Minnesota, for example, the City Academy is a year-round charter school serving forty at-risk students. Metro Deaf serves deaf students, while the Teamsters Union and the Minnesota

A Harvard graduate and Rhodes scholar, Jonathan Kozol had no idea "what it was like to be a poor kid in America." He quickly learned. In 1964 the Klu Klux Klan in Mississippi murdered three young civil rights workers. The injustice ignited a need to act.

I'd never been involved with racial issues. I was not particularly political. In fact, I wasn't political at all. But this event had an extraordinary effect. I volunteered to spend the summer teaching at a black church which had set up a freedom school. When September came, I walked into the Boston school department and said, "I'm going to be a teacher."[1]

He was assigned to the fourth grade of an urban school in Boston, a school so impoverished he didn't have a classroom. Kozol and his disenfranchised students camped out in an auditorium. In an effort to resuscitate their interest in learning, he shared his favorite poetry. Students recited lines, asked questions, even cried as they identified with the words of Langston Hughes. While the words of the black poet may have inspired students, the author was not on the school's approved reading list. Kozol was fired. He chronicled his first year teaching in *Death at an Early Age* (1967), which alerted the nation to the wrenching injustices found in impoverished schools and the resiliency of their students.

For almost four decades, Kozol's compassionate spirit has given voice to the poor. In his best-selling book, *Savage Inequalities* (1991), he describes life in destitute schools from East St. Louis to the Bronx. Kozol writes of schools so overcrowded that students only get desks when other students are absent. Of students who go for part, most, or all of the year without textbooks. While decrying this tragedy, Kozol does not find an answer in voucher programs.

[T]he idea behind choice (within the district), basically, is that if you let people choose, everybody will get the school they want. [But] people very seldom have equal choices, and even when they theoretically have equal choices, they rarely have equal access.

People can't choose things they've never heard of, for example. And lots of the poorest folks in our inner cities are functionally illiterate. In many of our inner cities, as many as 30 percent of our adults cannot read well enough to understand the booklets put out by school systems delineating their choices.

Even if they can understand and even if the school system is sophisticated enough to print these things in five different languages for all the different ethnic groups in cities like New York or Chicago, there's a larger point that those who hear about new schools, good schools, first are almost always the well connected.

And so, what often happens is that while everybody theoretically has the right to choose any school, the affluent, the savvy, the children of the academics, the children of the lawyers, the children of the doctors, the children of the school superintendent tend to end up in the same three little boutique elementary schools. And I call them boutique schools because they're always charming, and the press loves them, and they always have enough racial integration so it looks okay for the newspaper or the TV camera. But, in fact, they are separated by both race and class, and more and more by class.

What happens is that the poorest of the poor often do not get into these schools or very small numbers get in. Large numbers of the kids who nobody wants end up concentrated in the schools that no one chooses except by default . . .

Now the dark, terrifying prospect of vouchers or a choice agenda, of a so-called market basis for our public schools, is that rather than encourage a sense of common loyalties among people, choice will particularize loyalties. It will fragmentize ambition, so that the individual parent will be forced to claw and scramble for the good of her kid and her kid only, at whatever cost to everybody else. There's a wonderful quote from John Dewey. He said "What the best and wisest parent wants for his own child, that must the community want for all its children. Any other ideal for our schools is narrow and unlovely. Acted upon, it destroys our democracy."

. . . The best known voucher advocate, John Chubb, of the Brookings Institute, in Washington, says something—I'm paraphrasing him—like this: "Democratic governance of schools is what's wrong with schools. We need a voucher plan in order to break the bonds of democratic education, because it hasn't worked." That's what he says.

When I hear that, I think to myself, "Wait a minute. We've never tried democratic education." We haven't yet given equal, wonderful, innovative, humane schools—at the level of our finest schools—to all our children. . . . I think we should try it first, see how it might work.[2]

[1]Mardell Raney. Interview with Jonathan Kozol. *Technos,* 7 no. 3 (Fall 1998), pp. 4–10.
[2]Reprinted with permission of *Educational Leadership* 50, no. 3 (November 1992), pp. 90–92.

REFLECTION: In your opinion, what American values are reflected—or undermined—in school choice?

www.mhhe.com/ sadker To learn more about Jonathan Kozol, click on *Profiles in Education.*

As states focus on charter schools and other educational priorities, political leaders can be seen taking a more active role in schooling. Here, Iowa Governor Tom Vilsack serves on a panel with middle school students.

VIDEO SEGMENT 11
A Tour of a Charter School

Business Partnership sponsor a vocational and technical school, called Skills for Tomorrow, that uses internship placements to educate students interested in becoming skilled workers. The City on a Hill charter in Boston was created by two veteran teachers committed to providing a more effective education for poor inner-city children.[24] Although charter schools operate differently in different states, the increase in the number of charter schools across the country has been spectacular. Why?

One reason is that charter schools are less controversial than voucher plans. They do not involve religious schools or competition between public and private schools. They appeal to people who support public schools but who have concerns about their quality. The enthusiasm generated by these supporters is contagious, and often translates into a robust educational effort, and a great deal of positive publicity. But is enthusiasm enough for the long haul? Are charters doing as well as some say?

While it is too early to reach a final assessment of charters, some problems are coming to light. Charters were created to experiment, promote innovation, and to trailblaze new educational approaches. This is not happening. Most charters, in fact, are mirroring the most traditional educational practices available. And they are teaching a very select student population. Critics point out that by doing this, they are actually segregating students, creating schools where all the children are similar and share similar goals, a far cry from the inclusive and democratic ideal of public education. Initially advocates proclaimed that the charters would cut the cost of education by eliminating a "bloated administration," but this has not been the case. Their low student enrollments and the need to duplicate resources like libraries and computers has translated into just the opposite, higher administrative costs than public schools. Added to these financial woes is the fact that many charters are located in inadequate buildings, either converted facilities or schools built with cheap materials, so we can include safety concerns to our list.[25] In Arizona, the state with the most charter schools, one out of every three charters is "underperforming," a rate twice as high as the state's noncharter public schools.[26] This does not appear to be only an Arizona problem. In 2003, a national study revealed that charter schools were plagued by problems. Nearly half of the teachers were unlicensed, poor and disabled students underfunded, black students isolated, and overcrowding common. Yet, in other instances, charters were performing far better than other public schools, fueling a movement that has seen amazing growth.[27]

Who are the people who create such schools? Tom Watkins, director of the Detroit Center for Charter Schools, describes three types of charter advocates: reformers, zealots, and entrepreneurs.[28] *Reformers* are those who want to expand public school options and create more teacher- and student-centered institutions. These are the most mainstream advocates, the ones who often engender positive reports in the press. Watkins also describes *zealots,* those who prefer private to public schools, who view teacher unions as the obstacle to change and many of whom are themselves politically quite conservative. The final group consists of *entrepreneurs,* those who view schools as untapped profit centers and charter schools as vehicles for combining business and education. In the next section, we will take a closer look at these educational entrepreneurs.

EMOs (Educational Maintenance Organizations): Schools for Profit

Wall Street calls them **EMOs,** paralleling the HMOs in the health maintenance industry. HMOs are big business, and many on Wall Street are predicting that EMOs will be too. During the past few years, for-profit businesses have contracted with local school districts to provide a wide range of services in an attempt to win a segment of the lucrative education market, a market that exceeds $300 billion a year. Not that the entrance of private companies onto the public educational scene is completely new. For years, school districts have contracted with private businesses to provide school lunches and bus transportation. But, to provide education itself, to be responsible for academic performance, *is* new.

The largest for-profit venture in public schools, the **Edison Schools,** took off after a chance encounter. In 1990, Benno Schmidt, the president of Yale University, was attending a party in the Hamptons, a posh section of Long Island. At that party, Schmidt met Chris Whittle, an entrepreneur who was involved with various education-related projects. Apparently, they hit it off. Whittle offered Schmidt a high salary, reported to be about $1 million a year, to leave Yale and assume leadership of the Edison Schools. Chris Whittle's vision called for creating a model school, one based on proven educational programs, and then franchising the model nationally.

Edison Schools lengthen the school day by one or two hours, while increasing the school year from 180 days to 210 days. In effect, these changes add about two more years of study before graduation. Curricular changes include devoting more school time to math and science, foreign language instruction starting from the early grades, and using proven programs, such as the University of Chicago approach to math and a reading program developed at Johns Hopkins University. Learning contracts are used to increase student accountability. Edison's plan calls for linking each student to the school by a company-provided home computer. The computer offers students a virtual library and gives both parents and students a dedicated communication link to teachers.

The project's start-up costs were enormous, and the franchise idea was not easy to implement. Whittle saw that opening charter schools would be an easier way to disseminate his plan.[29] The charter school movement was a wonderful opportunity

FOCUS QUESTION 5
Do the laws of the marketplace belong in public education?

OVERHEAD 54
Educational Maintenance Organizations

CRITICAL THINKING QUESTION
The performance of EMOs is often debated from the point of view of a special interest group. Assist students to analyze studies by first asking, "What's in it for the research team?"

for education companies like Edison. The company could work with an entire school district or deal directly with parents and neighborhood groups, selling its Edison concept as a charter school. By 2001, more than 100 Edison Schools were up and running with a total student enrollment equivalent to Atlanta or Cincinnati. As Edison schools multiplied, the key question remained unanswered: Are these schools effective? A Columbia University study of Edison found that there was high teacher morale, enthusiasm for the curriculum, and satisfied parents and several public schools bought into the Edison concept. Some Edison employees reported that the company was hiding its problems from the public and that the needs of special education students, among others, were not being met. The American Federation of Teachers and the National Education Association undertook studies that found Edison students doing no better than regular public school students, and sometimes, worse. Questions persisted, financial backing tumbled, and in 2003 Chris Whittle decided to take the company private.[30] The future of Edison Schools remains rocky.

Other companies have harbored less grandiose plans than the Edison Schools. Rather than redesigning schools and creating entirely new school programs, these companies have focused on improving school performance through greater efficiency. A pioneer in this effort, **Tesseract** (formerly **Educational Alternatives Incorporated,** or EAI), began contracting with schools as early as 1990. A contract with Miami schools was followed by contracts with schools in Baltimore, Maryland (1992), and Hartford, Connecticut (1994). Tesseract made national news by providing new school managers dedicated to efficiency. The costs of maintenance, supplies, security, transportation, food contracts, and even consultant salaries were scaled back, producing a leaner school budget overall. But student performance did not improve. Tesseract complained that it lacked the power to make real changes, and all of these contracts were eventually terminated. By the late 1990s, the company had changed its name and direction, focusing instead on operating charter schools, turning a profit in the process.[31]

The business community has not been timid about investing in public education. The Edison Project, for example, spent at least $40 million in just the start-up phase, and John Walton, son of Wal-Mart founder Sam Walton, invested heavily in Tesseract, two strong signs indicating the size of the potential profits to be made in the **privatization** of public schools.[32] Private-sector education companies continue to multiply. Advantage Schools, a Boston-based company, focuses on urban school districts, hires nonunion teachers, and promotes direct instruction, a program that relies on intense and frequent teacher-student interactions, and like other private companies, does not have a stellar record with special education students. Sylvan Learning Systems, known for its after-school learning centers, now provides services to several large school districts, including after-school instruction for students who are performing below expectations.[33]

Brand Name Education: Should Schools Be "Open" for Business?

RAP 2.4
Visit a "Choice" School,
p. 275

Is school choice a good idea? Is even asking the question somehow undemocratic? Choice supporters are quick to point out that vouchers and charters give poor families the kind of school choice that wealthy families already enjoy. Even a brief visit to an impoverished urban neighborhood public school underscores this sad reality:

Are a Good Idea Because . . .

COMPETITION LEADS TO BETTER SCHOOLS

For-profit schools will break down the public school monopoly by creating competition and choice. As schools compete, parents (particularly poor parents) will finally have a choice, and not be forced to place their children in the neighborhood school. Just like in business, the weak schools will lose students and declare "bankruptcy." The stronger schools will survive and prosper.

SCHOOLS WILL BE ABLE TO REWARD GOOD TEACHERS, AND REMOVE WEAK ONES

The current public school bureaucracy protects too many incompetent teachers through the tenure system, and does not recognize teaching excellence. Using sound business practices, for-profit schools will reward superior teachers through profit-sharing incentives, retain competent teachers, and terminate ineffective teachers.

BUSINESS EFFICIENCY WILL IMPROVE SCHOOL PERFORMANCE

Education needs the skills and know-how of the business community. For-profit schools will implement the most effective educational strategies in a business culture. The top-heavy management of today's schools will be replaced by only a handful of administrators, and teachers will be driven to greater productivity through the profit incentives.

FOCUSED PROGRAMS AND INVESTOR OVERSIGHT LEAD TO ACADEMIC SUCCESS

For-profit schools will do a better educational job because they provide a focused and proven instructional plan. These schools avoid the public school pitfall of trying to offer "something-for-everyone." And if they falter and profits disappear, investor pressure will put them back on track.

Are a Bad Idea Because . . .

COMPETITION LEADS TO WEAKER SCHOOLS

Transplanting businesslike competition into the education arena would be a disaster. Competition is not all that business brings: false advertising, "special" promotions, a "feel-good" education—all the hucksterism of the marketplace to mislead students and their parents. Worse yet, the local public school, which holds a community together, will be lost.

TEACHERS WILL LOSE THEIR INFLUENCE AND ACADEMIC FREEDOM

Teachers who speak out against the company, or teach a controversial or politically sensitive topic, will have a brief career. The business community is quite vocal about teachers sharing in the profits, but strangely silent about what will happen during economic hard times.

PROFITS AND EDUCATION DO NOT MIX

For-profit schools are exactly that, "for profit," and when the interests of children and investors clash, investor interests will prevail. If investors demand better returns, if the stock market drops, if the economy enters hard times, the corporate executives will sacrifice educational resources. After all, while students enjoy little leverage, stockholders can fire business executives.

FOCUSED PROGRAMS MEANS KEEPING SOME STUDENTS OUT

Their one-size-fits-all approach practiced by these schools might be good for efficiency, but it is bad for students. The more challenging students, those with special needs, non-native speakers of English, or those who need special counseling, will be left to the underfunded public schools to educate.

 YOU BE THE JUDGE

Do you believe that business and schools are a good or a bad match? Explain. Do you believe that profits can be made in schooling the nation's children? As a teacher, would you want to work for a for-profit school?

Many of these schools are doing a woefully inadequate job. Little wonder that many urban parents support choice plans, and would view a new charter school as an oasis in an educational desert.[34] But we need to look more carefully, for the charter oasis may turn out to be little more than an educational mirage.

CLASS ACTIVITY
Business Code of Ethics
IM, Activity 4:10

It is convenient to group all choice options together. That is a big mistake. Choice options and charter schools vary greatly. One of the fundamental differences is whether a school is a nonprofit, public institution, or there to make a profit.[35] Along with a number of other writers and educators, the authors of this text have deep reservations about what happens to children when schools are turned into profit centers. Opening minds should be the goal of public education, not turning a profit. To ensure that we provide you with the other side of the issue, this chapter's *You Be the Judge* includes a business perspective. However, to be true to our beliefs, in this section, we will share some of our concerns.

Do the laws of the marketplace belong in public education? Should we give private companies access to public institutions? Business supporters answer in the affirmative and believe competition is the key to creating more efficient and effective schools. Not everyone agrees. Alex Molnar, for example, studied the economics of for-profit charter schools and discovered that they simply replace a public bureaucracy with a private one, are less efficient, less equitable, and less accountable than public schools.[36] Studies reveal that for-profit schools too often reject special needs students who may be more challenging and more costly to educate. Molnar finds the HMO-EMO analogy troubling:

> The only reason that the health care industry can make a profit is that it has nothing to do with [social] equity. We've got 40 million Americans who on any given day don't have health insurance. Now that's a social catastrophe. The same thing would happen in education. If you cut the schools loose from any concern about equity, you could carve out schools that you could run for a profit. However, it would be at an enormous social cost.[37]

The competitive business model is all about mining a market segment, finding the consumers likely to buy the product, and shunning others. Under a choice program, even nonprofit schools can be drawn into this marketplace strategy. Boulder, Colorado is a case in point. Half of Boulder's schools were turned into choice schools during the 2000–2001 school year, and each school's survival depended on drawing students by convincing parents of the school's wonderful qualities. Even in Boulder, a well-to-do community with an affluent and educated parent base, choice led to trouble. Lack of information and transportation reduced the opportunities of many families to truly choose their preferred school. Parents noted that some schools managed to attract more educational resources than others. And when all the choice schools were compared, there was a "tendency of academically strong students to move to high-achieving schools" (called *skimming*). It was clear that "stratification by race and income" became more rigid as white students chose schools outside of predominantly minority areas.[38] Although choice trumpeted equality, the ideals of Thomas Jefferson and Horace Mann were submerged by "niche" schools serving a narrowly focused clientele. Choice promoted societal fracture.[39]

If clever ads can convince Americans to pay $150 for athletic shoes or $100 for designer jeans, imagine the power of advertisements in hyping something really important, like education. Critics already complain that educational resources are being spent on questionable advertising rather than on improving educational programs. Will brand name schools be the designer clothes of the next decade? How far away are we from having our children attend Nike Elementary School or Dunkin' Donuts High? Perhaps closer than many imagine.

In Frederick, Maryland, students at Oakdale Elementary School won $10,000 for performing the best interpretation of Oscar Mayer's wiener song. This award was followed up by another $10,000 prize for writing and performing other songs devoted to bologna, ham and cheese, and included dressing up as "lunchable" meats and cheeses. Not to be outdone, Angel Soft toilet paper makes awards to schools to promote community service. The award includes money, a year's supply of toilet paper, and a teacher's guide to help the students differentiate among competing toilet papers. Consumer critic Jean Kilbourne decries such school commercialization, advertising to impressionable children who are likely to believe what corporate sponsors promote. Despite these concerns, as budgets tighten, thousands of schools a year now compete in contests sponsored by Dunkin' Donuts, Nestlé chocolate, Pizza Hut, and others. For the business community, such contests are far less expensive than television ads, and as a company spokesman explains, still provide children with "the brand experience."[40]

Brand naming is growing as schools enter "exclusive agreements" with companies to ensure that no competitive products are sold on school grounds. Coca-Cola promised Oakland, California half a million dollars to support a community youth program in return for a ten-year agreement banning the sale of competing soft drinks on city property. These exclusive "pouring rights" contracts may turn out to be a very bad business deal as school officials find themselves targeted by lawsuits blaming them, along with fast-food and soft drink companies, for contributing to America's obesity epidemic.[41] Schools are also borrowing business practices of professional sports, selling naming rights to school property. When Brooklawn, New Jersey needed funds for a new school gymnasium, the school board sold the name to the local supermarket, ShopRite. For this nonstop advertisement, ShopRite agreed to pay $100,000, prorated to $5,000 a year, a figure that only covered maintenance and operation costs. Naming rights was a smart business move since ShopRite Gym did not have to pay even a single penny of actual construction cost.

Branding schools does not stop with athletic facilities. School districts now sell the naming rights of school buildings, offer companies the opportunity to put their corporate logos on textbooks and other curricular material, and hang advertising banners from school buildings. Sometimes the corporation simply pays a bounty to the school for getting students and parents to buy their products. General Mills donates funds to schools based on the number of box-tops turned in or other coupons showing proof of purchase. Television commercials now air during school time to a captive audience of future consumers. Channel One, for example, broadcasts commercials in school and other media companies, including CNN, are exploring similar opportunities.

Business interests have moved beyond commercials to prime time, working to inculcate business values into the curriculum. The paper company Weyerhauser pays teachers during the summer to join their "company science center," and the industry group Pacific Logging Congress provides photos and brochures explaining why clear-cutting forests is environmentally sound. Should cell phones be part of the curriculum?

IN THE NEWS

Commercializing Schools: A Hidden Curriculum

The Center for Commercial-Free Public Education is concerned about marketing products to captive student audiences. Here are some examples of their concern:

- Exxon teaches children that the *Valdez* oil spill was an example of environmental protection.
- In Colorado, Burger King and 7-Up advertise on school buses.
- A Texas school roof is painted with a Dr. Pepper logo to capture the attention of passengers flying overhead.
- McDonald's teaches about deforestation, but fails to include the negative impact of cattle ranching on the rain forest.
- Clairol distributes free shampoo to students leaving school, along with a survey asking if they had a bad hair day.
- To teach the "practical applications" of algebra, Glencoe/McGraw-Hill publishers will be using articles and graphics from *USA Today* in their leading high school mathematics textbooks. Part of the agreement is that the books prominently display the *USA Today* logo.

SOURCE: *Educational Leadership*, October 1998; *San Francisco Chronicle*, June 6, 2001; *Education Week*, May 1, 2002.

 What's new in education? Click on *News Feeds.*

What does a school's name, mascot, message board, and presentation say about what's happening inside the classroom? What do these school signs tell you? Are there ways to identify a good school by its sign? How would your high school sign fit in the photo gallery?

MULTIPLE INTELLIGENCE CONNECTION
This photo montage of school signs integrates many of the key terms in this chapter. What other mosaic of educational images could enhance chapter content? Have students design a similar product.

They already are as students learn proper cell phone use behind the wheel, courtesy of Verizon. As one critic noted, if you teach business values early enough, children accept it as truth.[42]

OVERHEAD 55
Debate on the School Choice Plan

Profits and corporate values are well represented in everyday school practices. As Linda Darling-Hammond notes:

> The short segmented tasks stressing speed and neatness that predominate in most schools, the emphasis on rules from the important to the trivial, and the obsession with bells, schedules, and time clocks are all dug deep into the ethos of late nineteenth-century America, when students were being prepared to work in factories on predetermined tasks that would not require them to figure out what to do.[43]

OVERHEAD 56
Who Has Your Vote?

Add to this analogy the impact of the current standards and testing movement, and we can more clearly see that we are in the midst of a major business incursion into public schools. The National Association of Manufacturers insists on more testing as well as "a national system of skills standards designed by industry." Today's testing industry is a two-prong profit center, funneling literally billions of dollars into corporate coffers. Profit Center #1: The sales and scoring of newly required standardized tests. Profit Center #2: Public schools that score poorly become prime targets to be replaced by for-profit companies. We discuss the current standards and testing movement in greater detail later in this text, and the business influence will once again become evident.

Whatever your personal belief about the importance of business in America, the growing influence of business in schools raises serious ethical and educational concerns. Is public education a venue for corporate profits? Is competition, advertising, and a commitment to materialism good for our children? We believe that schools should promote creative thinking, reflection, care for others and a commitment to improve the quality of life on this planet. These goals are not only more important than profits and crass materialism, they are in conflict with them.

Home Schools, Home Teachers

FOCUS QUESTION 6
Why are so many families choosing home schooling?

CLASS ACTIVITY:
HOME SCHOOLING
INVESTIGATION
IM, Activity 4:7

Thirteen-year old Taylor is working at the kitchen table, sorting out mathematical exponents. At 10, Travis is absorbed in *The Story of Jackie Robinson,* while his brother Henry is practicing Beethoven's Minuet in G on his acoustical guitar. The week before, the brothers had attended a local performance of a musical comedy, attended a seminar on marine life and participated in a lively debate about news reports concerning corporal punishment in Singapore. These boys are part of a growing number of students being educated at home. What makes their story somewhat unusual is that their father is unable to participate in their education as much as he might like, because he must spend time at his own work: teaching English at a local public high school.[44]

Why would a schoolteacher choose to educate his own children outside of school? It is ironic that, while some educators view the world as a classroom, others see education as a cottage industry. Today between one and two million children in the United States are believed to participate in **home schooling;** twenty years earlier, only 12,500 students were home schooled.[45] Why the huge increase? Most people credit the explosion in the number of home-schooled children to the growth of fundamentalist Christianity, many of whose adherents choose to educate their children at home. While religious motivation is the reason that most families choose home schooling, it is not the only reason.[46]

Some historical perspective might be helpful. Home schooling is not new; it predates schools and has always been around in one form or another. As recently as the 1970s, "romantic" critics—such as John Holt, Ivan Illich, and Jonathan Kozol—were advocating home schooling as a way to avoid the oppressive, dehumanizing public school practices. It is fascinating that home schooling appeals to liberals, who view schools as too conservative, as well as to conservatives, who view schools as too liberal. But conservatives, liberals, and middle-of-the-roaders can be drawn to home schooling for a number of reasons.

RELATED READING
*The Teenage Liberation
Handbook: How to Quit
School & Get a Real Life &
Education* by Grace
Llewellyn (1997).

In urban areas, the lack of school safety may motivate some parents to educate their children in the security of their own homes, away from the dangers of guns and violence. Other parents are disenchanted with the quality and lack of responsiveness of schools, and home schooling provides them with a base from which to launch their ideas about education, and to test their own teaching skills, in an intimate and nurturing environment. Economics can play a role as well. In some two-parent working families, the income earned by one parent is consumed by the high cost of child care. In such cases, one parent can readily give up the "outside" job to become a home teacher—and the family may not lose any real income. But not all home schools are initiated for positive motivations. Sometimes racism, anti-Semitism, or another hateful reason can inspire an ideologue to withdraw his or her children from a public school and initiate home instruction.

Researcher Van Galen divides home schoolers into two groups: ideologues and pedagogues. **Ideologues** are very focused on imparting their values and view the

FIGURE 4.4

Who are home schoolers?

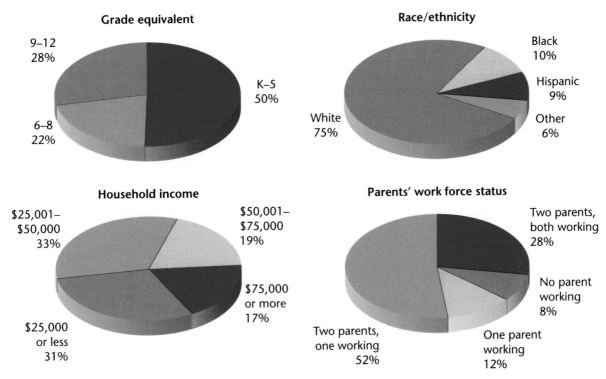

Grade equivalent

9–12
28%

K–5
50%

6–8
22%

Race/ethnicity

Black
10%

Hispanic
9%

White
75%

Other
6%

Household income

$25,001–
$50,000
33%

$50,001–
$75,000
19%

$75,000
or more
17%

$25,000
or less
31%

Parents' work force status

Two parents,
both working
28%

No parent
working
8%

Two parents,
one working
52%

One parent
working
12%

SOURCE: "Homeschooling in the United States: 1999." July 2001, National Center for Education Statistics.

REFLECTION: These percentages are based on under a million home schoolers. Some believe that the true number may be at least twice that. Why do you believe so many home schoolers are not counted? How might these statistics change if those left out were included?

home as their school, a place where they choose the curriculum, create the rules, and enforce the schedules. Van Galen classifies most religiously motivated home schoolers as ideologues. **Pedagogues** are motivated by more humanistic educational goals; they are interested in the process as much as the end product of learning. As a group, they are considered more open to various educational strategies. Pedagogues emphasize intrinsic motivation and experiential activities. While ideologues and pedagogues share a dissatisfaction with schools, they agree on little else.[47] (See Figure 4.4.)

As home schools' philosophies vary, so does their quality. Some parents are incredibly talented and dedicated teachers, while others are less than competent. Even when parents fall short of teaching excellence, individualized instruction is powerful. This may be one reason home-schooled children generally score quite well on standardized tests, averaging between 15–30 percentile points above their peers.[48] A number of home-schooled children have even achieved national acclaim. Grant Colfax was taught by his parents, never attending elementary or secondary school. He won admission to Harvard, graduated *magna cum laude,* became a Fulbright scholar, and eventually graduated from Harvard Medical School. His home-schooled brothers enjoyed similar success—all endorsements of home schooling.

Home schooling was more the norm than the exception in times past. Among wealthier British and U.S. families in the seventeenth and eighteenth centuries, parents and home tutors were the educators of choice. Home-schooling traditions exist in other cultures as well. In many Native American cultures, for example, the elders served—and often still serve—as teachers. Contemporary advocates often dip into the well of history to claim the success of home-schooled people, such as

- Woodrow Wilson
- Margaret Mead
- Florence Nightingale
- John Quincy Adams
- Franklin Roosevelt
- Thomas Edison
- The Wright Brothers

- Andrew Carnegie
- Abraham Lincoln
- Pearl Buck
- Agatha Christie
- Benjamin Franklin
- Sandra Day O'Connor

These success stories indicate that home schooling can be effective. Then again, the student's needs and the teacher's talents—at home or at school—are more important than any list of home-schooled achievers.

SOURCE: R. S. Moore and D. N. Moore, *Better Late Than Early: A New Approach to Your Child's Education* (New York: Reader's Digest Press, 1975); Gary Knowles, James A. Muchmore, and Holly W. Spaulding, "Home Education as an Alternative to Institutionalized Education," *The Education Forum 58* (Spring 1994), pp. 238–43; see also issues of *Growing Without Schooling* magazine; Linda Dobson, *Homeschoolers Success Stories* (Roseville, CA: Prima Publishing, 2000).

REFLECTION: What kind of student is a candidate for home schooling? Would students need a teacher at all? If so, what particular skills would a teacher for the home-schooled need?

Home-schooling critics are more concerned with potential abuses than with success stories, such as that of the Colfax family. Do children educated in isolation from their peers suffer any negative consequences? What is lost by not working and learning with other children of diverse beliefs and backgrounds? Since Americans were originally motivated to build schools in order to promote Americanization, to meld a single nation, it is logical to wonder, will home schooling adversely affect our national cohesion?[49]

Home-schooling families hold different views as to the importance of socialization. Some point out that much of what passes for socialization in school is negative, including everything from unhealthy competition to gang violence. They believe that, in the final analysis, their children come out ahead by remaining at home. Other home-school families believe that socialization is important and create their own social groups, such as book clubs, with like-minded others. Some forge a relationship with local school districts, so that their children, although instructed at home, can participate in district schools' sports and other extracurricular activities. School districts vary in their receptivity to such "dual" enrollments. In Virginia, for example, home schoolers are allowed to participate only unofficially in after-school sports. In Ames, Iowa, on the other hand, home schoolers participate in athletics equally, have access to school textbooks and standardized tests, and may take enrichment classes designed specifically for them. District policies on home schooling vary widely. Some school districts view home schoolers as educational partners; other districts see them as competitors.[50] When seen as competitors, schools do not readily provide assistance. This has led to usually successful litigation by home schoolers to acquire selected school resources and support.[51]

Advances in technology have provided a catalyst for the home-schooling movement, particularly the proliferation of personal computers and increasing access to the Internet. America Online, for example, offers a home-schooling forum, complete with lesson plans, tutoring, legislative updates, and the capability for networking with others interested in group work. In Michigan, the Noah Webster charter school

In *Deschooling Society,* Ivan Illich compared schools to a medieval church, performing more a political than an educational role. The diplomas and degrees issued by schools provide society's "stamp of approval," announcing who shall succeed, who shall be awarded status, and who shall remain in poverty. By compelling students to attend, by judging and labeling them, by confining them, and by discriminating among them, Illich believed that schools harm children. He would replace schools with learning "networks," lifelong and compulsory. To Illich, the notion of waking up to a world without schools would be a dream fulfilled.

SOURCE: Ivan Illich, *Deschooling Society* (New York: Harper & Row, 1973).

REFLECTION: How are schools more a political than an educational institution? What would your community be like if it were de-schooled?

offers a "school-less school," one that connects children and parents to teachers and the curriculum through telephone lines and terminals. Technology is radically altering education, and the school of the future may be less a place than a password onto the information superhighway. In the future, home schooling may be far less exotic and far more prevalent.[52]

This chapter asks the deceptively simple question, What's a school for? This deceptively easy question invites many possible answers. Ivan Illich, for example, questions the role of *any* school. While the elimination of schools is both radical and unlikely, it is evident that schools are undergoing serious transition. The traditional neighborhood school is reshaping itself, moving from a public monopoly into the profit arena, from a single neighborhood institution into the wider community, from the cookie-cutter similarities of the past to different models and approaches. Today's teachers will have the opportunity to choose their future career settings from a greater variety of teaching options than ever existed before.

CRITICAL THINKING QUESTION
What's a school for? How will students *now* synthesize an answer?

SUMMARY

1. What are the various expectations Americans hold for their schools?

   Since their inception, public schools have tried to meet society's academic, vocational, social, civic, and personal goals. Perhaps no other institution is the focus of such intense community values and conflict. Schools are expected to protect the national defense, prepare "world class" workers, unify a multicultural society while celebrating diversity, improve academic competence, and provide social and economic mobility.

2. Should schools transmit the American culture or change it?

   Two fundamental, often opposing, purposes of schools, are (1) to transmit society's knowledge and values, passing on the cultural baton, and (2) to reconstruct society, empowering students to promote social progress. More recently, a traditional Eurocentric cultural legacy has underpinned the school's curriculum, with a concurrent emphasis on standards and tests. Social issues and concerns have been de-emphasized.

3. What school purposes are emphasized by educational reform?

   In 1983, *A Nation at Risk* triggered a renewed interest in increased testing of a back-to-basics school curriculum. A second wave of reports by Sizer, Goodlad, Boyer, and others, focused on strategies to strengthen the teaching profession and restructure education. The third wave of reform reports viewed the school as a comprehensive institution providing

CHAPTER REVIEW

Go to the Online Learning Center to take a chapter self-quiz, practice with key terms, and review concepts from the chapter.

CURRENT NEWS FROM POWERWEB

To access PowerWeb, go to Chapter 4 on the Online Learning Center to read current articles and to access news feeds about:

- The Future of Education
- Education Reform
- School Vouchers
- Urban Schools
- Schools
- Federal Policy and Schools
- Public Perceptions of Schools

social, medical, and other services to children. The first reform wave continues to be the most enduring with its emphasis on a back-to-basics curriculum, standards and testing.

4. How are magnet and charter schools, open enrollment, and vouchers reshaping our concept of the neighborhood public school?

Conservative economist Milton Friedman and others applied a free-market economy to education, with the belief that only the best schools will survive the competition. The use of vouchers allows parents to choose public or private, secular or religious schools, and to pay for these schools with taxpayer monies. Open enrollments permit students to attend any available public school, even if the school is not in their neighborhood. For example, a magnet school is a public school with a unique focus, from musical talents to gifted education. The charter school movement, which started in 1991, encourages groups to contract with school boards and open their own public school. Charter schools enjoy greater freedom in deciding what and how to teach, but their effectiveness has not yet been proven.

5. Do the laws of the marketplace belong in public education?

For-profit education companies, Edison Schools, Advantage, Sylvan Learning, and Tesseract, also referred to as Educational Maintenance Organizations (EMOs), argue that they are more effective and efficient than public schools. Charter schools, vouchers, and other choice plans are based on the idea that competition will lead to better schools. But many parents and educators are concerned about the loss of academic freedom, social fragmentation through niche schools, inculcation of business values at the cost of educational goals and student independence, and giving private companies access to public institutions. They argue that profiteering and commercialism are compromising public education.

6. Why are so many families choosing home schooling?

Home schooling has grown dramatically in recent years. While many home-school for religious reasons, others choose home schooling because they believe that they can provide a more effective education than public or private schools.

EXTENDED LEARNING

Go to Chapter 4 on your *Resources for Exploring Education* CD-ROM to access Case Studies and Readings.

CASE STUDIES

- Alison Cohen: A teacher opens a resource room at a school that has never had any special education classrooms and believes the teachers are colluding to make the mainstreaming program fail.
- Amy Rothman: A high school resource room teacher is confronted by a parent during a staffing meeting about a gifted, autistic student in her resource room for whom the parent wants a service not provided by the school district.

READINGS

- Elliot Eisner. "The Kind of Schools We Need."
- Michael Romanowski. "Common Arguments About the Strengths and Limitations of Home Schooling."

KEY TERMS AND PEOPLE

acculturation, 138

Americanization, 138

Ernest Boyer, 136

charter schools, 145

children's boards, 142

children's policy, 142

James Coleman, 143

Edison Schools, 149

educational vouchers, 144

EMOs (Educational Maintenance Organizations), 149

empowering teachers, 141

Paulo Freire, 134

Milton Friedman, 143

full service schools, 142

John Goodlad, 135

home schooling, 156

ideologues, 156

Jonathan Kozol, 147

Lemon v. Kurtzman, 145

magnet schools, 144

A Nation at Risk, 140

National Commission on Excellence in Education, 139

open enrollment, 144

pedagogues, 157

The Pedagogy of the Oppressed, 134

A Place Called School, 135

privatization, 150

reconstructionists, 133

school choice, 144

service credit, 133

Theodore Sizer, 141

social action curriculum, 133

Tesseract (Educational Alternatives Incorporated), 150

three waves of reform, 140

Zelman v. Simmons-Harris, 145

DISCUSSION QUESTIONS AND ACTIVITIES

1. Discuss your list of school goals that you recorded with your classmates. Which goals seem to be most important to your peers? to your instructor? Which do *you* consider most important? Give reasons for your priorities.

2. Summarize the last decade of education reform. Predict what the next big reform report will propose. Consider both concerns and suggestions.

3. Imagine you are a school board member and your district is debating whether to move to an open enrollment or to a voucher system. Defend your opinion in a brief memo.

4. What do you think of private businesses contracting to run schools? What factors would cause you to seek or avoid teaching for a corporation? Would you feel secure in your job, even without tenure?

5. Does your local public school district have an official (or unofficial) policy concerning home schooling? Do home-schooled students participate in any school activities or receive any school resources? How do you feel about these (un)official policies?

 WEB-*TIVITIES*

Go to www.mhhe.com/sadker7e to do the following activities:

1. The Purposes of Schools
2. Paulo Freire and Reconstructionism
3. Educational Vouchers and School Choice
4. Educational Maintenance Organizations (EMOs)
5. Home Schools, Home Teachers

REEL TO REAL TEACHING

SCHOOL TIES (1992)
Run Time: 110 minutes

Synopsis: A working-class Jewish quarterback is offered a senior year scholarship to a prestigious New England academy. It's his ticket to an Ivy League education, but there is one condition: The school's administration asks him to hide his religious identity.

Reflection:

1. What is the purpose of education at St. Matthew's Academy, according to the school administration? Teachers? Students? Parents? Alumni? Describe the similarities and differences you discover.

2. Would the school's mission have been different if David Greene were allowed to express his religious identity? How?

3. What characteristics, other than religion, do students formally or informally hide in schools?

4. School choice programs, similar to a private school like St. Matthew's, may be selective about who is admitted to a school. How is a school's purpose reflected in selective inclusion policies?

5. Who should have the final authority to determine a school's purpose? Who had the ultimate authority in *School Ties*?

Follow-up Activity: Using words and pictures, create a school logo that reflects St. Matthew's school mission in *School Ties*. Revisit the *Where Do You Stand* section in the chapter (pages 136–139). What school goals did you mark as very important? Design a logo that reflects these goals.

www.mhhe.com/
sadker7e

How do you rate this film? Go to *Reel to Real Teaching* in the Critics' Corner to review this film.

FOR FURTHER READING

Choosing Schools, by Mark Schneider, Melissa Marshall, and Paul Eric Teske (2000). What parents value in education, how satisfied they are with their children's schools, and the impact of choice are analyzed.

The Great School Debate: Choice, Vouchers, and Charters, by Thomas Good and Jennifer Braden (2000). Drawing on a comprehensive research review of vouchers and charter schools, the authors discuss why contemporary choice programs have yet to fulfill the expectations of their advocates.

Inside Charter Schools: The Paradox of Radical Decentralization, by Bruce Fuller (2001). This book takes readers into six strikingly different schools, from an evangelical home-schooling charter in California to a back-to-basics charter in a black neighborhood in Lansing, Michigan.

The Irony of Early School Reform: Educational Innovation in Mid-Nineteenth Century Massachusetts, by Michael B. Katz, 2nd edition (2001). Maps out the origins of school reform and locates the source of educational inequalities and bureaucracies in patterns established in the nineteenth century.

Powerful Reforms with Shallow Roots, by Larry Cuban and Michael Usdan (2003). Featuring close-up case studies of six urban districts (Philadelphia, Baltimore, Chicago, Boston, San Diego, and Seattle), this book explores the reasons why these cities chose to alter their traditional school governance structures and analyzes what happened when the reforms were implemented.

Schools for Sale: Why Free Market Policies Won't Improve America's Schools, and What Will, by Ernest R. House (1998). Debunks the myth connecting economic productivity and educational excellence.

Life in Schools

5

FOCUS QUESTIONS

1. What rituals and routines shape classroom life?
2. How is class time related to student achievement?
3. How does the teacher's gatekeeping function influence classroom roles?
4. What is tracking, and what are its advantages and disadvantages?
5. Why has "detracking" become a popular movement?
6. How do peer groups impact elementary school life?
7. In what ways does the adolescent culture shape teenage perceptions and behaviors?
8. What steps can educators take to create a more supportive school environment?
9. What are the characteristics of effective schools?

 WHAT DO YOU THINK? What Was Your School Experience Like? See how it compares to that of your colleagues.

CHAPTER PREVIEW

School is a culture. Like most cultures, it is filled with its own unique rituals and traditions, and its own set of norms and mores. In school even the familiar, like time, is made new. Time is told by subjects ("Let's talk before math") or periods ("I'm going home after seventh period"). Teachers and administrators decide the "what" and "when" of students' lives. Students are pinched into passive roles, following schedules created by others, sitting still rather than being active, and responding to teacher questions, but seldom asking any of their own. Such a system challenges both teachers and students, and forces each into confining roles for five or more hours a day. For many, it is an uncomfortable fit.

Friendships and popularity take on enormous significance during school years. Peer groups create strong subcultures that make winners and losers of us all—at least for a brief time. Adults pick up where children leave off, assigning students to what amounts to an academic caste system through *de facto* tracking or ability grouping. Students begin to sense who are the "haves" and the "have-nots," and detect how classism and racism influence American life. Finally, adolescents and pre-adolescents are entering the new and confusing world of relationships, romance, and sexuality. While adults may focus on academics in school, many students are most concerned with the social side of school life.

In this chapter we take you beyond academics to the lesser-known three Rs (rules, rituals, and routines). We ask you to analyze the subtle dynamics of classroom communication and the role of peer groups. We also want you to think about some of the political realities of schools, such as ability grouping, and to consider what impact these may have on students. Finally, we look at five factors traditionally associated with effective schools, then take you beyond these factors to explore new arenas of effective schools research.

CHAPTER FOCUS
From the moment children first enter school, they are immersed in an informal and subtle network of interactions that forms a big part of school culture. This chapter takes readers beyond academics to the lesser-known three Rs (rules, rituals, and routines). School tracking practices assign students to high and low ability groups, and an academic caste system may emerge. The chapter summarizes major factors traditionally associated with effective schools. For a chapter outline, see the IM.

CHAPTER

Rules, Rituals, and Routines

GRABBER: CLASSROOM
PATTERNS
IM

FOCUS QUESTION 1
What rituals and routines
shape classroom life?

TEACHING TIP
Can students recall
classroom management
strategies that made *time
fly* or at least used time
effectively? What
judgments about past
teachers are also revealed
in the memories
("awesomely organized,"
"type A compulsive,"
"messier than the kids")?

Schools create their own cultures, replete with norms, rituals, and routines. Even simple tasks, like distributing textbooks, are clothed with cultural cues, but they are cues that differ for students and teachers.

"Come Right Up and Get Your New Books": A Teacher's Perspective

Dick Thompson looked at the pile of poetry anthologies stacked on his desk and sighed. Getting texts distributed and starting a new unit always seemed like such a chaotic ordeal, particularly with seventh-graders. But worrying over possible mishaps wouldn't get this poetry unit launched. Besides, his students were getting restless, so he had better get things started.

"Okay, class, quiet down. As you can see, the poetry books we've been waiting for have finally arrived. All right, you can cut out the groans. Give the books a fair trial before you sentence them. I'd like the first person in each row to come up, count out enough books for his or her row, and hand them out."

Six students charged to the front and made a mad grab for the books. In the ensuing melee, one stack of books went crashing to the floor.

"Hey, kids, take it easy and stop the squabbling. There are plenty of books to go around. Since this procedure obviously isn't working, we'll just have to slow down and do things one row at a time. Bob, you hand out the books for row 1 first; then Sally will come up and get the books for row 2. It will take a little longer this way, but I think things will go more smoothly. When you get your texts, write your name and room number in the stamped box inside the cover."

Since the dispensing of books now seemed to be progressing in an orderly fashion, Mr. Thompson turned his attention to the several hands waving in the air.

"Yes, Jessica?"

"I can't fill in my name because my pencil just broke. Can I sharpen it?"

"Go ahead. Jamie?"

"My pencil's broken too. Can I sharpen mine?"

"Yes, but wait until Jessica sits down. Let me remind you that you're supposed to come to class prepared. Now there will be no more at the pencil sharpener today. Scott?"

"Can I use the hall pass?"

"Is this absolutely necessary? All right then [responding to Scott's urgent nod]. Now I think we've had enough distraction for one morning. The period's half over and we still haven't gotten into today's lesson. After you get your book and fill in the appropriate information, turn to the poem on page 3. It's called 'Stopping by Woods on a Snowy Evening,' and it's by Robert Frost, one of America's most famous poets. Yes, Rosa?"

"I didn't get a book."

"Tomàs, didn't you hand out books to your row? Oh, I see. We're one short. Okay, Rosa, go down to the office and tell Mrs. Goldberg that we need one more of the new poetry anthologies. Now, as I was about to say, I'd like you to think about the questions that I've written on the board: How does the speaker in this poem feel as he looks at the snow filling up the deserted woods? Why does he wish to stop, and what makes him realize that he must go on? The speaker says, 'I have miles to go before I

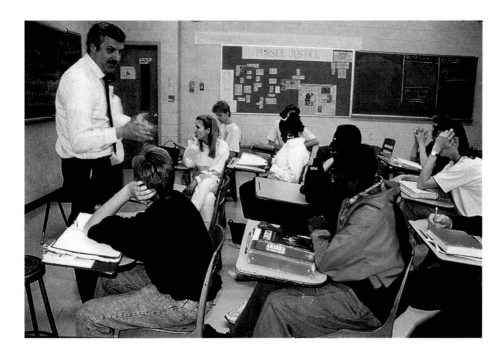

What is the hidden curriculum in this teacher-dominated classroom, where teachers actively talk and move about while students passively sit and listen?

sleep.' He may be talking about more than going to bed for the night. What else may 'sleep' mean in this poem? Yes, Timothy, do you have a comment on the poem already?"

"My glasses are being fixed and I can't read the board."

"All right. Take the seat by my desk. You'll see the board from there. April! Maxine! This is not a time for your private chat room. This is a silent reading activity—and I do mean silent. Okay, class, I think most of you have had enough time to read the poem. Who has an answer for the first question? Jordan?"

"Well, I think the guy in this poem really likes nature. He's all alone, and it's private, with no people around to interrupt him, and he thinks the woods and the snow are really beautiful. It's sort of spellbinding."

"Jordan, that's an excellent response. You've captured the mood of this poem. Now for the second question. Maxine?"

"I think he wants to stop because . . . "

Maxine's answer was cut short by the abrasive ring of the fourth-period bell.

"Class, sit down. I know the bell has rung, but it isn't signaling a fire. You'll have time to make your next class. Since we didn't get as far into our discussion as I had hoped, I want to give you an assignment. For homework, I'd like you to answer the remaining questions. Alice?"

"Is this to hand in?"

"Yes. Any other questions? Okay, you'd better get to your next-period class."

As the last student left, Dick Thompson slumped over his desk and wearily ran his fingers through his hair. As he looked down, he spotted the missing poetry anthology under his desk, a victim of the charge of the book brigade. The whole lesson was a victim of the book brigade. He had been so busy getting the books dispensed and fielding all the interruptions that he had forgotten to give his brief explanation on the differences between prose and poetry. He had even forgotten to give his motivating speech on how interesting the new poetry unit was going to be. Well, no time for a postmortem now. Stampedelike noises outside the door meant the fourth-period class was about to burst in.

"Come Right Up and Get Your New Books": A Student's Perspective

From her vantage point in the fourth seat, fifth row, Maxine eyed the stack of new books on the teacher's desk. She knew they were poetry books because she had flipped through one as she meandered into the room. She didn't care that it wasn't "in" to like poetry; she liked it anyway. At least it was better than the grammar unit they'd just been through. All those sentences to diagram—picking out nouns and pronouns—what a drag that was.

Maxine settled into her seat and began the long wait for her book. Her thoughts wandered: "Mr. Thompson seems like he's in some kind of daze, just staring at the new books like he's zoned out. Wonder what's bugging him. Good enough, the first kids in each row are heading up to get the books. Oh, right, they're getting into a brawl over handing out the stupid books. What a bunch of jerks; they must think they're funny or something. Now it'll be one row at a time and will take forever. I suppose I can start my math homework or write some letters."

Maxine got several of her math problems solved by the time her poetry anthology arrived, along with instructions to read the poem on page 3. She skimmed through the poem and decided she liked it. She understood how Robert Frost felt, watching the snowy woods and wanting to get away from all the hassles. It sure would be nice to read this poem quietly somewhere without listening to kids going on about pencil sharpeners and hall passes and seat changes. All these interruptions made it hard to concentrate.

As she turned around to share her observation about hassles with April Marston, Mr. Thompson's sharp reprimand interrupted her. She fumed to herself, "Private chat room. What's with him? Half the class is talking, and old Eagle Eyes Thompson has to pick on me. And they're all talking about the football game Saturday. At least I was talking about the poem. Oh well, I'd better answer one of those questions on the board and show him that I really am paying attention."

Maxine waved her hand wildly, but Jordan got called for question 1. Maxine shot her hand in the air again for a chance at question 2. When Mr. Thompson called on her, she drew a deep breath and began her response. Once again, she was interrupted in midsentence, this time by the fourth-period bell. Disgruntled, she stuffed her poetry book under her arm and fell into step beside April Marston.

"I really knew the answer to that question," she muttered under her breath. "Now we have to write all the answers out. Boring. Well, next period is science and we're supposed to be giving lab reports. Maybe we'll have a chance to finish the English homework there."

 ## Delay and Social Distraction

CRITICAL THINKING QUESTION
Challenge individuals to relate a personal classroom experience but now from two distinct points of view: the student and the teacher.

You have just read two capsular replays of a seventh-grade English lesson, one from the vantage point of the teacher, the other from the vantage point of a student. Mr. Thompson and Maxine play different roles, which cause them to have very different experiences in this class. In what ways is the same class experienced differently by teacher and student?

One difference you may have detected is that while Mr. Thompson was continually leapfrogging from one minor crisis to the next, Maxine was sitting and waiting. In his perceptive book *Life in Classrooms,* **Philip W. Jackson** describes how time is spent in elementary school.[1] He suggests that, whereas teachers are typically very busy, students are often caught in patterns of delay that force them to do nothing. Jackson notes that a great deal of teachers' time is spent in noninstructional busywork, such as keeping time and dispensing supplies. In the slice of classroom life you just read, Mr. Thompson spent a substantial part of the class time distributing new texts. Indeed, most teachers spend a good deal of time giving out things: paper, pencils, art materials, science equipment, floppy disks, exam booklets, erasers, happy faces, special privileges—the list goes on and on. The classroom scene described also shows Mr. Thompson greatly involved in timekeeping activities. Within the limits set by school buzzers and bells, he determines when the texts will be distributed, when and for how long the reading activity will take place, and when the class discussion will begin.

What do students do while teachers are busy organizing, structuring, talking, questioning, handing out, collecting, timekeeping, and crisis hopping? According to Jackson's analysis, they do little more than sit and wait.[2] They wait for the materials to be handed out, for the assignment to be given, for the questions to be asked, for the teacher to call on them, for the teacher to react to their response, and for the slower class members to catch up so that the activity can change. They wait in lines to get drinks of water, to get pencils sharpened, to get their turn at the computer, to go to the playground, to get to the bathroom, and to be dismissed from class. If students are to succeed in school, they must be able to cope with continual delay as a standard operating procedure.

One plea that is rarely granted is that of talking to classmates beyond controlled learning activities. Like the character from Greek mythology, Tantalus, who was continually tempted with food and water but was not allowed to eat or drink, students are surrounded by peers and friends but are restrained from communicating with them. In other words, students in the classroom are in the very frustrating position of having to ignore social temptation, of acting as though they are isolated despite the crowd surrounding them. Furthermore, while trying to concentrate on work and to ignore social temptations, students are beset by frequent interruptions—the public address system blaring a message in the middle of an exam, the end-of-class bell interrupting a lively discussion, a teacher's reprimand or a student's question derailing a train of thought during silent reading.

Consider how Maxine in Mr. Thompson's English class had to cope with delay, denial of desire, social distraction, and interruptions. She waited for the delivery of her new text. She waited to be called on by the teacher. Her attempt to concentrate on reading the poem was disturbed by frequent interruptions. Her brief communication with a classmate was interrupted by a reprimand. Her head was filled with ideas and questions. In short, there was a lot she would like to have said, but there was almost no opportunity to say it.

Watching the Clock

Educators concerned about school improvement have called attention to the inefficient use of time in school, claiming that we lose between one-quarter and one-half of the time available for learning through attendance problems, noninstructional

CRITICAL THINKING QUESTION
Do students see themselves as *inherently* organized? Efficient? Timekeepers? Are these natural traits of an effective teacher? Can they (or should they) be learned?

CLASS ACTIVITY: RULES, RITUALS, AND ROUTINES
IM, Activity 5:2

FOCUS QUESTION 2
How is class time related to student achievement?

FIGURE 5.1
School time.

SOURCE: From John Goodlad, *A Place Called School* (New York: McGraw-Hill, 1984).

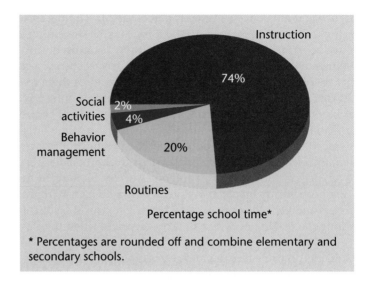

* Percentages are rounded off and combine elementary and secondary schools.

REFLECTION: About three-fourths of class time is spent in instruction. Does that seem high, low, or about right? The instruction category is quite broad. How might you break it down into more meaningful subcategories?

activities (such as class changes and assemblies), administrative and organizational activities, and disruptions caused by student misbehavior.[3]

In a classic study of schools, **John Goodlad** found a fair degree of consistency in how time is spent in different activities as children go through the grades. As Figure 5.1 illustrates, about 2 percent of time is spent to social activities, 2 to 5 percent to behavior management, 20 percent to routines, and 75 percent to instruction.

In Goodlad's study, although there was a general consistency in how time was spent at different levels of schooling, one of the most astonishing findings was the enormous variation in the *efficiency* with which different schools used time. When examining the hours per week allocated to subject-matter learning, time ranged from a low of 18.5 hours in one school to a high of 27.5 hours in another. Goodlad was also surprised at the limited amount of time spent on the academic staples, such as reading and writing. He found that only 6 percent of time in elementary school was spent on reading. This dropped to a minuscule 2 percent at the high school level. In contrast, the amount of time students spent listening to teacher lectures and explanations increased from approximately 18 percent in elementary school to more than 25 percent in high school.[4] Many schools have responded by adopting alternative or block scheduling and special focus activities, such as sustained silent reading, to make better use of time in school.

While the business world may suggest "time is money," for educators, time is learning. As one teacher points out,

> Time is the currency of teaching. We barter with time. Every day we make small concessions, small trade-offs, but, in the end, we know it's going to defeat us. After all, how many times are we actually able to cover World War I in our history courses before the year is out? We always laugh a little about that, but the truth is the sense of the clock ticking is one of the most oppressive features of teaching.[5]

There is a limited amount of time set aside for the school day. Research shows that, when more time is allocated to subject-matter learning, student achievement

Part of the hidden curriculum of schools is the "culture of waiting" that accompanies the many transition periods throughout the day. And often, waiting seems to be a gender-segregated activity.

increases.[6] When this valuable resource is spent handing out supplies or reprimanding misbehavior, it is lost for learning. Looked at from this perspective, Mr. Thompson's class was not only frustrating, but it also deprived students of a precious and limited resource—the time to learn.

 ## The Teacher as Gatekeeper

Philip Jackson reports that teachers are typically involved in more than one thousand verbal exchanges with their students every day.[7] Count the number of verbal exchanges Mr. Thompson had with his students during our abbreviated classroom scene and you will get some idea of how much and how often teachers talk. One of the functions that keeps teachers busiest is what Philip Jackson terms **gatekeeping.** As gatekeepers, teachers must determine who will talk, when, and for how long, as well as the basic direction of the communication.

In Chapter 3, "Teacher Effectiveness," we presented some of the findings about classroom interaction. Consider what effect these patterns of classroom interaction have on both teachers and students:

- Roughly two-thirds of classroom time is taken up by talk; two-thirds of that talk is by the teacher.[8]
- In the typical "pedagogical cycle," teachers structure (lecture and direct), question, and react to student comments. Teachers initiate about 85 percent of these verbal cycles.[9]
- While questioning signals curiosity, it is the teachers, not the learners, who do the questioning, asking as many as 348 questions a day.[10] The typical student rarely asks a question.[11]
- Most classroom questions require that students use only rote memory.[12]

FOCUS QUESTION 3
How does the teacher's gatekeeping function influence classroom roles?

CLASS ACTIVITY: ANALYZING OUR OWN CLASSROOM
IM, Activity 5:5

RAP 2.5
Rules, Rituals and Routines, p. 276

The Patterns of the Classroom

After observing in more than one thousand classrooms, John Goodlad and his team of researchers found that the following patterns characterize most classrooms:

- Much of what happens in class is geared toward maintaining order among twenty to thirty students restrained in a relatively small space.
- Although the classroom is a group setting, each student typically works alone.
- The teacher is the key figure in setting the tone and determining the activities.
- Most of the time, the teacher is in front of the classroom, teaching a whole group of students.
- There is little praise or corrective feedback; classes are emotionally neutral or flat places.
- Students are involved in a limited range of activities—listening to lectures, writing answers to questions, and taking exams.

- A significant number of students are confused by teacher explanations and feel that they do not get enough guidance on how to improve.
- There is a decline in the attractiveness of the learning environment and the quality of instruction as students progress through the grades.

Goodlad concluded that "the emotional tone of the classroom is neither harsh and punitive nor warm and joyful; it might be described most accurately as flat."

SOURCE: John Goodlad, *A Place Called School* (New York: McGraw-Hill, 1984).

REFLECTION: Goodlad's classic study is now two decades old. How many of these findings continue to characterize classroom life?

- Students are not given much time to ask, or even answer, questions. Teachers usually wait less than a second for student comments and answers.[13]
- Teachers interact less and less with students as they go through the grades.[14]

Ironically, while a major goal of education is to increase students' curiosity and quest for knowledge, it is the teachers, not the students, who dominate and manage classroom interaction. Classroom interaction patterns do not train students to be active, inquiring, self-reliant learners. Rather, students are expected to be quiet and passive, to think quickly (and perhaps superficially), to rely on memory, and to be dependent on the teacher. Silent, passive students have less positive attitudes and lower achievement. Perhaps the challenge new teachers should keep before them is finding a way to turn their gatekeeping role into a benefit for students, instead of a hindrance.

The Other Side of the Tracks

FOCUS QUESTION 4
What is tracking and what are its advantages and disadvantages?

OVERHEAD 57
Tracking

We have seen that teachers function as gatekeepers, controlling the amount and flow of student talk in the classroom. Let's step back a moment, and consider an even more basic question: Which students sit (for sit they mainly do) in which classrooms? That very crucial, political decision falls on teachers, counselors, and administrators. Many believe that it is easier for students with similar skills and intellectual abilities to learn together, in **homogeneous** classes. Educators following this belief, screen, sort, and direct students based on their abilities, and as a result, send them down different school paths, profoundly shaping their futures. Students of different abilities (low, middle, and high) are assigned to different "tracks" of courses and programs (vocational, general, college-bound, honors, and AP). **Tracking** is the term given to this process, and while some teachers believe that tracking makes instruction more manageable, others believe that it is a terribly flawed system.

In the 1960s, sociologist **Talcott Parsons** analyzed school as a social system and concluded that the college selection process begins in elementary school and is virtually sealed by the time students finish junior high.[15] Parsons's analysis has significant implications, for he is suggesting that future roles in adult life are determined by student achievement in elementary school. The labeling system, beginning at an early age, determines who will wear a stethoscope, who will carry a laptop computer, and who will become a low-wage laborer.

Several researchers consider students' social class a critical factor in this selection system. Back in 1929, Robert and Helen Lynd, in their extensive study of Middletown (a small midwestern city), concluded that schools are essentially middle-class institutions that discriminate against lower-class students.[16] Approximately fifteen years later, **W. Lloyd Warner** and his associates at the University of Chicago conducted a series of studies in New England, the deep South, and the Midwest and came to a similar conclusion.

The classroom language game, in which teachers talk and students listen, may encourage passivity and boredom.

> One group [the lower class] is almost immediately brushed off into a bin labeled "nonreaders, first grade repeaters," or "opportunity class," where they stay for eight or ten years and are then released through a chute to the outside world to become hewers of wood and drawers of water.[17]

In his classic analysis of class and school achievement, **August Hollingshead** discovered that approximately two-thirds of the students from the two upper social classes but fewer than 15 percent of those from the lower classes were in the college preparatory program.[18] In midwestern communities, **Robert Havinghurst** and associates reported that nearly 90 percent of school dropouts were from lower-class families.[19] The unfortunate tracking by class is one of the oldest of school traditions.

Parents and peers may influence academic choices even more than guidance counselors do.[20] When family and friends encourage children with similar backgrounds to stay together, students of the same race and class typically find themselves on the same school tracks. When school norms and children's culture clash, the result can also lead to racially segregated tracks. For example, some students of color devote time and attention to "stage setting." Stage setting may include checking pencils, rearranging sitting positions, and watching others—all part of a pattern of readiness before work can begin. To a teacher unfamiliar with this learning style, such behavior may be interpreted as inappropriate or as avoidance of work. Some racial and ethnic groups value cooperation and teamwork, yet school norms frequently stress individual, competitive modes of learning. Such cultural clashes work to the detriment of certain groups, relegating them to lower-ability classes and tracks.[21]

Several studies document differences in how students in high-ability and low-ability tracks are treated. In a classic study done in the 1970s, Ray Rist observed a kindergarten class in an all-black urban school. By the eighth day of class, the kindergarten teacher, apparently using such criteria as physical appearance, socioeconomic status, and language usage, had separated her students into groups of "fast learners" and "slow learners." She spent more time with the "fast learners" and gave them more instruction and encouragement. The "slow learners" got more than their fair share of control and ridicule. The children soon began to mirror the teacher's behavior. As the "fast learners" belittled the "slow learners," the low-status children began to exhibit attitudes of self-degradation and hostility toward one another. This

RELATED READING
"Why Are All the Black Kids Sitting Together in the Cafeteria?" And Other Conversations about Race. by Beverly D. Tatum (1999).

The Anti-Achievement Dilemma

Many students avoid academic excellence, because they fear their peers will label them nerds. According to B. Bradford Brown and Laurence Steinberg, who sampled eight thousand high school students in California and Wisconsin, this fear is warranted. Unlike athletes, who are offered adulation, high academic achievers often get resentment instead of respect.[1] To avoid the "nerd" label and the social rejection that comes with it, students learn that they should do well, but not too well. This brain-nerd connection causes students to put the brakes on academic achievement, cut corners, and do only what is necessary to get by. The anti-achievement climate is even stronger for African American students. Signithia Fordham and John Ogbu reported the results of a fascinating ethnographic study in a Washington, DC, high school, where the student population was 99 percent black.[2] They found that the students actively discouraged each other from working to achieve because attaining academic success was seen as "acting white." "Acting white" was understood to include speaking standard English, listening to white music and radio stations, being on time, studying in the library, working hard, and getting good grades. Students who did well in school were called "brainiacs," a term synonymous with jerk. The students who managed to achieve academic success and still avoid the "brainiac" label developed ingenious coping strategies. Some students camouflaged high achievement by "acting crazy," as class clowns or comedians. Others chose friends who would protect them in exchange for help with homework. Female achievers were more likely to hide out, keeping a low profile, so their peers would not know they were smart.

[1]B. Bradford Brown and Laurence Steinberg, "Academic Achievement and Social Acceptance," *The Education Digest* 55 (March 1990), pp. 57–60. Condensed from *National Center on Effective Secondary Schools Newsletter* 4 (fall 1989), pp. 2–4.
[2]Signithia Fordham, *Blacked Out: The Dilemmas of Race, Identity, and Success at Capital High* (Chicago: University of Chicago Press, 1996); Signithia Fordham and John Ogbu, "Black Students' School Success: Coping with the Burden of 'Acting White,'" *Urban Review* 18, no. 3 (1986), pp. 176–205.

REFLECTION: What can teachers do to break the brainiac-jerk association? How can the power of peer pressure be unleashed for success instead of mediocrity or failure? What do you think?

teacher's expectations, formed during eight days at the beginning of school, shaped the academic and social treatment of children in her classroom for the entire year and perhaps for years to come. Records of the grouping that had taken place during the first week in kindergarten were passed on to teachers in the upper grades, providing the basis for further differential treatment.[22]

FOCUS QUESTION 5
Why has "detracking" become a popular movement?

Jeannie Oakes's *Keeping Track* (1985) was a scathing indictment of tracking, adding momentum to the effort to **detrack,** or eliminate tracking practices from the nation's schools. Oakes found that race more than ability determined which students were placed in which tracks, and that the lower-tracked students had fewer learning opportunities.[23] Other studies confirmed that low demands were placed on students in low-ability groups, and teachers expected little from them and offered fewer constructive comments to students in low ability groups. Low tracks suffered from more classroom management problems, and focused more on social rather than academic matters. Over the course of a year, a child in the highest group moved ahead as much as five times more quickly than a child in the lowest group. By the fourth grade, an achievement spread of a full four grades separated children at the top and the bottom of the class, a difference that increased with time.[24] (See Frame of Reference: Tracking and Race.)

"True," tracking advocates argue, "it would appear more democratic to put everyone in the same class, but such idealism is destined to fail." They contend that it is unrealistic to think everyone can or should master the same material or learn it at the same pace. Without tracking we have **heterogeneous,** or mixed ability classes. Tracking advocates are quick to point out that mixed ability classes have their own set of problems: In heterogeneous classes, bright students get bored, while slower

- Minority students are 3 times as likely as white students to be enrolled in low-track math classes and whites are more than 1.5 times more likely to be in high-track classes.

- Schools with predominately poor and minority populations offer fewer advanced and more remedial courses in academic subjects.

- When parents intervene, counselors place middle- and upper-class students with comparably low grades and test scores into higher groups.

- African American and Hispanic students are under-represented in programs for the gifted.

- Asian students are more likely than Hispanic students to be recommended for advanced classes, even with equivalent test scores.

- Teachers with the least experience and the lowest levels of qualifications are assigned to students in the lowest tracks.

- Students are more likely to "choose" their friends from their ability groups and tracked classes in elementary through high school. The social network and peer status sorting system is linked to the academic sorting system.

- 73 percent of students completing an academic program are white, 10 percent are black, and 7 percent are Hispanic.

- 63 percent of Advanced Placement exam takers are white, 5 percent are black, and 10 percent are Hispanic.

SOURCE: "Race/Ethnicity of Students Taking Advanced Placement Exams, 2000," *The 2000 National Summary Report on Advanced Placement Program* (New York: College Board, 2000); "1994 High School Transcript Study," National Center on Educational Statistics (Washington, DC: U.S. Department of Education, September 1998); Jeannie Oakes, "Ability Grouping and Tracking in Schools," in T. Husen and T. Neville Postlethwaite (eds.), *The International Encyclopedia of Education,* 2nd edition (Tarrytown, NY: Pergamon Press), 1994; Jeannie Oakes, Adam Gamoran, and Reba Page, "Curriculum Differentiation: Opportunities, Outcomes, and Meanings," in Phil Jackson (ed.), *Handbook of Research on Curriculum* (New York: Macmillan, 1992).

REFLECTION: Can a tracking or ability grouping program avoid segregating children by race and ethnicity? How would you create such a program?

students have trouble keeping up, and we lose our most talented and our most needy students. Teachers find themselves grading the brighter students on the quality of their work, and the weaker ones on their "effort," which is a big problem (especially with parents!). Teachers get frustrated trying to meet each student's needs, and hardly ever hitting the mark. Putting everyone in the same class simply doesn't work.[25]

Detracking advocates, as you might imagine, offer a different take on the issue. "No sorting system is consistent with equality of opportunity. Worse yet, the tracking system is not based on individual ability. It is badly biased in favor of white middle-class America. We must face the reality that poor children, often children of color, come to school far from being ready to learn. And the school, whose job it is to educate all our children, does little to help. The built-in bias in instruction, counseling, curricular materials, and testing must be overcome. Students get shoveled into second-rate courses that prepare them for fourth-rate jobs. Their track becomes 'a great training robbery,' and the students who are robbed may be ones with great abilities."

While the social pitfalls of tracking have been well documented, its efficacy has not. With little hard evidence supporting tracking, and a growing concern about its negative fallout, it is little wonder that the term "tracking" has fallen out of favor. By the 1990s, only 15 percent of schools had official tracking policies, down from 93 percent in 1965, a quiet but persistent change that has been termed the **unremarked revolution.**[26]

Most schools today work hard to avoid using the term "tracking." Middle and high schools are taking their cue from elementary schools, where "ability grouping" has been in favor. **Ability grouping** sorts students based on capability, but the

MULTIPLE INTELLIGENCE CONNECTION

Tracking: "A Great Training Robbery" could be the title of an essay describing a writer's well-grounded opinion on tracking. Brainstorm other clever yet informative essay titles that represent students' points of view on tracking.

TEACHING TIP

Have students complete the following analogy: Tracking is to ability grouping as _____ is to _____.

groupings may well vary by subject. While tracks suggest permanence, ability grouping is more transitory. One year, a student might find herself in a high-ability math group and a low-ability English group. The following year, that same student might be reassigned to a new set of groups. Today, many middle and high schools talk about "ability grouping," but sometimes it is only the label that has been changed. (You may want to think of school tracking as a take-off on the federal "witness protection program": a reality functioning under an assumed identity.) By seventh grade, two-thirds of all schools have ability grouping in some classes, and about 20 percent have tracking or grouping in every subject.[27] Many educators charge that the United States relies more on tracking than any other nation in the world.[28]

Critics argue that we really can eliminate *de facto* tracking, whatever name it is given. They believe that detracking can work, if it is implemented correctly. Teachers, parents, and students should realize that although students arrive at school from very different backgrounds, learning from each other and together has great advantages. Instruction is best offered through individualized and cooperative learning, rather than the traditional approach of trying to teach all students simultaneously. Alternative assessments work far better than testing everyone with the same test (compare this view to the current emphasis on standardized tests). In fact, detracked schools can be authentic places of learning, academically challenging to all while teaching a living lesson in democracy. What is needed is time, careful planning, and adequate training for teachers so that they can succeed and all students can learn.[29]

As these arguments suggest, tracking is likely to remain an area of controversy in the years ahead, especially for educators who find it "the most professionally divisive issue" in the field.[30] One of the ironies of tracking is that it simply builds on an already divided school culture. What educators do not do to divide students, students often do to themselves.

 ## The Power of Elementary Peer Groups

Educational researcher Raphaela Best wanted to capture a portrait of life in school as a group of elementary school children experienced it. During a multiyear study, she played the role of participant observer, working with children during class time, playing with them at recess, eating lunch with them in the cafeteria, talking with them, observing them, and taking notes. She found that the children "organized their own intense, seething little world with its own frontiers, its own struggles, its own winners and losers. It was a world invisible to outsiders, not apparent to the casual observer,"[31] where the peer group became increasingly important in the children's lives—eventually competing with and even eclipsing parental influence.

In the first grade, when so much about school seems gigantic and fearful, children look to adults for safety: What am I supposed to do in the classroom? Where do I get lunch? How do I find the bus to ride home from school? Both girls and boys look to the teachers and to the principal for answers and for emotional support. In her study, Best found that the children ran to their first-grade teacher not only for this practical information but also for hugs, praise, and general warmth and affection. They climbed onto the teacher's lap and rested, secure, and comforted.

Their relationship to the teacher was far more important than their interactions with one another. For example, when Anne and Matthew were fighting over how to put a puzzle together, the teacher encircled them in her arms and asked, "Can't we find another way to play?" The children nodded affirmatively. "Good! You're so good

CLASS ACTIVITY: FORCED CHOICE GAME
IM, Activity 5:1

CRITICAL THINKING QUESTION
It could be rather rare or totally typical for you, as a professor, to take a clear stand in your class. In your opinion, is tracking *the most professionally divisive issue in the field?* What personal insights can you offer to your students? What do they think?

RAP 2.2
Scoping School Culture, p. 274

FOCUS QUESTION 6
How do peer groups impact elementary school life?

Jeannie Oakes never dreamed of being a schoolteacher. "It was just too ordinary. I wanted adventure, unconventionality." So she embraced her passion for reading, earned a degree in American Literature, married, and had children. "It turned out that I was a lot more conventional than I thought I was!" While raising her children at home in the 1960s, Oakes decided that, she would become a teacher for the "same old-fashioned reasons for which women have always taught—I wanted to be with my children when they came home from school every day."[1] But the unconventional spirit in Jeannie Oakes hadn't disappeared. She championed the Civil Rights movement and anti-Vietnam war activities. And she realized that teaching was a vehicle for social justice, that teaching could be far from ordinary.

Her first day in the classroom made a lasting impression. She didn't announce to students they were taking basic English, but recalls how within five minutes they knew and announced, "Oh, we're in the dumb class!" During the seven years Oakes taught middle and high school English in suburban Los Angeles, she struggled to be as good a teacher to low track classes as to the high ones, and was astonished how her own instruction and expectations changed for students placed in honors, average, and basic classes. She also witnessed how tracking dictated disparate lives in schools. "In a very public way, adults make judgments about students' current and future abilities that take on a hierarchical nature: We talk about top groups and bottom groups. And in the culture of schools, the top group becomes the top kids and the bottom group the bottom kids in a very value-laden and defining way."[2]

Creating innovative classrooms that unlocked successful learning for diverse students became her challenge. Each new school year, Oakes developed new curriculum and instructional strategies, hoping to invigorate enthusiasm for learning in students and fellow teachers. Her calls for change met with administrative resistance and her voice was increasingly silenced.

Her voice was heard as a doctoral student at UCLA, as Oakes researched with John Goodlad the varied aspects of life in schools. Oakes specifically explored how tracking and ability grouping limit the school experiences of low-income students and students of color. In 1985, her landmark book *Keeping Track: How Schools Structure Inequality* brought the inequities of tracking into the national spotlight, casting a riveting portrayal of how tracking creates segregation within schools and shortchanges quality learning and resources. Yet despite the attention, tracking remains one of the most entrenched school practices, relegating students to separate classrooms based less on ability and more on race and socioeconomic status.

Oakes believes the persistence is rooted in a cultural notion that intelligence is immutable and that there is virtually nothing schools can do to alter a student's fundamental capability. She doesn't buy such a limited view.

> Kindergartners show an enormous interest in learning, and this cuts across socioeconomic, racial, and ethnic lines. But as kids go through school, if they don't have successful experiences, they learn their efforts do not pay off. So by high school, we see disinterest unjustly interpreted by teachers as low ability.[3]

For Oakes, then, the fundamental goal of equalizing opportunity is not simply to detrack but to increase the quality of curriculum and instruction for everybody in schools, so that success is not limited to those in the high track. This requires a powerful shift in conventional norms, one that defines intellectual capacity as not fixed, but learned through interaction, problem solving, and critical thinking.

Oakes recognizes that the process of detracking schools is not easy. School reform efforts are often met with resistance by those who benefit from the current system. This political dimension of inequality cannot be underestimated. Parents of high-achieving students exert considerable pressure to ensure that their children have access to honors and AP classes. Moreover, teachers of high-track students often resist efforts to detrack, enjoying the intellectual challenge and prestige that come from teaching these students. School administrators and teachers who have undertaken detracking efforts often tell her it is their most difficult undertaking—and most rewarding. Oakes understands why: "It's about fairness and creating better schools. And getting there is half the fun."[4]

A conventional career, perhaps. But Jeannie Oakes is an unconventional advocate for equity and change.

[1] Carlos Alberto Torres, *Education, Power, and Personal Biography: Dialogues with Critical Educators* (New York: Routledge, 1998), pp. 224–25.
[2] John O'Neill, "On Tracking and Individual Differences: A Conversation with Jeannie Oakes," *Educational Leadership, 50, no. 2* (October 1992), p. 18.
[3] Ibid, p. 20.
[4] Torres, *Education, Power, and Personal Biography: Dialogues with Critical Educators,* p. 230.

REFLECTION: How has Jeannie Oakes made teaching an act of social justice? Why does tracking persist? How have you experienced or witnessed the impact of tracking?

www.mhhe.com/sadker   To learn more about Jeannie Oakes, click on *Profiles in Education.*

That's what researchers at the University of Michigan wanted to find out as they compared the activities of American 3- to 12-year-olds in 1981 and 1997. Can you identify these changing trends? (In comparing the early 1980s to the late 1990s, indicate whether you believe that children are spending *more* or *less* time in each of the following activities.)

	More	Less
1. Studying	_____	_____
2. Watching television	_____	_____
3. Playing sports	_____	_____
4. Reading	_____	_____
5. Enjoying leisure time	_____	_____
6. Hours in day care	_____	_____
7. Hours in school	_____	_____
8. Involved in religious activities	_____	_____
9. Involved in personal care	_____	_____

Answers: If you said "More" to the following, you are correct: (1) studying, (3) sports, (4) reading, (6) hours in day care, (7) hours in school, (9) involved in personal care. The survey reported "Less" time in the following activities: (2) watching television, (5) enjoying leisure time, and (8) involved in religious activities.

SOURCE: Sandra L. Hofferth and John F. Sandberg, 2001. "Changes in American Children's Time, 1981–1997," pages 193–229 in S. L. Hofferth and T. J. Owens (eds), *Children at the Millennium: Where Have We Come From, Where Are We Going? Advances in Life Course Research*, vol. 6. Oxford, England: Elsevier Science (JAI).

REFLECTION: Were your perceptions on target—or off? What factors do you see as contributing to these changes? How might this information impact your classroom teaching? Check online for the full findings at www.umich.edu/~newsinfo/Releases/1998/Nov98/r110998b.html.

and I'm so happy with the way you've been playing, but you know that accidents can happen and someone might have to stay out of school. We wouldn't want that to happen, now would we?"[32] Both children solemnly shook their heads and indicated that they would comply with the teacher's request.

By the second grade, the boys had begun to break away from teacher dependence and to place more importance on their peer group. Though loosely structured, this group was largely sex-segregated, with its own leadership hierarchy. In the first grade, the boys and girls had sat side-by-side in the lunchroom, but, by the second grade, the boys had claimed one end of a lunchroom table for themselves. To ensure privacy from the female world, the group's meeting place became the boys' bathroom, where the boys talked about kids at school and decided what to play at recess.

By the third grade, the boys were openly challenging teacher authority. They banded together to organize an all-male club, complete with pecking order, assignments, secrets, and anti-establishment pranks, such as stuffing the locks with paper so the teachers could not get into the building in the morning. Also, by the third grade, the boys' territorial rights had increased, and they had staked out an entirely male lunchroom table for themselves. The playground also became increasingly sex-segregated, as blacktop and grassy areas were reserved for active boys' ball games, and the girls were relegated to the fringe areas, where they stood talking, played hop-scotch, and jumped rope. The girls used their time to chat, giggle, and re-create game rules to discourage cut-throat competition. Occasionally, an athletic girl breached the cultural divide and played with the boys, yet her status as tomboy was always a limiting and noninclusive role. A powerful male culture had evolved, with the entitlement and rights of the privileged.

TEACHING TIP

Can students offer examples, from their own experience, of males who breached this *boy code*? How does being the *right kind of guy* impact masculinity? How do male stereotypes impact sex role stereotypes for females and gender equity?

Social exclusion occurs in mixed sex or same sex peer groups. In either setting, rejection and isolation can be painful.

Excluded from this all-male society were not only the girls but also some boys who were considered sissies. For these rejected boys, the consequences of being left out of the **dominant male peer group** were painful and severe. As they progressed through their elementary school years, these excluded male students exhibited an increasing number of social, emotional, and academic problems. Afraid of being teased by the male club, they avoided playing with the girls, even though they might have been very happy doing so. Belonging nowhere, they banded together loosely, not out of liking but out of need.

The girls spent the first few years of school helping the teacher, not switching their allegiance to the peer group until the fourth grade. Throughout their school years, this allegiance was rewarded, in part with good report card grades. Then, instead of joining a club, they formed best-friend relationships, in which pairs of girls pledged devotion to one another. Sometimes fights broke out, when two girls argued over having a third as best friend. In the upper elementary grades, the girls also began to fantasize about the "cute" boys in their class and about what being married and having a family would be like. Being a good student and having a pleasing personality were seen as important, but, by the upper elementary grades, appearance had become the key to social status.

The **gender wall** blocking boys and girls from interacting is stronger than barriers to racial integration; there is more cross-race than cross-sex communication during the elementary school years. When Best asked students why there was not more friendship between boys and girls, they reacted with embarrassment. "Everyone would make fun of you," said one girl. Another commented,

> If you say you like someone, other kids spread it all over the school and that's embarrassing. . . . If you even sit beside a boy in class, other kids say you like him. And they come to you in the bathroom and tease you about liking the boy. Once some of the girls put J. S. and B. B. on the bathroom walls. That was embarrassing.[33]

Some public schools have simply given up trying to teach girls and boys in a caring coeducational climate, and established single sex schools and classes.[34] Rather than solve the relationship challenge, these schools have chosen to avoid it. This may

FIGURE 5.2

Sociogram: A teacher's tool.

Sociograms provide insights into the social life of a class. In this sociogram, circles represent students, and colors indicate gender. Lines are drawn connecting circles when students interact with one another. Each line reflects a verbal communication: the more lines, the greater number of interactions. In this sociogram it appears that Anne and Patrice are friends; Julia, Susan, and Joyce may form a clique; while Matthew and Claire appear to be isolates. Charting several sociograms of these children over time would confirm or refute these initial perceptions.

> **REFLECTION:** Construct your own sociogram, drawing a circle for each person in your class or in a class that you are observing, or even in a lunchroom or during recess. During a specific period of time, draw a line every time there is an interaction. Can you detect friends, cliques, and isolates? How does class seating impact relationships? What might you do as a teacher to influence these patterns?

not be the best long-term strategy for teaching girls and boys how to learn, and work, and live together.

Every day, teachers must work to create humane and caring classrooms.

"If you hate Graham, sign here." The petition was making the rounds in one fourth-grade classroom not long ago. Fortunately, the teacher intercepted the paper just before it reached Graham's desk. This time, at least, Graham was spared.[35]

In one sense, Graham is not alone. Many children share his predicament. When students respond to questions designed to measure their friendship patterns, 10 percent of them emerge as not being anybody's friend (isolates). About half of these are just ignored. The other half become the victims of active peer group rejection and hostility. In fact, elementary school sociometric measures predict social adjustment better than most other personality and educational tests do.[36] These social preferences can be graphically presented in **sociograms** (see Figure 5.2).

Most friendless children are aware of their problem and report feeling lonely and unsuccessful in relating to others. Children without friends are more likely to experience adjustment problems in later life. Rejection by the child's peer group is a strong indicator of future problems.

GUEST COLUMN: Haunted by Racist Attitudes

As graduation time approaches, I am supposed to get nostalgic about my community and my school. I should be thankful for how they have enriched my life, and I should expect to reminisce later on the "great things" about living here. Frankly, in my case, that will not be possible; I'll be trying to forget the bigotry here. Elementary school fostered my negative first impressions. One kid tried to insult me in the halls by calling me "African." My classmates told me to "go back where you came from." (Obviously they had no idea what country this was, but cultural education is another essay.) Often, I was used as an object in a "cooties" game. I was the contaminated one who had to touch all the other pure white-skinned kids. One day after school I was tied to a tree by some boys. The girls just stood around to laugh. They were the friendly ones because at least they did not inflict bodily pain. Wasn't I the naive buffoon to underestimate the burn of psychological humiliation?

Summer meant parks and recreation day camp, and that was hellish. Each day, I was de-pantsed by some fifth-grade boys in front of the amused campers. I was too embarrassed to tell my parents, and the counselors paid no attention to the foolish games all little boys play. Adult ignorance was by far the most agonizing injustice. In middle school, I sat in front of a boy who constantly whispered, "You f — nigger, black, disgusting" in my ear. Racism was intolerable. The teacher, I guess, disagreed. At least kids are honest. Isn't it amusing how they are little reflections of a community's attitudes? Today, the same people who tormented me as a child walk down the halls faceless. Once a racist reaches a certain age, he realizes that prejudice is not an outright verbal contract. It is subtle and "understood."

Just yesterday my five-year-old sister came home from her preschool and complained, "A girl said she didn't wanna play with me because I'm black." I said, "That's terrible! Did you tell the teacher?" My sister responded, "My teacher said, 'Just ignore her.'"

Yes, I'll have no trouble trying to forget this place.

Student letter to the school paper[37]

The elementary school culture is driven by blatant and subtle peer group dynamics. An insightful teacher can structure a classroom to minimize negative and hurtful interaction and maximize the positive power of peer group relations. For instance, eliminating social cliques and race- and gender-based segregation is a precursor to successful cooperative groups. An "intentional" teacher often assigns students to seats or to group work to counter pupil favoritism and bias. A teacher's perceptiveness and skill in influencing the social side of school can mean a world of difference in the student's environment.

 ## High School's Adolescent Society

Rock singer Frank Zappa said, "High school isn't a time and a place. It's a state of mind." Sociologist James Coleman says that high school is "the closest thing to a real social system that exists in our society, the closest thing to a **closed social system.**" Sociologist Edgar Friedenberg points out that most high schools are so insular that they have their own mechanism for telling time—not by the clock but by periods, as in "I'll meet you for lunch after fourth period." Author Kurt Vonnegut says that "high school is closer to the core of the American experience than anything else I can think of." In his inaugural speech before Congress, President Gerald Ford confided, "I'm here to confess that in my first campaign for president—at my senior class at South High School—I headed the Progressive party ticket and I lost. Maybe that's why I became a Republican." More than forty years later, Gerald Ford still remembered high school. No matter where we go or who we become, we can never entirely run away from high school. It is an experience indelibly imprinted on our mind.[38]

FOCUS QUESTION 7
In what ways does the adolescent culture shape teenage perceptions and behaviors?

INTERACTIVE ACTIVITY
How Cool Are You?
Test how much of today's slang you understand.

More than 13 million students arrive at twenty thousand public high schools every day. These schools run the gamut from decaying buildings plagued by vandalism and drugs to orderly, congenial places with educators who hold positive expectations and high standards for their students. They vary in size from fifty to five thousand students, who spend days divided into either six or seven 50-minute periods or perhaps fewer, longer blocks of time.

In his book *Is There Life After High School?* Ralph Keyes stirs up the pot of high school memories and draws a very lively picture of what life was like during that time and in that place and state of mind. In researching his book, he asked many people, both the famous and the obscure, about their high school experiences. He was amazed at the vividness and detail with which their memories came pouring out—particularly about the status system, that pattern of social reward and recognition that can be so intensely painful or exhilarating. High school was remembered as a caste system of "innies" and "outies," a minutely detailed social register in which one's popularity or lack of it was continually analyzed and contemplated. In **The Adolescent Society,** James Coleman notes that a high school "has little material reward to dispense, so that its system of reward is reflected almost directly in the distribution of status. Those who are popular hold the highest status."[39]

OVERHEAD 58
Middle Schoolers'
Self-Perception

In a major study conducted almost a quarter of a century after Coleman wrote *The Adolescent Society,* John Goodlad reached a similar conclusion; the junior and senior high school students he researched were preoccupied not with academics but, rather, with athletics, popularity, and physical appearance. Only 14 percent of the junior high and 7 percent of the senior high students said that "smart students were the most popular." Thirty-seven percent of the junior high students said that the "good-looking" students and 23 percent said the athletes were the most popular. (See Figure 5.3.) In senior high, 74 percent of the students said that the most popular kids were "good-looking" and "athletes."[40]

When junior and senior high school students were asked to identify the one best thing about their school, they usually said, "My friends." Sports activities ranked second. "Nothing" ranked higher than "classes I'm taking" and "teachers." In some secondary schools, peer group interests bubbled so close to the surface that they actually pushed attention to academic subjects aside and almost took over the classroom. When asked to describe her school, one high school junior said,

> The classes are okay, I guess. Most of the time I find them pretty boring, but then I suppose that's the way school classes are supposed to be. What I like most about the place is the chance to be with my friends. It's nice to be a part of a group. I don't mean one of the clubs or groups the school runs. They're for the grinds. But an informal group of your own friends is great.[41]

**CLASS ACTIVITY:
SCHOOL LIFE (IN THE
LUNCH ROOM)**
IM, Activity 5:3

Most informal groups are rigidly homogeneous, as becomes apparent in the seating arrangements of the secondary school cafeteria. A student in one high school described the cafeteria's social geography like this: "Behind you are the jocks; over on the side of the room are the greasers, and in front of you are the preppies—white preppies, black preppies, Chinese preppies, preppies of all kinds. The preppies are the in group this year; jocks of course are always in and greasers are always out."[42]

In some cases, entire sections of the school are staked out by special groups. In a suburban high school near Chicago, the vice principal easily identified the school's different cliques. The "scums" were the group of students who partied all the time and were rebelling against their parents. Next to the cafeteria was "Jock Hall," where the male athletes and their popular girlfriends could be found. Close to the library was the book foyer, where the bright kids got together.[43]

PERCENTAGE OF MIDDLE SCHOOLERS WHO . . .

Look forward to school — 74%

Say most people think they're cool — 57%

Think they are attractive — 54%

Don't feel like they fit in — 48%

Are not concerned about their appearance — 30%

FIGURE 5.3
Middle schoolers' self-perception.

SOURCE: Roper Youth Report, Question 22, Self-Perception, 1999.

REFLECTION: Why are peer group opinions such a powerful influence on how adolescents view themselves?

Perhaps high school students flock to others most like themselves because making their way in the adolescent society is so difficult. David Owen is an author who wanted to find out what life in high school was like in the 1980s. Although he had attended high school from 1969 to 1973, he returned undercover, almost a decade later. Posing as a student who had just moved into the area, he enrolled in what he calls a typical American high school, approximately two hours out of New York City. During his experience, he was struck by the power of the peer group and how socially ill at ease most adolescents are. He likened adolescents to adults who are visiting a foreign country and a strange culture. Experimenting with new behavior, they are terrified of being noticed doing something stupid:

> Relationships among teenagers are founded on awkwardness more than most of them realize. When a typical high school student looks around at his classmates, he sees little but coolness and confidence, people who fit in better than he does. That was certainly the way I thought of my old high school classmates much of the time; no matter how well adjusted I happened to feel at any particular moment, other people seemed to be

IN THE NEWS

Honors Bathroom

At Northgate High School near Pittsburgh, integrity and honesty pay off in unusual ways. Students who pledge not to smoke or damage the fixtures will be issued magnetized cards that admit them to an *honors bathroom.* Smoke free lavatories are predicted to be the in thing, according to senior Rob S. *Most kids will want to be there,* he says. *I don't think the honors bathroom kids will be nerds.*

SOURCE: *Newsweek,* October 19, 1998.

 What's new in education? Click on *News Feeds.*

doing better. At Bingham, though, I saw another picture. Everyone seemed so shy. The kids hadn't learned the nearly unconscious social habits that adults use constantly to ease their way through the world. When kids bumped into each other in the halls, they almost never uttered the little automatic apologies—"Oops," "Sorry"—that adults use all the time. They just kept plowing right ahead, pretending they hadn't noticed. One day, when I was hurrying to my history class, I realized I was on a direct collision course with a girl coming the other way. Each of us made a little sidestep, but in the same direction. Just before we bumped, an expression of absolute horror spread across the girl's face. She looked as though she were staring down the barrel of a gun. The bubble of coolness had been burst. She probably brooded about it for the rest of the day. . . . Being an adolescent is a full-time job, an all-out war against the appearance of awkwardness. No one is more attentive to nuance than a seventeen-year-old. . . . When a kid in my class came to school one day in a funny-looking pair of shoes that one of his friends eventually laughed at, I could see by his face that he was thinking, "Well, that does it, there goes the rest of my life."[44]

INTERACTIVE ACTIVITY
The Popular Crowd?
Match celebrities with their high school profiles.

RAP 2.9
Reflections of a High School Yearbook, 2:9, p. 280

RELATED READING
Our Guys: The Glen Ridge Rape and the Secret Life of the Perfect Suburb by Bernard Lefkowitz. (1998).

The memory of high school rejection is powerful, even for generations of the rich and famous. Actress Mia Farrow recalls a high school dance at which every girl was on the dance floor except her. Cartoonist Charles Schulz never forgot the day the yearbook staff rejected his cartoon, and actress Eva Marie Saint recalls the time she did not get a part in the class play. No matter where we were in the high school system, few of us have egos so strong or skins so tough that we fail to get a psychological lift when we learn that beautiful actress Ali McGraw never had a date during high school, that actor Gregory Peck was regarded as least likely to succeed, that singer John Denver was called "four-eyes," or that no one wanted to eat lunch with former Secretary of State Henry Kissinger.[45]

For those who remember jockeying unsuccessfully for a place within the inner circle of the high school social register, it may be comforting to learn that the tables do turn. No study shows any correlation between high status in high school and later achievement as an adult. Those who are voted king and queen of the prom or most likely to succeed do not appear to do any better or any worse in adult life than those whose yearbook description is less illustrious. What works in that very insular adolescent environment is not necessarily what works in the outside world. One researcher speculates that it is those on the "second tier," those in the group just below the top, who are most likely to succeed after high school. He says, "I think the rest of our lives are spent making up for what we did or did not do in high school."[46]

Most students know the feeling of being judged and found wanting by high school peers, and some spend the rest of their lives trying to compensate or get even. Comedian Mel Brooks sums it up well:

> Thank God for the athletes and their rejection. Without them there would have been no emotional need and . . . I'd be a crackerjack salesman in the garment district.[47]

For some students, the impact of rejection does not lead to such positive outcomes. These students struggle to break through clique walls that are invisible but impervious. As one student stated: "I've never really been part of any group. I suppose I don't have anything to offer."[48]

Being part of a group continues to be a challenge for today's adolescents. While historically, entire communities participated in child care, and extended families guided and monitored children, today this social fabric of adult supervision has disappeared. With increased mobility, the generations have been separated, and traditional child care is gone. Two-parent wage earners provide less supervision, and the absence of widespread quality day care has added to the stress of growing up in America. These societal shifts demand a restructuring of the nation's approach to raising children—but that has not happened. In this social vacuum adolescents have created their own, separate culture.

In *A Tribe Apart: A Journey Into the Heart of American Adolescence* (1999), Patricia Hersch shares the story of three years she spent with seventh through twelfth graders in suburban Reston, Virginia.[49] What Hersch discovered was troubling: the development of a more isolated, intense, and perilous adolescent culture, where drugs, alienation, and violence represent ongoing threats. It is a teenage society unknown to many parents. Today's teenagers are less likely to form the tight teenage cliques that adults remember from their own childhood. Contemporary adolescent friendships appear to be more fluid: teenagers may have one group of friends in a drama club, another from math class, and a third set from sports activities. Today cross-gender friendships are also more common as boys and girls do a better job of developing relationships without the need for a romantic attachment.

But even as the number of friendships grows, the quality of adolescent relationships remains a problem (Figure 5.4). Today's teenagers, both girls and boys, report that although they have many friends, they lack intimate, close friends. Teenagers say that there is no one that they can really confide in, no one with whom to share their deepest thoughts. In the midst of a crowd, they feel alone. It is a disturbing admission, and some educators believe that schools can and should do something about it.

The Affective Side of School Reform

The message to children in this period of standards, testing, and competition, is that the school is a place of academics, and that the non-academic needs of students receive low priority. Students get this message. Students report that when they are feeling sad or depressed, overwhelmingly they turn for help to friends (77 percent) or

FIGURE 5.4
Adolescent angst
(What teens say).

SOURCE: *Are We Preparing
Students for the 21st Century?
Metropolitan Life Survey of The
American Teacher* (2000), p. 46

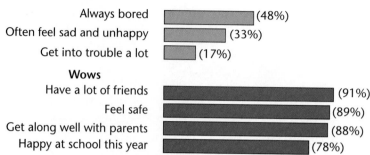

ADOLESCENT ANGST (WHAT TEENS SAY)

Woes

Always bored	(48%)
Often feel sad and unhappy	(33%)
Get into trouble a lot	(17%)

Wows

Have a lot of friends	(91%)
Feel safe	(89%)
Get along well with parents	(88%)
Happy at school this year	(78%)

REFLECTION: Where would you be on this graph? Why the contradiction between the high number of negatives and positives? How can you organize your class so that more students are actively and happily involved in learning?

family (63 percent); far less frequently do they seek out educators (33 percent).[50] Yet many teachers despair over the unmet **affective student needs** of today's children.[51] As a kindergarten teacher from an urban school system points out,

VIDEO SEGMENT 12
Teaching: It's Not All
Academic

> The difficult part of teaching is not the academics. The difficult part is dealing with the great numbers of kids who come from emotionally, physically, socially, and financially stressed homes. Nearly all of my kindergarten kids come from single-parent families. Most of the moms really care for their kids but are young, uneducated, and financially strained. Children who have had no breakfast, or who are fearful of what their mom's boyfriend will do to them—or their moms—are not very good listeners or cooperative partners with their teachers or their peers. We are raising a generation of emotionally stunted and troubled youth who will in turn raise a generation of the same. What is the future of this country when we have so many needy youngsters?[52]

RELATED READING
*Everyday Courage:
The Lives and Stories of
Urban Teenagers* by
Niobe Way (1998).

Those who teach in urban settings warn us that the future of poor and minority children is at risk. But all is not well in suburbia, either. Consider this comment from a teacher in suburban New Jersey: "In the large, efficient suburb where I teach the pressure is on kids from kindergarten to high school to get good grades, bring up the test scores, and be the best on the test."[53] Another teacher says that there is such pressure to get high test scores that students are rushed from one workbook to another. There is no time for anything not directly related to cognitive achievement. "We feel guilty," she says, "doing an art lesson or having a wonderful discussion."[54]

In another study, **Frances Ianni** describes the affluent lifestyle in the suburb of Sheffield (name fictitious), a place where families keep well-manicured lawns and push their children to succeed. Students are groomed to be good at everything—athletics, social skills, academic achievement. "People in Sheffield will tell you," Ianni says, "that the two things you never ask at a cocktail party are a family's income and the Scholastic Assessment Test scores of their children."[55] Virginia English teacher Patrick Welsh tells of teenagers who take the SATs four or five times, pushed on by their parents' promises of new cars if they score well:

I've had kids in class with their fingernails bitten to the quick and looking miserable, feeling they have to get As, and their parents going to the point of rewriting their papers for them. Every fall T.C. is gripped by "Ivy League Fever." Sweatshirts marked "Harvard" or "Princeton" start appearing. . . . I got so fed up, that one day in class I horrified everybody by saying I have yet to see anybody wearing an Ivy League sweatshirt get into an Ivy League school. The sweatshirts went back to the drawer after that.[56]

Pushed beyond their abilities and alienated from family, friends, and community, some teenagers develop a "delusion of uniqueness," a sense that "no one knows how I feel, no one else faces these problems, no one cares about me." When children feel cut off from what Urie Bronfenbrenner calls "the four worlds of childhood"—family, friends, school, and work—the situation can become serious and even life-threatening.[57] Sara Lawrence Lightfoot describes the following incident that took place in an elite school in a wealthy suburb in the Midwest:

A student with a history of depression . . . had been seeing a local psychiatrist for several years. For the last few months, however, she had discontinued her psychotherapy and seemed to be showing steady improvement. Since September, her life had been invigorated by her work on *Godspell*—a student production that consumed her energies and provided her with an instant group of friends. After *Godspell,* her spirits and enthusiasm declined noticeably. In her distress, she reached out to a teacher who had given her special tutorial support in the past, and the school machinery was set in motion. A meeting was scheduled for the following day to review her case. That night, after a visit to her psychiatrist, she killed herself.

The day after, the school buzzed with rumors as students passed on the gruesome news—their faces showing fear and intrigue. . . . But I heard only one teacher speak of it openly and explicitly in class—the drama teacher who had produced *Godspell.* Her words brought tears and looks of terror in the eyes of her students.

"We've lost a student today who was with us yesterday. We've got to decide where our priorities are. How important are your gold chains, your pretty clothes, your cars? . . . Where were we when she needed us? Foolish old woman that I am, I ask you this because I respect you. . . . While you still feel, damn it, feel . . . reach out to each other."[58]

This "reaching out" is what Ianni recommends in her **youth charter** network. "Communities," she says, "can create youth charters that encourage youngsters to move from dependence to independence, from the ethnocentrism of early adolescence to the social competence of young adulthood." She urges the community to move from benign neglect or outrage at the young to an organized system of positive involvement and guidance.[59] Many other child advocates are calling for a coordinated system of school-based social services to replace the existing maze of bureaucratic agencies.[60]

CLASS ACTIVITY: SCHOOL'S SOCIAL SYSTEM
IM, Activity 5:4

Alfie Kohn is one educator who claims that the social and affective sides of school must become an explicit part of the formal curriculum: "It is possible to integrate prosocial lessons into the regular curriculum. . . . Indeed to study literature or history by grappling with moral or social dilemmas is to invite a deeper engagement with these subjects." According to Kohn, such schools as the California-based Child Development Project, a long-term effort in prosocial education, teach children to take responsibility and care for one another.[61]

While most reform reports emphasize increased academic achievement, only a few recognize the social and emotional needs of children. The Carnegie Council on Adolescent Development report, ***Turning Points: Preparing American Youth for the 21st Century,*** warned that one in four adolescents were in serious jeopardy. Their basic human needs—caring relationships with adults, guidance in facing sometimes overwhelming biological and psychological changes, the security of belonging to constructive peer groups, and the perception of future opportunity—went unmet at this critical stage of life. Millions of these young adolescents will never reach their full potential.[62] Pointing to a society dangerous to adolescent health—one of drug abuse, poor school performance, alienation, and sexual promiscuity—the report called for comprehensive middle school reform to help protect these youngsters.

> Middle-grade schools—junior high, intermediate or middle schools—are potentially society's most powerful force to recapture millions of youth adrift. Yet all too often they exacerbate the problems youth face. A volatile mismatch exists between the organization and curriculum of middle-grade schools and the intellectual, emotional, and interpersonal needs of young adolescents.[63]

VIDEO SEGMENT 13
Immigrant Students

Describing the trauma students face when they shift from a neighborhood elementary school, where they spent most of the school day with one or two teachers who knew them well, to a larger, colder institution, where they move through six or seven different classes daily, the Carnegie report made the following recommendations:

- Divide large schools into smaller "communities" for learning.
- Create a core curriculum.
- Eliminate tracking.
- Emphasize cooperative learning.
- Develop stronger partnerships between schools and communities.
- Assign teams of teachers and students, with an adult adviser for each student.
- Emphasize the link between education and good health.
- Strengthen teacher preparation for dealing with the adolescent age group.

CRITICAL THINKING
QUESTION
Can students envision a
school that works?
Reflective thinkers suggest
that if we cannot create a
clear image, we will not be
able to realize the
recommendations.

Imagine life in a school that implements these recommendations. You would see a smaller middle school or high school, one emphasizing community activities and moving away from an atmosphere that produces "large-school alienation." Health issues would become more central, linking diet and exercise more directly to education, enhancing the longevity and quality of students' lives well into adulthood. But, to create such a caring and healthful school, teacher education itself would need to be changed. As you examine your own teacher education program, can you identify ways that these recommendations are being promoted? How does your teacher education program prepare you to develop school-community partnerships, promote cooperative learning, and respond more effectively to the needs of adolescents? Significant changes in many teacher education programs across the nation will need to be made if the recommendations of the Carnegie report are to be implemented.

 ## What Makes a School Effective?

FOCUS QUESTION 9
What are the characteristics
of effective schools?

The Carnegie Council's *Turning Points* recommendations were designed to create more sensitive and humane school climates. While some educators continue to be concerned with the personal, social, and psychological world of children, in recent years, the press, public and politicians have focused almost exclusively on standards, test scores and replacing curricular choices with required courses. While we believe you should become familiar with the current research on effective schools, we want to share our concerns as well. We are not comfortable with the current push toward more tests and increased academic stress. We believe that the current movement takes too narrow a view of education, overlooking students' personal needs and individual differences and strengths. We lament that loss. There are many exciting ways to view and measure school life, but too often these days, it comes down to test scores. As we review the salient issues in school effectiveness studies, let's keep in mind that these studies often emphasize academics to the exclusion of other important aspects of a child's life.[64]

The challenge facing teachers and school administrators in the years ahead may well be the thoughtful integration of the research on effective schools and effective teaching with the research on the social and psychological needs of children. How can we improve schools so that they enhance both psychological well-being and academic success? This will not be easy.

Consider the following situation: Two schools are located in the same neighborhood. They are approximately the same size, and the student populations they serve are similar in all characteristics, including socioeconomic level, racial, and gender composition, achievement scores on school entry, and parental education and occupation. However, in one school, the students have high dropout rates and low scores on national achievement tests. In the other school, the students' test scores are at or above the national average, and the students are more likely to stay in school. Why should such differences emerge?

Puzzled by situations such as this, researchers attempted to determine what factors have made some schools more effective in encouraging student achievement. As early as 1971, George Weber studied four schools that seemed successful in teaching reading.[65] Through research such as his, the more effective schools have been identified as those in which achievement, especially for students of color and of poverty, is at a uniformly successful level of mastery. One of the best-known studies, conducted by Ronald Edmonds and his colleagues, concluded that, in an effective school, students with a working-class background score as high as middle-class students on tests of basic skills.[66] Other groups around the country, from the Connecticut School Effectiveness Project to the Alaska Effective Schooling program, have conducted research to figure out what makes good schools work. In study after study, researchers have found a common set of characteristics, which has resulted in a **five-factor theory of effective schools.**[67] Researchers say that effective schools are able, by means of the five characteristics, to reduce the harmful effects of poor socioeconomic background. Let's start with these classic five factors, and then move on to some more recent studies.

Factor 1: Strong Leadership

In her book ***The Good High School,*** Sara Lawrence Lightfoot drew portraits of six effective schools.[68] Two, George Washington Carver High School in Atlanta and John F. Kennedy High School in the Bronx, were inner-city schools. Highland Park High School near Chicago and Brookline High School in Brookline, Massachusetts, were upper middle-class and suburban. St. Paul's High School in Concord, New Hampshire, and Milton Academy near Boston were elite preparatory schools. Despite the tremendous difference in the styles and textures of these six schools, ranging from the pastoral setting of St. Paul's to inner-city Atlanta, they all were characterized by strong, inspired leaders, such as Robert Mastruzzi, principal of John F. Kennedy High School.

When Robert Mastruzzi started working at Kennedy, the building was not yet completed. Walls were being built around him as he sat in his unfinished office and contemplated the challenge of not only his first principalship but also the opening of

INTERACTIVE ACTIVITY
What Makes Schools Effective? Rate what you think makes schools effective. Compare your responses to those of your colleagues.

OVERHEAD 60
Factors Supporting Effective Schools

TEACHING TIP
The need for new school site administrators is increasing. Do any of your students intend to become principals? What factors encourage and discourage them?

a new school. During his years as principal of John F. Kennedy, his leadership style has been collaborative, actively seeking faculty participation. Not only does he want his staff to participate in decision making, but he gives them the opportunity to try new things—and even the right to fail. For example, one teacher made an error about the precautions necessary for holding a rock concert (800 adolescents had shown up, many high or inebriated). Mastruzzi realized that the teacher had learned a great deal from the experience, and he let her try again. The second concert was a great success. "He sees failure as an opportunity for change," the teacher said. Still other teachers describe him with superlatives, such as "he is the lifeblood of this organism" and "the greatest human being I have ever known."[69]

Mastruzzi seems to embody the characteristics of effective leaders in good schools. Researchers say that students make significant achievement gains in schools in which principals

- Articulate a clear school mission
- Are a visible presence in classrooms and hallways
- Hold high expectations for teachers and students
- Spend a major portion of the day working with teachers to improve instruction
- Are actively involved in diagnosing instructional problems
- Create a positive school climate[70]

Factor 2: A Clear School Mission

MULTIPLE INTELLIGENCE CONNECTION
Focusing on the characteristics of strong leadership, have students develop a classified ad for a new school principal.

A day in the life of a principal can be spent trying to keep small incidents from becoming major crises. But the research is clear: In effective schools, good principals somehow find time to develop a vision of what that school should be and to share that vision with all members of the educational community. Successful principals can articulate a specific school mission, and they stress innovation and improvement. In contrast, less effective principals are vague about their goals and focus on maintaining the status quo. They make such comments as, "We have a good school and a good faculty, and I want to keep it that way."[71]

It is essential that the principal share his or her vision, so that teachers understand the school's goals and all work together for achievement. Unfortunately, when teachers are polled, more than 75 percent say that they have either no contact or infrequent contact with one another during the school day. In less effective schools, teachers lack a common understanding of the school's mission, and they function as individuals charting their own separate courses.

The need for the principal to share his or her vision extends not only to teachers but to parents as well. When teachers work cooperatively and parents are connected with the school's mission, the children are more likely to achieve academic success.

Factor 3: A Safe and Orderly Climate

OVERHEADS 61–62
School Related Violence

Factors Responsible for School Safety

Certainly before students can learn or teachers can teach, schools must be safe. An unsafe school is, by definition, ineffective. Despite the attention-grabbing headlines and the disturbing incidents of student shootings, schools today are safer than they have been in years.[72] (See Figure 5.5.) Nearly all public school teachers (98 percent) and most students (93 percent) report feeling safe in schools.[73] Yet the image of unsafe schools persists, and for more than two decades, opinion polls have shown that

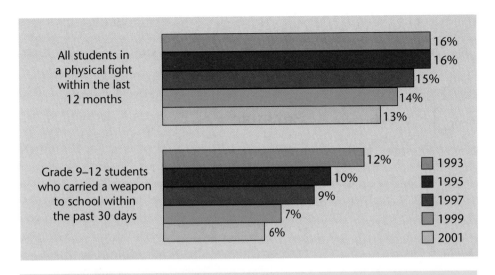

FIGURE 5.5
School-related violence:
On the decrease

SOURCE: U.S. Department of
Health and Human Services,
Public Health Service, Centers for
Disease Control and Prevention,
National Center for Health
Statistics. National Health
Interview Survey—Youth Risk
Behavior Survey, 1993, 1995, 1997,
1999, and 2001.

REFLECTION: How do you explain the popular perception of a more violent society contrasted with these statistics reflecting a decrease in school violence?

the public considers lack of discipline to be among the most serious problems facing schools.[74]

The vast majority of schools provide safe learning environments. This is accomplished by more than metal detectors and school guards. Safe schools focus on academic achievement, the school mission, involving families and communities in school activities, and creating an environment where teachers, students and staff are treated with respect. Student problems are identified early, before they deteriorate into violence. School psychologists, special education programs, family social workers, and schoolwide programs increase communication and reduce school tension.

GLOBAL VIEW
Compared to children in 25 other industrialized countries combined, U.S. children under age 15 are: 12 times more likely to die from gunfire; 16 times more likely to be murdered by a gun; 11 times more likely to commit suicide with a gun; 9 times more likely to die in a firearm accident. [Children's Defense Fund (2001) www.childrensdefense.org/ factsfigures_america.htm]

A positive, energizing school atmosphere characterized by accepting relationships between students and faculty often begins and ends with the principal.

A Major Part of a Student's Life Because . . .

THERE IS TOO MUCH MATERIAL TO BE MASTERED ONLY DURING SCHOOL TIME

Given demands on students to learn more and to increase their test scores, much study and learning needs to take place at home. After all, students are in school for just five hours of a 24-hour day.

IT BRINGS PARENTS INTO THE LEARNING PROCESS

School cannot accomplish its goals alone. Students achieve much more when academics are reinforced at home. By providing guidance and monitoring homework, parents demonstrate their support of learning, becoming true partners with teachers. Closing the school-home gap fosters competent and attentive students.

MANY STUDENTS DO NOT USE THEIR TIME WISELY

The average student comes home from school, talks on the phone with friends, "hangs out" at the mall, watches television for hours, and then plays a computer game or two before going to bed. Homework at least gives students something meaningful to do with their time.

Limited and Brief Because . . .

TOO MUCH STRESS IS PLACED ON STUDENTS AS IT IS

Schools have been taken over by this growing obsession with tests. The last thing we need to do is extend this angst to home life. Besides, homework is mostly busywork, unrelated to real learning.

IT FAVORS SOME STUDENTS AND PENALIZES OTHERS

Some children have highly educated parents, home computers, and the resources needed to produce quality homework. Other students have poor and uneducated parents, who may not even speak English, and who may be working two or more jobs. All too often homework is simply a measure of family resources.

MANY STUDENTS DO NOT HAVE THE LUXURY OF EXTRA TIME

Many students go directly from school to their part-time job. Their families may need the money. Other students must care for younger siblings at home while parents are at work. Increasing homework would place an enormous burden on these families.

 YOU BE THE JUDGE

Will you be assigning homework? If so, how much do you think is appropriate, and how will homework factor into your assessment of student work? Do you have a plan to handle differences in family resources?

In some of America's most distressed neighborhoods, safe schools provide a much needed neighborhood refuge. Sara Lawrence Lightfoot tells of the long distances that urban students travel to reach John F. Kennedy High School in the Bronx. One girl, who did not have money to buy a winter coat or glasses to see the chalkboard, rode the subway 1 hour and 40 minutes each way to get to school. She never missed a day, because for her school was a refuge—a place of hope where she could learn in safety.[75]

Factor 4: Monitoring Student Progress

As the researcher walked through the halls of a school we will call Clearview Elementary School, she noted attractive displays of student work mounted on bulletin boards and walls. Also posted were profiles clearly documenting class and school progress toward meeting academic goals. Students had a clear sense of how they were doing in their studies; they kept progress charts in their notebooks. During teacher interviews, the faculty talked about the individual strengths and weaknesses of their students. Teachers referred to student folders that contained thorough records of student scores on standardized tests, as well as samples of classwork, homework, and performance on weekly tests.

A visit to Foggy Bottom Elementary, another fictitious school with a revealing name, disclosed striking differences. Bulletin boards and walls were attractive, but few student papers were posted, and there was no charting of progress toward academic goals. Interviews with students showed that they had only a vague idea of how they were doing and of ways to improve their academic performance. Teachers also seemed unclear about individual student progress. When pressed for more information, one teacher sent the researcher to the guidance office, saying, "I think they keep some records like the California Achievement Tests. Maybe they can give you what you're looking for."

Following the visit, the researcher wrote her report: "A very likely reason that Clearview students achieve more than Foggy Bottom students is that one school carefully monitors student progress and communicates this information to students and parents. The other school does not."

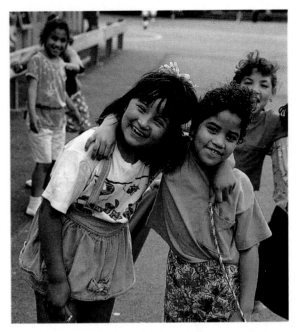

Good schools have safe environments.

Effective schools carefully monitor and assess student progress in a variety of ways:

- **Norm-referenced tests** compare individual students with others in a nationwide norm group (e.g., the SAT or ACT).
- **Objective-referenced tests** measure whether a student has mastered a designated body of knowledge (e.g., state assessment tests used to determine who has "mastered" the material).

Other measures may be less formal. Teacher-made tests are an important (and often overlooked) measure of student progress. Some teachers ask students to track their own progress in reaching course objectives as a way of helping them assume more responsibility for their own learning.[76] Homework is another strategy to monitor students. Researcher Herbert Walberg and colleagues found that homework increases student achievement scores from the 50th to the 60th percentile. When homework is graded and commented on, achievement is increased from the 50th to nearly the 80th percentile. Although these findings suggest that graded homework is an important ingredient in student achievement,[77] how much homework to assign, and what kinds of homework tasks are most effective, continue to be points of contention. (See the *You Be the Judge* feature in this chapter.)

Factor 5: High Expectations

The teachers were excited. A group of their students had received extraordinary scores on a test that predicted intellectual achievement during the coming year. Just as the teachers had expected, these children attained outstanding academic gains that year.

Now for the rest of the story: The teachers had been duped. The students identified as gifted had been selected at random. However, eight months later, these randomly

1800–1900	Memorization is the mark of an educated person, and homework consumes many hours
1900–1940	Homework is considered a form of child labor, and a health risk; memorization and homework are de-emphasized
1940–1957	Creative, individualized assignments usher in a more humane return to homework
1957–1967	The launch of *Sputnik* sparks increased homework, especially in math and science
1968–1982	Social concerns and civil rights take precedence over academics and homework
1982–present	*A Nation at Risk* reports that homework is an effective counter to falling test scores, and homework increases dramatically, despite the concern of many parents

SOURCE: Laurel Graeber, "More Work, Less Play," in Education Life, *The New York Times*, January 3, 1999.

REFLECTION: Where do you predict the homework pendulum will be during your time in the classroom? Do you have a preference?

selected children did show significantly greater gains in total IQ than did another group of children, the control group.

In their highly influential 1969 publication, ***Pygmalion in the Classroom,*** researchers **Robert Rosenthal** and **Lenore Jacobson** discussed this experiment and the power of teacher expectations in shaping student achievement. They popularized the term **self-fulfilling prophecy** and revealed that students may learn as much—or as little—as teachers expect.[78] Although methodological criticisms of the original Rosenthal and Jacobson study abound, those who report on effective schools say that there is now extensive evidence showing that high teacher expectations do, in fact, produce high student achievement, and low expectations produce low achievement.[79]

Too often, teacher expectations have a negative impact. An inaccurate judgment about a student can be made because of error, unconscious prejudice, or stereotype. For example, good-looking, well-dressed students are frequently thought to be smarter than their less attractive peers. Often, male students are thought to be brighter in math, science, and technology, while girls are given the edge in language skills. Students of color are sometimes perceived as less capable or intelligent. A poor performance on a single standardized test (perhaps due to illness or an "off" day) can cause teachers to hold an inaccurate assessment of a student's ability for months and even years. Even a casual comment in the teachers' lounge can shape the expectations of other teachers.

When teachers hold low expectations for certain students, their treatment of these students often differs in unconscious and subtle ways. Typically, they offer such students

- Fewer opportunities to respond
- Less praise
- Less challenging work
- Fewer nonverbal signs (eye contact, smiles, positive regard)

In effective schools, teachers hold high expectations that students can learn, and they translate these expectations into teaching behaviors. They set objectives, work toward mastery of those objectives, spend more time on instruction, and actively monitor student progress. They are convinced that students can succeed.

Do high expectations work if students do not believe they exist? Probably not, and that is too often the case. While a majority of secondary school principals believe that their schools hold such expectations for their students, only 39 percent of teachers believe this to be true, and even more discouraging, only one in four students believe their school holds high expectations for them.[80] We need to do a better job of communicating these expectations to students, and making certain that these expectations truly challenge students.

And it is not only students who benefit from high expectations. In *The Good High School*, Sara Lawrence Lightfoot reported that when teachers hold high expectations for their own performance, the entire school benefits. At Brookline High School, "star" teachers were viewed as models to be emulated. Always striving for excellence, these teachers felt that no matter how well a class was taught, next time it could be taught better.

A Note of Caution on Effective Schools Research

Although the research on what makes schools effective has had a direct impact on national reform movements, it has limitations.[81] First, there is disagreement over the definition of an effective school. Researchers use varying descriptions, ranging from "schools with high academic achievement" to schools that foster "personal growth, creativity, and positive self-concept." Although the five factors we have described are helpful, they do not really provide a prescription for developing successful schools.

Another problem is that much of the research has been conducted in elementary schools. Although some researchers suggest applicability to secondary and even higher education, caution must be used in carrying the effective-schools findings to higher levels of education. The generalizability of the research is also limited, since several of the studies were conducted in inner-city schools and tied closely to the achievement of lower-order skills in math and science. If one wanted to develop a school that nurtures creativity rather than basic skills, another set of characteristics might be more appropriate.

OVERHEAD 63
Student Observations of Effective School Practices

RAP 2.7
Effective Schools, p. 278

CLASS ACTIVITIES
Field Observation: Effective Schools
IM, Activity 5:6
Building an Effective School
IM, Activity 5:7

IN THE NEWS

School Uniforms and School Safety

In 1994, Long Beach, California became the first school district to require school uniforms for elementary and middle school students. Eagle Pass, Texas did them one better, requiring such uniforms for high schoolers as well. Baltimore, Chicago, Miami and Phoenix now allow individual schools to require uniforms. Why this growing popularity? Many parents and educators believe that a connection exists between safety and dress. Long Beach educators assert that gang clothing and designer sports clothes led to violence, fights, and overall delinquency. After the school uniform policy was initiated, school crime dropped by 76 percent, assaults dropped by 85 percent, and weapons offenses dropped by 83 percent. Meanwhile, attendance figures hit 94 percent, an all-time high. Parents supported the change, reporting that uniforms save them both money and time.

But not everyone agrees that uniforms are the reason for these encouraging figures. Critics indicate that dropping crime figures nationally are at least partially responsible for these positive changes. Educator Ray Rist believes that treating students in a special way affects their behavior. He believes it is not the uniforms, but the special attention that they are receiving that is responsible for the improved behavior. While some students like the uniform requirements, others do not. *I think it's stupid,* says ninth grader Jamie P., *What does school have to do with uniforms?*

SOURCE: *Teacher Magazine on the Web,* March 1998.

 What's new in education? Click on *News Feeds.*

Many schools, public and private, have opted for official uniforms. Even when dress remains a student choice, peer pressure may create "unofficial" uniforms. Based on the appearance of these students, what assumptions might you make about their schools?

It is more difficult to find a teaching position in Connecticut than in most places. Tough standards include entrance exams and video "shakedown" exercises, all designed to select the best teachers for Connecticut's classes. And this may be one important reason why the state's students are doing so well. Connecticut ranks first on several critical measures of student performance. While many credit Connecticut's academic success to its wealth and high level of parent education, student scores have been on the rise, while state wealth and parental education remain unchanged. So what's happening in Connecticut?

Many attribute Connecticut's success to the years of effort improving many of the school effectiveness factors discussed in this chapter: high expectations, hard work, high standards, close monitoring of student progress, and a string of talented educational leaders.

For the classroom teacher, the state's commitment is evident. Each new teacher is assigned a mentor, and then undergoes continual testing. If a problem is uncovered, in a classroom or a school, extra resources are devoted to remedy it. Rather than threaten to withhold diplomas from students or punish teachers in "failing schools," the state provides additional help for students and teachers. Teachers also get the message when their salary checks arrive: Connecticut pays the highest teacher salaries in the nation.

SOURCE: Jay Mathews, "Connecticut's Education Success Story," *The Washington Post,* July 18, 2000, p. A11; National Center for Educational Statistics.

REFLECTION: Before you run off to apply for a teaching job in Connecticut, tell us what factors would draw you to that state, and what might keep you away. While all this sounds grand, Connecticut's test scores are still being used to measure school effectiveness. Can you create your own nontest indicators of school effectiveness? How do you explain the public's fixation on test scores?

Beyond Five Factors

OVERHEAD 64
Beyond the Five Factors
Practices

New effective-schools findings offer us insights beyond these original five factors of effective schooling:

- *Early start.* The concept that there is a particular age for children to begin school needs to be rethought. The earlier schools start working with children, the better children do. High-quality programs during the first three years of life include parent training, special screening services, and appropriate learning opportunities for children. While such programs are rare, those that are in operation have significantly raised IQ points and have enhanced language skills. It is estimated that $1 spent in an early intervention program saves school districts $7 in special programs and services later in life.

- *Focus on reading and math.* Children not reading at grade level by the end of the first grade face a one-in-eight chance of ever catching up. In math, students who do not master basic concepts find themselves playing catch-up throughout their school years. Effective schools identify and correct such deficiencies early, before student performance deteriorates.

- *Smaller schools.* Students in small schools learn more, are more likely to pass their courses, are less prone to resort to violence, and are more likely to attend college than those attending large schools. Disadvantaged students in small schools outperform their peers in larger schools, as achievement

IN THE NEWS

The Expectation Gap

Sixty percent of middle and high school students believe that they will achieve their life goals, but only 19 percent of their teachers agree. Almost three out of four students believe that they will go to college, while their teachers believe that fewer than one in three will make it.

SOURCE: "Extra Credit," *The Washington Post,* October 10, 2000, p. A11.

What's new in education? Click on *News Feeds.*

differences for the rich and poor are less extreme. Many large schools have responded to these findings by reorganizing themselves into smaller units, into schools within schools. Research suggests that small schools are more effective at every educational level, but they may be most important for older students.

- *Smaller classes.* Although the research on class size is less powerful than the research on school size, studies indicate that smaller classes are associated with increased student learning, especially in the earlier grades. Children in classes of fifteen outperform students in classes of twenty-five, even when the larger classes have a teacher's aide present.

- *Increased learning time.* While not an amazing insight, research tells us what we already suspect: more study results in more learning. Longer school days, longer school years, more efficient use of school time, and more graded homework are all proven methods of enhancing academic learning time and student performance.

- *Assessment.* Investing time is useful, but assessing how effectively the time is spent is also important. Testing student performance has been tied to greater achievement, and some districts have gone so far as to pay teachers incentives for improvements in student test scores.

- *Teacher training.* Researcher Linda Darling-Hammond reports that the best way to improve school effectiveness is by investing in teacher training. Stronger teacher skills and qualifications lead to greater student learning. Conversely, students pay an academic price when they are taught by unqualified and uncertified teachers.

- *Trust.* Trusting relationships among parents, students, principals and teachers is a necessary ingredient to govern, improve, and reform schools. As trust levels increase, so does academic performance.

- *And what about technology?* School districts that are hesitant to spend funds on teacher training, class size reductions, or early childhood education programs nevertheless are quick to invest significant sums in computers and upgraded technology. Research says very little about the impact of technology on school effectiveness and student performance. Studies are few, sometimes contradictory, and long-term results are still unknown. It is a sad commentary that the glamour of cyberspace is more persuasive than decades of research.[82]

SUMMARY

1. **What rituals and routines shape classroom life?**

   Although teachers are enormously busy in the classroom, students spend much of their time sitting still and waiting, denying their needs, and becoming distracted.

2. **How is class time related to student achievement?**

   John Goodlad and others have documented that while some teachers use instructional time efficiently, others are sidetracked by behavioral problems and administrative routine. Efficient teachers advance student learning.

3. **How does the teacher's gatekeeping function influence classroom roles?**

   Ned Flanders found that two-thirds of the classroom time is talk; two-thirds of that talk is from the teacher. Teachers also initiate about 85 percent of Bellack's "pedagogical cycles,"

 CHAPTER REVIEW

Go to the Online Learning Center to take a chapter self-quiz, practice with key terms, and review concepts from the chapter.

CURRENT NEWS FROM POWERWEB

To access PowerWeb, go to Chapter 5 on the Online Learning Center to read current articles and to access news feeds about:

- Academic Performance
- Aims of Education
- Classroom Climate
- Education Reform
- Excellence and Education
- High School
- Schools

although the majority of questions they ask require only rote memory. Ironically, while a major goal of education is to increase students' curiosity, it is the teachers, not the students, who are the gatekeepers of what will be learned and which students will be allowed to actively participate.

4. What is tracking, and what are its advantages and disadvantages?

The practice of placing students into a specific class based on ability is called tracking. Jeannie Oakes found that a disproportionate number of poor children and students of color are labeled as slow learners, even when their achievement levels are strong. Students tracked into slower classes have weaker teachers, fewer opportunities, lower self-esteem and achievement. Yet many educators and parents believe that heterogeneous classes are also problematic, and some type of ability grouping is needed.

5. Why has "detracking" become a popular movement?

Supporters of detracking call for more individualization of instruction, more authentic learning, and less reliance on a "one size fits all" view of teaching. By 2000, only a small number of schools continued to use the term "tracking," although many continued the practice under terms such as "ability grouping."

6. How do peer groups impact elementary school life?

Peer pressure wields great power in and out of school. A gender wall rigidly segregates young children, with boys forming hierarchic societies and girls creating pairs of best friends. Compared to children in the early 1980s, in the late 1990s, elementary children spent more time in day care, in school, studying, reading, playing sports, and involved in personal care, while spending less time watching television, enjoying leisure time, or in religious activities.

7. In what ways does the adolescent culture shape teenage perceptions and behaviors?

Sociologist James Coleman described adolescence as an intense, almost "closed" social system, where peer status dominates. Ralph Keyes suggests that those socially frustrated in high school may be more motivated to succeed as adults. Patricia Hersch describes the lack of community or parental monitoring in contemporary culture, a practice that contributes to additional adolescent problems.

8. What steps can educators take to create a more supportive school environment?

Frances Ianni calls for schools to create "youth charters," a coordinated network of social services and psychological resources to nurture at-risk children. The Carnegie Foundation recommends more humane and caring structural changes, such as detracking, cooperative learning, and smaller school units.

9. What are the characteristics of effective schools?

Ron Edmonds set forth a "five-factor theory" of effective schools: (1) strong administrative leadership, (2) clear school goals shared by faculty and administration, (3) a safe and orderly school climate, (4) frequent monitoring and assessment of student progress, and (5) high expectations for student performance. Newer research connects effective schools with early intervention programs, an emphasis on reading and math, smaller schools, smaller classes, increased learning time, assessment of student progress, and expanded teacher training.

EXTENDED LEARNING

CASE STUDIES

- Bonnie Bradley: We spend two successive periods watching a first-year science teacher as she presents a lab to her students and then observes the students as they engage in the lab itself.
- Richard Carlton: We follow a second-grade teacher during his morning routine, which focuses on literacy instruction.
- Anne Holt: This case follows an experienced teacher through her morning routine with a diverse group of first-grade children.

Go to Chapter 5 on your *Resources for Exploring Education* CD-ROM to access Case Studies, Readings, and Media Observations.

READINGS

- Joyce Baldwin. "Meeting the Challenge of the Urban High School."
- Reece Peterson and Russell Skiba. "Creating School Climates that Prevent School Violence."
- David Strahan, et al. "Profiles in Caring: Teachers Who Create Learning Communities in Their Classrooms."

KEY TERMS AND PEOPLE

ability grouping, 173
The Adolescent Society, 180
affective student needs, 184
closed social system, 179
detrack, 172
dominant male peer group, 177
five-factor theory of effective schools, 187
gatekeeping, 169
gender wall, 177
The Good High School, 187
John Goodlad, 168

Robert Havinghurst, 171
heterogeneous, 172
August Hollingshead, 171
homogeneous, 170
Frances Ianni, 184
Philip W. Jackson, 167
Lenore Jacobson, 192
Life in Classrooms, 167
norm-referenced tests, 191
Jeannie Oakes, 172, 175
objective-referenced tests, 191
Talcott Parsons, 171

Pygmalion in the Classroom, 192
Robert Rosenthal, 192
self-fulfilling prophecy, 192
sociograms, 178
tracking, 170
Turning Points: Preparing American Youth for the 21st Century, 185
unremarked revolution, 173
W. Lloyd Warner, 171
youth charter, 185

DISCUSSION QUESTIONS AND ACTIVITIES

1. Observe in a local elementary school. What are the rules and regulations that students must follow? Do they seem reasonable or arbitrary? Do students seem to spend a large amount of time waiting? Observe one student over a 40-minute period and determine what portion of those 40 minutes she or he spends just waiting.

2. Do you think that tracking is a valid method for enhancing student performance? Or do you think it is a mechanism for perpetuating inequality of opportunity based on social class, race, or sex? Debate someone in your class who holds an opposing point of view.

3. We have noted the vividness and detail with which many people recall their high school years. Try to answer the following:

- Who was voted most likely to succeed in your high school class? (Do you know what he or she is doing today?)
- What was your happiest moment in high school? your worst?
- Name five people who were part of the "in crowd" in your class. What were the "innies" in your high school like?
- Is there any academic experience in high school that you remember vividly? If so, what was it?

4. Research the issue of adolescent alienation. Make some recommendations on how secondary schools could get students to become more involved in academic and extracurricular activities.

5. Based on the characteristics of effective schools, would you consider your elementary, middle, and high schools effective? If not, why? Share your responses with your classmates.

WEB-TIVITIES

1. The Anti-Achievement Dilemma
2. Preventing School Violence
3. Monitoring Student Progress
4. Gender Equity: The Work of Myra Sadker

REEL TO REAL TEACHING

ELECTION (1999)
Run Time: 103 minutes

Synopsis: This satirical comedy takes an uncommon look at ambition, ethics, the power of peer groups, and the hidden curriculum of student elections. Jim McAllister is a popular teacher and student government adviser, but he will risk his reputation and career to stop the school's consummate overachiever from winning the school's election. As campaign fever sets in, both teachers and students blur the lines of right and wrong.

Reflection:

1. What purpose(s) did the election have for Tracy Flick? Paul Metzler? Tammy Metzler? Mr. McAllister?

2. Do you agree with Tammy Metzler that student government should be abolished? Can student government ever help create effective schools?

3. Some believe that school elections actually hurt democratic principles, teaching students to vote on popularity rather than substance, and to not expect any real change after the elections. Do student elections actually do more harm than good?

4. Recall your own experiences with high school student elections. Did you run for an office? Why or why not? In your high school, what was the social status of students serving in student government?

5. How were race, gender, and socioeconomic status represented in *Election*? In your own high school elections?

6. What personal boundaries will you establish with your students? Are teacher-student friendships appropriate? Teacher-student sexual relationships? How might the grade level of students influence your answers?

Follow-up Activity: You are Mr. McAllister's successor as student council adviser at George Washington Carver High. After this major election foul-up, it is up to you to spark participation, confidence, and enthusiasm for student government. You must propose election guidelines:

Who is eligible to run for office? What power (if any) will each elected position wield? What are acceptable campaign platforms? Are candidates allowed to spend money? Where and when are candidates permitted to campaign? How will ballots be collected and counted?

www.mhhe.com/
sadker7e

How do you rate this film? Go to *Reel to Real Teaching* in the Critics' Corner to review this film.

FOR FURTHER READING

Becoming Good American Schools, by Jeannie Oakes, Karen H. Quartz, Martin Lipton, and Steve Ryan (1999). Tells the story of fifteen schools working to create caring, socially just, and academically rigorous climates.

Bullying, by Sharon Sharp, David Thompson, and Tiny Aroda (2001). An overview of research describing the causes of bullying coupled with practical strategies to prevent harassment in schools.

Caring Classrooms/Intelligent Schools: The Social Emotional Education of Young Children, by Jonathan Cohen (Editor) (2001). A collection of essays on the development of emotional intelligence and social competence. Includes practical strategies and curriculum for affective education.

Class Dismissed: A Year in the Life of an American High School, A Glimpse into the Heart of a Nation, by Meredith Maran (2000). Examines with incredible detail academic tracking, school safety, peer relationship, and the everyday trials of being a teenager—and a teacher—in today's high school.

Fires in the Bathroom: Advice for Teachers from High School Students, by Kathleen Cushman (2003). This collection of interviews conveys a uniform message: students do want to learn. They also have ideas for teachers on how to best make learning happen: from getting to know students, to earning their trust, to judging their behavior, to what to do when things go wrong.

kids are doing a great job, and the drama teacher is very creative. Kids who are participating in that play are learning a tremendous amount—music, theater, Shakespeare. Other students participate in band, in chorus, in sports. There are several computer clubs. We even have a Special Friends Club that some students use for their service requirement. The students work with kids who have disabilities—take them bowling, play with them during lunch, tutor them. Children learn a lot through these experiences. I think extracurricular activities are an important part of what students learn in school."

"You're right, Jim. I was thinking about the formal academic curriculum. And what children learn in school is broader than that. I also remember one of my education professors talking about a hidden curriculum. I wasn't quite sure what he meant at the time, but, over the years I've been teaching, I've grown more and more aware of just how powerful this hidden curriculum is."

"I couldn't agree with you more." Jim Battersea leaned forward. "What Carol and I are talking about, Mary Jean, is all that subtle, incidental learning that occurs as children interact with each other, with the teacher, with all the different sides and angles of this thing we call school. For example, those kids in the drama club are learning so much more than Shakespeare. How does it feel to be on stage in front of 500 people? Are they nervous? How do they handle stage fright? What do they do if they forget their lines? Can they improvise? Do they help each other and cooperate, or do they compete? And think what a tremendous amount students learn about themselves and human nature when they work with kids with disabilities in the Special Friends Club. This hidden curriculum is an undercurrent of the formal class structure too. What do kids learn when they're playing a game in class and no one chooses them for the team? What do they take away if a teacher treats them unfairly or explodes in anger? Or think of all a youngster will learn from that teacher who sits down to talk with him or her about hobbies, goals, and problems."

"I know just what you're talking about." Mary Jean put down her pencil. "Like right now. I've learned a lot more than formal definitions of the curriculum. I know what the teachers' room is like early in the morning. I know how early you get here, and that you take time out of your busy schedules to talk with someone who wants to be a teacher. I've learned about curriculum and about teaching as well."

• • •

TEACHING TIP
Have students imagine they were Mary Jean and just completed the faculty room interview. What quick notes would they record in answer to the question, "What's a curriculum?"

In 1962, highly regarded educator **Hilda Taba** said, "Learning in school differs from learning in life in that it is formally organized. It is the special function of the school to arrange the experiences of children and youth so that desirable learning takes place. If the curriculum is to be a plan for learning, its content and learning experiences need to be organized so that they serve the educational objectives."[1] Today, most educators regard the **formal curriculum** as the organization of intended outcomes for which the school takes responsibility.

OVERHEAD 65
Three Faces of the Curriculum

In *A Place Called School,* one of the most important and influential studies of school life, **John Goodlad** refers to an explicit and an implicit curriculum.[2] The **explicit curriculum** is reflected in curriculum guides, courses offered, syllabi describing courses, tests given, materials used, and teachers' statements of what they want students to learn. When you study geometry or U.S. history, you are studying the explicit curriculum. But sometimes the most powerful curricular lessons are the ones not taught. What is "left out" is also a curriculum, one we call the **null curriculum.** If your American History classes never went beyond World War II, then your null curriculum included the Korean and Vietnam Wars, the fall of communism, two wars in

Iraq, the Civil Rights and Women's Rights movements, an assassination and an impeachment, the disaster in Somalia, large-scale corporate corruption, the technology revolution, and the reasons behind the September 11 attack. While you may have been required to take geometry, a course in creative thinking was probably not even offered. Does this mean that geometry is more important than creative thinking or what happened after World War II is irrelevant? Of course not, but these examples suggest that much of the explicit curriculum is taught out of habit and inertia, not thoughtful analysis.

But there are other curriculums as well. The **implicit,** or **hidden, curriculum** emerges incidentally from the interaction between the students and the physical, social, and interpersonal environments of the school. The third curriculum has been called the **extracurriculum** and includes student activities, such as sports, clubs, governance, and the student newspaper. Before we look at the formal, or explicit, curriculum of elementary and secondary schools, perhaps we should examine these powerful, less formal, curricula first.

The Extracurriculum

"The Battle of Waterloo was won on the playing fields of Eton," said the Duke of Wellington, perhaps becoming the first to highlight the importance of extracurricular activities. Students seem to agree. In the early 1990s, 83 percent of all high school seniors participated in at least one extracurricular activity, with students from smaller schools and with stronger academic records most likely to be involved.[3] Varsity sports attracted the most students, with 44 percent of the high school boys and 28 percent of the high school girls participating. Students who participate in athletics typically learn leadership, teamwork, persistence, diligence, and fair play. Twenty-eight percent of students were involved with music and drama, developing their creativity and talents. Academic clubs were the third most popular activity, with about one-quarter of all students taking part by senior year, rates that have not changed since the early 1970s. Academic clubs—science, languages, computers, debate—enhance not only

FOCUS QUESTION 2
What is the place of the extracurriculum in school life?

Sports and varsity athletics comprise an important and influential part of school life.

Female athletic participation has been associated with healthier lifestyles, including lower incidences of breast cancer,[1] reduced rates of teen pregnancy, lower usage of drugs, and higher graduation rates.[2] While the percentage of girls participating in sports grew dramatically after Congress passed Title IX (1972), a law prohibiting gender discrimination, this increase has slowed in recent years. Just over 40 percent of high school athletes are female, and if the current trend continues, it will take high schools until the year 2033 to achieve gender parity in their sports programs.[3]

[1] J. Raloff, "Exercising Reduces Breast Cancer Risk," *Science News* 149, no. 14 (1 October 1994), p. 215.

[2] Feminist Majority Foundation, *Empowering Women in Sports* (Washington, DC: Feminist Majority Foundation, 1995); *Research Report: Health Risks and the Teen Athlete* (2001), www.womenssportsfoundation.org.
[3] Women's Sports Foundation. East Meadow, NY. Based on information in *Women's Sports Facts*, 2002.

REFLECTION: Consider your own high school athletic program. Were there inequities between male and female programs? Are you a staunch advocate of varsity sports in schools? For whom? Why or why not?

academic learning but social skills as well. Nationwide programs, such as Odyssey of the Mind and Future Bowl, promote cross-curricular interests and creative problem-solving skills. Advocates see these activities as so important that they refer to them not as the extracurriculum but as the *cocurriculum.*

Advocates proclaim the value of the extracurriculum to life both during and far beyond the high school years.

- Extracurricular activities enhance student self-esteem, school completion, and encourage civic participation.
- The extracurriculum, especially athletics, improves race relations.
- Participating students have higher SAT scores and grades.
- Involvement in the extracurriculum is related to high career aspirations, especially for boys from poor backgrounds.[4]

Not everyone is so sanguine about the extracurriculum. The underrepresentation of low socioeconomic students is evident in many programs, as are gender differences in the performing arts, school government and literary activities, which are populated by significantly more females.[5] Skeptics suggest that the best we can say "is that the effects of extracurricular participation on secondary school students' personal development and academic achievement are probably positive, but very modest, and are definitely different among students with different social or intellectual backgrounds."[6]

If you think back to your own high school days, you may remember both high- and low-profile students: the extracurricular superstar so involved in everything from the student council to the yearbook that she walked around with a little calendar in her backpack to keep activities straight; the nominal participants, involved in a few activities (this is where most students fall); and the nonparticipants, those who were alienated and excluded from the extracurricular side of school.

High-profile students have a complex network of reasons for participating. For some, there is genuine interest and enjoyment. Others see the extracurriculum as a path to social success. One study found that only 16 percent of students surveyed said getting good grades increases status among peers. However, 56 percent of students

Is the school's soccer team washing cars to raise money for a homeless shelter? Are the students in Spanish 3 tutoring children at the elementary school? Directing adolescent time and energy to benefit others can help students connect with each other and the real meaning of civic duty. Since many consider service such a worthy cause, it is frequently a requirement for graduation.

What works? When schools invest their resources to develop and schedule community service projects, student participation rates surge.

Who cares? About half of U.S. secondary students participate in service activities, and about half of those students are involved on a regular basis. Participants in extracurricular programs (student government and other school activities) and students who work for pay outside school are the most likely to contribute their time. The busiest young people are the most likely to be involved!

SOURCE: *The Condition of Education 1998,* Indicator 25: Community Service Participation of Students in Grades 6–12. U.S. Department of Education.

REFLECTION: Two questions are considered in this Frame of Reference. If you are (or have been) involved in any service project, *what has worked* to motivate you? How are you like (or unlike) a student *who cares?*

said that extracurricular activities can lead to popularity.[7] Other calculating students base their choice of activities not on their own interests but, rather, with an eye to the interests of admissions officers, who select the chosen few for the nation's most prestigious colleges and universities.

Controversies about the extracurriculum often focus on its uneasy relationship with the academic side of school. For example, the current emphasis on a rigorous academic curriculum has spilled over in the form of policies that bar students from extracurricular participation if they fail a course. In Texas and other states, "no pass, no play" rules deny students in poor academic standing the right to participate in varsity sports. In some communities, budget tightening has led to "pay to play" rules, in which a fee is required for sports participation, posing a serious problem for low-income families and students.

Such policies raise puzzling questions and issues. Should academic performance and financial constraints be factors in deciding who participates in extracurricular activities? If the extracurriculum is a vital part of the learning offered in school, should any students be denied access? According to data from the classic study *High School and Beyond,* African American and Latino males are most likely to be affected by these policies, since one-third fail to maintain a 2.0 grade point average.[8] Since the top academic students, more likely to be wealthy and white, already dominate the extracurriculum, will "pay to play" regulations make this curriculum even more exclusive, driving deeper divisions between the haves and have-nots and further segregating racial and ethnic groups?

An ongoing concern is that, to many, the extracurriculum means only one thing—varsity sports. (See Figure 6.1.) On any autumn Friday evening or Saturday afternoon in thousands of towns across the United States, entire communities—accompanied by bands, parades, and pep rallies—cheer the hometown football team with a level of adulation that can only be dreamed of by academic stars. For small town or large city athletes, the media hype and possibility of multimillion-dollar contracts can lead hopeful high school athletes down a treacherous road. While more than 5 million students across the nation play interscholastic varsity sports, 49 out of 50 will never make a college team. For every 100 male college athletes, only 1 will play professional sports. Many critics worry that the tail is wagging the dog in a system in which athletics get the resources, the hope, and the attention, while academics slide into the shadows.

CRITICAL THINKING QUESTION

What messages did students hear about extracurricular programs from the media, their family, friends, college counselors, club advisors, and inner voice?

RELATED READING

Friday Night Lights: A Town, A Team and a Dream by H. G. Bissinger (2000).

OVERHEADS 66–67

High School Seniors' Attitudes and Aspirations

The Importance of Extracurricular Activities and Academic Subjects

FIGURE 6.1

High school seniors' attitudes and aspirations.

SOURCE: University of Michigan, Institute for Social Research. Monitoring the Future Survey: 1998.

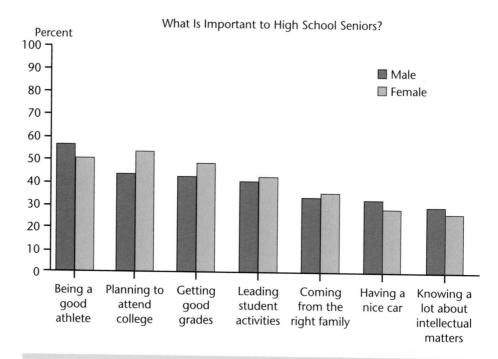

What Is Important to High School Seniors?

REFLECTION: How might these student priorities influence your teaching? How would you explain the gender gap?

 The Hidden or Implicit Curriculum

FOCUS QUESTION 3
How do the formal and the hidden curriculum differ?

OVERHEAD 68
Hidden Curriculum?

While the relationship between the formal curriculum and the extracurriculum is occasionally controversial, they have one thing in common: Both have goals and methods that are explicit and intentional. Although the hidden curriculum is absent from the official school catalog, it still teaches powerful lessons.

Jules Henry is an anthropologist who has analyzed the hidden curriculum of the elementary school and has studied the values and behavior it teaches. He concludes that students are capable of learning many things at one time and that the school teaches far more than academic content. The hidden curriculum consists of implicit learnings that are not always intended. For example, Henry described a fourth-grade classroom in which a spelling bee was taking place. Team members were chosen by two team captains. When a student spelled a word correctly on the board, a "hit" was scored. When three spelling errors were made, the team was "out." Students cheered or groaned, depending on the outcome for their team. According to Henry, these students were learning about more than spelling. They were learning about winning and losing, competition, and the feelings that accompany success and failure. If they were chosen early for a team, they learned about

IN THE NEWS

Lettering in Academics

Michael K., a senior at Westchester High School in Los Angeles, has earned the right to wear a football letter on his school jacket. He chose instead to wear the academic letter. The school awards letters to students with a 3.5 or higher GPA. *I worked harder for the academic jacket than the one for football,* he explained.

SOURCE: *The American School Board Journal,* August 1998.

 What's new in education? Click on *News Feeds.*

Strengthens Education Because It . . .

BEATS THE STREETS

Students need meaningful activities and a place to spend their time and energy. After-school programs, sponsored by caring adults, keep students out of trouble.

IS A POSITIVE SOCIAL SCENE

Interpersonal and intrapersonal skills, developed in extracurricular activities, provide the real foundation of successful adulthood. Students, especially those with unstable home lives, need the caring relationships found in after-school activities.

PROVIDES SKILLS FOR A LIFETIME

Academics alone don't do enough to support well-rounded individuals. Especially for students whose skills and talents lie outside the formal curriculum, extracurricular activities may keep some students in school.

FURNISHES CAREER OPPORTUNITIES

After-school programs are a place to see the rewards of persistent effort and build a disciplined work ethic. Students' experiences in music, technology or service clubs can lead to part-time employment and valuable careers.

DIMINISHES SOME INEQUITIES

For families with minimal resources, after-school programs may be the only chance some students get to visit a theater, play on a team, or rewire a computer.

Weakens Education Because It . . .

TAKES TIME OFF THE TASK

Students need to focus on their schoolwork. That's what a school is for! Too many distractions from studying put students' academic potential at risk.

IS A PROBLEMATIC SOCIAL SCENE

The social scene students experience in extracurriculars is bleary. Between the cliques and the clubs, students learn who's in and who's out. Team rituals create environments that promote negative behaviors like drinking and bullying.

ADDS A COSTLY FRILL

When dollars are at a premium, every penny needs to be put into the academic arena. Squandering resources on coaches, equipment, and travel means taking money away from what students really deserve: the best education.

CAN BE A CAREER CRUSHER

Athletic success misleads players into believing that college scholarships and professional sports are within their grasp. The demanding and singular focus of activities such as sports takes students away from everything else schools have to offer. Students' dreams get crushed.

SPOTLIGHTS ECONOMIC DIFFERENCES

Poorer students who cannot afford extracurricular fees (pay to play) are denied educational opportunities.

 YOU BE THE JUDGE

What do you believe is the best extracurricular program for students? What's the worst? Why? What interests and skills do you possess that make you a valuable sponsor, coach or advisor to the extracurricular world?

group support and recognition. If they were chosen late, they learned about embarrassment and rejection. Some of the more thoughtful students also learned about the absurdity of a spelling lesson being taught as a baseball game.[9]

Here is another example. The formal academic curriculum stresses the importance of preparing students to become active citizens in a democracy. Courses in government, civics, and history are offered to meet this goal. In the extracurriculum, elections to student government schoolwide and to offices in individual classes and clubs supposedly promote democratic participation. But the subtle and powerful message of the hidden curriculum may lead to some very different learning, learning entirely opposite to that which is intended. As they are run in most schools, elections may teach students that, rather than "selecting the best person for the job," they are merely casting a vote in a popularity contest or that the candidate with the best posters, rather than the best platform, is most likely to win. They may be learning that it does not matter if the winner has intelligent positions on issues, or the snazziest posters, or the most friends, because nothing changes, anyway. Perhaps the fact that a large segment of the adult electorate fails to vote in national elections is a testament to the power of the hidden curriculum.

 ## The Formal or Explicit Curriculum

FOCUS QUESTION 4
How do social forces shape curriculum development over time?

Although many of you left high school just a few years ago, the curriculum you knew has changed even in that short span of time, responding to new needs and new perspectives. To see how social forces change the curriculum, we have created a curriculum time machine. Because Chapter 8, "The History of American Education," offers you a look at U.S. schooling from colonial times through the progressive era, this time machine will only briefly review this period, while emphasizing curricular issues from the 1950s to the present (see Figure 6.2). In fact, we will even begin to explore the future, setting the context for what and how you will teach.

 ## The Curriculum Time Machine: A Historical Perspective

Time Capsule 1: The Two Rs in the Seventeenth Century

GLOBAL VIEW
Educational isolationism is the term used to describe students' lack of knowledge about worldwide events. Are there any educational (political, religious, economic or other) connections students can make with this curricular timeline?

In the seventeenth century, religion underlay all human activity. Reading the Scriptures provided the route to salvation, and the "two *Rs*" curriculum, a blend of reading and religion, prevailed. A white elementary student in those times would have acquired the rudiments of reading and religion from the **hornbook,** parchment attached to a paddle-shaped board and covered with a piece of transparent horn. If you were a white student toward the end of the century, you would be treated to a fear-inspiring dose of Puritan morality from America's first basal reader, ***The New England Primer.*** After elementary school, you would put away your hornbook if you were female. Secondary schooling was not offered to girls, while African Americans and Native Americans were routinely denied any formal education. If you were male and financially well off, you might go to the **Latin grammar school.** There you would learn Latin, Greek, and more Latin. If you grew weary of conjugating Latin verbs and translating Greek, you could always get a change of pace by reading the Bible and other religious texts.

CLASS ACTIVITY:
STATEMENT
COMPLETION
IM, Activity 6:5

Time Capsule 2: Curricula in the Eighteenth Century

The 1700s saw an upsurge in trade and commerce; the boundaries of the frontier stretched westward. These were changing times, with great faith in the progress and potential of humanity, dreams of fortunes to be made, and a growing commitment to life in the present instead of salvation after death. The shift from the spiritual to the

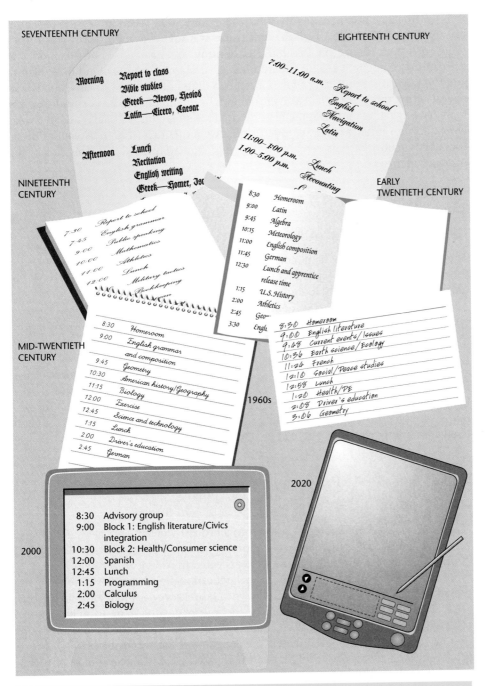

SEVENTEENTH CENTURY

Morning   Report to class
Bible studies
Greek—Aesop, Hesiod
Latin—Cicero, Caesar

Afternoon   Lunch
Recitation
English writing
Greek—Homer, Is...

EIGHTEENTH CENTURY

7:00–11:00 a.m.   Report to school
English
Navigation
Latin

11:00–1:00 p.m.   Lunch
1:00–5:00 p.m.   Accounting

NINETEENTH CENTURY

7:30   Report to school
7:45   English grammar
9:00   Public speaking
10:00   Mathematics
11:00   Athletics
12:00   Lunch
Military tactics
Bookkeeping

EARLY TWENTIETH CENTURY

8:30   Homeroom
9:00   Latin
9:45   Algebra
10:15   Meteorology
11:00   English composition
11:45   German
12:30   Lunch and apprentice release time
1:15   U.S. History
2:00   Athletics
2:45   Geo...
3:30   Engl...

MID-TWENTIETH CENTURY

8:30   Homeroom
9:00   English grammar and composition
9:45   Geometry
10:30   American history/geography
11:15   Biology
12:00   Exercise
12:45   Science and technology
1:15   Lunch
2:00   Driver's education
2:45   German

1960s

8:30   Homeroom
9:00   English literature
9:48   Current events/Issues
10:36   Earth science/Ecology
11:24   French
12:10   Social/Peace studies
12:58   Lunch
1:20   Health/PE
2:08   Driver's education
3:06   Geometry

2000

8:30   Advisory group
9:00   Block 1: English literature/Civics integration
10:30   Block 2: Health/Consumer science
12:00   Spanish
12:45   Lunch
1:15   Programming
2:00   Calculus
2:45   Biology

2020

REFLECTION: In the space provided, create a student schedule for the year 2020.

FIGURE 6.2
Student class schedules throughout time.

MULTIPLE INTELLIGENCE CONNECTION
Assign student groups to each of the class schedules. How does the visual presentation of the schedule offer clues to the curriculum content for each era?

secular began to free the curriculum from the tight bonds of religion. White elementary students still worked with *The New England Primer.* Studies focused on reading, religion, and morality, although writing and arithmetic were beginning to get more attention.

For white secondary students, there were some new alternatives to the Latin grammar school. At the **English grammar school,** you could learn vocational skills, such as surveying, bookkeeping, accounting, and navigating. By the middle of the century, you could attend the **academy.** Academies were a blend of the Latin and the English schools, and they housed two different courses of study. You could choose either the traditional Latin curriculum or the English course of study, which included English grammar, some history, and foreign languages. The academy broke with tradition in another way, for its doors were open to women as well as men, though the color barriers remained, denying education to Native Americans and African Americans.

Time Capsule 3: A Secularized Curriculum for Students in the Nineteenth Century

VIDEO SEGMENT 14
Saving Souls

The forces of nationalism, democratization, and industrial development spread across the land. As a result, universal literacy, vocational competence, and preparation for citizenship became curricular aims.

As an elementary school student, you would have traded in your *New England Primer* for McGuffey's readers. The course of study expanded to include writing, arithmetic, spelling, geography, and good behavior. As a secondary student, you would probably be enrolled in the academy, which by the middle of the century had become the dominant form of secondary school in America. You could choose either the Latin curriculum, which continued to focus on Latin, Greek, and arithmetic, or the expanding English curriculum, which included English grammar, public speaking, geography, history, and sometimes science, geometry, algebra, and a modern language—a long way from the two Rs of the 1600s!

Time Capsule 4: Progressive Education in the First Half of the Twentieth Century

GLOBAL VIEW
How does the peopling of America impact schools? Visit the *Americans All* website at www.americansall.com/ to see their large and inclusive electronic database on our immigration history.

Migration changed our agrarian nation into a primarily urban one. New and diverse waves of immigrants (Irish, Polish, German, Jewish, Italian, Slovak, Greek, and Finnish) poured ashore; the schools were expected to Americanize them into a homogeneous and productive workforce. New educational philosophies were being explored, such as the progressive movement with John Dewey as its chief spokesperson.

As an elementary student, you would have time for creative expression in the form of drawing, painting, music, dance, and craftwork. Moreover, the rigid distinctions that had separated content fields were breaking down. Rather than studying history, geography, and civics, you would face an integrated course called *social studies.* *Language arts* encompassed reading, writing, speaking, and listening.

As a secondary student, you might attend the **junior high school,** which grew in popularity during the 1920s. Here a core curriculum stressed the integration of various subject areas, studying topics from "conservation in the development of American civilization" to "how I can use my spare time." During this period, high school changed from a college-oriented institution organized to meet the needs of the elite to a secondary school for most white Americans. By 1918, vocational courses, such as typing, stenography, bookkeeping, domestic science, and industrial arts, had joined the curriculum.

Immigrant children such as these were expected to be "Americanized" by the schools of the late nineteenth and early twentieth centuries.

Time Capsule 5: *Sputnik* in Space and Structure in Knowledge, 1940s–1960s

After World War II, the vocational and service-oriented courses of progressivism became known as **life-adjustment education.** As a student, you might have enrolled in such courses as "developing an effective personality" or "common learning," in which you would have studied your own social and personal problems. In the 1950s, the life-adjustment curriculum was ridiculed as anti-intellectual and undemocratic, and progressive education was under attack from many sides.

In 1957, the iciest of Cold War fears seemed to be realized, with the launching of the Soviet ***Sputnik,*** the first artificial satellite. The schools were made the scapegoat for the U.S. failure in the race for space. *Life* magazine urged an end to the "carnival" in the schools; Congress passed the National Defense Education Act (NDEA) and appropriated nearly a billion dollars for programs in science, math, modern languages, and guidance. Academicians and the lay public alike decried the schools' lack of intellectual rigor.

As students after *Sputnik,* you and your classmates would have studied a foreign language and enrolled in rigorous math and science courses. Prestigious academics became involved in curriculum development, particularly in math and science. One of these scholars was **Jerome Bruner,** a Harvard psychologist, who served as secretary of a conference of scholars, scientists, and educators at Woods Hole, Massachusetts. Bruner's report on this conference, ***The Process of Education*** (1960), had a major impact on curriculum. Translated into twenty languages and read by educators worldwide, this report put forward the premise that "any subject can be taught effectively in some intellectually honest form to any child at any stage of development."[10] Bruner conceptualized a discipline not as a collection of facts but, rather, in terms of its structure—the principles and methods of inquiry most central to its study. Bruner believed that if students could learn these methods of inquiry, they could then study a field at different levels of sophistication. He envisioned the curriculum as a spiral in which students would return to the principles at the heart of the discipline and study them in progressively more complex and advanced forms.

In terms of teacher training, Bruner advocated the **discovery method,** in which teachers would assist students in uncovering meanings for themselves. The result of this curriculum revolution was an array of discipline-oriented curricula, particularly in science and math.

Time Capsule 6: Social Concern and Relevance, 1960s–1970s

During the late 1960s and early 1970s, Cold War competition seemed less pressing, as racial strife and the war in Vietnam tore at the very fabric of our society. As a student of the times, you might have thought that the discipline-oriented curricula of the past decade were out of touch with the needs of disadvantaged children and alienated youth, the movement for civil rights, and the devastation of war overseas.

Once again, school curricula became the object of critical scrutiny, and once again they were found lacking—this time by critics who have been variously labeled the "radical," "compassionate," or **"romantic" critics.** Whatever their label, these critics were concerned about the irrelevance of curricula that emphasized academics at the expense of social reality.

New courses and topics burgeoned, spinning the curriculum into new and exciting areas. As you read about these topics, consider how your own education may have been influenced by these curricular innovations.

Today's recycling efforts have their roots in the environmental education programs that emerged in the 1970s.

Women's Studies and Multicultural Curricula During the 1970s, curriculum developers began to design lessons, units, even entire programs, around the needs and contributions of women. These **women's studies** programs generally focused on patterns of sex bias and sought to compensate for the omissions of history and literature books, in which women and their contributions were systematically ignored. Responding to a similar exclusion of racial and ethnic groups, educational institutions developed a **multicultural approach** to the curriculum, particularly incorporated in social studies, language arts, and humanities.

Individualized Education Programs for Children with Disabilities Public Law 94-142, the 1975 Education for All Handicapped Children Act, mandated an **individualized education program (IEP)** for each child who is eligible for special education. The IEP consists of (1) assessment of the child's present achievement levels, (2) identification of goals and of the services needed to achieve those goals, and (3) systematic progress checks to see if the goals are being met or if they need to be revised. PL 94-142, renamed the Individuals with Disabilities Education Act (1990), remains controversial, as educators debate spiraling costs, accurate identification, and the impact of mainstreaming.

Social Issues: Death, War and Peace, the Environment During the 1970s, some educators, psychologists, and parents opened up the curriculum to formerly taboo subjects, such as death and dying:

> There is a need for guidance and knowledge about dying, grief, and bereavement [so that each child develops] an acceptance of death as a fact of life.[11]

Educators, also responding to the pervasive impact of violence and war, developed a peace curriculum through which students could analyze the conditions of peace, the causes of war, and the mechanisms for the nonviolent resolution of conflict. Courses in **peace studies** were first instituted in the 1960s, and, by 1974, twenty-nine colleges and universities had instituted either a certificate or an academic major in peace studies. In some cases, elements from these courses filtered down to secondary and elementary schools.

The 1970s ushered in an invigorated concern for the environment. Programs in ecology and **environmental education** stressed our planet's delicate environmental balance, and they continue to influence today's curricular materials.

The Open Classroom In 1967, a Parliamentary commission in Great Britain encouraged English primary schools to adopt a child-centered approach called the **open classroom.** Based on the work of Swiss child psychologist Jean Piaget, the open classroom created **interest,** or **learning centers.** Children were encouraged to select activities they wished to pursue in these learning centers.

Classrooms in the 1970s were exciting places, with students discussing topics ranging from war to changing sex roles; learning about the culture and heritage of various ethnic groups; studying sexuality, peace, drug, and consumer education; and moving freely from one interest center to another within the classroom. However, even as these innovations were occurring, newspaper editorials and articles in professional journals reflected a disenchantment with schools. The comments went something like this: "National tests show that our students are having trouble with reading, writing, and math. In view of this, what business do schools have dabbling in all these curricular frills? It's time to get back to the basics."

Time Capsule 7: Back to Basics, Standards and Testing, 1980s–2004

There was no unifying manifesto for those who advocated **"back to basics."** The meaning of this movement varied from one individual and school to another. In the early 1980s, a composite of what many back-to-basics advocates wanted schools to do looked something like this:

1. Devote most of the elementary school day to reading, writing, and arithmetic.
2. Place heavy secondary school emphasis on English, science, math, and history.
3. Give teachers more disciplinary latitude, including the authority to use corporal punishment.
4. Use instructional procedures that stress drill, homework, and frequent testing.
5. Adopt textbooks that reflect patriotism and reject those that challenge traditional values.
6. Eliminate electives, frills, and innovations, such as peace education programs.
7. Test, test, and test. Tie student promotion from grade to grade and graduation from high school to demonstrated proficiency on specific examinations. Issue

traditional report cards frequently to communicate and monitor student progress.[12]

The conservative *National Review* summed it up this way: "Clay modeling, weaving, doll construction, flute practice, volleyball, sex education, laments about racism, and other weighty matters should take place on private time." The public defined *back to basics* more succinctly as attention to the traditional subject areas of reading, writing, and arithmetic.[13]

The issue of declining test scores gave the movement its major impetus. Between 1952 and 1982, student scores dropped 50 points on the verbal part of the SAT and almost 30 points on the mathematics part. Many researchers focused with alarm on the burgeoning number of electives as a cause for achievement decline. Philip Cusick found a mushrooming curriculum at the high schools he studied. For example, one high school had thirty-one separate courses in English; another had twenty-seven. There was a proliferation of easy electives, such as "girl talk," "what's happening?" "personal relations," and "trouble shooter." Also, activities that used to be extracurricular—yearbook, student council, newspaper, band, glee club—were often given academic credit.[14] Sara Lawrence Lightfoot, in her study *The Good High School,* also found a bewildering array of electives. One of the schools she visited had a 188-page catalog with more than 500 course descriptions. Career courses alone took up 23 pages.[15]

Even though the proliferation of electives may reflect academic richness, there is no doubt that students began to avoid the more rigorous courses. A U.S. Department of Education study showed that, between 1964 and 1980, students flocked from academic study to "personal service and social development" courses. In the 1960s, 12 percent of high school students were enrolled in these more open-ended electives. By the 1970s, enrollment had skyrocketed to 42 percent.

When faced with the question of whether to tilt in the direction of student choice or of a curricular core, most reform reports opted for the latter. For example, the National Commission on Excellence in Education report, *A Nation at Risk* (1983), called for new basics—four years of English, three years of mathematics, three years of science, three years of social studies, and one-half year of computer science.

In his book *High School* (1983), **Ernest Boyer** also called for a **core curriculum,** with the proportion of required courses increased from one-half to two-thirds of the total number of units necessary to graduate. He said that this core should include literature, history, math, science, foreign languages, the arts, civics, non-Western studies, technology, the meaning of work, and health. He advocated the abolition of the three traditional high school tracks (academic, general, and vocational), calling instead for the integration of all students into one track, with a pattern of electives radiating from the center of a common core of learning. Boyer also advocated a service requirement, which would involve students in volunteer work in their communities.[16]

Influential in the reform movement, John Goodlad's *A Place Called School* also recommended a core but stated that a common set of topics should not form the basis of the core. Rather, the core should comprise "a common set of concepts, principles, skills and ways of knowing."[17] Theodore Sizer's *Horace's Compromise* (1984) fueled the movement to reform public schools; it, too, emphasized the process of knowing. Arguing that less is more, Sizer believed that only certain essentials, such as literacy, numeric ability, and civic understanding, should be mandated.[18]

The reform report that placed the most stringent emphasis on core requirements was developed by philosopher and educator **Mortimer Adler,** in his controversial

CLASS ACTIVITIES: ANALYZING CURRICULUM CONTENT
IM, Activity 6:1

CURRICULUM AND THE FUTURE
IM, Activity 6:2

CURRICULUM DEBATE
IM, Activity 6:4

TEACHING TIP
Have students develop a content review strategy (key term flash cards, guess the time frame game, jeopardy quiz) to check their knowledge of the curriculum time capsules.

OVERHEADS 69–70
Educational Time Line

LANGUAGE ARTS

Grades K–4: Students communicate using standard English grammar including usage, sentence structure, punctuation, capitalization, spelling, and handwriting in final drafts of writing assignments. (Louisiana)

Grades 3–4: Write informational reports that include facts, details, and examples that illustrate an important idea. (Ohio)

Grade 8: Read, interpret, and critically analyze literature. Identify the defining features and structure of literary texts, such as conflict, representation of character, and point of view. Analyze the effect of characters, plot, setting, language, topic, style, purpose, and point of view on the overall impact of literature. (Wisconsin)

Grades 9–12: The student constructs meaning from a wide range of texts through a variety of reference materials, including indexes, magazines, newspapers, and journals; and tools, including card catalogs and computer catalogs, to gather information for research topics. (Florida)

MATHEMATICS

Grade 1: Identify and classify two- and three-dimensional shapes. Classify two- and three-dimensional figures according to characteristics (e.g., square, rectangle, circle, cube, prism, sphere, cone, and cylinder). (Mississippi)

Grade 5: Select and use appropriate statistical methods to analyze data. Compare two related sets of data using measures of center—mean, median, and mode—and range. (Oregon)

Grade 7: The student will solve consumer application problems involving tips, discounts, sales tax, and simple interest, using whole numbers, fractions, decimals, and percents. (Virginia)

Grades 8–12: Students apply basic factoring techniques to second-degree and simple third-degree polynomials. These techniques include finding a common factor for all terms in a polynomial, recognizing the difference of two squares, and recognizing perfect squares of binomials. (California)

SOCIAL STUDIES

Grade 2: Rules and Law: Students know why society needs rules, laws, and governments. Students know and are able to participate in class decision making. (Nevada)

Grade 3: Identify contributions of individuals to U.S. history, such as George Washington, Thomas Jefferson, Abraham Lincoln, Theodore Roosevelt, Franklin D. Roosevelt, Abigail Adams, Sacajawea, Frederick Douglass, Clara Barton, Jackie Robinson, Rosa Parks, Archbishop Patrick Flores, Jaime Escalante, Sally Ride, Tiger Woods, Cal Ripken, Jr., Sammy Sosa. (Pennsylvania)

Grades 5–8: The student uses maps, globes, graphs, charts, models, and databases to answer geographic questions. The student is expected to create thematic maps, graphs, charts, models, and databases depicting various aspects of world regions and countries such as population, disease, and economic activities. (Texas)

Grades 9–12: Discusses the limitations of the Articles of Confederation and the reasons for the calling of the Constitutional Convention. (Georgia)

SCIENCE

Grades 1–3: Describe the basic earth materials (rocks, soils, water, and gases) and their physical properties. (Arizona)

Grades 5–8: Students will understand that cells are the basic units of life. The functions performed by organelles (specialized structures found in cells) within individual cells are also carried out by the organ system in multicellular organisms. This standard requires that students be conversant with magnifying devices, cell structure and function, body systems, and disease causes and the body's defense against them. (Maine)

Grades: 12: The student will apply skills, processes, and concepts of biology, chemistry, physics, and earth/space science to societal issues. (Maryland)

Grades 9–12: Students will use chemical formulas and equations to obtain and communicate information about chemical changes. (Connecticut)

Source: Education World. Online at www.education-world.com/standards.

REFLECTION: Do you think these standards represent what and who is worth knowing? Why or why not? What content standards would you promote in our nation's schools?

The Paideia Proposal. Adler advocated a required course of study that was the same for every child through the first twelve years of schooling. The only choice was the selection of which second language to study. Adler thought that electives only allow students "to voluntarily downgrade their own education."[19]

E. D. Hirsch, Jr., brought the issue of a core curriculum into the national spotlight with his best-selling **Cultural Literacy** (1987). According to Hirsch, the core cultural milestones can be identified. He extracted these markers and compiled them as lists of what literate Americans know.[20] "When the schools of the nation cease to transmit effectively the literate language and culture, the unity and effectiveness of the nation will necessarily decline."[21]

The emphasis on a more rigorous core curriculum inevitably led to a growing standards movement across the nation. By the second Bush administration, states and the national government promoted standards and curricular alignment for each discipline, testing students, schools, and teachers. If state-mandated standards were not being met, "failing" schools would be closed and students transferred to other schools. The curriculum had become a state-regulated and tested vehicle to ensure that a fixed body of skills and knowledge were attained by all students, a development we will explore in greater detail in the next chapter.

 # The Subjects of the Formal Curriculum

In the following sections, we offer a synopsis of what is taught in the formal curriculum in today's schools. We also summarize current tension points and trends that may shape what is taught in the schools of tomorrow.

Language Arts and English

Topics Language arts programs emphasize literacy development which includes reading, writing, speaking, listening, viewing, and media study. In elementary school, the language arts curriculum addresses the essentials of how to use language—reading, grammar, spelling, speaking, handwriting, composition, capitalization, punctuation, word processing, peer editing, and research skills. At the secondary level, language arts instruction (or simply, English class) shifts the focus to literature, and senior high school students read both classics and contemporary works by such authors as Shakespeare, Whitman, Austen, and Tan.

Tension Points and Trends Reading experts often divide along two camps, phonics and whole language. The **phonics** approach breaks down words into smaller units—phonemes. Sounding out (decoding) these phonemes leads to reading. The **basal readers** relied on phonics and dominated reading instruction for decades. The **whole language** movement gained popularity in the 1970s and 1980s and integrates the reading and writing of whole texts before analyzing words and individual letter sounds. The emphasis here is on the joy of reading good literature. Unfortunately, these pedagogical differences have taken on political overtones, with many conservatives promoting phonics and a number of liberals endorsing whole language. Research suggests both are useful, and that an awareness of the role of word sounds within the context of good literature provides the foundation of an effective reading program.[22]

Selecting "good literature" has become political as well. Classic literature, sometimes referred to as the **canon,** is European and American, written from a white, male perspective, and dominates schools. In 1907, thirty-one of the forty most frequently assigned authors were from other countries and cultures; by the end of the century, twenty-nine of the forty were American.[23] To create more diverse perspectives, some communities and states require that non-Western and female authors and perspectives be included.[24] While some charge "political correctness," others argue that it is time to recognize that great writers come in all colors and both genders.[25]

Teaching is a Delpit family tradition. As a child in Baton Rouge, Louisiana, Lisa Delpit played school as soon as she learned something new, eager to share her latest idea or fact with friends. Lisa didn't have to look far to find educational role models: her mother was a high school teacher; her father was a restaurant owner who donated meals to local elementary schools for children who couldn't afford lunch. So it was much to Delpit's surprise that her family discouraged her from pursuing a teaching career. Impressed with her academic talent, they wanted her to forge new opportunities for young black women, opportunities beyond "just being a teacher." But Lisa Delpit felt a calling to enrich the lives of students, especially those of color.

Delpit is an ardent supporter of public schools, where she believes an appreciation of diversity should be commonplace. But it is not. Too often American education fails to include, or even see, the vision of those outside the white mainstream culture. Even in the most diverse classrooms, Delpit often witnesses a prevailing tunnel vision—the richness of a multicultural lens obscured by calls for uniform standards based on traditional Eurocentric ideas. The perspectives and needs of students of color are sidelined. Delpit shares her insights:

> I have come to understand that power plays a critical role in our society and in our educational system. The worldviews of those with privileged positions are taken as the only reality . . . It is others who determine how students of color should act, how they are to be judged. When one "we" gets to determine the standards for all "wes," then some "wes" are in trouble![1]

Delpit has felt this cultural tension in her own language arts classrooms. In her teacher training, she embraced the ideas that open, progressive classrooms are the most humanizing environments, that children should be in control of their own learning, and that students will learn to read and write when they are ready. Determined to use all she had learned to benefit children of color, she accepted a teaching position in inner-city Philadelphia. She put her whole-language teaching approach into action. Little attention was given to basic writing skills, like grammar, punctuation, and paragraph structure. Students instead learned to write in meaningful contexts related to their lives and culture.

Delpit knew her students were fluent. In their stories, in jump rope chants on the playground, and in their classroom discussions, she heard their verbal creativity. But they were failing academically, fluent in a language often met with silence in schools. "Whether it is known as Ebonics, jive, or street talk, it is the language spoken by many of our African American children. It is the language through which they first encountered love, nurturance and joy and one that does not lead to success in schools or society."[2]

Lisa Delpit was in a quandary. While she believed in a whole-language approach that embraced diversity, her students were struggling, unable to grasp the language skills they needed, the keys to the language of the mainstream culture. She believes that mainstream ways of speaking and writing represent a language of power that *all* students need to master for success in the larger society. Like a captain who realized that she was sailing in the wrong direction, she charted a new instructional voyage, one that used more traditional methodology. Students diagrammed sentences, learned grammar rules, and memorized verbs. And their performance improved.

But Delpit's traditional approach does not suffer from cultural amnesia. In *Other People's Children,* she shares a vision of classrooms where teachers let the voices of all students come alive and transform the traditional canon to include the knowledge of our multicultural world. For Lisa Delpit, basic skills free students to hear how the language of their culture shapes their thinking, to understand the social realities of their lives, and to become intelligent caretakers of the future. It is a language arts curriculum for all students, including "other people's children."

[1]Lisa Delpit, *Other People's Children: Cultural Conflict in the Classroom* (1995), p. xv.
[2]Lisa Delpit, "Ebonics and Culturally Responsive Schools," *Rethinking Schools* 12 (Fall 1997).

REFLECTION: What images does the phrase "other people's children" evoke in your mind? What is the opposite of "otherness"? How has the school curriculum, both formal and hidden, shaped your definitions? How would you define Delpit's phrase "the language of power"? Other than language arts, choose a content area discussed in this chapter. What is its language of power?

www.mhhe.com/ sadker To learn more about Lisa Delpit, click on *Profiles in Education.*

Writing has been called the *neglected 'R'* (our first clue to the problem). Most students are not proficient writers, and observers blame poor writing performance on sheer lack of attention in schools. At the elementary level, students spend less than three hours a week on writing, and term papers in high school have become rare indeed. There is plenty of blame to go around, from the use and (misuse) of e-mail to emphasis on standards and testing, where correctly "filling in the bubbles" has become the measure of learning.[26]

Social Studies

Topics Social studies includes history, government, geography, economics, sociology, anthropology, and psychology. History remains paramount, yet, like the conflict over the literary canon, multiculturalists and traditionalists disagree on what to include, and what to leave to the null curriculum. The battle over history standards, discussed in Chapter 7, details this conflict. Although history has moved from a narrow emphasis on political and economic landmarks toward a broader perspective of social life and daily human struggles, it has become a victim of *No Child Left Behind,* President Bush's education program. As a result, schools across the nation have been trimming social studies classes and using this time for more reading and mathematics instruction.[27]

The early elementary school social studies program emphasizes self, family, and community. Upper elementary school students begin the study of history, geography, and civics. At the high school level, the focus is on U.S. history and government, but a wide array of electives, such as economics, sociology, law, world history, anthropology, and current events, may be offered.

Tension Points and Trends The inclusion of so many social sciences in this one curricular area means that there is a rich null curriculum. Let's look at geography, for example. One in ten Americans cannot find their own country on a map. Even after two wars with Iraq, only 13 percent of Americans between the age of 18 and 24

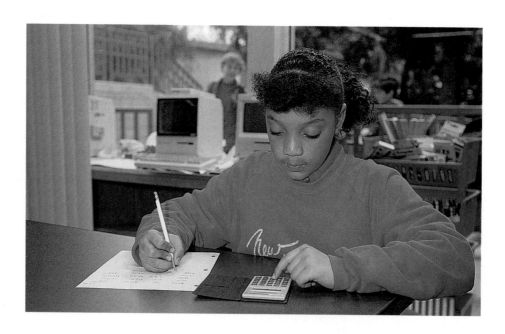

A major focus of current curriculum reform is how to improve girls' mathematics test scores.

(prime age for military service) could even find that country on a map.[28] Civics education (preparing effective citizens) is also central to social studies, yet when twelfth graders were asked to list two ways the American system of government is designed to prevent "absolute arbitrary power," 43 percent could not provide an acceptable answer.[29] As a result of the 9-11 attack, some educators have called for a more patriotic social studies curriculum, while others believe that this is the time for social studies to be less jingoistic and far more analytical. [30]

Mathematics

Topics *No Child Left Behind* has placed mathematics (along with reading) on a curricular pedestal, and schools are investing available resources to improve student test scores in math. The National Council of Teachers of Mathematics (NCTM) has issued and revised mathematics standards that emphasize problem solving and reasoning. In 2000, the NCTM published *Principles and Standards for School Mathematics,* which advocated eliminating ability grouping and tracking to ensure mathematical thinking and problem solving for all. The report endorsed real-world applications of math and the use of technology and computer graphics.[31]

Tension Points and Trends According to the **NAEP (National Assessment of Educational Progress),** average mathematics performance improved over the past few decades, but continues to be among the weakest academic areas on both national and international assessments. By twelfth grade, fewer than one in five Americans attain a proficient score on NAEP (See Figure 6.3). American seniors do not score well

OVERHEADS 74–75
Calculator Use in
Math Class

Advanced Math Courses

FIGURE 6.3
NAEP Achievement: Percentage of students attaining a score test makers consider at or above proficient.

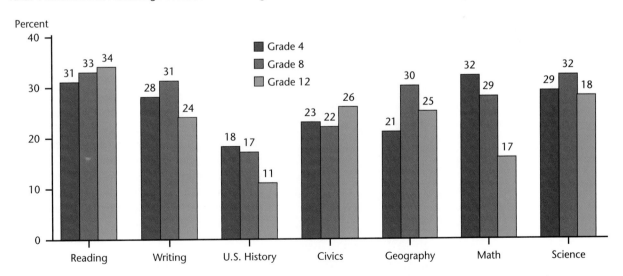

SOURCE: National Center for Education Statistics. NAEP Achievement Scores, 2000, 2001, 2002, 2003) Available at www.nces.ed.gov/nationsreportcard.

REFLECTION: Why do you believe scores drop in the 12th grade? Why is reading an exception? Why does poor performance in U.S. History receive so little attention?

in either general or advanced math when compared to students in other developed nations.[32] American girls have made striking gains in mathematics performance in the past decades, closing the gender gap, yet race and ethnic differences persist, posing a continuing challenge for educators.

Science

Topics At the elementary level, science instruction consists of a variety of topics, from animal and plant studies to astronomy, weather, light, heat, and sound. By middle school, topics are organized into courses like earth science, life science, and physical science. In high school, biology, chemistry, and physics comprise the science core, with earth science, astronomy, and other science courses also available. There are dramatic differences in the quality of high school science courses, with college-bound students receiving a far more rigorous science experience.

OVERHEAD 76
NAEP Achievement Scores

OVERHEAD 77
High School Course
Completion

FIGURE 6.4
Sample problem on the NAEP test of basic science knowledge.

SOURCE: National Assessment of Educational Progress.

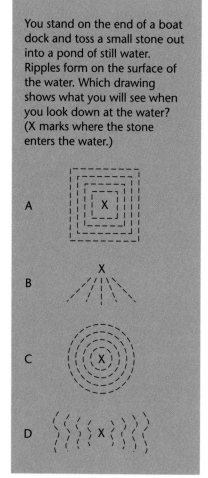

You stand on the end of a boat dock and toss a small stone out into a pond of still water. Ripples form on the surface of the water. Which drawing shows what you will see when you look down at the water? (X marks where the stone enters the water.)

A

B

C

D

REFLECTION: Two in five fourth graders didn't know the answer was C. How did you do?

RAP 2.1
State and National
Curricular Standards, p 273

Tension Points and Trends *Blueprints of Reform,* issued in 1998 by the American Association for the Advancement of Science (AAAS), stressed learning science through investigation, inquiry, discovery, and higher-order thinking. Despite this and similar recommendations, science instruction often relies on rote memorization. The report also recommended that the number of science topics and concepts be reduced, and deeper understanding of key scientific principles be encouraged. The proponents of this "deeper is better" approach collide with those who believe "more is better."[33] Some educators believe that the science core should be rethought, and suggest that a revised physics course offered early in high school would boost student interest in all sciences.[34] Science performance on national and international exams is disappointing, especially at the high school level. (You may want to try your hand at the sample problem in Figure 6.4.) Race, cultural, and gender differences in science enrollments and achievement represent an ongoing challenge. Improving science education often depends on a school's ability to hire well-prepared teachers and purchase costly lab equipment and technology.[35]

Foreign Languages

Topics Changing demographics and increased globalization have fueled foreign language enrollments. A majority of America's students take a foreign language (and almost one-third are enrolled for at least three years), yet fluency is rare. Lessons in grammar and vo-cabulary are giving way to immersion experiences, where students can speak in a more natural setting. While Spanish, French, and German are the most studied, Chinese, Japanese, Russian, Arabic and other languages are finding their way into some public and private schools.[36]

Tension Points and Trends America's power and influence has made English the most common second language around the world—the language of business, science, and diplomacy. Yet, fueled by its geographic isolation, the United States remains one of the most monolingual of all the developed countries. Today's increased international and multicultural interests may overcome this isolation as high schools and colleges re-establish foreign language requirements. Educators are calling for earlier emphasis on the study of foreign language, by the early elementary grades, when learners are more adept at language acquisition, and for instructional periods that are longer than forty or fifty minutes a day.[37]

The Arts

Topics Visual arts, dance, theater, and music constitute the four comprehensive arts, but three out of four students receive no instruction in theater or dance.[38] In elementary school, regular classroom teachers do most of the arts instruction, and it is rarely given serious time or attention. Arts in elementary school includes coloring, painting, cutting out forms, singing, and participation in school plays. The secondary school arts program is more robust, where the facilities support orchestras, graphic arts, ceramics, theater and dance, and the extracurricular program can draw many additional students to these artistic endeavors.

Tension Points and Trends Many educators consider the arts to be shamefully neglected—the last to be included and the first to be cut when the budget ax falls. Less than 5 percent of a school week is typically spent on arts education, and the majority of the teachers are untrained in this field. Increased academic testing and core requirements has further diminished the time available for art education, although research suggests that the arts positively influence academic performance, especially for poorer students.[39] Art standards call for a basic level of competency in each of the four arts disciplines—dance, music, theater, and visual arts, but many criticize the lack of creativity or aesthetic appreciation in today's programs.[40]

Physical Education

Topics High-quality physical education programs emphasize not only physical competence, enjoyment and lifetime activity but also social and psychological development, including leadership, teamwork, and cooperation. In recent years, there has been an emphasis on fitness, aerobics, flexibility, and well-being. Elementary programs are structured around skill development,

---

IN THE NEWS

Better Late Than Early

Minneapolis teenage students are sleeping about an hour later these days. Sleep authorities suggest that adolescent bodies can't manage early morning wake-up calls. The school district changed the 7:15 A.M. high school start time to 8:30 A.M. Middle schoolers don't start school until 9:40 A.M. What are the results of letting students sleep later? According to researchers at the University of Minnesota, these students are sleeping more, earning better grades, and experiencing less depression. And one more advantage: They are less likely to oversleep and miss school.

SOURCE: *The Startribune.com*, November 1998, *The Washington Post*, August 29, 2001.

 What's new in education? Click on *News Feeds*.

Across the nation, music programs range from grandiose spectacles to the sounds of silence. How does a school's music program amplify its culture?

and classes vary dramatically in quality. Middle school programs are often the first time students have certified PE specialists and a more structured course of study. By high school, the curriculum is governed by electives from aerobics and basketball to soccer and yoga.

Tension Points and Trends Obesity has become a major health concern in America, with 15 percent of six- to nineteen-year-olds overweight.[41] Yet physical education accounts for less than 100 minutes of the school week.[42] The testing and standards movement along with tight school budgets have taken resources from physical education. Although Title IX requires coeducational classes, many physical education programs continue to be gender-segregated.[43] By high school, boys are twice as likely as girls to be enrolled in physical education.[44]

Health

INTERACTIVE ACTIVITY
Create a Class Schedule.
What do you think your
students' week should
consist of?

Topics Years ago, health education meant little more than learning about the four basic food groups and routine dental care. A film on sex education at the high school level might "round out" the health program. Today, instruction includes tobacco, alcohol, and drug abuse; use of steroids; dietary patterns that contribute to disease; sedentary lifestyle; and sexual behaviors that result in unintended pregnancy, HIV or STD infection.[45]

Tension Points and Trends The dangers presented by teen pregnancy, AIDS, and STDs have created strong support for health programs, with over 90 percent of adults favoring such programs in high school, and over 80 percent supporting these programs at the middle school.[46] Despite this support, in what has been termed the "Culture Wars," traditionally minded individuals advocate an abstinence-only program, and seek to bar any other sex information from school. These critics argue that sex education promotes sexual activity. Those who support comprehensive sex education argue that such programs save lives and do not promote promiscuity.[47]

IN THE NEWS

Backpackless

Public schools are getting serious about student backpacks.

- At North Carroll High School in Hampstead, MD, students may take backpacks to and from school but not to and from class. Teachers were having difficulty navigating the halls around the bulging packs, and administrators complained that food hidden in the packs was adding to the rodent problem.

- Other schools were instituting backpack lessons out of a concern that the weighty packs were contributing to back and neck problems. Keep both shoulder straps on at all times or use a wheelie.

- Cumberland and neighboring Robeson County (NC) require that student backpacks be clear or transparent mesh to protect against drugs and weapons being brought to school.

SOURCES: *The American School Board Journal,* November 1998; *Back Pack Troubles from Back-to-School Backpacks* Lesson Tutor Online (March 29, 2001), www.lessontutor.com; Fayetteville (NC) *Observer-Times* (August 15, 1999).

  What's new in education? Click on *News Feeds.*

Career Technical Education

Topics Career technical education (formerly vocational education) occurs informally in elementary school, but in high school is clearly targeted to specific skills and careers, ranging from cosmetology and auto body repair to graphic arts and computer science. Surprisingly, virtually all high school students in America take at least one course considered to be vocational in nature, and nearly half of these students are college bound.[48] Despite the derogatory assumption that career technical education is for low-ability students, it is a valued and highly selected program in countries like Germany. America's programs lack this recognition and enrollments have been declining.[49]

Tension Points and Trends Critics charge that the standards and testing movement is fueled by the belief that all high school graduates should be ready for college, whether they choose to attend or not. They see this as an elitist movement that has contributed to the decline of career technical education and predict a negative impact on the economy. The lack of modern equipment and well-trained staff represent a continuing problem.[50]

In 1990, Congress passed the **Carl D. Perkins Vocational and Applied Technology Act** (amended in 1998 and 2004), signaling a shift from the traditional job-skills orientation of vocational education to a broader integration with academic instruction. Proponents of this approach argue that higher-order thinking skills should be emphasized in all vocational courses in order to adequately prepare students for today's job market. The original Perkins Act also channeled federal funds to school districts with the highest proportions of poor students, promoted nonsexist career choices, assisted displaced homemakers as they re-entered the job market, and offered support for post–high school vocational training programs. The government has backed away from these programs and certain groups, especially women, have lost out as states take over these efforts.[51]

 # New Directions for the Curriculum

Technological developments have shifted the focus of the U.S. economy from the production of goods (industrial) to information processing (postindustrial), as new careers in technology, computers, and communications emerge. This accelerated rate of change is also impacting the school curriculum. The tremendous knowledge explosion has produced more information than schools can teach, and many believe that schools need to turn away from the traditional curriculum and emphasize the thinking skills needed in the new information society.

What are these more relevant thinking skills? One of the pioneering works, *Teaching for Thinking: Theory and Application,* identified "thinking operations," **critical thinking skills,** that should be taught directly: comparing, interpreting, observing, summarizing, classifying, decision making, creating, and criticizing. *Teaching for Thinking* incorporates these critical thinking skills into such subjects as mathematics

INTERACTIVE ACTIVITY
Create a Class Schedule Using Standards.
Now organize your students' week based on a set of standards.

FOCUS QUESTION 6
What current curriculum directions may impact you?

CLASS ACTIVITY: TIME CAPSULE
IM, Activity 6:6

Curriculum can use activities that are innately interesting to foster a variety of learning activities. Here, students performing in this play might incorporate literature and history lessons, artistic expression, and social learnings among others.

RELATED READING
How People Learn: Brain, Mind, Experience, and School, John D. Bransford, Ann L. Brown, and Rodney R. Cocking, *editors* (1999).

CRITICAL THINKING QUESTION
What are the relevant thinking skills for today's students? Can respondents cite examples that strengthen their suggestions?

VIDEO SEGMENT 15
Integrating Diversity into the High School Curriculum

OVERHEAD 78
Curriculum Development

CLASS ACTIVITY:
CURRICULUM TRENDS
IM, Activity 6:3

and history, in which teachers ask higher-order questions that prompt students to analyze and evaluate data. Research indicates that not only do students learn critical thinking skills in such programs, but their knowledge of the content also increases when they apply these skills in the classroom.[52]

Teaching for Thinking is just one of several approaches. David Perkins of Harvard University's Project Zero emphasizes thinking frames, so that students develop a framework for acquiring information, internalizing practices, and transferring information.[53] Another approach, developed by Robert Marzano and his colleagues, stresses **metacognition** which enables students to monitor and control their commitment, attitudes, and attention during the learning process. Important traits for creative thinking include the ability to push one's own limits, the willingness to look at situations in new ways, and an ability to focus intensely on tasks. If these behaviors can be taught to students, they will become independent learners for the rest of their lives. Some educators are confident that these critical thinking skills are useful beyond the schoolhouse walls. **Critical pedagogy** is the term given to applying such analytic tools to society at large, and merges teaching and learning with social improvement. The purpose of critical pedagogy is for students and teachers to work on authentic social challenges such as eliminating pollution in a local lake or promoting consumer education in a poor community. Critical pedagogy connects schooling with actions to enhance the quality of life.[54]

As you have read about today's curriculum and how it has changed during the past decades, you may have felt a sense of déjà vu, with many recurring themes. There seems to be a timeless struggle among educators who hold differing visions of what schools should do. While other professions demonstrate steady, long-term progress, researcher Robert Slavin says that "education resembles such fields as fashion and design, in which change mirrors shifts in taste and social climate and is not usually thought of as true progress."[55] Many educators yearn for a more stable time when the radical curricular swing will be fine-tuned, so that innovation will depend more on research about what works than on the politics of who is in power. Only then can we best meet the needs of our students.

 ## The Saber-Tooth Curriculum

How can the curriculum prepare for tomorrow while preserving the past? Here is how curriculum scholar Michael Apple puts it:

> The curriculum must simultaneously be both conservative and critical. It must preserve the ideals that have guided discourse in the U.S. for centuries: a faith in the American people, a commitment to expanding equality, and a commitment to diversity and liberty. Yet it must also empower individuals to question the ethics of their institutions and to criticize them when they fail to meet these ideals.[56]

Unless we carefully consider what a school is for and what kind of curriculum can meet those goals, we might end up with a "saber-tooth curriculum." Since many of you may never have read this classic satire on Paleolithic curriculum written by Abner Peddiwell, known in real life as Harold Benjamin, we will summarize the story of **The Saber-Tooth Curriculum** for you here. This clever parody reveals the flaws of a saber-tooth curriculum. Are there any positive aspects of this kind of curriculum?

• • •

New-Fist was a brilliant educator and thinker of prehistoric times. He watched the children of his tribe playing with bones, sticks, and brightly colored pebbles, and he speculated on what these youngsters might learn that would help the tribe derive more food, shelter, clothing, security, and, in short, a better life.

Eventually, he determined that in order to obtain food and shelter, the people of his tribe must learn to fish with their bare hands and to club and skin little woolly horses; and in order to live in safety, they must learn to drive away the saber-tooth tigers with fire. So New-Fist developed the first curriculum. It consisted of three basic subjects: (1) "Fish-Grabbing-with-the-Bare-Hands," (2) "Woolly-Horse-Clubbing," and (3) "Saber-Tooth-Tiger-Scaring-with-Fire."

New-Fist taught the children these subjects, and they enjoyed these purposeful activities more than playing with colored pebbles. The years went by, and by the time New-Fist was called by the Great Mystery to the Land of the Setting Sun, all the tribe's children had been systematically schooled in these three skills; the tribe was prosperous and secure.

All would have been well and the story might have ended here had it not been for an unforeseen change—the beginning of the New Ice Age, which sent a great glacier sliding down upon the tribe. The glacier so muddied the waters of the creeks that it was impossible for people to catch fish with their bare hands. Also, the melted water of the glacier made the ground marshy, and the little woolly horses left for higher and drier land. They were replaced by shy and speedy antelopes with such a scent for danger that no one could get close enough to club them. And finally, as if these disruptions were not enough, the increasing dampness of the air caused the saber-tooth tigers to contract pneumonia and die. The tigers, however, were replaced by an even greater danger: ferocious glacial bears, who showed no fear of fire. Prosperity and security became distant memories for the suffering tribe.

Fortunately, a new breed of brilliant educators emerged. One tribesman, his stomach rumbling with hunger, grew frustrated with fruitless fish-grabbing in cloudy waters. He fashioned a crude net and in one hour caught more fish than the whole tribe could have caught had they fish-grabbed for an entire day. Another tribesman fashioned a snare with which he could trap the swift antelope, and a third dug a pit that captured and secured the ferocious bears.

As a result of these new inventions, the tribe again became happy and prosperous. Some radicals even began to criticize the school's curriculum and urged that net-making, snare-setting, and pit-digging were indispensable to modern life and should be taught in the schools. But the wise old men who controlled the schools objected:

> With all the intricate details of fish-grabbing, horse-clubbing, and tiger-scaring—the standard cultural subjects—the school curriculum is too crowded now. We can't add these fads and frills of net-making, antelope-snaring, and—of all things—bear-killing. Why, at the very thought, the body of the great New-Fist, founder of our Paleolithic educational system, would turn over in its burial cairn. What we need to do is to give our young people a more thorough grounding in the fundamentals. . . . The essence of true education is timelessness. It is something that endures through changing conditions like a solid rock standing squarely and firmly in the middle of a raging torrent. You must know that there are some eternal verities, and the saber-tooth curriculum is one of them.[57]

• • •

The Saber-Tooth Curriculum was written in 1939, but it has meaning today. Clearly, educators need to avoid a curriculum out of touch with the reality of today's students and thoughtlessly programmed for obsolescence. No educator worth his or her salt wants to be caught waving unnecessary firebrands at tigers long extinct. Today's debate over curricula for various ethnic groups versus a common, Eurocentric core is related to issues raised in *The Saber-Tooth Curriculum*. Is Latin a "saber-tooth" subject? What about the ancient history of the Romans and Greeks? Should these topics make way for subjects more relevant, useful, or culturally inclusive? If we omit these, do we lose an important part of the nation's cultural heritage? Is there room for everything? If not, how do we establish priorities? These are the kinds of questions thoughtful teachers face on a daily basis.

MULTIPLE INTELLIGENCE CONNECTION

Could students illustrate *The Saber-Tooth Curriculum* with a political cartoon? Are there other chapter themes that could be similarly drawn?

SUMMARY

CHAPTER REVIEW

Go to the Online Learning Center to take a chapter self-quiz, practice with key terms, and review concepts from the chapter.

1. **What curriculum is taught in schools?**

   The explicit or formal curriculum includes objectives, tests, materials, standards and syllabi, and transmits the culture or anticipates societal needs. The extracurriculum includes sports, clubs, student government, and school publications, while the implicit, or hidden, curriculum, emerges incidentally from the interaction between the students and school environment. The null curriculum includes many rich learning possibilities not part of the school curriculum.

2. **What is the place of the extracurriculum in school life?**

   Eighty percent of all students participate in this voluntary curriculum, which advocates argue builds self-esteem, civic participation, positive race relations, and professional and academic aspirations. Skeptics doubt these claims, and argue that the huge resources devoted towards athletics could be better spent on academics. Some states have instituted "no pass, no play" rules, excluding low-achieving students from participating in varsity sports.

3. How do the formal and the hidden curriculum differ?

Test scores, curricular standards, public and political pressure are only some of the forces shaping the formal curriculum. But in addition to these intentional lessons, schools teach a hidden or implicit curriculum. The norms and mores of the hidden curriculum can reinforce formal learnings, or contradict them.

4. How do social forces shape curriculum development over time?

Literacy and religion dominated the colonial curriculum, and sexism, classism and racism kept education in the hands of the few. As the idea of freedom grew in the eighteenth-century, the curriculum shifted toward the secular and opened the schoolhouse doors to white girls and poorer children. As a result of nationalism, democratization, and industrial development, the curriculum in the nineteenth century moved toward universal literacy, vocational competence, and preparation for citizenship. In the first half of the twentieth century, John Dewey and the progressive movement promoted creative expression, social skills, and a more integrated study of subject areas. The mission of high schools was to meet the needs of all the students, not only the college-bound. In 1957, the Soviets launched *Sputnik,* and the poor performance of American schools was blamed for the country's "defeat" in the race for space. As a result, there was an increased focus on content performance, particularly in math and science. The curriculum in the late 1960s and the 1970s reflected the nation's social concerns, including peace studies, ecology and the contributions of women and minorities, and led to the dissemination of open classrooms. By the 1980s and 1990s, the social scene had changed dramatically, triggered by a more conservative national administration and *A Nation at Risk,* decrying the nation's mediocre schools. Spurred on by charges of poor standardized test scores, back-to-basics, a core curriculum and cultural literacy grew in importance. This traditional approach is reflected in the current standards and testing movement.

5. What are contemporary subject matter trends and tension points?

National standards and testing continue to drive the curriculum, and *No Child Left Behind* has placed reading and math instruction on a curricular pedestal. While some advocate a phonics approach to reading, others support whole language instruction, and many teachers find themselves using elements of both. The recent emphasis on the traditional canon comes at the expense of women and non-Western authors. Although reading scores have improved, poor student writing remains a problem. Social studies curriculum has been criticized for lacking international perspective and doing a poor job in preparing students for their civic responsibilities. National math standards emphasize both an understanding of critical concepts and their application to real world situations, yet student performance here is another area of concern. U.S. students lag behind in foreign language instruction, and many educators prefer foreign language instruction to begin at an earlier age. Art education receives little emphasis in most schools, with three out of four students receiving neither theater nor dance instruction. The current emphasis to promote lifelong health benefits and enjoyment is compromised because fewer than one in three high school students participates in daily physical education programs. Health and sex education programs are receiving more public support due to the health threats confronting today's students.

6. What current curriculum directions may impact you?

The knowledge explosion has produced more information than teachers or students can master. Some educators believe that we should now focus on *how* we learn and use

CURRENT NEWS FROM POWERWEB

To access PowerWeb, go to Chapter 6 on the Online Learning Center to read current articles and to access news feeds about:

- Curriculum
- Education Standards
- Future of Education
- Education Reform

knowledge, including critical thinking skills, metacognition, and critical pedagogy. Robert Slavin believes education is too much like "fashion and design," and looks to a time when the curriculum will emerge from research and reasoning, not popular opinion. *The Saber-Tooth Curriculum* teaches us that a curriculum should preserve the past, but not be limited by it.

EXTENDED LEARNING

Go to Chapter 6 on your *Resources for Exploring Education* CD-ROM to access Case Studies, Readings, and Media Observations.

CASE STUDIES

- Tyler Johnson: An experienced teacher expresses his frustration with applying the NCTM Standards in his second-grade class as he details a lesson he taught.

- Chris Kettering: A teacher finds to his dismay that his white, middle-class students are not interested in social activism and that he is unable to promote awareness and openmindedness in them.

- Sarah Stewart: A first-year teacher trained in whole language is hired two weeks into the school year to teach fourth grade. After beginning her job, she finds that everyone else is teaching traditionally, and she begins to have second thoughts about the feasibility of applying a radical new approach.

READINGS

- Marge Scherer. "How and Why Standards Can Improve Student Achievement: A Conversation with Robert J. Marzano."

- Hilda Taba. Selection from *Curriculum Development: Theory and Practice.*

KEY TERMS AND PEOPLE

academy, 212

Mortimer Adler, 216

"back to basics", 215

basal readers, 218

Ernest Boyer, 216

Jerome Bruner, 213

canon, 218

career technical
   education, 226

core curriculum, 216

critical pedagogy, 228

critical thinking skills, 227

Cultural Literacy, 217

curriculum, 203

Lisa Delpit, 219

discovery method, 214

English grammar school, 212

environmental
   education, 215

extracurriculum, 205

formal or explicit
   curriculum, 204

John Goodlad, 204

Jules Henry, 208

High School, 216

E. D. Hirsch, Jr., 217

hornbook, 210

implicit or hidden
   curriculum, 205

individualized education
   program (IEP), 214

interest (learning)
   centers, 215

junior high school, 212

Latin grammar school, 210

life-adjustment
   education, 218

metacognition, 228

multicultural
   approach, 214

National Assessment of
   Educational Progress
   (NAEP), 221

*The New England
   Primer,* 221

null curriculum, 204

open classroom, 215

The Paideia Proposal, 217

peace studies, 215

DISCUSSION QUESTIONS AND ACTIVITIES

1. For some students, the hidden curriculum and the extracurriculum are most central to their school experience. Define the roles of these unofficial curricular experiences in your own education. If you were placed in charge of a school today, how would you change these hidden and extracurricular experiences? How might your changes be evident in elementary, middle, and high schools? Why?

2. Discuss your reactions to the current curriculum with your classmates. Were there any topics you studied that you now see as irrelevant? What subjects should be taught differently? Are there any subjects that are not included in the curriculum but that should be?

3. If you were given the job of developing a core curriculum for elementary school, what would it look like? What would you include in a core curriculum for middle and secondary school? for postsecondary education?

4. Reconsider your high school curriculum experience. Estimate the proportion of required courses versus electives. Did students perceive the electives as an opportunity to explore areas of interest or to avoid more rigorous courses? If you were in charge of a school's offerings, would you increase or decrease electives? Why? What particular electives would you want to design and teach?

5. Consider past and present curricular developments and think about the changes in contemporary society. Then, with the help of your instructor and classmates, predict what the school curriculum may be like in the year 2020.

 WEB-*TIVITIES*

1. The Formal or Explicit Curriculum
2. The Curriculum Time Machine
3. New Directions for the Curriculum

REEL TO REAL TEACHING

MR. HOLLAND'S OPUS (1995)
Run Time: 142 minutes

Synopsis: Glenn Holland is an aspiring composer who takes a teaching job to support his family. As the years unfold, the joy of sharing his passion for music with his students becomes his new definition of success.

MUSIC OF THE HEART (1999)
Run Time: 124 minutes

Synopsis: This is a true story of Roberta Guaspari and her fight against the board of education. Her effort to teach music to underprivileged students in East Harlem involved an innovative violin program.

Reflection:

1. *Mr. Holland's Opus* chronicles a 30-year teaching career. What changes in the music curriculum did you observe? In Mr. Holland's instructional style? What personal and institutional factors influenced these changes?

2. How did gender, race, and socioeconomic status influence the curriculum, teaching and efforts to save music education in *Music of the Heart?* In *Mr. Holland's Opus?*

3. How did the arts influence the education and life experiences of Gertrude and Sadler in *Mr. Holland's Opus?* Guadalupe and Naeem Adisa in *Music of the Heart?* What role did the fine arts play in your elementary and secondary education? In your life? Do your experiences parallel those of the films' characters?

4. Consider Mr. Holland's comment: "The day they cut the football budget in this state, that will be the end of Western Civilization as we know it!" Why do you think extracurricular athletics are often given priority in school budgets over music, art, and even physical education?

Follow-up Activity: It's time to take a stand! You are a colleague of Mr. Holland at John F. Kennedy High or Ms. Guaspari in East Harlem (or choose any school where the fine arts are targeted for elimination).* The local school board is holding finance hearings and you decide to share your opinion. In 500 words or less, create talking points. Use scenes from the films, information from the chapter, and your own life experiences as supporting evidence.

*If you feel strongly for or against another course potentially threatened by budget cuts (sign language, computer animation, child care) use this example for the position paper.

How do you rate this film? Go to *Reel to Real Teaching* in the Critics' Corner to review this film.

www.mhhe.com/
sadker7e

FOR FURTHER READING

Connecting Girls and Science: Constructivism, Feminism, and Science Education Reform, by Elaine V. Howes (2002). Describes the powerful results that can occur in secondary science classrooms when students' interest and curiosity about science are brought firmly to the center of the curriculum.

Critical Pedagogy: Notes from the Real World, by Joan Wink (1999). Personal stories about real teachers and students bring the complex theories of critical pedagogy and literacy into today's classroom. Lessons and activities model social justice practices in action.

Developing Personal, Social and Moral Education through Physical Education, by Anthony Laker (2001). Provides practical suggestions for teaching about culture, cooperation, spirituality, and emotional development in the physical education classroom. Activities that focus on fitness and lifetime sports are emphasized.

Issues in Social Studies: Voices from the Classroom, by Cameron White (2000). Trends in social studies content, such as multicultural education, citizenship, and social justice, are explored. Emphasizes strategies to create reflective students.

Radical Equations: Organizing Math Literacy in America's Schools, by Robert Moses and Charles Cobb (2001). Chronicles the success of the Algebra Project, a civil rights program in schools. Founded on the belief that math literacy is a prerequisite for full citizenship in society, the Project works with parents, teachers, and students to foster achievement for all students, especially those of color.

Standards, Testing, and the Controversy over Who Controls the Curriculum

CHAPTER 7

FOCUS QUESTIONS

1. What forces shape the school curriculum?
2. What are the provisions and criticisms of *No Child Left Behind*?
3. How does the standards movement influence what is taught in school?
4. What are the concerns with high-stakes testing?
5. How can we rethink curriculum and testing?
6. How do textbook publishers and state adoption committees "drive" the curriculum?
7. What are the seven forms of bias in instructional materials?
8. How do religious differences impact curricular materials?
9. Why are schoolbooks so frequently the targets of censorship?
10. Should the curriculum focus on teaching a core knowledge, or focus on the demands of a changing world?

 WHAT DO YOU THINK? The Cheating Problem. Answer the online poll and see where your responses fall in relation to those of your colleagues.

CHAPTER PREVIEW

"We shape our buildings and afterwards our buildings shape us," said Winston Churchill. Had the noted statesman been a noted educator, he might have rephrased this epigram, substituting curriculum for buildings, for what children learn in school today will affect the kind of adults they will become and the kind of society they will eventually create. In fact, it is the power of curriculum to shape students and, ultimately, society that takes curriculum development out of the realms of philosophy and education and into the political arena.

In buildings from the little red schoolhouse to the White House, adults (and occasionally their charges) discuss what is supposed to be learned in school. Two trends are pushing all schools toward a similar curriculum: the indomitable textbook and the recent emphasis on state standards and testing. While the current standards movement stresses the importance of students doing well on high-risk tests, it is teachers and schools that are also feeling the pressure to "perform." Protests (perhaps better titled "antitests") have been growing against the increasing influence of standardized tests in determining how teachers and students invest their time. The *No Child Left Behind* Act has raised the stakes in high-stakes testing, so not only students, but entire schools can now "fail." The benefits of standards, and the many problems with high-stakes tests, are explored in this chapter. We also consider some of the more positive and creative ways of looking at the school curriculum and testing options.

Many believe that even before the emergence of this new "unofficial national curriculum," we already had a de facto national curriculum: the textbook. For decades, publishers have happily crafted texts to market demands, even if they were not always the best texts for students. And if all that were not enough, the continuing threat of censorship makes the teacher's role in selecting materials to supplement textbooks a constant challenge.

Who controls the curriculum? Let's find out.

CHAPTER FOCUS
The power of curriculum to shape students and eventually society invites controversy over who controls the curriculum. Many groups that have a role in curriculum formation are described. Related issues of standards, testing, bias, and censorship are explored. For a chapter outline, see the IM.

The Faculty Room

TEACHING TIP
Give students a few
minutes to discuss the
scenario that opens this
chapter. Which character
do they suspect best
represents their own view?

A casual conversation in the faculty room opens this chapter door on the teacher's role in curricular decisions:

JO: Were you at yesterday's faculty meeting? The sales reps from the publishing company showed their new textbook series.

MAYA: No, I had an emergency dentist appointment—a root canal. That was painful enough! What's the new series like?

JO: Fabulous. It must be worth big money—superslick covers, beautiful photos, and graphics. And talk about supplementary materials. They have everything! It's got a website, which they promise to update regularly, that includes practical student projects. They went online for us yesterday, and it looks great. The objectives are totally spelled out, and there's a step-by-step teacher's guide saying exactly how to cover each objective. There are discussion questions after reading assignments and a student workbook with activities for the kids to do after we've finished the reading. They even have huge banks of test questions for weekly tests and unit exams on CD-ROM.

MAYA: What's got you so excited?

JO: Excited? The prep time alone is endless. Anything that saves me hours, I'm for. And these books look like a time-saving resource.

MAYA: Jo, we've been through so many TGIF afternoons—you know I need more "quality and quantity" time in my life. But some of these new comprehensive textbook systems make me nervous.

JO: What do you mean?

MAYA: I'm not so sure the people in slick offices (who do the slick covers) know what's best for our kids. What makes them so smart that they can determine what we should tell our students? I know my kids! What kind of expertise do they have to tell us how to teach? When was the last time those textbook writers were in a classroom, anyway? I'm a professional, and I am not ready to relinquish my control over what and how I teach.

JO: Sounds like you. But they can save you a lot of grief. You don't want to step on anyone's toes, or get the "Parents for an American Curriculum" breathing down your neck. Those textbooks sidestep a lot of those controversies for you.

MAYA: The other day I was talking with Jena, the new teacher who works across the hall from me. She just graduated from college a few years ago, and she has some terrific ideas. She's using an individualized reading program, and she's really got the kids into it. Instead of the basal reading selections, she's got the class reading everything from Judy Blume to Tolkien. And the kids are loving it. It's a tremendous success. But, instead of being psyched, she's in panic mode—afraid she's harming her students' reading development, because she's not following the official basal reader or the new state standards. The upcoming state reading assessment worries her. If her kids don't do well on that state exam, she's toast.

JO: You're kidding!

MAYA: I wish I were.

Who and What Shape the Curriculum?

From state standards to parental expectations, the curriculum is shaped by a pressure cooker of different interest groups (See Figure 7.1). Everyone from the president of the United States to a single parent can impact what is taught in your classroom. Here is a brief tour of some of the hands in the curricular pie.

Teachers

Teachers develop curriculum both formally and informally. They may serve on textbook selection committees that determine what texts the school will purchase, or they may actually work on writing a district's curriculum. In a less formal but no less powerful way, classroom teachers interpret and adapt whatever official text or curriculum guide has been assigned, stressing certain points in a text while giving scant attention to others; supplementing with teacher-made materials or directing students to the Internet.

Parental and Community Groups

Parents can be quite forceful in impacting the curriculum. They might advocate for more rigorous academic courses, concerned about poor student performance on standardized tests, or they may desire more practical vocational training, such as an increase in computer science courses. Banning certain books or videos from the curriculum is also not unusual. In more conservative communities, religious fundamentalists have objected to the absence of Christian values, while liberal communities have objected to books that use racial, ethnic or gender slurs and stereotypes.

Students

During the 1960s and 1970s, students demanded curricular relevance. Although students have not seemed particularly interested in influencing curriculum policy recently, they have been active in protests against standardized testing. Typically, students are given some freedom to select topics for independent projects, research papers, book reviews, and even authentic learning.

Administrators

Principals, in their role as instructional leaders, can wield substantial influence in shaping the curriculum. For example, a principal announces at a faculty meeting that the school's scores on the state standardized test in mathematics were disappointing, and this year's priority is to raise those scores. The result might well be a math curriculum that "teaches to the test." Sometimes central-office personnel, such as a language arts coordinator or a social studies supervisor, might create a new or revised school or district curriculum.

The State Government

States are now assuming a stronger leadership role in education, and their interest in curriculum matters has sharpened through the creation of state standards, curriculum

FOCUS QUESTION 1
What forces shape the school curriculum?

TEACHING TIP
As a preview to this section, have students brainstorm some of the "hands" in the curricular pie.

CLASS ACTIVITY: FORCES THAT SHAPE THE CURRICULUM
IM, Activity 7:2

OVERHEADS 79–81
Shaping the Curriculum

Who and What Shape the Curriculum?

Decision-Making Power

Figure 7.1
A pressure cooker of groups shaping the curriculum.

REFLECTION: What groups today exert the most influence? Do you see all these groups as a mark of democratic participation, or an inappropriate intrusion in curricular decision making?

guides and frameworks for all state schools to follow. In more conservative states, the role of religion and the treatment of evolution versus creationism are hot-button issues. In more liberal states, instructional materials are expected to include diversity.

Local Government

Local school boards make a variety of curriculum decisions, requiring courses from AIDS education to technology. Supporters feel that local school boards should have a strong voice in the curriculum, because they are closest to the needs of the local community and the interests of the students. Others feel that school board members lack the training and broad perspective needed to make curricular decisions.

Colleges and Universities

Institutions of higher learning influence curricula through their entrance requirements, which spell out courses high school students must take to gain admittance. As A. Bartlett Giamatti noted when he was president of Yale University,

> The high schools in this country are always at the mercy of the colleges. The colleges change their requirements and their admissions criteria and the high schools . . . are constantly trying to catch up with what the colleges are thinking. When the colleges don't seem to know what they think over a period of time, it's no wonder that this oscillation takes place all the way through the system.[1]

Standardized Tests

The results of state and national tests, from the state subject matter tests needed for graduation to the SATs, influence what is taught in the school. If students perform poorly in one or more areas of these standardized tests, the government or public pressure pushes school officials to strengthen the curriculum in these weak spots.

Schools of education are not immune from the current focus on test performance. Because an increasing number of states are requiring new teachers to take qualifying tests, such as the National Teacher Exam (NTE, Praxis series), these tests influence what is covered in teacher education programs. For example, if Benjamin Bloom's Taxonomy of Educational Objectives is emphasized on such tests, teacher education colleges will teach more about Bloom in their own programs.

Education Commissions and Committees

From time to time in the history of U.S. education, various committees, usually on a national level, have been called upon to study an aspect of education. Their reports often draw national attention and influence elementary and secondary curricula. The 1983 report, *A Nation at Risk,* and the National Education Summit in 1989 led to a more uniform core of courses, and a program for testing student progress.

Professional Organizations

Many professional organizations such as the National Education Association (NEA), the American Federation of Teachers (AFT), the National Association for the Education of Young Children (NAEYC), and numerous subject area associations (teacher groups in English, math, science, and the like)—publish journals and hold conferences that emphasize curriculum needs and developments. Their programs and materials may focus on teaching with technology, multicultural education, or authentic learning. Teachers, inspired by these presentations, might choose to modify their curriculum and implement new approaches and ideas.

Special Interest Groups

Major business and professional organizations—from labor unions to media conglomerates—have educational outreach programs, replete with curricular materials and instant lesson plans. These "how to" pieces range from using a daily newspaper for social studies to bringing the Olympics to your gymnasium. They are often so current and well-framed that they are easily added to a teacher's agenda, and may become part of the formal curriculum. It pays to be wary; citizen and business groups with wholesome names can have quite partisan purposes.

MULTIPLE INTELLIGENCE CONNECTION
The text refers to a pressure cooker in describing the forces that shape the curriculum. What other images come to mind? Can students develop a website, concept map, or other graphic illustration that informs their classmates? Discuss how the shapes, connecting lines, and colors of their graphic might be improved.

Publishers

The major goal of textbook publishers is—not surprisingly—to sell books. That is why textbooks are attractively packaged and chock full of terms and names, but unfortunately, do less well in providing depth or conflicting points of view. Textbooks come to market meeting the demands not of scholars, but of purchasers. Today's increasing emphasis on state standards and high-stakes tests are also influencing publishers.

The Federal Government

The federal government influences the curriculum through judicial decisions and legislation designed to promote a specific goal. For example, since 1965, the Elementary and Secondary Education Act (ESEA) has promoted education for children from low-income families. In 2001, ESEA was reauthorized under a new name, *No Child Left*

Behind, a very different kind of law that has become the center of a growing school controversy.

 ## No Child Left Behind

FOCUS QUESTION 2
What are the provisions and criticisms of *No Child Left Behind?*

OVERHEAD 82
No Desire to Turn Back

VIDEO SEGMENT 16
Explaining Standardized Test Scores to Parents: A Dramatization

OVERHEAD 83
When Students Do Poorly

Both Democrats and Republicans rallied round President Bush's **No Child Left Behind (NCLB)** legislation in 2001, a law that promised to radically change the federal-state approach to schooling. In addition, the law pledged that special attention would be paid to the performance of underachieving groups. Advocates spoke of the quiet bias of "low expectations" that allowed poor and minority students to fail. *NCLB* would change all that by creating standards that would inspire academic progress for all students. Education Secretary Rod Paige described the legislation this way: "Only if we hold schools and school districts accountable for the improved achievement of all students will we meet the goal of leaving no child behind."[2]

NCLB made it clear that progress would be measured by tests, and failing schools would either improve or be closed. Nationwide polls conducted by Public Agenda (2002) found a stunning 87 percent of Americans approve the Bush plan to test all third- through eighth-graders. Most Americans (53 percent) believe that test results are usually accurate and reliable. Only 11 percent of public school parents report that their child's school requires too many standardized tests. And when strikingly poor results come in, the public (57 percent) is also clear on who to blame: schools. (See Figure 7.2.) Both Democrats and Republicans have clamored aboard the legislation. Representative George Miller (D-CA), a leading education advocate, remarked: "This bill will help return our school system to the original goals of the Elementary and Secondary Education Act—to ensure that all children have the opportunity to learn regardless of income, background, or racial or ethnic identity. But unlike the laws on the books for over thirty-five years, we will back our commitment with a set of unambiguous expectations, time lines, and resources."[3]

Figure 7.2
When students do poorly.

SOURCE: Public Agenda, September 2000.

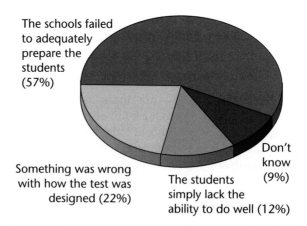

If you heard that many students in your school district did poorly on a standardized test, which of the following would be your most likely reaction?

The schools failed to adequately prepare the students (57%)

Something was wrong with how the test was designed (22%)

The students simply lack the ability to do well (12%)

Don't know (9%)

REFLECTION: Do you believe that schools have more to lose or to gain in the testing culture? Why is the public so ready to equate test scores with school performance?

But after only one year, Representative Miller and many others were attacking this key piece of education legislation. Let's take a look at the major provisions of *NCLB*, and then explore what the criticism is all about.

- *Annual Testing.* By the 2005–06 school year, reading and math assessments from grades 3–8 are required, with each state deciding on which test to use and what a passing or "proficient" grade is. By 2007–08, science assessments begin in elementary, middle and high school. Schools must report not only individual test scores, but also scores by race, ethnicity, disability, social class, and limited English proficiency to ensure that no group is left behind. Underperforming schools must improve—or they will be closed.

- *Academic Improvement.* States must define academic proficiency for all students, and all students must be proficient in reading and mathematics by 2013–14. The progress of each state and each school will be measured annually, and schools that fail to make **adequate yearly progress (AYP)** for two consecutive years are labeled "underperforming." Such schools are entitled to special assistance, but they must also give parents the option of sending their children to "successful" schools, and pay transportation costs. If the school does not achieve AYP for three years, additional supplemental services must be provided to children, including private tutoring, also paid for by the school. After four years of unsatisfactory test grades, the state institutes major staff and curricular changes. After five years, the school is closed and is either reconstituted by the state or reopened as a charter school.

- *Report Cards.* States and school districts must provide the public with "Report Cards" of district and school progress—or lack of progress. Underperforming schools must be made public.

- *Faculty Qualifications.* All teachers hired by 2005–06 must be "highly qualified," licensed with an academic major in the field they are teaching. Paraprofessionals must have at least two years of college or pass a rigorous test. Parents must be informed if their child's teacher is not "highly qualified."

Much of the criticism of *NCLB* has been leveled at the testing provisions and the impact those provisions will have on public schools. Critics argue that deciding if a school is successful or not based on a single test score is fundamentally unsound. Worse yet, the way this legislation is written, even schools that improve on most measures are likely to find themselves labeled "underperforming." This is possible because schools are rated not only on schoolwide test scores, but on the performance of particular groups. For example, if African Americans do poorly one year and improve the second year, but another group, let's say disabled students, do poorly the second year, that amounts to two years of poor scores, and the entire school is labeled "underperforming." In a small school or in a school with small numbers of these special groups, a change in scores of only a few students can make the difference. Even those who crafted the legislation believe that the majority of the nation's schools will be cited as underperforming, although they predict this will motivate schools to become more effective. But that's not what happened in Michigan.[4]

When Michigan initially tested its schools, 1,513 were labeled underperforming by the state, and "failing" by the media. Michigan took decisive action to reverse this problem: it lowered the passing grade from 75 percent to 42 percent, and *voilà*, only 216 schools were problematic. Michigan is not alone; other states have also lowered standards, some to the point where there is not a single underperforming school in

OVERHEAD 84
No Child Left Behind

CLASS ACTIVITY
A New Standardized Test
IM Activity 7.3

the entire state. "The severe sanctions may hinder educational excellence," explained University of Colorado Professor Robert Linn, "because they implicitly encourage states to water down their content and performance standards in order to reduce the risk of sanctions." A few states are considering giving up federal funds entirely rather than join the costly testing culture. It is estimated that to comply with the law, the states will spend between $1.9 and $5.3 billion to produce 460 new tests.[5]

But the Department of Education is committed to the testing culture and to giving parents educational options. As one official explains, "Public school choice and supplemental services should be part of how we see public education in America." In fact, the law obliges school districts to transfer students from failing schools to better schools, and to offer supplementary services, but this is not as easy as it sounds. In rural areas, transferring students to a more effective school that is hours away is not a realistic option. While urban or suburban areas may have a number of successful schools nearby, those schools are typically filled to capacity. In such cases, the government advises school districts to enlarge these schools by building more classrooms and hiring more teachers. If that doesn't work, the federal government recommends sending students to other school districts, although adequate funds to pay for all these recommendations are not provided. Moreover, as one commentator pointed out, even if the funds were provided to enlarge effective schools, adding new teachers and more classrooms may turn a successful school into a problematic one. Sending students to another school may create rather than solve a problem. Transferring inner-city students to a successful middle-class suburban school could be a disaster. Inner-city students may depend on many school programs missing from suburbia, including a free breakfast, an in-school medical clinic, remedial reading classes, and perhaps English as a Second Language instruction. Successful suburban schools may lack the experience and resources to serve poorer, urban youth. These are the kinds of problems that lead critics to charge that *NCLB* is a Trojan horse: when public schools, teachers, and students fail, vouchers and private educational companies will be presented as the solution.[6]

Another point of contention is the requirement that all students be taught by skilled and competent teachers. Secretary Paige describes reaching this goal as "challenging"; others see it as unattainable. The law defines a "highly qualified teacher" as holding a bachelor's degree from a four-year college, a state teacher's license, and demonstrated competency in the subject being taught. The intent is a strong focus on content mastery. Although highly qualified teachers are required for all core subjects (English, history, science, and math) by 2005, nearly half of the nation's teachers in 2002 did not meet this standard. Small rural schools can't afford to enlarge their faculties to include specialists in each subject area. Will rural communities lose their federal funds because they lack "highly qualified teachers"? Urban schools and poorer communities will also be at a disadvantage. It is likely that highly qualified teachers will be drawn to the most attractive and wealthiest school districts, leaving those schools most in need with the least trained teachers. Without increased funding to improve teacher salaries and working conditions, it is difficult to imagine how nearly two million "highly

---

IN THE NEWS

Blue Ribbon Failures

At least nineteen schools recognized by the federal government for their excellence as "Blue Ribbon" schools were also labeled "failing" under the *No Child Left Behind* Act. At least seven schools were simultaneously the "best" and the "worst" in the same school year. While federal officials explain that these programs measure different aspects of schooling, critics point out that such convoluted grading systems only confuse the public.

SOURCE: *USA Today*, August 5, 2002.

 What's new in education? Click on *News Feed.*

qualified" teachers will be drawn to teaching, or even more challenging, stay in teaching.[7]

Although these aspects of *NCLB* are often in the news, the law covers a number of areas, including reading, bilingual education, charter schools, and technology. Some less publicized areas have caused considerable consternation. For example, *NCLB* requires schools report personal student information to military recruiters, which critics argue violates students' privacy rights. The law calls for federal support for educational research, which is "scientifically based," but detractors point out that ideology more than science is driving this agenda, as research programs politically attractive to the administration are funded, and others are not. The legislation also requires that school buildings be opened to Boy Scout meetings. This became an issue because the Boy Scouts do not allow homosexuals to join, and some schools do not open their facilities to groups that practice discrimination. *NCLB* requires schools to ignore such local antidiscrimination regulations. The law also requires school officials to certify in writing that every student has the right to pray, and to submit this certification to the federal government every two years. Detractors charge that such politically motivated provisions do not improve the nation's schools. While the specifics of *NCLB* are likely to undergo continuing scrutiny, the standards and testing movement continues to impact the nation's schools.[8]

 ## The Standards Movement

Ah, the beauty, simplicity, and allure of standards! What can be more rational (let's face it, even honorable) than setting educational standards? Standards are like guiding stars that enable us to chart our course, locate our position, and navigate our educational vessels. Students can "see" what they know and need to learn, educators can improve their teaching strategies, and the public can evaluate their schools. Little surprise that the nation's governors responded positively when the first President Bush called them to meet in Charlottesville, Virginia in 1989 to develop educational standards. Out of this highly publicized "National Education Summit" came a set of educational goals, goals that were supposed to be reached within the decade.[9] The result of that effort, "Education 2000" (modified as "Goals 2000" under the Clinton administration), was a list of worthy, if unrealistically optimistic goals. The first goal stated, "All children will start school ready to learn," but only half of the nation's youth were enrolled in preschool by 2000, and many of those programs were of poor quality. "We will be first in the world in math and science by the year 2000," also missed the mark. In retrospect, the Education Summit was a transition between *A Nation at Risk* (1983), and today's emphasis on state standards and testing.

While the national goals were never attained, they did put the nation on a course of self-examination, and developing standards of learning dominated much of the education literature of the 1990s. The National Education Standards and Improvement Council was formed to harness the ideas of experts in mathematics, history, English, physical education, and other fields. The federal government funded organizations like the National Council for Geographic Education, the National Council of Teachers of Mathematics, and the National Academy of Sciences to develop content standards. Professional education associations, business leaders, and citizen groups got into the content standards business as well. **Content standards** detailed precisely what students should know and be able to do in each

FOCUS QUESTION 3
How does the standards movement influence what is taught in schools?

CLASS ACTIVITY
Developing Curriculum Standards
IM Activity 7:4

subject at each grade level. States echoed the call for better schools by adopting and adapting many of these national standards, and in some cases, developing their own. This step was crucial, for in the end the states have the major responsibility for creating the school curriculum.

But the federal government, which funded the standards development, was not always happy with the standards developed by scholars. When the content standards in history were presented, dissatisfied political leaders rejected them. Conservative commentators argued that the standards developed by history scholars slighted white men and maligned business leaders. The critics were led by Lynne Cheney, a former official in the first Bush administration, who characterized the new standards as "a warped view of American history."[10] No such outburst had accompanied the publication of the national standards for mathematics five years earlier. Forty-one states quickly adopted the mathematics standards, and math textbooks were modified accordingly. For mathematics, a national curriculum began to take shape.[11] Why was the process of adopting standards relatively easy for math but difficult for history? The basic reason is that mathematics raises fewer values questions, while other disciplines, such as history, live and breathe values. Here are just some of the questions raised by history standards:

- Should traditional heroes, sometimes called "DWM" (dead white males)—such as Washington, Jefferson, and other revered Americans—be the sole focus of the curriculum, or should the experiences and contributions of other groups, women and people of color, be researched and included?

- Should history continue to emphasize European roots, or should Afrocentric issues be included? What about the views of other groups? For instance, should schools teach a penetrating view of European settlement of the Americas as seen through the eyes of Native Americans and Mexicans?

- Should U.S. history tell only a story of victors and triumphs, or should it also relate varied views of social, cultural, and economic issues?

The new history standards did not please traditionalists. Familiar names like Daniel Webster, Paul Revere, and the Wright brothers were missing while unfamiliar names of women and people of color were now included. The Civil War received a different perspective as well, going beyond a chronology of battles to include an account of Northern riots by poor laborers who were being drafted for the deadliest war in American history, while rich men simply paid $300 and avoided the draft. It is clear that American history was in the eye of the beholder, and those funding the standards held a very different view of what children should be taught.[12] Political pressure rejected the scholars' proposals and traditional history standards were reinstated. Some suggest that over time, such pressure will create remarkably similar standards in all states.[13]

OVERHEAD 85
Three Types of Standards

By 2000, teachers reported that standards promoted higher student expectations and created a more demanding curriculum.[14] The second Bush administration passed legislation that required states to complete their work in creating science and history standards, and then went on to pass *No Child Left Behind*. The focus now was on **performance standards,** assessing how well students meet the content standards. While content standards initially proved to be quite popular, federally mandated testing and school punishments became problematic. A curious and difficult corner was turned when the standards movement became a testing movement.

Test Problems: Seven Reasons Why Standardized Tests Are Not Working

In a New York City middle school, the principal asked teachers to spend fifteen minutes a day with students practicing how to answer multiple-choice math questions in preparation for the state-mandated test. One teacher protested, explaining she taught Italian and English, not math. But the principal insisted, and she followed his directive. As you might suspect, the plan failed, and in the end, fewer than one in four New York City middle schoolers passed the exam. While the importance of the test dominated the formal curriculum, the lessons learned through the hidden curriculum were no less powerful. Students learned that test scores mattered more than English or Italian, and that teachers did not make the key instructional decisions. In fact, once the test was over, one-third of the students in her class stopped attending school, skipping the last five weeks of the school year.[15]

Inner-city schools aren't the only ones experiencing testing woes; rural communities and wealthy suburbs have their own complaints. In Scarsdale, New York, an upscale, college-oriented community, parents organized a boycott of the eighth-grade standardized tests. Of 290 eighth-graders, only 95 showed up for the exam.[16] In Miami protests erupted when over 12,000 Florida seniors were denied their high school diploma, and in Massachusetts, local school boards defied the state and issued their own diplomas to students they believed were being unfairly denied their high school graduation because of the state-mandated test. Teachers in California and Chicago refused to give tests and faced disciplinary action.[17] Why are teachers, students, and parents protesting? What's wrong with measuring academic progress through standardized tests? Here are some reasons why high-stake tests are problematic:

1. *At-Risk Students Placed at Greater Risk.* Using the same tests for all students, those in well-funded posh schools along with students trying to learn in underfunded, ill-equipped schools is grossly unfair, and the outcome is quite predictable. Since students do not receive equal educations, holding identical expectations for all students places the poorer ones at a disadvantage. State data confirm that African Americans and Hispanics, females, poor students and those with disabilities are disproportionately failing "high-stakes" standardized tests. In Louisiana, parents requested that the Office for Civil Rights investigate why nearly half the students in school districts with the greatest numbers of poor and minority children had failed Louisiana's test, even after taking it for a second time. In Georgia, two out of every three low-income students failed the math, English, and reading sections of the state's competency tests. No students from well-to-do counties failed any of the tests and more than half exceeded standards. Even moderate income differences could result in major test score differences. In Ohio, almost half of the students from families with incomes below $20,000 failed the state exams, while almost 80 percent of students from families earning more than $30,000 passed those same exams.

A third kind of standard called an opportunity-to-learn standard, was supposed to remedy these social and economic challenges. **Opportunity-to-learn standards** were to ensure a level playing field by providing all students with appropriate educational resources, competent teachers and modern technology. Differences in student learning styles were to be accommodated and additional time provided for students to relearn material if they failed the test. Teachers were to be given quality in-service training. Yet half the states did not earmark money to remedy dramatic educational

FOCUS QUESTION 4
What are the concerns with high-stakes testing?

CRITICAL THINKING QUESTION
What role do teachers have in protesting tests?

OVERHEAD 86
Seven Reasons Why Standardized Tests Are Not Working

As national, state, and district decision makers require more testing, for students and even their teachers, many have protested or boycotted these exams. What perspectives on curriculum do you think the protesters hold? Explain your convictions on testing. What policies would cause you to *take to the streets?*

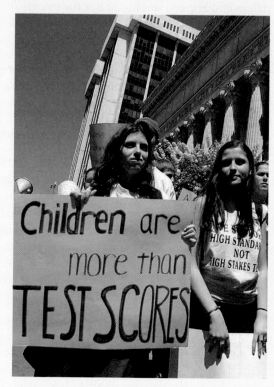

differences between school districts, and real barriers to achievement—racism, poverty, sexism, low teacher salaries, language differences, inadequate facilities—were lost in the sea of testing. Although the rhetoric of the standards movement is that a rising tide raises all ships, in fact, without the adequate resources, some ships do not rise. In the current standards and testing movement, opportunity-to-learn is the forgotten standard.[18]

2. *Lower Graduation Rates.* Grade-by-grade testing and graduation tests actually increase school dropouts. A Harvard University study found that students in the bottom 10 percent of achievement were 33 percent more likely to drop out of school in states with graduation tests. The National Research Council found that low-performing elementary and secondary school students who are held back do less well academically, are much worse off socially, and are far likelier to drop out than equally weak students who are promoted. Retention in grade is the single strongest predictor of which students will drop out—stronger even than parental income or mother's education level.

Education Secretary Paige was given credit for dramatic improvement of test scores in Houston, where he was superintendent. Houston was the centerpiece of the "Texas

Miracle" and the foundation for *No Child Left Behind*. But by 2003, it became clear that underreported dropouts contributed to test score gains. Houston reported a dropout rate of just over 1 percent a year, but that statistic was put in doubt by later studies that found the dropout rate was closer to 40 percent. When poor students, Latinos, African Americans, and Native Americans fail to meet graduation testing requirements, they are retained in grade and then likely to drop out. When their low scores disappear, the school's average test score improves, giving a picture of success when the real picture is failure.[19]

3. *Higher Test Scores Do Not Mean More Learning.* Evidence is mounting that for a growing number of schools, teaching is being redefined as test preparation. Seventy-nine percent of teachers surveyed by *Education Week* said they spent "a great deal" or "somewhat" of their time instructing students in test-taking skills, and 53 percent said they used state practice tests a great deal or somewhat. In Texas, James V. Hoffman and his colleagues asked reading teachers and supervisors to rate how often they engaged in test preparation. The study used a scale of 1 to 4, in which 1 stood for never, 2 for sometimes, 3 for often, and 4 for always. Most of those surveyed said that teachers engaged in the following activities "often" or "always":

- Teaching test-taking skills—3.5
- Having students practice with tests from prior years—3.4
- Using commercial test preparation materials—3.4
- Giving general tips on how to take tests—3.4
- Demonstrating how to mark an answer sheet correctly—3.2

In one school, for example, students were taught to cheer "Three in a row? No, No, No!" The cheer was a reminder that if students answered "c" three times in a row, probably at least one of those answers is wrong since the test maker is unlikely to construct three questions in a row with the same answer letter.[20]

Although this kind of test preparation may boost scores, it does not necessarily produce real gains in understanding that show up on other tests or performance measures or that students can apply in a nontesting situation. Consider these findings:

- A study of eighteen states with high-stakes testing compared trends in state test scores with long-term trends on other standardized tests. When state tests were given, other test scores often dropped. In more than half of these states, performance went down on the ACT, SAT, and the math test of the National Assessment of Educational Progress (NAEP). The study concluded that higher state test scores were most likely due to direct test preparation rather than increased student learning, and to differences in how many students were excluded from testing based on disabilities or limited English proficiency.

- Three-quarters of fourth-grade teachers surveyed by RAND in Washington State, and the majority of principals, believed that better test preparation (rather than increased student knowledge) was responsible for most of the score gains.

- In Kentucky's state assessment, scores went up on test items that were reused, then dropped when new items were introduced. This discrepancy between new and reused items was larger in schools that had greater overall test score gains, a relationship that suggests students were being coached on reused items.[21]

FIGURE 7.3
Teaching to the test.

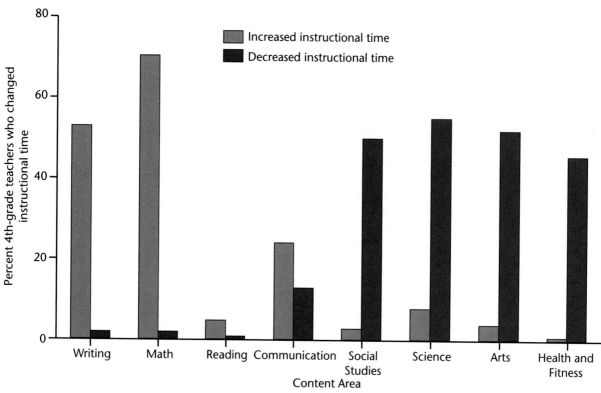

REFLECTION: What would the curriculum be like if you planned the instructional schedule?

4. *Standardized Testing Shrinks the Curriculum*. Educator Alfie Kohn advises parents to ask an unusual question when a school's test scores increase: "What did you have to sacrifice about my child's education to raise those scores?"[22] As schools struggle to avoid the "underperforming" label, entire subject areas—such as music, art, social studies, and foreign languages—are de-emphasized. What is not tested does not count, and 85 percent of teachers believe that their school gives less attention to subjects that are not on the state test. One teacher had this to say about how the timing of state tests drives teaching: "At our school, third- and fourth-grade teachers are told not to teach social studies and science until March."[23] As "real learning" takes a backseat to "test learning," challenging curriculum is replaced by multiple choice materials, individualized student learning projects disappear, and in-depth exploration of subjects along with extracurricular activities are squeezed out of the curriculum.[24] (See Figure 7.3.)

5. *When Tests Fail*. Tests themselves are often flawed, and high-stakes errors become high-stakes disasters. When Martin Swaden's daughter failed the state math test by a single answer, Swaden requested to see the exam so that he could help his daughter

correct her errors and pass the test next time around. It took a threatened lawsuit before he was able to meet with a state official to examine the answers. Together they made an amazing discovery: six of the sixty-eight answers were keyed incorrectly, not only for his daughter, but for all the students in Minnesota. Jobs had been lost, summers ruined, the joy of graduation turned to humiliation for those students who were misidentified as having failed. Suits followed and $7 million in damages were eventually paid, but the testing company argued that it was not liable for "emotional damages."

Unfortunately, such stories continue to mount as the crush of millions of new tests overwhelms the handful of testing companies. In Massachusetts, a senior spotted an alternative answer to a math question, and the scores of 449 students were suddenly propelled over the passing mark. A Massachusetts teacher spotted a question with two correct answers, and when the scores were adjusted, 666 more students passed. A flawed answer key incorrectly lowered multiple-choice scores for 12,000 Arizona students, erred in adding up scores of essay tests for students in Michigan and forced the re-scoring of 204,000 essay tests in Washington. Another error resulted in nearly 9,000 students in New York City being mistakenly assigned to summer school, and $2 million in achievement awards being denied to deserving students in Kentucky.[25] By 2003, the National Board on Educational Testing and Public Policy reported that fifty high-profile testing mistakes had occurred in twenty states from 1999 through 2002.[26]

Test materials also have been delivered late, or with missing pages, or errors have been found in scoring. Raters complained that they are given inadequate training and little time to grade essays, and at $9 an hour, many doubt the accuracy of their ratings. Many question the wisdom of rewarding and punishing students, teachers, and schools based on the flawed history of the testing industry.[27]

6. *Teacher Stress.* While teachers support high standards, they object to learning being measured by a single test.[28] Not surprisingly, in a national study, nearly seven in ten teachers reported feeling test-stress, and two out of three believed that preparing for the test took time from teaching important but nontested topics.[29] Fourth-grade veteran teachers were requesting transfers, saying that they could not stand the pressure of administering the high-stakes elementary exams, and teachers recognized for excellence were leaving public schools, feeling their talents were better utilized in private schools where test preparation did not rule the curriculum.[30] When eighty Arizona teachers and teacher educators were asked to visually depict the impact of standardized tests, their drawings indicated test-driven classrooms where boredom, fear, and isolation dominate. Teachers feel that they are shortchanging schoolchildren from a love for learning. Figure 7.4 presents one of those drawings. (For others, visit Mr. Tirupalavanam Ganesh's website at ganesh.ed.asu.edu/aims.)

7. *What's Worth Knowing?* The fact that history, drama, the arts and a host of subjects are given less attention in the current testing movement raises intriguing curricular questions: What is really important to teach? What is worth knowing? While it may sound pretty obvious, thinking beyond the obvious is often a good idea. Much of what is taught in schools is tradition and conventional wisdom, curricular inertia rather than careful thought. To see how society's notion of what is important can change, try your hand at the following test questions that were used to make certain that eighth graders in Kansas knew "important information." We have shortened the exam, but all these questions are from the original. (Hint: Brush up on your orthography.) See if you would qualify to graduate from elementary school in 1895.[31]

OVERHEAD 88
Teacher Stress

VIDEO SEGMENT 17
Teachers' Opinions about High-Stakes Testing

FIGURE 7.4

A teacher's impression of the testing movement.

SOURCE: A female teacher with a literature specialty teaching in a suburban elementary school. http://ganesh.ed.asu.edu/aims/view_image.php?image_id=72&grade_range_id=3

REFLECTION: Try your own hand at drawing an image of how you feel when you are about to take a high-stakes test.

8TH GRADE EXAMINATION GRADUATION QUESTIONS

SALINE COUNTY, KANSAS
APRIL 13, 1895

Reading and Penmanship—The Examination will be oral and the Penmanship of Applicants will be graded from the manuscripts.

Grammar

1. Give nine rules for the use of Capital Letters.
2. Define Verse, Stanza, and Paragraph.
3. What are the Principal Parts of a verb? Give Principal Parts of do, lie, lay, and run.

Arithmetic

1. District No. 33 has a valuation of $35,000. What is the necessary levy to carry on a school seven months at $50 per month, and have $104 for incidentals?
2. What is the cost of a square farm at $15 per acre, the distance around which is 640 rods?
3. Write a Bank Check, a Promissory Note, and a Receipt.

U.S. History

1. Give the epochs into which U.S. History is divided.
2. Tell what you can of the history of Kansas.
3. Describe three of the most prominent battles of the Rebellion.

Orthography

1. What are the following, and give examples of each: Trigraph, subvocals, diphthong, cognate letters, linguals?
2. Give four substitutes for caret "u."
3. Mark diacritically and divide into syllables the following, and name the sign that indicates the sound: card, ball, mercy, sir, odd, cell, rise, blood, fare, last.

Geography

1. Name and describe the following: Monrovia, Odessa, Denver, Manitoba, Heela, Yukon, St. Helena, Juan Fernandez, Aspinwall, and Orinoco.
2. Name all the republics of Europe and give capital of each.
3. Describe the movements of the earth. Give inclination of the earth.

Physiology

1. How does nutrition reach the circulation?
2. What is the function of the liver? Of the kidneys?
3. Give some general directions that you think would be beneficial to preserve the human body in a state of health.

How did you do? Well, if you bombed it, don't feel too badly, few of today's PhDs would pass. So what does this teach us? Are today's schools far weaker than earlier ones? If we failed are we not truly educated? Or perhaps what we consider "important knowledge" is less enduring than we believe. How much of today's "critical" information will be a curious and unimportant footnote in the years ahead?

 ## An Alternative Curriculum

Imagine that you are in charge of taking the schools down an educational path. What path would you trailblaze? What standards and assessments would you promote?

FOCUS QUESTION 5

How can we rethink curriculum and testing?

While literacy and numeracy are important, even a casual glance at today's challenges suggests the need for a strategic educational realignment. Our world is marked by hatred and misunderstanding, cultural and religious warfare, massive poverty, physical deprivation, and interpersonal conflicts. All these issues scream for the attention of not only political leaders, but educators and students as well. How can schools focus on more meaningful values, values that go beyond test scores and even academics, values that will not become tomorrow's orthography but will always be timely. Perhaps we can call this curriculum one of "enduring lessons." Here is a sample of what we would teach.

Enduring Lesson Number 1: Understand Our Roots There is a fundamental, even driving need to more deeply understand ourselves both as individuals, and as part of the wider community. We often learn only a few salient aspects of our backgrounds, such as personal and family history, cultural and religious beliefs, gender differences and challenges, and a single view of our national heritage. But these are incomplete lessons. We lack a healthy appreciation of how these key forces have shaped lives and limited our world view. Only through greater self-insight can we begin to understand our perceptions and motivations, our strengths and weaknesses, and the way we behave and think. In so doing, we develop a realistic and healthy self-esteem, and learn the first enduring lesson: "know yourself."

Enduring Lesson Number 2: Celebrate Others Once we are comfortable and secure with ourselves, we can reach out and seek insights from other peoples and cultures. While some have called this *teaching tolerance,* we do not believe that diversity should be *tolerated*. Today, we tolerate things from sleazy business practices to shoddy home repairs. Tolerance of diversity falls woefully short, and we believe that diversity should be celebrated. Cultural, racial and ethnic, and religious differences offer us wondrous insights into the human experience. We can learn so much from each other. Our challenge is to learn from our differences, not fear them.

Enduring Lesson Number 3: Encourage Individual Talents and Contributions High test scores predict high test scores, but not much else: not problem-solving skills, not good work habits, not honesty, not dependability, not loyalty, nor any cherished virtue. Schools should prepare students to live purposeful and satisfying lives. To do this, students need to learn and develop their own unique interests and abilities, skills, and talents. By measuring all students against the same yardsticks of literacy and numeracy, individual creativity and differences are lost or denigrated. Contrary to the current testing wave, we support less standardization and more individualization.

Enduring Lesson Number 4: Promote Purposeful Lives At the Antioch College commencement in 1859, Horace Mann advised the graduates, "Be ashamed to die until you have won some victory for humanity." While it is easy to forget Mann's words in this period of test mania, the real measure of an education is not what a student receives as a test grade or even does while in school; the real measure is what people do after graduation. Are students living higher lessons and working for noble purposes, or have they succumbed to baser temptations? Are adults honest and caring with one another, treating their children, families, colleagues, and even strangers with love, compassion, and forgiveness? The way we choose to live our lives as adults, and not our test scores, will be the true measure of our schooling.

One day in 1967, fifth-grader Alfie Kohn received a class assignment. As expected, he wrote his name and the date at the top of the paper. The title he chose, though, was unanticipated: "Busywork." He doesn't remember the announced purpose of the assignment. He does remember that it was busywork. Over three decades later, Alfie Kohn still discriminates between genuine learning and mindless school routine. As a teacher, researcher, and journalist, his work carries a common theme: Educational excellence comes from personalized learning, from recognizing the uniqueness of each student, not from a lockstep curriculum. As a teacher, he remembers:

> I lovingly polished lectures, reading lists, and tests. I treated the students as interchangeable receptacles—rows of wide-open bird beaks waiting for worms.
>
> Finally I realized I was denying students the joy of exploring topics and uncovering truths on their own.[1]

In his own education, Kohn adopted this personalized approach to learning. As an undergraduate at Brown University, he created an interdisciplinary major, and dubbed it normativism. He again took an unbeaten path at the University of Chicago, writing his graduate thesis on humor. "Learning was meaningful because I started with the question and then drew from whatever fields were useful in exploring it, rather than being confined to the methods and topics of a particular discipline."[2] When he visits classrooms today, Kohn is often disheartened. Rarely does he witness such engaged learning. Instead, he sees students usually learning just to pass a test.

Kohn challenges today's popular clamor for higher standards and increased testing. "Standardized testing has swelled and mutated, like a creature in one of those old horror movies, to the point that it now threatens to swallow our schools whole."[3] He passionately warns educators, policymakers, and parents that raising standardized test scores is completely different from helping students to learn. And the pressurized culture of testing exacts a high cost. Every hour spent on such exam preparation is an hour not spent helping students to think creatively, to tackle controversial issues, and to love learning.

Common standards often begin with "all students will be able to . . . " and Kohn sees a harmful message in such wording: Individual differences don't exist or are unimportant. Often justified in the name of accountability or rigor, standards turn schools into fact factories. Students may recite Civil War battles, distinguish between phloem and xylem, and memorize prime numbers in hopes of meeting predetermined standards of excellence. Will they? Kohn doesn't think so.

With a focus on standards of outcome rather than standards of opportunity, real barriers to achievement—racism, poverty, low teacher salaries, language differences, inadequate facilities—are lost in the sea of testing. "[A]ll students deserve a quality education. But declaring that everyone must reach the same level is naïve at best, cynical at worst, in light of wildly unequal resources."[4] Equally troublesome is testing's unbalanced reward system. As a bonus for good scores, more money is often given to successful schools and less to those already deprived. Callous is how he describes such a retreat from fairness and the implication that teachers and students need only be bribed or threatened in order to achieve.

Alfie Kohn also knows that change in schools can be slow. Standardized curriculum and testing are fueled by concerns of competition in our global economy and reinforced by a tradition of teacher-centered instruction. "I am not a utopian. I am as aware as anyone of the difficulties of creating schools that are genuinely concerned about learning and about meeting children's needs, but that causes me to redouble my efforts rather than throw up my hands."[5]

[1] Jay Matthews, "Education's Different Drummer," *The Washington Post* (January 9, 2001), p. A10. [2] Ibid. [3] Alfie Kohn, "Standardized Testing and Its Victims," *Education Week* (September 27, 2000). [4] Alfie Kohn, "One-Size-Fits-All Education Doesn't Work," *Boston Globe* (June 10, 2001), p. C8. [5] Jay Matthews, "Education's Different Drummer."

REFLECTION: Do you agree with Kohn that standardized testing undermines learning? In the next decade, do you think schools in the United States will become more or less reliant on standardized tests? Justify your answer.

www.mhhe.com/sadker To learn more about Alfie Kohn, click on *Profiles in Education.*

Alternatives to High-Stakes Testing

RAP 2.8
Memoirs of a Time Tested Student, p. 279

The testing guidelines issued by the American Psychological Association specifically prohibit basing any consequential decisions about individuals on a single test score.[32] Most educational organizations and measurement experts agree that a better gauge of student performance is multiple assessments: tests, portfolios, formal exhibitions, independent student projects, and teacher evaluations. Standardized tests are popular because they are relatively inexpensive compared to other assessments, offer clear results, and can be rapidly implemented. Many educators are working to create tests that more fully and precisely assess learning. **Authentic assessment** (also called alternative or performance-based assessment) captures actual student performance, encourages students to reflect on their own work, and is integrated into the student's whole learning process. Such tests usually require students to synthesize knowledge from different areas and actively use that knowledge. The student might demonstrate what has been learned through a portfolio (like the ones we encourage you to develop in the *RAP*s found in this text), or a journal, or by undergoing an interview, conducting an experiment, or giving a presentation. Authentic assessment offers a focused and intense insight into what the student has learned, and requires evidence quite different from what is required by responding to questions on a typical high-stakes test.[33] Comparisons are often made with sports, in which participants are expected to demonstrate in a game what they have learned in practice. A tennis player works on her backhand, so that she can demonstrate mastery of it in a game; similarly, when students know that they will be called on to demonstrate and use their knowledge, they are more motivated to practice their academic skills. Many states are exploring authentic methods of assessment, especially the writing sample.[34]

VIDEO SEGMENT 18
Alternative Assessment: Portfolios

Authentic assessment is used in the Coalition of Essential Schools, led by prominent educator Theodore Sizer. The coalition encourages schools to define their own model for successful reform, guided by nine basic principles that emphasize the personalization of learning. These principles include the requirement that students complete "exhibitions," tasks that call on them to exhibit their knowledge concretely. The high school curriculum is structured around these demanding, creative tasks, which may include:

- Completing a federal Internal Revenue Service Form 1040 for a family whose records you receive, working with other students in a group to ensure that everyone's IRS forms are correct, and auditing a return filed by a student in a different group

- Designing a nutritious and attractive lunch menu for the cafeteria within a specified budget and defending your definitions of nutritious and attractive

RELATED READING
Bail Me Out!: Handling Difficult Data and Tough Questions about Public Schools by Gerald W. Bracey (2000).

- Designing and building a wind instrument from metal pipes, then composing and performing a piece of music for that instrument

- Defining one human emotion in an essay, through examples from literature and history, and in at least three other ways (through drawing, painting, or sculpture; through film, photographs, or video; through music; through pantomime or dance; or through a story or play that you create)[35]

An increase in authentic testing may contribute to a greater classroom focus on critical thinking and personal development. Authentic assessments may help us go beyond the current dependence on high-stakes standardized tests in determining the competence of students and the success of schools.

Are Desirable Because . . .

SCHOOLS AND EDUCATORS ARE NOT BEING HELD ACCOUNTABLE FOR STUDENT FAILURE

"If they don't want to learn, we can't make them," has been the modus operandi of educators. As a result, we have high school graduates who cannot read or write, and college graduates who do little better. Standards and tests will finally hold educators accountable. We will be able to see what students know, and how well they know it. We can reward successful schools, help troubled schools, and finally close failing schools.

THEY MAKE US EDUCATIONALLY AND ECONOMICALLY COMPETITIVE

Many of today's high school graduates must be retrained in basic literacy skills by the corporations that hire them, because they are unable to do the work that is required. This is a sign that schools are failing. This sort of educational inefficiency leads to technically incompetent workers, and weakens our ability to compete in world markets. We must have standards and tests to educate a first class labor force and maintain our standard of living.

TEACHERS WORK COLLABORATIVELY RATHER THAN IN ISOLATION

A common set of standards promotes cooperation. Teachers and principals will work together to identify problems, develop instructional solutions, and collaborate as a professional team working to ensure that all the standards are met.

THEY WILL BIND THE NATION

National standards offer a unifying experience, as children learn about our common heritage. Without such standards, we become dangerously pluralistic and suffer the risk of becoming not one nation but several. There are already examples of countries that have lost this common thread and whose cultures have disintegrated.

LOCAL PAROCHIALISM WILL BE ELIMINATED

National standards will bring new insights and diverse points of view to the nation's children. Rather than being held hostage to the desires and views of local school boards, students will be able to consider broader perspectives. National standards can end debilitating local parochialism and broaden students' horizons.

Are a Mistake Because . . .

HIGH-STAKES TESTS REPRESENT A TERRIBLE ACCOUNTABILITY

Taking time from studies to prepare for a high-stakes test is not an effective demonstration of educational progress or school accountability. In fact, schools simply replace real learning with test preparation programs. One test is a terribly unreliable way to assess a person's knowledge, and flies in the face of all that we have learned about multiple intelligences, individual differences, and authentic assessment.

NATIONAL STANDARDS AND TESTS ARE A STEP BACKWARD FOR MANY STUDENTS AND SCHOOLS

National standards represent a step down for the nation's strongest school districts. The nation's best schools are well beyond such standards, yet must invest time and resources preparing for the state tests. Our schools prepare very competent scientists and engineers, many of whom are the first to be "downsized" by the same business executives who complain about educational quality. In fact, given our service economy, we may be overeducating our workforce.

TEACHERS WORK IN ISOLATION RATHER THAN COLLABORATIVELY

The pressure of tests and standards will drive teachers away from cooperative planning on educational goals, and into the trap of drilling their students to ensure that their class does well. Teachers will become competitors in a survival of the fittest scenario.

NATIONAL STANDARDS WILL DIVIDE THE NATION

We simply cannot agree on a single set of standards, on which facts to remember (and which to forget). What is important to one group of Americans may be unimportant or offensive to another. The effort to create unifying standards and tests will divide our people.

CENTRAL CONTROL OF OUR LIVES WILL GROW

The authors of the Constitution had it right, local communities and individuals know their children best, and they hold the practical wisdom that made this nation great. All we need is faith in the common sense of Americans, because they do know what's best for their children.

continued

Are Desirable Because . . .

NATIONAL TESTS WILL GIVE US CRITICAL INFORMATION AND DIRECTION

Standardized tests will enable us to compare student performance, and to understand what it takes to earn an "A" in one school, versus an "A" in another. We will discover who is really learning, and who is not. Finally, we will be able to make sense out of what is going on in almost 100,000 school buildings.

Are a Mistake Because . . .

NATIONAL TESTS WILL HURT EDUCATION

High-stakes tests hurt students who are bright, but simply don't test well. Such standardized tests encourage a school curriculum based on test preparation, drive away talented teachers, increase pressure to cheat, and create the kind of boring, predictable, "one-size-fits-all" curriculum that is a disservice to a true democracy.

 YOU BE THE JUDGE

Where do you stand on the standards and the testing issue? Can you separate standards from testing? How might you determine if standards are being met—without using a standardized test? Some educators assert that test development should precede standards development. Do you agree or disagree? Why?

 ## The Textbook Shapes the Curriculum

While some argue that the development of standards may lead to a national curriculum, others believe that we already have a *de facto* national curriculum: the textbook.[36] Students spend from 70 to 95 percent of classroom time using textbooks, and teachers base more than 70 percent of their instructional decisions on them. Given this heavy reliance on texts, there is no doubt that they have a major practical influence on what is taught in schools.

FOCUS QUESTION 6
How do textbook publishers and state adoption committees "drive" the curriculum?

Before 1850, textbooks were made up of whatever educational materials children had in their homes. Students took these textbooks to school, and instruction was based on them. Picture yourself trying to teach a class with the wide array of random materials children have in their homes. Although today we might use these personal resources to supplement instruction, back then it was difficult to teach with such disparate materials. In fact, despairing teachers appealed for common texts, so that all students could use the same materials. Local legislators responded by requiring schools to select appropriate books, and then parents were required to buy them. When families moved, they often had to buy new books. Concerned about the costly burden this lack of consistency placed on families, legislators mandated commonly used textbooks across larger geographic areas.

OVERHEAD 89
Textbook Adoption States

Today, the process of textbook development and adoption has come under intense criticism. One of its chief critics, Harriet Tyson Bernstein, says,

> Imagine a public policy system that is perfectly designed to produce textbooks that confuse, mislead, and profoundly bore students, while at the same time making all the adults in the process look good, not only in their own eyes, but in the eyes of others. Although there are some good textbooks on the market, publishers and editors are virtually compelled by public policies and practices to create textbooks that confuse students with non sequitors, that mislead them with misinformation, and that profoundly bore them with pointedly arid writing.
>
> None of the adults in this very complex system intends this outcome. To the contrary, each of them wants to produce good effects, and each public policy regulation or

Figure 7.5

Textbook adoption states. While some school districts are free to choose any text, others are limited to state-approved textbooks.

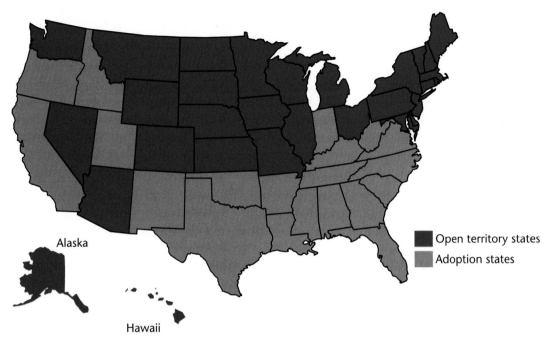

Alaska

Hawaii

Open territory states

Adoption states

SOURCE: American Association of Publishers, Washington, DC, 2003.

REFLECTION: What patterns do you notice in the states that require texts be selected from an approved list? Would such state adoption procedures be a factor in deciding where you might teach? Visit the site for updates at www.publishers.org.

conventional practice was intended to make some improvement or prevent some abuse. But the cumulative effects of well-intentioned and seemingly reasonable state and local regulations are textbooks that squander the intellectual capital of our youth.[37]

Here's how the system works and why Bernstein and other opponents are so angry. In 1900, when our current textbook system was designed, twenty-two states enacted laws that put in place a centralized adoption system. More than twenty states, located mainly in the South and the West, are **textbook adoption states.** (These states are indicated in Figure 7.5.)

Under a state adoption system, local school districts typically select their texts from an official, state-approved list. Those in favor of statewide adoption claim that this process results in the selection of higher-quality texts. This system creates a common, statewide curriculum, which unites educators and makes school life easier for students who move to different schools within the state. State adoptions also save time and work for educators at the local level, and, because of the large numbers of books purchased, the per book cost is kept low.

Criticism of statewide adoptions focuses on what has been called the **Texas and California effect,** which might more accurately be termed the "Four States Effect" (including Florida and North Carolina). Together these four states exert an enormous influence on what is included—or omitted—from the texts. These states draw up plans for what they would like to see in a textbook, and the publishers design books to meet the states' "wish list." These four populous states account for a billion dollars of annual textbook sales.³⁸ As you can well imagine, a publisher's dream is to be selected as one of the few approved sources of textbooks, especially in populous states such as these. Because major publishers design their books to meet these state adoption standards, the leading texts available to all states are the ones designed for the adoption states.

Criticism of textbook adoption does not stop with the influence of large states. Many textbook evaluators have limited training for their role. Often, severe time constraints hamper careful decision making. Reviewing large numbers of books in brief periods of time, harried committee members sometimes flip through a book to determine its merit. Publishers are well aware of this "flip phenomenon" and make sure that their books have "eye appeal." Teachers and administrators asked to select a textbook, whether from a state-approved list or not, can be influenced by the cosmetics—the cover, the graphics, the headings, the design. While visual attractiveness can enhance learning, it is no substitute for well-written and accurate content.

Frequently, adoption committees are given criteria sheets to assist them in determining textbook quality. Some criteria sheets are incredibly brief and general; others, in a well-intentioned attempt to be comprehensive, are long and unwieldy, too cumbersome to be used efficiently.³⁹

Criteria sheets often include information on the books' readability, yet another problematic area. By sampling several passages, **readability formulas** assess word difficulty and sentence length to determine the reading skill level for the book. Initially, the use of readability formulas seemed a promising development. What could be more reasonable than making sure the books' reading level was grade-appropriate? But readability formulas have created their own problems. Readability levels vary widely from passage to passage, so it is possible to find eleventh-, eighth-, seventh-, and fourth-grade passages in a single book designated as fifth-grade level. Worse yet, the different readability formulas give different results. For one text, the Spache readability formula indicated a 3.1 grade level, the Dale-Chall 4.2, and the Gunning 4.0, and the Fry put the text at the seventh-grade (7.0) level.⁴⁰

Since some states will buy texts only if they have a specified reading level, publishers are under pressure to develop books that meet this criterion. Often, authors avoid difficult words and long sentences, so that, for example, esophagus becomes food tube and protoplasm becomes stuff. The result, according to former secretary of education Terrell Bell and other critics, is the **dumbing down** of the textbook. Ironically, readability formulas may make books harder, not easier, to read. When authors simplify vocabulary, they replace precise and clear terminology with simple, vague, even ambiguous words. When authors shorten sentences, they often leave out the connective issue—and, but, therefore—words that clarify the relationships between events and ideas. Shortening sentences to make reading simple can make understanding challenging ideas even more difficult.

Writing to the readability level not only hurts comprehension but "squeezes the juice out of some very fine tales."⁴¹ For example, the following is one such distorted reading text version of "The Tortoise and the Hare":

CLASS ACTIVITY: TEXTBOOK ADOPTION COMMITTEE
IM, Activity 7:5

MULTIPLE INTELLIGENCE CONNECTION
Challenge students to create a short verse, rap, or limerick, using the terms *readability formula, dumbing down,* and *mentioning phenomenon.* If that's too tough (which is *dumbing down*), can they mention (*mentioning phenomenon*) all three terms in a sentence that is grade-level appropriate (*readability formula*)?

IN THE NEWS

Stronger Glue Needed?

David B., a member of the Texas State Board of Education, objected to the content in an algebra textbook. When his objection was considered inadequate, he pointed out that the book also had manufacturing defects, additional grounds for rejection. He demonstrated the manufacturing defects by ripping the book apart.

SOURCE: *The American School Board Journal,* January 1998.

 What's new in education? Click on *News Feeds.*

Rabbit said, "I can run. I can run fast." "You can't run fast," Turtle said. "Look Rabbit. See the park. You and I will run. We'll run to the park."

Rabbit said, "I want to stop. I'll stop here. I can run, but Turtle can't. I can get to the park fast." Turtle said, "I can't run fast. But I will not stop. Rabbit can't see me. I'll get to the park."[42]

In this textbook version, the characterization is gone. So is the moral. So is the enjoyment.

As textbooks skim over content, simply to cover it, the student loses information necessary for comprehension. Critics are frustrated by this **mentioning phenomenon,** and charge that texts typically include too many subjects and gloss over them to such a degree that students do not really understand what is going on.[43]

One reason for the mentioning phenomenon is the knowledge explosion. But another cause can be traced to the adoption process. In their quest for higher scores on standardized tests, many states have called for aligning the curriculum in textbooks with what is on standardized tests. Adoption committees have delineated in minute detail all the names, dates, and places they want included, and what skills they want students to attain. Frequently, in-depth analysis and clarifying examples are lost in favor of mentioning lots of names, places, and dates.

Researchers have also found that basal readers and other texts, in attempting to be inoffensive to potential purchasers, include only a limited range of story types, often devoid of interpersonal and internal conflict.[44] In their efforts to satisfy local and regional groups, some companies even publish alternative versions of the same book. For example, in some texts, Thanksgiving is truly a "movable feast": if you grew up in Massachusetts, your social studies book may have told you that the first Thanksgiving took place in Plymouth; if you went to school in Virginia, you may have learned that this great celebration occurred in Jamestown.

The lack of depth that characterizes U.S. texts does not keep them immune from errors, as a parent in Pennsylvania discovered. He was working with his daughter on a homework assignment when he found an error in her middle school science text, a best seller. By the time he was done analyzing the text, over 200 errors were documented. Worse yet, Prentice Hall, the publisher, was slow to correct any of them.[45] Nor was this an isolated incident. Another study found science textbooks that had Newton's first law of physics wrong, another had the wrong formula for finding the volume of a sphere, and the wrong definition for absolute zero. One text had a picture of singer Linda Ronstadt labeled as a silicon crystal.[46] Eventually the publishers set up a website (www.publishers.org) so that people could quickly communicate the errors as they found them.

Today's trend is a comprehensive textbook package, with a highly sophisticated instructional design, student materials, classroom visuals, and even website support. Obviously, there are positive elements in these comprehensive, commercially developed textbook systems. If you recall from the conversation in the faculty room at the start of this chapter, comprehensive packages can save overburdened teachers (especially new teachers) a great deal of time, which the teachers can then devote to individualized instruction, as well as a variety of classroom management duties. Some teachers enjoy this "freedom" from making curricular choices. Researcher Allan Odden has found that, the "more programs are ready made," the less teachers are worn out, reinforcing his belief that packages are more effective than teacher- or school-devised programs.[47]

"Knowledge is power," the saying goes, and in the final analysis the degree of power and talent you exert as an architect of the curriculum will depend on your own

VIDEO SEGMENT 19
Try Teaching 5 Classes a Day, 5 Days a Week

knowledge and skills. If you are supposed to teach a unit on the Civil War but you know little about it, it will be all you can do to implement commercially prepared materials. If you are to teach a unit on poetry but avoided literature classes in college, you will be at the mercy of whatever the publishers or the test makers tell you to do and say. If your knowledge of science is limited to that terrible memory of when you tried to dissect a frog, you may gratefully follow to the last dot on the i whatever instructions are in the teacher's manual (and beg for the science specialist to come in and do it for you). Your own knowledge about content and teaching skills is a classroom asset, giving you the power to put into action one of the most creative functions of teaching: shaping what your students learn in school.

But even when you have a solid intellectual handle on a topic, other challenges emerge. One such continual challenge is the subtle bias that permeates textbooks. Although women and people of color are included more frequently than in the past, they still suffer from tokenism, and American society as a whole is presented in an unrealistic, even idealized manner. What does this bias look like? Glad you asked, because it is an important question, one we explore in the next section.

Seven Forms of Bias

While many of yesterday's textbooks were racist and sexist, many of today's authors work hard to create more realistic and balanced portrayals. Unfortunately, they do not always succeed. Following is a description of **seven forms of bias** which can be used to assess instructional materials.[48] These categories identify bias not only against females and various racial and ethnic groups, but can also identify bias directed at the elderly, people with disabilities, limited and non-English speakers, gays and lesbians, and other groups.

Invisibility

The most fundamental form of bias is exclusion. Prior to the 1960s, African Americans, Latinos, Asian Americans, women, and Native Americans were largely absent from educational resources. Today, those with disabilities or gays and lesbians are among those underrepresented or invisible.

Stereotyping

When rigid roles or characteristics are assigned to all members of a group, a stereotype is born. Examples of stereotypes include presenting all African Americans and Mexican Americans as manual workers or troublemakers, women as passive and defined only in terms of their home and family roles, and all middle-class Americans as white Anglo-Saxon, and Protestant.

Imbalance and Selectivity

Curriculum often perpetuates bias by presenting only one side of an issue or a narrow view of a group. Such imbalanced accounts simplify and distort complex issues by omitting different perspectives. Describing how women were "given" the vote while omitting the physical abuse and sacrifices suffered by suffragettes who "won" the

FOCUS QUESTION 7
What are the seven forms of bias in instructional materials?

OVERHEAD 90
Forms of Bias

TEACHING TIP
Ask students to cite specific examples of curricular bias against other individuals or groups, such as those listed here.

CRITICAL THINKING QUESTION
When obligated to use resources that are biased, how can teachers redirect learning in a positive way?

GLOBAL VIEW
What stereotypes exist for national, racial and ethnic groups living outside the United States? What stereotypes persist when these individuals immigrate to the United States?

CLASS ACTIVITIES IDENTIFYING BIAS IN INSTRUCTIONAL MATERIALS
IM, Activity 7:6

Teachers serving on textbook adoption committees apply specific criteria to determine text suitability for their curriculum.

vote is one example. Another is selecting literature primarily from European male authors.

IDENTIFYING BIAS AGAINST MALES
IM, Activity 7:7

Unreality

Curricular materials too often ignore unpleasant facts or opinions that put the nation or political leaders in a negative light. By pretending that prejudice, racism, exploitation, and other persistent problems do not exist, we deny children the information they need to recognize, understand, and perhaps some day conquer these problems. Examples of unreality include statements that all Americans enjoy the same rights in the legal system, or that technology will one day resolve persistent social problems.

Fragmentation and Isolation

Have you ever seen a chapter or section focusing on one group, perhaps entitled "Ten Famous Asian Americans." When texts isolate groups in this way, they ignore dynamic group relationships and suggest that these groups are of less importance and out of society's mainstream.

INTERACTIVE ACTIVITY
What Is the Bias?
Match scenarios with the bias being displayed.

RAP 2.3
Curriculum Bias Detectors, 2:3, p. 275

Linguistic Bias

Language is a powerful conveyor of bias, in both blatant and subtle forms. For example, using words like "roaming," "wandering," or "roving" to describe Native Americans suggests nondirected behavior and relationships. Such language implicitly justifies the seizure of native lands by "more goal-directed" white Americans, who "traveled" or "settled" their way westward. More subtle examples include word orders and word choices that place males in a primary role, like "men and their wives."

CRITICAL THINKING QUESTION
The Forms of Bias could also be applied to instructional behaviors. Teacher actions can be biased and reflect stereotyping, invisibility, and so on. Can students transfer this curricular tool and identify or imagine teaching that is biased?

Cosmetic Bias

Cosmetic bias offers the "illusion of equity" as a marketing strategy to lure educators into purchasing books that appear current, diverse, and balanced. The problem is that it may be superficial and misleading. A science textbook that features a glossy pullout of female scientists but precious little on female scientists is an example. So is a music book with a multiethnic cover that belies the traditional white male composers lurking behind the cover.

 ## Religious Fundamentalism

FOCUS QUESTION 8
How do religious differences impact school curricular materials?

Some parents and educators argue that publishers have not gone far enough in producing nonsexist, multicultural books, but others believe that the publishers have gone much too far. While censorship attacks can originate from either liberals or conservatives, since the 1980s, they have been much more likely to come from conservative quarters. One such conservative group is Christian fundamentalists. **Christian, Bible,** or **religious fundamentalists** (sometimes called the **religious right**), generally believe in a strict interpretation of the Bible and advocate a conservative social agenda. Such issues as abortion and evolution can spark a strong reaction from these groups.

> Pressures from the politically organized religious Right have made it risky for publishers to discuss evolution. If evolution is discussed at all, it is often confined to a chapter in the book. Students are conducted on a forced march through the phyla, and given no understanding of the overarching theory (evolution) that gives taxonomy life and meaning. Touchy subjects like dinosaurs, the fossil record, genetics, natural selection, or even the scientific meanings of the words "theory" and "belief" are treated skimpily or vaguely in order to avoid the ire of the Bible fundamentalists.[49]

Here are two examples of the nature of these controversies.

Case 1. A 1986 case in eastern Tennessee made headlines when a group of fundamentalist Christian families objected to a series of Holt, Rinehart & Winston readers. They objected to an illustration in a first-grade reader showing a kitchen scene with a girl reading while a boy cooks (he is making toast). The plaintiffs argued that "the religion of John Dewey is planted in the first graders [sic] mind that there are no God-given roles for different sexes.[50] The plaintiffs also objected to *The Diary of Anne Frank,* which was cited as being antireligion in its acceptance of diversity in religious belief and practice. Consider the following passage:

TEACHING TIP
Research or share similar case studies involving religion and the curriculum.

ANNE: (Softly) I wish you had a religion, Peter.

PETER: No, thanks! Not me.

ANNE: Oh, I don't mean you have to be Orthodox . . . or believe in heaven and hell and purgatory and things . . . I just mean some religion . . . it doesn't matter what. Just to believe in something! When I think of all that's out there . . . the trees . . . the flowers . . . and seagulls . . . when I think of the dearness of you, Peter . . . and the goodness of the people we know . . . Mr. Kraler, Miep, Dirk, the vegetable man, all risking their lives for us every day. . . . When I think of these good things, I'm not afraid anymore.[51]

It is not only Anne Frank or nontraditional gender roles that capture attention. Other categories called "offensive" included "futuristic supernaturalism, one-world government, situation ethics or values clarification, humanistic moral absolutes, pacifism, rebellion against parents or self-authority, role reversal, role elimination, animals are equal to humans, the skeptic's view of religion contrasting belief in the supernatural with science, false views of death and related themes, magic, other religions, evolution, godless supernaturalism . . . and specific humanistic themes."[52]

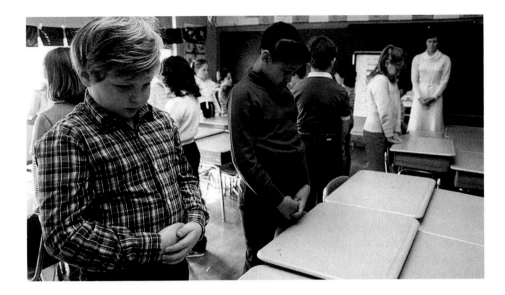

Scenes like this one involving overt religious prayer have been banned from the school curriculum. Should the study of religion as a vital social force also be banned or watered down because it is politically dangerous?

Case 2. During the spring of 1988, an assignment from Robert Marzano's *Tactics for Thinking* unleashed a storm of controversy in southern Indiana. Protesters charged that the following exercise could induce a self-hypnotic trance:

> Have students focus their attention on some stimulus (e.g., a spot on the wall). Explain to them that you want them to focus all of their energy for about a minute and ask them to be aware of what it is like when they are really trying to attend to something.[53]

Many community members were persuaded that the book was brainwashing children into believing in a one-world government and religion. In Battle Ground, Washington, a group of citizens claimed that *Tactics for Thinking* was teaching the occult. Thomas McDaniel, dean of Converse College, reported that, in one county, *St. George and the Dragon, Puss in Boots,* and *Sylvester and the Magic Pebble* were dropped from the reading curriculum. Parents objected because they were about magic.[54] In at least a dozen other states, there were protests against these and other books connected with the New Age movement or secular humanism.

It is hard to define what conservative religious leaders call the **New Age movement** and **secular humanism.** Humanists define themselves as living ethically without recourse to organized religions, or necessarily to a supernatural being. Christian fundamentalists and other opponents contend that "secular humanists" are anti-religion, deny God, a creator, or any divinity by promoting global education, the occult, values clarification, Eastern mysticism, and a belief in a one-world government. Critics charge that secular humanists are *pseudoreligious,* and promote "agnosticism, various forms of feminism, environmentalism, political liberalism and conservatism, various ethnic or sexual identities. . . ."[55]

To respond to this perceived secular threat, several public school systems have developed programs that not only teach, but also promote basic Christian beliefs. For example, in the 2000 academic year, a Virginia public school system used the following exam questions:

1. List six proofs that the Bible is God's word.

2. God is supreme ruler and has given man free choice. This shows that God is:

   A. Omniscient   B. Good   C. Sovereign   D. Merciful[56]

By no means is such inappropriate instruction confined to one region of the country. In Belridge, California, for example, the public school system was forced to abandon its Christian education program as a result of a suit by the American Civil Liberties Union. In 1999, Belridge was using textbooks that described non-Christian religions as "cults," taught that God helped Columbus discover America, that Native American accomplishments were "worthless" since they had no knowledge of the "true" God, and asked students to punctuate a sentence that read: "The Hebrew people often grumbled and complained." Clearly the separation of church and state is an ongoing challenge.[57]

While many people are disturbed by these unconstitutional school practices that promote religious beliefs, teachers can overreact. Many teachers shy away from teaching about religion at all for fear that the topic should not be taught in public schools.[58] Actually, teaching *about* different religions is important, but *promoting* or *disparaging* religious beliefs is inappropriate. Although states frequently require that students be taught about the world's great religions by the time they reach the tenth grade, what is taught is less than adequate. Religious topics taught during the elementary years are often quite superficial, while the high school courses rarely cover religious issues beyond the Civil War.[59] Religious ignorance and bigotry are at least partially responsible for the increasing number of censorship attacks on books used in public schools, attacks that can tie a school system into knots and pose a genuine threat to academic freedom.[60]

 # Censorship and the Curriculum

FOCUS QUESTION 9
Why are schoolbooks so frequently the targets of censorship?

Ruth Sherman lived just outside New York City, in a Long Island neighborhood known for its Italian community and easy commute to the city. Although she traveled only a short distance to P.S. 75, where she taught third grade, she might as well have been teaching in another country. P.S. 75 was in the Bushwick section of Brooklyn, a graffiti-filled neighborhood populated by poor black and Hispanic families living in the midst of a rampant drug culture. "Why there?" her friends asked her. "Because I want 'to turn things around,'" she responded. She was that kind of teacher. But, in just three months, it was Ruth Sherman, and not her students, who was turned around.

Her problems started in September, although she did not learn about it until later, when she assigned a book called *Nappy Hair*, by African American author Carolivia Herron. Her students loved the book, about a little black girl with "the nappiest, fuzziest, the most screwed up, squeezed up, knotted hair," and clamored for copies to take with them. By Thanksgiving, the parents in Ruth Sherman's class had also discovered the book, which considered racially insulting. At a parents' meeting, she was confronted by fifty parents (most of them parents of children not in her class), who shouted racial epithets and eventually threatened her. The superintendent sent Ruth home, for her own protection. A review of the book followed. The review brought only praise for a book that promoted positive images for children and presented stories that appealed to them. Within a few days, the superintendent wrote her a letter, commending her performance, inviting her back to the school, and promising security escorts to protect her. But, by then, it was too late. Ruth Sherman, the teacher who wanted to make a difference, did not want to work in a climate that required "escorts" to ensure her safety. She transferred to another school.[61]

CLASS ACTIVITY: HOW TO HANDLE CENSORSHIP
IM, Activity 7:1

This incident occurred in 1998 in New York, but it could occur anywhere at anytime. Nearly everyone—teachers, parents, the general public, and various special interest groups—wants some say as to what is and is not in the school curriculum. No matter what content is found in a particular textbook or course of study, someone is likely to consider it too conservative or too liberal, too traditional or too avant-garde, racist, sexist, anti-Semitic, violent, un-Christian, or pornographic.[62] When this happens, pressure to **censor** the offending materials soon follows.

There is no such thing as a totally safe, acceptable, uncontroversial book or curriculum. Each of the following has been subjected to censorship at one time or another:

OVERHEAD 91
Examples of Censorship

- Mary Rodgers's *Freaky Friday:* "Makes fun of parents and parental responsibility"
- Plato's *Republic:* "This book is un-Christian"
- Jules Verne's *Around the World in Eighty Days:* "Very unfavorable to Mormons"
- William Shakespeare's *Macbeth:* "Too violent for children"
- Fyodor Dostoyevsky's *Crime and Punishment:* "Serves as a poor model for young people"
- Herman Melville's *Moby Dick:* "Contains homosexuality"
- Anne Frank's *Diary of a Young Girl:* "Obscene and blasphemous"
- E. B. White's *Charlotte's Web:* "Morbid picture of death"
- J. R. R. Tolkien's *The Hobbit:* "Subversive elements"
- Roald Dahl's *Charlie and the Chocolate Factory:* "Racist"
- Mark Twain's *The Adventures of Huckleberry Finn:* "Racism, insensitivity, and offensive language"
- *Webster's Dictionary:* "Contains sexually explicit definitions"[63]

According to the American Library Association, between 1990–2000, there were 6,364 challenges reported.[64] But the incidences of **self-censorship,** which some term **stealth censorship,** is considered much higher.[65] Stealth censorship occurs when educators or parents quietly remove a book from a library shelf or a course of study in response to an informal complaint—or in order to avoid controversy. Teachers practice the same sort of self-censorship when they choose not to teach a topic or not to discuss a difficult issue. Numbers on the frequency of self-censorship are impossible to obtain. Tallying up the number of books that were officially removed or placed on restricted-access shelves in libraries is far easier.[66] Frequently challenged authors include J. K. Rowling, Judy Blume, Robert Cormier, Mark Twain, Phyllis Reynolds Naylor, Stephen King, Lois Duncan, S. E. Hinton, Maya Angelou, Roald Dahl, and Toni Morrison. On today's list of challenged books, you often find:

RELATED READING
Not in Front of the Children: "Indecency," Censorship, and the Innocence of Youth by Marjorie Heins (2001).

1. *Harry Potter* series, by J. K. Rowling: "Wizardry and magic"
2. *Alice* series, by Phyllis Reynolds Naylor: "Sexually explicit, using offensive language and being unsuited to age group"
3. *The Chocolate War* by Robert Cormier: "Using offensive language and being unsuited to age group"
4. *I Know Why the Caged Bird Sings* by Maya Angelou: "Sexual content, racism, offensive language, violence and being unsuited to age group"
5. *Taming the Star Runner* by S. E. Hinton: "Offensive language"[67]

At the heart of the case against censorship is the First Amendment, which guarantees freedom of speech and of the press. Those who oppose censorship say that

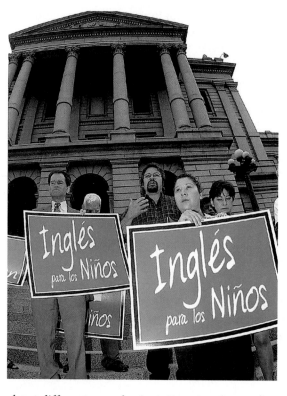

our purpose as educators is not to indoctrinate children but to expose them to a variety of views and perspectives. The case for censorship (or, perhaps in a more politically correct phrase, *mature judgment and selection*) is that adults have the right and obligation to protect children from harmful influences. But "harmful influences" are in the eye of the beholder. For instance, challenges to books that include homosexuality have become commonplace. Critics say that these books promote homosexuality, and that is not acceptable in school. Others believe that such books teach tolerance of sexual differences, and serve a positive purpose for both heterosexual and homosexual students. Moreover, they argue, reading about different sexual orientations is a far cry from promoting any particular sexual outlook.[68] The censorship controversy is symbolic of how politicized the curriculum debate has become.

 ## Cultural Literacy or Cultural Imperialism?

Both George Orwell and Aldous Huxley were pessimists about the future. "What Orwell feared were those who would ban books," writes author Neil Postman. "What Huxley feared was that there would be no one who wanted to read one."[69] Perhaps neither of them imagined that the great debate would revolve around neither fear nor apathy but, rather, deciding which books are most worth reading.

Proponents of **core knowledge,** also called **cultural literacy,** argue for a common course of study for all students, one that ensures that an educated person knows the basics of our society. Novelist and teacher John Barth laments what ensues without core knowledge:

> In the same way you can't take for granted that a high school senior or a freshman in college really understands that the Vietnam War came after World War II, you can't take for granted that any one book is common knowledge even among a group of liberal arts or writing majors at a pretty good university.[70]

Allan Bloom's ***The Closing of the American Mind*** (1987) was one of several books that sounded the call for a curricular canon. A canon is a term with religious roots, referring to a list of books officially accepted by the church or a religious hierarchy. A **curricular canon** applies this notion to schools by defining the most useful and valued books in our culture. Those who support a curricular canon believe that all students should share a common knowledge of our history and the central figures of our culture, an appreciation of the great works of art and music and, particularly, the great works of literature. A shared understanding of our civilization is a way to bind our diverse people.

Allan Bloom, professor of social thought at the University of Chicago, took aim at the university curriculum as a series of often unrelated courses lacking a vision of what an educated individual should know, a canonless curriculum. He claimed that his university students were ignorant of music and literature, and charged that too many students graduate with a degree but without an education.[71] One of the criticisms of Bloom's vision was that his canon consisted almost exclusively of white, male, European culture.

E. D. Hirsch, Jr., in his book ***Cultural Literacy,*** was more successful than Bloom in including the contributions of various ethnic and racial groups, as well as women. This is a rarity among core curriculum proponents. In fact, Hirsch believes that it is the poorer children and children of color who will most benefit from a cultural literacy curriculum. He points out that children from impoverished homes are less likely to become culturally literate. A core curriculum will teach them the names, dates, places, events, and quotes that every literate American needs to know in order to succeed. In 1991, Hirsch published the first volume of the core knowledge series, *What Your First Grader Needs to Know.* Other grades followed in these mass-marketed books directed not only at educators but at parents as well.[72]

Not everyone is enamored with the core curriculum idea. A number of educators wonder who gets included in this core, and, just as interesting, who gets to choose? Are Hirsch, Bloom, and others to be members of a very select committee, perhaps a blue-ribbon committee of "Very Smart People"? Why are so many of these curricular canons so white, so male, so Eurocentric, and so exclusionary?

Many call for a more inclusive telling of the American story, one that weaves the contributions of many groups and of women as well as of white males into the textbook tapestry of the American experience. Those who support **multicultural education** say that students of color and females will achieve more, will like learning better, and will have higher self-esteem if they are reflected in the pages of their textbooks. And let's not forget white male students. When they read about people other than themselves in the curriculum, they are more likely to honor and appreciate their diverse peers. Educator and author James Banks calls for increased cultural pluralism:

INTERACTIVE ACTIVITY

Do You Know the "Basics"? See how you do on this hypothetical quiz created to test your cultural literacy. Get a first-hand feel for the testing issue.

What balance should schools seek between teaching a common core curriculum that binds all Americans together and teaching a curriculum that celebrates the many cultures that have been brought to the United States?

GLOBAL VIEW

How could the enormous diversity of this nation be evident in any school curriculum? Have students provide positive (or negative) examples of multicultural education in their current studies.

RELATED READING

K–12 Teachers in the Midst of Reform: Common Thread Cases by Traci Bliss and Joan Mazur (2002).

People of color, women, and other marginalized groups are demanding that their voices, visions, and perspectives be included in the curriculum. They ask that the debt Western civilization owes to Africa, Asia, and indigenous America be acknowledged. . . . However, these groups must acknowledge that they do not want to eliminate Aristotle and Shakespeare, or Western civilization, from the school curriculum. To reject the West would be to reject important aspects of their own cultural heritages, experiences, and identities.[73]

Advocates of a core curriculum claim that it will empower the poor and the disadvantaged. Opponents say it will rob them of the chance to see their experiences reflected in history and literature. What some call *cultural literacy* others see as *cultural imperialism.* "Whose knowledge is of most worth?" is the question of the day. And, as America becomes a nation of growing diversity, the argument will continue to drive the debate about what is core, what is fair, and what should be in the curriculum.

SUMMARY

CHAPTER REVIEW

Go to the Online Learning Center to take a chapter self-quiz, practice with key terms, and review concepts from the chapter.

CURRENT NEWS FROM POWERWEB

To access PowerWeb, go to Chapter 7 on the Online Learning Center to read current articles and to access news feeds about:

- Curriculum
- Education Standards
- Future of Education
- Education Reform
- Politics
- Schools and Federal Policy
- Testing and Evaluation

1. What forces shape the school curriculum?

   Publishers, teachers, students, parents, administrators, the federal, state, and local governments, colleges and universities, national tests, education commissions and committees, professional organizations, and special interest groups all influence the curriculum. In recent years, standards and statewide testing have been dictating much of what is taught in school.

2. What are the provisions and criticisms of *No Child Left Behind*?

   One of the most far-reaching federal education plans, *No Child Left Behind,* includes annual testing in reading and math in grades 3–8. Schools must report all student scores as well as the subscores of certain groups based on poverty, race, ethnicity, disability, and limited English proficiency. Underperforming schools must make adequate yearly progress—or they can be closed. All teachers hired by 2005–06 must be "highly qualified," licensed with an academic major in the field they are teaching. Paraprofessionals must have at least two years of college or pass a rigorous test. Parents must be informed if their child's teacher is not "highly qualified." Critics of the program point out many problems: trying to grade an entire education program by standardized tests, measuring wealthy and poor schools with the same test while not providing the necessary resources to improve the poorer schools, lowering state standards to make passing tests easier, and how scores of only a small number of students can "fail" an entire school.

3. How does the standards movement influence what is taught in school?

   The effort to create subject matter standards, or content standards, gained momentum with the National Education Summit held in Charlottesville in 1989, and provided the states with direction in terms of what should be included in the curriculum. In mathematics, national standards were quickly developed. But in more value-laden disciplines like history, arguments and disagreements erupted over what should be included. While most Americans believe standards will enhance learning, by the beginning of the twenty-first century, concern arose regarding performance standards and standardized testing.

4. What are the concerns with high-stakes testing?

   There are numerous criticisms aimed at high-stakes tests. At-risk students are placed at greater risk, errors on tests persist, dropouts increase, high scores do not necessarily reflect greater learning, teachers teach-to-the-test and the curriculum is narrowed, teacher stress increases and what is considered critical information varies over time.

5. How can we rethink curriculum and testing?

The reader is invited to consider what knowledge endures and should be the focus of schools, and the authors suggest a four-tier curriculum that promotes self-understanding, human relations, and greater individualization. Rather than "high-stakes" tests, a variety of assessment tools is recommended. One of these, authentic assessment, evaluates students by asking them to synthesize what they have learned in a final product or "exhibit."

6. How do textbook publishers and state adoption committees "drive" the curriculum?

More than twenty states, mainly located in the South and West, are textbook adoption states, and local school districts must select their texts from an official, state-approved list. A few populous states exert considerable influence as these books are developed. Textbooks represent a compromise, and many believe they are poorly written and do not reflect the subtleties of controversies in a subject area.

7. What are the seven forms of bias in instructional materials?

Seven forms of bias can characterize textbooks: invisibility, stereotyping, imbalance and selectivity, unreality, fragmentation and isolation, linguistic bias, and cosmetic bias. These forms of bias can work against a group's race, ethnicity, gender, age, or (dis)ability.

8. How do religious differences impact school curricular materials?

Controversies over religious fundamentalism and secular humanism have characterized textbook adoption in recent years. In some communities, these controversies have led to book banning and censorship. Teachers do not always appreciate the difference between teaching about religion and promoting a religious belief. As a result, some teachers promote their beliefs, while many others avoid the topic entirely.

9. Why are schoolbooks so frequently the targets of censorship?

Censorship can emanate from the political left or right. Liberals argue against books that defame or omit certain racial, ethnic, or other groups. Conservatives, particularly religious fundamentalists, target books and ideas that conflict with their values. The censors have targeted even some of the most popular books, from Shakespeare to the *Harry Potter* series. The line between "selecting" and "censoring" is not always clear. Many teachers, fearful of censorship attacks, follow a path of stealth or self-censorship, avoiding books and topics that could be controversial.

10. Should the curriculum focus on teaching a core knowledge or focus on the demands of a changing world?

Proponents of a core curriculum and cultural literacy, such as E. D. Hirsch, feel that it will benefit the disadvantaged and transmit the culture essential for well-educated citizens. Multiculturalists, such as James Banks, argue that most examples of cultural literacy minimize the roles, experiences, and contributions of women and people of color.

EXTENDED LEARNING

CASE STUDIES

- Elaine Adams: A student teacher near the end of her assignment observes her cooperating teacher giving students help while administering the district-mandated standardized tests.

- Therese Carmen: A second-year teacher is presented with a new district-wide science curriculum that she finds difficult to teach because she relies on the objectives found in the teacher's manual.

- Jim Colbert: A third-grade teacher in an inner-city school is trying his best to teach language arts using basal readers and a district-required curriculum.

Go to Chapter 7 on your *Resources for Exploring Education* CD-ROM to access Case Studies, Readings, and Media Observations.

- Melinda Grant: A teacher who has developed an innovative curriculum is concerned because another teacher continually warns her that she will be held responsible for her students' end-of-year standardized test scores.

READINGS

- Linda Nathan. "The Human Side of the High Stakes Testing Story."
- Alan Jones. "Welcome to Standardsville."

KEY TERMS AND PEOPLE

adequate yearly progress (AYP), 241

authentic assessment, 254

Allan Bloom, 266

censor, 265

Christian, Bible, or religious fundamentalists, 262

The Closing of the American Mind, 266

content standards, 243

core knowledge, 262

Cultural Literacy, 267

curricular canon, 266

dumbing down, 258

E. D. Hirsch, Jr., 267

Alfie Kohn, 253

mentioning phenomenon, 259

multicultural education, 267

New Age movement, 263

No Child Left Behind (NCLB), 240

opportunity-to-learn standards, 245

performance standards, 244

readability formulas, 258

religious right, 262

secular humanism, 263

self-censorship, stealth censorship, 265

seven forms of bias, 260

Texas and California effect, 257

textbook adoption states, 257

DISCUSSION QUESTIONS AND ACTIVITIES

 WEB-*TIVITIES*

1. Censorship and the Curriculum
2. The Textbook Shapes the Curriculum
3. Is the United States Going Test Crazy?
4. The Teacher as the Curriculum Developer

1. What subject areas spark the greatest debate and controversy over creating a single, national curriculum? Are there strategies to help reach a consensus on these issues? How might a national history curriculum written today differ from one written a century from now? A century ago? Why?

2. Do you believe that children's educational materials should be censored? Are there any benefits to censorship? Any dangers? What kinds of materials would you refuse to let elementary school students read? Middle or high school students? Postsecondary students?

3. Collect textbooks from your local elementary and secondary schools and analyze them according to the following criteria:

   - Do they include instructional objectives? Do these require students to use both recall of factual information and analytical and creative thinking skills?

   - Were readability formulas used in the preparation of the textbooks? If so, did this appear to have a negative or positive impact on the quality of the writing?

   - Are underrepresented group members included in the textbooks' narrative and illustrations? Are individuals with disabilities included?

- When various individuals are included, are they portrayed in a balanced or a stereotyped manner?

4. Consider the materials and textbooks used on your campus in your major courses. Do you think a traditional or a multicultural perspective is reflected? What testing strategies are used in your courses? What are the strengths and weaknesses of these strategies?

5. Your course instructor probably used this textbook as a framework for curriculum development in this course. How has this text served as a foundation for content, testing, discussion, and activities?

REEL TO REAL TEACHING

INHERIT THE WIND (1960)
Run Time: 127 minutes

Synopsis: A small Tennessee town gained national attention in 1925 when a biology teacher was arrested for violating state law by teaching Darwin's theory of evolution. The explosive battle between science and religion continues to this day.

Reflection:

1. Bertram Cates is the character of what real life person? What happened to his teaching career following the trial? Who do Henry Drummond and Matthew Harrison Brady represent in real life?

2. Who should control what is taught in schools? Government? School boards? Teachers? Parents? Why?

3. In which court was Bertram Cates tried: a court of law or the court of public opinion? Who won the trial? Support your answer with specific quotes and scenes from the film.

4. Should there be a difference between the type of control exerted by state legislatures over what teachers can teach in public elementary and secondary schools as opposed to what professors teach in publicly supported universities? Why or why not?

5. Research recent attempts to ban the teaching of evolution. Who or what sparked the debate? What were the outcomes? Why is evolution still considered a controversial theory?

6. Where do professional teaching associations stand on the issues of teaching religion versus teaching about religion, teaching evolution versus teaching creationism? You may want to start with the National Science Teachers Association, National Council for Social Studies, American Federation of Teachers, and National Education Association.

7. Explain the meaning of the phrase "inherit the wind."

Follow-up Activity: Create your own *You Be the Judge: Voices of Human Origin*. Develop arguments for and against the question "Should alternative theories of human origin be taught along with evolution?" After presenting 5–6 well-supported points on both sides of the issue, you be the judge and hand down a definitive ruling.

www.mhhe.com/
sadker7e

How do you rate this film? Go to *Reel to Real Teaching* in the Critics' Corner to review this film.

FOR FURTHER READING

The Case Against Standardized Testing: Raising Scores, Ruining Schools, by Alfie Kohn (2000). Argues that standardized tests undermine quality learning and reflect the interests of politicians and business leaders rather than students and educators.

Caught in the Middle: Nonstandard Kids and a Killing Curriculum, by Susan Ohanian (2001). Describes how curriculum standards impart a singular definition of success that fails many students. The lives of eight students who "think outside the box" are detailed.

Political Agendas for Education: From the Religious Right to the Green Party, by Joel Spring (2002). The political and religious background to the many controversies over American education today are explained. Topics include the Republican agenda for the twenty-first century, the meaning of "compassionate conservative," creationism, and commercialization of schools.

Put to the Test: An Educator's and Consumer's Guide to Standardized Testing, by Gerald Bracey (2002). This nationally recognized author leads readers through the often confusing landscape of standardized testing, describing what tests are and aren't. Bracey covers, in easy-to-understand language, how to interpret test scores, different types of standardized tests, and specific standardized tests. An in-depth analysis of the *No Child Left Behind* Act's impact on standardized testing is also included.

Protecting the Right to Learn: Power, Politics, and Public Schools, by James Daly, Patricia Schall, and Rosemary Skeele (2001). Investigates how censorship stifles the ability of schools and teachers to educate students in meaningful ways through a case study of one school district embroiled in a legal battle over control of the curriculum.

REFLECTIVE ACTIVITIES AND YOUR PORTFOLIO

Part II: Schools and Curriculum

2:1 State and National Curricular Standards

Purpose: Many of today's schools are immersed in standards and testing, and being familiar with these policies can be enormously helpful. A knowledge of standards and testing can guide you during the hiring process, in deciding where to teach, and also in crafting and presenting effective lessons.

INTASC PRINCIPLE 1
Knowledge of
Subject Matter

Activity: Perform an Internet search of "curriculum standards" at both the national and state level. For state curriculum standards, choose a particular state that interests you. As you get closer to the hiring process, you may want to investigate curriculum standards for specific school districts. Standards are typically broken into curricular areas, so choose at least one subject area for your focus. A useful resource for this activity is: www.educationworld.com/standards.

Artifact: "Venn Diagram: Curricular Standards" After reading through the curriculum standards at both the national and state level, complete the following Venn Diagram. Venn Diagrams are useful for examining similarities and differences. They help us to compare the elements of one or more items. Compare and contrast at least three standards.

Venn Diagram

Subject and Standard (*example* Math—numbers and operations grades 3–5):

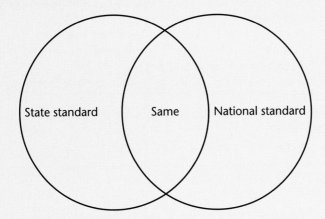

Reflection: What did you learn from this activity? Any surprises? In your opinion, are these standards realistic? Useful? Support your opinion. What kind of similarities

273

and differences do you find between the national curriculum standards and the state level curriculum standards? How do you envision using curriculum standards in planning lessons? Attach your reflections to your Venn Diagram and include in your portfolio.

2:2 Scoping School Culture

Purpose: Have you ever wanted to "stop the world" and, rather than get off, take the time to really observe people's behavior? Here's your chance with the added bonus that this experience will help you better understand your future teaching environment. Your inherent curiosity, coupled with some directed observations, can offer a rich opportunity to study the growth and development of students.

Activity: Visit an elementary, middle, or high school campus, preferably at the level you envision teaching one day. Set yourself up to the side of the major thoroughfares with notepad, laptop, or sketchbook and make "notes." Consider three public and informal spaces: cafeteria, hallways, open space quad, blacktop/field, or recess areas.

Artifact: Create a "School Observation Diary" by taking notes on what you observe. Below are some questions to guide you. Feel free to add your own thoughts, questions, and observations.

 FORM:
School
Observation Diary

INTASC PRINCIPLE 2
Human
Development and
Learning

School Observation Diary
<ul><li>What does the "scene" look like? How are individuals and groups dressed? What else do you see?</li><li>Focus on students and their body language. Who's talking, touching, or teasing? Describe the behavior. Are groups divided along racial, gender, and/or economic lines?</li><li>Focus on staff or faculty in the area. What are their roles? Are they detached, integrated, or "in charge"? Describe their actions. What is the ratio of male teachers to female teachers?</li><li>What noise is evident—music, varied languages, general chatter, or the "sounds of silence"?</li><li>Compare and contrast school geography to see if cliques dominate certain areas or activities?</li><li>What other behaviors, in general, do you observe?</li></ul>

Reflection: Did the students' behavior appear to vary by such factors as gender, race, physical size, language fluency, and clothing? What insights did you have about this student body and individual pupils? How did their use of time and space in the halls, cafeteria, and open areas interest and inform you? What insights about student and teacher behavior might you draw from your observations? How might these observations help you understand human development? Has this observation experience influenced your opinion about a career in teaching? Attach your reflection to the "School Observation Diary" and include both in your portfolio.

2:3 Curriculum Bias Detectors

Purpose: The way curricular materials portray different groups can promote either knowledge or stereotypes. In this activity, you will refine your skills for detecting bias. As a teacher, once you recognize this problem, you can select or adapt materials to counter such biases.

Activity: Review the seven forms of bias discussed in Chapter 7. Borrow a K–12 textbook (appropriate for your subject major or grade level) from your college's curriculum resource center, a local school, or a teaching friend. Look for an example of each form of bias.

FORM:
Bias Busters

INTASC PRINCIPLE 3
Diversity in
Learning

Bias Busters		
Book Title/Author/Reference Information:		
Brief description of text:		
Type of Bias	**Page #**	**Example**
1. Invisibility		
2. Stereotyping		
3. Imbalance and selectivity		
4. Unreality		
5. Fragmentation and isolation		
6. Linguistic bias		
7. Cosmetic bias		

Reflection: What did you learn from this experience? Was there more or less evidence of bias than you thought? What surprised you about this activity? Will this experience influence how you use materials in your classroom? Why or why not? How will you teach your students to become "Bias Detectors"? Attach your "Forms of Bias" notes to your reflection and include in your portfolio.

2:4 Visit a "Choice" School

Purpose: As Chapter 4 illustrates, public education is moving beyond the neighborhood school. An abundance of school choices now exist: magnet schools, charter schools, for-profit schools, voucher programs, and home schooling to name a few. If

INTASC PRINCIPLE 4
Variety of
Instructional
Strategies

you choose to become a teacher you may find yourself working in a very different setting than the one you attended. For this reason it is important that you become familiar with the changing face of America's public schools.

Activity: Arrange to visit at least one "choice" school. Spend time not only in the classrooms but also in the halls and on the playground. Speak with administrators, teachers, students, and (if possible) parents. What is the educational environment like? Is it conducive to learning? Is the curriculum innovative? Feel free to use the observations questions from 2.2 above.

Artifact: Create a "Choice School Observation Diary" that includes your notes and observations. Find out what each group likes or doesn't like about this "choice" school. Create a Venn Diagram comparing this school to a nonchoice school. You can compare it to the school you attended as a student or to the "Scoping School Culture" activity in 2.2.

Venn Diagram

Type of Choice School (*example* charter):

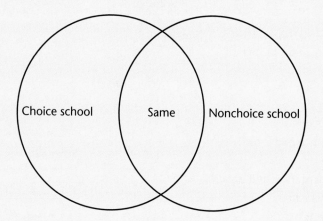

Reflection: What did you learn from this Venn Diagram? Would you want to teach in such a setting? Why or why not? Would you want your children to attend such a school? Do you believe that this "choice" will become more or less attractive over time? Attach your notes and Venn Diagram to your reflection and include in your portfolio.

2:5 Rules, Rituals, and Routines

INTASC PRINCIPLE 5
Motivation and
Management

Purpose: Most teachers struggle to balance motivating students with managing them. Sometimes, in an attempt to keep it "all together and in control" teachers overregulate a class. At other times, they wait too long to rein in exuberant students. Consider behavior techniques along with your study of school, because as a prospective teacher, it is never too early to begin sorting out how you will manage your classroom.

Activity: Arrange to visit a few classrooms of the age of children you want to teach. Use the chart below to record your observations. You may find it helpful to review the section on classroom management and the findings of classroom management expert Jacob Kounin prior to your observations.

Artifact:

Management/Motivation Observation
Examples
Group alerting
Withitness
Overlapping
Least intervention
Flip flops
Overdwelling
Fragmentation
Thrusts
Dangles

FORM:

Management/
Motivation
Observation

Reflection: Were you able to find evidence/examples of all the categories on the chart? What successful management and motivation strategies and techniques did you see? How might you employ what you learned from this teacher in your own classroom? What, if any, evidence of the hidden or implicit curriculum did you witness? If you observed a teacher struggling with management and motivation, what lessons did you take from this experience? What do you believe is the most difficult aspect of motivation? What do you believe is the most difficult aspect of management? Attach your artifact to your reflection and include in your portfolio.

2:6 A Public Service Announcement: The Purpose of School

Purpose: Chapter 4 details two diverse purposes of education: to transmit society's knowledge and values (passing the cultural baton); and to reconstruct society (schools as tools for change). Your ability to formulate and express your vision for education can guide your formal application for a teaching position. Communicating your goals clearly and concisely will let you practice verbal language skills, a foundation of effective instruction.

INTASC PRINCIPLE 6
Communication
Skills

Activity: Develop a public service announcement (PSA) supporting one of these purposes of education. Think of it as a radio spot (thirty to forty-five seconds long) that tells the listening public just what *they* need to know.

Artifact: "Public Service Announcement for Schools." Write, edit, and practice your script with a stopwatch. Rewrite, edit again, and rehearse until it's right. You may not always be able to practice and tighten your lessons this thoroughly, but the strategies you use to develop and refine your PSA are a necessary part of your communication repertoire. Deliver your PSAs in small groups during a class session, maybe as a series of "commercial breaks." Perhaps you can record and broadcast your PSA. Challenge: Develop a second PSA supporting the other purpose of education.

Reflection: What did you learn from this activity? How were your peers' messages similar or different? Which PSAs appealed to you the most? Did you find yourself supporting the other purpose of education? Is it really possible to support only one of these purposes of education? Attach your PSA artifact to your reflection and include in your portfolio.

2:7 Effective Schools

INTASC PRINCIPLE 7
Instructional
Planning Skills

Purpose: Chapter 5, "Life in Schools," detailed five factors of effective schools: strong leadership, a clear school mission, a safe and orderly climate, the monitoring of student progress, and high expectations.

Activity: Visit one or more elementary, middle, or high schools in an effort to find evidence of these factors. Walk the halls of these schools. Spend time in a variety of classrooms. Look for both positive and negative examples of the five factors of effective schools. Keep in mind that it is difficult to get a complete picture of a school from a few short visits. Use the chart below to record your observations.

Artifact:

FORM:
Effective Schools
Observation

Effective Schools Observation	
	Positive or Negative Examples
Strong Leadership	
Clear School Mission	
Safe and Orderly Climate	
Monitoring of Student Progress	
High Expectations	

Reflection: Was it easy to identify these five factors? Were some factors easier to spot than others? What other factors might be used to gauge school effectiveness? As a student, did your schools exhibit some or all of these characteristics? What did you learn from this experience? Attach your reflection to your artifact and store in your portfolio.

2:8 Memoirs of a Time-Tested Student

Purpose: National, state, and district tests are a huge part of school culture, yet few teachers analyze their own role in the current testing climate. The following activity will help you define that role.

INTASC PRINCIPLE 8
Assessment

Activity: Think about the quizzes and tests you took as a student. Looking back, would you rate your teachers as helpful, or not so helpful? Either through your own journal entry or a conversation with a partner (live, taped, or online), consider the following questions below as you consider your testing experiences.

- What's an early memory of a "big deal" test? (Sharpening your number 2 pencil? unsealing special pamphlets in elementary school? being tucked in a cardboard "cubby" for privacy? proctors milling through rows, looking for cheating?) Consider thoughts from your classmates and see if more recollections are sparked.

- What did the teacher do that encouraged and supported you during the test?

- Do you remember any words or behaviors that distracted or annoyed you during the test?

Artifact: Review the *You Be the Judge* format that you find in this text, and create two columns that would be useful for your teacher-testing role. Prepare a *You Be the Judge* feature on testing by brainstorming what teachers can do to ensure a positive climate for student testing in one column, and list actions teachers should definitely avoid in the other.

You Be the Judge: "Testing Do's and Don'ts"	
What Teachers SHOULD Do . . .	**What Teacher Should NOT Do . . .**
1. Describe the purpose of the test*	1. Leave the room*
2.	2.
3.	3.
etc.	etc.

*Sample items.

FORM:

You Be the Judge: "Testing Do's and Don'ts"

Reflection: What have you learned from this activity? Based on your analysis, what are some of the most critical factors in a testing climate? How can you remember to implement effective testing practices? Attach the *You Be the Judge* sheet to your reflection and store in your portfolio.

2:9 Reflections of a High School Yearbook

Purpose: Part 2 of this text looked at all aspects of the school scene, from the student role to a teacher's reality. While you may have shifted perspective as you walked away

INTASC PRINCIPLE 9
Reflection and
Responsibility

from your high school graduation ceremony, the purpose of this activity is to look back and assess some of your choices and actions. Your high school yearbook symbolizes a snapshot of your school and a view of yourself in the social system. What does it show you about your school, yourself, and others?

Activity: Dig out your high school yearbook or see if it is posted on the Internet. Many schools now have their own web pages. Read through the questions below before starting the artifact.

- Find yourself. Are you included? What is the caption under your senior photo? Did you get caught in candid shots? Are you with clubs, in activities, and on teams? Are you surrounded by your friends or often on your own? Which images recall emotions: pride, embarrassment, sadness? Did your school have an FTA (Future Teachers of America) organization? Were you pictured with them? How does being a future teacher or a member of that club look today? Were your curricular strengths evident by achievements, awards, and participation? (You were an officer for the Model UN and you're now a social studies major; you belonged to the Storyteller Society and you want to be an elementary teacher; you lettered in many sports and plan to teach physical education.) In what ways are you the same or different today?

- Find your friends. In what ways were you similar or different from them? When and where do they appear?

- Find lesser-known faces. Stop and really stare at students you may have walked by for years. What of their stories do you suspect or know? What groups were they in? What labels described their lives?

- Who is invisible or missing? Are there students who appear only in their "mug shot" and never as part of the campus culture? Do female or male students, from varied racial and ethnic groups, dominate particular activities or campus locales?

Artifact: Write a paragraph entitled "My High School Days" or "The Story Behind the Story" describing what really was going on with you socially, physically, and psychologically during this year in high school. Include both positive and negative experiences and feelings. (You can even compose a song or poem to share your high school years.)

Reflection: What do you notice about your school and yourself? How does it compare with the student cultures described in this text? Would you want to teach there or at a very different site? What stories from your yearbook pages would be valuable to share with classmates? Attach your reflection to your artifact and store in your portfolio.

2:10 Support Staff Interview

Purpose: When you have a teaching job, you become part of a learning community. Knowing about the roles and responsibilities of support personnel will enhance your

INTASC PRINCIPLE 10
Relationships and Partnerships

understanding of the way schools work. Nonteaching employees contribute significantly to a well-functioning school. Bus drivers, clerical personnel, media and custodial staff, instructional aides, playground and lunch supervisors, resource specialists, medical and psychological professionals, and security and safety personnel all do their part. They befriend alienated kids, clean up after trashy nutrition breaks, reset chairs in an auditorium as many as eight times a day, frisk students with clothes baggy enough to cover goods and evils, know most students' names when they step up to the office counter, make lunchrooms smell like fresh cookies (maybe not quite often enough), find media materials with the leanest of hints from teachers and students, toss balls in one direction and *bench* students in another, and provide one-on-one practice for the most unique of tasks and talents. And these support personnel have their own special view of students, schools, and teachers. Fostering relationships with these colleagues is a way to create a valuable extension of your classroom community.

Activity: Try to schedule a 20-minute interview with one of the nonteaching employees at a local school. Here are some questions to ask, but feel free to add your own to the list.

- Describe your job duties.
- What do you like best about your job?
- What is the most challenging aspect of your job?
- How do students, teachers, and administrators impact your job?
- What is one thing about your job that you would like students to know about?
- What is one thing about your job that you would like teachers to know about?
- What is one thing about your job that you would like administrators to know about?
- Recount your best day on the job.

Artifact: Write a brief description entitled "A Day in the Life of _____." How do teachers support the support personnel, and more specifically, what can you do to create a positive relationship with school support personnel?

FORM:

Support Staff Interview

Reflection: What did you learn from this experience? How might this interview affect your rapport and behavior with support staff? Attach your reflection to your artifact and store in your portfolio.

III

PART

Foundations

CLASS ACT

A chilly morning in early September 1952. My parents walked me down the dirt road to the state highway, where the No. 3 school bus passed by our farm. I boarded the faded yellow bus with no idea where I was going. Half an hour later, I was deposited in front of an old brick building: Dardanelle Elementary School.

I walked into a school that had been constructed in 1869, and had once housed both elementary and secondary students. Now grades one through six filled the school. Greeting me at the schoolhouse door, the principal escorted me to my first grade class. Stepping inside the classroom, it seemed as if I had entered the nineteenth century. The two-seat student desks were bolted to the floor, facing the teacher's desk that rested upon a wooden platform. A cracked chalkboard stood behind the teacher's desk. My assigned seat was next to a "town girl" on the first row.

After printing her name on the chalkboard, Mrs. "T" began the year-long process of teaching academic skills to students who had had no preparation for the first grade. We had no preschool, no kindergarten, and no educational television in those days. It was Mrs. T's job to fill our minds with basic academic knowledge. For seven hours each day, she lectured, recited, dictated, directed, questioned, and criticized. If we broke any of her many rules, we could expect a tongue-lashing or a public spanking, for physical punishment was not unusual back then.

Though she was a harsh taskmaster, Mrs. T proved an effective teacher. Using textbooks from the 1930s, she taught us how to read, write, and cipher. Our favorite class was spelling, because the textbooks were new, and it was also our last class of the day. At three o'clock every afternoon, the dismissal bell freed us. Mrs. T, who had been a member of the Woman's Army Corps during World War II, was a warrior on the educational front lines in 1952. This massive wave of children, which we now call the "baby boom," would strain the resources of America's educational system. It was left to the well-educated but ill-paid American teachers to cope with this flood of students. Mrs. T created a nineteenth-century style classroom climate to allow her to cope with thirty illiterate, rambunctious children, who came from the county seat, outlying hamlets, and scattered rural farms. She narrowed the curriculum to four essential subjects—reading, writing, spelling, and mathematics. Teaching the essential subject in time-honored fashion, she tolerated no "misbehavior" and ruled her classroom with an iron hand.

In retrospect, I admire Mrs. T's accomplishments during the 1952–1953 school year. In one year, she taught us the basic academic skills we needed for success in the upper grades. Most of her students not only completed high school, but they also finished college. Several even managed to earn post-graduate degrees. However, her harsh classroom climate left its mark. Today, when I walk into a classroom, I feel the old fear that I experienced in her class fifty years ago. Mrs. T taught me about the lifelong influence that a powerful first grade teacher can have. And she taught me something about myself as well: my personal commitment to create a classroom without fear.

John Solomon Otto
American University

Read more *Class Acts* at Sadker.com.

www.mhhe.com/
sadker7e

CHAPTER 8

The History of American Education

FOCUS QUESTIONS

1. What was the nature and purpose of colonial education?
2. How did the Common School Movement influence the idea of universal education?
3. How did teaching become a "gendered" career?
4. How did secondary schools evolve?
5. How have twentieth century reform efforts influenced schools?
6. What were the main tenets of the Progressive Education movement?
7. What role has the federal government played in American education?
8. Who are some of the key individuals who have helped fashion today's schools?

 WHAT DO YOU THINK? How Much Do You Already Know about the History of Education? Before reading the chapter, take a quiz that includes some "basics" and fun facts.

CHAPTER PREVIEW

Understanding the history of America's schools offers you perspective—a sense of your place in your new profession. Your classroom is a living tribute to past achievements and sacrifices.

In this chapter, we will trace American education from colonial times to the present. Education during the colonial period was intended to further religious goals and was offered primarily to white males—typically, wealthy white males. Over time, educational exclusivity diminished, but, even today, wealth, race, and gender continue to impact educational quality. To a great extent, the story of American education is a battle to open the schoolhouse door to more and more of our citizens. In this chapter, we share the story of the struggle to have America honor its commitment to equality.

The complex network of expectations surrounding today's schools is the product of a society that has been evolving for over three centuries. Individuals, groups, and the government all have contributed to making public schools more accessible. Benjamin Franklin, Horace Mann, Emma Hart Willard, and Mary McLeod Bethune, for example, fought to free America from historical biases. New federal laws were designed to create more equitable and effective educational opportunities. Today, the federal focus is to increase school competition, identify failing schools, and either "fix" them or replace them. But the notion of competition and standards is only the most recent chapter in the story of our nation's schools. In the colonial era, the goals were simpler: to teach the Scriptures and to develop a religious community. We will begin by looking into the classroom of Christopher Lamb, a New England teacher in one of the earliest American schools, over three centuries ago.

Christopher Lamb's Colonial Classroom

The frigid wintry wind knifed through Christopher Lamb's coat, chilling him to the bone as he walked in the predawn darkness. The single bucket of firewood that he lugged, intended to keep his seventeenth-century New England schoolroom warm all day, would clearly not do the job. Once the fire was started, Christopher focused on his other teaching tasks: carrying in a bucket of water for the class, sweeping the floor, and mending the ever so fragile pen points for the students. More than an hour after Christopher's predawn activities had begun, Margaret, the first student, arrived. Although Margaret, like most girls, would stay in school for only a year or two, Christopher believed that she should learn to read the Bible, so that she could be a better wife and mother. With any luck, she might even learn to write her name before she left school. But that was really not all that important for girls. As other students trickled in, they were directed to either the boys' bench or the girls' bench, where, in turn, they read their Testament aloud.

Those who read the Scriptures without error took their place at the table and wrote on their slates. Christopher was amazed at how poorly some students read, tripping over every other word, whereas others read quite fluently. The last student to finish, Benjamin, slowly rose from the bench, cringing. Christopher called out, "Lazy pupil," and a chorus of children's voices chimed in: "Lazy pupil. Lazy pupil. Lazy pupil." Benjamin, if not totally inured to the taunts, was no longer crushed by them, either. He slowly made his way to the end of the student line.

After the recitation and writing lessons, all the children were lined up and examined, to make certain they had washed and combed. A psalm was sung, and Mr. Lamb exhorted the students to walk in God's footsteps. For ten minutes, the class and teacher knelt in prayer. Each student then recited the day's biblical lesson. Those who had memorized their lessons received an *O*, written on their hand, a mark of excellence. Those who failed to recite their lessons correctly after three attempts once again were called "lazy pupil" by the entire class, and this time their names were written down. If by the end of the day they had finally learned the lesson, their names were erased from the list, and all the children called out "Diligent!" to those students.

Christopher Lamb had been an apprentice teacher for five years before accepting this position. He rejected the rod approach used so frequently by his master teacher. Using the children to provide rewards and punishments was far more effective than welts and bruises, marks left by a teacher's rod. Yes, Christopher was somewhat unorthodox, perhaps even a bit revolutionary, but the challenges of contemporary seventeenth-century society demanded forward-thinking educators, such as Christopher Lamb.

 # Colonial New England Education: God's Classrooms

One of the striking differences between Christopher Lamb's colonial classroom and today's typical public school is the role of religion in education. The religious fervor that drove the Puritans to America also drove them to provide religious education for their young, making New England the cradle of American education. In Christopher Lamb's time, school was meant to save souls. Education provided a path to heaven, and reading, writing, and moral development all revolved around the Bible.

CHAPTER FOCUS
Understanding the history of America's schools offers students perspective—a sense of their place in education. In a very real way, today's classrooms are living tributes to past achievements and sacrifices. This chapter traces American education from colonial times to the present and the ongoing struggle to open the schoolhouse door to more and more of our citizens. For a chapter outline, see the IM.

GRABBER: PRIMING YOUR CLASS
IM

FOCUS QUESTION 1
What was the nature and purpose of colonial education?

CLASS ACTIVITIES
GROUP REPORTS
IM, Activity 8:1
MEDIA PRESENTATION
IM, Activity 8:2

OVERHEADS 92–95
The Development of America's Schools

Educational Milestones

Recitation lesson in a colonial classroom.

Early colonial education, both in New England and in other colonies, often began in the home. (Today's home schooling movement is not a *new* approach.) The family was the major educational resource for youngsters, and the first lessons typically focused on reading. Values, manners, social graces, and even vocational skills were taught by parents and grandparents. Home instruction eventually became more specialized, and some women began to devote their time to teaching, converting their homes into schools. These "dames" taught reading, writing, and computation, and their homes became known as **dame schools.** A "dame," or well-respected woman with an interest in education, became (for a fee) the community's teacher.

An **apprenticeship** program rounded out a child's colonial education. While boys, sometimes as young as 7 years of age, were sent to live with masters who taught them a trade, girls typically learned homemaking skills from their mothers. Apprenticeship programs for boys involved not only learning skilled crafts but also managing farms and shops. Many colonies required that masters teach reading and writing as well as vocational skills. The masters served **in loco parentis**—that is, in place of the child's parent. The competencies of the masters guiding apprentices varied greatly, as did the talents of family members, dames, ministers, and others fulfilling the teaching role. Not surprisingly, this educational hodgepodge did not always lead to a well-educated citizenry; a more formal structure was needed.

Twenty-two years after arriving in the New World, the Puritans living in the Commonwealth of Massachusetts passed a law requiring that parents and masters of apprentices be checked periodically to ensure that children were being taught properly. Five years later, in 1647, Massachusetts took even more rigorous measures to ensure the education of its children. The Massachusetts Law of 1647, more commonly known as the **Old Deluder Satan Law**—the Puritans' attempt to thwart Satan's trickery with Scripture-reading citizens—required that

- Every town of 50 households must appoint and pay a teacher of reading and writing.
- Every town of 100 households must provide a (Latin) grammar school to prepare youths for the university, under a penalty of £5 for failure to do so.[1]

By 1680, such laws had spread throughout most of New England. The settlement patterns of the Puritans, who lived in towns and communities rather than scattered throughout the countryside, made establishing schools relatively uncomplicated. After learning to read and write, most girls returned home to practice the art of housekeeping. Boys who could afford to pay for their education went on to a **Latin grammar school.** In 1635, only fifteen years after arriving in America's wilderness, the Puritans

TEACHING TIP

Throughout this chapter, students will see many new key terms in bold. Can they envision a study strategy, in "keeping with the times," that would help them learn these new words? For example, in the colonial classroom they would recite and spell new terms repeatedly—with some fear of the teacher's rod for an error.

established their first Latin grammar school in Boston. The Boston Latin Grammar School was not unlike a "prep" school for boys and was similar to the classical schools of Europe. The Boston Latin Grammar School was a rather exclusive school for boys of wealth, charging tuition to teach boys between the ages of 7 and 14.

Many consider the Boston Latin Grammar School to be the first step on the road to creating the American high school, although the school's curriculum reflected European roots. Students were expected to read and recite (in Latin, of course) the works of Cicero, Ovid, and Erasmus. In Greek, they read the works of Socrates and Homer. (Back to basics in colonial times meant back to the glory of Rome and Greece.) By the eighteenth century, the grammar school had incorporated mathematics, science, and modern languages. Classes started at 7 A.M., recessed at 11 A.M., and picked up from 1 P.M. until 5 P.M. Graduates were expected to go on to college and become colonial leaders, especially ministers.

Within a year of the founding of the Boston Latin Grammar School, Harvard College was established specifically to prepare ministers. Founded in 1636, Harvard was the first college in America, the jewel in the Puritans' religious and educational crown.[2]

For attendance at exclusive schools, such as Boston Latin Grammar, or at college, wealth was critical. The least desirable educational and apprenticeship opportunities were left to the poor. Some civic-minded communities made basic education in reading and writing more available to the poor, but only to families who would publicly admit their poverty by signing a "Pauper's Oath." Broadcasting one's poverty was no less offensive in colonial times than today, and many chose to have their children remain illiterate rather than sign such a public admission. The result was that most poor children remained outside the educational system.

Blacks, in America since 1619, and Native Americans were typically denied educational opportunities. In rare cases, religious groups, such as the Quakers, created special schools for children of color.[3] But these were the exceptions. Through racism and slavery, whites denied formal schooling to most Native Americans and blacks; they also eventually passed laws prohibiting their education. (See Chapter 12, "The Struggle for Educational Opportunity," for a more complete review of these issues.) Girls did not fare much better. After they had learned the rudiments of reading and writing, girls were taught the tasks related to their future roles as mother and wife. They were taught various handicrafts. Girls memorized the alphabet and then learned to stitch and display their accomplishments. They also learned to reproduce and attractively display religious sayings, on the road to becoming good Christian wives and mothers. As much as we value these beautiful samplers today, they are a sad reminder of a time when they marked the academic finish line for girls, the diploma of a second-rate education, a depressing denial of equal educational rights.

Location greatly influenced educational opportunities. The northern colonies were settled by Puritans who lived in towns and communities relatively close to one another. Their religious fervor and proximity made the creation of community schools dedicated to teaching the Bible a predictable development.

In the middle colonies, the range of European religious and ethnic groups (Puritans, Catholics, Mennonites, the Dutch, and Swedes) created, if not a melting pot, a limited tolerance for diversity.[4] Various religious groups established schools, and apprenticeships groomed youngsters for a variety of careers, including teaching. In the middle colonies, the development of commerce and mercantile demands promoted the formation of private schools devoted to job training. By the 1700s, private teachers and night schools were functioning in Philadelphia and New York, teaching accounting, navigation, French, and Spanish.

CRITICAL THINKING QUESTION

Is a public admission of poverty still evident in today's programs, such as free and reduced lunch? In what ways can parents request financial assistance? Or, are families protected from signing a modern-day "Pauper's Oath"?

The first city in North America was St. Augustine, Florida, where there is evidence that the Spanish settlers established schools. In terms of education, the southern English colonies trailed behind. The rural, sparsely populated southern colonies developed an educational system that was responsive to plantation society. Wealthy plantation owners took tutors into their homes to teach their children not only basic academic skills but also the social graces appropriate to their station in life. Plantation owners' children learned the proper way to entertain guests and "manage" slaves, using such texts as *The Complete Gentleman*. Wealthy young men seeking higher education were sent to Europe. Girls made do with just an introduction to academics and a greater focus on their social responsibilities. Poor white children might have had rudimentary home instruction in reading, writing, and computation. Black children made do with little if any instruction and, as time went by, encountered laws that actually prohibited their education entirely.[5]

Education has come a long way from colonial days and from Christopher Lamb's class—or has it? Consider the following:

1. The colonial experience established many of today's educational norms:
    -   Local control of schools
    -   Compulsory education
    -   Tax-supported schools
    -   State standards for teaching and schools

2. The colonial experience highlighted many of the persistent tension points challenging schools today:
    -   What is the role of religion in the classroom?
    -   How can we equalize the quality of education in various communities?
    -   How can the barriers of racism, sexism, religious intolerance, and classism be eliminated, so that all children receive equal educational opportunity?
    -   How can we prepare the most competent teachers?

TEACHING TIP
Has education come a long way? Give students a chance to *write-pair-share* their thoughts on this question by a) individually making some notes, b) conversing with a partner, and c) speaking to the full class.

Old school buildings remind us of how much schools have changed—and how much they have not.

The Development of Colonial Higher Education

Many of today's colleges and universities began as small, religiously sponsored institutions founded to train the clergy. The first fifteen institutions of higher education established in the colonies were all affiliated with a religious denomination.

Year	Institution	Year	Institution
1636	Harvard University	1769	Dartmouth University
1693	College of William and Mary	1782	Washington College
1701	Yale University	1782	Washington and Lee University
1746	Princeton University	1783	Hampton-Sidney College
1754	King's College (Columbia University)	1783	Transylvania College
1755	University of Pennsylvania	1783	Dickinson College
1764	Brown University	1784	St. John's College
1766	Queen's College (Rutgers University)		

REFLECTION: What religious artifacts, if any, exist on these campuses today? Do you know when your campus was founded? Did that period influence the culture of your college?

A New Nation Shapes Education

The ideas that led to the American Revolution revolutionized our schools. European beliefs and practices, which had pervaded America's schools, were gradually abandoned as the new national character was formed. None of these beliefs had been more firmly adhered to than the integration of the state and religion.

In sixteenth- and seventeenth-century England, the Puritans' desire to reform the Church of England was viewed as treason. The Puritans encountered both religious and political opposition, and they looked to the New World as an escape from persecution. However, they came to America *not* to establish religious freedom, as our history books sometimes suggest, but to establish their own church as supreme, both religiously and politically. The Puritans were neither tolerant of other religions nor interested in separating religion and politics. Nonconformers, such as the Quakers, were vigorously persecuted. The purpose of the Massachusetts colony was to establish the "true" religion of the Puritans, to create a "new Israel" in America. Schools were simply an extension of the religious state, designed to teach the young to read and understand the Bible and to do honorable battle with Satan.

During the 1700s, American education was reconstructed to meet broader, nonsectarian goals. Such leaders as **Thomas Jefferson** wanted to go beyond educating a small elite class or providing only religious instruction. Jefferson maintained that education should be more widely available to white children from all economic and social classes. Public citizens began to question the usefulness of rudimentary skills taught in a school year of just three or four months. They questioned the value of mastering Greek and Latin classics in the Latin grammar schools, when practical skills were in short supply in the New World.

In addition to serving two terms as president, Thomas Jefferson was the colonial era's most eloquent spokesperson for education and was the founder of the University of Virginia.

In 1749, **Benjamin Franklin** penned *Proposals Relating to the Youth of Pennsylvania,* suggesting a new kind of secondary school to replace the Latin grammar school—the **academy.** Two years later, the **Franklin Academy** was established, free of religious influence and offering a variety of practical subjects, including mathematics, astronomy, athletics, navigation, dramatics, and bookkeeping. Students were able to choose some of their courses, thus setting the precedent for elective courses and programs at the secondary level. In the late 1700s, it was the Franklin Academy and not the Boston Latin Grammar School that was considered the most important secondary school in America.[6]

The Franklin Academy accepted both girls and boys who could afford the tuition, and the practical curriculum became an attractive innovation. Franklin's Academy sparked the establishment of six thousand academies in the century that followed, including Phillips Academy at Andover, Massachusetts (1778), and Phillips Exeter Academy in Exeter, New Hampshire (1783). The original Franklin Academy eventually became the University of Pennsylvania.

Jefferson's commitment to educating all white Americans, rich and poor, at government expense, and Franklin's commitment to a practical program of nonsectarian study offering elective courses severed American educational thought from its European roots. Many years passed before these ideas became widely established practices, but the pattern for innovation and a truly American approach to education was taking shape.

The Common School Movement

FOCUS QUESTION 2
How did the Common School Movement influence the idea of universal education?

During the early decades of the nineteenth century, education was often viewed as a luxury. However, even parents who could afford such a luxury had limited choices. The town schools still existed in Massachusetts, and some charity schools served the poor and orphans. Dame schools varied in quality. In some areas, religious schools of one denomination prevailed, while, in rural areas and the South, few schools existed at all. The United States was a patchwork quilt of schools, tied together by the reality that money was needed to attain a decent education.

During the early decades of the nineteenth century, the democratic ideal became popular as many "common people"—immigrants, small farmers, and urban laborers—demanded greater participation in the democracy. With the election of Andrew Jackson in 1828, the voices of many poor white people were heard, particularly their demands for educational access. Many more decades would pass before additional voices—particularly those of people of color—would also be heard.

VIDEO SEGMENT 20
The Common School and the Teaching Profession

Horace Mann became the nation's leading advocate for the establishment of a **common school** open to all. Today we know this common school as the public **elementary school.** Historians consider Horace Mann to be the outstanding proponent of education for the common person (the common school movement), and he is often referred to as "the father of the public school." (More about Mann appears in The Education Hall of Fame, later in this chapter.) Mann helped create the Massachusetts State Board of Education and in 1837 became its secretary, a position similar to today's state superintendent of schools. In this role, Mann began an effort to reform education, believing that public education should serve both practical and idealistic goals. In practical terms, both business and industry would benefit from educated workers, resulting in a more productive economy. In idealistic terms, public schools should help us identify and nurture the talents in poor as well as wealthy

A rich variety of textbooks, media, library books, and computer software provide today's teachers with curricular resources unimaginable just a few years ago. As a teacher, you will come across references to some of the limited but influential curriculum materials of the past. Here is a brief profile of the best-known instructional materials from yesterday's schools.

HORNBOOK

The most common teaching device in colonial schools, the **hornbook** consisted of an alphabet sheet covered by a thin, transparent sheet made from a cow's horn. The alphabet and the horn covering were tacked to a paddle-shaped piece of wood and often hung by a leather strap around the student's neck. Originating in medieval Europe, the hornbook provided colonial children with their introduction to the alphabet and reading.

NEW ENGLAND PRIMER

The first real textbook, the **New England Primer** was a tiny 2½- by 4½-inch book containing 50 to 100 pages of alphabet, words, and small verses accompanied by woodcut illustrations. First published in 1690, it was virtually the only reading text used in colonial schools until about 1800. The *Primer* reflected the religious orientation of colonial schools. A typical verse was

In Adam's Fall
We sinned all.
Thy Life to mend,
This Book attend
The idle fool
Is whipt at School.

AMERICAN SPELLING BOOK

The task undertaken by Noah Webster was to define and nourish the new American culture. His **American Spelling Book** replaced the *New England Primer* as the most common elementary textbook. The book contained the alphabet, syllables, consonants, rules for speaking, readings, short stories, and moral advice. The bulk of the book was taken up by lists of words. Royalty income from the sale of millions of copies of this book supported Webster in his other efforts to standardize the American language, including his best-known work, which is still used today, the *American Dictionary*.

MCGUFFEY READERS

William Holmes McGuffey was a minister, professor, and college president who believed that clean living, hard work, and literacy were the virtues to instill in children. He wrote a series of readers that emphasized the work ethic, patriotism, heroism, and morality. It is estimated that more than 100 million copies of *McGuffey Readers* educated several generations of Americans between 1836 and 1920. **McGuffey Readers** are noteworthy because they were geared for different grade levels and paved the way for graded elementary schools.

> **REFLECTION:** Can you detect the morals and traditional values being promoted in today's texts? Can you cite any examples?

children, and schools should ameliorate social disharmony.[7] Mann decried the rifts between rich and poor, Calvinists and religious reformers, new Irish immigrants and native workers. A common school instilling common and humane moral values could reduce such social disharmony (a popular belief today as well). Mann attempted to promote such values, but he encountered strong opposition when the values he selected revealed a distinct religious bias, one that offended Calvinists, atheists, Jews, Catholics, and others. His moral program to create a common set of beliefs had the opposite impact, igniting a dispute over the role of religion in school.

The idea of public education is so commonplace today that it seems difficult to imagine another system. But Horace Mann, along with such allies as Henry Barnard of Connecticut, fought a long and difficult battle to win the acceptance of public elementary schools. The opposition was powerful. Business interests predicted disaster if their labor pool of children were taken away. Concerned taxpayers protested the additional tax monies needed to support public education. There was also the competition. Private schools and religious groups sponsoring their own schools protested the establishment of free schools. Americans wondered what would become of a nation

GLOBAL VIEW
The United States has signed (but not yet ratified) the *Convention on the Rights of the Child,* which does include free compulsory primary education and equal treatment regardless of gender, race or cultural background. www.unicef.org/crc/convention.htm.

Contributing to the school reforms of the nineteenth century were the poor physical conditions that characterized most U.S. schools.

in which everyone received an elementary education. Would this not produce over-educated citizens, questioning authority and promoting self-interest? The opposition to public elementary schools was often fierce, but Horace Mann and his allies prevailed.

As he fought for public schools for all, Mann also waged a battle for high-quality schools. He continually attempted to build new and better schools, which was a problem, since so many Massachusetts schools were in deplorable condition. By publicly disseminating information about which communities had well-built or poorly built schools, he applied public pressure on districts to improve their school buildings. He worked for effective teacher training programs as well and promoted more stringent teacher licensing procedures. As a result of his efforts, several **normal schools** were founded in Massachusetts, schools devoted to preparing teachers in pedagogy, the best ways to teach children. He also championed newer teaching methods designed to improve and modernize classroom instruction. He opposed the routine practice of corporal punishment and sought ways to positively motivate students to learn. Mann emphasized practical subjects useful to children and to adult society, rather than the mastery of Greek and Latin. Mann saw education as a great investment, for individuals and for the country, and he worked for many years to make free public education a reality. He worked for the abolition of slavery, promoted women's educational and economic rights, and even fought alongside the temperance movement to limit the negative impact of alcohol. He was not only a committed educator but a committed reformer as well.

By the time of the Civil War, this radical notion of the public elementary school had become widespread and widely accepted. Educational historian Lawrence Cremin summarized the advance of the common school movement in his book *The Transformation of the School:*

> A majority of the states had established public school systems, and a good half of the nation's children were already getting some formal education. Elementary schools were becoming widely available; in some states, like Massachusetts, New York, and Pennsylvania, the notion of free public education was slowly expanding to include secondary schools; and in a few, like Michigan and Wisconsin, the public school system was already capped by

The Development of American Schools

ELEMENTARY SCHOOLS

Dame schools (1600s) These private schools taught by women in their homes offered child care for working parents willing to pay a fee. The dames who taught here received meager wages, and the quality of instruction varied greatly.

Local schools (1600s–1800s) First started in towns and later expanded to include larger districts, these schools were open to those who could afford to pay. Found generally in New England, these schools taught basic skills and religion.

Itinerant schools (1700s) and tutors (1600s–1900s) Rural America could not support schools and full-time teachers. As a result, in sparsely populated New England, itinerant teachers carried schooling from village to village; they lived in people's homes and provided instruction. In the South, private tutors taught the rich. Traveling teachers and tutors, usually working for a fee and room and board, took varying levels of education to small towns and wealthy populations.

Private schools (1700s–1800s) Private schools, often located in the middle colonies, offered a variety of special studies. These schools constituted a true free market, as parents paid for the kind of private school they desired. As you might imagine, both the curricula and the quality of these schools varied greatly.

Common schools (1830–present) The common school was a radical departure from earlier ones in several ways. First, it was free. Parents did not have to pay tuition or fees. Second, it was open to all social classes. Previously, schools usually taught either middle-class or upper-class children. Horace Mann's common school was intended to bring democracy to the classroom. By the mid-nineteenth century, kindergarten was added. In the past few decades, many common schools, now called *elementary schools,* have added Head Start and other prekindergarten programs.

SECONDARY SCHOOLS

Latin grammar schools (1600s–1700s) These schools prepared wealthy men for college and emphasized a classical curriculum, including Latin and some Greek. From European roots, the curriculum in these schools reflected the belief that the pinnacle of civilization was reached in the Roman Empire.

English grammar schools (1700s) These private schools moved away from the classical Latin tradition to more practical studies. These schools were viewed not as preparation for college but as preparation for business careers and as a means of instilling social graces. Some of these schools set a precedent by admitting white girls, thus paving the way for the widespread acceptance of females in other schools.

Academies (1700s–1800s) The academies were a combination of the Latin and English grammar schools. These schools taught English, not Latin. Practical courses were taught, but history and the classics were also included. Some academies emphasized college preparation, while others prepared students to enter business and vocations.

High schools (1800s–present) These secondary schools differed from their predecessors in that they were free; they were governed not by private boards but by the public. The high school can be viewed as an extension of the common school movement to the secondary level. High schools were open to all social classes and provided both precollege and career education.

Junior high schools (1909–present) and middle schools (1950s–present) Junior high schools (grades 7–9) and middle schools (grades 5–8) were designed to meet the unique needs of preadolescents and to prepare them for the high school experience.

REFLECTION: If you were responsible for creating a new school based on contemporary needs, what kind of school would you create?

membership, (3) command of fundamental academic skills, (4) vocation, (5) citizenship, (6) worthy use of leisure time, and (7) ethical character. The high school was seen as a socializing agency to improve all aspects of a citizen's life.

Since the publication of the *Cardinal Principles* in 1918, not a decade has passed without a committee or commission reporting on reforms needed to improve U.S. schools. During the 1930s, the Progressive Education Association (PEA) provided suggestions to promote social adjustment as well as individual growth. Similar findings reported in the 1940s and 1950s noticeably influenced the evolution of our high schools. More electives were added to the high school curriculum. Guidance counselors were added to the staff. Vocational programs were expanded. The result was the formation of a new, comprehensive institution.

In time, the United States has come full circle, echoing the original call for intellectual rigor first voiced by the Committee of Ten in 1893. In 1983, the federal government's National Commission on Educational Excellence issued ***A Nation at Risk: The Imperative for Educational Reform,*** maintaining that mediocrity, not excellence, characterized U.S. schools. The commission declared that the inadequate rigor of U.S. education had put the nation at risk, losing ground to other nations in commerce, industry, science, and technology. The commission called for fewer electives and a greater emphasis on academic subjects.

**CRITICAL THINKING
QUESTION**

Are recent educational reform reports, shaped by public relations firms, market researchers and media spinners, still an indication of our "faith in education"?

Reports on the status of education and recommendations for school reform have become a U.S. tradition. These reports have underscored a built-in dichotomy in public education, a conflict between intellectual excellence and basic education for the masses, between college preparation and vocational training, between student-centered education and subject specialization. Some of the reports have called for more focus on the student, on programs to enhance the student's entrance into society and the workplace. Others have cited the need for more emphasis on academic and intellectual concerns, as well as for programs to enhance the student's preparation for college. This dichotomy has been and continues to be an integral feature of American education. Regardless of the particular reforms advocated, all the reports, from the 1890s to the present, have had a common theme: a faith in education. The reports have differed on solutions but have concurred on the central role of the school in maintaining a vibrant democracy.

 # John Dewey and Progressive Education

FOCUS QUESTION 6

What were the main tenets of the Progressive Education movement?

John Dewey was possibly the most influential educator of the twentieth century—and probably the most controversial one. Some saw him as a savior of U.S. schools; others accused him of nearly destroying them. Rather than become engrossed in the heated controversy surrounding Dewey, however, let us look at *progressivism,* the movement with which he is closely associated, and later in this text, explore the philosophy behind progressivism.

As early as 1875, Francis Parker, superintendent of schools in Quincy, Massachusetts, introduced the concepts of progressivism in his schools and by 1896, John Dewey had established his famous **laboratory school** at the University of Chicago. But it was not until the 1920s and 1930s that the progressive education movement became more widely known. During the 1920s and 1930s, the Dalton and Walden schools in New York, the Beaver Country Day School in Massachusetts, the Oak Lane Country Day School in Pennsylvania, and laboratory schools at Columbia and Ohio State universities began to challenge traditional practices. The progressive education approach soon spread to suburban and city public school systems across the country. Various school systems adapted or modified progressive education, but certain basic features remained constant, and elements of progressive education can still be found in many schools.

Progressive education included several components. First, it broadened the school program to include health concerns, family and community life issues, and a concern for vocational education. Second, progressivism applied new research in psychology and the social sciences to classroom practices. Third, progressivism emphasized a more democratic educational approach, accepting the interests and needs of an increasingly diverse student body.

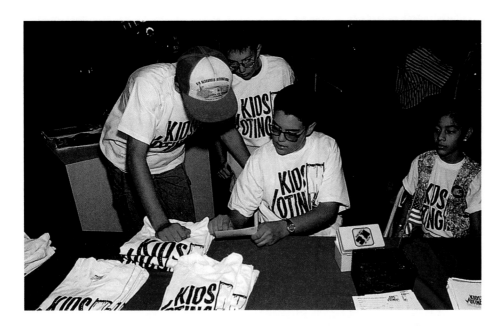

Progressive educators, such as John Dewey, believed that participation in democratic decision making developed rational problem-solving abilities and social skills.

This model of education assumed that students learn best when their learning follows their interests. Passively listening to the teacher, according to the progressive movement, is not the most effective learning strategy. The role of the teacher is to identify student needs and interests and provide an educational environment that builds on them. In fact, progressive education shares some characteristics with problem-based and authentic learning, popular innovations in some of today's schools.

Although not involved in all the progressive education programs, John Dewey, in many minds, is the personification of progressive education, as well as its most notable advocate. (See "The Education Hall of Fame" later in this chapter for a description of Dewey and his achievements.) In no small part, this is due to the tens of thousands of pages that Dewey wrote during his long life. (Dewey was born on the eve of the Civil War in 1859 and died during the Korean War in the early 1950s.) Toward the end of Dewey's life, both he and progressive education came under strong attack.

The criticism of Dewey and progressive education originated with far-right political groups, for it was the era of Senator Joseph McCarthy and his extremist campaign against communism. While McCarthy's hunt for communists was primarily directed at the government and the military, educators were not immune. Some viewed progressive education as an atheistic, un-American force that had all but destroyed the nation's schools. Because students were allowed to explore and question, many critics were able to cite examples of how traditional values were not being taught. Although these critics were generally ignorant of Dewey's ideas and progressive practices, a second group was more responsible in its critique.

This second wave of criticism came not from the radical right but from individuals who felt that the school curriculum was not academically sound. Hyman Rickover, a famous admiral and developer of the nuclear submarine, and Arthur Bestor, a liberal arts professor, were among the foremost critics decrying the ills of progressive education. They called for an end to "student-centered" and "life-adjustment" subjects and a return to a more rigorous study of traditional courses. While the arguments raged, the launching of *Sputnik* by the Soviet Union in 1957 put at least a temporary closure on the debate. The United States was involved in a space race with the Soviets, a race

TEACHING TIP

Introduce students to primary source commentary by educators who made history. "To *learn from experience* is to make a backward and forward connection between what we do to things and what we enjoy or suffer from things in consequence."
Have students interpret Dewey's comments (or those of other selected authentic voices) about *learning from experience* in their own words.

OVERHEAD 97
John Dewey Quotation

to educate scientists and engineers, a race toward the first moon landing. Those arguing for a more rigorous, science- and math-focused curriculum won the day. Although many still argued vociferously over the benefits and shortcomings of progressive education, traditionalists were setting the direction for the nation's curriculum.

Before leaving progressive education, however, it will be beneficial to examine one of the most famous studies of the progressive movement. The Progressive Education Association, formed in 1919, initiated a study during the 1930s that compared almost three thousand graduates of progressive and of traditional schools as they made their way through college. The study, called the **Eight-Year Study,** was intended to determine which educational approach was more effective. The results indicated that graduates of progressive schools:

1. Earned a slightly higher grade point average

2. Earned higher grades in all fields except foreign languages

3. Tended to specialize in the same fields as more traditional students

4. Received slightly more academic honors

5. Were judged to be more objective and more precise thinkers

6. Were judged to possess higher intellectual curiosity and greater drive

 The Federal Government

FOCUS QUESTION 7
What role has the federal government played in American education?

As World War II drew to a close, the United States found itself the most powerful nation on earth. For the remainder of the twentieth century, the United States reconstructed a war-ravaged global economy while confronting world communism. In fact, the United States viewed education as an important tool in accomplishing these strategic goals. When the Soviets launched *Sputnik,* for example, the government enlisted the nation's schools in meeting this new challenge. Consequently, Congress passed the **National Defense Education Act (NDEA)** in 1958 to enhance "the security of the nation" and to develop "the mental resources and technical skills of its young men and women." The NDEA supported the improvement of instruction and curriculum development, funded teacher training programs, and provided loans and scholarships for college students that allowed them to major in subjects deemed important to the national defense (such as teaching). However, looking back in history, it is not at all clear how the federal government was legally able to do this. After all, the framers of the Constitution made their intentions clear: Education was to be a state responsibility, and the federal government was not to be involved. How did the NDEA and other federal acts come to pass?

Many people are unaware that the responsibility for educating Americans is not even mentioned in the Constitution. Under the **Tenth Amendment,** any area not specifically stated in the Constitution as a federal responsibility is automatically assigned to the states. Why was education a nontopic? Some historians believe that, since the individual colonies had already established disparate educational systems, the framers of the Constitution did not want to create dissension by forcing the states to accept a single educational system. Other analysts believe that education was deliberately omitted from the Constitution because Americans feared control of the schools by a central government, any central government, as had been the case in Europe. They saw central control as a possible threat to their freedom. Still others

The Supreme Court decision in *Brown v. Board of Education of Topeka,* followed by the 1964 Civil Rights Act, made it possible for students of all races, cultures, and disabling conditions to receive a desegregated education.

suggest that the framers of the Constitution, in their haste, bartering, and bickering, simply forgot about education (what a depressing thought!). Whatever the reason, distinct colonial practices continued, as each state created its own educational structure—its own approach for preparing teachers and funding schools.

Over time, however, the federal government discovered ways to influence education. As early as the revolutionary period, the new nation passed the **Land Ordinance Act** of 1785 and the **Northwest Ordinance** of 1787. These acts required townships in the newly settled territories bounded by the Ohio and Mississippi Rivers and the Great Lakes to reserve a section of land for educational purposes. The ordinances contained a much-quoted sentence underscoring the new nation's faith in education: "Religion, morality, and knowledge being necessary to good government and the happiness of mankind, schools and the means of education shall forever be encouraged."

The federal government also exerted its influence through targeted funding, or **categorical grants.** By using federal dollars for specific programs, the government was able to create new colleges and universities, to promote agricultural and industrial research efforts, and to provide schools for Native Americans and other groups. During the Great Depression of the 1930s, the federal government became even more directly involved with education, constructing schools, providing free lunches for poor children, instituting part-time work programs for high school and college students, and offering educational programs to older Americans. With unemployment, hunger, and desperation rampant in the 1930s, states welcomed these federal efforts. More and more Americans were coming to realize that some educational challenges were beyond the resources of the states.

Court action also provided an avenue for federal involvement in schools, as in the landmark ***Brown v.***

RELATED READING

A Lesson Before Dying by Ernest J. Gaines (1993).

IN THE NEWS

KKK Wizard Honored

School board member Roberta W. is trying to change the name of Nathan Bedford Forrest middle school in Gadsden, Alabama. Named for the Confederate general who went on to become the first grand wizard of the Ku Klux Klan, Ms. Roberta W. feels the time to change the name is long overdue. Her request to explore a new name was defeated when no one seconded her motion.

SOURCE: *The American School Board Journal,* April 1998.

What's new in education? Click on *News Feeds.*

The following is a partial list of legislation indicating the long history of federal involvement in education.

1. *Land Ordinance Act* and *Northwest Ordinance* (1785 and 1787). These two ordinances provided for the establishment of public education in the territory between the Appalachian Mountains and the Mississippi River. In these new territories, 1 square mile out of every 36 was reserved for support of public education, and new states formed from these territories were encouraged to establish "schools and the means for education."

2. *Morrill Land Grant College Acts* (1862 and 1890). These acts established sixty-nine institutions of higher education in the various states, some of which are among today's great state universities. These acts were also called simply the *Land-Grant College Acts,* since public land was donated to establish these colleges.

3. *Smith–Hughes Act* (1917). This act provided funds for teacher training and program development in vocational education at the high school level.

4. *Servicemen's Readjustment Act* (G.I. Bill of Rights, 1944). This act paid veterans' tuition and living expenses for a specific number of months, depending on the length of their military service.

5. *National Defense Education Act* (1958). In response to the Soviet launching of *Sputnik,* the NDEA provided substantial funds for a variety of educational activities, including student loans, the education of school counselors, and the strengthening of instructional programs in science, mathematics, and foreign languages.

6. *Elementary and Secondary Education Act* (1965). This law provided financial assistance to school districts with low-income families, to improve libraries and instructional materials, and to promote educational innovations and research. In the 1970s, this legislation was expanded to include funding for bilingual and Native American education, drug education, and school lunch and breakfast programs.

7. *Project Head Start* (1964–1965). This act provides medical, social, nutritional, and educational services for low income children 3 to 6 years of age.

8. *Bilingual Education Act* (1968). In response to the needs of the significant number of non-English-speaking students, Congress authorized funds to provide relevant instruction to these students. The primary focus was to assist non-English speakers, particularly Spanish-speaking students, almost 70 percent of whom were failing to graduate from high school. Although many other languages besides Spanish are included in this act, a relatively limited percentage of non-English-speaking students participate in these programs, due to funding shortfalls.

9. *Title IX of the Education Amendments* (1972). This regulation prohibits discrimination on the basis of sex. The regulation is comprehensive and protects the rights of both males and females from preschool through graduate school, in sports, financial aid, employment, counseling, school regulations and policies, admissions, and other areas. Title IX enforcement has been lax and many schools violate one or more parts of the regulation.

10. *Individuals with Disabilities Education Act* (1975, 1991). This act provides financial assistance to local school districts to provide free and appropriate education for the nation's 8 million children with disabilities who are between 3 and 21 years of age.

11. *No Child Left Behind Act* (2001). This act revises the Elementary and Secondary Education Act (ESEA, 1965) and calls for state standards and annual testing of math and reading in grades 3–8. Schools that test poorly may receive additional funds for improvement, but also face the possibility of being closed. Parents are given greater freedom to select schools, with increased federal support for charter schools. The act also attempts to improve teacher quality, assist students with limited English skills, and encourage tutoring and supplemental educational services, even when carried out by private and religious organizations.

REFLECTION: Current federal initiatives promote standards and testing. How is this a departure from the general history of federal legislation?

OVERHEAD 98
Selected Federal Legislation

Board of Education of Topeka (1954). In this case, the U.S. Supreme Court ruled that separating children "from others of similar age and qualifications solely because of their race generates a feeling of inferiority as to their status in the community that may affect their hearts and minds in a way unlikely to ever be undone." By the 1970s, courts had ruled that discrimination based on gender or directed at students with disabilities was a violation of the U.S. Constitution.

As the twentieth century drew to a close, more conservative administrations reduced federal financial support of education, but not federal influence. Through presidential and congressional leadership, the U.S. government continues to help shape the nation's schools by promoting increased school standards and student testing.

The World We Created at Hamilton High: A Schoolography

In 1988, Gerald Grant published a fascinating book describing life at Hamilton High School (real school, fictitious name) from the 1950s to the 1980s. Like a biography that helps us understand the forces shaping and directing individual lives, *The World We Created at Hamilton High* may be thought of as a "schoolography," offering powerful insights into the forces that have shaped today's schools. The events at Hamilton probably mirror many of the developments in the life of the school you attended, or the one in which you will be teaching. The biography of Hamilton High offers a microcosm of the roots of and reasons behind the current demand for educational reform.[15]

RELATED READING
Growing up with Dick and Jane: Learning and Living the American Dream by Carole Kismaric with Marvin Heiferman (1996).

A Super School (If You're on the Right Side of the Tracks), 1953–1965

In 1953, Hamilton High opened its doors to students growing up in one of the new suburban developments, a prototype of those that were sprouting up all across postwar America. Carefully coifed girls in sweaters and skirts and neatly dressed boys with crewcuts and baggy khakis relished their new school, with its tennis courts, modern design, and strong academic offerings. The social life of the Northern, all-white, middle-class school was driven by fraternities and sororities that prohibited or limited the membership of Catholics and Jews. The principal, a former coach, did not provide instructional leadership but certainly did run a tight ship. The purpose of the school was college preparation, and an evaluation of Hamilton written in 1960 reported that a "strong, almost pathological resistance to taking noncollege preparation courses exists in this school community." While letters in the school paper debated whether school spirit was dwindling and what would happen if girls were allowed to wear miniskirts, the school board was approving a desegregation plan that would bring the "southern problem" to Hamilton and open a second, more volatile chapter of the school's history.

MULTIPLE INTELLIGENCE CONNECTION
The Hamilton High *schoolography* is historical fiction at its best. Invite students to select a significant educational era and develop a similar piece. Their final products could be in the form of a dramatic monologue, videotaped interview, journal entry, student newspaper, or TV news segment—each detailing historical events at a fictional school.

Social Unrest Comes to School, 1966–1971

Northern desegregation was as difficult as southern desegregation, with white teachers unprepared to teach black students and both black and white students encountering the reality of racism. SAT scores fell, racial incidents and conflicts rose, and white families began leaving the neighborhood. The proportion of African American students in the school system jumped from 15 to 33 percent. As racial confrontations grew, Hamilton was forced to close several times because of bomb threats and the cloud of threatened violence. Fear gripped the school, teachers became physically ill trying to survive the tension, and several principals, unable to control or eliminate

For over one hundred years, many classrooms have looked strikingly similar. What does each of these rooms say about the roles of teachers and students? How would you describe the aesthetic of these spaces? Design the classroom you would like to have when you begin teaching.

the problems, came and went during this period. By the fall of 1971, more than 70 percent of the teachers who had taught at Hamilton in 1966 had left the school.

The Students' Turn, 1972–1979

The old world of fraternities, sororities, and a social structure that was discriminatingly clear disintegrated in the race riots of the 1960s and split the faculty: some were sympathetic to the curricular change and goals of the student protests; others opposed such changes. The administration used uneven standards of discipline, with white children penalized less harshly than black children. There was a lack of trust between the old and the young, parents and the school, and even between the students and administration at all levels as protests over the Vietnam War and the draft grew more intense. As America's social fabric unraveled, the Supreme Court handed down influential decisions awarding greater liberties to students, including grievance procedures and due process rights. Many teachers and administrators were unclear about what constituted legal or illegal discipline. As a result, they found it legally smarter not to discipline students. An abyss was created, with power unclear and the rules in limbo.

From this maelstrom, student leaders (with some faculty supporters) emerged, and student demands began to reshape the world at Hamilton. While teachers and the administration tolerated student infractions of the rules (for fear of being drowned in litigation), students suffered no such inhibitions. They flexed their legal muscles by bringing suits against parents, guardians, and teachers. In class, students felt free to play their radios—that is, when they attended; most students reported that they regularly skipped classes. Drinking and gambling became a part of the school parking-lot landscape, and the students even published an underground newspaper that kept

SEVENTEENTH CENTURY

Informal family education, apprenticeships, dame schools, tutors

1635	Boston Latin Grammar School
1636	Harvard College
1647	Old Deluder Satan Law
1687–1890	*New England Primer* published

EIGHTEENTH CENTURY

Development of a national interest in education, state responsibility for education, growth in secondary education

1740	South Carolina denies education to blacks.
1751	Opening of the Franklin Academy in Philadelphia
1783	Noah Webster's *American Spelling Book*
1785, 1787	Land Ordinance Act, Northwest Ordinance

NINETEENTH CENTURY

Increasing role of public secondary schools, increased but segregated education for women and minorities, attention to the field of education and teacher preparation

1821	Emma Willard's Troy Female Seminary opens, first endowed secondary school for girls.
1821	First public high school opens in Boston.
1823	First (private) normal school opens in Vermont.
1827	Massachusetts requires public high schools.
1837	Horace Mann becomes secretary of board of education in Massachusetts.
1839	First public normal school in Lexington, Massachusetts
1855	First kindergarten (German language) in United States
1862	Morrill Land Grant College Act
1874	*Kalamazoo case* (legalizes taxes for high schools)
1896	*Plessy v. Ferguson* Supreme Court decision supporting racially separate but equal schools

TWENTIETH CENTURY

Increasing federal support for educational rights of under-achieving students; increased federal funding of specific (categorical) education programs

1909	First junior high school in Columbus, Ohio
1919	Progressive education programs
1932	New Deal education programs
1944	G.I. Bill of Rights
1950	First middle school in Bay City, Michigan
1954	*Brown v. Board of Education of Topeka* Supreme Court decision outlawing racial segregation in schools
1957	*Sputnik* leads to increased federal education funds.
1958	National Defense Education Act funds science, math, and foreign language programs.
1964–1965	Job Corps and Head Start are funded.
1972	Title IX prohibits sex discrimination in schools.
1975	Public Law 94-142, Education for All Handicapped Children Act (renamed Individuals with Disabilities Education Act, 1991), is passed.
1979	Cabinet-level Department of Education is established.
1990– present	Increased public school diversity and competition through charter schools, for profit companies, open enrollment and technological options. Promotion of educational goals, standards and testing.
2001	Passage of *No Child Left Behind* Act.

SOURCE: Compiled from Edward King, *Salient Dates in American Education, 1635–1964* (New York: Harper & Row, 1966); National Center for Education Statistics, U.S. Department of Education, *Digest of Education Statistics, 1994.*

REFLECTION: What milestones do you believe may occur in the years ahead?

them up-to-date on their legal rights, as well as strategies for cutting classes without being caught—not that the classes themselves were difficult or demanding. In fact, course requirements were reduced significantly. Electives were the choice of the day. Some students were revitalized by the new curriculum, but others took easy classes (called "gut" courses) and graduated from Hamilton without much to show for their high school years.

YOU BE THE JUDGE
SCHOOL MASCOTS

Should Change with the Times Because . . .

MASCOT NAMES CAN BE HURTFUL

A pep rally featuring chanting "Indians" shaking rubber tomahawks trivializes meaningful rituals and cultural differences. Names such as the "Lady Bucks" or "Tigerettes" perpetuate an image of female inferiority and the second-class status of their sports.

MASCOT NAMES PROMOTE VIOLENCE

Stands filled with "Pirates" wielding sabers and chanting insults bring us all closer to potential violence and injury. Mascots should build a positive climate, not a destructive one.

WE SHOULD SET AN EXAMPLE FOR STUDENTS

We must teach by example, and changing offensive mascot names gives us that opportunity. By adopting names like "Freedom" or "Liberty," we teach our children how names can model our historical best, not our historical bigotries, and how adults can learn from past mistakes.

Should Not Change over Time Because . . .

IT'S JUST A NAME

There are more important issues to address than changing names of athletic teams. Exaggerated complaints about mascot names consume hours of school board meetings, and only show how political correctness is driving the times.

MASCOT NAMES BUILD SCHOOL SPIRIT

Proud mascot names like the "Patriots" highlight courage and bravery. Mascot names instill school spirit, a trait sorely needed by today's young people.

TRADITION MATTERS

Some things really do need to stay the same. Building a positive and stable school community is hard enough with people constantly moving and families splitting. School mascot names provide stability, and do not mindlessly mirror every passing fad.

YOU BE THE JUDGE

You and your classmates may want to share your own experiences on this hot-button issue. Should any mascot names be changed? Which names and why (or why not)? Brainstorm positive team names and mascots. This may be more challenging than you think. To understand more about mascots and American Indians, visit www.racismagainstindians.org.

In 1978, a new principal came to the high school, a veteran educator considered tough enough to handle the problems. A uniform discipline code for blacks and whites was established, administrators were taught to back up teachers in their discipline efforts, and the avalanche of easy courses was replaced by a more demanding curriculum. Student suspensions soared. That year, thirty seniors who had cut too many classes were prohibited from participating in graduation. Ever so slowly, adult authority was re-established, and Hamilton's experiment in rule by students came to an end.

New Students, Old School, 1980–1985

Racial desegregation and student protests radically changed Hamilton during the 1970s; the enrollment of students with disabilities sparked the school's second transformation. Although a new federal law (PL 94-142) required that special education students be mainstreamed and taught in regular classes, the teachers were unprepared to respond to their needs, and a number of Hamilton's students were hostile to the new arrivals. Students with disabilities were mainstreamed—and taunted. Mentally retarded, emotionally disturbed, and physically disabled students both experienced and caused frustration when placed in regular classrooms.

During these years, immigrants from Southeast Asia were introduced to Hamilton through the English as a Second Language (ESL) program. Tension between the newly arrived Vietnamese and Cambodian students and African Americans at Hamilton led to fights. While Hamilton searched for peace and consensus with its new student populations, some students escaped from reality through drug use. By 1984, a third of Hamilton's students were experimenting with drugs, typically marijuana. However, an increase in adult authority had checked the escalation of black-white tensions and had increased academic demands. The decline in national test scores at Hamilton had stabilized, and "white flight" had ceased. The school was settling down, but Hamilton was not a particularly inspiring or dynamic institution. The academic star of the 1950s had become an academic has-been of the 1980s. Many people were disappointed in their school.

The disappointment at Hamilton High has been felt in other communities. In 1983, *A Nation at Risk* was published, and it initiated a national evaluation of schools. How effective is our educational system? Is it accomplishing its goals? (These and other questions were considered in Chapter 4, "Schools: Choices and Challenges.")

While Grant's account of Hamilton High ends in 1985, schoolographies continue. If you were to author the most recent period of school history, what title and description might you give to this latest, and as yet unwritten chapter, of *The World We Created at Hamilton High?*

INTERACTIVE ACTIVITY
When Did That Happen?
Place important educational events on a timeline to test your knowledge.

RAP 3.9
Publication of the Month, p. 436

_____ **1985–2005**

_____

_____

_____

_____

_____

_____

_____

_____

_____

 ## Hall of Fame: Profiles in Education

FOCUS QUESTION 8
Who are some of the key individuals who have helped fashion today's schools?

A "hall of fame" recognizes individuals for significant contributions to a field. Football, baseball, rock and roll, and country music all have halls of fame to recognize outstanding individuals. We think education is no less important and merits its own forum for recognition. In fact, Emporia State University in Kansas is currently developing a Teachers' Hall of Fame. Following are the nominations we would offer to honor educators who we believe should be in a hall of fame.

Obviously, not all influential educators have been included in these brief profiles, but it is important to begin recognizing significant educational contributions. Indirectly or directly, these individuals have influenced your life as a student and will influence your career as a teacher.

RAP 3.1
Self-Fulfilling
Prophecy, p. 429

For his pioneering work in identifying developmental stages of learning and his support of universal education—

Comenius, born Jan Komensky (1592–1670). A teacher and administrator in Poland and the Netherlands, Comenius' educational ideas were revolutionary for his day. Abandoning the notion that children were inherently bad and needed corporal punishment to encourage learning, Comenius attempted to identify the developmental stages of learners and to match instruction to these stages. He approached learning in a logical way and emphasized teaching general principles before details, using concrete examples before abstract ideas, sequencing ideas in a logical progression, and including practical applications of what is taught. He believed that education should be built on the natural laws of human development and that caring teachers should gently guide children's learning. Comenius supported universal education, and his ideas were later developed by Rousseau, by Pestalozzi, and, nearly 400 years later, by the progressive education movement in the United States.

For his work in distinguishing schooling from education and for his concern with the stages of development—

Jean-Jacques Rousseau (1712–1778). French philosopher Rousseau viewed humans as fundamentally good in their free and natural state but corrupted as a result of societal institutions, such as schools. Like Comenius, he saw children as developing through stages and believed that the child's interests and needs should be the focus of a curriculum. In *Emile,* a novel he wrote in 1762, Rousseau described his educational philosophy by telling the story of young Emile's education, from infancy to adulthood. Emile's education took place on a country estate, under the guidance of a tutor and away from the corrupt influences of society. The early learnings came through Emile's senses and not through books or the words of the teacher. The senses, which Rousseau referred to as the *first teachers,* are more efficient and desirable than learning in the schoolroom. Nature and related sciences were acquired through careful observation of the environment. Only after Emile reached age 15 was he introduced to the corrupt influences of society to learn about government, economics, business, and the arts. Rousseau emphasized the senses over formalized teaching found in books and classrooms, nature over society, and the instincts of the learner over the adult-developed curriculum of school. Rousseau's visionary education for Emile can be contrasted with the sexist education he prescribed for Sophie, the book's female character. Sophie's education amounted to little more than obedience school, because Rousseau expected women to be totally subservient to men. (This terribly restricted view of the role of women is an indication that even members of the Education Hall of Fame have their limitations.)

Rousseau was a pioneer of the contemporary deschooling movement, as he separated the institution of the school from the process of learning. His work led to the

CLASS ACTIVITIES
HALL OF FAME ROLE-PLAYS
IM, Activity 8:3
LANDMARKS IN HISTORY
OF AMERICAN EDUCATION
IM, Activity 8:4

child study movement and served as a catalyst for progressive education. Rousseau's romantic view of education influenced many later reformers, including Pestalozzi.

For his recognition of the special needs of the disadvantaged and his work in curricular development—

Johann Heinrich Pestalozzi (1746–1827). Swiss educator Pestalozzi read, agreed with, and built on Rousseau's ideas. Rather than abandoning schools, Pestalozzi attempted to reform them. He established an educational institute at Burgdorf to educate children, as well as to train teachers in more effective instructional strategies.

He identified two levels of effective teaching. At the first level, teachers were taught to alleviate the special problems of poor students. Psychological, emotional, and physical needs should be remediated by caring teachers. In fact, the school environment should resemble a secure and loving home, contributing to the emotional health of the child. At the second level, teachers should focus on teaching students to learn through the senses, beginning with concrete items and moving to more abstract ideas, starting with the learner's most immediate surroundings and gradually moving to more complex and abstract topics.

Pestalozzi's ideas are seen today in programs focused on the special needs of the disadvantaged student. His curricular ideas emerge in today's expanding-horizons social studies curriculum, where children learn first about their family, then their community, their state, and eventually the national and world community. Pestalozzi's ideas influenced Horace Mann and other U.S. educators committed to developing more effective school practices.

For establishing the kindergarten as an integral part of a child's education—

Friedrich Froebel (1782–1852). Froebel frequently reflected on his own childhood. Froebel's mother died when he was only 9 months old. In his recollections, he developed a deep sense of the importance of early childhood and of the critical role played by teachers of the young. Although he worked as a forester, chemist's assistant, and museum curator, he eventually found his true vocation as an educator. He attended Pestalozzi's institute and extended Pestalozzi's ideas. He saw nature as a prime source of learning and believed that schools should provide a warm and supportive environment for children.

In 1837 Froebel founded the first **kindergarten** ("child's garden") to "cultivate" the child's development and socialization. Games provided cooperative activities for socialization and physical development, and such materials as sand and clay were used to stimulate the child's imagination. Like Pestalozzi, Froebel believed in the importance of establishing an emotionally secure environment for children. Going beyond Pestalozzi, Froebel saw the teacher as a moral and cultural model for children, a model worthy of emulation (how different from the earlier view of the teacher as disciplinarian).

In the nineteenth century, as German immigrants came to the United States, they brought with them the idea of kindergarten education. Margaretta Schurz established a German-language kindergarten in Wisconsin in 1855. The first English-language kindergarten and training school for kindergarten teachers were begun in Boston in 1860 by Elizabeth Peabody.

For his contributions to moral development in education and for his creation of a structured methodology of instruction—

Johann Herbart (1776–1841). German philosopher Herbart believed that the primary goal of education is moral education, the development of good people. He believed that through education, individuals can be taught such values as action based on personal conviction, concern for the social welfare of others, and the positive and negative consequences associated with one's behavior. Herbart believed that the development of cognitive powers and knowledge would lead naturally to moral and ethical behavior, the fundamental goal of education.

Herbart believed in the coordinated and logical development of all areas of the curriculum. He was concerned with relating history to geography and both of these to literature—in short, in clearly presenting to students the relationships among various subjects. Herbart's careful and organized approach to the curriculum led to the development of structured teaching. His methodology included preparing students for learning (readiness), helping students form connections by relating new material to previously learned information, using examples to increase understanding, and teaching students how to apply information.

Herbart's concern for moral education paved the way for contemporary educators to explore the relationship between values and knowledge, between a well-educated scientist or artist and a moral, ethical adult. His structured approach to curriculum encouraged careful lesson planning—that is, the development of a prearranged order of presenting information. Teachers who spend time classifying what they will be teaching and writing lesson plans are involved in the kinds of activities suggested by Herbart.

CRITICAL THINKING QUESTION
Some of your students, along with a few professors and politicians, may ask "Why do future teachers need to know the history of education?" As your class considers this question, have them imagine how several of our *Hall of Famers* might answer the question as well. Can they support their suppositions with evidence drawn from the profiles?

For opening the door of higher education to women and for promoting professional teacher preparation—

Emma Hart Willard (1787–1870). The sixteenth of seventeen children on a farm in Connecticut, Willard was fortunate enough to be born of well-educated and progressive parents who nurtured new ideas. At a time when it was believed that women could not learn complex subjects, Willard committed her life to opening higher education to women. In her own education, she pursued as rigorous an academic program as was permitted women at the time. She had mastered geometry on her own by the age of 12. At 17, she began her career in teaching. In 1814, she opened the Middlebury Female Seminary. In reality, the seminary offered a college-level program, but the term *college* was avoided and *seminary* was used so as not to offend the public. Although she herself was denied the right to attend classes at nearby Middlebury College, she learned college-level material on her own and incorporated this curriculum into the subjects she taught her female students at the seminary.

She put forth her views on opening higher education to women in a pamphlet entitled *An Address to the Public; Particularly to the Members of the Legislature of New York, Proposing a Plan for Improving Female Education* (1819). The pamphlet, written and funded by Willard, won favorable responses from Thomas Jefferson, John Adams, and James Monroe, but not the money she sought from the New York State Legislature to open an institution of higher learning for women. Eventually, with local support, she opened the Troy Female Seminary, establishing a rigorous course of study for women, more rigorous than the curriculum found in many men's colleges. Moreover, the seminary was devoted to preparing professional teachers, thus providing a teacher education program years before the first normal (teacher training) school was founded. To disseminate her ideas and curriculum, Willard wrote a number of textbooks, especially in geography, history, and astronomy. In 1837, she formed the Willard Association for the Mutual Improvement of Female Teachers, the first organization to focus public attention on the need for well-prepared and trained teachers.

Emma Hart Willard was a pioneer in the struggle for women's intellectual and legal rights. She wrote and lectured in support of the property rights of married women and other financial reforms, and she dedicated her life to promoting the intellectual and educational freedom of women. Her efforts promoted the recognition of teaching as a profession and the creation of teacher education programs. In the years that followed, colleges, graduate schools, and the professions opened their doors to women. It was Emma Hart Willard's commitment to providing educational opportunities for women that has shaped the past two centuries of progress, not only for women but for all Americans.

For establishing free public schools and expanding the opportunities of poor as well as wealthy Americans, and for his visions of the central role of education in improving the quality of American life—

Horace Mann (1796–1859). Perhaps the most critical factor in shaping the life of Horace Mann was not what he was given but what he was denied. Although he proved to be an able and gifted student, he was not afforded very much in the way of formal schooling. Forced to learn on his own, he acquired an education and was eventually admitted to Brown University. Before him was a career in law as well as a career in politics, but neither influenced his life as much as his struggle to gain an education. He worked to ensure that others would not be denied educational opportunities. That struggle directed his life and altered the history of U.S. education.

As an educator and a member of the Massachusetts House of Representatives, he worked to improve the quality of education. Corporal punishment, floggings, and unsafe and unsanitary school buildings were all denounced by Mann in speeches, letters, and his lobbying efforts before the state legislature and the U.S. Congress. Of the numerous challenges Mann confronted, he was probably most violently denounced for his efforts to remove religious instruction from schools. He also worked to lengthen the school term; to increase teacher salaries; and, by establishing the first public normal school in 1839, to prepare better teachers. He organized school libraries and encouraged the writing of textbooks that included practical social problems. Mann's efforts resulted in the establishment of the Massachusetts Board of Education, and he became the board's first secretary of education, a position equivalent to a state superintendent of schools.

Of the many achievements attributed to Mann, he is probably best remembered for his leadership in the common school movement, the movement to establish free, publicly supported schools for all Americans. He viewed ignorance as bondage and education as a passport to a promising future. Through education, the disadvantaged could lift themselves out of poverty, blacks could achieve freedom, and children with disabilities could learn to be productive members of society. Mann's credo was that social mobility and the improvement of society could be attained through a free education for all.

However, Mann's fervor was not confined to establishing quality public education. As a member of Congress, he denounced slavery, child labor, worker exploitation, workplace hazards, and the dangers of slum life. Later, as president of Antioch College, he provoked further controversy by admitting women and minority members as students. In the 1850s, this was not only a radical move; for many, it suggested the imminent collapse of higher education. Mann did more than verbalize the importance of freedom and education; his life and actions were a commitment to these principles. The fruits of Mann's efforts are found in our public school system; the education of minorities, the poor, and women; and efforts to provide well-trained teachers working in well-equipped classrooms.

For her integrity and bravery in bringing education to African American girls—

Prudence Crandall (1803–1889). Born of Quaker parents, Prudence Crandall received her education at a school in Providence, Rhode Island, founded by an active abolitionist, Moses Brown. Her upbringing within Quaker circles, in which discussions of abolition were common, may have inspired her interest in racial equality, an interest that led her to acts of personal courage as she strove to promote education among people of all colors.

After graduating from the Brown Seminary around 1830, Crandall taught briefly in Plainfield, Connecticut, before founding her own school for girls in the neighboring town of Canterbury. However, her decision to admit a black girl, Sarah Harris, daughter of a neighboring farmer, caused outrage. While African Americans in Connecticut were free, a large segment of the white population within Canterbury supported the efforts of the American Colonization Society to deport all freed blacks to Africa, believing them to be inherently inferior. Many were adamant that anything but the most basic education for African Americans would lead to discontent and might encourage interracial marriage. The townspeople voiced fears that Crandall's school would lead to the devaluation of local property by attracting a large number of blacks to the area. Prudence Crandall was pressured by the local population to expel Sarah Harris. However, she was determined to defy their wishes. When the wife of a prominent local clergyman suggested that, if Harris remained, the school "could not be sustained," Crandall replied, "Then it might sink then, for I should not turn her out."

When other parents withdrew their children, Crandall advertised for pupils in *The Liberator,* the newspaper of abolitionist William Lloyd Garrison. A month later, the school reopened with a student body comprising fifteen black girls. However, the townspeople made life difficult for Crandall and her students. Supplies were hard to obtain, and Crandall and her pupils faced verbal harassment, as well as being pelted with chicken heads, manure, and other objects. Nonetheless, they persisted.

In 1833, only one month after Crandall had opened her doors to African American girls, the Connecticut legislature passed the notorious "Black Law." This law forbade the founding of schools for the education of African Americans from other states without the permission of local authorities. Crandall was arrested and tried. At her trial, her counsel advised the jury, "You may find that she has violated an act of the State Legislature, but if you also find her protected by higher power, it will be your duty to acquit." Her conviction was later overturned on appeal, but vandalism and arson continued. When a gang stormed the school building with clubs and iron bars, smashing windows and rendering the downstairs area uninhabitable, the school finally was forced to close.

Prudence Crandall's interest in education, racial equality, and women's rights continued throughout her life. Several of her students continued her work, including her first African American student, Sarah Harris, who taught black pupils in Louisiana for many years.[16]

For her work in identifying the educational potential of young children and crafting an environment in which the young could learn—

Maria Montessori (1870–1952). Montessori was no follower of tradition, in her private life or in her professional activities. Shattering sex-role stereotypes, she attended a technical school and then a medical school, becoming the first female physician in Italy. Her work brought her in contact with children regarded as mentally handicapped and brain-damaged, but her educational activities with these children indicated that they were far more capable than many believed. By 1908, Montessori had established a children's school called the Casa dei Bambini, designed to provide an education for disadvantaged children from the slums of Rome.

Montessori's view of children differed from the views held by her contemporaries. Her observations led her to conclude that children have an inner need to work at tasks that interest them. Given the right materials and tasks, children need not be rewarded and punished by the teacher. In fact, she believed that children prefer work to play and are capable of sustained periods of concentration. Young children need a carefully prepared environment in order to learn.

Montessori's curriculum reflected this specially prepared environment. Children learned practical skills, including setting a table, washing dishes, buttoning clothing, and displaying basic manners. They learned formal skills, such as reading, writing, and arithmetic. Special materials included movable sandpaper letters to teach the alphabet and colored rods to teach counting. The children developed motor skills as well as intellectual skills in a carefully developed sequence. Montessori worked with each student individually, rather than with the class as a whole, to accomplish these goals.

The impact of Montessori's methods continues to this day. Throughout the United States, early childhood education programs use Montessori-like materials. A number of early childhood institutions are called **Montessori schools** and adhere to the approach she developed almost a century ago. Although originally intended for disadvantaged students, Montessori's concept of carefully preparing an environment and program to teach the very young is used today with children from all social classes.

For his work in developing progressive education, for incorporating democratic practices in the educational process—

John Dewey (1859–1952). John Dewey's long life began before the Civil War and ended during the Korean War. During his 93 years, he became quite possibly the most influential educator of the twentieth century. Dewey was a professor at both the University of Chicago and Columbia University, as well as a prolific writer whose ideas and approach to education created innovations and provoked controversies that continue to this day.

Dewey's educational philosophy has been referred to as *progressivism, pragmatism,* and *experimentalism.* Dewey believed that the purpose of education is to assist the growth of individuals, to help children understand and control their environment. Knowledge is not an inert body of facts to be committed to memory; rather, it consists of experiences that should be used to help solve present problems. Dewey believed that the school should be organized around the needs and interests of the child. The learner's interests serve as a springboard to understanding and mastering contemporary issues. For example, a school store might be used to teach mathematics. Students involved in the store operation would learn mathematics by working with money and making change. Dewey was committed to child-centered education, to learning by doing, and to the importance of experience. Classrooms became laboratories in which students could experiment with life and learn to work together.

Dewey's philosophy was founded on a commitment to democratic education. The student should be free to explore and test all ideas and values. Basic American beliefs and institutions should be investigated and restructured when necessary. Education consists of change and of reconstructing experiences. Children, like adults, should learn how to structure their lives and develop self-discipline. Autocratic governments and authoritarian schools are disservices to democracy, for students should participate in shaping their education. Not only should school be a preparation for democracy, but also it should be a democracy. Students should continue this process and shape their world as adults.

The disciples of Dewey's philosophy became a powerful force in education. They founded the Progressive Education Association, which influenced education well into the 1950s. Today, Dewey's writings and ideas continue to motivate and intrigue educators, and there still exist educational monuments to Dewey, both in a variety of school practices and in professional organizations, such as the John Dewey Society. Dewey's philosophy helped open schools to innovation and integrated education with the outside world.

For her contributions in moving a people from intellectual slavery to education—

Mary McLeod Bethune (1875–1955). The first child of her family not born in slavery, Bethune rose from a field hand, picking cotton, to an unofficial presidential adviser. The last of seventeen children born to South Carolina sharecroppers, she filled the breaks in her fieldwork with reading and studying. She was committed to meeting the critical need of providing education to the newly freed African Americans, and, when a Colorado seamstress offered to pay the cost of educating one black girl at Scotia Seminary in Concord, New Hampshire, she was selected. Bethune's plans to become an African missionary changed as she became more deeply involved in the need to educate newly liberated American blacks.

With $1.50, five students, and a rented cottage near the Daytona Beach city dump in Florida, Bethune founded a school that eventually became Bethune-Cookman College. As a national leader, she created a number of black civic and welfare organizations, serving as a member of the Hoover Commission on Child Welfare, and acting as an adviser to President Franklin D. Roosevelt.

Mary McLeod Bethune demonstrated commitment and effort in establishing a black college against overwhelming odds and by rising from poverty to become a national voice for African Americans.

For his creation of a theory of cognitive development—

Jean Piaget (1896–1980). As a student at the University of Paris, Swiss psychologist Piaget met and began working for Alfred Binet, who developed the first intelligence test (a version of which we know today as the Stanford-Binet IQ test). Binet was involved in standardizing children's answers to various questions on this new test, and he enlisted Jean Piaget to assist. Piaget not only followed Binet's instructions, but he went beyond them. He not only recorded children's answers but also probed students for the reasons behind their answers. From the children's responses, Piaget observed that children at different age levels see the world in different ways. From these initial observations, he conceptualized his theory of cognitive, or mental, development, which has influenced the way educators have viewed children ever since.

Piaget's theory outlines four stages of cognitive development. From infancy to 2 years of age, the child functions at the *sensorimotor stage.* At this initial level, infants explore and learn about their environment through their senses—using their eyes, hands, and even mouths. From 2 to 7 years of age, children enter the *preoperational stage* and begin to organize and understand their environment through language and concepts. At the third stage, *concrete operations,* occurring between the ages of 7 and 11, children learn to develop and use more sophisticated concepts and mental operations. Children at this stage can understand numbers and some processes and relationships. The final stage, *formal operations,* begins between 11 and 15 and continues through adulthood. This stage represents the highest level of mental development, the level of adult abstract thinking.

Piaget's theory suggests that teachers should recognize the abilities and limits at each stage and provide appropriate learning activities. Children should be encouraged to develop the skills and mental operations relevant to their mental stage and should be prepared to grow toward the next stage. Teachers, from early childhood through secondary school, need to develop appropriate educational environments and work with students individually according to their own levels of readiness.

Piaget revealed the interactive nature of the learning process and the importance of relating the learner's needs to educational activities. His work led to increased attention to early childhood education and the critical learning that occurs during these early years.

For his contributions in establishing a technology of teaching—

Burrhus Frederick (B. F.) Skinner (1904–1990). When poet Robert Frost received a copy of young B. F. Skinner's work, he encouraged the author to continue writing. But Skinner's years of serious writing in New York's Greenwich Village were unproductive. As Skinner explained, "I discovered the unhappy fact that I had nothing to say, and went to graduate study in psychology, hoping to remedy that short-coming."

Skinner received his doctorate from Harvard, where he eventually returned to teach. He found himself attracted to the work of John B. Watson, and Skinner's ideas became quite controversial. One critic described him as "the man you love to hate."

Skinner's notoriety stemmed from his belief that organisms, including humans, are entirely the products of their environment; engineer the environment, and you can engineer human behavior. Skinner's view of human behavior (called **behaviorism**) irked individuals who see it as a way of controlling people and enslaving the human spirit. Skinner's response was that he did not create these principles but simply discovered them and that a constructive environment can "push human achievement to its limits."

Skinner's early work included the training of animals. During World War II, in a secret project, Skinner trained, or conditioned, pigeons to pilot missiles and torpedoes. The pigeons were so highly trained that they were capable of guiding a missile right down the smokestack of an enemy ship.

Skinner believed that children could be conditioned to acquire desirable skills and behaviors. By breaking down learning into small, simple steps and rewarding children after the completion of each step, learning mastery is achieved. By combining many of these steps, complex behaviors can be learned efficiently. To advance his ideas, he developed the "teaching machine," a device that used these principles of step-by-step instruction requiring and rewarding student responses. This approach laid the foundation for the later development of behavior modification and computer-assisted instruction.

Skinner's creative productivity resulted in both inventions and numerous publications. The "Skinner box" enabled researchers to observe, analyze, and condition pigeons and other animals to master tasks, while teaching machines translated these learning principles into human education. Skinner's books, including *Walden Two, The Technology of Teaching,* and *Beyond Freedom and Dignity,* spread his ideas on the importance of environment and behaviorism to educators, psychologists, and the general public. He provided guiding principles about the technology of learning, principles that can be used to unleash or to shackle human potential.

For her creative approaches placing children at the center of the curriculum—

Sylvia Ashton-Warner (1908–1984). Sylvia Ashton-Warner began her school career in her mother's New Zealand classroom, where rote memorization constituted the main avenue for learning. The teaching strategies that Ashton-Warner later devised, with their emphasis on child-centered learning and creativity in the classroom, stand in opposition to this early experience.

Ashton-Warner was a flamboyant and eccentric personality; throughout her life, she considered herself to be an artist rather than a teacher. She focused on painting, music, and writing. Her fascination with creativity was apparent in the remote New Zealand classrooms, where she encouraged self-expression among the native Maori children. As a teacher, she infuriated authorities with her absenteeism and unpredictability, and in official ratings she was never estimated as above average in her abilities. However, during the peak years of her teaching career, between 1950 and 1952, she developed innovative teaching techniques that influenced teachers around the world and especially in the United States.

Realizing that certain words were especially significant to individual pupils because of their life experiences, Ashton-Warner developed her "key vocabulary" system for teaching reading to young children. Words drawn from children's conversations were written on cards. Using these words, children learned to read. Ashton-Warner asserted that the key to making this approach effective lay in choosing words that had personal meaning to the individual child: "Pleasant words won't do. Respectable words won't do. They must be words organically tied up, organically born from the dynamic life itself. They must be words that are already part of the child's being."

Bringing meaning to children was at the center of Ashton-Warner's philosophy. This belief provided the foundation of several reading approaches and teaching strategies used throughout the United States. Her work brought meaning to reading for millions of children. In her best-selling book, *Teacher,* she provided many future teachers with important and useful insights. Her emphasis on key vocabulary, individualized reading, and meaningful learning is evident in classrooms today in America and abroad.

For his work in identifying the crippling effects of racism on all American children and in formulating community action to overcome the educational, psychological, and economic impacts of racism—

Kenneth Clark (1914–). Born in the Panama Canal Zone, Clark was influenced by a forceful mother, who relocated the family to New York City when Clark was 5 years of age in order to provide better educational opportunities for her children. Working as a seamstress in a New York sweatshop, she helped organize the International Ladies' Garment Workers Union. Clark attributes the lessons he learned concerning the importance of "people doing things together to help themselves" to his mother.

Clark attended schools in Harlem, where he witnessed an integrated community become all black and felt the growing impact of racism. He attended Howard University and received his doctorate from Columbia University, but his concern with the educational plight of African Americans generally, and the Harlem community in particular, was always central in his professional efforts.

Clark participated in the landmark study of racial segregation undertaken by Gunnar Myrdal, which resulted in the publication of *An American Dilemma* in 1944. In his own work, he investigated the impact of segregated schools in New York City, concluding that black students receive an education inferior to that of whites. To counter this problem, he established several community self-help projects to assist children with psychological and educational problems. One of those programs, called HARYOU (Harlem Youth Opportunities Unlimited), was designed to prevent school dropouts, delinquency, and unemployment. His efforts served as a catalyst for government action, with both New York City and the federal government providing funds to enhance educational opportunities for minority students.

Kenneth Clark was the first African American appointed to a faculty position at the City College of New York. In books such as *Prejudice and Your Child*, he analyzed the impact of racism on both whites and blacks. The Supreme Court, in its 1954 *Brown* decision, cited Clark's work as psychological evidence for the need to desegregate U.S. schools. His psychological studies and community efforts represented pioneering achievements in desegregating U.S. schools and enhancing U.S. education. As Clark noted decades ago, "A racist system inevitably destroys and damages human beings; it brutalizes and dehumanizes blacks and whites alike."

For his contribution in establishing an American school of cognitive psychology and for his insights in shaping the school curriculum—

Jerome Bruner (1915–). As a graduate student in psychology at Harvard, Jerome Bruner found himself deeply involved in the study of animal perceptions and learning. Psychology was then a new field, and U.S. psychologists, heavily influenced by the behaviorist tradition, turned a deaf ear to studying anything as "unscientific" as human thinking and learning. But Bruner's involvement in World War II altered the direction of his efforts and helped initiate an American school of cognitive psychology, a movement to study human behavior.

During the war, Bruner worked in General Eisenhower's headquarters, studying psychological warfare. His doctoral dissertation concerned Nazi propaganda techniques. After the war, he published works showing how human needs affect perception. For example, poor children are more likely to overestimate the value of coins than are richer children. Adult values and needs affect the way they see the world as well, and realities that do not conform to these needs and beliefs are mentally altered. Bruner showed that human behavior can be observed, analyzed, and understood in an objective way. By 1960, he had helped found Harvard University's Center for Cognitive Studies. Bruner helped legitimize the systematic, objective, and scientific study of human learning and thinking.

Bruner's thoughtful and practical approach to issues was applied to the study of the school curriculum. He was a leader of the Woods Hole conference, a summit of scientists, educators, and scholars interested in reforming education. (The conference followed the Soviet success in launching *Sputnik*.) His report on the conference was published in ***The Process of Education*** (1960), hailed as a practical and readable analysis of curriculum needs. The Process of Education has been translated into twenty-two languages and is studied by teachers around the world. In his book, Bruner argued that schools should not focus on facts but should attempt to teach the "structure," the general nature, of a subject. He also stressed the need for developing intuition and insights as a legitimate problem-solving technique. Finally, in his best-known quotation from *The Process of Education,* Bruner stated, "Any subject can be taught effectively in some intellectually honest form to any child at any stage of development." Bruner has cogently argued for more problem solving and direct involvement in the process of education for all learners, from young children to adults.

For his global effort to mobilize education in the cause of social justice—

Paulo Reglus Neves Freire (1921–1997). Abandoning a career in the law, Brazilian-born Freire committed himself to the education of the poor and politically oppressed. His efforts moved literacy from an educational tool to a political instrument.

Freire denounced teacher-centered classrooms. He believed that instructor domination denied the legitimacy of student experiences and treated students as secondary objects in the learning process. He termed such instruction "banking" education, since the students become little more than passive targets of the teacher's comments. Freire championed a *critical pedagogy,* one that places the student at the center of the learning process. In Freire's pedagogy, student dialogues, knowledge, and skills are shared cooperatively, legitimizing the experiences of the poor. Students are taught how to generate their own questions, focus on their own social problems, and develop strategies to live more fruitful and satisfying lives. Teachers are not passive bystanders or the only source of classroom wisdom. Freire believed that teachers should facilitate and inspire, that teachers should "live part of their dreams within their educational space." Rather than unhappy witnesses to social injustice, teachers should be advocates for the poor and agents for social change. Freire's best known work, ***Pedagogy of the Oppressed,*** illustrated how education could transform society.

Freire's approach obviously threatened the social order of many repressive governments, and he faced constant intimidation and threats. Following the military overthrow of the Brazilian government in 1964, Freire was jailed for "subversive" activities and later exiled. In the late 1960s, while studying in America, Freire witnessed racial unrest and the antiwar protests. These events convinced Freire that political oppression is present in "developed nations" as well as third world countries, that economic privilege does not guarantee political advantage, and that the pedagogy of the oppressed has worldwide significance.

INTERACTIVE ACTIVITY
Who Am I?
Using hints, determine the identity of famous educational figures.

SUMMARY

 CHAPTER REVIEW

Go to the Online Learning Center to take a quiz, practice with key terms, and review concepts from the chapter.

 CURRENT NEWS FROM POWERWEB

To access PowerWeb, go to Chapter 8 on the Online Learning Center to read current articles and to access news feeds about:

- Aims of Education
- Comparative Education
- Education
- The Future of Education
- High School
- Schools and Federal Policy

1. What was the nature and purpose of colonial education?

   Much of colonial education took place in the home through dame schools, in the church, and through apprentice programs, with instruction dominated by religious teachings. In 1647, Massachusetts passed the "Old Deluder Satan Law," requiring every town to provide for education; although throughout the colonies, whites, males, and wealthier individuals were most likely to be schooled. Thomas Jefferson and Benjamin Franklin viewed the new nation's schools as a continuation of democratic principles and as a break from classist European traditions. By omitting any mention of education as a federal responsibility, the Constitution left schooling to the states, and so each state developed its own educational culture—although textbooks, from the rudimentary hornbook to the *McGuffey Reader*—created a minimal national curriculum. From colonial times to the present, continuing educational disputes include: the role of religion in schools, local control and state standards, and inequities in educational opportunities for women, people of color, and the poor.

2. How did the Common School Movement influence the idea of universal education?

   Nineteenth-century leader Horace Mann fought for the establishment of the common school, today's elementary school, and also for quality teacher education through normal schools. He believed that education should develop the talents of the poor as well as the wealthy.

3. How did teaching become a "gendered" career?

   Although teaching was initially "gendered" male, the advent of the common school created a demand for a large number of inexpensive teachers, and women were recruited. Since the late nineteenth century, teaching positions have been dominated by women, and teaching "re-gendered" female. Both female and male teachers continue to confront issues of sexuality and sexism. Gendered enclaves persist in today's schools, as women dominate elementary teaching, and men dominate certain academic specialties and leadership positions.

4. How did secondary schools evolve?

   The first publicly supported secondary school was the English Classical School in Boston. As America became more industrial and urban, public support for high schools grew, and the Kalamazoo case (1874) created the legal basis for high school funding. By the twentieth century, junior high schools and middle schools were established.

5. How have twentieth century reform efforts influenced schools?

   From the Committee of Ten in 1892 to the 1989 National Education Summit, waves of educational reform have become part of the American landscape. While the purpose of reform movements vary, one idea remains key: Schools should have a central role in maintaining a vibrant democracy.

6. What were the main tenets of the Progressive Education movement?

   Progressivism, led by John Dewey, emphasized learning by doing and shaping curricula around children's interests, but has frequently been attacked. Extremists of the 1950s saw progressivism as communistic, and after the 1957 Soviet *Sputnik* launching, progressivism was blamed for America's poor science and math performance.

7. What role has the federal government played in American education?

   While the Constitution leaves the responsibility for schooling to the states, the federal government has played an increasing role in education over the past century, promoting teacher training, science and math instruction, and desegregation. More recently, the emphasis has been on school standards and testing.

8. Who are some of the key individuals who have helped fashion today's schools?

Each of the chapters in this text highlights a significant educator through the *Profile in Education* feature. In this chapter, seventeen noted educators from sixteenth-century Comenius to twentieth-century Paulo Freire are profiled.

EXTENDED LEARNING

READINGS

- Horace Mann. Selection from *The Education of Free Men.*
- Elizabeth Cady Stanton. Selection from *Eighty Years and More.*

Go to Chapter 8 on your *Resources for Exploring Education* CD-ROM to access Case Studies and Readings.

KEY TERMS AND PEOPLE

KEY TERMS

academy, 290, 297

American Spelling Book, 291

apprenticeship, 286

behaviorism, 316

Brown v. Board of Education of Topeka, 301

Cardinal Principles of Secondary Education, 296

Carnegie unit, 296

categorical grants, 301

Committee of Ten, 296

common school, 290, 297

dame schools, 286, 297

Eight-Year Study, 300

elementary school, 290

English Classical School, 294

Franklin Academy, 290

gendered career, 293

hornbook, 291

in loco parentis, 286

junior high schools, 296, 297

Kalamazoo, Michigan case, 295

kindergarten, 310

laboratory school, 298

Land Ordinance Act, 301

Latin grammar school, 286, 297

McGuffey Readers, 291

middle schools, 296, 297

Montessori schools, 314

A Nation at Risk: The Imperative for Educational Reform, 298

National Defense Education Act (NDEA), 300

New England Primer, 291

normal schools, 292

Northwest Ordinance, 301

Old Deluder Satan Law, 286

Pedagogy of the Oppressed, 319

The Process of Education, 318

progressive education, 298

secondary school, 294

Tenth Amendment, 300

KEY PEOPLE

Sylvia Ashton-Warner, 317

Mary McLeod Bethune, 315

Jerome Bruner, 318

Kenneth Clark, 318

Comenius, 309

Prudence Crandall, 313

John Dewey, 314

Benjamin Franklin, 290

Paulo Reglus Neves Freire, 319

Friedrich Froebel, 310

Johann Herbart, 311

Thomas Jefferson, 289

Horace Mann, 312

Maria Montessori, 314

Johann Heinrich Pestalozzi, 310

Jean Piaget, 315

Jean-Jacques Rousseau, 309

Burrhus Frederick (B. F.) Skinner, 316

Emma Hart Willard, 311

DISCUSSION QUESTIONS AND ACTIVITIES

1. In the colonial period, a number of factors influenced the kind of education you might receive. Describe how the following factors influenced educational opportunities:
   - Geography
   - Wealth
   - Race/ethnicity
   - Gender

2. "New England, more than any other region, was the birthplace of educational innovation." Support this statement, using examples from elementary, secondary, and postsecondary education.

3. Progressive education has sparked adamant critics and fervent supporters. Offer several arguments supporting the tenets of progressivism, as well as arguments against this movement.

4. Identify the contributions made by the following educators, whom some might consider candidates for the Hall of Fame: Septima Poinsette Clark, Madeline C. Hunter, Charlotte Hawkins Brown, Johnetta Cole, Joyce Ladner, Henri Mann.

5. Some teacher preparation programs do not consider or discuss the history of education, while other programs devote courses reviewing and analyzing educational history. Set up a debate (or use another *academic controversy* strategy) arguing the pros and cons of the following proposition. Resolved: Teacher preparation programs should focus on current issues and not consider the history of education.

REEL TO REAL TEACHING

You can find a wealth of classic movies with an education twist. Watch one of the four oldies but goodies described here, or visit the classics section of your local video store and check out a film "new" to you.

BLACKBOARD JUNGLE (1955)
Run Time: 101 minutes

Synopsis: The story of an idealistic teacher on his first job in a tough, urban, all male high school. A shocking film for its time, *Blackboard Jungle* was banned in some cities for its multiracial content and fear that it would spark violence.

THE MIRACLE WORKER (1962)
Run Time: 107 minutes

Synopsis: The true story of Anne Sullivan's devotion to teaching Helen Keller, a girl whose childhood illness caused her to become blind and deaf, how to communicate.

TO KILL A MOCKINGBIRD (1962)
Run Time: 129 minutes

Synopsis: Atticus Finch, a lawyer and single parent in a small Southern town during the Great Depression, defends an African American man wrongfully accused of raping a white woman. During the trial, his children and the community learn lessons of racial and disability tolerance.

TO SIR, WITH LOVE (1967)
Run Time: 105 minutes

Synopsis: Unable to find work as an engineer, an African American engineer accepts a teaching job in the slums of London. To motivate his rebellious students, he rejects traditional textbooks and lectures, and endeavors to earn their trust through unorthodox instruction.

Reflection:

1. Does the film you viewed remind you of a current issue? Which one(s)? Describe the similarities and differences.

2. What elements of effective teaching did you observe in the film? Is good teaching in the 1950s and 1960s still considered good teaching today?

3. Would you like to teach in the school depicted in the film? Why or why not?

Follow-up Activity: If there were an Education History Movie Hall of Fame, which classic film would you honor? Visit the *Reel to Real Teaching* on our website and post your nomination. Tell us why this film is a timeless winner!

How do you rate these films? Go to *Reel to Real Teaching* in the Critics' Corner to review these films.

www.mhhe.com/
sadker7e

FOR FURTHER READING

American Education, by Wayne Urban and Jennings Wagoner, Jr. (3rd ed., 2004). Chronicles the history of American education from precolonial times to the present, setting the discussion against the broader backdrop of national and world events.

The American School 1642–2000, by Joel Spring (2000). A critical analysis of the economic, political, and multicultural forces that have shaped education from colonial times to the present.

Cultural History and Education, by Thomas Popkewitz, Barry Franklin, and Miguel Pereyra (2001). Traces historical changes in the definitions of student, teacher, school, and community across Europe, Latin America, and North America.

Images of Schoolteachers in America, by Pamela Bolotin Joseph and Gail Burnaford (Editors) (2001). The question "What does it mean to be a teacher during the past 100 years?" is explored through a variety of media including film, television, portraits, photographs, fiction, comic strips, oral histories, and poetry.

Pedagogies of Resistance: Women Educator Activists, 1880–1960, by Margaret Smith Crocco, Petra Munro, and Kathleen Weiler (1999). Chronicles the lives of women who resisted conventional gender roles to make education and society more equitable.

The White Architects of Black Education: Ideology and Power in America, 1865–1954, by William H. Watkins (2001). Describes how corporate power and private wealth shaped unequal race relations and structured segregated education.

CHAPTER 9

Philosophy of Education

FOCUS QUESTIONS

1. What is a philosophy of education, and why should it be important to you?
2. How do teacher-centered philosophies of education differ from student-centered philosophies of education?
3. What are some major philosophies of education in the United States today?
4. How are these philosophies reflected in school practices?
5. What are some of the psychological and cultural factors influencing education?
6. What were the contributions of Socrates, Plato, and Aristotle to Western philosophy, and how is their legacy reflected in education today?
7. How do metaphysics, epistemology, ethics, political philosophy, aesthetics, and logic factor into a philosophy of education?

 WHAT DO YOU THINK? What Is Your Philosophy of Education? Take an electronic version of the quiz on pages 327–329. Then, submit your responses to see how they compare to those of your colleagues.

CHAPTER PREVIEW

The root for the word **philosophy** is made up of two Greek words: *philo*, meaning "love," and *sophos*, meaning "wisdom." For thousands of years, philosophers have been wrestling with fundamental questions: What is most real—the physical world or the realm of mind and spirit? What is the basis of human knowledge? What is the nature of the just society? Educators must take stances on such questions before they can determine what and how students should be taught.

Since educators do not always agree on the answers to these questions, different philosophies of education have emerged. Although there are some similarities, there are also profound differences in the way leading educators define the purpose of education, the role of the teacher, the nature of the curriculum and assessment, and the method of instruction.

This chapter is intended to start you on a path of thoughtfully considering your values and beliefs. Five influential philosophies will be described, and you will see how each can shape classroom life. We invite you to consider how psychological and cultural beliefs can also affect schools. We then revisit the roots of Western philosophy with three ancient Greeks as our guides: Socrates, Plato, and Aristotle. Finally, we briefly examine the building blocks of philosophy, the divisions within philosophy that focus on questions pertinent to educators (what is of worth? how do we know what we know?). The ideas in this chapter will spark some very basic questions about your role in the classroom, and the school's role in society. Your answers to these questions will help you frame your philosophy of education.

CHAPTER FOCUS

Philosophical questions have always influenced education. Since educators do not agree on the answers to these questions, different philosophies of education have emerged. This chapter introduces the foundations of educational philosophy and illustrates how each of five major philosophies appears in practice. Although there are similarities, there are also profound differences in the way leading educators define the purpose of education, the role of the teacher, the nature of curriculum and assessment, and the method of instruction. For a chapter outline, see the IM.

Finding Your Philosophy of Education

What is a philosophy of education? Do you have one? Do you think it matters? If you are like most people, you probably have not given much thought to philosophy, in education or elsewhere. Being a practical person, you may be more concerned with other questions: Will I enjoy teaching? Will I be good at it? How will I handle discipline problems? Believe it or not, underlying the answers to these practical questions *is* your philosophy of education.

At this point, your philosophy may still be taking shape (not a bad thing). Your beliefs may reflect an amalgam of different philosophies. Unfortunately, they may also be filled with inconsistencies. In order to help you shape a coherent and useful educational philosophy, you must consider some basic—and very important—questions, such as:

What is the purpose of education?

What content and skills should schools teach?

How should schools teach this content?

What are the proper roles for teachers and students?

Still not sure what a philosophy of education is all about, or how it shapes classroom and school life? Let's listen to some teachers discussing the direction a new charter school should take. You'll see that each teacher has very clear ideas about what schools are for, what students should learn, and how teachers should teach.

Hear that noise coming from the faculty room down the hall? Your potential colleagues sometimes get a bit loud as they debate the possible directions for the new charter school. As you listen in, try to sort out which of these educational directions appeals to you.

JACKIE POLLACK: I am so excited! This new charter school can be just what we need, a chance to reestablish a positive reputation for the quality of public education! Let's face it, we are competing in a global economy, against nations whose students outscore ours on all the standardized tests that matter. It's embarrassing. If we can create a rigorous school (I'd prefer to call it an "Academy") with tough standards and a real commitment to learning, then look out! We'll make those "preppie" kids from Country Day School sorry they ever opted out of the public school system. I'd love to see a school with a strict code of conduct and core courses, like literature, history, math, and science, without those silly electives like "mass media." I would love to see our students wear uniforms and enroll in courses at the Advanced Placement level. What a great school not only for kids to learn, but for us to teach! It's all about rigorous standards.

ROBIN MILLER: Jackie, you and I both would like to teach in a more rigorous school, one with a tougher curriculum. But I am getting tired of standards and testing. I'll tell you a secret: I don't much care whether South Korean kids score better than Americans on some silly short answer test. I'm interested in a school committed to learning, not testing or competing. The new school should replace these boring textbooks with Great Books, books that intrigue, entice, and teach. Kids thirst for meaningful ideas. The school I envision would focus on classic works of literature and art. We would teach through intellectual questioning, a "Socratic dialogue." What exciting discussions we could have about *The Old Man*

GRABBER: A CHANGE OF SPACE
IM

FOCUS QUESTION 1
What is a philosophy of education, and why should it be important to you?

CLASS ACTIVITY: ANOTHER CHANGE OF SPACE
IM, Activity 9:1

and the Sea, Plato's *Republic* and Homer's *Iliad.* Maybe we can re-invent the all-but-extinct American student: One who knows not only how to read, but a student who actually *wants* to read, *enjoys* reading and best of all, knows how to *think.* Jackie, I like the name you came up with—"Academy"—but I want our new charter school to create great minds, not just great test scores.

MARK WASHINGTON: I agree with Robin that we need to move beyond today's tyranny of testing, but Hemingway and Homer are not the answers. Problem is, we have more relevant issues and skills to deal with, issues never dreamed of in Plato's or Shakespeare's day. Our job as teachers is to make certain that our students can do well in the real world. We must be practical. Let me give you an example: When I was in eighth grade, my class took a three-week trip around the Midwestern states by train. Most of the semester was spent planning this trip. We worked together, researching different areas of the region and deciding where to go. We learned how to read train schedules and maps because we had to. We had to be organized and run meetings effectively. Math, history, geography, writing . . . talk about an integrated curriculum! We learned by doing. I still remember that trip and what went into it as a high point in my life. I want all students to have that kind of intense experience, to learn how to solve real world problems, not just answer test questions or discuss books.

TED GOODHEART: I want students to do more than simply fit into society; I want them to leave the world a better place than they found it. Behind our community's pretty façade are people in pain. We need to educate kids to care more about these people than we did. One out of six children is born into poverty here. One out of six! I want to teach kids to make a difference, and not let books and homework insulate them from real world concerns. The new charter school must equip children to tackle issues like poverty, violence, pollution, bigotry, and injustice. We need to prepare students with both a social conscience and the political skills needed to improve our society. I want to teach students whose actions will make me, and all of us, proud. Teaching in a socially responsible charter school would be my dream.

ALICIA CAMUS: Everyone in this room has been trying to design a charter school backwards, thinking mostly about what we teachers think. Here's a revolutionary idea: Let's build an education around the students. Why not have the students decide what they will learn? Students must assume primary responsibility for their own learning. I would like our charter school staffed by teachers who are skilled in facilitating and counseling children to reach their personal goals. Believe it or not, I trust students, and I would give every child (even the youngest or least able) an equal voice in decision making. It's not enough to slowly reform education; we need to rebuild it from the center, from where the students are.

CLASS ACTIVITY: THE
FISHBOWL
IM, Activity 9:4

As you might have suspected, these teachers are not only discussing different approaches to a proposed charter school, they are also shedding light on five major educational philosophies. Do any of these diverse views sound attractive to you? Do any sound particularly unappealing? If so, note which of these teachers you thought reflected your own beliefs, and which were really off the mark. If you found that you had strong opinions—pro or con—about one or more of these teachers' positions, then you are beginning to get in touch with your educational philosophy. Let's leave the faculty room conversation, and take a closer, more orderly look at your own philosophical leanings. The following inventory can help you sort out tenets of your educational philosophy.

 # Inventory of Philosophies of Education

As you read through each of the following statements about schools and teaching, decide how strongly you agree or disagree. In a bit, we will help you interpret your results. Write your response to the left of each statement, using the following scale:

5   Agree strongly

4   Agree

3   Neither agree nor disagree

2   Disagree

1   Disagree strongly

_____   1.   A school curriculum should include a common body of information that all students should know.

_____   2.   The school curriculum should focus on the great ideas that have survived through time.

_____   3.   The gap between the real world and schools should be bridged through field trips, internships, and adult mentors.

_____   4.   Schools should prepare students for analyzing and solving the social problems they will face beyond the classroom.

_____   5.   Each student should determine his or her individual curriculum, and teachers should guide and help them.

_____   6.   Students should not be promoted from one grade to the next until they have read and mastered certain key material.

_____   7.   Schools, above all, should develop students' abilities to think deeply, analytically, and creatively, rather than focus on transient concerns like social skills and current trends.

_____   8.   Whether inside or outside the classroom, teachers must stress the relevance of what students are learning to real and current events.

_____   9.   Education should enable students to recognize injustices in society, and schools should promote projects to redress social inequities.

_____ 10.   Students who do not want to study much should not be required to do so.

_____ 11.   Teachers and schools should emphasize academic rigor, discipline, hard work, and respect for authority.

_____ 12.   Education is not primarily about workers and the world economic competition; learning should be appreciated for its own sake, and students should enjoy reading, learning, and discussing intriguing ideas.

_____ 13.   The school curriculum should be designed by teachers to respond to the experiences and needs of the students.

_____ 14.   Schools should promote positive group relationships by teaching about different ethnic and racial groups.

_____ 15. The purpose of school is to help students understand themselves, appreciate their distinctive talents and insights, and find their own unique place in the world.

_____ 16. For the United States to be competitive economically in the world marketplace, schools must bolster their academic requirements in order to train more competent workers.

_____ 17. Teachers ought to teach from the classics, because important insights related to many of today's challenges and concerns are found in these Great Books.

_____ 18. Since students learn effectively through social interaction, schools should plan for substantial social interaction in their curricula.

_____ 19. Students should be taught how to be politically literate, and learn how to improve the quality of life for all people.

_____ 20. The central role of the school is to provide students with options and choices. The student must decide what and how to learn.

_____ 21. Schools must provide students with a firm grasp of basic facts regarding the books, people, and events that have shaped the nation's heritage.

_____ 22. The teacher's main goal is to help students unlock the insights learned over time, so they can gain wisdom from the great thinkers of the past.

_____ 23. Students should be active participants in the learning process, involved in democratic class decision making and reflective thinking.

_____ 24. Teaching should mean more than simply transmitting the Great Books, which are replete with biases and prejudices. Rather, schools need to identify a new list of Great Books more appropriate for today's world, and prepare students to create a better society than their ancestors did.

_____ 25. Effective teachers help students to discover and develop their personal values, even when those values conflict with traditional ones.

_____ 26. Teachers should help students constantly reexamine their beliefs. In history, for example, students should learn about those who have been historically omitted: the poor, the non-European, women, and people of color.

_____ 27. Frequent objective testing is the best way to determine what students know. Rewarding students when they learn, even when they learn small things, is the key to successful teaching.

_____ 28. Education should be a responsibility of the family and community, rather than delegated to formal and impersonal institutions, such as schools.

Interpreting Your Responses

RAP 3.6
Putting Your Philosophy into the Classroom, p. 434

Write your responses to statements 1 through 25 in the columns on the next page, tally up your score in each column. (We will return to items 26 to 28 in a bit.) Each column is labeled with a philosophy and the name of the teacher who represented that view in this chapter's opening scenario (the charter school discussion). The highest possible score in any one column is 25, and the lowest possible score is 5. Scores in the 20s indicate strong agreement, and scores below 10 indicate disagreement with the tenets of a particular philosophy.

A	B	C	D	E
			Social	
Essentialism (Jackie)	Perennialism (Robin)	Progressivism (Mark)	Reconstructionism (Ted)	Existentialism (Alicia)
1. _____	2. _____	3. _____	4. _____	5. _____
6. _____	7. _____	8. _____	9. _____	10. _____
11. _____	12. _____	13. _____	14. _____	15. _____
16. _____	17. _____	18. _____	19. _____	20. _____
21. _____	22. _____	23. _____	24. _____	25. _____
Scores _____	_____	_____	_____	_____

Your scores in columns A through E, respectively, represent how much you agree or disagree with the beliefs of five major educational philosophies: essentialism, perennialism, progressivism, social reconstructionism, and existentialism. Check back to see if your scores reflect your initial reactions to these teachers' points of view. For example, if you agreed with Jackie's proposal to create an "Academy," then you probably agreed with a number of the statements associated with essentialist education, and your score in this column may be fairly high.

Compare your five scores. What is your highest? What is your lowest? Which three statements best reflect your views on education? Are they congruent and mutually supporting? Looking at the statements that you least support, what do these statements tell you about your values? You may notice that your philosophical leanings, as identified by your responses to statements in the inventory, reflect your general outlook on life. For example, your responses may indicate whether you generally trust people to do the right thing, or if you believe that individuals need supervision. How have your culture, religion, upbringing, and political beliefs shaped your responses to the items in this inventory? How have your own education and life experiences influenced your philosophical beliefs?

Now that you have begun to examine varying beliefs about education, you may even want to lay claim to a philosophical label. But what do these philosophical labels mean? In the following pages we will introduce you to all five of these educational philosophies, and look at their impact in the classroom.

INTERACTIVE ACTIVITY

Where Do You Stand on the Philosophy Spectrum? Note where you think your philosophy of education falls, and compare where you stand to where your colleagues do.

Five Philosophies of Education

Essentialism, perennialism, progressivism, social reconstructionism, and existentialism. Taken together, these five schools of thought do not exhaust the list of possible educational philosophies you may consider, but they present strong frameworks for you to refine your own educational philosophy. We can place these five philosophies on a continuum, from teacher-centered (some would say "authoritarian"), to student-centered (some would characterize as "permissive").

Are you politically conservative or liberal? (Great, now we are bringing politics into this discussion.) Actually, your political stance is one predictor of your

IN THE NEWS

Reflection

After a hectic school year, Kentucky High school graduate Juan C. avoided the beach graduation celebration and chose instead to spend the week in reflection at a Trappist monastery. The student explained: We spend a lot of time nourishing our bodies, but we spend little time nourishing our souls.

SOURCE: *American School Board Journal,* 1998.

What's new in education? Click on *News Feeds.*

FIGURE 9.1
Teacher- and student-centered philosophies of education.

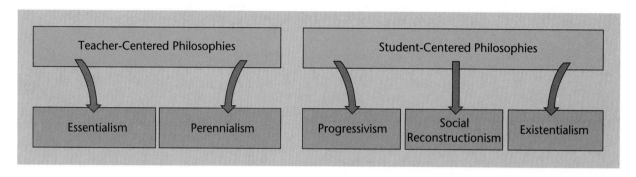

REFLECTION: Check back with your scores on the Inventory of Philosophies in Education (p. 329). Now consider your scores in terms of teacher- or student-centered philosophies. What does this tell you about your own educational priorities?

TEACHING TIP
The coverage of five educational philosophies will integrate three focus questions.

FOCUS QUESTION 2–4
How do teacher-centered philosophies of education differ from student-centered philosophies of education? What are some major philosophies of education in the United States today? How are these philosophies reflected in school practices?

educational philosophy. Conservatives often champion teacher-centered philosophies and practices that emphasize the values and knowledge that have survived through time, while liberals find student-centered approaches more to their liking. (See Figure 9.1).

Let's begin our discussion with the teacher-centered philosophies, for they have exerted significant influence on American education during the past two decades.

 Teacher-Centered Philosophies

Traditionally, **teacher-centered philosophies** emphasize the importance of transferring knowledge, information, and skills from the older (presumably wiser) generation to the younger one. The teacher's role is to instill respect for authority, perseverance, duty, consideration, and practicality. When students demonstrate through tests and writings that they are competent in academic subjects and traditional skills, and through their actions that they have disciplined minds and adhere to traditional morals and behavior, then both the school and the teacher have been successful. (If you recall from Chapter 4, "Schools: Choices and Challenges," these philosophies view the primary purpose of schools as "passing the cultural baton.") The major teacher-centered philosophies of education are essentialism and perennialism.

Essentialism

OVERHEAD 99
Essentialism

Essentialism strives to teach students the accumulated knowledge of our civilization through core courses in the traditional academic disciplines. Essentialists aim to instill students with the "essentials" of academic knowledge, patriotism, and character development. This traditional or **back-to-basics** approach is meant to train the mind, promote reasoning, and ensure a common culture among all Americans.

American educator **William Bagley** popularized the term *essentialism* in the 1930s,[1] and essentialism has been a dominant influence in American education since World War II. Factors such as the launching of *Sputnik* in 1957, the 1983 report *A Nation at Risk,* intense global economic competition and increased immigration into the United States have all kept essentialism at center stage. Some educators refer to the present period as **neoessentialism** because of the increased core graduation requirements, stronger standards and more testing of both students and teachers.

Whether they call themselves essentialists or neoessentialists, educators in this camp are concerned that the influx of immigrants threatens American culture. In response, they call for rigorous schools teaching a single, unifying body of knowledge for all Americans. One of the leading essentialists, **E. D. Hirsch, Jr.,** authored *Cultural Literacy: What Every American Needs To Know,* and *The Schools We Need and Why We Don't Have Them.* Hirsch provides lists of people, events, literature, historical facts, scientific breakthroughs and the like, lists that specify what students at every grade level should know to be "culturally literate."

Most of you reading this chapter have been educated in essentialist schools. You were probably required to take many courses in English, history, math, and science, but were able to enroll in only a few electives. Such a program would be typical in an essentialist school.

The Essentialist Classroom   Essentialists urge that traditional disciplines such as math, science, history, foreign language, and literature form the foundation of the curriculum, which is referred to as the **core curriculum.** Essentialists frown upon electives that "water-down" academic content. Elementary students receive instruction in skills such as writing, reading, measuring, and computing. Even when studying art and music, subjects most often associated with the development of creativity, students master a body of information and basic techniques, gradually moving to more complex skills and detailed knowledge. Only by mastering the required material are students promoted to the next higher level.

RAP 3.5
What You See and What
You Get, p. 432

VIDEO SEGMENT 23
Essentialism in Action

Essentialists maintain that classrooms should be oriented around the teacher, who should serve as an intellectual and moral role model for the students. The teachers or administrators decide what is most important for the students to learn and place little emphasis on student interests, particularly when such interests divert time and attention from the academic curriculum. Essentialist teachers rely on achievement test scores to evaluate progress. Essentialists expect that students will leave school possessing not only basic skills and an extensive body of knowledge, but also disciplined, practical minds, capable of applying schoolhouse lessons in the real world.

Essentialism in Action: The Coalition of Essential Schools   The **Coalition of Essential Schools,** headed by Theodore Sizer, offers several tangible examples of essentialism in action. The 200 coalition schools pledge to promote intellectual rigor, test students for mastery of information and skills, have teachers and students work closely together, and develop strong thinking skills across subjects. But is the Coalition of Essential Schools purely essentialist? Not entirely. Coalition schools recognize and promote individual student differences, a clear departure from a strict essentialist interpretation. In fact, schools in the coalition do not share a fixed core curriculum, but each school continually analyzes and can alter core contents. The coalition also stresses "less is more," since Sizer believes that teachers and students should focus on fewer topics, but go into them more deeply. In fact, these essential schools also incorporate components of perennialism, which happens to be the next teacher-centered philosophy that we will discuss.

Perennialism

Perennialism is a cousin to essentialism. Both advocate teacher-centered classrooms. Both tolerate little flexibility in the curriculum. Both implement rigorous standards.

OVERHEAD 100
Perennialism

CLASS ACTIVITY: GREAT
BOOKS IN EVERY
PHILOSOPHY
IM, Activity 9:5

Both aim to sharpen students' intellectual powers and enhance their moral qualities. So what are the differences?

Perennialists organize their schools around books, ideas and concepts, and criticize essentialists for the vast amount of factual information they require students to absorb in their push for "cultural literacy." Perennial means "everlasting"—a perennialist education focuses on enduring themes and questions that span the ages. Perennialists recommend that students learn directly from the **Great Books**—works by history's finest thinkers and writers, books as meaningful today as when they were first written.

Perennialists believe that the goal of education should be to develop rational thought and to discipline minds to think rigorously. Perennialists see education as a sorting mechanism, a way to identify and prepare the intellectually gifted for leadership, while providing vocational training for the rest of society. They lament the change in universities over the centuries, from institutions where a few gifted students (and teachers) rigorously pursued truth for its own sake, to a glorified training ground for future careers.

Those of you who received a religious education might recognize the perennialist philosophy. Many parochial schools reflect the perennialist tradition with a curriculum that focuses on analyzing great religious books (such as the *Bible, Talmud,* or *Koran*), discerning moral truths, and honoring these moral values. In the classroom description that follows, we will concentrate on secular perennialism as formulated in the twentieth-century United States by such individuals as Robert Hutchins and Mortimer Adler.

The Perennialist Classroom As in an essentialist classroom, students in a perennialist classroom spend considerable time and energy mastering the three "Rs," reading, 'riting and 'rithmetic. Greatest importance is placed on reading, the key to unlocking the enduring ideas found in the Great Books. Special attention is given to teaching values and character training, often through discussion about the underlying values and moral principles in a story. (Former Secretary of Education Bill Bennett wrote a collection of such stories in 1993, entitled *Book of Virtues*.) High school marks an increase in academic rigor as more challenging books are explored, including works of Darwin, Homer, and Shakespeare. Few elective choices are allowed. In an extreme example, in his ***Paideia Proposal,*** published in 1982, **Mortimer Adler** proposed a single elementary and secondary curriculum for all students, with no curricular electives except in the choice of a second language.

Electives are not the only things perennialists go without. You find few if any textbooks in a perennialist class. **Robert Hutchins,** who as president of the University of Chicago introduced the Great Books program, once opined that textbooks "have probably done as much to degrade the American intelligence as any single force."[2] Because perennialist teachers see themselves as discussion seminar leaders and facilitators, lectures are rare. Current concerns like multiculturalism, gender stereotypes, or computer technology would find no place in a perennialist curriculum.

While critics chastise perennialists for the lack of women, people of color, and non-Western ideas in the Great Books they teach, perennialists are unmoved by such criticism. To them, "training the mind" is ageless, beyond demographic concerns and transient trends. As Mortimer Adler wrote,

> The Great Books of ancient and medieval as well as modern times are a repository of knowledge and wisdom, a tradition of culture which must initiate each generation.[3]

While both essentialism and perennialism promote a conservative, status quo approach to education and schools, these teacher-centered philosophies draw their curricula from different sources. The first column includes excerpts from a typical essentialist list (we included a few of the words and phrases under the letter "c"); the second column provides selections from the perennialists' *Great Books* curriculum. Remember, these are only a few suggestions from very long lists!

The List

centigrade	Calvary
center of gravity	cast pearls before swine
cerebellum	Cascade Mountains
carry coals to Newcastle	cadre
capital expenditure	catharsis
Cèzanne	carbon dioxide
Canberra	carte blanche
Cain and Abel	Caruso, Enrico
Caesar Augustus	cathode ray tube
Candide	

Great Books

Aristotle, *Sense and Sensible*

The Bible

Geoffrey Chaucer, *Canterbury Tales*

Charles Darwin, *On the Origin of Species*

Charles Dickens, *Oliver Twist*

F. Scott Fitzgerald, *The Great Gatsby*

Homer, *The Iliad*

Henry James, *In the Cage*

James Joyce, *Ulysses*

The Koran

Thomas Mann, *Death in Venice*

Karl Marx, *Das Kapital*

Herman Melville, *Moby Dick*

George Orwell, *Animal Farm*

Thomas Paine, *Common Sense*

Plato, *Charmides*

Jonathan Swift, *Gulliver's Travels*

Virginia Woolf, *Night and Day*

Leo Tolstoy, *War and Peace*

REFLECTION: How many of these names and terms can you identify? Does this list make you feel culturally literate—or illiterate? Do you believe that lists like this one should be important? Why or why not?

Perennialism in Action: St. John's College The best-known example of perennialist education today takes place at a private institution unaffiliated with any religion: St. John's College, founded in 1784 in Annapolis, Maryland (www.sjcsf.edu). St. John's College adopted the Great Books as a core curriculum in 1937 and assigns readings in the fields of literature, philosophy and theology, history and the social sciences, mathematics and natural science, and music. Students write extensively and attend seminars twice weekly to discuss assigned readings. They also complete a number of laboratory experiences and tutorials in language, mathematics, and music, guided by the faculty, who are called *tutors*. Seniors take oral examinations at the beginning and end of their senior year and write a final essay that must be approved before they are allowed to graduate.

Although grades are given in order to facilitate admission to graduate programs, students receive their grades only upon request and are expected to learn only for learning's sake. Since the St. John's experience thrives best in a small-group atmosphere, the college established a second campus in 1964 in Santa Fe, New Mexico to handle additional enrollment.

 ## Student-Centered Philosophies

Student-centered philosophies are less authoritarian, less concerned with the past and "training the mind," and more focused on individual needs, contemporary relevance, and preparing students for a changing future. Progressivism, social reconstructionism, and existentialism place the learner at the center of the educational process: Students and teachers work together on determining what should be learned and how best to learn it. School is not seen as an institution that controls and directs

RELATED READING
The View from Saturday by E. L. Konigsburg (1998).

Teacher-Centered Approaches Are Best Because . . .

AFTER CENTURIES OF EXPERIENCE, WE KNOW WHAT TO TEACH

From Plato to Orwell, great writers and thinkers of the past light our way into the future. We must pass our cherished cultural legacy onto the next generation.

TEACHERS MUST SELECT WHAT IS WORTH KNOWING

The knowledge explosion showers us with mountains of new, complex information on a daily basis. Selecting what students should learn is a daunting challenge. Teachers, not students, are trained and best equipped to determine what is of value. To ask students to choose what they should learn would be the height of irresponsibility.

SCHOOLS MUST BE INSULATED FROM EXTERNAL DISTRACTIONS

Students can be easily distracted by the "excitement" of contemporary events. While academic and rigorous school-based learning may be less flashy and less appealing, in the long run, it is far more valuable. Once schoolwork has been mastered, students will be well prepared to leave the sanctuary of learning and confront the outside world.

WE ARE FALLING BEHIND OTHER NATIONS

U.S. student performance on international tests lags behind that of students from other nations. We have grown "educationally soft," lacking the challenging teacher-centered curriculums that other nations use. Only by creating a tough and demanding curriculum can we hope to compete with other nations.

COMPETITION AND REWARDS ARE IMPORTANT FOR MOTIVATING LEARNERS

Most people want and need to be recognized for their effort. Students are motivated to earn good report card grades and academic honors, to "ace" the SATs and be admitted to a prestigious college. Competition to earn high grades is the engine that drives successful school performance. Competition and rewards also drive the nation's productive workforce.

Student-Centered Approaches Are Best Because . . .

GENUINE LEARNING ORIGINATES WITH THE LEARNER

People learn best what they want to learn, what they feel they should or need to learn. Students find lessons imposed "from above" to be mostly irrelevant, and the lessons are quickly forgotten.

THEY BEST PREPARE STUDENTS FOR THE INFORMATION AGE

The knowledge explosion is actually a powerful argument for student-directed learning. Teachers can't possibly teach everything. We must equip students with research skills, then fan the flames of curiosity so they will want to learn for themselves. Then students can navigate the information age, finding and evaluating new information.

EDUCATION IS A VITAL AND ORGANIC PART OF SOCIETY

The most important lessons of life are found not on the pages of books or behind the walls of a school, but in the real world. Students need to work and learn directly in the community, from cleaning up the environment to reducing violence. Social action projects and service learning can offer a beacon of hope for the community, while building compassionate values within our students.

MULTIPLE CHOICE TESTS ARE NOT AN OLYMPIC EVENT

Education is not a competition, and academic tests are not a new Olympic event where youngsters have to get the highest score to please the cheering crowd. National success will come from living up to our beliefs, not "beating" the children of some other nation on a multiple choice test.

MEANINGFUL REWARDS DO NOT COME FROM ACADEMIC COMPETITIONS

Grades, funny stickers, and social approval are poor sources of motivation. Authentic learning rests on a more solid foundation: intrinsic motivation. Real success comes from an inner drive, not from artificial rewards. Schools need to develop students' inner motivation and stress student cooperation, not competition.

continued

Teacher-Centered Approaches Are Best Because . . .

DISCIPLINED MINDS, RESPECTFUL CITIZENS

Students who listen thoughtfully and participate respectfully in classroom discussions learn several important lessons. For one, they learn the worth and wisdom of Western culture. They also learn to appreciate and to honor those who brought them this heritage, the guardians of their freedom and culture: their teachers.

Student-Centered Approaches Are Best Because . . .

HUMAN DIGNITY IS LEARNED IN DEMOCRATIC CLASSROOMS

Democracy is learned through experience, not books. Students flourish when they are respected; they are stifled when they are told what and how to think. As students manage their own learning, they master the most important lesson any school can teach: the importance of the individual's ideas.

 YOU BE THE JUDGE

Do you find yourself influenced more by the arguments supporting teacher-centered approaches, or those advocating student-centered approaches? Are there elements of each that you find appealing? How will your classroom practices reflect your philosophy?

---

youth, or works to preserve and transmit the core culture, but as an institution that works with youth to improve society or help students realize their individuality.

Progressivism

Progressivism organizes schools around the concerns, curiosity, and real-world experiences of students. The progressive teacher facilitates learning by helping students formulate meaningful questions and devise strategies to answer those questions. Answers are not drawn from lists or even Great Books; they are discovered through real world experience. Progressivism is the educational application of a philosophy called pragmatism. According to **pragmatism,** the way to determine if an idea has merit is simple: test it. If the idea works in the real world, then it has merit. Both pragmatism and progressivism originated in America, the home of a very practical and pragmatic people. John Dewey refined and applied pragmatism to education, establishing what became known as progressivism.

John Dewey was a reformer with a background in philosophy and psychology who taught that people learn best through social interaction in the real world. Dewey believed that because social learning had meaning, it endured. Book learning, on the other hand, was no substitute for actually doing things. Progressivists do not believe that the mind can be disciplined through reading Great Books, rather that the mind should be trained to analyze experience thoughtfully and draw conclusions objectively.

Dewey saw education as an opportunity to learn how to apply previous experiences in new ways. Dewey believed that students, facing an ever-changing world, should master the scientific method: (1) Become aware of a problem; (2) define it; (3) propose various hypotheses to solve it; (4) examine the consequences of each hypothesis in the light of previous experience; and (5) test the most likely solution. (For a biography of John Dewey, see the Hall of Fame: Profiles in Education in Chapter 8.)

Dewey regarded democracy and freedom as far superior to the political ideas of earlier times. Dewey saw traditional, autocratic, teacher-centered schools as the

OVERHEAD 101
Progressivism

antithesis of democratic ideals. He viewed progressive schools as a working model of democracy. Dewey wrote:

> To imposition from above is opposed expression and cultivation of individuality; to external discipline is opposed free activity; to learning from texts and teachers, learning through experience; to acquisition of isolated skills and techniques by drill is opposed acquisition of them as means of attaining ends which make direct vital appeal; to preparation for a more or less remote future is opposed making the most of the opportunities of present life; to statistics and materials is opposed acquaintance with a changing world.[4]

The Progressive Classroom Walk into a progressivist classroom, and you will not find a teacher standing at the front of the room talking to rows of seated students. Rather, you will likely see children working in small groups, moving about and talking freely. Some children might be discussing a science experiment, while another group works on a model volcano, and a third prepares for a presentation. Interest centers would be located throughout the room, filled with books, materials, software, and projects designed to attract student interest on a wide array of topics. Finally you notice the teacher, walking around the room, bending over to talk with individual students and small groups, asking questions and making suggestions. You sense that the last thing on her mind is the standardized state test scheduled for next week.[5]

VIDEO SEGMENT 24
Progressivism in Action

Progressivists build the curriculum around the experiences, interests, and abilities of students, and encourage students to work together cooperatively. Teachers feel no compulsion to focus their students' attention on one discrete discipline at a time, and students integrate several subjects in their studies. Thought-provoking activities augment reading, and a game like Monopoly might be used to illustrate the principles of capitalism versus socialism. Computer simulations, field trips, and interactive websites on the Internet offer realistic learning challenges for students, and build on students' multiple intelligences.

Progressivism in Action: The Laboratory School In 1896, while a professor at the University of Chicago, Dewey founded the Laboratory School as a testing ground for his educational ideas. Dewey's writings and his work with the **Laboratory School** set the stage for the progressive education movement. Based on the view that educators, like scientists, need a place to test their ideas, Dewey's Laboratory School eventually became the most famous experimental school in the history of U.S. education, a place where thousands observed Dewey's innovations in school design, methods, and curriculum. Although the school remained under Dewey's control for only eight years and never enrolled more than 140 students (ages 3 to 13) in a single year, its influence was enormous.

Dewey designed the Lab School with only one classroom but with several facilities for experiential learning: a science laboratory, an art room, a woodworking shop, and a kitchen. Children were likely to make their own weights and measures in the laboratory, illustrate their own stories in the art room, build a boat in the shop, and learn chemistry in the kitchen. They were unlikely to learn through isolated exercises or drills, which, according to Dewey, students consider irrelevant. Since Dewey believed that students learn from social interaction, the school used many group methods such as cooperative model-making, field trips, role playing, and dramatizations. Dewey maintained that group techniques make the students better citizens, developing, for example, their willingness to share responsibilities.

Children in the Laboratory School were not promoted from one grade to another after mastering certain material. Rather, they were grouped according to their individual interests and abilities. For all its child-centered orientation, however, the Laboratory School remained hierarchical in the sense that the students were never given a role comparable to that of the staff in determining the school's educational practices.

Social Reconstructionism

Social reconstructionism encourages schools, teachers, and students to focus their studies and energies on alleviating pervasive social inequities, and as the name implies, reconstruct society into a new and more just social order. Although social reconstructionists agree with progressivists that schools should concentrate on the needs of students, they split from progressivism in the 1920s after growing impatient with the slow pace of change in schools and in society. **George Counts,** a student of Dewey, published his classic book, *Dare the Schools Build a New Social Order?*, in which he outlined a more ambitious, and clearly more radical, approach to education. Counts's book, written in 1932, was no doubt influenced by the human cost of the Great Depression. He proposed that schools focus on reforming society, an idea that caught the imagination and sparked the ideals of educators both in this country and abroad.

Social challenges and problems provide a natural (and moral) direction for curricular and instructional activities. Racism, sexism, environmental pollution, homelessness, poverty, substance abuse, homophobia, AIDS and violence are rooted in misinformation and thrive in ignorance. Therefore, social reconstructionists believe that school is the ideal place to begin ameliorating social problems. The teacher's role is to explore social problems, suggest alternate perspectives, and facilitate student analysis of these problems. While convincing, cajoling, or moralizing about the importance of addressing human tragedy would be a natural teacher response, such adult-led decision-making flies in the face of reconstructionist philosophy. A social reconstructionist teacher must model democratic principles. Students and teachers are expected to live and learn in a democratic culture; the students themselves must select educational objectives and social priorities.

The Social Reconstructionist Classroom A social reconstructionist teacher creates lessons that both intellectually inform and emotionally stir students about the inequities that surround them. A class might read a book and visit a photojournalist's exhibit portraying violent acts of racism. If the book, exhibit and the class discussion that follows move the students, the class might choose to pursue a long-term project to investigate the problem. One group of students might analyze news coverage of racial and ethnic groups in the community. Another student group might conduct a survey analyzing community perceptions of racial groups and race relations. Students might visit city hall and examine arrest and trial records in order to determine the role race plays in differential application of the law. Students might examine government records for information about housing patterns, income levels, graduation rates and other relevant statistics. The teacher's role would be as facilitator: assisting students in focusing their questions, developing a strategy, helping to organize visits, and ensuring that the data collected and analyzed meet standards of objectivity. Throughout, the teacher would be instructing students on research techniques, statistical evaluation, writing skills, and public communications.

OVERHEAD 102
Social Reconstructionism

GLOBAL VIEW
The Council on Global Education is dedicated to the development of a new model of education for the child in the 21st century. Its four building blocks are universal values, global understanding, excellence in all things, and service to humanity. www.globaleducation.org

"Domephobia," the fear of things domestic, is Jane Roland Martin's word for gender bias in schools and in society. She coined the term when she compared the distinct educations Jean-Jacques Rousseau designed for his fictitious students Emile and Sophie. Martin was frustrated that while the boy, Emile, was said to revel in intellectual exploration, Sophie was to receive second-rate training—to be a wife and mother.

Martin deplores the disconnect between intellectual development and the development of abilities to love and care for a family. She recognizes that today's schools continue to craft different expectations for males and females. In fact, she knows this inequity firsthand. Teaching philosophy at the University of Massachusetts at Boston for over thirty years, Martin found herself fighting to have her intellectual voice heard in a traditional male discipline. Her experience of bias fueled her anger that equal opportunity education is still so far from reality.

Yet, Jane Roland Martin knows "women are barometers of change." Feminism today, like Sophie's education 300 years ago, gives men and women a special gift—a new perspective on gender roles. At the dawn of a new millennium, women's roles at work and in the family are indeed changing. Not only are women wives and mothers, they are corporate CEOs, medal-winning soccer players, and Supreme Court justices. Yet even as society may

champion the greater earning power and talents of women, we are seeing a backlash against the more liberated roles of women. The trouble? The changes have cast as fiction the rosy Norman Rockwell portrait of the American family: More than half of all mothers work outside the home and single-parent homes number 1 in 5. These numbers stir concern that day care is bad, working mothers are neglectful and the well-being of the nation's children is threatened.

What society may see as problematic, Jane Roland Martin envisions as opportunity. Historically the physical, emotional, and social needs of children have been met by family, primarily mothers. Today, women are drawn by economic need and personal desire to enter the workforce. Martin sees these changes as a defining moment for schools, a chance to recreate within schools the nurturing tasks traditionally performed at home.

Martin's critics say no, schools should focus only on intellectual development. Not Martin. A social reconstructionist, she challenges schools to open their doors to what she calls the 3Cs—caring, concern, and connection. As more children are cared for outside the home, she fears the 3C curriculum is in danger of being lost. And American society has paid a heavy price for ignoring such domestic needs. Social inequalities continue and children are often the victims. Martin has an antidote: transform schoolhouses into "schoolhomes."

The schoolhome is far different from traditional "factory-model schooling which views children as raw material, teachers as workers who process their students before sending them on to the next station on the assembly line, [and] curriculum as the machinery that forges America's young into marketable products."[1] Instead, Martin's schoolhome focuses on students' individual

emotional and cognitive needs. It embraces the experience of all learners and welcomes racial, cultural, and gender diversity. Martin's vision of schools reflects her vision of American society as everyone's home:

> Instead of focusing our gaze on abstract norms, standardized tests, generalized rates of success and uniform outcomes, the ideas of the schoolhome direct action to actual educational practice. Of course a schoolhome will teach the 3Rs. But it will give equal emphasis to the 3Cs—not by designating formal courses in these but by being a domestic environment characterized by safety, security, nurturance and love. In the schoolhome, mind and body, thought and action, reason and emotion are all educated.[2]

The schoolhome will incorporate the 3Cs into our very definition of what it means for males and females to be educated. Creating such nurturing and equitable schools will require "acts of both great and small, strategic and utterly outrageous. The cause demands no less, not one whit less."[3]

[1] Jane Roland Martin. *The Schoolhome: Rethinking Schools for Changing Families* (Cambridge, MA: Harvard University Press, 1992), p. 41. [2] Jane Roland Martin. "Women, School, and Cultural Wealth." In Connie Titone and Karen Maloney (eds.). *Thinking Through Our Mothers: Women's Philosophies of Education* (Upper Saddle River, NJ: Merrill, 1999), pp.161–62. [3] Jane Roland Martin. *Coming of Age in Academe: Rekindling Women's Hopes and Reforming the Academy* (New York: Routlege, 2000), p. 182.

REFLECTION: Do you agree with Jane Roland Martin that the 3Cs should be an integral part of the curriculum? Explain. Describe what a 3C curriculum might look like in schools today.

www.mhhe.com/ sadker To learn more about Jane Roland Martin, click on *Profiles in Education.*

In a social reconstructionist class, a research project is more than an academic exercise; the class is engaged in a genuine effort to improve society. In this case, the class might arrange to meet with political leaders, encouraging them to create programs or legislation to respond to issues the students uncovered. The students might seek a *pro bono* attorney to initiate legal action to remedy a social injustice they unmasked. Or perhaps the students might take their findings directly to the media by holding a press conference. They might also create a Web page to share their findings and research methods with students in other parts of the country, or other parts of the world. How would the teacher decide if the students have met the educational goals? In this example, an objective, well-prepared report would be one criterion, and reducing or eliminating a racist community practice would be a second measure of success.

Social Reconstructionism in Action: Paulo Freire **Paulo Freire** believed that schools were just another institution perpetuating social inequities while serving the interests of the dominant group. Like social reconstructionism itself, Freire's beliefs grew during the Great Depression of the 1930s, when he experienced hunger and poverty firsthand. Influenced by Marxist and neo-Marxist ideas, Freire accused schools of perpetuating the status quo views of the rich and powerful "for the purpose of keeping the masses submerged and content in a culture of silence."[6] Schools were endorsing **social Darwinism,** the idea that society is an ingenious "sorting" system, one in which the more talented rise to the top, while those less deserving find themselves at the bottom of the social and economic pecking order. The conclusion: Those with money deserve it, those without money deserve their lot in life, and poverty is a normal, preordained part of reality.

Freire rejected this conclusion. He did not believe that schools should be viewed as "banks," where the privileged deposit ideas like social Darwinism to be spoon fed into the limited minds of the dispossessed. He envisioned schools as a place where the poor can acquire the skills to regain control of their lives and influence the social and economic forces that locked them in poverty in the first place. Freire engaged the poor as equal partners in dialogues that explored their economic and social problems and possible solutions. Freire believed in **praxis,** the doctrine that when actions are based on sound theory and values, they can make a real difference in the world. (It is no accident that the term praxis is also the name given to the teacher competency tests required by many states.) Freire's ideas took hold not only in his native Brazil, but in poor areas around the globe. As poor farm workers became literate and aware, they organized for their self-improvement, and began to work for change. It is not surprising that the autocratic leaders of his country eventually forced him into exile, for he had turned schooling into a liberating force. (For a biography of Paulo Freire, see the Hall of Fame: Profiles in Education in Chapter 8.)

Existentialism

Existentialism, the final student-centered philosophy we will discuss, places the highest degree of importance on student perceptions, decisions, and actions. **Existentialism** rejects the existence of any source of objective, authoritative truth other than the individual. Individuals are responsible for determining for themselves what is true or false, right or wrong, beautiful or ugly. In short, it is up to the student to make all relevant educational decisions, and to evaluate those decisions.

Noted philosopher **Jean-Paul Sartre**'s (1905–1980) classic formulation of existentialism is "existence precedes essence." What does this mean? One interpretation

OVERHEAD 103
Existentialism

CLASS ACTIVITY:
OBSERVATION
IM, Activity 9:2

TABLE 9.1
Five philosophies of education.

	Underlying Basis: Metaphysics	Underlying Basis: Epistemology	Focus of Curriculum	Sample Classroom Activity	Role of Teacher	Goals for Students	Educational Leaders
Student-Centered Philosophies							
Progressivism	The physical world is the basis of reality; the world inevitably progresses over time	We learn best from meaningful life experiences, social interaction, and scientific experimentation	Flexible; integrated study of academic subjects around the needs, and experiences of students	Learning by doing—for example, students plan a field trip to learn about history, geography, and natural science	Guide and integrate learning activities so that students can find meaning	To become intelligent problem solvers, socially aware citizens who are prepared to live comfortably in the world	John Dewey, Nel Noddings
Social Reconstructionism	The physical world is the basis of reality; world progresses, but slowly	We learn best from meaningful social experiences that improve society	Focus on social, political, and economic needs; integrated study of academic subjects around socially meaningful actions	Learning by reconstructing society—for example, students work to remove health hazards in a building housing the poor	Provide authentic learning activities that both instruct students and improve society	To become intelligent problem solvers, to enjoy learning, to live comfortably in the world while also helping reshape it	George S. Counts, John Brameld, Jane Roland Martin
Existentialism	Reality is individually determined; people shape their innermost nature in accordance with their free will	Each individual determines learning strategies; learning engages emotional as well as intellectual faculties	Each student determines the pace and direction of his or her own learning	Students choose their preferred medium—such as poetry, prose, or painting—and evaluate their own performance	One who seeks to relate to each student honestly; skilled at creating a free, open, and stimulating environment	To accept personal responsibility; to understand deeply and be at peace with one's own unique individuality	A. S. Neill, Maxine Greene

goes as follows: We did not ask to be born into this world; so we "exist" before we are anything. We also are powerless at the other end of the life cycle, when we die. In between those two uncontrollable events, we shape our essence.

Existentialists believe that each person needs to define life's meaning. To become an authentic individual, one who values and practices free choice, we must struggle free of the influences of our parents, teachers, schools, religion, and culture. Existentialists

TABLE 9.1
(concluded)

	Underlying Basis: Metaphysics	Underlying Basis: Epistemology	Focus of Curriculum	Sample Classroom Activity	Role of Teacher	Goals for Students	Educational Leaders
Teacher-Centered Philosophies							
Essentialism	The physical world is the basis of reality	We learn through reasoning, primarily empirical reasoning	Core curriculum of traditional academic topics and traditional American virtues	Teacher focuses on "essential" information or the development of particular skills	Model of academic and moral virtue; center of classroom	To become culturally literate individuals, model citizens educated to compete in the world	William Bagley, E. D. Hirsch, Jr., William Bennett
Perennialism	The realm of thought and spirit rooted in the physical world; all human beings are by nature rational animals	We learn through reasoning—particularly through creative, deep, and logical analysis	Core curriculum analyzing enduring ideas found in Great Books	Socratic dialogue analyzing a philosophical issue or the meaning of a great work of literature	Scholarly role model; philosophically oriented, helps students seek the truth for themselves	To increase their intellectual powers and to appreciate learning for its own sake	Robert Hutchins, Mortimer Adler

REFLECTION: How many of these philosophies have you experienced in your own education? Describe the circumstances. Would you like to encounter others as a student? a teacher? Explain.

believe education should be about helping each of us answer the fundamental questions: Why am I here? What is my purpose?

The Existentialist Classroom   Existentialism in the classroom is a powerful rejection of traditional, and particularly essentialist thinking. In the existentialist classroom, subject matter takes second place to helping the students understand and appreciate themselves as unique individuals. The teacher's role is to help students define their own essence by exposing them to various paths they may take in life and by creating an environment in which they can freely choose their way. Existentialism, more than other educational philosophies, affords students great latitude in their choice of subject matter and activity.

The existentialist curriculum often emphasizes the humanities as a means of providing students with vicarious experiences that will help unleash their creativity and self-expression. For example, existentialists focus on the actions of historical individuals, each of whom provides a model for the students to explore. Math and the

YESTERDAY'S VOICES

William Bagley (1874–1946) *Essentialism* Bagley believed that the major role of the school is to produce a literate, intelligent electorate; argued against electives while stressing thinking skills to help students apply their academic knowledge.

Robert M. Hutchins (1899–1979) *Perennialism* During the sixteen years he served as president of the University of Chicago, Hutchins abolished fraternities, football, and compulsory attendance, and introduced the Great Books program.

John Dewey (1859–1952) *Progressivism* A founder of progressivism, Dewey not only worked to democratize schools, he also fought for women's suffrage and the right of teachers to form unions.

George S. Counts (1907–1974) *Social Reconstructionism* Counts viewed education as an important tool to counter social injustices, and, if educators questioned their own power to make critical decisions, Counts's plea was to "Just do it!"

A. S. Neill (1883–1973) *Existentialism* Neill's attitude toward education stemmed from his own problems as a student, problems which fueled his creation of Summerhill, a school that encouraged youngsters to make their own decisions about what and when to learn.

TODAY'S VOICES

E. D. Hirsch, Jr. (1928–) *Essentialism* He established the Core Knowledge Foundation to develop a prescribed curriculum in subject areas, including technology. Visit your local bookstore and browse through his books delineating what educated people should know.

Mortimer Adler (1902–2001) *Perennialism* He renewed interest in perennialism with the publication of *The Paideia Proposal* (1982). Adler advocated that all students be educated in the classics and that education be a lifelong venture.

Nel Noddings (1929–) *Progressivism* She believes that an ethic of care can best be cultivated when the curriculum is centered around the interests of students. Schools are challenged to nourish the physical, spiritual, occupational, and intellectual development of each child.

bell hooks (1952–) *Social Reconstructionism* Her theory of education, *engaged pedagogy*, helps students and teachers develop a critical consciousness of race, gender, and class biases. A prolific writer, her books include *Ain't I a Woman: Black Women and Feminism* (1981) and *Teaching to Transgress: Education as the Practice of Freedom* (1994).

Maxine Greene (1917–) *Existentialism* She believes that it is crucial for students and teachers to create meaning in their lives. Greene sees the humanities and the arts as catalysts for moving people to critical awareness and conscious engagement with the world.

REFLECTION: The ideas of Dewey and Counts were particularly popular in the 1930s, 1960s, and 1970s, while the teacher-centered philosophies were popular in the other decades of the twentieth century. Existentialism drew a few influential supporters, but never many adherents. How did historical events during the twentieth century influence which of these voices were heard?

REFLECTION: How do these spokespersons reflect current political trends? Which voices are being heard in public policy circles today, and which are not? Why is this the case?

natural sciences may be de-emphasized because their subject matter is less fruitful for promoting self-awareness. Career education is regarded more as a means of teaching students about their potential than of teaching a livelihood. In art, existentialism encourages individual creativity and imagination more than it does the imitation of established models.

Existentialist learning is self-paced, self-directed, and includes a great deal of individual contact with the teacher. Honest interpersonal relationships are emphasized; roles and "official" status de-emphasized. According to philosopher Maxine Greene, teachers themselves must be deeply involved in their own learning and questioning: "Only a teacher in search of his freedom can inspire a student to search for his own." Greene asserts that education should move teachers and students to "wide awakeness," the ability to discover their own truths.[7]

Although elements of existentialism occasionally appear in public schools, this philosophy has not been widely disseminated. In an age of high-stakes tests and standards, only a few schools, mostly private, implement existentialist ideas. Even Summerhill, the well-known existentialist school founded in England by **A. S. Neill** in 1921, struggles to persevere with its unusual educational approach.

Existentialism in Action: The Sudbury Valley School Visit Sudbury Valley School just outside of Boston, Massachusetts, look around, look closely, and you still may not see the school. The large building nestled next to a fishing pond on a ten-acre campus looks more like a mansion than a school. Walk inside, and you will find students and adults doing pretty much as they please. Not a "class" in sight. Some people are talking, some playing, some reading. A group is building a bookcase over there, a student is working on the computer in the corner, another is taking a nap on a chair. All ages mix freely, with no discernable grade level for any activity. In fact, it is even difficult to locate the teachers. If there is a curriculum, it is difficult to detect. Instead, the school offers a wide variety of educational options, including field trips to Boston, New York, and the nearby mountains and seacoast, and the use of facilities that include a laboratory, a woodworking shop, a computer room, a kitchen, a darkroom, an art room, and several music rooms.

Sudbury Valley provides a setting, an opportunity, but each student must decide what to do with that opportunity. Students are trusted to make their own decisions about learning. The school's purpose is to build on the students' natural curiosity, based on the belief that authentic learning takes place only when students initiate it. The school operates on the premise that all its students are creative, and each should be helped to discover and nurture his or her individual talents.

Sudbury Valley is fully accredited, and the majority of Sudbury Valley's graduates have continued on to college. The school accepts anyone from 4-year-olds to adults and charges low tuition, so as not to exclude anyone. Evaluations or grades are given only on request. A high school diploma is awarded to those who complete relevant requirements, which mainly focus on the ability to be a responsible member of the community at large.

Psychological Influences on Education

FOCUS QUESTION 5
What are some of the psychological and cultural factors influencing education?

While essentialism, perennialism, progressivism, social reconstructionism, and existentialism are influential philosophies of education, they are far from the only forces shaping today's schools. Teachers who take their profession seriously pay attention to work in other fields, such as psychology, and may modify their teaching based on

Each of these photographs reflects a major tenet of the five educational philosophies described in this chapter. See if you can match the picture with the philosophy it best represents.

A

B

C

D

E

models proposed there. The following descriptions offer a glimpse into some of these forces guiding current school practices.

Constructivism

Constructivism, like existentialism, puts the learner at the center of the educational stage. **Constructivism** asserts that knowledge cannot be handed from one person to another (from a teacher to a learner), but must be *constructed* by each learner through interpreting and reinterpreting a constant flow of information. Constructivists believe that people continually try to make sense and bring order to the world.

Built on the work of Swiss and Russian psychologists, Jean Piaget and Lev Vygotsky, constructivism reflects the cognitive psychologists' view that the essence of learning is the constant effort to assimilate new information. Let's take a brief spin in your car to see how this works. You are driving happily along the highway and don't you

OVERHEAD 104
Constructivism

know it—you hear an odd noise. No, it's not your passenger, it is coming from the engine. Just before panic sets in, you remember that your friend Karen mentioned that the air pressure looked low in your left front tire. You suspect that is causing the noise. You are doing just what a constructivist would expect you to do: looking for a pattern, a meaning to explain the noise. You step out of the car, look at the tires, but they all seem just fine. Now you need to figure out another explanation for the noise, another meaning. You open the hood, look around the engine, and find the fan belt waving wildly, hitting everything in sight. You back off, relieved that you have "learned" what is making the noise. You have reconstructed your thoughts based on new information. Next time you hear that noise, you might look first for that pesky fan belt. If that is not the problem, you will start the process again, and build more knowledge about what could go wrong in your car.

In a constructivist classroom, the teacher builds knowledge in much the same way, gauging a student's prior knowledge and understanding, then carefully orchestrating cues, penetrating questions, and instructional activities that challenge and extend a student's insight. Teachers can use **scaffolding,** that is, questions, clues or suggestions that help a student link prior knowledge to the new information. The educational challenges facing students in a constructivist classroom could be creating a new way to handle a math problem, letting go of an unfounded bias about an ethnic group, or discovering why women's contributions seem all but absent in a history textbook. In a constructivist classroom, students and teachers constantly challenge their own assumptions. (If you check back to the philosophy inventory, see how you responded to item 26, which captured this aspect of constructivism.)

While constructivism runs counter to the current emphasis on uniform standards and testing, it is enjoying popularity, especially among school reformers. Perhaps part of the reason for its growing acceptance is that constructivism dovetails with authentic learning, critical thinking, individualized instruction, and project-based learning, ideas popular in reform circles.

Behaviorism

OVERHEAD 105
Behaviorism

In stark contrast to both existentialism and constructivism, **behaviorism** is derived from the belief that free will is an illusion, and that human beings are shaped entirely by their environment. Alter a person's environment, and you will alter his or her thoughts, feelings, and behavior. People act in response to physical stimuli. We learn, for instance, to avoid overexposure to heat through the impulses of pain our nerves send to our brain. More complex learning, such as understanding the material in this chapter, is also determined by stimuli, such as the educational support you have received from your professor or parents and the comfort of the chair in which you sit when reading this chapter.

INTERACTIVE ACTIVITY

What Philosophy or Approach Is This? Read scenarios and match the philosophy or approach being exhibited.

Harvard professor **B. F. Skinner** became the leading advocate of behaviorism, and he did much to popularize the use of positive reinforcement to promote desired learning. (For a biography of B. F. Skinner, see the Hall of Fame: Profiles in Education in Chapter 8.) Behaviorists urge teachers to use a system of reinforcement to encourage desired behaviors, to connect learning with pleasure and reward (a smile, special privilege, or good grades). In a program termed **behavior modification,** extrinsic rewards are gradually lessened as the student acquires and masters the targeted behavior. By association, the desired behavior now produces its own reward (self-satisfaction). This process may take minutes, weeks, or years, depending on the complexity of the learning desired and on the past environment of the learner. The teacher's goal is to move the learner from extrinsic to intrinsic rewards. (If you check the inventory at the chapter's opening, behaviorism was represented by statement 27. How did you respond?)

Behavior modification is perhaps most commonly used to manage student behavior. One well-known program is **assertive discipline,** developed by Lee and Marlene Canter. "The key to assertive discipline is catching students being good, recognizing and supporting them when they behave appropriately, and letting them know you like it, day in and day out."[8]

Critics of behaviorism decry behaviorists' disbelief in the autonomy of the individual. They ask, Are people little more than selfish "reward machines"? Can clever forces manipulate populations through clever social engineering? Are educators qualified to exert such total control of students? Those who defend behaviorism point to its striking successes. Behaviorism's influence is apparent in the joy on students' faces as they receive visual and auditory rewards via their computer monitor, or in the classroom down the hall where special needs learners make significant progress in a behaviorist-designed curriculum.

CLASS ACTIVITY: SMALL GROUP ACTIVITY: DESIGNING A SCHOOL
IM, Activity 9:3

 ## Cultural Influences on Education

Most of the ideas and philosophies discussed in this chapter are drawn from Western culture. As a nation, we rarely identify or reflect on the ideas that derive from many parts of Asia, Africa, and Latin America. We are guilty of **ethnocentrism,** the tendency to view one's own culture as superior to others, and (perhaps worse) a failure to consider other cultures at all. Let's broaden our view, and examine education as practiced in other cultures.

In much of the West, society's needs dictate educational practices, with statewide standards, national goals, and high-stakes testing. In the rest of the world, that is to say, in most of the world, the child's education is primarily a concern of the family, not the society. A child's vocational interests, for example, might mirror the occupation of a parent or be built around the unique interest or talent of the child, rather than respond to the broader employment market or societal priorities. Family and community are foremost; the nation is a weaker influence.

In Western society, formal schools, formal certification and degrees are valued; in other societies, more credence is placed on actual knowledge and mastery rather than educational documentation. The notion of *teachers* and *nonteachers* is foreign in many cultures, since all adults and even older children participate in educating the young. Children learn adult roles through observation, conversation, assisting and imitating, all the while absorbing moral, intellectual, and vocational lessons. This shared educational responsibility is called **informal education.**[9] (What does calling this practice "informal education" reveal about Western values and assumptions? Would someone in a culture practicing this integrated education call it "informal education"?) In the process, adults also learn a great deal about the children in the community.

GLOBAL VIEW
S. G. Summer introduced the concept of *ethnocentrism* early in the 1900s. Culture tends to encompass national character/basic personality, perception, time and space concepts, thinking, language and nonverbal communication, values, behavior (norms, rules, manners), social groupings and relationships.
www.ic.intermundo.net

IN THE NEWS

Towards Enlightenment: Are Schools *Feng Shui*?

Décor makes a difference, at least that's what some researchers say about the link between school architecture and student achievement. As classroom daylight increases, so does student performance in math and reading. In windowless classrooms (typical of the energy efficient 70s and security conscious 90s) students experience a kind of jet lag, which contributes to a lag in academic success.

SOURCE: *The New York Times,* August 5, 2001.

 What's new in education? Click on *News Feeds.*

CRITICAL THINKING QUESTION

Many of your students are between the roles of children or parents. Who are the significant *noneducators* providing an *informal education* in their current world?

Strong bonds are forged between the generations. (As you probably already concluded, item 28 on our opening inventory describes informal education. You might want to check your answer to that statement.)

Oral traditions enjoy particular prominence in many parts of the world, even in literate societies where reading and writing are commonplace and valued. In the **oral tradition,** spoken language becomes a primary method for instruction: Word problems teach reasoning skills; proverbs instill wisdom; and stories, anecdotes, and rhymes teach lessons about nature, history, religion, and social customs. The oral tradition refines communication and analytical skills, and reinforces human connections and moral values. Not infrequently, religious and moral lessons were passed on initially through oral communication, only later to be written. In fact, the word Qur'an (Koran) is often translated as "the Recitation."

The practices and beliefs of peoples in other parts of the world offer useful insights for enhancing—or questioning—our own educational practices, but they are insights too rarely considered, much less implemented. Perhaps this will change in the years ahead as immigration continues to bring these ideas to our communities, while technological advances bring all world cultures closer together. For now, however, our education philosophies are rooted in the ideas and thoughts of Western thinkers. Let's visit some of these powerful thinkers and their influential, enduring contributions.

The Three Legendary Figures of Classical Western Philosophy

FOCUS QUESTION 6

What were the contributions of Socrates, Plato, and Aristotle to Western philosophy, and how is their legacy reflected in education today?

To understand Western philosophy, we must look back to the birthplace of Western philosophy—ancient Greece. Specifically, we must begin with a trio of philosopher-teachers: Socrates, Plato, and Aristotle. Together they laid the foundation for most of Western philosophy. It is likely that you are familiar with at least their names. Let's review their lasting contributions to the world of philosophy.

The name of **Socrates** is practically synonymous with wisdom and the philosophical life. Socrates (469–399 B.C.E.) was a teacher without a school. He walked about Athens, engaging people in provocative dialogues about questions of ultimate significance. Socrates is hailed as an exemplar of human virtue whose goal was to help others find the truths that lie within their own minds. In that regard, he described himself as a "midwife"; today we call his approach the **Socratic method.** By repeatedly questioning, disproving, and testing the thoughts of his pupils on such questions as the nature of "love" or "the good," he helped his students reach deeper, clearer ideas.

TEACHING TIP

Assist students to make learning connections to Socrates, Plato, and Aristotle. If the three were currently teaching *just down the hall,* what might be happening (both content and process) in their classrooms?

Socrates's method did not just promote intellectual insights in his students; it also challenged the conventional ideas and traditions of his time. Socrates offended many powerful people and was eventually charged with corrupting the youth of Athens. Even in this, Socrates provides a lesson for today's teachers: challenges to popular convention may lead to community opposition and sanctions. (Luckily, sanctions today are less severe than those meted out to Socrates, who was condemned to death for his "impiety.")

RAP 3.4

The Great Lecture Theory of Learning, p. 431

We know about Socrates and his teachings through the writings of his disciples, one of whom was **Plato** (427–347 B.C.E.). Plato's writing is renowned for its depth, beauty and clarity. His most famous works were dialogues, conversations between two or more people, that present and critique various philosophical viewpoints. Plato's dialogues feature Socrates questioning and challenging others and presenting

TEACHER: Today we will try to understand what we mean by the concepts of right and wrong. What are examples of conduct you consider wrong or immoral?

STUDENT: Lying is wrong.

TEACHER: But what if you were living in Germany around 1940 and you were harboring in your house a certain Jewish man named Nathan Cohen, who was wanted by the Nazis? If asked by a Nazi if you knew the whereabouts of that Mr. Cohen, wouldn't it be acceptable, even obligatory, to lie?

STUDENT: I suppose so.

TEACHER: So could you rephrase what you meant when you said that lying is wrong or immoral?

STUDENT: I think what I meant is that it is usually wrong to lie. But it is true that there are times when lying is acceptable, because the overall effects of the lie are good. Look at how much your Mr. Cohen was helped; the lie about where he was may have saved his life.

TEACHER: So you are saying that it is okay to lie, as long as the consequences of the lie are positive. But consider this hypothetical situation: I am a business tycoon who makes millions of dollars selling diamonds to investors. I sell only to very rich people who can afford to lose the money they invest in my diamonds. I tell my customers that my diamonds are worth $10,000 each, but they really are fakes, worth only $2,000 each. Rather than keeping the profits myself, I give all the money to the poor, helping them obtain the food and shelter they need to live. If you look at the obvious consequences of my business—the rich get slightly poorer and the needy are helped out immensely—you may conclude that my business has a generally positive effect on society. And, yet, because the business is based on fraud, I find it immoral. Do you agree?

STUDENT: Yes, I find it immoral. I suppose I was wrong in saying that whenever a lie has generally good results it is morally acceptable. In your diamond example, unlike the Nazi example, the lie was directed at innocent people and the harm done to them was significant. I want to change my earlier statement that a lie is acceptable whenever it has generally good results. What I want to say now is that you should never lie to innocent people if that would cause them significant harm.

As is typical of Socrates' dialogue, this one could go on indefinitely, because there is no simple, "correct" solution to the issues being discussed—the meaning of right and wrong and, more specifically, the contours of when a lie is morally acceptable. By asking questions, the teacher is trying to get the student to clarify and rethink his or her own ideas, to come eventually to a deep and clear understanding of philosophical concepts, such as right and wrong.

REFLECTION: Have you ever experienced the Socratic Dialogue as a student? What were your reactions? Would you like to develop this teaching technique? Why or why not?

his own philosophy. After Socrates was put to death, Plato became disillusioned with Athenian democracy and left the city for many years. Later, he returned to Athens and founded **The Academy,** considered by some to be the world's first university.

Plato held that a realm of eternally existing "ideas" or "forms" underlies the physical world. In Plato's philosophy, the human soul has three parts: intellect, spirit, and appetite (basic animal desires). Plato believed that these faculties interact to determine human behavior. Plato urged that the intellect, the highest faculty, be trained to control the other two. For a look at Plato's famous "Parable of the Cave," from *The Republic*, setting out his political philosophy (he envisioned a class of philosopher-kings that would rule over the warriors and the common people) visit the Online Learning Center.

Just as Plato studied under Socrates, **Aristotle** (384–322 B.C.E.) studied under Plato. Aristotle entered Plato's Academy at age 18 and stayed for twenty years. In 342 B.C.E., Aristotle went to northern Greece and, for several years, tutored a young boy named Alexander, later known as Alexander the Great. After educating Alexander, Aristotle returned to Athens to set up his own school, the **Lyceum,** adjacent to Plato's Academy.

- **Socrates.** His philosophical lifestyle; the Socratic method, in which students are provocatively questioned so that they can rethink what they believe; his noble death
- **Plato.** Discussions of philosophy through eloquent dialogues; the theory of "forms," or "ideas," that exist in an eternal, transcendent realm; a vision of utopia, where an elite group of philosopher-kings rules over other members of society
- **Aristotle.** The breadth of his knowledge; the synthesis of Plato's belief in the eternal "forms" and a

scientist's belief in the "real" world that we can see, touch, or smell; the theory of the Golden Mean (everything in moderation)

REFLECTION: How might your current classroom instruction change if your education professor was Dr. Socrates, Plato, or Aristotle? Detail aspects of a "typical" lesson.

The depth and breadth of Aristotle's ideas were unsurpassed in ancient Western civilization. In addition to tackling philosophical questions, Aristotle wrote influential works on biology, physics, astronomy, mathematics, psychology, and literary criticism. Aristotle placed more importance on the physical world than did Plato. Aristotle's teachings can, in fact, be regarded as a synthesis of Plato's belief in the universal, spiritual forms, and a scientist's belief that each animal, vegetable, and mineral we observe is undeniably real.

Aristotle also won renown for his ethical and political theories. He wrote that the highest good for people is a virtuous life, fully governed by the faculty of reason, with which all other faculties are in harmony. Aristotle promoted the doctrine of the **Golden Mean,** or the notion that virtue lies in a middle ground between two extremes. Courage, for example, is bordered on the one side by cowardice and on the other side by foolhardiness.

Many of the ideas first formulated by Socrates, Plato, and Aristotle have long been integrated into Western culture and education.

FOCUS QUESTION 7
How do metaphysics, epistemology, ethics, political philosophy, aesthetics, and logic factor into a philosophy of education?

CRITICAL THINKING QUESTION
What is education's role in society? This question has been introduced earlier in pragmatic and now in philosophical terms. In conversation with a partner, can students answer the question using the vocabulary and understanding from this chapter?

 Basic Philosophical Issues and Concepts

Philosophy has many subdivisions that are of particular significance to educators: metaphysics, epistemology, ethics, political philosophy, aesthetics, and logic. (See Figure 9.2.) These fields are where key educational questions are raised, including: How do we know what we know? What is of value? What is education's role in society? As you ponder these questions, you should find elements of your philosophy of education coming into sharper focus.

Metaphysics and Epistemology

Metaphysics deals with the origin and structure of reality. Metaphysicians ask: What really is the nature of the world in which we live? **Epistemology** examines the nature and origin of human knowledge. Epistemologists are interested in how we use our minds to distinguish valid from illusory paths to true knowledge. It may be easiest to remember the scope of these closely related disciplines by considering that epistemology and metaphysics address, respectively, *how* we know (epistemology) *what* we know (metaphysics) about reality.

FIGURE 9.2
Branches of philosophy.

OVERHEAD 106
Branches of Philosophy

Is Reality Composed Solely of Matter? One of the most basic metaphysical issues is whether anything exists other than the material realm that we experience with our senses. Many philosophers assert the existence only of the physical, affirming fundamentally the existence of matter, a philosophy called **materialism.** By emphasizing in their curriculum the study of nature through scientific observation, modern public schools clearly deem that the material world is real and important. Other philosophers contend that the physical realm is but an illusion. They point out that matter is known only through the mind. This philosophy is called spiritualism or **idealism.** Educators responding to ideals might focus on students' relationships with each other or with a more spiritual world. A third group of philosophers asserts that reality is composed of both materialism and idealism, body and mind, a belief associated with French philosopher René Descartes and called **Cartesian dualism.**

Is Reality Characterized by Change and Progress? Metaphysicians question whether nature is constantly improving through time. The belief that progress is inevitable is widely held in the United States. On the other hand, some philosophers hold that change is illusory and that a foundation of timeless, static content underlies all reality. Still others believe that change is cyclical, swinging widely from one side of center to the opposing side.

Teachers who believe in the inevitability of progress seek new approaches to teaching and new subjects to be taught, thereby "keeping up with the times." Other teachers, less enamored with change, pay little heed to current trends and technologies. They may prefer to teach everlasting, timeless truths discovered by great thinkers, such as Plato and Aristotle. Finally, some teachers suggest that, with change such a constant, it is pointless to try to keep pace. They choose to ignore these cycles and to simply select the teaching methods they find most comfortable.

What Is the Basis of Our Knowledge? Empiricism holds that sensory experience (seeing, hearing, touching, and so on) is the source of knowledge. Empiricists assert that we experience the external world by sensory perception; then, through reflection, we conceptualize ideas that help us interpret that world. For example, because we have seen the sun rise every day, we can formulate the belief that it will rise again tomorrow. The empiricist doctrine that knowledge is gained most reliably through scientific experimentation may be the most widely held belief in Western culture. People want to hear the latest research or be shown documentation that something is true. Teachers expect students to present evidence before drawing conclusions. Even children demand of one another, "Prove it."

MULTIPLE INTELLIGENCE CONNECTION
Have students create (alone or in small teams) a visual organizer that incorporates all these terms: metaphysics, epistemology, materialism, idealism, Cartesian dualism, empiricism, rationalism, ethics, political philosophy, aesthetics, deductive reasoning, and inductive reasoning. Compare and contrast their designs with classmates. Does comprehension grow as the drawings get clearer?

Rationalism emphasizes the power of reason—in particular, logic—to derive true statements about the world, even when such realities are not detected by the senses. Rationalists point out that the field of mathematics has generated considerable knowledge that is not based on our senses. For example, we can reason that 7 cubed equals 343 without having to count 7 times 7 times 7 objects to verify our conclusion experientially. Whereas educational empiricists would support hands-on learning activities as the primary source for discovery and validation of information, rationalists would encourage schools to place a greater emphasis on teaching mathematics, as well as such nonempirical disciplines as philosophy and logic.

Ethics, Political Philosophy, and Aesthetics

Whereas metaphysics focuses on what "is," ethics, political philosophy, and aesthetics are concerned with what "ought to be." In these disciplines, philosophers grapple with the issue of what we should value. As you read on, consider the place of ethics, political philosophy, and aesthetics in the classroom.

RELATED READING
*Tuesdays with Morrie:
An Old Man, a Young
Man and The Five People
You Meet in Heaven* by
Mitch Albom (2003).

Ethics is the study of what is "good" or "bad" in human behavior, thoughts, and feelings. It asks, What is the good life? and How should we treat each other? (What should schools teach children about what is "good" and what is "bad"?)

Political philosophy analyzes how past and present societies are arranged and governed and proposes ways to create better societies in the future. (How might schools engage in an objective evaluation of current governments, including our own?)

RAP 3.3
Philosophy on The Big
Screen, p. 43

Aesthetics probes the nature of beauty. It asks, What is beauty? Is beauty solely in the eyes of the beholder? Or are some objects, people, and works (music, art, literature) objectively more beautiful than others? (How can teachers help students understand how their personal experiences, peer group values, and cultural and ethnic history shape their standards of what is beautiful?)

Logic

Logic is the branch of philosophy that deals with reasoning. Logic focuses on how to move from a set of assumptions to valid conclusions and examines the rules of inference that enable us to frame our propositions and arguments. While epistemology defines reasoning as one way to gain knowledge, logic defines the rules of reasoning.

Schools teach children to reason both deductively and inductively. When teaching **deductive reasoning,** teachers present their students with a general rule and then help them identify particular examples and applications of the rule. Inductive reasoning works in the opposite manner. When teaching **inductive reasoning,** teachers help their students draw tentative generalizations after having observed specific instances of a phenomenon.

A teacher who explains the commutative property of addition (a + b = b + a) and then has the student work out specific examples of this rule (such as 3 + 2 = 2 + 3) is teaching deductive reasoning. Contrast this with a teacher who begins a lesson by stating a series of addition problems of the form 3 + 2 = 5 and 2 + 3 = 5, then asks, "What do you notice about these examples?" If students can draw a generalization about the commutative property of addition, they are reasoning inductively. While math is a natural field to isolate examples of deductive and inductive reasoning, logic equips students to think more precisely in virtually any field.

Your Turn

[I]n modern times there are opposing views about the practice of education. There is no general agreement about what the young should learn either in relation to virtue or in relation to the best life; nor is it clear whether their education ought to be directed more towards the intellect than towards the character of the soul. . . . [A]nd it is not certain whether training should be directed at things useful in life, or at those conducive to virtue, or at nonessentials. . . . And there is no agreement as to what in fact does tend towards virtue. Men [sic] do not all prize most highly the same virtue, so naturally they differ also about the proper training for it.[10]

Aristotle

More than 2,300 years later, we still find that reasonable people can come to entirely different points of view on all kinds of issues in education. (Remember the charter school discussion in the faculty room at the beginning of the chapter?) If everyone agreed on what should be taught, and how to teach it, there might be just one philosophy of education. But it is not so simple.

Rereading the inventory statements at the beginning of this chapter can help you determine if one of the five major philosophies speaks for you. You may be more eclectic in your outlook, picking and choosing elements from different philosophies. Your responsibility as an educator is to wrestle with tough questions, to bring your values to the surface and to forge a coherent philosophy of education.

You might say a clear philosophy of education is to a teacher what a blueprint is to a builder—a plan of action; reassurance that the parts will fit together in a constructive way. With a clear philosophy of education, you will not ricochet from one teaching method to another, and will not confuse students, parents and administrators with conflicting messages about the role of students and teacher in the classroom. If you have a well-honed philosophy of education, you will be better able to assess whether you will find a comfortable fit in a school and a community. Simply put, a philosophy brings purpose and coherence to your work in the classroom.

RELATED READING
The Courage to Teach: Exploring the Inner Landscape of a Teacher's Life by Palmer Parker (1998).

SUMMARY

1. What is a philosophy of education, and why should it be important to you?

   Behind every school and every teacher is a set of related beliefs—a philosophy of education—that influences what and how students are taught. A philosophy of education answers questions about the purpose of schooling, a teacher's role, what should be taught and by what methods.

2. How do teacher-centered philosophies of education differ from student-centered philosophies of education?

   Teacher-centered philosophies, like essentialism and perennialisim, are more conservative, emphasizing the values and knowledge that have survived through time. Student-centered philosophies focus on individual needs, contemporary relevance, and a future orientation. Progressivism, social reconstructionism, and existentialism place the learner at the center of the educational process.

3. What are some major philosophies of education in the United States today?

   Essentialists urge that schools return to the basics through a strong core curriculum and high academic standards. Perennialists value the Great Books and the philosophical

 CHAPTER REVIEW

Go to the Online Learning Center to take a quiz, practice with key terms, and review concepts from the chapter.

concepts that underlie human knowledge. The curriculum of a progressivist school is built around the personal experiences, interests, and needs of the students. Social reconstructionists more directly confront societal ills. Existentialism is derived from a powerful belief in human free will, and the need for individuals to shape their own futures.

4. How are these philosophies reflected in school practices?

Essentialism and perennialism give teachers the power to choose the curriculum, organize the school day, and construct classroom activities. The curriculum reinforces a predominantly Western heritage. Progressivism, social reconstructionism, and existentialism focus on contemporary society, student interests and needs, while teachers serve as guides and facilitators.

5. What are some of the psychological and cultural factors influencing education?

Constructivist teachers gauge a student's prior knowledge, then carefully orchestrate cues, classroom activities, and penetrating questions to push students to higher levels of understanding. According to Skinner, behavior can be modified through an extrinsic reward system that motivates students even if they do not fully understand the value of what they are learning. The practices and beliefs of peoples in other parts of the world, such as informal and oral education, offer useful insights for enhancing our own educational practices, but they are insights too rarely considered, much less implemented.

6. What were the contributions of Socrates, Plato, and Aristotle to Western philosophy, and how are their legacies reflected in education today?

Socrates is hailed today as the personification of wisdom and the philosophical life. He used persistent questions to help students clarify their thoughts, a process now called the Socratic method. Plato, Socrates' pupil, crafted eloquent dialogues that present different philosophical positions on a number of profound questions. Aristotle, Plato's pupil, provided a synthesis of Plato's belief in the universal, spiritual forms and a scientist's belief in the physical world. He taught that the virtuous life consists of controlling desires by reason and by choosing the moderate path between extremes.

7. How do metaphysics, epistemology, ethics, political philosophy, aesthetics, and logic factor into a philosophy of education?

Metaphysics deals with the nature of reality, its origin and its structure, and poses curricular choices: Should we study the natural world, or focus on spiritual or ideal forms? Epistemology examines the nature and origin of human knowledge, and influences teaching methods. "How we know" is closely related to how we learn and therefore, how we should teach. Ethics is the study of what is "good" or "bad" in human behavior, thoughts, and feelings. Political philosophy proposes ways to create better societies in the future, and asks: How will a classroom be organized, and what will that say about who wields power? Aesthetics is concerned with the nature of beauty, and raises the issue: What works are deemed of value to be studied or emulated?

EXTENDED LEARNING

CASE STUDIES

- Brenda Forester: A teacher who has developed an innovative curriculum is concerned because another teacher continually warns her that she will be held responsible for her students' end-of-year standardized test scores.

- Michael Watson: A teacher finds that the assistant principal's evaluation of his class calls into question his teaching style as well as his philosophy of education.

READINGS

- John Dewey. Selection from *Experience and Education* (Macmillan, 1938).
- Maxine Greene. Selection from "The Passions of Pluralism: Multiculturalism and the Expanding Community," *Educational Researcher.*
- Carl Rogers. Selection from *Freedom to Learn in the Eighties.*

KEY TERMS AND PEOPLE

KEY TERMS

The Academy, 349
aesthetics, 352
assertive discipline, 347
back-to-basics, 330
behavior modification, 346
behaviorism, 346
Cartesian dualism, 351
Coalition of Essential Schools, 331
constructivism, 344
core curriculum, 331
deductive reasoning, 352
empiricism, 351
epistemology, 350
essentialism, 330
ethics, 352
ethnocentrism, 347
existentialism, 339
Golden Mean, 350
Great Books, 332
idealism, 351
inductive reasoning, 352

informal education, 347
Laboratory School, 336
logic, 352
Lyceum, 349
materialism, 351
metaphysics, 350
neoessentialism, 331
oral tradition, 348
Paideia Proposal, 332
perennialists, 332
philosophy, 324
political philosophy, 352
pragmatism, 335
praxis, 339
progressivism, 335
rationalism, 352
scaffolding, 346
social Darwinism, 339
social reconstructionism, 337
Socratic method , 348
student-centered philosophies, 333

teacher-centered philosophies, 320

KEY PEOPLE

Mortimer Adler, 332, 342
Aristotle, 349
William Bagley, 330, 342
George Counts, 337, 342
John Dewey, 335, 342
Paulo Freire, 339
Maxine Greene, 342
E. D. Hirsch, Jr., 331, 342
bell hooks, 342
Robert Hutchins, 332, 342
Jane Roland Martin, 338
A. S. Neill, 342
Nel Noddings, 342
Plato, 348
Jean-Paul Sartre, 339
B. F. Skinner, 346
Socrates, 348

DISCUSSION QUESTIONS AND ACTIVITIES

1. Suppose that you are a student who must choose one of five schools to attend. Each reflects one of the five major philosophies. Which would you choose and why? Which school would you choose to work in as a teacher? Why?

2. Interview a teacher who has been teaching for several years. Find out what that teacher's philosophy was when he or she started teaching and what it is today. Is there a difference? If so, try to find out why.

3. Reread the five statements by the teachers in the faculty room at the beginning of the chapter. In what areas do you think these teachers could agree? In what areas are their

philosophies distinct and different? What do you predict will be the result of their meeting? Which of the statements by the five teachers do you agree with most? Are there elements of each teacher's philosophy that could combine to form your own philosophy of education?

4. How would you describe your own philosophy of education? Imagine you are a teacher. Create a 3-minute speech that you would give to parents on back-to-school night that outlines your philosophy of education and identifies how it would be evident in the classroom.

5. The key terms and people in this chapter could be dramatically expanded by including Far Eastern and Middle Eastern philosophy. Consider the following additions: Buddhism, Confucius, Hinduism, Islam, Jainism, Judaism, Mohammed, Shinto, Taoism, Zen Buddhism. Research and briefly describe each of these. What has been (or might be) the impact of these religions, principles, and individuals on our present school philosophy?

REEL TO REAL TEACHING

QUIZ SHOW (1992)
Run Time: 130 minutes

Synopsis: By giving answers to the players they wanted to win, the producers of the popular 1950s game show *Twenty-One* had their trump card for capturing huge audience ratings. Charles Van Doren, college professor and scion of a great literary family, was the "perfect" game show contestant. The fact that the handsome and genteel Van Doren was prepared to participate in the cheating was an extra benefit. Based on a true story, the film probes the fault lines between knowledge, privilege, and scandal, and raises serious questions about what is most worth knowing.

Reflection:

1. What hooks you into a good game show or causes you to quickly flip channels? How is your educational philosophy reflected in your passion (or distaste) for game shows?

2. Which educational philosophy is best represented in *Quiz Show*? What elements of the classroom are seen on the game show stage?

3. How did factors such as race, religion, gender, and socioeconomic class determine who knew the answers on *Twenty-One*? Compare how these same factors shape how we define who is intelligent in schools.

4. After the scandal, Charles Van Doren noted that he believed the difference between good and evil was "not cut and dried." How is this statement revealed in the motives of the *Twenty-One* producers? Contestant Herb Stempel? Charles Van Doren? What power did each have? What power did each believe he had? How is this "winning at all costs" attitude reflected in schools and the testing culture?

5. What accounts for the popularity of quiz shows in the 1950s? Today? Consider the events, people, and values of each time period. How do game shows reflect American society and the value it places on knowledge?

Follow-up Activity: It's Game Night at your school. Choose a subject area and design your own "quiz show" based on one of the five philosophies discussed in the chapter. How will you define winning? How will the host, contestants, questions/answers, interactions, seating arrangements, and prizes reflect the key principles of the philosophy? Consider the many variables, such as the "facts"; the roles of gender, race, and class; and political motivations, among other things, that go into creating a "quiz show."

www.mhhe.com/
sadker7e

How do you rate this film? Go to *Reel to Real Teaching* in the Critics' Corner to review this film.

FOR FURTHER READING

Approaches to Teaching, by Gary Fenstermacher and Jonas Soltis (3rd ed., 1998). Through an interactive, case studies approach, the authors explore the strengths and weaknesses of various philosophical perspectives. Readers are challenged to critically assess their own philosophical positions on education and to unpack the meaning of teaching.

Children as Philosophers, by Joanna Haynes and Tony Brown (2001). This book was written with the belief that philosophy can assist with children's thinking, speaking, and listening skills as well as provide a stimulus and structure for moral inquiry.

Historical and Philosophical Foundations of Education: A Biographical Introduction (2nd ed., 1997). A comprehensive account of the competing schools of educational philosophy and their applications to schooling. This book provides thumbnail sketches of significant figures and guides readers in investigating their own philosophies.

In the Deep Heart's Core, by Michael Johnston (2002). When the author signed up for a two-year stint with Teach for America, he hoped to make a difference in the lives of the poor children of the Mississippi Delta. What he hadn't planned on was the impact they would have on him; his experience makes for riveting reading.

Variations on a Blue Guitar, by Maxine Greene (2001). For twenty-five years, Maxine Greene has been the philosopher-in-residence at the innovative Lincoln Center Institute, where her work forms the foundation of the Institute's aesthetic education practice. Each summer she addresses teachers from across the country, representing all grade levels. This book contains selected lectures on aesthetic education, imagination and transformation, educational renewal and reform, standards, and cultural diversity—powerful ideas for today's educators.

10

Financing and Governing America's Schools

CHAPTER

FOCUS QUESTIONS

1. Why do teachers need to know about finance and governance?
2. How is the property tax connected to unequal educational funding?
3. What is the distinction between educational equity and educational adequacy?
4. What are the sources of state revenues?
5. How does the federal government influence education?
6. What current trends are shaping educational finance?
7. How do school boards and superintendents manage schools?
8. What is the "hidden" government of schools?
9. How does the business community influence school culture?
10. How are schools being made more responsive to teachers and the community?

 WHAT DO YOU THINK? What Costs More? Try your hand at ranking the cost of several items on a state education budget.

CHAPTER PREVIEW

Do you know who pays for U.S. schools, and how? You might be surprised. In this chapter we introduce you to the decentralized, politically charged systems of school funding and school governance in the United States. You will become familiar with the sources of financial inequity in schooling, and, more important, learn how reformers are pursuing strategies to keep effective education within the reach of all, not just the very wealthy. Both the formal structure of power in school governance (school boards, school superintendents, and the like) and the informal, hidden government will impact your life in the classroom. By understanding the mechanics behind school finance and governance, you will be more empowered as a classroom teacher, and better able to influence decisions that shape the education of our nation's children.

Local and state governments have long grappled with the difficult proposi-

tion of raising enough public funds to adequately support education while dodging taxpayer ire over high taxes. Students in wealthy neighborhoods attend modern, well-equipped schools; poorer children make their way to decaying, ill-equipped school buildings in impoverished communities. Courts have forged solutions aimed at reducing these glaring disparities and bringing a measure of fairness to education. Many states are now focusing on guaranteeing that every student receives an adequate and appropriate education.

Day-to-day classroom life is influenced not only by economic issues but also by the ways in which schools are governed. In this chapter, you will learn how schools are managed, officially and unofficially. Your knowledge of educational decision making can be a powerful ally in shaping a successful teaching career.

Follow the Money: Financing America's Schools

Why Should Teachers Care Where the Money Comes from?

Why should a teacher be concerned much about school finance? (Put another way, why should I want to read this chapter?) Doesn't a teacher's responsibility pretty much start and end at the classroom door?

Sounds reasonable, but here is where the authors jump in. We believe that it is unwise, and even dangerous, for teachers to invest their time and talent in a career where the key decisions are considered beyond their knowledge or influence. Educational finance may well determine not just the quality of life you experience as a teacher, but the very futures of the students you teach. Common sense tells us that the amount of money spent in a school is directly related to how well students learn, but not everyone agrees. What is the wisest way to invest educational dollars—and who should decide?

In the Watergate scandal that toppled Richard Nixon from the presidency, the *Washington Post* reporters who broke the story were given invaluable advice from a strange and still anonymous source: "Deep Throat." Deep Throat advised the reporters to "Follow the money." He explained that in politics, the money trail reveals what is happening and who is benefiting. Money is the key to what is happening in schools as well.

We believe that teachers should be major participants in financial and governance policy decisions. The current trend toward testing teachers and developing school standards is an example of what happens when teachers are left out of policy circles. The emphasis on standards and testing too often casts the teacher in the role of a technician, implementing other people's goals with the resources other people decide they should have. And in the end, other people evaluate how well teachers (and students) perform. We believe that this system serves neither teachers nor students well. We see teachers as advocates for children, children who themselves are excluded from policy decisions. Teachers and students find themselves the victims of rising educational expectations but limited educational resources. Teachers should have a voice, and be a voice for children as well. Consider this chapter a step in that direction, and a primer on both the economics and governance of schools.

The Property Tax: The Road to Unequal Schools

> The method of financing public schools . . . can be fairly described as chaotic and unjust.
>
> *Supreme Court Justice Potter Stewart*

To someone from another country, the way the United States funds its schools must seem bizarre, and certainly unfair. Unlike many other nations, which use a centralized funding system, we have a very decentralized system. In fact, we have three levels of government—local, state, and federal—all raising and distributing funds. Currently, the local and state governments share the biggest burden of funding schools, with the federal government responsible for just 6 to 8 percent of the total. What a tangled web we weave when fifty states, fifteen thousand local governments, and one enormous federal government become involved in funding and managing 90,000 schools.

How did this financial hodgepodge begin? In colonial America, schools were the concern of local communities. Then, at the birth of our nation, the Constitution did

GRABBERS 1, 2
Quotable
IM
Savage Inequalities
IM

FOCUS QUESTION 1
Why do teachers need to know about finance and governance?

TEACHING TIP
Many of your students are transitioning (we hope) from a life with limited financial awareness to one that is self-sufficient and fiscally sound. Be on the alert. They may know a lot more about education (after all, they have been in schools for a dozen or more years) than they do about dollars.

CRITICAL THINKING QUESTION
As your students ponder all the issues in this chapter, is the financial voice of a teacher (or other decision makers) always, often or rarely the *voice for children*?

FOCUS QUESTION 2
How is the property tax connected to unequal educational funding?

Steadily increasing property taxes have led to taxpayer revolts in such states as California, Texas, and Massachusetts, where voters have passed propositions limiting such taxes.

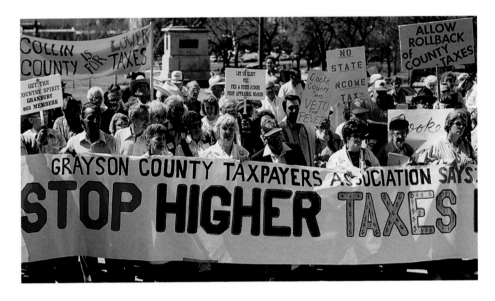

GLOBAL VIEW
Most poor countries spend more on servicing foreign debt than on educating their own children. See Oxfam Community Aid Abroad at www.caa.org.au/index.html

not designate a federal role in education, effectively leaving it the responsibility of the states. "Local control" of schools became a well-established tradition, one that still holds sway today.

In the agrarian society of colonial times, wealth was measured by the size of people's farms. So to raise money for schools, colonial towns and districts assessed a **property tax.** Although today only 2 percent of Americans still work the land, the property tax continues to be the major source of school revenue. Today's property taxes are levied on real estate (homes and businesses) and sometimes personal property (cars and boats). Whether a school district will find itself rich in resources, or scrambling to make ends meet, depends largely on the wealth of the community being taxed. Not surprisingly, a tax on a Beverly Hills mansion raises many more thousands of dollars than a tax on a house in South Central Los Angeles. Communities blessed with valuable real estate can easily raise funds for their schools. Impoverished communities are not so fortunate. Urban areas struggle the most, suffering not only from lower property values, but also the need to use those limited resources to fund more police officers, hospitals, subways, and other services than their suburban counterparts, a phenomenon known as **municipal overburden.**[1]

Reforming Education Finance

Unequal school funding results in stark differences, sometimes in close quarters. In 1968, 48-year-old sheetmetal worker Demetrio Rodriguez looked with despair at his children's school in a poor Latino section of San Antonio, Texas. Not only did Edgewood Elementary School lack adequate books and air conditioning, the top two floors were condemned and barely half the teachers were certified.[2] Ten minutes away, in affluent Alamo Heights, children were taught by certified teachers, in comfortable surroundings with ample materials. The educational cards were stacked against Rodriguez and his neighbors: even though Edgewood residents paid one of the highest tax rates on their property of any Texas community, the property itself was not worth much. Edgewood raised only $37 per student; Alamo Heights raised $412 per student. Rodriguez went to court, claiming that the system violated the U.S. Constitution's guarantee for equal protection under the law.

In a landmark decision, ***San Antonio v. Rodriguez*** (1973), the Supreme Court ruled against Rodriguez, deferring to the long history of local communities funding neighborhood schools. The Court declared that education was not a "fundamental right" under the U.S. Constitution, and that preserving local control was a legitimate reason to use the property tax system. While the Court recognized that educational funding through the property tax was a seriously flawed system, it was left up to the states to change it. It took sixteen more years before the Texas Supreme Court would act on the Rodriguez case. By the mid-1980s, Edgewood had neither typewriters nor a playground, but affluent Alamo Heights had computers and a swimming pool. Throughout Texas, per-pupil expenditures ranged from $2,112 in the poorest community to $19,333 in the wealthiest. In ***Edgewood v. Kirby*** (1989) the Texas Supreme Court issued a unanimous decision that such differences violated the Texas constitution, and ordered Texas to devise a fairer plan.

Reformers had more courtroom success under state constitutions' equal protection clauses. The California Supreme Court, in ***Serrano v. Priest*** (1971), struck down the state's financing system as unconstitutional. The court, faced with the glaring differences between Beverly Hills spending $1,232 per student, and nearby Baldwin Park spending only $577 a student, declared that education was a fundamental right under the California constitution and that the property tax system violated equal protection of that right. The court found that heavy reliance on the local property tax "makes the quality of a child's education a function of the wealth of his parents and neighbors. . . . Districts with small tax bases simply cannot levy taxes at a rate sufficient to produce the revenue that more affluent districts produce with a minimum effort." The *Serrano v. Priest* decision ushered in both a wave of litigation in other states and an increase in the state share of school funding.[3] (See Figures 10.1 and 10.2.) **Robin Hood reformers,** as they were called, won a victory as they took funds from wealthy districts and redistributed the monies to the poorer districts, much like the Robin Hood hero of Sherwood Forest fame. States have used different programs to try to equalize funding. In the **foundation program,** the state provides funds to ensure that each student receives a minimal or "foundation" level of educational services. Unfortunately, the established minimum is frequently far below actual expenditures. Another approach is the **guaranteed tax base program,** which adds state funds to poorer districts, helping to reduce economic inequities.

The Serrano victory in California was short-lived. Many voters feared tax increases, and wealthy voters revolted as their tax dollars were transported from their own children's schools to faraway poor schools. **Proposition 13** was passed to limit the property tax. With decreased tax revenue, California saw its schools go into a rapid decline. California schools were finally becoming equal, but equally bad.

Robin Hood's New Arrow: Adequacy

California provided an early example of the growing opposition to Robin Hood laws. In New Jersey, for example, the legislature was dominated by wealthy interests and middle-class communities who fought the Robin Hood idea. The state court shut down the schools to force the legislature to distribute more funds to poorer districts. In ***Abbott v. Burke*** (1990, 1998), the state court identified twenty-eight failing districts (known as "Abbott districts") where the rights of poor students were being denied. The court mandated that significantly greater funds be spent to transform their students into "productive members of society."[4] For school districts like Camden, with buildings in disrepair and students failing, Robin Hood funds were seen as the

OVERHEAD 107

School Segregation and Poverty

TEACHING TIP

By the way, Beverly Hills Unified remains on top of the Los Angeles County list, spending $7,343 per pupil. Baldwin Park is well behind, spending $5,205 per student. www.losangelesalmanac. com/topics/Education/ ed04n.htm

OVERHEADS 108–109

The Public Education Dollar: Where the Money Comes From

The Public Education Dollar: Where the Money Goes

FOCUS QUESTION 3

What is the distinction between educational *equity* and educational *adequacy*?

FIGURE 10.1

The public education dollar:
Where the money comes from.

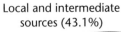

Local and intermediate
sources (43.1%)

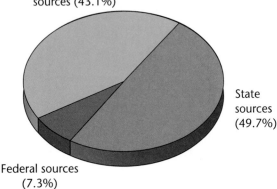

State
sources
(49.7%)

Federal sources
(7.3%)

SOURCE: *Digest of Education Statistics,* National Center for Educational
Statistics Common Core Data, "National Public Education Financial Survey"
U.S. Department of Education 2000–01.

> **REFLECTION:** Is the proportion of revenue spent by
> local, state, and federal governments on education
> different from your initial perceptions? If you were able
> to suggest changes in this pie graph, what would they
> be? Why?

FIGURE 10.2

The public education dollar:
Where the money goes.

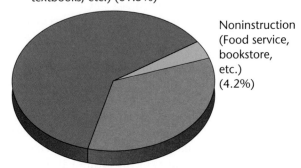

Instruction (teacher salaries,
textbooks, etc.) (61.5%)

Noninstruction
(Food service,
bookstore,
etc.)
(4.2%)

Support services (school maintenance,
nurses, administration, library, etc.) (34.3%)

SOURCE: U.S. Department of Education, National Center for Education
Statistics, Common Core of Data (CCD). "National Public Education Financial
Survey" 2000–01.

> **REFLECTION:** Does the distribution of educational funds
> surprise you? Are there changes that you would suggest?

solution. But even after Camden received tens of millions of dollars in additional aid, academic statistics remained dismal. Critics of Robin Hood charged that increased funding could not turn failing school districts into successful ones. Redistributing tax dollars was not only politically unpopular, now it was considered ineffective.[5] (No wonder Robin Hood chose Sherwood Forest instead of New Jersey.)

CRITICAL THINKING QUESTION

How would your students describe a *failing school?* Does the Court's use of the term *adequate education* alter their grasp on this language?

The *Abbott* cases in New Jersey contributed to a new line of litigation focusing on **educational outcome** (student achievement) rather than **financial input** (per-pupil expenditures). State constitutions do not guarantee that every student receive either an equal education or equal funding, but they do guarantee education. With different words, states guarantee an "efficient" education, or a "thorough" education, or the need for all schools to be "free and uniform." These constitutional guarantees are referred to as **adequate education** so that all students have equal opportunities to play roles as citizens and to compete in the labor market.[6] States also differ dramatically in how they interpret adequate education. In Kentucky, an activist court ruled that the state's "entire system of common schools was infirm."[7] The court defined an "efficient" education as one that provides students with oral and written communications skills; knowledge of economics, history, and social systems; and sufficient preparation for academic and career success. To meet these goals, the state legislature enacted the Kentucky Education Reform Act in 1990, launching a new curriculum, statewide performance tests, preschool programs for at-risk students, multiple grades in the same class, and economic incentives for educational progress. New York took a minimalist approach, requiring all schools to provide students with

YOU BE THE JUDGE
"EQUITY" OR "ADEQUACY"

We Should Seek Educational "Equity" Because . . .

MONEY TALKS

The gap between wealthy and poor communities makes a mockery of democracy and fairness. Poor students attend schools with leaking roofs and uncertified teachers; wealthy students learn in schools with computers, swimming pools, and well-paid and qualified teachers. No real democracy can ignore such glaring inequities.

EQUALIZING INPUT IS CRUCIAL

Isn't it strange that those who advocate business values like choice and competition ignore the most fundamental business value of all: money. Wealth creates good schools; poverty creates weak ones. Invest money wisely over a period of time, and watch those once poor schools thrive.

EQUITY IS POWERFUL

Democracy and equity are powerful words representing powerful ideals. Adequacy is a feeble word subject to interpretation and compromise. What's adequate? Is it the ability to read at a high school level, or at an eighth grade level? Does an adequate education lead to a minimum wage job? Only "Equity" can serve as a rallying cry.

We Should Seek Educational "Adequacy" Because . . .

MONEY DIVIDES

Robin Hood is dead. Wealthy communities are not going to fund poor ones, happily sending their hard earned dollars to fund someone else's school. The cornerstone of democracy is local control, and trying to redistribute wealth is fundamentally unfair, and smacks of the approach used by Communists (another failed system).

EQUALIZING INPUT IS INEFFECTIVE

We will never make schools more effective by throwing dollars at them. When California moved toward equitable input, the quality of its public schools deteriorated. Our goal is not to increase school budgets and per pupil expenditures, but to increase student achievement.

ADEQUACY IS ATTAINABLE

Equity is a powerful dream, but adequacy is an attainable one. We are unlikely to achieve a completely equitable school system, but we can demand reasonable and reachable educational standards. Moreover, we are on firmer legal footing, since state constitutions guarantee not identical expenditures, but an adequate education for all.

 YOU BE THE JUDGE

Do you believe that adequacy or equity provides the best foundation for reforming schools? Explain. Can these approaches be blended, or are they mutually exclusive?

---

desks and pencils, but not up-to-date science textbooks.[8] States from Wyoming to Ohio endured years of litigation as they struggled to define adequate education.

Perhaps the purest example of the adequacy approach is found in Maryland. Historically, states decided how much money they could afford to spend on education, and then decided how best to distribute those funds. Maryland turned that approach upside down. The state appointed a commission that defined adequate education, then computed how much money was needed to achieve it. Adequate education was defined as a school with at least 94 percent student attendance, less than a 4 percent dropout rate, and 70 percent or more of the students passing state achievement tests. Then the state commission studied successful schools that were meeting these goals, and found that they were spending about $6,000 per pupil. At the other end of the spectrum, low performing schools had high numbers of poor children, non-English speakers, and children with special needs. Maryland determined that those schools

CRITICAL THINKING QUESTION

How would your students define an adequate education?

would require an additional $4,500 per pupil to reach the goals of an adequate education. Final bill: Maryland would need an additional $1.1 billion. Although Maryland struggles to find these funds, the state tackled the problem voluntarily, and without litigation.[9]

Does Money Matter?

To my knowledge, the U.S. is the only nation to fund elementary and secondary education based on local wealth. Other developed countries either equalize funding or provide extra funding for individuals or groups felt to need it.[10]

Why do Americans tolerate such dramatic inequities in school funding? Here are a few explanations:[11]

1. *Local Control.* In colonial times, it was left to individual communities in rural America to support their local schools. The Constitution codified this practice, and even after urbanization and suburbanization, Americans continue to believe that local taxes should be used to educate neighborhood children.

2. *Horatio Alger.* The rags to riches story of fictional Horatio Alger symbolizes the strongly held American belief that wealth and success are the fruits of individual effort, and that an individual's circumstances are merely obstacles to be overcome. It stands to reason, therefore, that if hard work and motivation alone are responsible for success, poverty comes from a lack of effort and a lack of talent. Individualism absolves communities from any collective responsibility for the poverty of others.

3. *Genetics.* For centuries, genetic differences have been used to explain why some succeed and others fail. The notion that certain groups are genetically deficient was promoted as recently as 1994 in Richard Hernstein and Charles Murray's book, *The Bell Curve*.

4. *Culture of Poverty.* Some believe that poor people live in and are shaped by the problems inherent in impoverished communities, problems that cannot be remedied through additional school funding.

5. *Flawed Studies.* Back in the 1960s, the classic Coleman study reported that school quality and funding had less of an effect on student achievement than family background or peer groups, and critics of equity efforts echo this notion that school funding is unrelated to student achievement. However, such studies have been cited for major methodological flaws.

6. *Previous Funding Increases Have Not Resulted in Achievement Gains.* Critics point out that although education spending has increased, test scores have not. However, most of these new funds were not for instructional improvement or test preparation, but to respond to targeted education needs, including special education, dropout prevention, expanded school lunch programs, and higher teacher salaries.

Does money matter? Of course it matters. Both common sense and a number of studies teach us that wealthier schools attract better-qualified teachers and have smaller class sizes. Both of these factors are associated with higher student achievement. Gaps in achievement between students from high and low socioeconomic-status homes are greater in poorly funded schools than in well-funded schools. Obviously, money alone will not cure all educational ills, and mismanagement or poor decisions can sabotage even well-funded education plans. But in the final analysis, money matters, and current practices perpetuate inequities both within the state and among the states. Many believe that this problem can only be resolved by the federal government, but a federal solution is at best unlikely. For now, it is up to each state to "find the money."

States Finding the Money

Let's assume that you have been asked by your (choose one or more of the following): (a) education professor, (b) teacher association, (c) favorite political candidate, or (d) spouse, to "follow the money" and find out how states raise their educational funds. States have a dizzying number of budget items to fund. But for our purposes, the basic question is: Where do we find the money for our schools?

At the state level, a common revenue source is the **sales tax,** which is simply a charge added to all sales. Consumers pay a few extra pennies for small purchases or a few extra dollars for large purchases. The sales tax accounts for 30 percent of the typical state's income.[12] More than forty states use a sales tax, usually collecting between 2 percent and 8 percent of the item's value. A problem with the sales tax is that some people may choose to avoid paying the tax by taking their business to a neighboring state with a lower tax rate. And the tax is regressive: poor families must spend most of their income purchasing necessities, and end up feeling the impact of the tax much more than wealthy people.

Another popular option is the **personal income tax,** used in more than forty states. The personal income tax brings in more than 25 percent of state revenues.[13] Like the federal income tax, the personal income tax is collected through payroll deductions, even before a worker receives his or her paycheck. The tax is a percentage of income, typically above a particular threshold of income, so how each state determines these percentages in the end will resolve how equally, or unequally, the tax burden falls on the poor, the middle class, and the rich.

In a relatively new funding source, state lotteries, poorer people once again bear the greatest burden. **State lotteries** offer holders of winning tickets the chance

FOCUS QUESTION 4
What are the sources of state revenues?

CLASS ACTIVITY:
FINANCE REPORTS
IM, Activity 10:2

The governor, working with the state legislature, is responsible for providing direction and financing for the state's schools.

FIGURE 10.3

Current per-pupil expenditures for elementary and secondary schools.

Current expenditures include salaries, employee benefits, purchased services, and supplies, but exclude capital outlay, debt service, facilities acquisition and construction, and equipment.

SOURCE: U.S. Department of Education, National Center for Education Statistics, Common Core Data, "National Public Education Financial Survey," School Year 2000–2001.

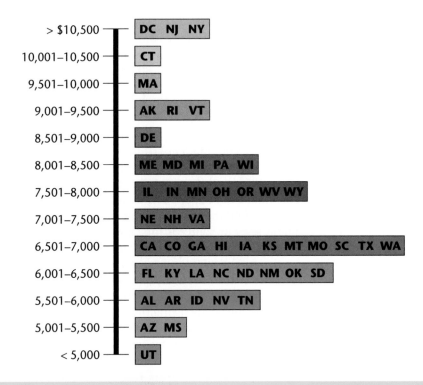

> $10,500	DC NJ NY
10,001–10,500	CT
9,501–10,000	MA
9,001–9,500	AK RI VT
8,501–9,000	DE
8,001–8,500	ME MD MI PA WI
7,501–8,000	IL IN MN OH OR WV WY
7,001–7,500	NE NH VA
6,501–7,000	CA CO GA HI IA KS MT MO SC TX WA
6,001–6,500	FL KY LA NC ND NM OK SD
5,501–6,000	AL AR ID NV TN
5,001–5,500	AZ MS
< 5,000	UT

REFLECTION: Do your teaching plans include any of the states at the top or bottom of this list? Will this spending information influence your decision on where to teach? For more information on how different states respond to the needs of children, visit www.childrensdefense.org/statesdata.htm.

CRITICAL THINKING
QUESTION
Ask your students what they think about funding schools (even a small portion) via lotteries. Are their beliefs and behaviors (buying or not buying tickets) in agreement?

CLASS ACTIVITY:
BRAINSTORMING
IM, Activity 10:1

to collect millions in prize money. But there are few winners and a disproportionate percentage of the poor purchase these long-shot lottery tickets. Roughly two-thirds of the states now have lotteries, and nearly half of those claim to dedicate at least a portion of the revenues to education. In reality, however, most states use lottery revenues to supplement, not fund, parts of an established education budget.[14]

Other common state sources of funding include: **excise taxes** (on tobacco, gasoline, and liquor, sometimes known as **sin tax); severance tax** (based on the state's mineral wealth); **motor vehicle license fee;** and **estate** or **gift taxes.**

Your brief course in "State Finance 101" is over. You can see some of the limits of state revenue sources. For extra credit, can you devise an entirely new scheme to raise state funds? As you can tell from Figure 10.3, states vary widely in how much money is invested in education.

The Federal Government's Role in Financing Education

FOCUS QUESTION 5
How does the federal government influence education?

At this point, some of you might be thinking: Even if every state provided every school district with adequate funding and a great education plan, the economic gaps among the states would still be enormous. If you thought about that, congratulations, you have put your finger on a systemic problem. For instance, in Connecticut, students throughout the state typically receive far more education dollars than students in Mississippi, regardless of what finance plans each of those states use. (See Frame of Reference: State Education Spending.) While we have been discussing *intrastate* equity, we have yet to explore *interstate* equity. Because of the Constitution, this is a problem the United States seems unable to correct.

RAP 3.2
Money Matters, p. 429

If the Constitution had assigned education as a federal responsibility, we might expect to see the federal government close the economic gap between states. U.S. schools might be centrally financed and governed; or at the very least, the Supreme Court might rule funding inequities among states unconstitutional. But this is not the case. The Supreme Court has ruled that education is not a "fundamental right" under the U.S. Constitution, and has left education to the states. Accordingly, the federal government's role in the financing of education is relatively small. In fact, the federal government typically pays only 6 to 8 percent of the nation's educational costs.

However, the federal government still manages to influence schools. How does it do this? One way has been through **categorical grants**—funds directed at specific categories and targeted educational needs. Categorical grants have provided funding for preschool programs for poor children, library construction, acquisition of new technology, educational opportunities for veterans, the training of teachers and administrators, educational research, lunches for low-income youth, and loans to college students. By targeting funds into these categories, federal aid, although limited, has had a significant impact on schools.

More recently, there has been a shift away from categorical grants to "block grants." The obligations, rules, and even competition associated with seeking federal dollars were greatly reduced in the 1980s and 1990s. States were awarded **block grants,** lump sums of money, and were given great latitude in how to spend this money. As a result, there were educational winners and losers in the quest for federal dollars:

Winners. Under the block grant system, more funds went to purchase instructional materials, including computers. Many rural communities that lacked the resources even to apply—much less compete—for federal dollars, received federal support. The paperwork for all districts was reduced.

Losers. Desegregation efforts were cut by two-thirds under the block grant approach. Programs for disadvantaged and urban students, women's equity, and many other targeted programs were reduced or eliminated. Long-range programs lost support, and accountability for how the funds were spent was greatly weakened.[15]

In 1979, President Jimmy Carter established the **United States Department of Education,** raising federal involvement in education to cabinet status. The Department of Education influences schools by conducting research, publishing information, proposing legislation, and disbursing targeted, if limited, federal funds. Expenditures for the Department of Education are dwarfed by other federal priorities. (See Figure 10.4.)

Although the federal government's financial role is limited, the federal government can exert tremendous influence on our schools through federal laws and court actions. For example, the 1954 *Brown* decision desegregated schools, and civil rights laws have increased educational opportunities for students of color, limited speakers of English, females, and others while *No Child Left Behind* (2001) brought high-stakes testing to center stage. (You will read about these laws and court cases, and more, in Chapter 11, "School Law and Ethics.")

FIGURE 10.4
Federal budget. Within the federal budget, education expenditures remain quite small.

SOURCE: Federal Role in Education, U.S. Department of Education (2002). www.ed.gov/about/overview/fed/role.html?src=ln

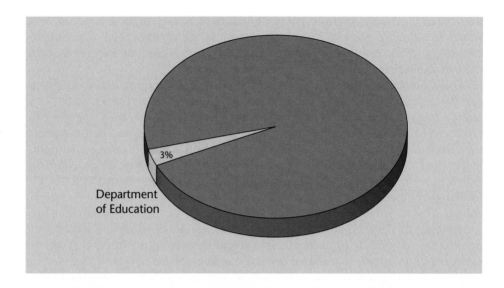

3%

Department
of Education

REFLECTION: Can you think of an area of the Federal budget that receives fewer dollars than education?

 ## What the Future May Hold for School Finance

FOCUS QUESTION 6
What current trends are shaping educational finance?

Today, we are in a period of shifting governmental responsibility for the financing of schools. Reformers are focusing less on financial inequity and more on educational inadequacy. What are some other trends in educational finance, and what issues are likely to surface in the years ahead?

Accountability

RAP 3.8
Assessing the Assessor, p. 435

The public wants to see academic progress for their tax dollars—in short, **accountability.** Students will be tested, and so will educators. Graduation will be based less on time spent in school and more on proven performance. Teachers may find tenure more difficult to obtain. Schools will be required to identify specific goals, such as minimum achievement levels on standardized tests, and will be held responsible for reaching these goals, as in *No Child Left Behind.*

Choice Programs

CLASS ACTIVITY:
CHOICE PLANS
IM, Activity 10:3

The neighborhood school, long a mainstay of public education, may be radically reshaped (or even eliminated) in the years ahead. As discussed in Chapter 4, "Schools: Choices and Challenges," many reformers are promoting a business culture and the value of competition as the keys to school improvement. Choice programs, charter schools, and vouchers are front burner issues in education.

The Economy's Impact on School Budgets

When our cyclical economy takes a downturn, state and local budgets are cut. This means fewer teachers are employed, class sizes increase, sports and extracurricular activities are eliminated, and courses like art and music are seen as "nonessential." School systems have even been known to end the school year early, or move to a four-day school week. Few governments maintain the public reserves necessary to avoid such cutbacks.[16]

Local Fundraising

Wealthier school districts are developing creative strategies to ensure that their schools are not endangered by funding redistribution plans. Through Parent Teacher Association donations, online fundraisers, cooperative agreements with local businesses, and tax-sheltered private educational foundations, additional dollars are collected for advanced science equipment, computers, special devices for disabled students, and college scholarships. Wealthy communities defend such practices as a way to prevent parents from fleeing "to private school if they don't perceive the public education to be excellent."[17]

Decaying Infrastructure

Here we are in the twenty-first century, using schools that were built in the nineteenth. When local governments need to replace these aging buildings, they usually resort to issuing bonds. A **bond** is a certificate of debt issued by a government guaranteeing payment of the original investment plus interest by a specified future date. Bonds give the local communities the money they need to build the schools and fifteen to twenty years to pay off the debt.

But for most schools, repair not replacement is the remedy for antiquated buildings. While keeping schools current means new wiring and electrical outlets for computer and Internet installation, teachers and principals give higher priority to "adequate" heating, lighting, acoustics, ventilation, and air conditioning. The Department of Education estimates that 25,000 schools need major repairs, at an estimated cost of over $112 billion.[18] One piece of good news: Polls indicate that the public recognizes the financial need of our schools suggesting that local bonds will be approved.

 Governing America's Schools

School Governance Quiz

The following quiz should help you focus on how schools are governed. If you are puzzled at some of these questions, fear not; the remainder of the chapter is organized around a discussion of these questions and their answers.

1. Most school board members are (choose only one)
   a. Conservative, white, male, and middle or upper class.
   b. Liberal, middle-class women, about half of whom have been or are teachers.
   c. Middle of the road politically, about evenly divided between men and women, and representing all socioeconomic classes.
   d. So diverse politically, economically, and socially that it is impossible to make generalizations.
2. State school boards and chief state school officers are
   a. Elected by the people.

INTERACTIVE ACTIVITY
Know Your School Finance Lingo! Match economic terms with educational definitions.

OVERHEADS 111–112
Public Opinion on Education Spending

Environmental Factors Impact the Condition of Schools

TEACHING TIP
Use the School Governance Quiz as pretest with your class. Poll students' answers to get a sense of their assumptions and interests.

INTERACTIVE ACTIVITY
School Governance Quiz. Take an electronic version of this quiz.

Students and staff arrive to very different school buildings. What attitudes might develop as a result of learning in these dissimilar facilities? What physical improvements would you make to the dilapidated school building? List the physical characteristics of a school building that you believe are needed to ensure an "adequate education."

371

    b. Elected by the people's representatives.

    c. Appointed by the governor.

    d. Appointed by officials other than the governor.

    e. All of the above.

    f. None of the above.

3. During the past two decades, the influence of local school boards has
    a. Increased.
    b. Decreased.
    c. Remained unchanged.

4. Local school district superintendents are (you may choose more than one):
    a. Often mediating conflicts.
    b. Civil service–type administrators.
    c. Elected officials.
    d. Sometimes powerless figureheads.

5. Who might be considered part of the "hidden school government" (you may choose more than one):
    a. The school principal.
    b. The state school superintendent.
    c. The U.S. secretary of education.
    d. The school secretary.
    e. Parents.
    f. The Teacher Arbitration and Labor Relations Board.

6. The influence of the business community in U.S. schools can best be characterized as
    a. Virtually nonexistent.
    b. Felt only in vocational and commercial programs.
    c. Extensive and growing.
    d. Usually illegal.

7. In most schools, teachers are expected to
    a. Design the policies guiding their schools.
    b. Collaborate with principals and district officials to create policies to suit their schools.
    c. Comply with policies made by principals and by district and state officials.
    d. Comply with policies that seem appropriate and change those that do not.

School Governance Answer Key

1. a   2. e   3. b   4. a, b, d   5. d, e   6. c 7. c

    0 to 1 wrong: You receive the Horace Mann Award.

    2 wrong: You may want to run for school board.

    3 wrong: Read the rest of the chapter carefully.

    4 or more wrong: Take detailed notes on this part of the chapter; become a frequent visitor to the text Web page; find a friend to quiz you; and whatever you do, stay away from T.V. quiz shows.

FOCUS QUESTION 7
How do school boards and superintendents manage schools?

The Legal Control of Schools

The following sections review and discuss the quiz you have just taken, beginning with the first two questions:

1. Most school board members are . . . *conservative, white, male, and middle or upper class.*

2. School boards and chief state school officers are . . . *elected by the people, elected by the people's representatives, appointed by the governor, or appointed by officials other than the governor.*

There is great diversity in school governance. In some states, school boards and chief state school officials are elected; in others, they are appointed. Depending on the state, chief state school officers may be called superintendent, commissioner, or secretary. Although some say that "variety is the spice of life," you are probably thinking, How did this strange system get started (and will I ever sort it out)?

By the time the Constitution was written, control of schools by local communities was well established. The Constitution recognized and reaffirmed the states' responsibilities in this area under the **Tenth Amendment:** "The powers not delegated to the United States by the Constitution [as education is not], nor prohibited by it to the States, are reserved to the states, respectively, or to the people."

Today, the United States is unusual in this respect. Whereas most nations have a national ministry of education, which determines what and how children are taught in all parts of those nations, in the United States the legal responsibility for public education resides within each of the fifty states, the District of Columbia, and several U.S. territories. Since few governors or state legislators possess special expertise in education, state governments have delegated much of their authority to state boards of education, state superintendents, and departments of education, and finally to local governments. Probably the best way for you to learn how school boards, superintendents, and the entire governance structure works, is to consider a specific example.

From an Idea to a Reality

A state-level policy decision usually begins when someone, a legislator, school board member, superintendent, or a citizens' group suggests a new educational program, such as the need to improve student writing skills or the desire to limit class size. For our example, let's assume that the testing craze has led to a new policy in your state: All new candidates for a teaching license must take a course in "Instructional Strategies for Improving Student Test Performance."

Perhaps you're wondering, Who thinks up these policies? Policy suggestions originate from all kinds of sources: professional educators, school board members, state legislators, superintendents, state and federal court decisions, federal laws or initiatives, special interest groups, and the general public. In short, the role of the state school board is to consider recommendations for educational policy and to vote for or against their implementation.

Policy implementation is the responsibility of the chief state school officer and the state department of education. The chief state school officer is given different titles in different states (superintendent, director, commissioner, or secretary of education) and is usually the executive head of the state department of education. Together, the superintendent and the state department enforce state laws, evaluate teachers and schools, plan for future educational developments, and provide training and information to educators throughout the state. In our example, the superintendent would inform all school districts in the state of the new course requirement. If you were to apply for a teacher's license in the state, someone in the state department

GLOBAL VIEW
The World Data on Education (WDE) website provides access to information for 144 national education systems. www.ibe. unesco.org/ International/Databanks/ Wde/wde.htm

MULTIPLE INTELLIGENCE
CONNECTION
Figure 10.5 is a visual or
concept map of a typical
state school system. Have
students create their own
model but limit them to the
equipment and items that
are currently in the
classroom (desks, chairs,
trash can, water bottles,
backpacks). With three-
dimensional items and a
broader array of space, they
should be challenged by
the task's intricacies.

OVERHEADS 113–115
Structure of a Typical State
School System

Who Controls What?

of education would review your transcript to make certain that you had successfully completed the new course on improving test scores. If this and other requirements were met, you would be issued your teacher's license.

What about a job? States issue teacher's licenses, but the hiring and firing of teachers is done by local education districts. The nearly fifteen thousand school districts across the country are the most visible agency of educational governance—the ones you read about most often in your local newspaper. These districts are actually agencies of state rather than local governments, but they exercise control over such local matters as recruitment of school staff, curriculum formulation, and budgets—including teacher salaries and school building programs.

Most local school districts look something like the state government, but on a smaller scale. They have a school board, a superintendent, and an education office that, like the state department of education, helps administer the schools. Most local **school boards** are elected, although a few local communities appoint them. Each local board then hires a local superintendent to provide educational leadership within the community. Thus, in any given state, educational governance involves not only a state superintendent with a department of education and a statewide board but also local school boards and local superintendents. In many instances, local administrators and board members influence education more than do their counterparts at the state level. In practice, each state is unique in the way it delegates and administers its educational program. Figure 10.5 shows an example of a state school system's structure. And the main agents of school governance are described in the following paragraphs.

State Board of Education The **state board of education** is responsible for formulating educational policy. The members are usually appointed by the governor, but sometimes they are chosen in a statewide election.

Chief State School Officer Called *superintendent, commissioner, secretary of education, or director of instruction,* the **chief state school officer** is responsible for overseeing, regulating, and planning school activities, as well as implementing the policies of the board of education. The state superintendent is usually selected by the board of education but sometimes campaigns for the position in an election.

State Department of Education The **state department of education** performs the administrative tasks needed to implement state policy. This includes licensing teachers, testing student progress, providing information and training to teachers, distributing state and federal funds, seeing that local school systems comply with state laws, and conducting educational research and development. The state superintendent usually manages state department of education activities.

VIDEO SEGMENT 25
School Board Meeting

School Districts—Local School Boards and Superintendents All states except Hawaii have delegated much of the responsibility for local school operations to local school districts. (Hawaii treats the entire state as a single school district.) School districts vary in size from those serving only a few students to those with more than a million. Sometimes, local school districts are grouped into intermediate units as a way to simplify management. Most local school districts mirror the state organization, with a local school board, **superintendent,** and office of education. Local school districts may be responsible for school construction, taxing, budgeting, the hiring of school personnel, curriculum decisions, local school policy, and the education of students. Although school districts operate at the local level, their authority derives from the

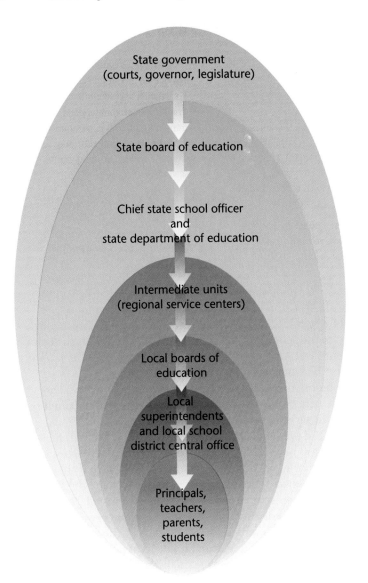

FIGURE 10.5
Structure of a typical
state school system.

State government
(courts, governor, legislature)

State board of education

Chief state school officer
and
state department of education

Intermediate units
(regional service centers)

Local boards of
education

Local
superintendents
and local school
district central office

Principals,
teachers,
parents,
students

REFLECTION: What are some of the difficulties in these many levels of governance? Do you favor elected or appointed school boards? Why?

state, and they must operate within the rules and regulations specified by the state. (The *Frame of Reference:* Who Controls What? Levels of Educational Power summarizes the relationships between state and local control of schools.)

State Influence Grows as School Boards Come under Fire

3. During the past two decades, the influence of local school boards has . . . *decreased.*

Forged in the hamlets of colonial New England, school boards have symbolized small-town democracy. School board meetings evoke the essence of Americana—the

INTERACTIVE ACTIVITY
Who Is in Control?
Test your knowledge of
who controls different
aspects of the school.

STATE GOVERNMENTS

- Levy taxes
- License teachers and other educators
- Set standards for school attendance, safety, etc.
- Outline minimum curricular and graduation standards (sometimes including specific textbooks to be used and competency tests for student graduation and teacher certification)
- Regulate the nature and size of local school districts

LOCAL SCHOOL DISTRICTS

- Implement state regulations and policies
- Create and implement local policies and practices for effective school administration

- Hire school personnel
- Provide needed funds and build appropriate facilities
- Fix salaries and working conditions
- Translate community needs into educational practice
- Initiate additional curriculum, licensing, or other requirements beyond state requirements
- Create current and long-range plans for the school district

REFLECTION: As a classroom teacher, offer some examples of the issues that would lead you to deal with state government. Which issues would send you down a path to the local government?

CRITICAL THINKING QUESTION

Ask your class if they would consider running for public office. Since their interest (and expertise) is education, would they contemplate a run for the school board? What presumptions impact their willingness or avoidance?

TEACHING TIP

A 2001 candidate for the Los Angeles School Board spent over $2 million to win the seat, making it the most costly school board seat in America. The job pays $24,000 per year. (*LA Weekly,* June 22–28, 2001)

kind painted by Norman Rockwell and made into a Frank Capra movie entitled "Mr. Deeds Elected to the School Board" (starring Jimmy Stewart as the beleaguered school board president). But Americana aside, many criticize school boards as unresponsive and entrenched bureaucracies.

Part of the problem is that there is little consensus on how school boards should operate.[19] Most school board members view themselves as **trustee representatives,** selected to serve because of their educational expertise and good judgment, and independent of ever-changing popular opinions. But others, including many voters, see school board members as **delegate representatives,** responsible for implementing the will of the public (or being voted out of office if they do not). The type of elections used to select school board members can shape the kind of school board that will emerge. When school boards are selected through "at-large" elections, in which the entire school district votes for all the members of the school board, the school board is expected to represent the interests of the entire community—in line with the notion of trustee representatives. But some school districts do not have at-large elections, instead choosing to have smaller geographic areas vote. In this type of election each of these smaller neighborhoods selects a board member to represent its interests (delegate representation).

While it might appear that at-large elections are less partisan, they do have serious drawbacks. Districtwide, at-large elections typically result in more elite, politically conservative and upper class individuals being elected to school boards. After all, it is the well-established individual who is likely to have the financial resources and educational and business background needed to win a big, districtwide election. Poorer citizens, people of color, and women are less likely to find themselves on school boards selected through at-large elections. Unfortunately, many citizens feel disenfranchised when it comes to school board elections.

Other criticisms of school boards run deeper. The Twentieth Century Fund and the Danforth Foundation conducted an intensive study of school boards, and recommended a total overhaul of the system, charging that

- School boards have become *immersed in administrative details,* at the expense of more important and appropriate policy issues. One study of West Virginia

. . . SCHOOL BOARDS BUT NEVER THOUGHT TO ASK

- The first school board was established in 1721 in Boston.
- In the United States, there are almost 15,000 school boards in charge of 53 million students in almost 93,000 schools.
- Three-quarters of the school districts are small, with fewer than 2,500 students in each.
- Fewer than 1 percent of the school districts in urban areas enroll 23 percent of all students in the United States.
- Eighty-five percent of local school boards are elected.
- School board members are typically white (81.3 percent), male (54.1 percent), financially secure (two-thirds earn more than $60,000 and almost half earn over $80,000).
- School boards hire superintendents who look much like themselves (96 percent of the superintendents are white, 88 percent are male, 95 percent are married).

SOURCE: Data compiled from Digest of Education Statistics, 2002; Characteristics of the 100 Largest Public Elementary and Secondary School Districts in U.S.: 1998–1999. NCES; C. Emily Feistritzer, "A Profile of School Board Presidents," in Patricia First and Herbert Walberg (eds.), *School Boards: Changing Local Control* (Berkeley: McCutchan, 1992); Jesse L. Freeman, Kenneth E. Underwood, and Jim C. Fortune, "What Boards Value," *American School Board Journal* 178 (January 1991), pp. 32–37.

REFLECTION: Can you think of other public institutions that are governed by a group similar to a school board? How does the school board in your community compare to the demographics of the typical board? To the demographics of your community?

school boards showed that only 3 percent of all decisions made concerned policy.

- School boards are *not representing local communities,* but only special interest groups. Elections to the school board receive little public support. In a New York City school board election, for instance, only 7 percent of the voters participated.

Superintendents (mostly white males) along with members of state and local boards of education comprise the official governance system of schools.

- The *politics of local school board elections* have a negative impact on attracting and retaining superintendents and lead to conflict with state education agencies.

- The composition of the boards is *not representative,* with individuals of color, women, the poor, and the young unrepresented or underrepresented.

- School boards have been in the *backseat when it comes to educational change and reform.* As a matter of fact, many school boards do not support current educational reform proposals, and members have lagged behind public opinion on such issues as school choice and educational vouchers.

- The education of children goes beyond school issues to include health, social, and nutritional concerns. School boards are *too limited in scope* to respond to all the contemporary concerns of children.

- If schools continue to be *financed less from local funds and more from* state funds, local boards could become less influential.

- Many of the new reforms call for *new governance organizations,* site-based management, or choice programs that relegate the school board to a less important, perhaps even unnecessary, role.[20]

CLASS ACTIVITY:
OVERVIEW AND GUEST
SPEAKER
IM, Activity 10:5

While these criticisms suggest a dismal future for school boards, preparing their obituary may be premature. School boards have endured a long time and may be around long after many of the reform recommendations are forgotten.

The School Superintendent and Principal

4. Local school district superintendents are: *often mediating conflicts, civil service–type administrators, and sometimes powerless figureheads.*

The first superintendents were hired to relieve school boards of their growing administrative obligations. The year was 1837, and these new superintendents worked in Buffalo and Louisville. As the nineteenth century progressed, more communities followed this example. Superintendents were expected to supervise and hire teachers, examine students, and buy supplies, which had become too burdensome for the school boards themselves. Superintendents also kept school records, developed examinations, chose textbooks, and trained teachers.

RELATED READING
If You Don't Feed the Teachers They Eat the Students! by Neila E. Connors (2000).

By the twentieth century, the superintendent's role had changed from the board's administrative employee to its most knowledgeable educational expert—from helper to chief executive officer. Today, the superintendent is the most powerful education officer in the school district, responsible for budgets, buildings, new programs, daily operations, long-term goals, short-term results, and recruiting, hiring, demoting, and firing personnel. When things are going well, the superintendent enjoys great popularity. But, when things are going poorly, or school board members are not pleased, or local community groups are angry, or teacher organizations turn militant, or . . . you get the picture. When there is a problem, it is usually the head of the system, the superintendent, who gets fired. The superintendent lives and works in a fishbowl, trying to please various groups while managing the school district. It is a very insecure existence of sidestepping controversies, pleasing school board members, responding to critics, juggling many different roles and goals, and living with conflict. Between 1990 and 2001, in thirty large urban school districts, superintendents served less than three years before they were fired, resigned, or retired.[21]

PROFILE IN EDUCATION   Anne Bryant

"Because they care about children and believe that all children can achieve. Most of [them] . . . serve with little or no remuneration. When you think of it, they are the one group who often makes a decision based on the needs of all children."[1]

Who are these community-oriented individuals? While few people consider them in this light, Anne Bryant, executive director of the National School Board Association (NSBA), is quick to underscore the service and commitment of the nation's school board members. Bryant believes that the strength of local school board leadership arises from school board members' capacity to represent the diversity of students and communities. The National School Board Association (NSBA) is a federation of 53 state and territorial organizations, representing 14,500 school districts, and almost 100,000 school board members. At the helm is Anne Bryant.

Bryant has long held a passion for public education, a commitment cultivated as a student teacher. Tapping into the intellectual curiosity of her students was a welcomed challenge. School bureaucracies and traditional teacher-centered instruction were not. Seeking to understand the political, economic, and social forces that shape education, Bryant became a student once again, pursuing graduate studies at the University of Massachusetts at Amherst. She wanted to unleash learning from the politics she believed stifled it. "With a doctorate in education, I felt prepared to reinvigorate life into teaching and learning and to lead schools in excellence and equity."[2]

Today Bryant is a seasoned school association executive. Prior to leading the NSBA, she served as executive director of the American Association of University Women (AAUW), a national organization advancing equity for women and girls in education, the workplace, and the family. With the release of AAUW's *How Schools Shortchange Girls* (1992), she brought attention to the academic, physical, and emotional losses females encounter in school. Bryant soon experienced the wrath of disgruntled constituents. Regressive political forces, ultraconservative parents, and sometimes even very traditional faculty and students denounced Bryant's call for gender equity, claiming that equal educational opportunities for females come at the expense of males. Bryant stood her ground.

As executive director of NSBA, Bryant understands such attacks, and appreciates how politics, special interests, and intensely traditional beliefs can derail school boards from meeting the contemporary needs of students. "My message is simple: Stop the power plays and personal vendettas and concentrate on improving student achievement."[3] While the national conversation about student achievement often focuses narrowly on students' abilities to perform well on standardized tests, Bryant contends that school boards must work to define achievement in ways that are meaningful to the communities they represent.

Demands on students are increasing as never before. The changing character of society and today's technology-based economy are driving new questions about what students should know and be able to do when they graduate.

Expectations are rising, not just for students but for schools and communities too. If we want students to succeed, school boards need to take action.[4]

Local governance of public education is, according to Bryant, a cornerstone of democracy. Yet, she believes that school boards are too often unrecognized partners in educational reform. As a link between the public and schools, she sees local boards uniquely positioned to lead efforts aimed to improve education. At the forefront of the NSBA's mission, then, is working with local boards to forge new partnerships with parents, teachers, and businesses. When tackling issues from school choice to school safety, building repairs to technology, Bryant encourages board members to imagine their entire community supporting the needs of students and to then make that vision a reality. And her message to board members is constant: Serving public schools is an honorable calling.

[1] Anne Bryant. Personal communication. (July 10, 2001). [2] Anne Bryant. Personal communication (July 16, 2001). [3] Jay Matthews. The Freedom Choice. *Washington Post* 10 July 2001. Online at www.washingtonpost.com [4] Anne Bryant. Technology on Board. *Technos Quarterly* 7 (Fall 1998), pp. 26–29.

REFLECTION: Do you agree with Anne Bryant that school boards go unrecognized for their ability to effect change in schools? Why or why not? What tensions have you witnessed between boards and local constituents? As a teacher, what role would you like local school boards to play in determining what schools can and should do?

www.mhhe.com/ sadker To learn more about Anne Bryant, click on *Profiles in Education.*

One need not look hard for the reasons for this turnover. Successful superintendents must win and maintain public support and financing for their schools. This involves forming political coalitions to back their programs and to ward off attacks from those more concerned with rising taxes than with the school budget. In an era in which most citizens in many communities do not have children in schools, this becomes a real test of political acumen. Superintendents find themselves serving on a number of civic committees, speaking to community groups, and being the public relations spokesperson for the school district.

School superintendents who survive and thrive are the politically savvy administrators who can "read" their school board. In *The School Managers: Power and Conflict in American Public Education,* Donald McCarty and Charles Ramsey provide a useful classification system that matches school board types with different superintendent styles.[22]

RAP 3.10
Get on Board
p. 436

School boards in communities that are . . .	*Prefer superintendent style that is . . .*
Dominated: School boards run by a few local elite who dominate community and school policies	*Functionary:* Follows wishes of the board
Factional: Divided community, competing factions	*Political:* Balances often opposing concerns, avoids appearance of favoritism
Pluralistic: Competition among interest groups	*Advisor:* Moves cautiously as advisor among shifting community coalitions
Inert: No visible power structure, little interest in schools	*Decision maker:* Board relies on superintendent for leadership and decision making

An effective superintendent must be an effective manager, and a number of new superintendents of large school districts have been selected for their management skills rather than their educational expertise. New York City, San Diego, Seattle, and Los Angeles have chosen generals, lawyers, and a former governor to lead their schools.[23] Because a large school district employs thousands of professionals and serves tens of thousands of students, these districts chose managers instead of educators. And good management is essential. Superintendents have been terminated when textbooks or teacher paychecks arrive late, or when the school days chosen for closing prove unpopular. And as if that were not enough, some school districts have adopted performance-based contracts that link superintendent compensation directly to student performance.[24]

While the superintendent is the focal point of district pressures, the principal bears the brunt of the school pressure. "Stress, testing, and social problems are all in the schools now. AIDS education, security, parenting classes, language programs. There are so many things that they are responsible for that they might not have control over, and it's led to concern about principal burnout."[25] Even at the elementary level, where many consider the stress most tolerable, a typical elementary principal supervises 30 teachers, 14 other staff members, 425 students, and works an average of nine or ten hours a day, 54 hours or more a week.[26] Amazingly, 20 percent of principals report spending five to ten hours a week in efforts aimed at a single purpose: avoiding lawsuits.[27] Principal recruiters struggle to overcome persistent racial and ethnic imbalances as well.[28] (Figure 10.6 provides insight into principal demographics.)

RELATED READING
Who Said School Administration Would Be Fun?: Coping with a New Emotional and Social Reality by Jane L. Sigford (1998).

OVERHEADS 116–118
Elementary and Secondary School Principals

Elementary Principals and Power

What Principals Earn

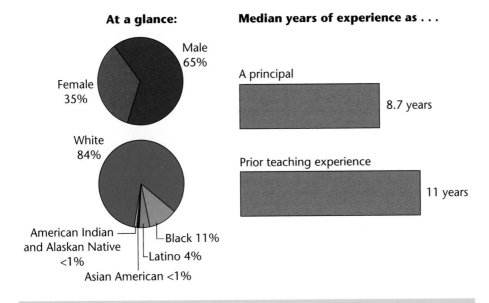

At a glance:

Median years of experience as . . .

Male 65%

Female 35%

White 84%

American Indian and Alaskan Native <1%

Black 11%

Latino 4%

Asian American <1%

A principal — 8.7 years

Prior teaching experience — 11 years

FIGURE 10.6

Elementary and secondary school principals.

SOURCE: National Center for Educational Statistics, "Principals in Public and Private Elementary and Secondary Schools, by Selected Characteristics, 1993–94," *Digest of Educational Statistics 2000* (Washington, DC: U.S. Department of Education, 2000).

REFLECTION: What are the potential challenges for schools with white principals and a majority of students of color?

Covert Power in Schools

5. Who might be considered part of the "hidden school government" . . . *the school secretary and parents.*

So you think that the school principal is the only one responsible for school personnel decisions, including hiring and firing? Think again. Parents, vocal individuals, the school secretary, and community groups have **covert power** and can bring significant pressure to bear on which teachers stay in a school, and which leave. These unofficial but highly involved persons and groups constitute the **hidden government** of schools.

The concept of hidden government is not unique to schools. In fact, most of our institutions, including the White House, have developed their own unique forms of hidden government. There, decision making is often influenced more by old colleagues back home (the "kitchen cabinet") than by the president's official advisers and cabinet members.

How does hidden government operate in schools? Following are some examples.

Example 1 A first-year teacher in a New England junior high school spent long hours after school, preparing lessons and working with his students. Admirable as all this appeared, the school secretary, Ms. Hand, advised the teacher not to work with female students after school hours, because "You may get your fingers burned." The teacher smiled, ignored the secretary's advice, and continued providing students with after-school help.

Within a week, the principal called the teacher in for a conference and suggested that the teacher provide extra help to students only if both male and female students were present. The teacher objected to the advice and to the secretary's complaining

FOCUS QUESTION 8
What is the "hidden" government of schools?

RELATED READING
Schools That Learn: A Fifth Discipline Fieldbook for Educators, Parents, and Everyone Who Cares About Education by Peter M. Senge (ed.) (2000).

TEACHING TIP
Have students *think-pair* and *share* similar examples that illuminate the hidden government of schools.

to the principal. The principal responded, "You're new here, and I can understand your concern. But what you have to learn is that Ms. Hand is more than a secretary. She knows this school better than I do. Follow her advice and you'll do just fine."

Lesson: You can't always tell which people hold the real power by their official position.

Lesson: The school secretary is often the eyes and ears of the principal. In some cases, the secretary manages the day-to-day operations of the school.

Example 2 A young teacher in an elementary school in the Midwest was called into the principal's office for a conference. The principal evaluated her teaching as above average but suggested that she maintain greater discipline. Her classroom was simply too noisy, and the students' chairs were too often left in disarray. The conference was over in ten minutes.

The teacher was offended. She did not feel her classroom was too noisy, and the chairs were always arranged in a neat circle. Moreover, the principal had visited her class for only five minutes, and during that time the students had said hardly a word.

The next day, in the teacher's lounge, all became clear when she discussed the conference with another teacher. The teacher nodded, smiled, and explained:

"Mr. Richards."

"The custodian?"

"Yup. He slowly sweeps the halls and listens for noisy classrooms. Then he tells the principal. He also hates it when the chairs are in a circle, since it makes sweeping harder. Nice straight rows are much easier. Just make sure your classroom is quiet when he's in the halls and have your students put the chairs in neat, straight rows at the end of the day. That's the ticket for getting a good evaluation!"

Lesson: School custodians are often a source of information for principals and of supplies for teachers. They make very helpful allies and powerful adversaries.

Example 3 An elementary school teacher in a rural southern community was put in charge of the class play. Rehearsals were under way when the teacher received a note to stop by the principal's office at 3:00 P.M.

The principal had received a call from a parent who was quite disappointed at the small part her daughter had received in the play. The principal wanted the teacher to consider giving the child a larger part. "After all," he explained, "her mother is influential in the PTA, and her father is one of the town's most successful businessmen. It's

The school secretary holds a position that can exert significant covert power in his or her pivotal role as the principal's "eyes and ears."

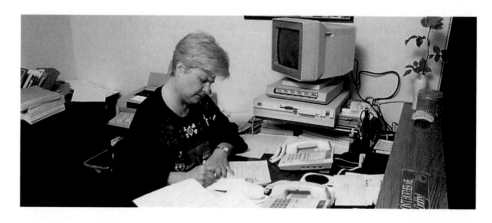

silly for you to alienate them. Give her a bigger part. Life will be easier for both of us, and we may be able to get her parents' support for the next school bond issue. That would mean a raise for all of us."

Lesson: Parents can also be influential in school decisions by applying pressure on principals, school boards, and community groups. When you decide to make a stand in the face of parental pressure, choose a significant issue and be able to substantiate your facts.

Business and Schools

6. The influence of the business community in U.S. schools can best be characterized as . . . *extensive and growing.*

Business values have long influenced school practices, and decades ago educators adopted a business vocabulary. *Superintendent,* the title originally given to a factory supervisor, was assigned to the school district leader. Both a factory and a school have been called a *plant. Quality control, accountability, management design,* and *efficiency* were also expropriated. Little surprise that a growing number of superintendents come from the business sector. School values often mirror those of business: hard work, competition, dependability, punctuality, neatness, conformity, and loyalty.[29] Companies that formalize a relationship with a school, by dedicating personnel or products or signing exclusive rights contracts, are said to have formed an **educational partnership.** A number of educators express concerns about these developments, an issue we explored earlier in this text. But whether we are comfortable or uncomfortable with this trend, "The most far-reaching initiative in education to emerge in recent years is the growing corporate interest in public schools."[30]

CLASS ACTIVITY: GOVERNANCE SIMULATION
IM, Activity 10:4

FOCUS QUESTION 9
How does the business community influence school culture?

Competition and other business-oriented values have become so familiar and pervasive in our schools that we have become inured to them.

Making Schools More Responsive

FOCUS QUESTION 10
How are schools being
made more responsive to
teachers and the
community?

CLASS ACTIVITY:
ADDITIONAL
GOVERNANCE ROLE-
PLAYS
IM, Activity 10:6

7. In most schools, teachers are expected to . . . *comply with policies made by principals and by district and state officials.*

While parents, community groups, and the business sector carve out their roles in schools, teachers traditionally have been omitted from meaningful involvement in school governance. To get a sense of what that might feel like, imagine that you are the senior faculty member at Someplace High School. Having taught there for thirty years, you know the school like the back of your hand. You are regarded as an excellent teacher, an expert at judging the needs of your students. Should you participate in making decisions affecting the management of your school?

To get a sense of how little say teachers have once they leave their own classrooms, let's join the first faculty meeting of the fall at Someplace High. The principal, Mr. Will E. Tell, is discussing the new teacher assessment forms with the faculty:

> MR. TELL: If you all look in your folders, you'll see the criteria on which you will be assessed when I observe in your classrooms. Look these forms over carefully, and let me know if you have any questions. I'll be scheduling my school observation visits with you shortly. Another issue I wanted to raise with you concerns our need to develop better relations with the community. I've passed around a sign-up sheet for a committee to turn around the low attendance at parent conferences. What I have in mind is a car wash or a bake sale or another fund-raising activity to bring the community together. Ms. Johnson, you have a question?

> MS. JOHNSON: Yes, Mr. Tell. I thought that we were going to talk about setting up a better school website, one that can pull parents into school conferences and activities, assist students with their homework, have links to resources, and address special interest topics for teachers and parents. We all indicated at last year's faculty meeting that this should be a top priority.

> MR. TELL: You're absolutely right, Louise, and I'm glad you raised the topic. That was going to be our first order of business, but I'm happy to report that the district office called yesterday and has promised us website support by the second semester. I'll be getting out my first newsletter to the faculty in a few weeks, and I'll be sure to include that information. I'll also be announcing the in-service training sessions for the fall semester. I heard some interesting speakers at the national convention I attended, and I think I'm going to be able to get some of them to come to our district. Before we end the meeting, I want to introduce our new faculty member. I hired Ms. Wetherby over the summer, and she'll join the teachers in our English department. I know you'll all do everything you can to make sure that Ms. Wetherby feels welcome. Now, if there are no further topics for discussion, let's all get back to our classrooms. Tomorrow the kids arrive. It's time for a new year.

IN THE NEWS

Bonus Pay

Governor Jeb Bush of Florida decided to give teachers and schools millions of dollars in "bonus pay" as a reward for high scores on standardized tests. But when two middle schools offered the cash bonuses directly to high scoring students, as much as $150 per student, the governor objected. The chair of the school board argued that if adults get bonuses, so should children. Florida Congressman Jim Davis characterized the episode as "a new and inevitable low in testing run amok."

Source: "Cash for Success," *The Washington Post,* August 21, 2001.

 What's new in education? Click on *News Feeds.*

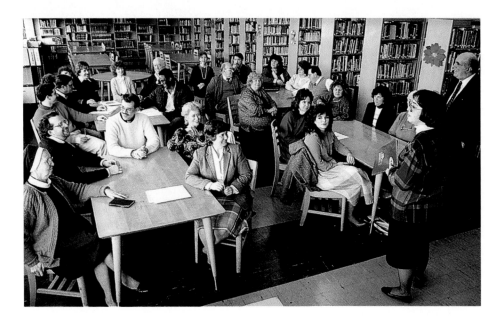

Teachers, who know more than most people in the educational chain about the needs and interests of individual students, have often been excluded from school management and policy-making.

From listening in on this faculty meeting, you can tell that many of the most crucial decisions were made by others. Whether a teacher will be assigned to advanced placement literature classes or remedial English is a decision usually made by the principal. Teachers, as a rule, do not participate in hiring new teachers, in developing criteria by which their teaching will be evaluated, in setting graduation requirements, or in scheduling classes.

One reason for unresponsive schools is sheer size: over the past centuries, schools and school districts continue to grow. Larger districts are considered more cost-effective because they lower the per pupil expenses, from preparing food to building maintenance, and bigger school districts are able to offer more courses, extracurricular activities, and sports programs.[31] Merging smaller schools and districts into larger ones is called **consolidation.** (See *Frame of Reference:* Consolidation in Action.) But larger schools and school districts also mean more red tape, greater student alienation, and reduced parent-teacher involvement; in other words, less responsive schools.[32] Many districts are now reversing the trend, creating smaller schools and smaller districts, a process called **decentralization.**

In addition to size, top-down decision making by principals and superintendents also contributes to a sense of teacher powerlessness.[33] Efforts to empower teachers include site-based or school-based management and collaborative decision making. **Site-based** or **school-based management** shifts decision making from the central district office to individual schools, while **collaborative decision making** creates teacher committees to share power between the principal and the faculty. While you may find yourself teaching in a school using one or both of these approaches, keep in mind that the results have been mixed. While some teachers enjoy making curricular and budgetary decisions, others feel such participation simply becomes "just another meeting you've got to go to."[34] To complicate these efforts even further, federally mandated tests have preempted many local decisions.[35] One of the challenges facing you as a teacher or administrator will be to create more responsive and humane school climates, both for yourself and your students.

MULTIPLE INTELLIGENCE CONNECTION

Speaking of *all over the country,* country music song titles have long been known to express the lyricists' deepest (albeit exaggerated) emotions. Can students suggest country music titles for themes (or key terms) in this chapter? Here are a few samples: *My Tax Dollars Renewal Bought Nuthin' for the School; Gotta Consolidate My Mind, It's Site-Based Management Time; Principals Don't Whine, They Ain't Got the Time.*

FRAME OF REFERENCE   Consolidation in Action

The following numbers show the dramatic reduction in school districts. Still, 75 percent of the remaining districts are fairly small, servicing fewer than 2,500 students each.

School Year	Number of Public School Districts
1939–1940	117,108
1949–1950	83,718
1959–1960	40,520
1970–1971	17,995
1980–1981	15,912
1989–1990	15,367
1999–2000	14,928

SOURCE: *Digest of Education Statistics 2002,* U.S. Department of Education, National Center for Education Statistics.

REFLECTION: While district size is difficult for a student to gauge, school size is far easier. In your opinion, what is the "ideal" size for a high school? What was the size of your high school? How does your experience influence the notion of an "ideal" size?

SUMMARY

CHAPTER REVIEW

Go to the Online Learning Center to take a quiz, practice with key terms, and review concepts from the chapter.

CURRENT NEWS FROM POWERWEB

To access PowerWeb, go to Chapter 10 on the Online Learning Center to read current articles and to access news feeds about:

- Government
- School Vouchers
- Schools and Federal Policy

1. Why do teachers need to know about finance and governance?

   For teachers to influence the direction of schools, they need to become more involved in finance and governance issues. Unfortunately, the insights of students and teachers are rarely heard in policy circles.

2. How is the property tax connected to unequal educational funding?

   Local communities generally fund their schools through a property tax, which many people consider outdated and unfair. Since some areas are wealthier than others, some school districts generate more than enough money for schools, while others must struggle to keep schools open. Robin Hood laws, built on the California *Serrano* decision, attempted to equalize educational funding between wealthy and poor communities. Resistance to these attempts led to passage of laws such as Proposition 13, which limited property taxes. Although the Supreme Court recognized that school financing is a flawed system, it did not rule the process unconstitutional. State courts continue to address these financial inequities.

3. What is the distinction between educational *equity* and educational *adequacy?*

   Opposition grew as state court decisions, for example *Abbott v. Burke* in New Jersey, directed funds be moved from wealthier districts to poorer communities. Because increased funding did not always lead to higher test scores, courts began to differentiate between financial input and educational outcome. Several state court decisions have cited state constitutional language guaranteeing adequate or efficient education, and focus on the educational skills of graduates, rather than per pupil expenditures. While critics of educational equity charge that money will not solve poor educational performance, well-funded schools draw more qualified teachers and have smaller classes, two factors associated with student achievement.

4. What are the sources of state revenues?

The most common state sources of school funding are property tax, sales tax, personal income tax, and state lotteries. Many of these revenue sources are regressive, putting most of the burden on the poorest citizens. Although states have experimented with different funding methods, such as foundation programs and a guaranteed tax base for all districts, none has proved very successful.

5. How does the federal government influence education?

According to the Tenth Amendment of the U.S. Constitution, education is the responsibility of the states. Still, the federal government exercises great influence through court actions, funding leverage, and specific programs sponsored by the U.S. Department of Education. Federal monies provide between 6 and 8 percent of K–12 educational costs, much of which is in block grants.

6. What current trends are shaping educational finance?

School financing in the future will be influenced by demands tying school performance to funding levels (accountability), the popularity of choice programs, the economy's impact on school budgets, the great need for repairing deteriorating school buildings (infrastructure), and the continuing effort of wealthy communities to retain their tax revenues in their own community, which perpetuates educational inequality.

7. How do school boards and superintendents manage schools?

At the state level, the legislature, state board of education, state superintendent, and state department of education administer schools, and delegate some of its power to local school boards and superintendents. Boards of education formulate education policy and can act as trustee representatives, serving the interests of the entire community, or as representative delegates, serving the interests of their neighborhoods. The chief state school officer, often called the superintendent, is responsible for implementing those policies of the state board of education, just as the local superintendent implements the policies of the local board of education. Several large school districts are turning to former lawyers, business executives, political leaders, and even military officers to lead their school districts.

8. What is the "hidden" government of schools?

Parents, school secretaries, and custodians influence school life, and are part of the hidden government of schools.

9. How does the business community influence school culture?

The business community significantly impacts schools through its ethos, vocabulary, and value system, which promote competitiveness, conformity, and punctuality. Many question the motivation, tactics, and commercialism involved in those efforts.

10. How are schools being made more responsive to teachers and the community?

Traditionally, teachers have not had a significant role in school governance. Recent trends of school-based management, also called site-based management, and collaborative decision making, may provide teachers with a more influential position in school governance. Consolidation has decreased the number of school districts while increasing the average size of schools. Supporters believe that this increases educational opportunities and efficiency by absorbing small school districts with limited educational resources and electives into larger districts. Critics claim that it increases alienation and red tape.

Go to Chapter 10 on your *Resources for Exploring Education* CD-ROM to access Case Studies and Readings.

EXTENDED LEARNING

CASE STUDIES

- Debby Bennett: An experienced high-school English teacher on hall duty challenges an obstreperous student without a pass. She is offended by the actions of an assistant principal who minimizes the student's offenses and remarks on her need to "hassle" students.

- Kate Sullivan: A principal faces the problems endemic to the students served by her school, which is located in a very low socioeconomic area.

- Jane Vincent: A teacher is asked by her principal to reconsider her grading of a student whose numerical average for the marking period is just below the department's cutoff score for that grade.

READINGS

- Jonathan Kozol. Selection from *Savage Inequalities: Children in America's Schools.*

- Elaine Wilmore and Cornell Thomas. "The New Century: Is It Too Late for Transformational Leadership?"

KEY TERMS AND PEOPLE

Abbott v. Burke, 361
accountability, 368
adequate education, 362
block grants, 367
bond, 369
Anne Bryant, 379
categorical grants, 367
chief state school officer, 374
collaborative decision making, 385
consolidation, 385
covert power, 381
decentralization, 385
delegate representative, 376
Edgewood v. Kirby, 361
educational outcome, 362

educational partnerships, 383
estate (or gift) taxes, 366
excise taxes, 366
financial input, 362
foundation program, 361
guaranteed tax base program, 361
hidden government, 381
motor vehicle license fee, 366
municipal overburden, 360
personal income tax, 365
property tax, 360
Proposition 13, 361
Robin Hood reformers, 361
sales tax, 365

San Antonio v. Rodriguez, 361
school boards, 374
Serrano v. Priest, 361
severance tax, 366
sin tax, 366
site-based (school-based) management, 385
state board of education, 374
state department of education, 374
state lotteries, 365
superintendent, 374
Tenth Amendment, 373
trustee representative, 376
United States Department of Education, 367

DISCUSSION QUESTIONS AND ACTIVITIES

1. Create a plan for (a) raising funds for education and (b) distributing funds equitably to all school districts within a state.

2. What is your opinion of the "adequacy" argument? Do you have any reservations about this approach? Do you believe that educational expenditures and educational quality are directly related? Support your position.

3. Research the average costs of educating a student in a local district. Discuss with classmates as you compare district programs, tax base, facilities, and student achievement.

4. Which of the four types of school boards would you prefer to serve on, or work for? Why? Which of the four types of school superintendents would you prefer to be, or to work for? Why?

5. Have you had any personal experience in an organization that had both a formal and a "hidden" government? Explain how these governments operated.

 WEB-*TIVITIES*

1. States to the Rescue
2. The Federal Government's Role in Financing Education
3. The Legal Control of Schools
4. Superintendents
5. School Boards Under Fire
6. The Business of America Is Business
7. Trends in School Governance: Educational Partnerships

REEL TO REAL TEACHING

OCTOBER SKY (1999)
Run Time: 108 minutes

Synopsis: The true story of Homer Hickam, a high school student seemingly destined to repeat his father's harsh life in the West Virginia coal mines, until the Soviet launch of *Sputnik* in 1957 sparks his own scientific aspirations. With the encouragement of a science teacher, Homer and his fellow "Rocket Boys" venture to launch their own homemade rockets.

Reflection:

1. This chapter emphasizes the financing and governing of schools. How did these two factors shape students' lives in Coalwood? Give examples from the film. How did your schooling reflect educational governance and financing?

2. Consider how inequitable funding is related to geography. How does school finance impact educational opportunities in rural, suburban, and urban schools?

3. *October Sky* is set in the late 1950s, prior to many of the landmark legal rulings on educational funding discussed in this chapter. How might these court decisions have altered educational opportunities at Coalwood High?

4. What student expectations are revealed in the principal's comment to Ms. Riley: "Our job is to give these kids an education, not false hopes. Once in a while a lucky one gets out on a football scholarship. The rest work in the mines."

5. What academic and social purposes do events such as science fairs, spelling bees, and music festivals play in schools and communities? How do these differ in wealthy and poor schools? Interview classmates who attended rural, suburban, and urban schools to learn about these differences.

Follow-up Activity: *October Sky* is a "coming of age" film. Homer Hickam wrestles with accepting life in the mines and pursuing his own dreams. It is a common theme not only in film, but also in life. Interview older friends or family members about whether they were ever expected to "follow in the footsteps" of others. How did they feel about it? Why did they choose to follow tradition or make a new path? Was their decision influenced by a pivotal schooling experience, a motivating teacher, or inspiring hero? What do they think now of the decisions they made then? Capture their stories by audiotaping, video recording, or taking notes on the interviews.

www.mhhe.com/
sadker7e

How do you rate this film? Go to *Reel to Real Teaching* in the Critics' Corner to review this film.

FOR FURTHER READING

Cultivating Leadership in Schools: Connecting People, Purpose, and Practice, by Gordon Donaldson, Jr. (2000). Enter the real-life world of decision making by administrators, teachers, parents, and school boards. "See" how interpersonal and intrapersonal skills are the keys to successful leadership.

Equal Resources, Equal Outcomes: The Distribution of School Resources and Student Achievement in California, by Julian R. Betts, Kim S. Rueben, and Anne Danenberg (2000). Debunks the myth that centralized funding of California public schools has equalized spending across districts and demonstrates how inequalities in school resources create inequalities in student achievement.

Reframing the Path to School Leadership, by Lee Bolman and Terrence Deal (2002). A rare blend of storytelling and analysis between teachers and principals, the authors give an optimistic view of what can go right in schools today, and what possibilities lie ahead for classroom and school leadership.

School Finance: A Policy Perspective, by Allan Odden and Larry Picus (3rd ed., 2003). Provides a roadmap through recent research on equity and adequacy, case studies on state plans for resource allocation, and a simulation allowing readers to manipulate school finance data and see the effects on resources and achievement.

Who Governs Our Schools? Changing Roles and Responsibilties, by David T. Conley (2003). Provides valuable insights on and implications for the current transfer of power from local and state school governments to the national level. Examines the new federal role, including the *No Child Left Behind* Act.

School Law and Ethics

FOCUS QUESTIONS

1. What are your legal rights and responsibilities as a teacher?
2. What legal rights do students enjoy (and do they have legal responsibilities)?

3. What are today's main approaches to moral education?

 WHAT DO YOU THINK? What Is Your Rights Quotient? Take an electronic version of the quiz on page 392.

CHAPTER PREVIEW

- An honors student sues the school district after being randomly stripped searched.
- A teacher is reprimanded for allowing a first grader to read a Bible story to the class.
- A school puts the senior yearbook on its Web page and finds that it helps pedophiles identify potential targets.
- A student complains that peer grading of assignments is a violation of privacy.
- A homosexual student sues a school district for discrimination.

Today, lawyers and judges are increasingly a part of school life. In this chapter, you will have the opportunity to respond to actual legal situations that have confronted teachers and students. (Get ready to determine your RQ—Rights Quotient.) Also included are some pragmatic steps for your legal self-defense, steps that you can take to avoid potential problems. But, beyond the nitty-gritty of these legal case studies, we will ask more penetrating questions about right and wrong, questions that go beyond the law, such as: How should teachers deal with ethical issues that emerge in the classroom? Should teachers take positions on moral issues? Or should they play a more neutral role? To handle these important but difficult ethical dilemmas, we will offer some suggestions for ways teachers can organize their classrooms, and themselves.

CHAPTER FOCUS

In this chapter, readers respond to actual legal situations that have confronted teachers and students. In fact, your class can test themselves to determine their RQ (Rights Quotient). Also included in the chapter are pragmatic steps that teachers can take for legal self-defense. Students are offered suggestions for organizing a classroom, and handling important but difficult ethical dilemmas in school. For a chapter outline, see the IM.

Classroom Law

You have probably heard it before: the United States is a litigious society. "Take them to court," "I'll sue," and "Have your lawyer call my lawyer" are phrases that have worked their way into the American lexicon. And actions match words. People sue companies. Companies sue people. Governments sue companies. Companies and people sue governments. We tend to seek redress in the courts for all kinds of problems, from divorce to physical injury, from protecting our beliefs to complying (or not complying) with laws.

Today, parents sue teachers. Students sue teachers. Teachers sue schools. Despite the growing importance and influence of school-related law, many educators are still unaware of their basic legal rights and responsibilities. This can be a costly professional blind spot.[1]

What rights do you have in the classroom? Consider this exchange between a college professor and a former associate superintendent of public instruction for California:

SUPERINTENDENT: "Teaching is a privilege, not a right. If one wants this privilege, he or she has to give up some rights."

PROFESSOR: "Just what constitutional rights do people have to give up in order to enter teaching?"

SUPERINTENDENT: "Any right their community wants them to give up."[2]

Although such simplistic attitudes still exist, recent years have seen extraordinary changes in the legal rights of both teachers and students. Once the victims of arbitrary school rules and regulations, today's teachers and students can institute legal action if they believe that their constitutional rights are being threatened. In an increasing number of cases, the courts are finding school administrators guilty of violating the rights of both teachers and students.

As a classroom teacher, what can you legally say and do? Can you let your students log freely onto the Internet? What disciplinary methods are acceptable? How does your role as teacher limit your personal life? Knowing the answers to these questions *before* you step into a classroom can help you avoid costly mistakes.

While teachers would like to know definitively what is legal and what is not, courts often set forth standards with such terms as "reasonable care" or "appropriately under the circumstances." Courts try to balance legitimate concerns that can be raised on both sides of an issue and to keep their options open. Staying legally up-to-date is an ongoing professional task.

 ## What Is Your Rights Quotient?

The following case studies focus on court cases or federal law.[3] The vignettes are divided into two parts: teachers' rights and students' rights. In each case, an issue is identified, a situation is described, and you are asked to select an appropriate (legal) response. After your selection, the correct response and relevant court decisions or laws are described. Keep track of your rights and wrongs; a scoring system at the conclusion will help you determine your RQ (rights quotient). Good luck!

Federal, state, and local governments all have a voice in education, although they don't necessarily speak in unison. To help you navigate the legal landscape, here's a brief look at how the different branches and levels of government influence school law.

THE U.S. CONSTITUTION

While the Constitution does not mention education, it does guarantee to individuals basic rights, rights that are of concern in schools. Three Constitutional Amendments are of special interest to teachers and students.

- **First Amendment** protects freedom of religion and speech. An important part of this Amendment is the **establishment clause,** which prohibits government (including school) advancement of religion.
- Fourth Amendment protects basic privacy and security.
- Fourteenth Amendment protects right to due process and equal protection.

FEDERAL LAWS

Many federal laws influence education. The Civil Rights Act of 1964 bars discrimination on the basis of race, color, or national origin. Title IX prohibits discrimination on the basis of sex. The Individuals with Disabilities Education Act expands educational opportunities to persons with disabilities. By funding certain programs, and withholding funds from others, from elementary school through college, the federal government exerts a significant influence on education.

STATE AND LOCAL LAWS

State constitutions as well as state and local laws influence education, so there are significant local differences throughout the nation. State and local laws (also known as statutes) often deal with school financing, collective bargaining, teacher certification, and compulsory attendance.

THE COURTS

A dual judicial system of state and federal courts exists in the United States. State courts initially hear most legal issues in education. Only cases challenging the U.S. Constitution or federal laws are heard in federal courts, including the U.S. Supreme Court.

SOURCE: Michael LaMorte, *School Law: Cases and Concepts* (Needham Heights: Allyn & Bacon, 2002).

REFLECTION: What are the advantages and disadvantages of these different government jurisdictions determining school law? Offer at least two benefits and drawbacks of this system.

I. Teachers' Rights and Responsibilities

Issue	*Situation 1*
Applying for a position	You did it! You finished student teaching (you were great!) and the school district you most want to teach in has called you for an interview. Mr. Thomas, from the personnel office, seems impressed with your credentials and the interview is going well. He explains that the school district is very committed to its teachers and invests a great deal of resources in training. He wants to make certain that this investment makes sense, so he asks you for your long-range plans with such questions as: "Do you see yourself teaching in this system for a long time?" and "Are you planning to get married or have children in the near future?"

_____ You answer the questions realizing that the district is entitled to know about your long-range plans.

_____ You avoid answering the questions. You think it's none of his business, but you are worried that you won't get the position.

Federal and State Laws, Court Decisions   Not too long ago, school districts regularly considered marital and parenthood status in employment decisions. For

TEACHING TIP
It is very possible that you and your students have stories of interviews where illegal or inappropriate questions were asked. Usually, when we are caught off guard, we respond instinctively—revealing more than an interviewer is entitled to know. Brainstorm several ways to successfully deflect or respond to inappropriate questions.

women these were critical factors in being offered a job, and the "right" answer was: "No, I am not going to get married or have children." For male candidates, the question was less important and rarely asked. Now a variety of federal and state laws and court decisions make such inquiries illegal. Interview questions must be related to the job requirements. Questions about race, creed, marital status, sex, religion, age, national origin, and physical or other disabilities and even a request for photographs along with an application are generally illegal. **Title IX of the Education Amendments (1972)** and **Title VII of the Civil Rights Act (1964)** are two federal laws that prohibit many of these practices. In situation 1, the questions are inappropriate and illegal, and you need not answer them. You may wish to notify the school district or even the Office for Civil Rights in order to stop the school district from asking such discriminatory questions in the future. The challenge, of course, is how you could answer such questions without ruining your chances for being offered a position—that is, if you still want the job.[4]

Issue	*Situation 2*
Sexual harassment	After surviving the gender discriminatory interview, you are offered a teaching position and decide to take it. After all, you like the community and the children, and with any luck you will never run into Mr. Thomas (the interviewer) again. You are very excited as you prepare for your first day. You are up an hour early, rehearsing your opening remarks. You enter the school, feeling hopeful and optimistic. Then it's your worst nightmare. You meet the new principal, Mr. Thomas, recently transferred from the personnel office. You spend the next year dodging his lewd comments, his unwanted touches, and his incessant propositions. At the end of the year, you find yourself in counseling and worried about your job. You decide that

_____ Your initial instincts were right. You should never have taken this job. Quit before things get worse.

_____ Enough is enough. You sue the district for damages.

MULTIPLE INTELLIGENCE CONNECTION
It can take a high degree of interpersonal intelligence to avoid inappropriate situations with students. Ask your class to imagine themselves as new teachers. Seated nearby in a restaurant is a group of high school seniors eating and drinking beer. They send over a pitcher of beer to you and watch closely for your reaction. How best might you handle this? Have students roleplay possibilities. Comment on their solutions with regard to legal standards and interpersonal skills.

Court Decision Anita Hill's charges against Supreme Court nominee Clarence Thomas, as well as similar charges against former President Clinton, a stream of Senators, and other officials have awakened millions of Americans to the issue of sexual harassment. The principal's behavior, both verbal and physical, is clearly an example of this problem. The Supreme Court ruled that victims of sexual harassment are also victims of sex discrimination and can recover monetary damages. Keeping a record of the principal's behavior and having witnesses will strengthen your case. You certainly can sue, and, if you are successful, you may be awarded significant monetary damages. You can also file a grievance with the Office for Civil Rights, without even having a lawyer. This grievance will launch an investigation of the school's practices.[5]

Issue	*Situation 3*
Personal lifestyle	After your first few months, your reputation is established: You are known as a creative and effective teacher and are well liked by students and colleagues (isn't that wonderful!). But your life outside the classroom is not appreciated by school officials. You are single and living with your

"significant other." Several school officials have strong feelings about this and believe that you are a poor role model for the students. The school system publicly announces that your cohabitation is having a negative influence on your elementary-age students and suspends you.

_____ You are the victim of an illegal action and should sue to be reinstated.

_____ The school board is within its rights in dismissing you and removing a bad role model from the classroom.

Court Decision   This case hinges on how much personal freedom an individual abandons as a teacher and role model for students. Although court decisions have varied, the following general standard should be kept in mind: Does your behavior significantly disrupt the educational process or erode your credibility with students, colleagues, or the community? If the school district can demonstrate that you have disrupted education or have lost credibility, then you may be fired.

In the case outlined here, the teacher sued the school district (*Thompson v. Southwest School District*). The court indicated that, until the school district took action to suspend the teacher on grounds of immorality, the public was generally unaware of the teacher's cohabitation with her boyfriend. The court decided that it was unfair of the board of education to make the issue public in order to gain community support for its position. Furthermore, the court ruled that the teacher's behavior had not interfered with her effectiveness in the classroom. With neither a loss of credibility nor a significant disruption of the educational process, the board lost its case and the teacher kept her job.

What if the teacher's "significant other" was of the same sex? Whether gay and lesbian teachers need legal protection from dismissal based on sexual orientation is a divisive and unsettled debate. Several states and more than 100 cities and counties prohibit sexual orientation discrimination in employment. Even in places without specific laws protecting gay and lesbian teachers, it is unlikely that they can be dismissed without direct evidence showing that a homosexual lifestyle negatively impacts their teaching.

Court decisions regarding the personal lifestyles of teachers have differed from state to state. Driving while intoxicated or smoking marijuana was found to be grounds for dismissal in one state but not in another, depending on whether the behavior resulted in "substantial disruption" of the educational process. On the other hand, an attempt to dismiss a teacher because she did not attend church was not upheld by the court. In fact, the teacher in this case actually won financial damages against the school district.

What about your personal appearance? What can a school district legally require in terms of personal grooming and dress codes for teachers? Courts have not been consistent in their decisions, although the courts may uphold the legality of dress codes for teachers if the dress requirements are reasonable and related to legitimate educational concerns.[6]

CRITICAL THINKING QUESTION
Personal appearance? This question has absorbed educational philosophers and student teaching supervisors for a long time. What is your program's policy? Do students see this as a legal issue, a matter of professionalism or an opportunity for self-expression?

OVERHEAD 119
Academic Controversy

Issue	*Situation 4*
Teachers' academic freedom	As a social studies teacher, you are concerned about your students' apparent insensitivity to racism in the United States. You have found a very effective simulation game that evokes strong student feelings on racial issues, but the school board is concerned by this activity and has asked you to stop

The courts are constantly asked to draw the line between a teacher's personal freedom and the community's right to establish teacher behavior standards. Historically, the scales have tilted toward the community, and teachers have been fired for wearing lipstick, joining a certain church, or getting married. Today's courts make more deliberate efforts to balance personal liberty and community standards. Although each case must be judged on its own merits, some trends do emerge. The courts have ruled that the community has the right to fire a teacher for

- Making public homosexual advances to nonstudents
- Incorporating sexual issues into lessons and ignoring the approved syllabus
- Inciting violent protest among students
- Engaging in sex with students
- Encouraging students to attend certain religious meetings
- Allowing students to drink alcohol
- Drinking excessively
- Using profanity and abusive language toward students
- Having a sex-change operation
- Stealing school property (even if it is returned later)
- Not living within his or her district if that is listed as a condition of employment

On the other hand, courts have ruled that teachers should not be fired for

- Smoking of marijuana
- Private homosexual behavior
- Obesity (unless it inhibits teaching performance)
- Adultery
- Use of vulgar language outside of school
- AIDS or disability

Why are teachers dismissed in some cases and not in others? Often, the standard the courts use is whether the behavior under question reduces teacher effectiveness. Public behavior, or behavior that becomes public, may compromise a teacher's effectiveness. In such cases, the courts find it reasonable and legal to terminate the teacher. If the behavior remains private, if the teacher shows discretion, the teacher's "right to privacy" often prevails.

SOURCE: These examples have been adapted from Louis Fischer, David Schimmel, and Cynthia Kelly, *Teachers and the Law* (New York: Longman, 2002).

REFLECTION: Courts have disagreed on whether the following three situations constitute grounds for dismissal of a teacher. If you were the judge, how would you rule on the following issues?
- Unwed cohabitation
- Unwed parenthood
- Conviction for shoplifting

using the game. The board expressed its concern over your discussion of controversial issues. Committed to your beliefs, you persist; at the end of the year, you find that your teaching contract is not renewed.

_____ Since you think your academic freedom has been violated, you decide to sue to get your job back.

_____ You realize that the school board is well within its rights to determine curriculum, that you were warned, and that now you must pay the price for your indiscretion.

Court Decision The right to **academic freedom** (that is, to teach without coercion, censorship, or other restrictive interference) is not absolute. The courts will balance your right to academic freedom with the school system's interests in its students' learning appropriate subject matter in an environment conducive to learning. Courts look at such factors as whether your learning activities and materials are inappropriate, irrelevant to the subjects to be covered under the syllabus, obscene, or substantially disruptive of school discipline. In the case of the simulation game involving racial issues, the activity appears to be appropriate, relevant, and neither obscene nor

Academic freedom protects a teacher's right to teach about sensitive issues, such as AIDS or other sex education topics, as long as the topic is relevant to the course, is not treated in an obscene manner, and is not disruptive of school discipline.

disruptive. If you were to sue on the grounds of academic freedom, you would probably get your job back.[7]

Issue	Situation 5
Legal liability (negligence)	You are assigned to cafeteria duty. Things are pretty quiet, and you take the opportunity to call a guest speaker and confirm a visit to your class. While you are gone from the cafeteria, a student slips on some spilled milk and breaks his arm. His parents hold you liable for their son's injury and sue you for damages.

_____ You will probably win, since you did not cause the fall and were on educational business when the accident occurred.

_____ The student's parents will win, since you left your assigned post.

_____ The student who spilled the milk is solely responsible for the accident.

_____ No one will win, because the courts long ago ruled that there is no use crying over spilled milk. (You knew that was coming, right?)

INTERACTIVE ACTIVITY
What Can a Teacher Be Fired For?
Test your knowledge of teachers' rights.

Court Decision   In recent years, litigation against teachers has increased dramatically. The public concern over the quality of education, the bureaucratic and impersonal nature of many school systems, and the generally litigious nature of our society have all contributed to this rising tide of lawsuits. Negligence suits against teachers are common. In the cafeteria example, you would be in considerable jeopardy in a legal action. A teacher who is not present at his or her assigned duty might be charged with negligence, unless the absence is "reasonable." The courts are very strict about what is "reasonable" (leaving your post to put out a fire is reasonable, but going to the telephone to make a call is unlikely to be viewed as reasonable). It is a good practice to stay in your classroom or assigned area of responsibility unless there is an emergency.

OVERHEAD 120
Standards to Determine Negligence

CLASS ACTIVITY: GUEST
SPEAKERS
IM, Activity 11:3

Teacher liability is an area of considerable concern to many teachers. Courts generally use two standards in determining negligence: (1) whether a reasonable person with similar training would act in the same way and (2) whether or not the teacher could have foreseen the possibility of an injury. Following are some common terms and typical situations related to teacher liability:

OVERHEAD 121
Teacher Liability

- *Misfeasance.* Failure to conduct in an appropriate manner an act that might otherwise have been lawfully performed; for example, unintentionally using too much force in breaking up a fight is **misfeasance.**

- *Nonfeasance.* Failure to perform an act that one has a duty to perform; for example, the cafeteria situation is **nonfeasance,** since the teacher did not supervise an assigned area of responsibility.

- *Malfeasance.* An act that cannot be done lawfully regardless of how it is performed; for example, starting a fistfight or bringing marijuana to school is **malfeasance.**

- *Educational malpractice.* Although liability litigation usually involves physical injury to students because of what a teacher did or failed to do, a new line of litigation, called **educational malpractice,** is concerned with "academic damage." Some students and parents have sued school districts for failing to provide an adequate education. Many courts have rejected these cases, pointing out that many factors affect learning and that failure to learn cannot be blamed solely on the school system.

Issue	*Situation 6*
Teachers' freedom of speech	As a teacher in a small school district, you are quite upset with the way the school board and the superintendent are spending school funds. You are particularly troubled with all the money being spent on high school athletics, since these expenditures have cut into your proposed salary raise. To protest the expenditures, you write a lengthy letter to the local newspaper, criticizing the superintendent and the school board. After the letter is published, you find that the figures you cited in the letter were inaccurate.
	The following week, you are called into the superintendent's office and fired for breaking several school rules. You have failed to communicate your complaints to your superiors and you have caused harm to the school system by spreading false and malicious statements. In addition, the superintendent points out that your acceptance of a teaching position obligated you to refrain from publicizing critical statements about the school. The superintendent says although no one can stop you from making public statements, the school system certainly does not "have to pay you for the privilege." You decide to

_____ Go to court to win back your position.

_____ Chalk it up to experience, look for a new position, and make certain that you do not publish false statements and break school rules in the future.

Court Decision   This situation is based on a suit instigated by a teacher named Marvin Pickering. After balancing the teacher's interests, as a citizen, in commenting on issues of public concern against the school's interests in efficiently providing public services, the Supreme Court ruled in favor of the teacher. It found that the disciplined operation of the school system was not seriously damaged by Pickering's letter and that the misstatements in the letter were not made knowingly or recklessly. Moreover, there was no special need for confidentiality on the issue of school budgets. Hence, concluded the Court, prohibiting Pickering from making his statements was an infringement of his First Amendment right to freedom of speech. You, too, would probably win in court if you were to issue public statements on matters of public concern, unless your statements were intentionally or recklessly inaccurate, disclosed confidential material, or hampered either school discipline or your performance of duties.[8]

Issue	*Situation 7*
Copying published material	You read a fascinating two-page article in a national magazine, and, since the article concerns an issue your class is discussing, you duplicate the article and distribute it to your students. This is the only article you have distributed in class, and you do not bother to ask either the author or the magazine for permission to reprint it. You have

_____ Violated the copyright law, and you are liable to legal action.

_____ Not violated any copyright law.

Federal Law   Initially, as copiers became commonplace in staff rooms, teachers could reproduce articles, poems, book excerpts, or whatever they pleased with virtually no fear of legal repercussions. But, in January 1976, Congress passed the **Copyright Act** (PL 94-553) and teachers' rights to freely reproduce and distribute published works were greatly curtailed. Under this law, in order to use a published work in class, teachers must write to the publisher or author of the work and obtain written permission. This sometimes requires the payment of a permission fee, something that teachers on a limited budget are usually unwilling to do. Under certain circumstances, however, teachers may still reproduce published material without written permission or payment. This is called **fair use**, a legal principle that allows the limited use of copyrighted materials. Teachers must observe three criteria in selecting the material: brevity, spontaneity, and cumulative effect.

1. *Brevity.* A work can be reproduced if it is not overly long. It is always wise to contact publishers directly, but typical limits might include the following criteria. Poems or excerpts from poems must be no longer than 250 words. Articles, stories, and essays of less than 2,500 words may be reproduced in complete form. Excerpts of any prose work (such as a book or an article) may be reproduced only up to 1,000 words or 10 percent of the work, whichever is less. Only one illustration (photo, drawing, diagram) may be reproduced from the same book or journal. The brevity criterion limits the length of the material that a teacher can reproduce and distribute from a single work. If you were the teacher in this example and you reproduced only a two-page article, you probably would not have violated the criterion of brevity.

2. *Spontaneity.* If a teacher has an inspiration to use a published work and there is simply not enough time to write for and receive written permission, then the

MULTIPLE INTELLIGENCE CONNECTION
Ask your students to imagine that they are explaining the criteria for fair use to a new teacher, who doesn't speak English. Can they create a pantomime (using their kinesthetic intelligence) that incorporates the three key terms—brevity, spontaneity, and cumulative effect—with the principle of fair use?

teacher may reproduce and distribute the work. The teacher in our vignette has met this criterion so is acting within the law. If the teacher wishes to distribute the same article during the next semester or the next year, written permission would be required, since ample time exists to request such permission.

3. *Cumulative effect.* The total number of works reproduced without permission for class distribution must not exceed nine instances per class per semester. Within this limit, only one complete piece or two excerpts from the same author may be reproduced, and only three pieces from the same book or magazine. Cumulative effect limits the number of articles, poems, excerpts, and so on that can be reproduced, even if the criteria of spontaneity and brevity are met. The teacher in our vignette has not reproduced other works and therefore has met this criterion also.

Under the fair use principle, single copies of printed material may be copied for your personal use. Thus, if you want a single copy for planning a lesson, that is not a problem. Whenever multiple copies are made for classroom use, each copy must include a notice of copyright.

What about videotapes, computer software, and mixed media? Without a license or permission, educational institutions may not keep copyrighted videotapes (for example, from a television show) for more than forty-five days. The tape should not be shown more than once to students during this period, and then it must be erased. The growing use of computers prompted the amendment of the Copyright Act in 1990 to prohibit the copying of software for commercial gain. In 1998, Congress further amended the Copyright Act and passed the Digital Millennium Copyright Act to protect the vast amount of material published on the World Wide Web. Text, graphics, multimedia materials, and even e-mail are copyright protected, and teachers must follow fair use guidelines when using information obtained from the Internet and gleaned from e-mail attachments. With so much information at our fingertips, both teachers and students need to be aware that all work posted on the Internet is copyright protected, whether or not a specific notice is included. It is always advisable to check with your local school district officials to determine school policy and procedures.[9]

Issue	*Situation 8*
Labor rights	Salary negotiations have been going badly in your school district, and at a mass meeting teachers finally vote to strike. You honor the strike and stay home, refusing to teach until an adequate salary increase is provided. During the first week of the strike, you receive a letter from the school board, stating that you will be suspended for fifteen days without pay at the end of the school year, owing to your participation in the strike. You decide

_____ To fight this illegal, unjust, and costly suspension.

_____ To accept the suspension as a legal action of the school board.

Court Decision   In a number of cases, courts have recognized the right of teachers to organize; to join professional organizations, such as the NEA (National Education Association) and the AFT (American Federation of Teachers); and to bargain collectively for improved working conditions. You cannot legally be penalized for these activities. On the other hand, courts have upheld teachers' right to strike in only about half the states. (In some states, the courts have determined that teachers

Strikes are legal for K–12 educators in Alaska, California, Colorado, Hawaii, Illinois, Louisiana, Minnesota, Montana, North Dakota, Oregon, Pennsylvania, and, in very limited cases, Wisconsin.

SOURCE: National Education Association, *Collective Bargaining Laws for Public Sector Education Employees* (Washington, DC: NEA, October 2001).

REFLECTION: Can you offer any generalizations about the states that permit K–12 teachers to strike? What specific circumstance would cause you to strike?

provide a vital public service and cannot strike.) You need to understand your state laws to know if you are breaking the law by honoring the strike. The school board may be within its rights to suspend, fine, or even fire you for striking.

Although about half of the states have laws that prohibit strikes, many communities choose not to prosecute striking teachers. Conversely, even though membership in teacher organizations and the right to collective bargaining have been upheld by the courts, some communities and school boards are adamantly opposed to such organizations and refuse to hire or to renew contracts of teachers who are active in them. Such bias is clearly illegal; nevertheless, it is very difficult to prove in court and, consequently, it is very difficult to stop.

In summary, law and reality do not always coincide. Legally speaking, teachers may be prohibited from striking by state law but are rarely prosecuted or penalized. In some communities, however, active involvement in teacher organizations may result in discriminatory school board actions. If you choose to strike, do so with the realization that such activity makes you liable to legal sanctions.[10]

OVERHEADS 123–124
Teachers' Bill of Rights
A Teacher's Right to Strike

Issue	Situation 9
Internet censorship	You have found a terrific website, one that really communicates recent changes and unique insights about the

CLASS ACTIVITY: LEGAL RIGHTS AND THE REAL WORLD
IM, Activity 11:1

Although many states have laws prohibiting teachers from striking, most communities choose not to penalize striking teachers.

401

learning more about your students will make you a more effective teacher. As you finish reviewing some of the folders, Brenda, a 16-year-old student of yours, walks in and asks to see her folder. Since you have several sensitive comments recorded in the folder, you refuse. Within the hour, the student's parents call and ask if they can see the folder. At this point, you

_____ Explain that the information is confidential and sensitive and cannot be shared with nonprofessional personnel.

_____ Explain that the parents can see the folder and describe the procedure for doing so.

Federal Law   The Family Rights and Privacy Act, commonly referred to as the **Buckley Amendment** (1974), allows parents and guardians access to their children's educational records. The amendment also requires that school districts inform parents of this right and establish a procedure for providing educational records on request. Moreover, written parental permission is needed before these records can be shared with anyone other than professionals connected with either the school the student attends or another school in which the student seeks to enroll, health or safety officials, or persons reviewing the student's financial aid applications. If the student has reached 18 years of age, he or she must be allowed to see the folder and is responsible for granting permission for others to review the folder. The Buckley Amendment was recently tested by the common teacher practice of asking students to exchange and grade others' papers. In *Owasso Independent School District v. Falvo* (2002), the Supreme Court ruled that students can grade their peers' academic work and even announce the results in class without violating the privacy act.

Under this law, you should have chosen the second option, for it is the parents' right to see this information.[12]

Issue	*Situation 11*
Distribution of scholarships	As a secondary teacher, you are concerned with the manner in which scholarships and other financial awards (donated by the local booster club and neighborhood businesses) are distributed at graduation. You notice that nearly all the awards are going to boys. You mention this to the principal, who explains that this has been the case for as long as anyone can remember. The groups donating the scholarship funds use such categories as leadership skills and sports abilities in choosing the recipients. The principal says that, although this is not exactly equitable, it is realistic, because future financial burdens hit males more than females. You decide that

_____ It is an unfortunate but realistic policy.

_____ It is unfair, unreasonable, and unrealistic. You file a complaint with the Office for Civil Rights.

FOCUS QU
What leg;
students enjoy (a
have legal respo

CLASS ACTIVITY:
STUDENTS FOR THE
DEFENSE
IM, Activity 11:2

Federal Law   Title IX prohibits using sex as a criterion by which to grant awards, scholarships, or financial aid. Scholarships and aid must be awarded by objective criteria fairly applied without regard to sex. If it turns out that the most qualified

FRAME OF REFERENCE   Is Corporal Punishment Legal?

Corporal punishment, the physical discipline of students, is deplored by most educators, yet it remains legal in approximately half the states.

The Children's Defense Fund estimates that a public school student is physically punished every 10 seconds.

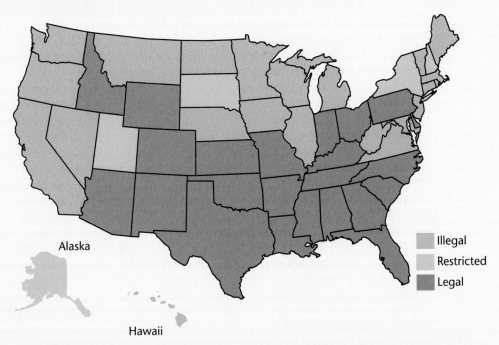

Alaska

Hawaii

Illegal
Restricted
Legal

SOURCE: Children's Defense Fund, "Moments in America for Children," *Children's Defense Fund Online*, March 2003; Louis Fischer, David Schimmel, and Cynthia Kelly, *Teachers and the Law* (New York: Longman, 2002).

REFLECTION: Knowing whether corporal punishment is legal in your state and in your school is only part of the issue; sorting out your philosophy on this issue is more to the point. As a teacher, would you use physical punishment against a student? Explain your reasoning.

students in a given year are predominantly or entirely of one sex, that is acceptable, as long as the procedures and criteria have been fairly applied. But sex itself should not be a criterion; this example is a violation of Title IX and should be corrected.[13]

Issue	*Situation 12*
Suspension and discipline	You are teaching a difficult class, and one student is the primary source of trouble. After a string of disorderly episodes on this student's part, the floppy disks for the entire class mysteriously disappear. You have put up with more than enough, and you send the student to the principal's office to be suspended. The principal backs you up, and the student is told not to return to school for a week. This action is

_____ Legal and appropriate (and probably long overdue!).

_____ Illegal.

Court Decision   Although troublesome and disorderly students can be disciplined, suspension from school represents a serious penalty, one that should not be taken lightly. In such cases, the Supreme Court has ruled (*Goss v. Lopez*) that teachers and administrators are required to follow certain procedures in order to guarantee the student's **due process** rights granted by the Fourteenth Amendment. In this case, the student must be informed of the rule that has been broken and of the evidence. The student is also entitled to tell his or her side of the story in self-defense. For suspensions in excess of ten days, the school must initiate more formal procedures. School officials can be held personally liable for damages if they violate a student's clearly established constitutional rights (*Wood v. Strickland*).

If you look back at this vignette, you will notice that you do not know for sure that this student is responsible for the missing floppy disks, nor is the student given the opportunity for self-defense. If you selected "illegal," you chose the correct response.

Many schools have adopted zero-tolerance policies in an attempt to create safe schools. A **zero-tolerance policy** typically sets out predetermined consequences or punishment for specific offenses, regardless of the circumstances or disciplinary history of the student involved. Nine out of ten schools report zero-tolerance policies for firearms. Many schools have zero-tolerance policies covering possession of alcohol, drugs, and tobacco, as well as incidents of violence. Courts have generally ruled that students' constitutional right to due process is not violated by zero-tolerance policies.

Zero tolerance sends a powerful message to the school community that violent, aggressive behavior is not acceptable. However opponents point out that zero-tolerance policies are inherently unfair and can backfire. For example, one six-year-old was expelled for bringing a weapon into school. His grandmother had placed a "weapon" in his lunch sack—a plastic knife for spreading peanut butter. The American Bar Association has denounced zero-tolerance policies that mandate expulsion or referral to juvenile court for minor offenses that do not compromise school safety.

While considering discipline, let us look at the legality of **corporal punishment**. In *Ingraham v. Wright* (1977), the Supreme Court ruled that physical punishment may be authorized by the states. The Court ruled that the corporal punishment should be "reasonable and not excessive," and such factors as the seriousness of the student offense, the age and physical condition of the student, and the force and attitude of the person administering the punishment should be considered. Although the courts have legalized corporal punishment, many states and school districts do not believe in it and have prohibited the physical punishment of students; other districts and states provide very specific guidelines for its practice. You should be familiar with the procedures and norms in your district before you even consider this disciplinary strategy.[14]

Issue	*Situation 13*
Freedom of speech	During your homeroom period, you notice that several of your more politically active students are wearing T-shirts with a red line drawn through "www." You call them to your desk and ask them about it. They explain that they are protesting censorship, the new school board policy that limits student access on the Internet. You tell them that you share their concern but that wearing the T-shirts is specifically forbidden by school rules. You explain that you will let it go this time, since they are not disturbing the class routine, but that if they wear them again, they will be suspended.

Sure enough, the next day the same students arrive at
school still wearing the T-shirts, and you send them to the
principal's office. The students tell the principal that,
although they understand the rule, they refuse to obey it.
The principal, explaining that school rules are made to be
followed, suspends them. The principal's action is

_____ Legally justified, since the students were given every opportunity to
understand and obey the school rule.

_____ Illegal, since the students have the right to wear T-shirts if they so desire.

Court Decision   In December 1965, three students in Des Moines, Iowa, demonstrated their opposition to the Vietnam War by wearing black arm bands to school.
The principal informed them that they were breaking a school rule and asked that
they remove the arm bands. They refused and were suspended.

The students' parents sued the school system, and the case finally reached the
Supreme Court. In the landmark *Tinker* case, the Court ruled that the students were
entitled to wear the arm bands, as long as the students did not substantially disrupt
the operation of the school or deny other students the opportunity to learn. Since
there was no disruption, the Court ruled that the school system could not prohibit
students from wearing the arm bands or engaging in other forms of free speech. The
school system in this vignette acted illegally; it could not prevent students from wearing the protest T-shirts. Does *Tinker* apply in cyberspace? Probably. Although the
courts have not definitely resolved the issue, early "cyberTinker" decisions support
First Amendment rights. One of the first lawsuits arose after a Missouri high school
suspended a student for creating an Internet homepage that criticized his school administration. The student, Brandon Buessink, created the homepage outside of school
on his home computer. The website caused no documented disturbance at this school

Courts have upheld
students' freedom of
speech in a number of
cases, so long as the
protests were not
disruptive of other
students' right to learn
and were not obscene.

and a federal district court reversed the suspension, citing the principal's simple dislike of the content as "unreasonable justification for limiting it."[15]

The issue of allegedly "obscene" speech has been considered by the Supreme Court. In a 1986 decision (*Bethel School District v. Fraser*), the Court evaluated the First Amendment rights of a high school senior, Matthew Fraser. Fraser presented a speech at a school assembly that contained numerous sexual innuendoes, though no explicit, profane language. After Fraser was suspended for his speech and told that he was no longer eligible to speak at his class's graduation, his father sued the school district. The Court upheld the suspension on the grounds that the language in the speech was indecent and offensive and that minors should not be exposed to such language. Obscene speech posted on the Internet from a student's home computer is also not constitutionally protected. A Pennsylvania district court upheld the suspension of a middle school student for posting inflammatory and perverse comments about his principal and algebra teacher.[16]

Issue	*Situation 14*
School prayer	A student on your team objects to the daily prayer recitation. You are sensitive to the student's feelings, and you make certain that the prayer is nondenominational. Moreover, you tell the student that he may stand or sit silently without reciting the prayer. If the student likes, he may even leave the gym while the prayer is being recited. As a teacher, you have

_____ Broken the law.

_____ Demonstrated sensitivity to individual needs and not violated the law.

Court Decision You were sensitive but not sensitive enough—you violated the law. As a result of leaving the gym, the student might be subjected to embarrassment, ostracism, or some other form of social stigma. The Supreme Court has ruled that educators must be completely neutral with regard to religion and may neither encourage nor discourage prayer. The Court has ruled that the separation of church and state prevents educators, but not necessarily students, from promoting religious activities. For example, students may engage in private prayer and religious discussion during school, and form religious clubs on school property if other, nonreligious clubs are also given school space. "Official" prayers given by school personnel are not permitted, even at graduation ceremonies (where they frequently are heard despite the law). State laws vary on whether a student can give a graduation speech when the speech becomes a platform for prayer. However, the Court has declared that student-led public prayers at athletic events constitute school sponsorship of religion, a violation of the establishment clause of the First Amendment. The Pledge of Allegiance also sparks controversy in public schools. Though many state and local school districts often champion the need for patriotism when requiring students to recite the pledge, students cannot be compelled to salute the

Student locker searches for contraband items are permissible since schools have parentlike responsibility for the safety of their students.

flag. Finally, the legality of observing a moment of silence in schools varies by state, and educators are encouraged to check their school policies.

No Child Left Behind legislation gives special attention to school prayer, requiring states to certify that their school policies do not prevent constitutionally protected prayer. If states fail to comply, they can lose funding, connecting for the first time federal money to student prayer rights. Such mandates will undoubtedly continue debate on the role of religion in public schools.[17]

Issue	Situation 15
Search and seizure	The drug problem in your school is spreading, and it is clear that strong action is needed. School authorities order a search of all student lockers, which lasts for several hours. Trained police dogs are brought in, and each classroom is searched for drugs. The dogs sniff suspiciously at several students, who are taken to the locker rooms and strip-searched.

_____ School authorities are well within their rights to conduct these searches.

_____ Searching the lockers is legal, but strip-searching is inappropriate and illegal.

_____ No searches are called for, and all of these activities present illegal and unconstitutional violation of student rights.

Court Decision   Courts have ruled that school authorities have fewer restrictions than do the police in search-and-seizure activities. Courts have indicated that school property (such as lockers or cars parked in the school lot) are actually the responsibility of the school. Moreover, the school has a parentlike responsibility (termed ***in loco parentis***) to protect children and to respond to reasonable concerns about their health and safety. Even random drug testing of students participating in extracurricular activities is permissible.

TEACHING TIP
Schools have responded differently to school locker concerns. Some have removed them entirely, requiring students to carry all books and coats. Yet for each solution, another problem follows. Overcrowded classrooms don't have the space for big kids and their equally large backpacks. Ask the class to brainstorm new and different solutions to the problem.

How might these students (and their teachers) feel as they begin the school day? How do search and seizure responsibilities in schools contrast with those for the general public?

 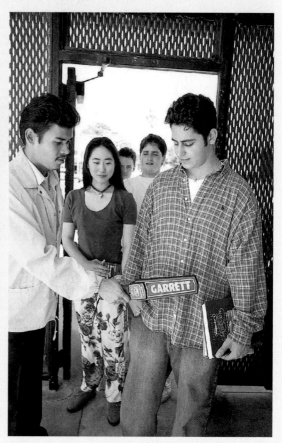

In situation 15, the search of lockers is legal. However, using police dogs to sniff students (rather than things) is allowable only if the dogs are reliable and the student is a reasonable suspect. The strip-search is illegal.

The second choice is the correct response. Although school personnel have great latitude in conducting school search and seizures, educators should be familiar with proper legal procedures and should think carefully about the related ethical issues.[18]

Issue	Situation 16
Freedom of the press	*The Argus* is the official student newspaper, written by students as part of a journalism course, but it has run afoul of school administrators. First the student newspaper ran a story critical of the school administration. In the next edition, the paper included a supplement on contraception and abortion. With their patience worn thin, school administrators closed the publication for the remainder of the school year.

_____ Closing the student newspaper is a legal action.

_____ Closing the student newspaper is an illegal action.

Court Decision   In 1988, a relatively conservative Supreme Court ruled in the *Hazelwood* case that student newspapers may be censored under certain circumstances. The Court held that student newspapers written as part of a school journalism course should be viewed as part of the official school curriculum. School administrators, according to the Court, can readily censor such a paper. In situation 16, since the publication is part of a journalism course, closing the school newspaper would be legal.

On the other hand, if the newspaper were financed by the students and not associated with an official school course, the students would enjoy a greater degree of freedom. Additional grounds for censoring a school newspaper include obscenity, psychological harm, and disruption of school activities.[19]

Issue	*Situation 17*
HIV-infected students	As you enter school one morning, you are met by a group of angry parents. They have found out that Randy, one of your students, is HIV positive, and hence can transmit the AIDS-related virus to others. There is no cure for AIDS, and there is no compromise in the voices of the parents confronting you. Either Randy goes, or they will keep their children at home. You listen sympathetically, but find your mind wandering to your own contact with Randy. You worry that you, too, may be at risk. In this case, you decide

RELATED READING
At Peril: Stories of Injustice
by Thomas J. Cottle (2000).

_____ It's better to be safe than sorry, so you ask Randy to return home while you arrange a meeting with the principal to discuss Randy's case. There is no cure for AIDS and no reason to put every child's life in jeopardy.

_____ It's probably okay for Randy to attend school, so you check with your principal and try to calm the parents down.

Court Decision   In a case very similar to this situation, Randy, a hemophiliac, and his brothers were denied access to De Soto County Schools in Florida when they tested positive for the HIV virus. The court determined that the boys' loss of their education was more harmful than the remote chance of other students' contracting AIDS. In fact, in this 1987 case, Randy's parents won an out-of-court settlement in excess of $1 million for the pain the school system inflicted on the family. In *Bragdon v. Abbott* (1998), the court determined that HIV-infected students are protected under PL 94-142, the Individuals with Disabilities Education Act. Clearly, medical guidelines direct the court. If some AIDS children present more of a public risk (for example, because of biting behavior, open sores, and

IN THE NEWS

Is It Fair?

Blair Hornstine achieved the highest GPA at her high school in Morristown, New Jersey, but the school board wanted her to share the valedictorian honors with two other students who had earned lower averages. Their reasoning: Blair had an immune deficiency illness, and spent only a few hours at school. The rest of the time she studied at home with tutors. She was excused from physical education because of her illness, and was able to enroll in more weighted academic classes. Several parents said that this gave her an unfair advantage, and the school officials agreed. Blair's family did not agree and sued the school system, pleading that she had earned the valedictorian selection by attaining the highest average in her school, despite her illness. How would you rule in this case? To find out how the case was settled, look below.

SOURCE: *The New York Times,* May 2003.

Decision: The judge ruled that Blair should be the sole valedictorian, and sharing that honor would be discrimination.

 What's new in education? Click on *News Feeds.*

fighting), more restrictive school environments may be required. To date, however, HIV-infected students and teachers are not viewed as a significant risk to the health of the rest of the population and cannot be denied their educational rights.[20]

Issue	*Situation 18*
Sexual harassment	One of your favorite students appears particularly upset. You are concerned, so you go over to Pat and put your arm around him. Pat stiffens his shoulder and pushes you away. He is obviously distressed about something. The next day, you offer to take Pat to a local fast-food restaurant after school, to cheer him up with a hot fudge sundae. He refuses to go but thanks you for the gesture. A few weeks later, the principal calls you into her office to explain that you have been charged with sexual harassment.

_____ You decide not to respond to the principal until you seek legal advice.

_____ You decide to apologize, realizing that you have overstepped the boundaries of propriety.

Court Decision   In **_Franklin v. Gwinnett_** (1992), the Supreme Court extended the reach of Title IX, allowing students to sue a school district for monetary damages in cases of sexual harassment. The Gwinnett County case involved a Georgia high school student who was sexually harassed and abused by a teacher, a case much more serious than the pat on the back and offer of a hot fudge sundae described in the vignette above. In Georgia, the teacher's behavior was extreme and the school district's response inadequate. The school district was instructed to pay damages to the student—establishing a precedent.

However, just a few years later the Court made collecting personal damages from school districts more difficult. The Court ruled that the school district had to show "deliberate indifference" to complaints about teacher and peer sexual harassment before the district would be forced to pay damages [*Gebser v. Lago Independent School District* (1998) and *Davis v. Monroe County Board of Education* (1999)]. In fact, just notifying the principal when sexual harassment occurred was insufficient, according to the Court. More powerful officials would need to know and not act on this information before damages could be collected—clearly, an extremely difficult standard. The school district could suffer Title IX penalties (lose federal funds), and the individual accused of harassment could be forced to pay personal damages, but the school district, the place where large funds are available, could not be sued.[21]

OVERHEADS 125–129
Who Harasses Whom?

Personal Experiences with
Harassment: Boys and Girls

Teachers have both a legal and ethical responsibility to prevent and respond to harassment. Sexual harassment is a pervasive, harrowing part of everyday school life for both males and females. (See Figure 11.1.) Four out of five students report being harassed at school. Harassment ranges from sexual comments and gestures, to inappropriate touching, to rape and the consequences are troubling. Students fear attending school, withdraw from friends and activities, and suffer sleep and eating difficulties.

Title IX protections against sexual harassment also apply to gay and lesbian students. Hostility and ridicule toward homosexual students may be actionable in court if they are sufficiently severe and pervasive. For example, a gay student in Wisconsin was awarded a $900,000 judgment when his school district failed to end the violence he endured at the hands of classmates from grades 7 through 11. This landmark case established that school districts must take action to protect gay and lesbian students. Title IX does not apply, however, to heckling about a person's sexual orientation. For

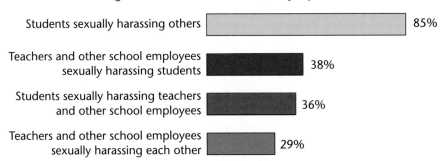

When students were asked for their perceptions of who is harassing whom in their own schools, they reported:

Students sexually harassing others — 85%

Teachers and other school employees sexually harassing students — 38%

Students sexually harassing teachers and other school employees — 36%

Teachers and other school employees sexually harassing each other — 29%

FIGURE 11.1
Who harasses whom?

SOURCE: Harris Interactive, *Bullying, Teasing and Sexual Harassment in School.* Commissioned by AAUW Educational Foundation (Washington, DC: American Association of University Women, 2001), p. 14.

REFLECTION: Girls' and boys' assessments of their school climate generally mirror their personal experiences, with one exception. Students perceive that teachers and other school adults harass students more than they personally have experienced. What reasons might you offer for this discrepancy? As a teacher, if you observed each of these four kinds of harassment, how would you respond?

example, Title IX does not prohibit comments like "Gay students not welcome here" or "We fear queers," although such comments might well violate other civil rights or school conduct policies. For example, a lesbian student in California was barred from gym class after her teacher learned of her sexual orientation. A federal court determined that the school violated the young woman's constitutional right to equal protection and could be sued for monetary damages.[22]

Sexual harassment complaints against teachers have been increasing. Teachers need to realize that **sexual harassment** laws protect individuals not only from extreme actions, as in the Georgia case, but from offensive words and inappropriate touching. The mild scenario of comforting words, touching, and an offer of ice cream can indeed lead to problems. While the teacher's intention might have been pure and caring, the student's perception might have been quite different. The threat of the legal broadside that can result from this gap between teacher intentions and student perceptions has sent a chill through many school faculties. Teachers now openly express their fears about the dangers of reaching out to students, and some teachers are vowing never to touch a student or be alone in a room with a student, no matter how honorable the intention. Many teachers lament the current situation, recalling earlier times, when a teacher's kindness and closeness fostered a caring educational climate, rather than a legal case.[23] In the above situation, the first course of action would be the most prudent, to seek legal advice.

Scoring

To determine your RQ (Rights Quotient), the following scoring guide may be useful:

15 to 18 correct:	Legal eagle
13 or 14 correct:	Lawyer-in-training
11 or 12 correct:	Paralegal
9 or 10 correct:	Law student
8 or fewer correct:	Could benefit from an LSAT prep course

CRITICAL THINKING QUESTION
For educators who desire to cultivate a caring classroom, touching students is more than a touchy subject. How do you and your students feel about *touch?* What definition (for how, when or why to touch students) could they provide that would be widely accepted?

CLASS ACTIVITY: AN EDUCATOR'S LEGAL BRIEF
IM, Activity 11:6

OVERHEADS 130–131
Sensible Suggestions to Avoid Groundless Lawsuits

Students' Bill of Rights

Teachers' and Students' Rights

The following summaries highlight the critical cases that have defined the boundaries of civil rights and liberties in American schools. You may not agree with all these Supreme Court decisions, but for now, they are the law of the land.

TEACHERS' RIGHTS

Freedom of Speech

Pickering v. Board of Education (1968)

A teacher's letter to the newspaper, a letter that criticized the school board, contained some false statements made because of incomplete research. The teacher was fired. The Court determined that the teacher's letter neither seriously damaged the disciplined operation of the school, disclosed confidential information, nor contained any misstatements that were made knowingly or recklessly. Under the First Amendment, a teacher has the same rights as all other citizens to comment on issues of legitimate public concern, such as a school board's decisions in allocating funds.

Separation of Church and State

Engel v. Vitale (1962)

A local school board instructed that a prayer composed by the New York Board of Regents be recited aloud every day by each class. The prayer was nondenominational and voluntary. Students who did not want to recite the prayer were permitted to remain silent or leave the classroom while the prayer was said. The Supreme Court held that the New York statute authorizing the prayer in school violated the First Amendment, particularly the establishment clause, and that official, organized prayer in school is not permitted.

Wallace v. Jaffree (1985)
Lee v. Weisman (1992)

Alabama enacted a law that authorized a 1-minute period of silence in all public schools for meditation or voluntary prayer. The Supreme Court held that the Alabama law violated the establishment clause. To determine whether the Alabama law was constitutional, the Court applied the three-part test established in *Lemon v. Kurtzman,* (1971): did the policy (1) have a secular purpose, (2) have a primarily secular effect, and (3) avoid excessive government entanglement with religion? In *Wallace,* the Alabama statute was found to have a religious rather than a secular purpose and was thus ruled unconstitutional, even though prayer was not required during the moment of silence. In *Weisman,* the court declared prayer led by school personnel at public school graduation to violate the establishment clause. However, Federal Courts are again reviewing the observance of a moment of silence.

McCollum v. Board of Education (1948);
Board of Education of the Westside Community Schools v. Mergens (1990);
Good News Club v. Milford Central Schools (2001)

In *McCollum,* an Illinois school district allowed privately employed religious teachers to hold weekly religious classes on public premises. The students who chose not to attend these classes in religious instruction pursued their secular studies in other classrooms in the building. The Court ruled that a program allowing religious instruction inside public schools during the school day was unconstitutional, because it violated the establishment clause. However, in 1990, the Court modified this somewhat by allowing the use of school facilities by student organizations after school hours if other student clubs had similar access. In *Milford,* the Court allowed adult-led religious organizations the use of school facilities, further lowering the figurative wall of separation between church and state.

Stone v. Graham (1980)

A Kentucky statute required the posting of a copy of the Ten Commandments, purchased with private contributions, on the wall of each public classroom in the state. Despite the fact that the copies of the Ten Commandments were purchased with private funds and had a notation describing them as secular, the statute requiring that they be posted in every public school classroom was declared unconstitutional. Under the three-part *Lemon* test, the Court concluded that the statute requiring posting of the Ten Commandments failed under part 1 of the test in that it lacked a secular purpose. Merely stating that the Ten Commandments are secular does not make them so.

Academic Freedom and Teaching Evolution

Epperson v. Arkansas (1968)
Edwards v. Aquillard (1987)

In *Epperson,* the Court ruled that the teaching of evolution does not violate the First Amendment's call for separation of church and state. During the 1980s, religious fundamentalists won state "balanced" rulings that required science teachers to give equal instructional time to Biblical creationism and evolution. But the Supreme Court did not agree. In *Edwards,* the Court declared that policies *requiring* instruction in creationism violate the First Amendment's establishment clause.

Sexual Harassment

North Haven Board of Education v. Bell (1982)

The Court affirmed that Title IX protects teachers from discrimination based on sex. Title IX joined two other federal statutes, Title VII of the 1964 Civil Rights Act and the 1963 Equal Pay Act, to protect employees from sex discrimination.

continued

STUDENTS' RIGHTS

Freedom of Speech (Symbolic)

Tinker v. Des Moines Independent Community School District (1969)

Unless there is substantial disruption in the school caused by student protest, the school board cannot deprive the students of their First Amendment right to freedom of speech. Students do not shed their constitutional rights at the school door. (See situation 13.)

West Virginia State Board of Education v. Barnette (1943)

A compulsory flag-salute statute in the public school regulations required all students and teachers to salute the U.S. flag every day. Two Jehovah's Witness students refused to salute the flag, because doing so would be contrary to their religious beliefs, and they were not permitted to attend the public schools. The Court determined that students cannot be compelled to pledge allegiance to the flag in public schools, a right protected by the First Amendment.

Freedom of Speech (Verbal)

Bethel School District v. Fraser (1986)

The Supreme Court, balancing the student's freedom to advocate controversial ideas with the school's interests in setting the boundaries of socially appropriate behavior, found that the First Amendment does not prevent school authorities from disciplining students for speech that is lewd and offensive.

Freedom of the Press

Hazelwood School District v. Kuhlmeir (1988)

Two articles about divorce and teenage pregnancy that were written in the student paper were deleted by the principal. The Supreme Court held that, since the student paper was school-sponsored and school-funded and was part of the school's journalism class, the school principal had the right to control its content. On the other hand, the courts have ruled that school authorities may not censor student newspapers produced at the students' own expense and those produced off school property, papers not part of any school's curriculum.

Freedom of Access to the Printed Word

Board of Education, Island Trees Union Free School District No. 26 v. Pico (1982)

A school board decided to remove nine books from the school library because the board members felt the books were objectionable and improper for students. The court ruled that school boards may not suppress ideas by removing books from a school library based on their feelings that the material contains controversial or unpopular viewpoints.

Right to Due Process

Goss v. Lopez (1975)
New Jersey v. T.L.O. (1985)

In *Goss,* several high school students were suspended from school for ten days. The Supreme Court held that before a principal can suspend a student, he or she must present the student with the charges and provide the student with a hearing or opportunity to defend against the charges. The Fourteenth Amendment's due process procedures mandated as a result of this decision can be compared to the "Miranda rights" required in criminal cases. In *T.L.O.* the Court determined that school officials are not necessarily bound by the Fourth Amendment but by reasonable cause when engaged in a search.

Ingraham v. Wright (1977)

Florida statute allowed corporal punishment. Two students were punished by being hit with a flat wooden paddle and later sued the schools. The Supreme Court held that corporal punishment, such as the paddling, is not cruel and unusual punishment and does not necessarily deprive the student of his or her rights.

Separation of Church and State

Santa Fe Independent School District v. Doe (2000)

In a 6–3 ruling, the Supreme Court held that student-led prayer at football games violated the U.S. Constitution's prohibition against a government establishment of religion. The majority said the Texas school district's authorization of a student vote on whether to have an invocation before games and the election of a student speaker amounted to government sponsorship of prayer.

School Attendance and Choice

Pierce v. Society of Sisters of the Holy Names of Jesus & Mary (1925)
Plyer v. Doe (1982)
Zelman v. Simmons-Harris (2002)

Although most of us take school for granted, the right to an education and freedom to choose a school often spark legal debate. School choice appeared on the legal landscape with *Pierce.* The Court deemed unconstitutional an Oregon law requiring parents to send their children to public schools. Such a law denied parents the right to control their children's education. *Plyer* extended the reach of public education. The Court ruled that Texas could not withhold free public education from illegal immigrants because "education provides the basic tools by which individuals might lead economically productive lives to the benefit of us all." *Zelman* ushered in a new era of school choice as the Court affirmed that parents could use public vouchers to send their children to private religious schools.

continued

Sexual Harassment

Franklin v. Gwinnett County Public Schools (1992) The *Franklin* case involved a Georgia high school student who alleged that a teacher-coach engaged in behavior toward her ranging from unwelcome verbal advances to pressured sexual intercourse on school grounds. The Court ruled that "victims of sexual harassment and other forms of sex discrimination in schools may sue for monetary damages" under Title IX of the Education Amendments of 1972.

Gebser v. Lago Vista Independent School District (1998) The Court limited the circumstances under which a school district can be held liable for monetary damages for a teacher's sexual harassment of a student. The court ruled 5–4 that a district cannot be held liable under Title IX unless a district official with the authority to take corrective action had actual knowledge of teacher misconduct and was deliberately indifferent to it.

Davis v. Monroe County Board of Education (1999) In a 5–4 ruling, the Court held that districts may be found liable under Title IX only when they are "deliberately indifferent" to information about peer harassment at school and when the harassment is so "severe, pervasive, and objectively offensive" that it bars the victim's access to an educational program or benefit.

Note: The section on legal landmarks was written by Nancy Gorenberg and Karen Zittleman.

> **REFLECTION:** Can you recall a time when you believe your rights as a student (or the rights of a classmate) were denied? Describe those events. What court cases and parts of the U.S. Constitution would apply to the situation?

INTERACTIVE ACTIVITY Practice with Court Cases. Match names of court cases with their description.

CLASS ACTIVITY: COURT OBSERVATION/ VISITATION

IM, Activity 11:4

This brief review of the legal realities that surround today's classroom is not meant to be definitive. These situations are intended to highlight the rapid growth and changing nature of school law and the importance of this law to teachers. It will be your responsibility to become informed, and stay current, on legal decisions that influence your actions inside and outside your classroom. Ignorance of the law, to paraphrase a popular saying, is no defense. More positively, knowledge of fundamental legal principles allows you to practice "preventive law"—that is, to avoid or resolve potential legal conflicts so that you can attend to your major responsibility: teaching.

Teaching and Ethics

FOCUS QUESTION 3

What are today's main approaches to moral education?

Sam, the new student, seems so awkward in school, and he is often late. You have asked him more than once why he can't get to class on time, but he is barely audible as he mumbles, "I dunno." What's more, his behavior is strange. He seems to have an aversion to chairs, and, whenever possible, he prefers to stand in the back of the room alone. His clothes are not the neatest or cleanest, which is unusual in your class, where most of the children come from middle-class homes and dress fairly well. You have never seen Sam laugh or even smile. Every day, even on the hot ones, he wears a long-sleeve shirt. What is that all about? What a puzzle.

Then, one day, Sam arrives in class with some bruises on his face, and you begin to suspect that there is more to this story. You ask Sam, who shrugs it off and says that he fell and bruised his face. But you are not so sure. You begin to put the puzzle pieces together: quiet . . . standing rather than sitting . . . wearing long-sleeve shirts all the time . . . late . . . no smiles . . . no real friends . . . and now bruises. You arrive at a frightening thought: Could Sam be an abused child? How horrible! Now, what do you do?

In this case, you are confronting both an ethical dilemma and a legal challenge. Maybe you should speak to Sam's parents. Or should you press Sam for more information?

Checking with other teachers makes sense, to see how they would handle the problem. Or perhaps it is time to go to the administration and let them find out what is going on.

Wait a second. What if you are wrong? Sam says he fell down and bruised himself. Maybe that is all it is. You should not go around accusing people without real evidence. Are you responsible for Sam's family situation? Is that a private concern rather than your business? Maybe the prudent course of action would be to monitor the situation for now and keep your suspicions to yourself. What would you do?

The ethical issue is pressing. If Sam is being injured, if his safety is in jeopardy, then waiting could be costly. Many would find that the most ethical course to follow would be to share your concerns with an appropriate person in your school, perhaps a school psychologist, counselor, or administrator, or to notify Child Protective Services, a report which can be confidential. The potential for injury is simply too great to remain silent. Sharing your concern is not the same as making an accusation of child abuse, which may be false. By bringing the situation to the school's attention, you start the wheels in motion to uncover facts.

The American Humane Institute states that very few child abuse reports come from educators, yet it is the ethical responsibility of teachers to report the abusive treatment of children. Fortunately, as far as suspicion of child abuse is concerned, this ethical responsibility is reinforced by the law. Every state requires that teachers report "suspected" cases of abuse, and failure to report such cases can result in the loss of a teacher's license. Most of these laws also protect teachers from any legal liability for reporting such cases.

As a teacher, you may well encounter child abuse. In the last twenty years, reports of child maltreatment more than doubled, although as many as two-thirds of these reports are never investigated.[24]

Child abuse and neglect include a range of mistreatment, such as the following:

- Physical abuse, evidenced by cuts, welts, burns, and bruises
- Sexual molestation and exploitation
- Neglect: medical, educational, or physical
- Emotional abuse

Some citizens believe that the most important issues that face U.S. schools are the ethical ones like how adults treat children. They believe that, beyond adhering to the law, teachers will need to teach more enduring and pervasive moral lessons. (See Figure 11.2.) Yet, while the public applauds moral lessons they are concerned about promoting a narrow set of beliefs.[25] So, how do schools respond to the public's demand for ethical, but not parochial, education?

Moral Education: Programs That Teach Right from Wrong

During the American colonial experience, schools transmitted a common set of values, an approach called **traditional inculcation.** Back then (and in many places today) it was the Protestant ethic: diligence, hard work, punctuality, neatness, conformity, and respect for authority. Those few individuals who received a college education during the eighteenth and nineteenth centuries received, above all, an experience in character development. The most important course in the college curriculum was moral philosophy, required of all students and often taught by the

OVERHEADS 132–133
Child Abuse: Warning Signs

Sexual Abuse: Warning Signs

VIDEO SEGMENT 26
Cheating: A Dramatization

FIGURE 11.2

The dishonor role.

SOURCE : "Rutgers Study Finds Extensive Cheating," *Baltimore Sun*, April 29, 2001, p. 15B.

Percentage of Students Polled Admitting They . . .

Cheated on a test by copying from another student or using a crib sheet — 74%

Plagiarized on a written assignment or handed in someone else's work — 72%

Used the Internet to plagiarize — 54%

Believed teachers ignore cheating — 47%

Turned in work done by parents or collaborated with peers on individual assignments — 23%

REFLECTION: This is from a recent study of 4,500 students in twenty-five high schools. Is cheating an acceptable norm in American schools? Why or why not? As a teacher, how might you approach the cheating dilemma?

OVERHEAD 134
The Dishonor rule

college president. Even those receiving a minimal education got a heavy dose of morality, perhaps illustrated best by McGuffey Readers, replete with tales and poems of moral elevation. The tremendous influx of immigrants in the early part of the twentieth century prompted a resurgence of this traditional approach in order to "meld" these new Americans by teaching core U.S. values.

RAP 3.7
A Real Inservice Program
p. 434

During the social and political uncertainty of the 1960s and 1970s, a more analytical and individual approach to moral education became popular. This **individual analysis** method emphasized the decision-making process of students and avoided prescribing a fixed set of beliefs or values. Students were encouraged to consider the moral implications of past and present events and to formulate a set of values based on their analyses. Today's schools can choose from several different approaches to moral education, ranging from student decision-making to the more traditional paths. Four of the most widely known are (1) values clarification, (2) character education, (3) moral stages of development, and (4) comprehensive values education.

OVERHEAD 135
Approaches to Moral Education

Values Clarification   The controversial **values clarification** program is designed to help students develop and eventually act on their values. Students might be asked to describe their preferences (select the ten things you most enjoy doing), analyze behavior (when did you last do each of these activities?), analyze reasons (what appeals to you about each of these activities?), and develop action plans (how can you schedule more time to do what you enjoy?). Students begin to bring their private values into a public light, where they can be analyzed, evaluated and eventually put into action.

Critics charge that values clarification is itself valueless. In this approach, all values are treated equally, and there is no guarantee that good and constructive values will be promoted or that negative ones will be condemned. If, for example, a student decides that anti-Semitism or fascism is a preferred value, values clarification might do little to contradict this view. This "value neutral" stance is troubling to some and has led to the barring of values clarification in several school districts.

Children who suffer physical abuse may

- Exhibit signs of frequent injury—burns, black eyes, and other bruises
- Refuse to change into gym clothes; wear long-sleeves even in very warm weather
- Not want to sit down
- Show unusually aggressive or unusually withdrawn behavior
- Not show emotion—no joy, pain, or anger
- Be frequently absent or tardy
- Be unusually eager to please
- Complain about pain, beating, or other abusive treatment
- Show a significant change in school attitude, behavior, or achievement

Children who suffer sexual abuse may

- Complain of pain or itching in the genital area
- Exhibit unusual odors or signs of trauma in the genital area
- Wear bloody, torn, or stained undergarments
- Create stories or drawings of an unusually sexual nature
- Exhibit unusually sophisticated knowledge of sexual behavior
- Have difficulty sitting or walking
- Talk about sexual involvement with an adult
- Try to run away from home
- Be extremely mature or seductive in dress and behavior
- Exhibit symptoms of sexually transmitted diseases
- Become pregnant

SOURCE: Childhelp USA, *Combating Child Abuse Across America,* www.childhelpusa.org (2003).

REFLECTION: If one of your students showed warning signs of abuse, whom in your school would you approach first? How would you phrase your concern?

Character Education **Character education** programs—currently legislated in more than half the states[26]—assume that there are core attributes of a moral individual that children should be directly taught in school. (To see if your state requires character education, visit www.character.org.) While still a form of moral inculcation, character education programs are less didactic and more analytic than some of the more traditional approaches.[27] What values are promoted? Core values include trustworthiness, respect, responsibility, fairness, caring, and good citizenship, and are encouraged through the school culture, conduct codes, curriculum, and community service.[28] Younger students may be asked to find examples of these qualities in literature and history, while older students may consider these values through ethical reasoning exercises. Some character education programs include training in conflict resolution to develop problem-solving skills and respect. School districts using character education report a drop in discipline problems and enhanced student responsibility.

Not everyone is enamored with character education. Opponents view this approach as superficial, artificially forcing a diverse student population into a simplistic and narrow set of unexamined values that does not really alter behaviors. Character education is often criticized for relying on testimonials to prove effectiveness. Although the federal government is committed to funding "scientifically based" programs, it has nevertheless distributed over $50 million to fund character education programs despite the lack of proven effectiveness.[29]

Other critics believe that character education is little more than the old-fashioned "fix-the-kids" approach, a return to the past conservative, religious agenda that simply rewards students who do what adults desire. Who selects the values or the way the values are taught are issues at the heart of the concerns expressed by these critics. Although character education attempts to walk a middle ground, not all Americans find the values or the approach appropriate.[30]

GLOBAL VIEW

Seeds of Peace is a nonprofit, nonpolitical organization that helps teenagers from regions of conflict learn the skills to end the cycles of violence and make peace. www.seedsofpeace.org

CLASS ACTIVITY: CHARACTER EDUCATION IM, Activity 11:5

419

Moral Stages of Development   Based on the work of Jean Piaget, the psychologist who identified stages of intellectual development (see "The Hall of Fame" in Chapter 8), a schema proposed by **Lawrence Kohlberg** identifies **moral stages of development.** The earliest stages focus on simple rewards and punishments. Young children are taught "right" and "wrong" by learning to avoid physical punishment and to strive for rewards. Most adults function at a middle, or conventional, stage, in which they obey society's laws, even laws that may be unjust. At the highest level, individuals act on principles, such as civil rights or pacifism, that may violate conventional laws. Kohlberg believes that teachers can facilitate student growth to higher stages of morality. In Kohlberg's curriculum, students are encouraged to analyze moral dilemmas presented in brief scenarios. For example, one such scenario might tell the story of someone breaking into a store and stealing, and the question is posed: isn't stealing always wrong, or could it ever be justified? What if the person was stealing medicine needed to save a life; would that justify the theft? The teacher's role in this curriculum is to help students move to higher stages of moral development.

RELATED READING

A Cry for Character: How a Group of Students Cleaned up Their Rowdy School and Spawned a Wildfire Antidote to the Columbine Effect by Dary Matero (2001).

Detractors express concern that traditional (what Kohlberg calls "conventional") values are attacked. Kohlberg pushes toward higher levels of moral development, principled beliefs that may run counter to current law. Other critics point out that Kohlberg's theory was developed on an all-male population and that females may go through different stages of moral reasoning. Harvard professor **Carol Gilligan,** for example, found that women and men react differently when responding to moral dilemmas. While males seem to strongly value those who follow the rules and laws, females value relationships and caring. Kohlberg rated males as reaching a higher level of moral development than females, because the scales he developed were male-oriented. Finally, Kohlberg's stages are intellectually based. Some critics believe that behavior, not intellect, is the real measure of one's morality.

Comprehensive Values Education   Now that we have reviewed three approaches to teaching about values and ethics, it is worth noting that some teachers "mix and match," creating what might be considered a hybrid or fourth approach. Howard Kirschenbaum suggests that both values clarification and traditional inculcation have important lessons for children. In his approach, **comprehensive values education,** traditional values such as honesty, caring, and responsibility are taught and demonstrated directly. However, since other values are less straightforward, such as favoring or rejecting the death penalty, students are taught the analytical skills that will help them make wise decisions. There is an appropriate place in the school curriculum for each approach, Kirschenbaum insists, and many teachers instinctively apply multiple approaches.[31]

Classrooms That Explore Ethical Issues

For many educators and parents, concerns about values are daily events, too important to be left solely to a specific program or curriculum. How should teachers handle matters of ethics that appear on a daily basis? Consider that as a teacher, you find

A student complains that her Vietnamese culture is being demeaned by the Christian and Western classroom activities.

A student is upset because his e-mail has been opened and read by classmates.

Your best student, the one you just recommended for a special award, is looking at a crib sheet during an examination.

Are Best Taught by Instilling American Values Through Character Education Because . . .

OUR YOUTH ARE BEING CORRUPTED BY THE MEDIA

Television, music, and videos bombard children with commercialism, violence, and sex. Schools must be proactive in helping families instill the moral attitudes and values needed to counteract our lax social mores.

CHILDREN ARE UNABLE TO MAKE THEIR OWN MORAL CHOICES

Throughout history, educators have recognized that children have "impressionable" minds. Without moral training at a young age, as Theodore Roosevelt once noted, they can quickly become "a menace to society."

SHARED VALUES AFFIRM A NATIONAL IDENTITY

Americans believe in a common code of values to teach our children: respect, patriotism, tolerance, and responsibility. Our national fabric is built on such values, and our nation's future depends on them.

Should Help Students Develop Their Own Values Because . . .

SOCIETAL INDIFFERENCE IS CORRUPTING OUR YOUTH

Traditional character education adopts a "blame the media" approach while neglecting real social needs. By ignoring poverty, racism, and sexism, traditionalists inculcate their own rosy picture of America, overlooking genuine if unattractive social injustices.

CHILDREN MUST LEARN TO MAKE MEANINGFUL MORAL CHOICES

Through character indoctrination, students are manipulated to adopt a narrow set of values. Far better is for teachers to help students become reflective thinkers, active citizens ready to work for social justice.

INDIVIDUAL VALUES HONOR DIVERSITY

In a nation of people with diverse cultural backgrounds, indoctrinating one set of fixed values is undemocratic and unwise. Respect for different cultural values will help create a safe and fair society marked by tolerance.

 YOU BE THE JUDGE

What role should character education play in public schools? Examine textbooks and curriculum used in a local school to determine the major values being taught to students. Are students expected to accept the values or to critically examine them? Which strategy do you support?

How are teachers to navigate this tricky moral minefield? Educators have offered several recommendations, summarized below:

The Setting

Climate. Create an environment that respects and encourages diverse points of view and that promotes the sharing of diverse opinions, by both the teachers and the students.

School and class rules. Requiring that students unquestioningly follow rules does not lead to democratic values. School and class rules need to be explained to students, and the reasons behind them understood. Many teachers go further and ask students to participate in formulating the rules they will live by.

Parents and community. Citizens and community leaders should participate with the school in developing mission statements and ethical codes of responsibility.

NATIONAL EDUCATION ASSOCIATION CODE OF ETHICS

Preamble

The educator, believing in the worth and dignity of each human being, recognizes the supreme importance of the pursuit of truth, devotion to excellence, and the nurturing of democratic principles. Essential to these goals is the protection of freedom to learn and to teach and the guarantee of equal educational opportunity for all. The educator accepts the responsibility to adhere to the highest ethical standards.

The educator recognizes the magnitude of the responsibility inherent in the teaching process. The desire for the respect and confidence of one's colleagues, of students, of parents, and of the members of the community provides the incentive to attain and maintain the highest possible degree of ethical conduct. The Code of Ethics of the Education Profession indicates the aspiration of all educators and provides standards by which to judge conduct. The remedies specified by the NEA and/or its affiliates for the violation of any provision of this Code shall be exclusive and no such provision shall be enforceable in any form other than one specifically designated by the NEA or its affiliates.

Principle I—Commitment to the Student

The educator strives to help each student realize his or her potential as a worthy and effective member of society. The educator therefore works to stimulate the spirit of inquiry, the acquisition of knowledge and understanding, and the thoughtful formulation of worthy goals.

In fulfillment of the obligation to the student, the educator—

1. Shall not unreasonably restrain the student from independent action in the pursuit of learning.
2. Shall not unreasonably deny the student access to varying points of view.
3. Shall not deliberately suppress or distort subject matter relevant to the student's progress.
4. Shall make reasonable effort to protect the student from conditions harmful to learning or to health and safety.
5. Shall not intentionally expose the student to embarrassment or disparagement.
6. Shall not on the basis of race, color, creed, sex, national origin, marital status, political or religious beliefs, family, social or cultural background, or sexual orientation, unfairly:
   a. Exclude any student from participation in any program;
   b. Deny benefits to any student;
   c. Grant any advantage to any student.
7. Shall not use professional relationships with students for private advantage.
8. Shall not disclose information about students obtained in the course of professional service, unless disclosure serves a compelling professional purpose or is required by law.

Principle II—Commitment to the Profession

The education profession is vested by the public with a trust and responsibility requiring the highest ideals of professional service.

In the belief that the quality of the services of the education profession directly influences the nation and its citizens, the educator shall exert every effort to raise professional standards, to promote a climate that encourages the exercise of professional judgment, to achieve conditions which attract persons worthy of the trust to careers in education, and to assist in preventing the practice of the profession by unqualified persons.

In fulfillment of the obligation to the profession the educator—

1. Shall not in an application for a professional position deliberately make a false statement or fail to disclose a material fact related to competency and qualifications.
2. Shall not misrepresent his/her professional qualifications.
3. Shall not assist entry into the profession of a person known to be unqualified in respect to character, education, or other relevant attribute.
4. Shall not knowingly make a false statement concerning the qualifications of a candidate for a professional position.
5. Shall not assist a noneducator in the unauthorized practice of teaching.
6. Shall not disclose information about colleagues obtained in the course of professional service unless disclosure serves a compelling professional purpose or is required by law.
7. Shall not knowingly make false or malicious statements about a colleague.
8. Shall not accept any gratuity, gift, or favor that might impair or appear to influence professional decisions or actions.

AMERICAN FEDERATION OF TEACHERS BILL OF RIGHTS

The teacher is entitled to a life of dignity equal to the high standard of service that is justly demanded of that profession. Therefore, we hold these truths to be self-evident:

I. Teachers have the right to think freely and to express themselves openly and without fear. This includes the right to hold views contrary to the majority.

II. They shall be entitled to the free exercise of their religion. No restraint shall be put upon them in the manner, time or place of their worship.

III. They shall have the right to take part in social, civil, and political affairs. They shall have the right, outside the classroom, to participate in political campaigns and to hold office. They may assemble peaceably and may petition any government agency, including their employers, for a redress of grievances. They shall have the same freedom in all things as other citizens.

IV. The right of teachers to live in places of their own choosing, to be free of restraints in their mode of living and the use of their leisure time shall not be abridged.

V. Teaching is a profession, the right to practice which is not subject to the surrender of other human rights. No one shall be deprived of professional status, or the right to practice it, or the practice thereof in any particular position, without due process of law.

VI. The right of teachers to be secure in their jobs, free from political influence or public clamor, shall be established by law. The right to teach after qualification in the manner prescribed by law is a property right, based upon the inalienable rights to life, liberty, and the pursuit of happiness.

VII. In all cases affecting the teacher's employment or professional status a full hearing by an impartial tribunal shall be afforded with the right to full judicial review. No teacher shall be deprived of employment or professional status but for specific causes established by the law having a clear relation to the competence or qualification to teach, proved by the weight of the evidence. In all such cases the teacher shall enjoy the right to a speedy and public trial, to be informed of the nature and cause of the accusation, to be confronted with the accusing witnesses, to subpoena witnesses and papers, and to the assistance of counsel. No teacher shall be called upon to answer any charge affecting his employment or professional status but upon probable cause, supported by oath or affirmation.

VIII. It shall be the duty of the employer to provide culturally adequate salaries, security in illness and adequate retirement income. The teacher has the right to such a salary as will: a) Afford a family standard of living comparable to that enjoyed by other professional people in the community; b) To make possible freely chosen professional study; c) Afford the opportunity for leisure and recreation common to our heritage.

IX. Teachers shall not be required under penalty of reduction of salary to pursue studies beyond those required to obtain professional status. After serving a reasonable probationary period a teacher shall be entitled to permanent tenure terminable only for just cause. They shall be free as in other professions in the use of their own time. They shall not be required to perform extracurricular work against their will or without added compensation.

X. To equip people for modern life requires the most advanced educational methods. Therefore, the teacher is entitled to good classrooms, adequate teaching materials, teachable class size and administrative protection and assistance in maintaining discipline.

XI. These rights are based upon the proposition that the culture of a people can rise only as its teachers improve. A teaching force accorded the highest possible professional dignity is the surest guarantee that blessings of liberty will be preserved. Therefore, the possession of these rights imposes the challenge to be worthy of their enjoyment.

XII. Since teachers must be free in order to teach freedom, the right to be members of organizations of their own choosing must be guaranteed. In all matters pertaining to their salaries and working conditions they shall be entitled to bargain collectively through representatives of their own choosing. They are entitled to have the schools administered by superintendents, boards or committees which function in a democratic manner.

REFLECTION: How do these two statements reflect the somewhat different philosophies of these organizations? Do you feel more comfortable with one or the other of these positions? Would you add or delete any items from the lists?

One way to encourage such cooperation is to plan joint efforts that tie the family and civic organizations into school-sponsored programs. The key is to reinforce ethical lessons in the school, the home, and the community.

The Teacher

Model. You need to demonstrate the ethical lessons you teach. Teacher behavior should reflect such values as tolerance, compassion, forgiveness, and open-mindedness. (Values are often *caught not taught.*)

Interpersonal skills. You need effective communication skills to encourage students to share their concerns. A critical component of interpersonal skills is empathy—the ability to see problems from more than one point of view, including through the eyes of students.

Commitment. It takes determination and courage on your part to confront ethical dilemmas, rather than to take the easier path of indifference or even inattention.

Reflection skills. To unravel moral questions, you must know how to analyze a dilemma objectively and how to evaluate its essential components. Teachers with effective and deliberate reasoning skills are best suited for this challenge.

Personal opinions. You should not promote or indoctrinate students with your personal points of view, nor should you shy away from showing students that you have strong beliefs. The key is to create a classroom in which individuals can freely agree or disagree, as they see fit.[32]

While laws direct us to what we can and cannot do, moral guidelines direct us in what we should and should not do. Professional associations have also suggested ethical guidelines for educators. (See the *Frame of Reference:* Code of Ethics and Bill of Rights.) Moral issues will continue to be a major concern in the years ahead, in many ways a measure of the quality of our culture. Indeed, even as our society grows in wealth and makes great scientific strides and technological breakthroughs, the final measure of our worth may not be our materialistic accomplishments but, rather, the way we treat each other.

SUMMARY

 CHAPTER REVIEW

Go to the Online Learning Center to take a quiz, practice with key terms, and review concepts from the chapter.

1. What are your legal rights and responsibilities as a teacher?

   When applying for a teaching position, you do not have to answer questions unrelated to the job. A teacher enjoys job security as long as the teacher's behavior and personal life do not disrupt or interfere with teaching effectiveness. However, academic freedom does not protect teachers who use obscene, irrelevant, inappropriate, or disruptive materials or instruction, and freedom of speech does not protect a teacher who uses malicious, intentionally inaccurate, confidential material, or whose speech hampers teaching performance. Teachers may copy material for classroom use by adhering to three criteria: brevity, spontaneity, and cumulative effect. While information on the Internet enjoys First Amendment protection, teachers may legally choose to limit student access to material that is vulgar or educationally inappropriate.

2. What legal rights do students enjoy (and do they have legal responsibilities)?

Parents and guardians have the right to see their child's educational record, and at 18 years of age, students become responsible for providing permission for others to see it. Title IX prohibits many forms of sexual harassment and sex discrimination, including treatment of students and faculty, financial aid, health care, scholarships, and counseling. Students have constitutionally protected rights to due process before they can be disciplined or suspended from school. As long as students do not disrupt the operation of the school or deny other students the opportunity to learn, they have the right to freedom of speech within the schools. Early "cyberTinker" cases have extended this right to the Internet. Schools can neither promote nor inhibit student prayer in honoring separation of church and state. The legality of a "moment of silence" varies from state to state. The school's *in loco parentis* responsibility allows it to search school lockers and cars in school parking lots and submit student athletes to random drug testing. Student publications can be censored if they are an integral part of the school curriculum, such as part of a course, or if they are obscene, psychologically damaging, or disruptive. Children with the HIV virus, like others who confront medical challenges, have their student status protected under the Individuals with Disabilities Education Act.

    The following suggestions for teachers are derived from court decisions and are intended to serve as a basic guide:

- Read school safety rules, regulations and handbooks
- Respect student confidentiality in records and forms
- Notify parents if curriculum materials might be objectionable
- Exercise forethought (due care) by anticipating dangerous situations
- Report suspected incidents of child abuse
- Know and follow due process when penalizing students
- Keep your meetings with students public
- Separate your personal and professional life
- Avoid offensive, sexual, and off-color comments
- Know and follow district policies regarding corporal punishment
- Seek medical assistance for student injuries or illness
- Avoid touching students
- Follow copyright laws

3. What are today's main approaches to moral education?

From detecting and reporting suspected cases of child abuse to helping students make ethical judgments, society expects teachers to provide moral education to students, but rejects the notion of promoting a particular or narrow set of beliefs. Historically, traditional values were imparted in a didactic style. Another approach, called values clarification, promotes values through personal reflection and individual analysis. Character education is a popular approach that promotes a core set of values, including respect, responsibility, citizenship, caring, and fairness. Lawrence Kohlberg and Carol Gilligan have attempted to map moral stages of development and build curricular materials based on these stages. Comprehensive values education combines both traditional and analytical approaches by directly teaching some values, like honesty and caring, while encouraging students to analyze their own positions on more controversial issues, like the death penalty. What teachers do and say provides a model for students, serving as an "informal" curriculum on ethical behavior.

CURRENT NEWS FROM POWERWEB

To access PowerWeb, go to Chapter 11 on the Online Learning Center to read current articles and to access news feeds about:

- Character Education
- Ethics and Teaching
- Morality and Schooling
- Politics
- Schools and Federal Policy
- Teachers' Attitudes

EXTENDED LEARNING

Go to Chapter 11 on your *Resources for Exploring Education* CD-ROM to access Case Studies and Readings.

CASE STUDIES

- David Burton: A teacher whose principal brooks no challenge to his authority discovers that two students who are thought to be guilty of crashing a systemwide computer program are being given unequal punishments by the principal.

- Amanda Jackson: A teacher discovers that her principal has a drinking problem, which is well known but never discussed among the staff.

- Ellen Norton: A teacher whose concern for a shy, underachieving student has led to the student becoming her 'shadow,' learns that another student may be the victim of child abuse at home.

READINGS

- Alfie Kohn. "How Not to Teach Values: A Critical Look at Character Education."
- Martha McCarthy. "Is the Supreme Court's Ruling 'Good News' for Public Schools?"
- Perry Zirkel. "Decisions That Have Shaped U.S. Education."

KEY TERMS AND PEOPLE

academic freedom, 396

Buckley Amendment, 404

character education, 419

child abuse, 417

comprehensive values
    education, 420

Copyright Act, 399

corporal punishment, 406

Morris Dees, 403

due process, 406

educational malpractice, 398

establishment clause, 393

fair use, 399

First Amendment, 393

Carol Gilligan, 420

in loco parentis, 409

individual analysis, 418

Lawrence Kohlberg, 420

malfeasance, 398

misfeasance, 398

moral stages of
    development, 420

nonfeasance, 398

sexual harassment, 413

Title VII of the Civil Rights
    Act (1964), 394

Title IX of the Education
    Amendments
    (1972), 394

traditional inculcation, 417

U.S. Supreme Court cases

Engel v. Vitale, 414

*Franklin v. Gwinnett
    County Public
    Schools,* 412, 416

Goss v. Lopez, 415

*Hazelwood School District
    v. Kuhlmeir,* 411, 415

Lee v. Weisman, 414

*Pickering v. Board of
    Education,* 414

*Tinker v. Des Moines
    Independent Community
    School District,* 407, 415

values clarification, 418

zero-tolerance policy, 406

DISCUSSION QUESTIONS AND ACTIVITIES

WEB-*TIVITIES*

1. Teachers' and Students'
   Rights and
   Responsibilities
2. Students' Rights: Title IX
   and Sexual Harassment

1. If you were to suggest a law to improve education, what would that law be? Would you make it federal, state, or local? Why?

2. The role of religion and prayer in schools has always been controversial, and teachers are advised to neither *encourage* nor *discourage* religious observances. As a teacher, what religious celebrations or practices might you encounter in your class? How would you respond to these issues while maintaining your neutrality?

3. Construct an argument to support the principle that students and their property should not be searched without the students' consent.

4. Which of the paths to moral education (values clarification, moral development, character education, or comprehensive values education) appeals to you most? Why?

5. Describe some steps you might explore to promote ethical student behavior in your classroom.

REEL TO REAL TEACHING

FINDING FORRESTER (2000)
Run Time: 133 minutes

Synopsis: *Finding Forrester* is a telling portrayal of ethics and expectations as an African American teen writing prodigy and star athlete finds a mentor in a reclusive author.

Reflection:

`1. What expectations did William Forrester, Dr. Crawford, and Clarie hold for Jamal? What social factors influenced these expectations? Did they change throughout the film. Why or why not?

2. How would you describe a successful student? An athlete? Did you picture this student as male or female? As a person of color or white? Now imagine that your successful student (and successful athlete) is the opposite sex or another race. Did your description change? What values are embedded in your answer?

3. As a teacher, how will you confront cheating and plagiarism in your classroom?

4. What lessons in character did Forrester and Jamal learn from each other?

Follow-up Activity: As part of a character education program, create an Honor Code to help students learn about academic integrity. You may want to consider the following questions: Is your Code a teacher's solo creation or a teacher-student partnership? What aspects of school life (such as bullying, lying, and punctuality) are included in the Code? Who will enforce the Code, and what are the rewards and punishments? What values will students learn from following (or breaking) the Honor Code?

How do you rate this film? Go to *Reel to Real Teaching* in the Critics' Corner to review this film.

**www.mhhe.com/
sadker**7e

FOR FURTHER READING

First Class Character Education Activities Program, by Michael Koehler and Karen Royer (2002). Provides coherent, nonreligious arguments in favor of character education, and then offers practical guidelines and resources of implementation.

Protecting the Right to Teach and Learn, by James Daly, Patricia Schall, and Rosemary Skeele (2001). Explores the legal and pedagogical implications of academic freedom in the face of political and religious challenges to what is taught in schools.

The Respectful School: How Educators and Students Can Conquer Hate and Harassment, by Stephen Wessler (2003). Teachers may not always see it, but every day, students are being harassed and intimidated because of their race, religion, gender, or other personal characteristics. This book draws on definite research and experiences of young victims to explain fundamental changes that every school should make to protect students.

School Law and the Public Schools: A Practical Guide for Educational Leaders, by Nathan Essex (2001). Summarizes educational laws and their impact on the organization of schools and daily classroom practices. Policy guidelines for issues such as school prayer, disability, sexual harassment, and freedom of speech are featured.

School Law: Cases and Concepts, by Michael LaMorte (2002). Designed for educators with little background in school law, this book provides an overview of the nation's legal structure. Details opinions and dissents on landmark cases include those on First Amendment protections, school finance, desegregation, and privacy.

REFLECTIVE ACTIVITIES AND YOUR PORTFOLIO

Part III: Foundations

3.1 Self-Fulfilling Prophecy

Purpose: Someday, at the end of your career in education, you will no doubt recall your early hopes and dreams. Will you have realized your goals? Project yourself into the future, and imagine you have accomplished all that you set out to do. An orientation toward the future can help you attain your goals.

Activity: Time flies: A new generation has decided to become teachers and they open *Teachers, Schools, and Society* (25th edition!), which they bought for only $1,284 and wondered if it was really worth it. They turn to the history chapter and begin reading the profiles in the "Hall of Fame." And you are there. Why? Let's find out.

Artifact: "My Hall of Fame Entry." Write yourself into *The Education Hall of Fame* by following the format in Chapter 8. Provide a graphic image, a statement of significant contribution, and about 250 words that detail your accomplishments in education. Be sure to include your unique skills and expertise to describe your achievement.

Reflection: The activity should help you define your professional values. What actions might help you reach your long-time goals? What steps should you consider now? Are there mentors and professional relationships that might help support your success? Keep this *Hall of Fame* entry in your portfolio. You could even seal and date it in an envelope to be opened when you teach your first class of students, receive your doctorate in education, are named U.S. Secretary of Education, or attend your retirement dinner. Attach your reflection to the artifact and include in your portfolio.

INTASC PRINCIPLE 1: Knowledge of Subject Matter

3.2 Money Matters

Purpose: Most state offices of education work to equalize per-pupil expenditures. Still, children live with very different financial realities at home and at school. A family's income influences a student's physical, social, emotional, moral, and cognitive growth.

Activity: To better understand and meet the needs of your learners, consider how economics has impacted you and your education.

Artifact: "Finances and Me." Under each developmental area, list ways your education was helped and/or hindered by money. While we all realize to one degree or another that money matters, we rarely take the time to consider specifically how it has shaped our own lives.

INTASC PRINCIPLE 2: Human Development and Learning

Developmental Areas and Socioeconomic Class
Physical (such as size, shape, fitness, health, medical resources):
Social (such as autonomy, civility, relationships):
Emotional (such as expressiveness, empathy, motivation):
Moral (such as ethics, honesty, good will):
Cognitive (such as intellectual resources, academic services, inherent abilities):

FORM

Developmental
Areas and Socio-
economic Class

Reflection: Consider how your childhood financial security (or lack thereof) contributed to your educational reality. How was your growth and development distinguished by economic class? How might your life have been different if you were raised with a very different financial base? What is the correlation between financial resources and academic success? Attach your reflection to the artifact and include in your portfolio.

3.3 Philosophy on the Big Screen

Purpose: The philosophies of education are captured not just in this section of the book, but in classic and contemporary films about schools. Movies reflect diverse (and sometimes overdramatized versions) of teaching philosophies, and watching these movies critically can help you analyze and explore your own philosophical preferences.

Activity: Before you choose a movie to watch, refresh your memory of the major philosophies by scanning the philosophy discussion in Chapter 9 (essentialism, perennialism, progressivism, existentialism, social reconstructionism). Select a video by reviewing the *Reel to Real Teaching* feature after each chapter, or browse through your local video rental store and choose a film about schools and teaching.

Artifact: "Philosophy in Action." Use the simple chart below to record evidence of the major philosophies that appeared in the film. As you watch (with or without pop-corn), attend to the various techniques the teachers use to meet the needs of the learners. Can you match the theories of philosophy to the cast of characters? Take notes and try to capture the indicators of educational philosophy that appear in the film.

Philosophy on the Big Screen	
Movie: _____	
Major Education Philosophy	**Cinematic Evidence**

FORM
Philosophy on the Big Screen

Reflection: What philosophy was most prevalent? Why do you think the filmmaker chose to highlight this philosophy? What appealed or disappointed you about the film? What did you learn about teaching and educational philosophies from this film? What traits of the cinematic teacher might you adapt . . . avoid? Attach your reflection to the artifact and include in your portfolio.

3.4 The Great Lecture Theory of Learning

Purpose: Most of us have attended, even been moved by, a great lecture, yet, when we learn about strategies for classroom instruction, the lecture is often relegated to the

INTASC PRINCIPLE 3:
Diversity in Learning

INTASC PRINCIPLE 4:
Variety of Instructional Strategies

least effective method or, simply, disparaged. Lecturing is not inherently evil. While it can be tiresome and boring, it can also be motivating, filled with information, clearly understood, and easily recalled. In some cases, the lecture format may be the best way to convey information. There are reasons that great lecturers are great, and the sooner you figure out some of those reasons, the sooner you will be able to give terrific lectures yourself.

Activity: Check around the campus with friends and acquaintances to find out which professors give great lectures. You may also want to inquire at a local elementary, middle or high school. Choose one teacher to observe and ask permission to attend a class. (Or, if necessary, check into television courses, videotapes from a distance learning course, or satellite seminar series.)

Artifact: "Effective Lecture Ideas." Take notes, but not on the specific lecture information—rather on presentation strategy and style. Ask some of the following questions about lecture technique:

OLC FORM:

Effective Lecture
Ideas

- What pulled you into the lecture? (a great story? a provocative question?)
- How did you know where the lecture was going? (Was the purpose or objective stated or implied?)
- How did the speaker use presentation or communication skills?
  Facial expressions?
  Gestures?
  Eye contact?
  Voice?
  Movement?
  Interaction with the audience?
  Other skills?
- What technical aids or materials (videotapes, PowerPoint presentation) enhanced your understanding and interest?
- Did the speaker use vivid examples, stories, metaphors, or role-play to enhance your comprehension?
- How might you assess the speaker's expertise in the lecture's content?

Reflection: All in all, was this lecturer worthy of his or her reputation? Why? How are you when it comes to public speaking? What's your comfort zone? Given what you know about yourself, which of the observed lecturer's strengths might be strengths of yours as well? Which might you want to add to your repertoire? Attach your reflection to the artifact and include in your portfolio.

3.5 What You See and What You Get

INTASC PRINCIPLE 5:
Motivation and
Management

Purpose: The philosophy of a classroom can be seen, felt, and heard, yet future teachers sometimes have a difficult time "getting" it, even when examples of educational philosophy surround us. This activity will help you connect with specific clues that signal a teacher's philosophy.

Activity: Arrange to observe several classrooms of the age of student you would like to teach. If this is not possible, do this activity in your college classrooms. Record observations on the following chart. Gather at least three different observations.

Artifact:

Philosophy-in-the-Classroom Observations

Indicators of Education Philosophy
Course: _____ Room arrangement: Teacher-student interactions: Student-initiated actions: Instructional grouping and organization (full class, individuals/groups, centers/stations):   Instructional resources: Other:

Reflection: What classroom indicators have you observed? What do these indicators suggest about the philosophy of your teachers, classes, program, or institution? What do your notes tell you about how faculty members manage instruction and motivate learning? Which elements do you want to include in your teaching? Which would you prefer to omit or avoid? Attach your reflection to the artifact and include in your portfolio.

INTASC PRINCIPLE 6:
Communication
Skills

3.6 Putting Your Philosophy into the Classroom

Purpose: What is your educational philosophy? Is it teacher-centered or student-centered? Do you subscribe to essentialism, perennialism, progressivism, existentialism, or social reconstructionism? Or do you prefer a cafeteria approach—that is, picking and choosing from several approaches? A strong sense of your educational philosophy will guide and shape your development as an educator. Refining and declaring your beliefs will allow you to sharpen your professional communication skills.

Activity: Using the discussion on educational philosophies from Chapter 9 as a guide, formulate your educational philosophy. Begin by brainstorming thoughts and ideas about your own beliefs. Work to hone your beliefs into a concise one-page declaration. It may be useful to begin a number of your philosophy statements with the phrase, "I believe . . ."

Artifact: "My Philosophy of Education." Using this one-page declaration as a guide, create a poster describing your philosophy. Use pictures and words (or be more creative) to convey your philosophy. Can the poster convey a sense of your personal commitment? Challenge classmates to guess your philosophy by viewing your poster. How can you adopt this poster idea for your classroom, and share with your students your educational philosophy when you begin teaching?

Reflection: Was it difficult to formulate a philosophy? How did your beliefs evolve during the course of this assignment? What surprised you about this activity? What did you learn about yourself from this activity? Do you have—or are you moving toward—a consistent philosophy? Were classmates able to guess your philosophy? Attach your one-page declaration and reflection to the artifact and include in your portfolio.

3.7 A Real Inservice Program

INTASC PRINCIPLE 7:
Instructional
Planning Skills

Purpose: Several districts and states, along with independent schools, are instituting a service obligation as a high school graduation requirement. The intent is to instill a contributory ethic in students. While an ongoing service requirement may be one way to meet this principled goal, you as a teacher can help by integrating this "service ethic" in your lessons.

Activity: Recall a lesson or unit you have seen. Brainstorm (alone or with others) how you might add a service component. Use the chart below as a guide.

Artifact: "A Service Component." Briefly outline a lesson or unit that you will be teaching, and then describe in (about 150 words) how you would integrate a service project or activity into your lesson. The following sample chart can offer some suggestions.

FORM

Service Integration
Ideas

Service Integration Ideas	
Lesson	**Sample Service Component**
Language arts	Read with special population students, children, or seniors
Science	Assist with student health appraisal
Math	Be a homework helper, one on one, with a student
Social studies	Work on a student or teacher rights campaign
Technology	Teach computer skills at a local shelter
Physical education	Referee or supervise a children's sport event or recess
Health	Bring the Great American Smoke Out to a local school
Vocational and career	Review career materials for bias
Foreign language	Assist bilingual parents with school visits and conferences
Arts	Volunteer with children in theater, art, dance, or music

Reflection: This reflection might better be called a projection. Project yourself into the future, actually teaching your lesson. Describe your service component. What goals do you hope to accomplish? Your service component teaches "higher lessons" about honoring each other and developing a caring community. How can you integrate these lessons of caring and compassion with your official curriculum? Attach your reflection to the artifact and include in your portfolio.

3.8 Assessing the Assessor

Purpose: With all the attention being given to the performance of American students on national and local tests, it makes sense for you to explore the promise and problems of districtwide evaluation.

INTASC PRINCIPLE 8:
Assessment

Activity: Invite a school district administrator with assessment responsibilities to your class or study group for one hour. (Create a class chat room on your department's website or conduct an interview, if that works better.) Ask your guest to describe the district's history and current evaluation procedures.

Artifact: "Testing Practices." Use the following questions (or your own) to expand your guest's commentary. Record the answers.

 FORM
Testing Practices

- What are the purposes behind these tests?
- Give examples of when these policies and procedures work effectively—and when there are problems.
- What is the best thing about these tests, and what is the worst?
- What is the biggest problem you face?
- What role does the public (parents, media, chamber of commerce) play?

- How do special interest groups influence testing policies?
- How do teachers, students, and parents react to these tests?
- Can you suggest other approaches to gauge achievement?

Bonus Artifact: Assume you are writing for a newspaper and turn the administrator's presentation and interview into a story for your local newspaper.

Reflection: What have you learned? What information surprised you? What do you still have on your "need to know" list? Do you support the current testing culture? What are the pros and cons? Attach your reflection to the artifact and include in your portfolio.

3.9 Publication of the Month

INTASC PRINCIPLE 9:
Reflection and
Responsibility

Purpose: While the Internet represents ready sources of information, not all of the information on the Internet is of high quality. Professional journals and magazines often include the best writing in our field. Journal articles are submitted and reviewed by educational experts, selected for their high standards of excellence. To be a reflective and responsible teacher, you will need to keep current by reading one or more professional journals.

Activity: Pick a journal or an educational magazine that is new to you. Try one at your professor's suggestion or use sources listed in the endnotes of this text. Spend at least one hour reading through the journal.

Artifact: "Journal Review." Harvest a sense of what this journal offers by analyzing its intended audience, format, content, style, policy, and readability. Write up your findings in a review format and present to the class or a small group of classmates. You may want to create a class scrapbook that describes these journals by sharing all the descriptions created by your classmates.

Refection: In describing this journal to your peers, what positive points would you stress? What are its weaknesses? If you could read only one journal a month, would it be this one, or perhaps another reviewed by a classmate? Why? Attach a sample article and your artifact to the reflection and include in your portfolio.

3.10 Get on Board

INTASC PRINCIPLE 10:
Relationships and
Partnerships

Purpose: One seemingly distant group, the school board, influences every teaching day. As an elected agency of the community, school boards hold regular meetings, usually open to visitors. Because their norms and procedures vary, you have to see one to understand one. The purpose of this activity is to better understand how school boards function and how they might impact your life in the classroom.

Activity: Attend a school board meeting or watch one on television (many are broadcast by local cable networks). Imagine you are covering the meeting for your district's teacher association. Note what is going on. Try to grasp the formal curriculum (old and new business and procedures). Look also at the hidden curriculum, the cultural cues and the nonverbal signals, that tell you what else is going on.

Artifact: "A School Board Column." Write your notes into a news column for a teachers' newsletter that might be distributed in a local school system. Limit your article to a single page. Read your article in class and lead a class discussion.

Reflection: What were your personal and professional impressions of the meeting? What rituals and routines did you observe? How were your assumptions about school boards and meetings altered by your attendance? Were underlying politics evident? How were attendees treated? Did any of the school board's decisions directly impact district teachers? How? Based on your observation of the school board meeting, would you consider teaching in this district? Would you consider running for a school board position? Why or why not? Attach your reflection to your article and include in your portfolio.

CLASS ACT

At this time of year, graduates may feel a little lost. We have been students for SO long, and now suddenly things are changing. At such time of transition, we need a larger purpose to guide us—why have we chosen these careers as educators? It certainly wasn't for the money! I would like to share some words that I have turned to for a sense of purpose.

Over thirty years ago, W.E.B. DuBois, the great African American writer and activist, said from his death bed: "One thing alone I charge you: As you live, believe in life! Always human beings will live and progress to greater, broader, and fuller life. The only possible death is to lose belief in this truth . . . "

Despite all the injustice he experienced, DuBois died believing that the future will be ever brighter. In our line of work, it is not always easy to believe in progress. Apparently, DuBois never tried to get licensed at the New York City Board of Ed.! I have had many discussions with other students, wondering how to tackle problems such as glaring educational inequity based on race and class, negative or indifferent attitudes toward bilingual and special education, international disparities in the quality of education, and a general lack of respect in this country for the work that we do. What impact can I have as one individual educator? True, one person alone cannot change society. But each of us does have the power to change other people, and collectively we are an impressive force. For example, think of a teacher or family member who has passed on a legacy to you.

I am imagining two people up here with me: my mother's mother and my father's father. My grandmother, Mercy Oduro, was a West African woman who touched hundreds as a teacher and headmistress of an elementary school. It's a testament to her life's work that, although she died six years ago, I am still called "Teacher Mercy's granddaughter" when I go back to Ghana. To me, she has passed on a flair for celebration and an unshakeable belief in her students, and I will pass these on to my own students.

My American grandfather, William Steel, 83 years old, is a retired teacher, but STILL tutoring daily at his local school. His legacy is so strong that on his eightieth birthday he got letters from people he taught over fifty years ago, acknowledging his influence on them. To me, he has passed on a fantastic curiosity about the world and a playful sense of humor, and I will pass these on when I teach.

Imagine now that all the people we will reach ARE crowded in this room today—hundreds, thousands of them. In each of these people there is a piece of one of us, continuing the legacy of those who came before. Look around. Can you see the ocean of possibility flowing from us here today? Together, how can we NOT create DuBois' vision of greater, broader, and fuller life? Let me tell you, we are powerful: We are educators.

Melissa Steel
Teachers College Graduation Speech
Columbia University

Read more Class Acts at Sadker.com.

**www.mhhe.com/
sadker7e**

The Struggle for Educational Opportunity

FOCUS QUESTIONS

1. How do deficit, expectation, and cultural difference theories explain disparate academic performance among various racial, ethnic, and cultural groups?
2. What major developments have marked the educational history of Native Americans, Hispanics, African Americans, Asian Americans/Pacific Islanders, and Arab Americans?
3. What educational barriers and breakthroughs have girls and women experienced?
4. What classroom strategies are appropriate for teaching culturally diverse learners?
5. What impact do changing family patterns and economic issues have on children and schools?
6. How can educators respond to social issues that place children at risk?

 What Do You Think? Estimate the social, racial, and ethnic backgrounds of today's students.

CHAPTER PREVIEW

CHAPTER FOCUS

This chapter describes two types of struggles. One struggle concerns the historical and continuing battle waged by students of color and women to open the schoolhouse door. We also consider the destructive social forces impacting children, including poverty, family patterns, and substance abuse. Both realms pose serious challenges to schools, teachers, and especially, children. For a chapter outline, see the IM.

Have you ever felt the cold slap of rejection because of race, religion, color, sex, language, national origin, social class, sexual orientation, or physical or learning disability? Have you ever denied a family history that included divorce, suicide, or abuse? Frequently, the dominant culture has little tolerance for those who are in any way "different." As most of us know from personal experience, when you happen to be the one who is outside—the one who is deprived even briefly of the privileges and status of the inside group—the feeling of being labeled "less worthy" can be more than painful.

Ideally, education should be for all children. In reality, education has repeatedly labeled, tracked, and excluded students who are in any way different. These children have met prejudicial treatment early, right at the schoolhouse door. This chapter will review the major developments that have pried open the school door and have brought these once excluded learners into the educational mainstream.

Intersecting with racism and sexism, considerable economic and social problems engulf our children and our schools. The recent past has not been kind to children, who now make up the poorest segment of society. Their survival and educational achievements are threatened by poverty, changing family patterns, substance abuse, depression, and even suicide. We will identify strategies that help keep the school door open for these troubled students as well.

Student diversity continues to increase dramatically. Teachers, schools, and society must respond, so that both equity and excellence can be achieved and maintained.

Educational Opportunity for All

"Welcome to class," says the professor as you take your seat. "I want you to respond to the following case study. Now it is, of course, fictional, but suspend belief, read the parable and tell me what you think."

As a student in this class, you think this sounds kind of interesting (and a good grade in this course would be really nice). So you settle down and read the brief story:

> You are a white person and are visited by an official who explains that a mistake has been made, and you were actually born to black parents who live far from where you grew up. The error has to be rectified. At midnight, you will become black, acquiring a darker skin, and body and facial features that reflect your African heritage. Your knowledge and ideas, your "inside," however, will remain the same.
>
> Now this is an unusual and rare problem, the official explains, but the error was not yours, and the organization that he represents is ready and able to offer you appropriate recompense. His records indicate that you are scheduled to live another 50 years.
>
> How much financial recompense would you request?

You look around and see your classmates settle into the task—considering what the possible compensation should be, each from their own unique perspective of race and ethnicity. You wonder: How much money will your white classmates ask for? How do the students of color respond to this controversial, some would say offensive, class exercise? Now the BIG question: How much money would *you* ask for?

While the parable is not true, the scenario is. Professor Andrew Hacker at Cornell put this question to white students in his class, and asked them to come up with a settlement figure: How much money would they want to offset the "error"? If you are wondering what figure Hacker's students came up with, most felt that a reasonable payment for the "mistake" would be fifty million dollars, a million dollars "for each coming black year."

The book that described this activity, *Two Nations: Black, White, Separate, Hostile, Unequal* (1992), received a great deal of media coverage in the 1990s, but we believed that it also left many questions unanswered.[1] What if Professor Hacker had continued the experiment with other groups? How much money would an Hispanic American, African American, and Asian American request if a mistake were made and they had to live the rest of their lives as a member of another race or culture? Would they request less compensation for the "administrative" blunder? The same fifty million? Would they want more money?

Certainly, just posing the problem underscores the American tendency to look to the courts to fix any "mistake," no matter how bizarre. And of course, in this story, money is the all-American panacea, a salve for any social injury. But despite these confounding issues, the parable is fascinating, and the questions it raises are intriguing.

Why did Professor Hacker construct this strange story, and how did he interpret the payment? He believed that the story unmasks America's hidden racism. Professor Hacker considers white privilege to be so commonplace that most of us are no longer able to "see" it. He uses the parable because it makes the hidden advantage of being white visible again. In Hacker's estimation, the fifty million dollars that his students thought "fair" represents the value that white people place on the color of their own skin.

How do you interpret the story? Would you seek a legal settlement and monetary damages? (Here's an idea, perhaps you might feel privileged to experience more than one culture or one race in a single lifetime.) Or like Hacker, do you believe that some

GRABBER: PREVIEW
IM

FOCUS QUESTION 1
How do deficit, expectation, and cultural difference theories explain disparate academic performance among various racial, ethnic, and cultural groups?

TEACHING TIP
For students just entering the field of education, opinions on this chapter could range from *too fascinating* to *too much*. Consider unique approaches to the content including class activities in the IM. Your teaching pace could be extended—providing enriched coverage with an extra session. This chapter is also situated at a time when students crank up (or fade out) at end of the term. As a good *teacher*, recognize the challenge of keeping student effort and energy high to the end of the semester.

RAP 4.2
Getting to Know Whom?,
p. 563

CLASS ACTIVITY: IT'S A
PRIVILEGE
IM, Activity 12:9

races and cultures are more valued in America? And perhaps a more basic question: Do you feel that just going through this exercise is an appropriate classroom activity? Or do you believe that it is too problematic?

When it comes to education, are certain groups more valued? If we ask Americans directly about race and schooling, how do you think they would respond? (And how would you respond?) Well, in fact, that's a question that the Gallup organization asked in 1978, and again in 2001.[2] In 1978, 80 percent of the public believed that the schooling opportunities for all American children, regardless of race or ethnicity, were equal. In 2001, that figure was 79 percent, virtually unchanged. But while most believe that educational opportunity is equal, they do not accept the notion that all students are achieving equally. Almost half said that whites are achieving at a higher rate than African Americans or Hispanics. Why this difference, and what should be done about it? Eighty percent surveyed said that while the achievement gap is not the fault of the schools, it is up to schools to close the gap.

The challenge we as educators face is figuring out exactly how this should be done. A number of theories have emerged to explain why some groups soar in school, while others flounder. Some of the explanations are fatalistic, others more hopeful. One argument would go something like this: Certain students do poorly in school because of their cultural, social, or linguistic backgrounds. The values, language patterns, and behaviors that these children learn at home do not mesh with the culture of U.S. schools, putting these students at a disadvantage. This explanation is known as the **deficit theory**. (Before the 1960s, the deficit theory held that genetic and IQ deficiencies of certain groups, especially people of color, were the root cause of academic underachievement. Deficit theory proponents today steer clear of such claims.)

Here's a second view: Some children do poorly because their teachers do not expect much of kids from certain racial and ethnic groups. As a result, they teach these students differently, the students' academic performance suffers, and the entire cycle becomes a self-fulfilling prophecy. This is called the **expectation theory**, which was first made popular by Rosenthal and Jacobson (their classic study is mentioned in Chapter 3, "Teacher Effectiveness"). Expectation theory holds that academic performance can be improved if teacher behavior is modified.

A third explanation argues for better cross-cultural understanding. **Cultural difference theory** asserts that academic problems can be overcome if educators study and mediate the cultural gap separating school and home. Let's consider one case in point, and then see how cultural difference theory works:

> Polynesian children in a Hawaiian village are performing poorly on the school reading tests. They seem unresponsive to the extra time and effort made by teachers to improve their reading performance. Why is this happening, and how can the situation be improved?

In this example, educators studied the Polynesian culture and discovered that older children, rather than adults, play a major role in educating the young. Accordingly, the school established a peer learning center, providing the opportunity for older children to teach younger ones. By recognizing and adopting cultural traditions, the school was able to dramatically improve students' reading scores.[3]

Creating effective classrooms for all children takes a deliberate and thoughtful process. In the first part of this chapter we continue on the road to bridging the cultural, racial, and ethnic divide, and creating a classroom climate that recognizes and honors differences. So you may better appreciate where your students are coming from, we provide brief histories of the U.S. experiences of several nondominant cultures and immigrant groups.

But race, culture and ethnicity are only some of the issues that teachers should consider in their classrooms. Gender is another. Does gender influence teaching—and achievement? You bet it does. How can teachers ensure that both girls and boys are treated fairly? In this chapter, we offer several specific suggestions for nonsexist, non-racist teaching.

As the chapter draws to an end, we will examine barriers to equal opportunity that come from social realities. In today's America, girls and boys from all racial, ethnic, and cultural backgrounds struggle with issues ranging from substance abuse to AIDS, from homophobia to teen pregnancy, from homelessness to being home alone. These issues are all part of today's social fabric, and they all have implications for your class-room. In fact, if the diverse characteristics of today's children were merged into your classroom of thirty students:[4]

MULTIPLE INTELLIGENCE CONNECTION
A musical tip: lyrics offer positive (and negative) messages regarding race, ethnicity and gender. "Drowning" (Hootie and the Blowfish: *Cracked Rear View*)
"Drowning in a sea of tears,
Hatred trying to hide your fears,
Living only for yourself,
Hating everybody else,
Cause they don't like you."

RELATED READING
The Third Culture Kid Experience: Growing Up Among Worlds by David C. Pollock and Ruth E. Van Reken (1999).

19 would be white.

17 will be living with their two biological or adoptive parents.

15 will live in a single-parent family at some point in childhood.

12 will never complete a single year of college.

10 were born to unmarried parents.

10 will be poor at some point in childhood.

10 are a year or more behind in school.

8 live with only one parent.

6 were born poor.

6 were born to a mother who did not graduate from high school.

6 would be Hispanic.

6 live in a family receiving food stamps.

6 have a foreign-born mother.

5 are poor today.

5 would be African American.

4 have no health insurance.

4 live with a working relative but are poor nonetheless.

4 were born to a teenage mother.

4 speak a language at home other than English.

4 will never graduate from high school.

3 might be questioning their heterosexuality or believing that they are gay, lesbian, bisexual, or transgendered.

3 have a disability.

2 live at less than half the poverty level.

2 have difficulty speaking English.

1 would be an Asian American.

1 might be Native American.

1 lives with neither parent.

Several might be biracial or bicultural.

And, for every 35 classrooms, 1 student will be killed by gunfire before age 20.

Native Americans: The History of Miseducation

In the beginning, God gave to every people a cup of clay, and from this cup they drank their life. They all dipped in the water, but their cups were different. Our cup is broken now. It has passed away.

Digger Indian proverb

FOCUS QUESTION 2
What major developments have marked the educational history of Native Americans, Hispanics, African Americans, Asian Americans/Pacific Islanders and Arab Americans?

Indian boarding schools were established to assimilate young Native Americans into the dominant European-American values: veneration of property, individual competition, European-style domesticity, toil, and European standards of dress.

OVERHEAD 136
Diversity and Education

TEACHING TIP
From 1879 to 1918, approximately 12,000 Native American children attended the Carlisle Indian Industrial School in Pennsylvania. They came (willingly and otherwise) from all corners of the US— and from more than 140 tribes. In 2000, a nationwide Powwow remembered the school and its goal—to ensure that Indian children be "educated in the ways of the European-American culture." http://home.epix.net/~landis/powwow.html.

TEACHING TIP
When urban Indians trace their ancestry (blood quantam levels) their analysis can determine tribal enrollments, availability of medical services and scholarship opportunities. Tribes and social and government agencies all use different standards for mixed-race peoples.

Over the centuries, the impact of white people on the tribal life of Native Americans has been one of conquest and the attempted and often successful destruction of tradition and culture.[5] The early attempt of whites to provide their own brand of education for Native Americans was carried out by church missionary societies. Many Native Americans responded enthusiastically to the white approach to their education—as long as this approach did not attempt to eradicate their cultures. The missionaries, however, often saw their goal as one of "civilizing" and Christianizing the tribes. They ignored or actively suppressed the languages of their pupils and tried to teach exclusively in English.[6]

Despite such adverse conditions, Native Americans achieved some extraordinary educational accomplishments that rejected white attempts to deny tribal heritages and languages. For example, in 1822, **Sequoyah** invented a Cherokee syllabary. This permitted the Cherokee language to be written; books were published in Cherokee; Cherokee schools became bilingual; and the Cherokee nation wrote, edited, and published the *Cherokee Phoenix*, a bilingual weekly newspaper. However, as federal interventions became more systematic, the tribes' control over their own education diminished.

After the Civil War, the federal government, through the **Bureau of Indian Affairs (BIA)**, dominated the education of Native Americans. Education became a tool of conquest, and the reservations saw more and more white superintendents, farm agents, teachers, inspectors, and missionaries. The largest of the tribes, the Navajos, despite their years of resistance, were assigned to a reservation. The treaty with the Navajos promised that schools would be built to educate their children. In 1892, almost twenty years after the treaty was signed, only seventy-five students attended the one and only school on the reservation. This represented less than 0.5 percent of the Navajo population.

Many Native Americans refused to send their children to reservation schools. Arrest and kidnapping were common practices in forcing Native American children to attend. Rations were often withheld from parents as a means of compelling them to send their children to school.

After 1920, there was an increase in political and legal activity as Native Americans fought for tribal and educational rights. Native Americans challenged the federal government for violating treaties, including failure to provide adequate education. The federal courts were not responsive. Greater gains at the state level were made, and in several court cases Native Americans won the right to attend public schools.[7]

Over half of the 2 million Native Americans in this country do not live on reservations, and their youngsters have become invisible children of color in urban centers. As the students have been desegregated across neighborhoods, they have lost their "critical mass," which is often associated with higher achievement.[8]

The recent decades have witnessed continued activity by Native Americans to win control of the reservations, including the schools. The tribes feel strongly that such control will maintain cultural identity, as well as increase the academic achievement of their children. The vast majority of Indian children are educated in public schools. Most other Native youth are clustered in programs under the advisory of the Bureau of Indian Affairs or private schools.

Black Americans: The Struggle for a Chance to Learn

Much of the history of African American education in the United States has been one of denial. The first law prohibiting education of slaves was passed in South Carolina in 1740. During the next hundred years, many states passed similar and even stronger compulsory-ignorance laws. For example, an 1823 Mississippi law prohibited six or more Negroes from gathering for educational purposes. In Louisiana, an 1830 law imposed a prison sentence on anyone caught teaching a slave to read or write. However, because education has always been integral to African Americans' struggle for equal opportunity, they risked the penalties of these laws and even the dangers of violence for a chance to learn. They formed clandestine schools throughout most large cities and towns of the South. Suzie King Taylor described what it was like to attend one of those secret schools in Savannah, Georgia:

> We went every day about nine o'clock with our books wrapped in paper to prevent the police or white persons from seeing them. We went in, one at a time, through the gate, into the yard to the L Kitchen which was the schoolroom.[9]

The Civil War brought an end to policies of compulsory ignorance and an affirmation of black people's belief in the power of education. Most of the schooling of African Americans immediately following the Civil War was carried out by philanthropic societies. These associations worked with the Freedmen's Bureau, a federal agency established to provide various services, including the establishment of schools. School staffs were usually a mixture of instructors from the North, blacks of Caribbean island heritage, and formerly enslaved literate blacks.

Many white Southerners responded to the education of blacks with fear and anger. Sometimes there was terrorism against black schools. In the end, however, politics replaced violence as the principal means of denying blacks equal educational opportunity. As conservatives began regaining political power, state after state passed laws that explicitly provided for segregated schools. With the 1896 ***Plessy v. Ferguson*** Supreme Court decision, segregation became a legally sanctioned part of the American way of life. In this landmark case, the Court developed the doctrine of **separate but equal.** Separate but equal initially legalized separate railway passenger cars for

VIDEO SEGMENT 31
Native American Education

TEACHING TIP
Mississippi often ranks very close to the bottom in per-pupil education expenditures. At $5,590 per student, they are $1,239 below the national average. What is the impact of routinely underfunded schools for children from all racial and ethnic groups? (Selected Statistics on Mississippi Education: 2001) www.mde.k12.ms.us/extrel/pub/stat.htm.

The famous Tuskegee Normal School founded by Booker T. Washington became a national symbol for the educational aspirations of African Americans.

VIDEO SEGMENT 28
Fighting for What's Fair

black and white Americans, and was also used to justify a legally segregated school system, which in many states lasted for more than half a century.

"Separate but equal" was not equal. In 1907, Mississippi spent $5.02 for the education of each white child but only $1.10 for each black child. In 1924, the state paid more than $1 million to transport whites long distances to schools. No money was spent for blacks, and for them a daily walk of more than twelve miles was not out of the question. Attending schools without enough books, seats, space, equipment, or facilities taught African American children the harsh reality of "separate but unequal." In the South, a dual school system based on race was in existence. This was ***de jure* segregation**—that is, segregation by law or by official action.

In the North, school assignments were based on both race and residence. ***De facto*** (unofficial) **segregation** occurred as the result of segregated residential patterns, patterns that were often prompted by discriminatory real estate practices. As housing patterns changed, attendance zones were often redrawn to ensure the separation of white and black children in schools. Even in schools that were not entirely segregated, black children were routinely placed in special classes or separate academic tracks, counseled into low-status careers, and barred from extracurricular activities. Whatever the obstacle, however, African Americans continued their struggle for access to quality education. As W.E.B. DuBois noted: "Probably never in the world have so many oppressed people tried in every possible way to educate themselves."[10]

Political gains by blacks followed their participation in World War II and the New Deal policies of Franklin Roosevelt. In May 1954, the Supreme Court handed down a groundbreaking decision. In ***Brown v. Board of Education of Topeka*** (Kansas), the Court unanimously ruled that "in the field of public education the doctrine of 'separate but equal' has no place. Separate educational facilities are inherently unequal." Indicating how quickly the **desegregation** of Southern schools was to take place, the Court used the phrase "with all deliberate speed." In effect, the Court established a vague timetable, one without a deadline of any kind, so yet another generation of black children experienced segregated education. Ten years after *Brown*, almost 91 percent of all African American children in the South still attended all-black schools.

CRITICAL THINKING
QUESTION
A Washington Post headline reads "A Path of Hostility in Belfast." "Elementary school girls in pleated blue skirts and starched white blouses learned a lesson in hate on the way to class this morning . . . " (September 5, 2001) Does the struggle for educational opportunity still put children at risk of their lives? How are the times, places, and people the same and different?

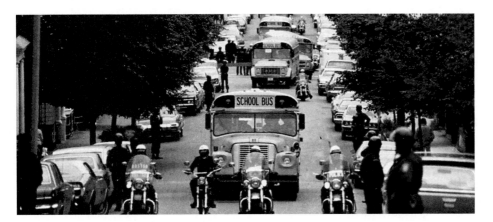

In 1964, Congress moved boldly to eradicate racial segregation and discrimination in schools by passing the **Civil Rights Act,** including two titles of particular importance to schools. **Title IV** gave the U.S. Commissioner of Education the power to help desegregate and the U.S. Attorney General the power to initiate lawsuits to force school desegregation. **Title VI** prohibited the distribution of federal funds to schools with racially discriminatory programs of any kind. Together, these two titles produced more desegregation in their first four years than the Supreme Court's decision in *Brown* had produced during the preceding decade.

During the late 1960s and early 1970s, the courts became the primary battleground in the African American communities' fight for equal educational opportunity. The Supreme Court handed down a series of decisions indicating its impatience with the slow pace of desegregation. The Court also began attacking *de facto* segregation stemming from racially imbalanced neighborhoods. In Charlotte-Mecklenburg County, North Carolina, a U.S. district judge ordered extensive **busing** of students to different schools to achieve integration. Courts later supported racial quotas and school pairing to eradicate school segregation in both the North and the South. But over time, many of these efforts were abandoned and racial segregation reappeared.

School districts began to experiment with other remedies more acceptable to school families. Typically, these procedures involved more freedom of choice and greater emphasis on improved instruction. Such remedies included magnet schools, choice plans, and voluntary metropolitan desegregation arrangements.

As schools became more racially balanced, students discovered a new barrier to equality. Although in the same school building, black and white students found themselves separated by race, a phenomenon called **second-generation segregation.** Tracking was a common method for second-generation segregation, but not the only one. While whites pursued certain extracurricular activities, blacks gravitated to others. Territoriality developed as areas of school buildings became informally segregated, and African American students also found themselves being treated differently.[11] As the famous Kerner Commission warned back in the 1960s: "Our nation is moving toward two societies, one black, one white—separate and unequal." The commission charged that white society must assume responsibility for the black ghetto. "White institutions created it, white institutions maintain it, and white society condones it."[12]

Although the middle of the century witnessed many difficult but hopeful efforts to desegregate the nation's schools, as the century drew to a close, a more conservative political tide was evident. Many affirmative efforts, such as busing, were abandoned,

VIDEO SEGMENT 29
Social Change: Desegregating Schools

OVERHEAD 137
Percentage of African American Students in Hyper-Segregated Schools

CRITICAL THINKING QUESTION
Many of your students have been schooled during these court-ordered geographic shifts. What have they heard (or said) about efforts to desegregate?

RAP 4.1
Nontraditional Hero, p. 562

RELATED READING
A Hope in the Unseen: An American Odyssey From the Inner City to the Ivy League by Ron Susskind (1998).

CLASS ACTIVITY: EXPERIENCING DISCRIMINATION
IM, Activity 12:2

and in the *Hopwood* (1996) and the *University of Michigan* decisions (2003), firm racial set-asides for college and law school admissions were eliminated. Although the courts said that race could be a factor in promoting student diversity, it could not be a major factor. The consequences of these actions are now evident in the nation's schools.[13]

Professor Gary Orfield at the Harvard Civil Rights Project reports a powerful trend toward school resegregation. Today's students are more segregated than they were three decades ago, with white students experiencing the most segregated educational environment. Yet those relatively few students attending diverse schools are more comfortable with other racial and ethnic groups and more understanding of diverse points of view. The Harvard Project points out that most students will not see these benefits. Orfield puts most of the responsibility for a resegregated school system on an increasingly conservative judiciary that has abandoned court-ordered integration plans. (See Figure 12.1.)[14]

Figure 12.1
Students in *de facto* minority schools.

SOURCE: Darryl Fears, "Schools' Racial Isolation Growing," *The Washington Post*, July 18, 2001, p. A3.

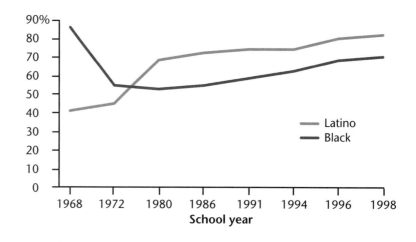

REFLECTION: Do you believe that desegregation of America's schools will ever be possible? Is desegregation important? Explain your position.

Magnet schools can offer students exceptional educational opportunities and often attract culturally diverse learners.

Past and present policies which made it extremely difficult for black Americans to achieve at the level of their ability are like dropping the baton. And black America is not another team in competition with white America. Black Americans are part of America's team. If America keeps running without the baton, no matter how fast or how far, we're going to lose.[15]

Hispanics: Growing School Impact

OVERHEAD 138
U.S. Hispanic Subgroups

Almost 40 million Hispanics live in the United States, including Puerto Rico, up over 75 percent since 1980. Over two-thirds of Hispanics living in the United States are U.S.-born citizens and constitute 13 percent of the nation's population, the largest minority group in the nation.[16] Because many Latinos immigrated to the United States to escape economic and political repression, not all of them entered the country legally. Consequently, their numbers may be underestimated. Ongoing legal and illegal immigration, together with high birth rates for young families in their child-bearing years, have made Hispanics the youngest and fastest-growing school-age population in the United States. By the year 2030, Hispanic children will represent one-fourth of the total school-age population.[17]

Hispanics consist of several subgroups, which share some characteristics, such as language, but differ in others, such as race, location, age, income, and educational attainment. The three largest Hispanic subgroups are Mexican Americans, Puerto Ricans, and Cuban Americans. There is also significant representation from other Latin American and Caribbean countries, such as the Dominican Republic, El Salvador, Nicaragua, and Honduras.[18] (See Figure 12.2.) In contrast to these new immigrants, many from war-torn or poverty-stricken countries, there is also an "old" population of Mexican and Spanish descent living in the Southwest with a longer history on this continent than those who trace their ancestors to the New England colonies.

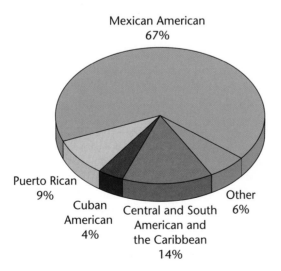

U.S. Hispanic subgroups

Figure 12.2
U.S. Hispanic subgroups.

SOURCE: The Hispanic Population in the United States, U.S. Census Bureau, March 2002.

REFLECTION: While many refer to Hispanics as a homogeneous community, they are not. What distinctions can you make for each of these segments? What similarities have you observed or studied?

By 2030, Hispanic children will comprise one quarter of the total school-age population.

Latino children confront numerous educational barriers. As early as kindergarten, Hispanic students are less able than their white peers to identify colors, recognize letters, count to fifty, or write their first name. Over a third of Hispanics drop out of school, a number more than twice as high as African Americans and more than three times as high for non-Hispanic whites.[19]

Mexican Americans

At the end of the United States' war with Mexico (1846–1848), the Mexicans who decided to stay in the new U.S. territories were guaranteed full citizenship. By 1900, approximately 200,000 Mexican Americans were living in the Southwest, having built the cities of Los Angeles, San Diego, Tucson, Albuquerque, Dallas, and San Antonio. The devices that were used to deny educational opportunity to Mexican Americans were similar to those imposed on African Americans. By 1920, a pattern of separate and unequal Mexican American schools had emerged throughout the Southwest. With the passage of Civil Rights legislation in the 1960s, Crystal City, Texas, became the flashpoint of the Chicano Movement. The Chicano students walked out of school, protesting inferior facilities and demanding bilingual/bicultural education.[20]

Then, as now, significant numbers of Mexican American families migrated once or twice a year, exploited as a source of cheap labor in rural, agricultural communities. With constant transitions, children's learning suffered. One superintendent in Texas, reflecting deeply engrained prejudice, argued that education was actually dangerous for Mexican Americans:

Most of our Mexicans are of the lower class. They transplant onions, harvest them, etc. The less they know about everything else, the better contented they are . . . so you see

In the late 1960s, Cesar Chavez led the fight of migrant Mexican American laborers to organize themselves into a union and to demand a more responsive education that included culture-free IQ tests, instruction in Spanish, smaller classes, and greater cultural representation in the curriculum.

it is up to the white population to keep the Mexican on his knees in an onion patch. . . . This does not mix well with education.[21]

Today, more than one in four public schools enroll migrant students, mostly Mexican Americans. The greatest numbers are in rural sections of California, Texas, and North Carolina.[22]

RELATED READING
Barefoot Heart: Stories of a Migrant Child by Elva Trevino Hart (1999).

Puerto Ricans

During the nineteenth century, many of the Puerto Ricans in the United States were highly respected political exiles striving for the independence of their homeland. But all that changed in 1898, when Puerto Rico was acquired from Spain and became a territory of the United States. Citizenship, through the Jones Act in 1917, provided free movement between the continent and the island. Migration to the mainland peaked during the 1950s, with the majority of Puerto Ricans settling in New York City. By 1974, there were more than a quarter of a million Puerto Rican students in the New York City public schools. Currently, about half the Puerto Rican population lives within the fifty states, and the other half lives in Puerto Rico.[23] The frequent passage between the island and the United States, as families search for a better economic life, makes schooling all the more difficult for Puerto Rican children.

Cuban Americans

Following the Castro-led revolution in the 1950s, Cuban immigration to the United States increased significantly. During the 1960s, Cubans who settled in the United States were primarily well-educated, professional, and middle- and upper-class. By 1980, 800,000 Cubans—10 percent of the population of Cuba—were living in the United States. For the most part, Cubans settled in Miami and other locations in southern Florida, but there are also sizable populations in New York, Philadelphia, Chicago, Milwaukee, and Indianapolis. Cubans, considered one of the most highly educated people in American immigration history, tend to be more prosperous and more conservative than most of the other Latino groups.[24]

In the second immigration wave, during the 1980s, there were many more black and poor Cubans, who have not been accepted as readily into communities in the United States.

GLOBAL VIEW
The 96 percent adult literacy rate in Cuba is often tied to the policies of President Fidel Castro. Go to UNICEF's website (www.unicef.org/statis/index.html) to find out national literacy rates.

Asian Americans and Pacific Islanders: The Magnitude of Diversity

The term "Asian Americans and Pacific Islanders" embraces peoples from nations as diverse as India, Vietnam, China, Pakistan, Korea, Samoa, Japan, and Native Hawaiian, about half the world's population. Over 10 million Americans have roots in Asia, although demographers predict that this figure will increase severalfold by the year 2050.[25] As a group these Americans have attained a high degree of educational and economic success. This section will describe the differing experiences of four of the largest Asian immigrant groups—Chinese, Filipinos, Asian Indians, and Japanese—as well as problems faced by refugees from Southeast Asia.[26]

Many of these cultures hold education in high esteem, and well-mannered, respectful and studious Asian American students have earned themselves the moniker of **model minority.** In kindergarten, Asian American children outscore their peers

RELATED READING
A White Teacher Talks About Race by Julie Landsman (2001).

in both reading and math.[27] Over 40 percent of Asian American/Pacific Islanders graduate from college. One year after graduation, they have a higher starting salary than any racial or ethnic group.[28] However, diversity within the Asian community is often overlooked, and as with many stereotypes, misconceptions abound. Fewer than half of Vietnamese and Samoan Americans graduate from high school, and Asian New Wavers reflect the current countercultural pattern, with baggy pants, combat boots and dyed hair, challenging the model minority stereotype.[29]

Chinese Americans

TEACHING TIP
From 1910–1940, Chinese immigrants were detained and interrogated at Angel Island station in San Francisco Bay. For further information on U.S. immigration history, visit the Angel Island website at www.angelisland.org. Ellis Island was the New York gateway for European immigration from 1900–1920 (www.ellisisland.com). An extension collection of primary resource photographs and immigration history for educators cans be found at *Americans All* (www.americansall.com).

When the Chinese first began immigrating to the West Coast in the 1850s, they were mostly young, unmarried men who left China, a country ravaged by famine and political turmoil, to seek their fortune in the "Golden Mountains" across the Pacific and then take their wealth back to their homeland. The California gold mines were largely depleted by the time they arrived, and, after the completion of the transcontinental railroad signaled a loss of jobs for Chinese laborers, many found that the hope of taking fortunes home to their families in China was an impossible dream.

By 1880, approximately 106,000 Chinese had immigrated to the United States, fueling a vicious reaction: "The Chinese must go." With the passage of the Immigration Act of 1882, along with a series of similar bills, further Chinese immigration was blocked. The Chinese already in this country responded to increasing physical violence by moving eastward and consolidating into ghettos called *Chinatowns*. Inhabited largely by male immigrants, these ghettos offered a grim and sometimes violent lifestyle, one with widespread prostitution and gambling. Chinatowns, vestiges of century-old ghettos, can still be found in many of America's cities.

In 1949, the institution of a Communist government in mainland China caused Congress to reverse more than a century of immigration quotas, naturalization, and antimiscengenation laws and grant refugee status to five thousand highly educated Chinese in the United States. Despite facing active prejudice and discrimination, Chinese Americans today have achieved a higher median income and educational level than that of white Americans.

Filipino Americans

After the 1898 Spanish-American War, the United States acquired the Philippines. Filipinos, viewed as low-cost labor, were recruited to work in the fields of Hawaii and the U.S. mainland. Thousands left the poverty of their islands to seek economic security.

With a scarcity of women (in 1930, the male–female ratio was 143 to 1) and the mobility of their work on farms and as fieldhands, the Filipinos had difficulty establishing cohesive communities. Like other Asian immigrants, they came with the goal of taking their earnings back to their homeland; like other Asian immigrants, most found this an impossible dream.

By the 1920s Filipinos were immigrating in greater numbers, and fear of the "yellow peril" became pervasive. Riots erupted, especially in California, where most of the Filipinos had settled. Because of their unique legal status (the United States had annexed the Philippines in 1898), Filipinos were not excluded as aliens under the Immigration Act of 1924. However, the Tydings-McDuffie Act of 1934 was a victory for those who wanted the Filipinos excluded from the United States. Promising independence to the Philippines, this act limited immigration to the United States to fifty per year.

All that changed in 1965, when a new immigration act allowed a significant increase in Filipino immigration. Between 1970 and 1980, the Filipino population in the United States more than doubled. The earlier presence of the U.S. military in Manila generated an educated elite who spoke English, studied the American school curriculum, and moved to the United States with professional skills, seeking jobs commensurate with their training.[30] Concentrated in urban areas of the West Coast, Filipinos are the second-largest Asian American ethnic group in the United States.

Asian Indian Americans

Traders from India arrived in New England in the 1880s, bartering silks and spices. Intellectuals Henry David Thoreau, Ralph Waldo Emerson, and E. M. Forester (*Passage to India*) gravitated to the culture, religion, and philosophy of the Eastern purveyors. On the West Coast, Indians from Punjab migrated to escape British exploitation, which had forced farmers to raise commercial rather than food crops. With farming conditions in California similar to those in India, Punjabees became successful growers and landowners. They were destined to lose their lands, however, and even their leasing rights, under the California Alien Land Law, which recalled the ownership of land held by Indians and Japanese.

In addition to legal restrictions, Indian laborers were attacked by racist mobs in Bellingham, Washington, in 1907, triggering other riots and expulsions throughout the Pacific region. U.S. government support for British colonial rule in India became the rationale to further restrict Indian immigration. It was not until 1946 that a law allowing Indian naturalization and immigration was passed.

During the 1980s and 1990s, tens of thousands of Indians arrived in America. Most Indians are extremely well educated, and many are professionals. More than 85 percent have graduated from high school, over 65 percent have college degrees, and 43 percent have graduate or professional degrees. Their educational and income levels are the highest of any group in the United States, including other Asians.[31]

Japanese Americans

Only when the Japanese government legalized emigration in 1886 did the Japanese come to the United States in significant numbers. For example, in 1870, records show only fifty Japanese in the United States, but, by 1920, the number had increased to more than 110,000.

With the immigration of the Chinese halted by various exclusion acts, Japanese immigrants filled the need for cheap labor. Like the Chinese, the early Japanese immigrants were males who hoped to return to their homeland with fortunes they earned in the United States. For most, this remained an unfulfilled dream.

Few women were among the early Japanese immigrants. However, the practice of "picture brides," the arrangement of marriages by the exchange of photographs, established Japanese families in the United States. Many researchers suggest that the strong Japanese family structure, maintained in the early system of picture brides, is key to the achievement of Japanese Americans today.

Praised for their willingness to work when they first arrived in California, the Japanese began to make other farmers nervous with their great success in agriculture and truck farming. Anti-Japanese feelings became prevalent along the West Coast. Such slogans as "Japs must go" and warnings of a new "yellow peril" were frequent. In 1924, Congress passed an immigration bill that halted Japanese immigration to the United States.

CRITICAL THINKING QUESTION

How could traditional values conflict with assimilation? Picture multiple generations of Japanese (and other Asian Americans and Pacific Islanders) discussing this question. What key points might be proposed and by whom?

After Japan's attack on Pearl Harbor on December 7, 1941, fear and prejudice about the "threat" from Japanese Americans were rampant. On February 19, 1942, President Franklin Roosevelt issued Executive Order No. 9006, which declared the West Coast a "military area" and established federal "relocation" camps. Approximately 110,000 Japanese, more than two-thirds of whom were U.S. citizens, were removed from their homes in the "military area" and were forced into ten **internment camps** in California, Idaho, Utah, Arizona, Wyoming, Colorado, and Arkansas. Located in geographically barren areas, guarded by soldiers and barbed wire, these internment camps made it very difficult for the Japanese people to keep their traditions and cultural heritage alive. Almost half a century later, the U.S. government officially acknowledged this wrong and offered a symbolic payment ($20,000 in reparations) to its victims.

Despite severe discrimination in the past, today's Japanese Americans enjoy both a high median family income and educational attainment. Their success is at least partially due to traditional values, a heritage some fear may be weakened by increasing assimilation.

Southeast Asian Americans

Before 1975, the United States saw only small numbers of immigrants from Southeast Asia, including Vietnam, Laos, and Kampuchea/Cambodia. Their arrival in greater numbers was related directly to the end of the Vietnam War and resulting Communist rule.

The refugees came from all strata of society. Some were wealthy; others were poverty stricken. Some were widely traveled and sophisticated; others were farmers and fishing people who had never before left their small villages. Most came as part of a family, and almost half were under age 18 at the time of their arrival. Refugee camps were established to dispense food, clothing, medical assistance, and temporary housing, as well as to provide an introduction to U.S. culture and to the English language.

By December 1975, the last refugee camp had closed and the U.S. government had resettled large numbers of Southeast Asians across the nation without too high a

INTERACTIVE ACTIVITY

Multicultural Literacy. Match multicultural terms with their descriptions.

Asian Americans and Pacific Islanders are the most culturally diverse group to enter the United States since the 1970s.

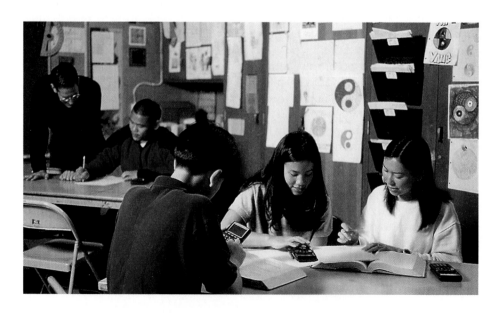

concentration in any one location. This dispersal was well intentioned but often left the refugees feeling lonely and isolated. In fact, many moved from original areas of settlement to cities where large numbers of Asian Americans were already located.

A second wave of Southeast Asian refugees followed in the years after 1975. Cambodians and Laotians migrated to escape poverty, starvation, and political repression in their homelands. Many tried to escape in small fishing boats not meant for travel across rough ocean seas. Called *boat people* by the press, almost half of them, according to the estimates, died before they reached the shores of the United States.

Similar to war refugees from Latin America, these children brought memories of terrible tragedy to school. For example, a teacher in San Francisco was playing hangman during a language arts lesson. As the class was laughing and shouting out letters, she was shocked to see one child, a newcomer, in tears. The girl spoke so little English she could not explain the problem. Finally, another child translated. The game had triggered a traumatic memory. In Cambodia, the girl had watched the hanging of her father.[32] Since the fall of Saigon in 1975, more than 1.4 million Southeast Asians have resettled in the United States. Their struggle to find a place in this society remains conflicted as most Americans associate Vietnam with war.

Arab Americans: Moving Beyond the Stereotype

Misunderstanding and intolerance have been all-too-common facts of life for three million Americans of Arab descent. Arab Americans' quality of life is often influenced by events taking place in other parts of the world. The Gulf War against Iraq, assaults on the terrorist camps in Taliban-ruled Afghanistan, the September 11, 2001 attacks on the World Trade Center and the Pentagon, and the continuing conflict between Israelis and Palestinians create tension and anxiety for Americans of Arab descent. While these news events are troubling enough, media portrayals can exacerbate the problem. Books and movies depict a strange melange of offensive Arab caricatures: greedy billionaires, corrupt sheiks, immoral terrorists, suave oil cartel magnates, and even romantic, if ignorant, camel-riding Bedouins. Nor are children's books immune from such characterizations. Caroline Cooney's *The Terrorist* (1999), a popular book for children in grades 5 through 10, is the fictional tale of an American teenager who tries to find the Arab terrorist responsible for her younger brother's death. It is not surprising that polls taken as far back as the 1980s reveal that most Americans perceive Arabs as anti-American, warlike, anti-Christian, and cunning.[33] The challenge to educators could not be clearer. Students and teachers need to learn about Arab Americans, as well as the Arab world.

The first wave of Arab immigrants, mostly from Syria and Lebanon, came to America at the end of the nineteenth century, for the same reasons that have driven so many immigrants: political freedom and economic opportunity. Toledo, Ohio, and Detroit, Michigan, became important centers of Arab immigration, and business became the economic mainstay of this first wave. Other waves of immigration followed, one just after World War II, and the third as a result of the Palestinian-Israeli conflict. Arabs arrived from over a score of countries, typically settling in major urban centers.

Many Americans confuse Arabs and Moslems, mistaking Islam, a religion, with Arabs, a cultural group. While Islam is the predominant religion of the Middle East, and most Arabs living there are Moslems, there are also millions of Christian Arabs (as well as those who are Jewish or Druse). In the United States, the vast majority of the three million Arab Americans are Christian. And, in contrast, the majority of America's eight million Moslems are not Arab. While Arabs practice different religions,

TEACHING TIP

Friendship Through Education is a consortium of groups linking U.S. students and students in countries with Moslem populations. Initially, three schools in U.S. communities most directly affected by the September 11, 2001 terrorist attacks will be linked with schools in Islamic nations. www.FriendshipThrough Education.org.

TEACHING TIP

African Americans represent about 25 percent of the U.S. Moslem population. Students at the Clara Muhammad School in Southeast Washington, D.C. begin their day reciting the *Koran*'s opening verse, the *Fatihah*, and then face the U.S. flag and pledge allegiance to "One nation under Allah . . . "

CLASSROOM ORGANIZATION

- *Segregation.* Avoid segregated seating patterns or activities. Sometimes teachers segregate: "Let's have a spelling bee—boys against the girls!" Other times, students segregate themselves. Gender, race, or ethnic groups that are isolated alter the dynamics of the classroom and create barriers to effective communication among students, as well as obstacles to equitable teaching. If necessary, you will need to move students around to create a more integrated class. Knowledgeable teachers know there are times when children need to be in same language, gender, or similar clusters. If there are only two or three students of a certain group in a class, separating them can actually increase the sense of isolation. Diversity and good judgment are both important as teachers group and organize students.

- *Mobility.* Students sitting in the front row and middle seats receive the majority of the teacher's attention. This is because the closer you get to students, the more likely you are to call on them. If you move around the room, you will get different students involved. By the way, students are mobile too. You may want to change their seats on a regular basis to disperse classroom participation more equally.

- *Cooperative education.* Collaboration, rather than individual competition, is a social norm for many groups, including African Americans, Native Americans, and females. When cooperation is less valued, research suggests, inequities emerge, especially when students choose their own partnerships. For instance, in cooperative learning groups, girls tend to assist both other girls and boys, while boys are more likely to help only other boys. Boys get help from everyone in the group, but girls must make do with less support. In addition, some students (usually boys) may dominate the group, while others (usually girls) are quiet. It is a good idea to monitor your groups, in order to intervene and stop these inequitable patterns.

- *Displays.* Check your bulletin boards, your displays, and your textbooks. Are women and other underrepresented groups evident? Should you find resources to supplement materials and create a more equitable classroom climate? Do you remember the phrase "If the walls could speak"? In a sense they do. What messages are the classroom walls and curriculum sending to your students?

CULTURAL CUES

- *Eye contact.* Teachers sometimes assume that children's nonverbal messages are identical to their own. But many factors can change the meaning of "eye" messages. A teacher's respectfully stated request to "Look at me when I am talking to you" anticipates a student will feel comfortable with the request. In fact, many Asian American, Pacific Islander, and Native American children lower their eyes as a sign of respect. For other children, lowered eyes is a sign of submission or shame, rather than respect. Consider the background of your students. Even silent eyes speak many languages.

- *Touching and personal space.* Our personal cultural history contributes to how "touchy" we are and how we reach out and touch others. Many Southeast Asians feel it is spiritually improper to be touched on the head. A similar touch, on an African American child's head, may be perceived as demeaning, rather than kind. Getting close or even "right up in someone's face" can be threatening, or caring. Some teachers, worried that any touch may be misconstrued as sexual harassment, avoid touching students at all, yet we know that touch which supports learning can be a powerful and positive force.

  Teachers need to be conscious and culturally sensitive when being near or touching students. Let students know you will respect their nonverbal comfort zones. In fact, many teachers "read the need" of a child, observing students' use of touch and space.

- *Teacher-family relationships.* Students, depending on their heritage, view teachers with varied degrees of attachment. Hispanics may include the teacher as an extension of family, with high expectations for contact and closeness. Asian Americans may seem more formal, or even distant, evidencing respect for adults and the teacher's role. Parents from certain cultural groups may see the teacher's job as independent of parental influence, so conferences or phone calls may appear unwanted or awkward. Wealthy parents may treat teachers as subordinates, part of a hardworking staff that serves their child's interests. The teacher's goal is to expand relationship skills and relate effectively with diverse student families and cultures.

INTERACTION STRATEGIES

- *Calling on and questioning students.* Do not rely on the "quickest hand in the West," which is usually attached to a male. Relying on the first hand raised will skew the pattern of classroom participation. Be aware that some students will feel intimidated anytime they are called on. Whether it is a lack of English language skill, a personal power strategy to shun the teacher's control or even a sign of respect, some students work to escape teacher contact. Asking a teacher for help can suggest a lack of understanding and may be avoided by Asian American and Native American children.

Develop other strategies for student participation besides hand raising—for example, writing each student's name on a card and using the cards to select students. Or set an expectation for full participation, and then call on students who don't raise their hands. Instead of a few students "carrying" the class, all students will be pulled into the learning process.

- *Wait time 1.* Wait time can be a big help in promoting equitable participation. Giving yourself 3 to 5 seconds before you call on a student allows more time to deliberately and thoughtfully choose which student to call on. The extra wait time also allows you more time to develop an answer. Research indicates that many females, students of color, and limited English speakers particularly benefit from this strategy.
- *Wait time 2.* Give yourself more wait time *after* a student speaks, as well. Research shows that boys get more precise feedback than girls do. Waiting will

give you the opportunity to think about the strengths and weaknesses of a student's answer, to be more specific in your reaction, and to provide all students with more specific feedback as well.

- *Assigning tasks.* Too often teachers stereotype classroom activities. Boys (especially bigger boys) are asked to tackle physical jobs or mechanical skills while girls are assigned to grade papers.
- *Discipline.* Boys are reprimanded more often (one study shows that they receive eight to ten times as many control messages as girls do) and are punished more harshly. Not only do teachers punish boys more, but they also talk to them more, listen to them more, and give them more active teaching attention.

REFLECTION: Why are these equitable instructional skills so often missed by teachers? What steps can you take to ensure that you will use them? (Here's a hint . . . these tips are not meant to be a teacher's secret. Explaining to your students why you are committed to equitable teaching skills can spark their interest and help.)

they do share the same language and culture, a culture that is at times in conflict with western values.[34]

Such differences can create friction, in and beyond school. For example, Arabs enjoy close social proximity, and members of the same sex often walk arm-in-arm or hold hands, behaviors at odds with American practice. Features of the Arabic language, including loudness and intonation, may be perceived in America as too loud, and even rude. While punctuality is considered a courtesy in the United States, being late is not considered a sign of disrespect in Arab culture. In addition to these cultural disconnects, more profound differences emerge, such as the disparity between the role of women in Arab society and the role of women in Western society. Many Arab nations cast women in an inferior position, denying them education, inheritance, and power. Saudi Arabia, for example, still forbids women to drive, prohibits coeducation, and requires that women wear veils in public. Arranged marriages and polygamy are practiced in several Arab nations. While the birth of a son is celebrated in conventional Arab families, the birth of a daughter may be met with silence.[35] Yet, change is also sweeping part of the Arab world. Several Arab states have opened schools and the workplace to women, with dramatic results.

Today, students of Arab heritage can be found in all fifty states, and as a group, do well in American schools. The proportion of Arab Americans who attend college is higher than the national average and Arab Americans earn postgraduate degrees at a rate nearly double the national average. Yet they still face challenges. They learn from textbooks that have little if anything to say about their history or experiences. American teachers lack basic information about Arab culture, which may present problems. For example, a traditional Arab student may be troubled or confused in an American school where women can be both teachers and principals. In a similar way,

OVERHEAD 139
Classroom Tips for Nonsexist, Nonracist Teaching

CLASS ACTIVITY: POINT-COUNTERPOINT: DEBATE
IM, Activity 12:3

Growing up in South Carolina (vintage 1940s), Marian Wright Edelman learned to counter the summer heat with a swim. African American children were not allowed in the public pool, so Marian and her friends did their summer swimming, diving, and fishing in the creek, despite the fact that it was polluted with hospital sewage. One of her friends decided that the bridge spanning the creek would be a good diving platform, but that decision turned out to be fatal: He broke his neck on impact. His death was one of several tragedies that taught Edelman early lessons on the deadly impact of race segregation. In recalling these tragedies, Edelman says: "You never, ever forget."[1]

Marian Wright Edelman's family provided a refuge from this racial hatred. Her father was a Baptist minister, her mother a devout Sunday schoolteacher, and both instilled a sense of service. Sharing a bed, a meal, or a pair of shoes with foster children or neighbors in need was a common event for Edelman and her four siblings. While public playgrounds were closed to black children, her parents made Shiloh Baptist Church a community resource center for black sports teams, Boys Scouts and Girl Scouts. Edelman learned that "[s]ervice is the

rent we pay for living. It is the very purpose of life and not something you do in your spare time."[2]

During the 1960s, Edelman worked as a volunteer at the National Association for the Advancement of Colored People (NAACP), campaigning for passage of the Voting Rights Act as well as finding legal assistance for students jailed during sit-ins and demonstrations. As she sorted through requests for NAACP assistance from poor black citizens, Edelman realized that law could be a vehicle to social justice. She attended Yale University Law School and became the first black woman to pass the bar exam in Mississippi. Although she practiced civil rights law, Edelman's work with poor children helped her to see that they were the most vulnerable and voiceless group in our society. Children "had no one to speak out on their behalf—no one to make sure that there were laws and government policies in place to protect them."[3] During the next four decades, Marian Wright Edelman became their voice.

Edelman founded the Children's Defense Fund (CDF) in 1973, with the mission to "Leave No Child Behind." The CDF works to ensure that every child has a Healthy Start, a Head Start, a Fair Start, a Safe Start, and a Moral Start in life. The CDF strives to protect all children—and particularly children of low-income and minority families—through research, community organization, federal and state government lobbying, and public education. Among those who worked for the CDF was a young Wellesley graduate named Hillary Rodham, who continued to advocate for children's rights later when she became the First Lady and then U.S. Senator from New York.

CDF also sponsors Freedom Schools that recruit college students to serve as mentors to over 12,000

students both after school and during the summer. Edelman understands the lasting influence mentors give students, and she has a message for all teachers:

> Teaching is a mission, not just a task or a job. I don't care how fancy the school, how low the student-teacher ratio (which I believe should be lower), how high the pay (which I think should be higher): If children don't feel respected by adults who respect themselves, and don't feel valued, then they lose and all of us lose. Make it a reality that all children, especially poor children, are taught how to read, write, and compute so they can have happy and healthy options in their future. We need to understand and be confident that each of us can make a difference by caring and acting in small as well as big ways."[4]

[1]Marian Wright Edelman, *The Measure of Our Success: A Letter to My Children and Yours* (Boston: Beacon Press, 1992), p. 8; [2]Ibid, p. 6; [3]Marian Wright Edelman, *Lanterns: A Memoir of Mentors* (Boston: Beacon Press, 1999), p. 28; [4]Ibid, p. 22.

REFLECTION: Surf the Children's Defense Fund website at www.childrensdefensefund.org and click on State Data. Compare the social problems and needs of children in your state with national averages. Which statistics surprised you? What responsibilities do you believe teachers have to ensure equal educational opportunity for children in poverty?

www.mhhe.com/ sadker To learn more about Marian Wright Edelman, click on *Profiles in Education*.

patience was wearing thin. He wanted to end these long, boring days, get a job, and get a car. He'd had enough of school.

OVERHEAD 143
Dropout Rates in the U.S.

Lamar is a good candidate to join the nation's dropouts. In fact, poor students are four times more likely to drop out than wealthy ones, and students whose parents do not value schooling are also on the "most-likely-to-drop-out" list. Typically, dropping out is a long-term process with academic warning signs. In a Baltimore study, more than half of the students who eventually dropped out did poorly even in the first grade. Seventy-one percent of students who repeated a grade once, and 80 percent of students who repeated a grade twice, eventually dropped out. On the other hand, students who reported being "engaged" in school did not drop out.[54]

In 1950, just over half of 25- to 29-year-olds completed high school. Today, the high school completion rate is approximately 90 percent. Ninety-three percent of white students, 89 percent of African American students, and 73 percent of Hispanic students now complete high school.[55] Teachers can encourage youngsters to stay in school through one-on-one instruction, mentoring and tutoring, more relevant curricular materials, early intervention and counseling, and advocacy programs.[56]

Sexuality and Teenage Pregnancy

OVERHEAD 144
At-Risk Responses

Who can blame today's adolescents for being confused about sexuality? On the one hand, they see a "green light," as they are bombarded with suggestive advertising, graphic movies, bawdy television shows and sexualized cable channels. Contraceptives, including the morning-after pill, offer pregnancy safeguards that did not exist just a few years ago. Then students see a bright "red light" of morality standards preaching abstinence and the looming threat of sexually transmitted diseases (STDs). So how do schools respond to this conflict? The short answer is not well. About a third of the school systems preach an "abstinence only until marriage" policy, which discourages sex outside of heterosexual marriage. Little if any other information is given. Other schools embrace comprehensive sex education, which stresses abstinence but also includes contraceptive information. What students are taught differs state to state, district to district, and school to school.

One thing is certain: the current fractured approach is not working. Rates of pregnancy and STDs in this nation are the highest in the industrialized world, and many attribute the problem to the lack of a coherent sex education curriculum. A study of nine abstinence-focused programs found that the information being taught was inaccurate, outdated, and biased against reproductive choice options. Some students have objected to the abstinence-only program, and demanded more complete information. A few states, including California, Oregon, Missouri, and Alabama, have passed laws requiring schools to teach up-to-date, judgment-free information about contraception, but these laws are difficult to enforce, and the majority of states simply look the other way, leaving sex education to local school systems. It is an approach that has not worked.[57]

AIDS: HIV Comes to School

For many communities, decades of opposition to sex education were unceremoniously cast aside with the emergence of the medical nightmare AIDS. Sexually active children represent a major

When families are headed by young mothers, they are six times as likely to be in poverty.

- Almost 1 million teenage women (11 percent) of those aged 15–19 become pregnant each year.
- One in five sexually active teen women becomes pregnant.
- Fifty percent of adolescents who have a baby become pregnant again within two years.
- Teenage mothers and their babies are more likely to suffer medical complications and have higher mortality rates than mothers over 20.
- Teen mothers are much more likely to come from low-income families.
- The children of adolescent mothers are at increased risk for being a teen parent themselves.
- About one in five infants born to unmarried minors are fathered by men five or more years older than the mother.

SOURCE: Alan Guttmacher Institute, *Issues in Brief* (2001); reports from the National Center for Health Statistics; National Vital Statistics Report, 2003.

REFLECTION: *The National Campaign to Prevent Teen Pregnancy* asked one thousand youth the primary reason for the decline in teen pregnancy over the last decade. Can you predict their top four answers? See how you did.

(Reflection answer: Worry about AIDS/STD (38 percent); More birth control available (24 percent); More attention to the issue (15 percent); More parental involvement (9 percent); Changing morals and values, fewer teens having sex, the improved economy and welfare reform combined for 14 percent.)

GLOBAL VIEW

Teen pregnancy rates remain much higher in the U.S. than in many other developed countries—twice as high as in England and Wales or Canada, and nine times as high as in the Netherlands or Japan.
www.agi-usa.org/pubs/ fb_teen_sex.html

at-risk population for the disease, and sex education has become a prime weapon against the spread of the virus. In the early 1990s, the House Select Committee on Children, Youth, and Families estimated that forty thousand teens each year contract the HIV virus.[58] A decade of very public attention resulted in a decline in AIDS incidence and deaths in 1996. One of the largest diagnosed populations with AIDS is men who have sex with men. But, even in this group, AIDS incidence and death are on the decline. The greatest decline is evident in younger children, following efforts to reduce perinatal transmission for pregnant HIV-infected women and their children.[59]

AIDS-related sex education is now an accepted part of some school programs, a controversial part of others, and something that was avoided in still other communities. To many, but not all Americans, the threat of this nearly always fatal disease was horrific enough to eliminate reservations concerning sex education programs in the schools.

Substance Abuse: Drinking, Drugs, and Smoking

CLASS ACTIVITY: EFFECTIVE SEX EDUCATION COURSES
IM, Activity 12:7

"I know personally kids who drink whole bottles of liquor on the weekends by themselves."

"You won't see the drug culture here unless you know what to look for. You'll get a lot of parent and school denial, but the reputation of this school is 'cocaine heaven.'"

"On an average week, I gross over $2,000 dealing drugs at this school."

These statements from high school students add a personal dimension to official reports indicating that the United States has the highest rate of teenage drug use of any industrialized nation in the world. **Substance abuse** ranges from alcohol and chewing tobacco to inhalants, cocaine and LSD. Sixty percent of high school students and 30 percent of middle schoolers say drugs are used, kept and sold in their schools.[60]

Alcohol abuse represents by far the most widespread form of substance abuse. In 2000, one-third of all high school seniors reported being drunk in the preceding

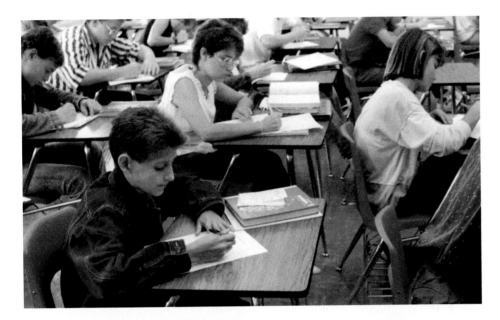

The widespread publicity surrounding Ryan White, a young AIDS victim who led a courageous fight to open school doors to young AIDS patients, did much to relieve the ignorance that surrounds this deadly disease.

The United States has the highest rate of teenage drug use of any industrialized nation in the world.

month.[61] Justice Department figures show that alcohol or drug use is associated with more unplanned pregnancies, more sexually transmitted diseases, and more HIV infection than is any other single factor.[62] The more teenagers drink, the more likely they are to be involved in violent crime, such as murder, rape, or robbery, either as victim or perpetrator.

Substance abusers suffer significant school problems. Marijuana users are twice as likely as nonusers to average *D*s and *F*s. A Philadelphia study showed that four out of five dropouts were regular drug users. Unfortunately, many parents and educators are unaware of the extent of the problem. In an Emory University study, although 3 percent of parents said that their children had used marijuana in the past month, 28 percent of those children reported that they had actually taken the drug.[63] "It's normal denial and suburban American dream denial. This isn't supposed to happen here."[64]

GLOBAL VIEW
Cigarette smoking and alcohol use is less prevalent for U.S. tenth graders than almost all European nations. The lifetime use of marijuana and other illicit drugs is higher in the U.S. than any European country. www.monitoringthefuture.org/pubs/espad_pr.pdf.

While smoking is down for the population as a whole, its use by teenagers, especially females, is on the rise. Each year, more than a million young people start smoking. Cigarette smoking provides a window on teen substance abuse:

- Teenagers who smoke are more likely to get poor grades, drink alcohol, fight, get drunk, and try marijuana than are nonsmokers.

- Teens who smoke hang out with friends after school, while nonsmokers are more apt to be involved in school sports and activities.

- Almost a third of teens who smoke report doing no homework, compared with 8 percent of their nonsmoking peers.

- Perceptions on smoke-free campuses vary greatly. While most teachers and administrators say their schools are smoke-free, most students do not agree.

- Although teens understand that smoking is bad for their health, nearly one-fourth admit they cannot quit because they are addicted. According to the Center for Disease Control, less than 5 percent of schools nationwide are implementing effective prevention programs.[65]

Youth Suicide

TEACHING TIP
Read parent Tony Salvatore's deeply personal letter to *Any Suicidal Young Person* following the death of his son Paul. www.members.tripod.com/LifeGard/memo.html.

A closely knit New Jersey community across the Hudson River from Manhattan was viewed as a model town. The high school frequently won the state football championship, the police department won awards for its youth-assistance programs, and the town was known for the beauty of its parks and safety of its streets. On an early Wednesday morning in March, the citizens of Bergenfield woke up to discover that four of their teenagers had locked themselves in a garage, turned on a car engine, and left a note requesting that they be buried together. The group suicide brought the total of teen suicides in Bergenfield to eight that year.

In the past twenty-five years, while the general incidence of suicide has decreased, the rate for those between the ages of 15 and 24 has tripled. Suicide is the third most common cause of death among adolescents, and many health specialists suspect it is seriously underreported. Every day fourteen adolescents (mostly males) will take their own lives. Particularly at risk are substance abusers, teens questioning their sexuality, and girls who have been physically or sexually abused.[66]

What should teachers look for? Depression often precedes suicide attempts. Manifestations include persistent sadness, boredom or low energy, loss of interests in favorite pastimes, irritability, physical complaints and illness, serious changes in sleeping and eating, and school avoidance or poor performance.[67] Impulsivity, which accounts for about one-fourth of all adolescent suicides, is particularly difficult for adults to deal with, since it may cause students to commit suicide in response to their first bout with depression. To date, teachers and parents have not done well in preventing youth depression and suicide.

IN THE NEWS

Get Away from the Starting Line

The year 2000 National Education Goal that pledged America's schools would be "safe, disciplined, and alcohol- and drug-free" has now been deemed a complete failure. Among students who have: *ever* tried cigarettes, 85.7 percent, 2.1 million, are still smoking in the twelfth grade; *ever* been drunk, 83.3 percent, 2.1 million, are still getting drunk in twelfth grade; *ever* tried marijuana, 76.4 percent, 1.4 million, are still using it in twelfth grade.

SOURCE: Press Release: *Malignant Neglect: Substance Abuse and America's Schools*, 5 September 2001. www.casacolumbia.org/newsletter1457/newsletter_show.htm?doc_id=80623.

 What's new in education? Click on *News Feeds.*

Gay, Lesbian, Bisexual, and Transgendered: Our Invisible Students

When I was 11, I started smoking dope, drinking alcohol, and snorting speed every day to make me feel better and forget I was gay. I would party with friends but get more and more depressed as the night would go on. They would always make antigay remarks and harass gay men while I would just stand there. Late at night after they went home, I would go down to the river and dive in—hoping I would hit my head on a rock and drown.[68]

Fear and intolerance toward homosexuals, labeled **homophobia**, characterize the culture of secondary schools and cause depression and suicidal feelings. Some schools have a climate that is actively hostile: Students and even faculty make jokes about "faggots," "dykes," "gays," and "queers," and antigay graffiti cover bathroom walls and school desks. At times, verbal abuse turns physical, as in the case of a black male student in Ohio who was dragged into a bathroom stall. There eight boys called him a faggot, bashed his head against a toilet, and threatened to kill him. As punishment, the eight boys were given demerits for the incident.[69]

Because homophobia is so prevalent and so virulent, most lesbian and gay students go into hiding and try to pass as "straight." Afraid to let other students, faculty, or even their families know, too many become painfully isolated.

The National Education Association (NEA) adopted a resolution advocating equal opportunity for students and staff regardless of sexual orientation and encouraging schools to provide counseling by trained personnel. It developed training materials and workshops on "Affording Equal Opportunity to Gay and Lesbian Students Through Teaching and Counseling." School districts have also responded. San Diego, Cincinnati, and St. Paul have issued antiharassment measures and policies designed to protect homosexual students. In New York City, the Harvey Milk High School was established in 2003 as the first publicly funded school for gay, lesbian, and transgendered students. The need to build such a safe haven signals the difficulty of creating safe schools for these students.[70]

Bullying

While metal detectors and extra security measures have sharply reduced school violence, the old-fashioned bully still stalks the hallways. Half of America's children report being bullied at least once a week, ten percent report being continually targeted, and ten thousand children stay home from school at least once a month because they fear a bully. The most likely targets are gay students, or students perceived as being gay.[71]

Bullying has been an accepted school tradition for decades, if not centuries, often because so many teachers accept the myths surrounding bullying: only a small number of children are affected, students are just "tattling, it's a natural behavior," and "boys will be boys." But these myths are dangerous. Bullying has been linked to depression, suicide, eating disorders and assaults, and schools are finally "getting it." The rise of lawsuits, and the creation of antibullying programs have helped to keep the bully in his (or her) place. Effective antibullying practices ask teachers to be involved and interested in students, set firm limits on unacceptable behavior, apply consistent nonpunitive, nonphysical sanctions, and act as authorities and positive role models. Creating a safe classroom climate is the first step in effective teaching.[72]

TEACHING TIP

The Gay, Lesbian and Straight Education Network (GLSEN), has a brief survey to help a school evaluate their current climate with regard to the safety and respect afforded gay, lesbian, bisexual and transgender students on campus. www.glsen.org.

- Confront directly school incidents of antilesbian and antigay prejudice.

  Name it: "That is homophobic harassment (or an appropriate age-level alternative)."

  Claim it: "That is not okay in our room (or school) because it is disrespectful."

  Stop it: "It cannot happen again. If it does (state the consequences)."

- Accurately portray and openly acknowledge the roles and contributions of gay, lesbian, and bisexual people.
- Include gay, lesbian, and bisexual concerns in prevention programs (pregnancy, dropout, suicide).

If a student comes to you to discuss gay, lesbian, bisexual or transgendered concerns,

- Be aware of your own feelings. Avoid making negative judgments that may cause the student even more pain.
- Use the terms the student uses. Say "homosexual" if that is the term used, or "queer," "lesbian," or "bisexual" if the student chooses these terms.

- Respect confidentiality. Let the student know you appreciate his or her trust.
- Be aware that the student may be feeling grief and emotional pain.
- Remember that gay and bisexual male students are particularly in need of information concerning protection from AIDS.

SOURCE: Adapted from *Affording Equal Opportunity to Gay and Lesbian Students Through Teaching and Counseling* (Washington, DC: National Education Association, 2000); "When Kids Don't Have a Straight Answer," *NEA Today Online:* Health (March 2001), www.nea.org/neatoday/0103/health.html.

REFLECTION: It has been said that the most powerful contribution to prejudice is not made by the oppressor, but by those who apathetically stand by. Try to recall a time when you said or did nothing about a bigoted or homophobic remark. What could you say *next time* that would identify you as an educator-advocate for gay, lesbian, bisexual, and transgendered students?

Tension Point: Are Equity and Excellence Compatible?

CLASS ACTIVITIES
SOCIAL ISSUES IN SCHOOLS
IM, Activity 12:8
SMALL GROUP ACTIVITY:
Statement Completion
IM, Activity 12:6

RAP 4.3
A Novel Read, p. 564

When 6000 young people are killed every year with a gun, when 5000 young people commit suicide every year, when over a million young people run away from home every year, when almost half a million young people drop out of school every year, and when hundreds of thousands of young people get into drugs and alcohol and tobacco and just mess up their lives, can we truly say we are a child-centered society . . . ?

Richard Riley, former U.S. Secretary of Education
The Washington Post, July 23, 1998

While not denying the importance of meeting these pressing social needs, critics question whether this is a proper role for schools. If schools are dispensing social services, at what cost? Promoting cultural sensitivity and responding to social problems are investments not devoted to raising school standards and student achievement.

Equity proponents counter that, without equity, without attending to these basic social needs, America can never be a truly great nation. Without equity and social justice, excellence becomes a hollow goal.

Are equity and excellence compatible? Should investments in equity be made, even at the possible cost of diverting resources from academic excellence? The basic question may be, Can education be excellent if it is not excellent for all?

YOU BE THE JUDGE
KEEP STUDENTS TOGETHER OR MIX THEM UP?

Teaching Kids in Segregated Settings . . .

BY GENDER, CAN FOCUS ON ACADEMIC NEEDS

Same gender classes help students focus on academics, not on each other. Girls can get extra encouragement in math and science; boys can get special assistance in reading and language arts.

BY COMMUNITY, PROMOTES RACIAL AND ETHNIC PRIDE

Let's eliminate the alienation caused by busing students out of their neighborhood. Students feel accepted and take pride in local schools, where they can study with friends, and learn from a curriculum that reflects and honors their heritage.

BY CIRCUMSTANCE, OFFERS PREGNANT MINORS A SAFE PLACE TO LEARN

Special facilities and separate programs can bring young women closer for needed encouragement, shielded from the judgment of their nonpregnant peers. And well-designed child care classes can prepare these women for parenthood.

BY NEED, OFFERS AN EDUCATIONAL HOME FOR THE HOMELESS

Special schools can help homeless students cope with their unique personal and academic circumstances. Being with homeless students protects them from comparisons and ridicule that might exist elsewhere.

Teaching Kids Together . . .

PROMOTES GENDER EQUALITY

Learning and succeeding together in the classroom prepares boys and girls to live and work together as adults. Equitable instruction and curriculum will teach students how to eliminate traditional gender barriers in society.

FOSTERS CULTURAL AND RACIAL UNDERSTANDING

We must not allow our nation to be fractured along racial, ethnic, and class lines. Integrating children of different backgrounds mirrors our ideal of a democratic society. Cross-cultural classrooms enrich the learning experience.

GIVES TEEN MOTHERS A REALISTIC SCHOOL EXPERIENCE

Pregnant teens deserve the genuine academic challenges of a regular school program. Modifications might be necessary in a physical education class; otherwise, pregnant teens should learn to participate on equal footing with their peers.

GIVES THE HOMELESS HOPE FOR THE FUTURE

Attending a regular school gives homeless students insight into more secure lifestyles. Clothing drives or free tickets to school events can help needy youngsters feel part of the school community.

OLC YOU BE THE JUDGE

Do you believe equal educational opportunity is best achieved in separate or integrated classrooms? Is your position consistent or does it vary depending upon the identified group? Extend this *You Be the Judge* feature by developing the arguments for either integrating or separating two other groups discussed in this chapter (or identify new groups).

SUMMARY

1. How do deficit, expectation, and cultural difference theories explain disparate academic performance among various racial, ethnic, and cultural groups?

   Most white Americans believe that schools offer equitable educational opportunities to all children, and do not "see" the invisible privileges that they enjoy. Deficit, expectation, and

CHAPTER REVIEW

Go to the Online Learning Center to take a quiz, practice with key terms, and review concepts from the chapter.

CURRENT NEWS FROM POWERWEB

Go to Chapter 12 on the Online Learning Center to read current articles and to access news feeds about:

- Bilingual Education
- Cultural Diversity in Education
- Prejudice in Education
- Prejudice in Schools
- School Integration
- Cultural Diversity in Schools
- Racial Integration in Schools
- Social Contexts of Multicultural Education

cultural difference theories offer different explanations for the academic gaps that characterize different group performance in America's schools.

2. What major developments have marked the educational history of Native Americans, Hispanics, African Americans, Asian Americans/Pacific Islanders, and Arab Americans?

Each ethnic and racial group in America shares a unique history. Despite a national commitment to educate all citizens, bias and discrimination characterize the histories of many of these groups. Native Americans have seen their culture attacked through forced schooling practices. Even educating African Americans during the colonial period was sometimes illegal, and, when schools were provided, they were inadequate and underfunded. The doctrine of "separate but equal" (Plessy v. Ferguson) legalized segregated schools, but, in 1954 (Brown v. Board of Education of Topeka), "separate but equal" was declared unconstitutional. Yet resegregation increases, due in large part to racially segregated neighborhoods. Hispanics (or Latinos) are now the largest minority group in the United States, comprising large proportion of Mexicans, Puerto Ricans, and Cubans. Hispanic immigration from Central America, including Nicaragua and El Salvador, is increasing. Asian is a broad label assigned to several billion people from a score of nations. Asian Americans and Pacific Islanders comprise another rapidly growing population, and like Hispanics, must adjust to a new culture and language. Students from China and India are stereotyped as model minorities, a label that often masks the impact of prejudice on these children. Misunderstanding and intolerance have been all-too-common facts of life for three million Americans of Arab descent. Many Americans confuse Arabs and Moslems, mistaking Islam, a religion, with Arabs, a cultural group.

3. What educational barriers and breakthroughs have girls and women experienced?

For much of this nation's history, females were denied access to or segregated within schools. Researchers continue to find subtle bias in classroom interactions, curriculum materials, and enrollment patterns. Title IX of the 1972 Educational Amendments Act prohibits sex discrimination in schools that receive federal financial assistance, and progress is evident by increased female participation in athletics and improved test scores in math and science. Compliance with Title IX, however, remains erratic.

4. What classroom strategies are appropriate for teaching culturally diverse learners?

Teachers can create more equitable classrooms through a variety of instructional techniques: ensuring that seating and grouping patterns are not segregated by gender, race or language, varying learning activities, increasing wait-time, using space and eye contact in a culturally sensitive manner, and using materials to meet individual student needs and interests.

5. What impact do changing family patterns and economic issues have on children and schools?

Nearly one in six U.S. children lives in poverty, a condition that frequently short-circuits educational promise. The traditional family unit of the past has undergone a radical transformation. Divorce, remarriage, wage earning, parenting, and alternative relationships have restructured the family and the home-school connection. Latchkey children are found throughout society; the more educated the parent, the more likely there is a latchkey child at home. Passage of the 1987 McKinney-Vento Homeless Assistance Act, amended in 1990, was strengthened in 2001 and is intended to lessen the impact of homelessness on Americans. This law protects the rights of children who have no permanent address to attend school and receive all necessary services and opportunities.

6. How can educators respond to social issues that place children at risk?

Today, approximately nine in ten white students complete high school; poor students, urban students, students of color and especially Hispanics are far more likely to drop out.

The mixed sexual messages sent to students in our society have contributed to an alarmingly high rate of teenage pregnancy. Many pregnant teenagers are destined for abbreviated educational careers, and ultimately poverty. Fear of AIDS and STDs has served as a catalyst for establishing sex education programs, but the quality of these programs varies tremendously. "Abstinence-only" programs compete with comprehensive sex education. The courts, contending that AIDS is a disability, do not allow schools to discriminate against students or teachers with HIV. Substance abuse by teens has generally declined since the 1970s, yet both alcohol and smoking remain major problems. For the general population, the suicide rate has decreased, yet youth suicide has tripled in the last quarter century, a warning sign of a persistent and undetected social problem. Gay, lesbian, bisexual, and transgender youth are more likely to commit suicide than are heterosexual youngsters, and face a generally hostile school climate. Today, bullying is being taken as a more serious problem than in the past, and schools and teachers are working to create safer school climates. Guidelines for teachers include taking an active role in recognizing and confronting bullying,

EXTENDED LEARNING

CASE STUDIES

Go to Chapter 12 on your *Resources for Exploring Education* CD-ROM to access Case Studies and Readings.

- Helen Franklin: A teacher who uses parents as volunteers to help with her unique classroom organization notices that a parent volunteer who has questioned the teachers' methods will work only with white students.

- Leigh Scott: A teacher gives a higher-than-earned grade to a mainstreamed student on the basis of the boy's effort and attitude and is confronted by a black student with identical test scores who received a lower grade and who accuses her of racism.

- Mark Siegel: A teacher is irritated by a black parent who visits him regularly, demanding better instruction for her son.

- Marsha Warren: A teacher is overwhelmed by the problems created by her students, including eight children who have unique home problems and personal situations that are affecting their schooling.

READINGS

- Janis Bullock. "Bullying Among Children."
- David Sadker. "An Educator's Primer to the Gender War."
- Karen Zittleman and David Sadker. "Teacher Education Textbooks: The Unfinished Gender Revolution."

KEY TERMS AND PEOPLE

alternative families, 465
Brown v. Board of Education of Topeka, 446
Bureau of Indian Affairs (BIA), 444

busing, 447
Civil Rights Act, 447
cultural difference theory, 442
de facto segregation, 446

de jure segregation, 446
deficit theory, 442
desegregation, 446
Marian Wright Edelman, 468
expectation theory, 442

DISCUSSION QUESTIONS AND ACTIVITIES

1. Observe a classroom, noting how many times teachers call on girls and boys. Compare the amount of attention boys and girls get to their representation in the classroom. Do boys or girls get more than their fair share of teacher attention? The online observation guide can be helpful in this activity.

2. How do you react to the various issues raised in this chapter? On a separate sheet of paper complete the following sentences as honestly as you can. If you wish, share your responses with your classmates.

   • To me, the phrase *invisible race privilege* means . . .

   • A great example of expectation theory is . . .

3. What can schools do to address each of the following issues?

   • Poverty

   • High divorce rates

   • Single-parent families

   • Alternative families

   • Parental income

4. Research some school-based programs used to prevent students from dropping out or using drugs. What alternatives might you suggest?

5. Do you think equity and excellence in the field of education are compatible? Why or why not?

 WEB-*TIVITIES*

1. Today's Students: Patterns of Diversity
2. Native American Education Today
3. Black Americans and Desegregation
4. Hidden America: Homeless Families
5. Children: At Promise or At Risk?

REEL TO REAL TEACHING

BEND IT LIKE BECKHAM (2002)
Run Time: 112 minutes

Synopsis: Jess Bhamra is an 18-year-old growing up in West London, where her family has taken every effort to stay in touch with its Indian heritage. Her father and mother want their daughter to go to law school, learn to cook a traditional Indian dinner, and settle down with a nice Indian boy. Much to her family's chagrin, however, Jess's talents and interests push her to pursue her love for soccer.

Reflection:

1. In the film, gender, culture, sexual orientation, religion, and ethnicity clash. How is Jess's identity impacted by each of these dimensions? How do Pinky, Jules, and Jules's and Jess's parents serve as advocates of roles in society? Which of these characters reflect views that you experienced as you grew and developed? How did you resolve these conflicting views of the world—or did you?

2. Although Jess's family held to tradition in food, dress, and celebrations, identify times when they embraced new ideas. How did the greater British society influence them? How did they affect that British society? Can an individual pursue his or her dreams and passions without giving up cultural values and traditions? What is the cost of giving up these traditional values? What is the cost of closely adhering to tradition? Can/should these differences be bridged?

3. In the United States in 2001, Ashley Martin became the first woman to score in a NCAA Division I football game. She kicked three extra points. Should women play football? Do you have limits for certain groups to participate in athletics, classrooms, and careers? What's "too far"?

Follow-up Activity: What barriers have you struggled through? Are you the only *male* or *female* in the stands, the only *non-major* in the hall, the only *straight* or *gay* person in the room? How does difference feel? What did you learn from such an experience? What can others learn? How might a difference in social class, religion, gender, ethnicity, or sexuality affect your life as a teacher or a student? Do you feel ready for the challenge and opportunity to teach students who are quite different from you? How can you prepare yourself for teaching in diverse classrooms?

How do you rate this film? Go to *Reel to Real Teaching* in the Critics' Corner to review this film.

www.mhhe.com/ sadker7e

FOR FURTHER READING

Brown v. Board of Education: A Civil Rights Milestone and Its Troubled Legacy, by James T. Patterson (2001). Details the racial segregation in schools that prompted this legal landmark, the debates surrounding the Supreme Court's decision, and the unfinished business of truly democratizing our educational system.

Ordinary Resurrections: Children in the Years of Hope, by Jonathan Kozol (2001). Kozol offers a hopeful vision of life in the South Bronx. Poverty and depravation are viewed through the eyes of the children who live there, and an admiring portrait is painted of the teachers, priests, parents, and grandparents who strive against all odds to ensure that these children grow up with a strong sense of hope and pride.

The Public Assault on America's Children: Poverty, Violence, and Juvenile Injustice, by Valerie Polakow (2001). Through personal narratives and national statistics, the violence, educational neglect, poverty and social disregard that shape the lives of poor children are detailed.

There Are No Shortcuts, by Rafe Esquith (2003). What's a Los Angeles middle-school teacher to do with fifth and sixth graders, none of whom speak English at home and most of whom are eligible for free lunches? If you're Esquith, you have them read Twain, perform Shakespeare, play classical guitar and study algebra. You take them camping and to concerts and the theater. And you teach them that "there are no shortcuts" to excellence.

Refusing Racism, by Cynthia Stokes Brown (2003). Why and how have whites joined people of color to fight against white supremacy in the United States? What have they risked and what have they gained? This book offers rich portraits of four contemporary white American activists who have dedicated their lives to the struggle for civil rights.

Technology in Education

FOCUS QUESTIONS

1. Has technology changed schools?
2. How does television affect children?
3. Why is computer technology difficult to implement in schools?
4. How can teachers effectively use computers and the Internet?
5. In what ways does global education refocus the curriculum?
6. How is teaching redefined by virtual schools?
7. Does technology exacerbate racial, class, geographic, and gender divisions?

 WHAT DO YOU THINK? How Tech-Savvy Are You? Take this quiz to see how much you know.

CHAPTER PREVIEW

In an earlier time, before there were factories, there were cottage industries. People manufactured products, not as a group of workers in a central place but individually, in their houses. Some believe that schools may be retracing these steps—in reverse. Today's factorylike schools may soon be replaced by children learning in their homes. "Cottage schools" may be created as technology brings the teacher, the curriculum, and the library onto our home computer screens. Rather than taking the yellow school bus to a large school building, students are now traveling to school on the Internet.

The Internet can transport students around the world (through virtual field trips) or instantly and inexpensively add millions of books and articles to school libraries. Simulations can bring realism into a classroom, personal tutors can patiently diagnose learning needs, and adaptive technology can help special needs students succeed in school. But not everyone is enamoured with the new technology. Will computers and technology make an important difference in education or will tomorrow's schools look remarkably similar to schools you attended as a child? The future, if nothing else, is unpredictable.

Technology raises other serious concerns for teachers, including the need to monitor inappropriate Internet material and to avoid the health risks associated with computer use. While these pitfalls are real, the potential of technology is also real but must be considered within the context of what we know about effective teaching. In this chapter, we explore how technology can be used with multiple intelligences, problem-based and cooperative learning, and direct and deep teaching. Whether or not it revolutionizes education, technology is likely to play a role in your classroom. We will explore how technology is currently modifying classroom life and how it may impact your teaching.

CHAPTER FOCUS
This chapter explores how technology has previously, and is currently, modifying classroom life. We review the impact on schools, our teaching procedures and the way we are digitally divided. Whether or not it revolutionizes education, technology is likely to play a role in the lives of your students and tomorrow's teachers. For a chapter outline, see the IM.

The Technology Revolution

FOCUS QUESTION 1
Has technology changed schools?

GRABBER:LIMERICK
IM

CLASS ACTIVITY: COMPUTER AND THE INTERNET
IM, Activity 13:4

TEACHING TIP
What technologies can students identify as they look around the room? (Or, are you teaching by oil lamp after hiking 3 miles uphill in the snow?) Take them back to photos from The History of American Education (Chapter 8) to distinguish the changes. Working cooperatively, can they list more than 10 advances? Can they list 25?

FOCUS QUESTION 2
How does television affect children?

In the twentieth century, education was forever changed. Human beings serving as teachers, the core of schooling for centuries if not millennia, were made technologically obsolete. The new invention was used at home and then in the more affluent schools. Eventually, all schools were connected. Slowly but surely, the classroom teacher was replaced. These new machines took students where they had never been before, did things no human could do, and shared an unlimited reservoir of information. Clearly, this technological breakthrough had potential to teach more effectively at a far lower cost than human teachers. Predictions varied from the replacement of all teachers to the replacement of most teachers. Some even predicted the replacement of schools themselves.

Sound familiar? While today's computer revolution has sparked these sorts of predictions, the machine described above is not a computer. These predictions were made in the 1950s about television. The popular perception back then was that educational television would reshape the classroom. If predictions about classroom innovations were exaggerated, predictions about television's impact on America were not. Television has reshaped America's cultural landscape.

Many of today's homes have multiple television sets, tied into satellite dishes, antennae, and cables, pulling hundreds of stations into our lives for an average of six hours a day. Some families turn on television sets in the morning and turn them off in the evening, imitating the waking and sleeping of another family member. Television has reduced our time for sleep, social gatherings, leisure activities, and even conversations with each other. By the time the average student has reached 18 years of age, he or she will have attended eleven thousand hours of school—and watched fifteen thousand hours of television. To ignore the impact of this medium is to ignore a major educational influence on children.

Television is not only a force; it is also a target. Television has been blamed for an array of crises and behavior problems, from a lack of school discipline to student passivity, from a decline in standardized test scores to an increase in family tensions and violence. It is unlikely that television, or any single factor, is responsible for all of society's ills. On the other hand, television does present a bizarre and disturbing view of the world. By the time the average child reaches age 15, he or she will have seen thirteen thousand murders on television, and television violence can influence behavior. Longitudinal data collected on television viewing and violence since 1960 present overwhelming evidence that higher levels of viewing violence on television correlate with increased aggressive behavior, in both children and adults.[1]

Television, our national storyteller, presents an image that is not only violent but distorted.[2] If television programs are to be believed, we are a nation destined for extinction. Less than 1 percent of television characters have children under 6. This is surprising, because, according to TV plot lines, caring for children is a snap. In almost half of the television families with young children, child care concerns are never mentioned, yet children are magically cared for anyway. Although two-thirds of the nation's mothers work for pay, only one-third of television's mothers do. America's population is 51 percent female, but not on television, where some calamity has evidently reduced females to less than half the population.

Family life is not the only subject suitable for television "make-overs," as ethnicity and race are jumbled as well. In televisionland, Asian Americans are servants, villains, detectives, and karate experts. Native Americans are presented without tribal distinctions and are often characterized as lazy, alcoholic, and humorless. African American criminals are a mainstay of many police and adventure shows, offset by a growing

RELATED READING
The Children Are Watching: How the Media Teach About Diversity by Carlos Cortés (2000).

number of African American police officers. Characters in children's after-school programs are overwhelmingly white. It is not surprising, therefore, that research indicates that television viewers have a garbled worldview, overestimating the percentage of the world population that is white and wealthy and underestimating the number of Americans living in poverty.

A distorted world scene is only part of the cost paid by the television audience; unregulated viewing robs children of both play and study time while teaching some abhorrent attitudes and behaviors. According to studies in the 1990s by the American Psychological Association and by Stanford University, television increases prejudice, obesity, aggressive behavior, and even drinking. For high school students, each hour of daily television watching corresponds to a 9 percent greater risk of alcohol consumption during the following 18 months. If music videos are watched, the drinking risk rises 31 percent.[3]

Children are more susceptible to, less knowledgeable about, and more naïve about the techniques and products promoted on television than are adults. Bombarded by twenty thousand TV commercials a year, children often have trouble distinguishing advertisements from the programs themselves.[4]

Some believe that the case against television may be both too convenient and overstated. Researchers Daniel Anderson and Patricia Collins found that television's impact depends greatly on who is watching and their general viewing habits, and that many of the bad practices and negative behaviors promoted by television can be prevented by attentive adults. [5] According to the American Psychological Association, when teachers and parents regulate television viewing, children improve their vocabulary, cognitive, and social skills.[6]

Educational television programming, like *Mister Rogers' Neighborhood,* has promoted more positive interpersonal relationships and greater persistence among young children. *Sesame Street* has been shown to improve verbal IQ test scores, school attitudes, and first-grade performance. *Sesame Street* accomplishes this in part by using brief, engaging episodes to capture children's attention while teaching them, a lesson learned from commercials.[7] But even those lessons are changing. The rapid rise of the Nickelodeon show *Blue's Clues* is built upon the concept that preschoolers can watch certain kinds of scenes and stories for a long time, an insight that is reshaping children's programming.[8]

Television is now a part of school life as well. Cable television stations, including A&E, C-Span, CNN, The History Channel, Bravo, The Learning Channel, and The Discovery Channel, join noncable Public Broadcasting to bring high-quality movies and plays, exciting biographies, historical re-enactments, and breaking news stories directly into the curriculum. Monthly television guides written specifically for teachers alert them to upcoming programs of special educational interest. The growing number of videotapes and videodiscs offers teachers a library of rich television resources. Advocates point out that television can be a valuable learning resource, a real asset to classroom instruction. Critics charge that watching television is an unproductive use of class time, an activity that at best should be used as an instructional supplement, to be viewed at home or in the school's media resource room.

Channel One takes the controversy over television in schools to another level. Thousands of participating schools receive several tangible benefits: programming, television monitors, and a satellite dish are provided at no charge. When all are in place, students get to watch ten minutes of news each day. And the cost? The children must also watch two minutes of commercials with each newscast. Studies suggest that students who watch *Channel One* do slightly better on a current events test

TEACHING TIP
"Children watch too much television—three or four hours a day. Poor and minority children watch even more, up to five hours a day," said Dr. Alvin Poussaint, clinical professor of psychiatry at Harvard Medical School (2000). www.hsph.harvard.edu/ats/Mar31/ mar31_02.html.

CLASS ACTIVITY: TELEVISION: WHAT SHOULD IT TEACH? IM, Activity 13:1

CLASS ACTIVITY:
TELEVISION ANALYSIS
IM, Activity 13:2

than do their nonviewing counterparts. Many students and teachers in *Channel One* schools report that they are satisfied with the program.[9]

Many researchers and educators are less pleased with *Channel One*, arguing that schools are not the place to be selling things to children. They estimate that *Channel One* costs the public almost two billion dollars a year, while the *Channel One* commercials alone cost students over 300 million dollars of lost instructional time, while offering content of questionable educational value.[10]

Even before *Sesame Street* and *Channel One*, controversy swirled around new technologies. Consider the following soothsayers:

> "The motion picture is destined to revolutionize our educational system, and . . . in a few years it will supplant largely, if not entirely, the use of textbooks."
>
> *Thomas Edison*

> "The time may come when a portable radio receiver will be as common in the classroom as is a blackboard."
>
> *William Levenson, director of Cleveland Public School's radio station*

> "With the help of teaching machines and programmed instruction, students can learn twice as much in the same time and with the same effort as in a standard classroom."
>
> *B. F. Skinner[11]*

Americans have a habit of overpredicting the impact of technology. But sometimes they underpredict. Consider the case of the frightening eighteenth century technological breakthrough that baffled educators: the chalkboard. Teachers were stunned: How could the chalkboard possibly be better than slate boards? How could teachers use this newfangled gizmo? Would chalkboards help or hinder learning? Not surprisingly, chalkboards were ignored and left to gather dust. And then instructional manuals were published, training programs launched, and as they say, "the rest is history." Now, 150 years later, chalkboards are history again, being replaced by whiteboards. Some whiteboards are simply shiny surfaces to be used with markers, but others are sophisticated and expensive touch-sensitive computer screens that can be written on, surf the Internet, and print a copy of class notes for each student.[12] Similar histories surround all kinds of "technology," from overhead projectors to the modest highlighter that you use to underline the scintillating sentences and important information in this text. Highlighters and the Internet are all part of the same technology stream.

Given the number of technological advances, it is reasonable to ask why today's schools look so remarkably similar to the schools of a century ago. Why has technology had such a modest impact on education? Will computers be the technological breakthrough, the magic bullet that finally revolutionizes education? The next sections, while skillfully sidestepping this question, attempt to capture some of the excitement, controversy, and captivating applications surrounding computers in the classroom.

Schools.com

FOCUS QUESTION 3
Why is computer technology difficult to implement in schools?

Bringing schools into the computer age has been expensive. Recognizing the sizable costs required to bring computer technology to students, Congress passed the Telecommunications Reform Act (1996), establishing a discounted school cost, or **E-Rate** (education rate), for using the Internet and access increased dramatically (see

Technological breakthroughs in satellite communications and increasing international trade suggest that global education will become a reality in the years ahead.

Figure 13.1). A 2003 law created a new Internet domain: kids.us. The **dot.kids** domain is adult supervised and G-rated, intended to protect children from inappropriate Internet material.[13] Many adults believe that such a kid-specific domain will provide the equivalent of a safe e-playground for children. But some critics believe that segregating youngsters from most of the Internet sends the wrong message: the Internet is not "safe." They would prefer to create blocks that stop pornography and inappropriate material while ensuring that the rest of the Internet is open to all.

While keeping schools flush with the latest technologies has been a monumental challenge, plugging in teachers has been no less daunting. While educational technology advocates encourage teachers to move from the "sage on the stage" to the "guide on the side," teachers initially were slow to apply for cyber-citizenship.[14] Teachers can teach effectively, even inspirationally, without computers. Long-time teachers unfamiliar with incorporating computer technology into their lessons can be wary of the investment of time and effort needed to become computer literate—and dismayed to realize that many students come to school far more tech savvy than their teachers. But as the technological revolution gains momentum, teachers will be expected to keep pace.

Each state and many school districts have technology plans that include standards for students and training and exams required of teachers. You should check with your individual state to see if you are up to speed, technologically speaking. As one example, to renew a teaching license in Virginia, you must be able to develop Web pages and create four lessons that integrate technology.[15]

The different attitudes and skills that teachers bring to using computers can make schoolwide implementation of new technology a challenge. Let's see how these concerns emerge in a fictitious faculty meeting, as principal Whyerd greets his staff:

PRINCIPAL WHYERD: Welcome back, although maybe welcome forward would be a better greeting. It's our first time to be together as the faculty of Bill Gates Middle School. With the new name and our new building, we have really opened up the latest window [he waits for a little laughter] on technology in education. We have a spectacular computer lab; in every classroom, we have three online

OVERHEAD 145
Internet Access in Schools and Classrooms

MULTIPLE INTELLIGENCE CONNECTION
Have students complete the following simile: *For me, being a tech savvy teacher in the classroom is like . . .*

VIDEO SEGMENT 31
A Guided Tour of Technology in Today's Classrooms

FIGURE 13.1

Internet access in schools and classrooms. U.S. public schools are approaching universal access, with classrooms and schools in high poverty areas closing the "digital divide" in recent years.

Note: High poverty schools are schools where 75 percent or more of the students are eligible for federal or reduced-price lunch program.

SOURCE: U.S. Department of Education, National Center for Education Statistics, "Internet Access in U.S. Public Schools and Classrooms: 1994–2001."

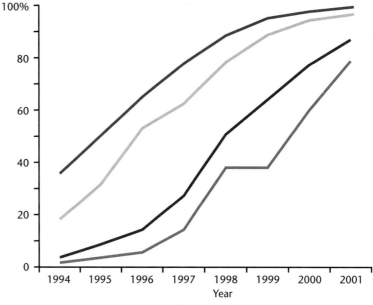

— School Internet access—all public schools

— School Internet access—high-poverty schools

— Classroom Internet access—all public schools

— Classroom Internet access—high-poverty schools

REFLECTION: Why have Americans been willing to fund Internet access in schools? In what ways might the "digital divide" between rich and poor reappear in the future?

computers, video monitors, and we've hired a full-time technology resource instructor. Have you all met Pat Blizzard? [Pat stands confidently]. Okay? We also got the grant for the video production lab with computer hookups for editing and enhancement, so the project-based learning activities at the core of the social science program should really take off. Let's see . . . our Tech Task Force, eleven of you, from six departments, took advantage of the T3 (that's Teacher Tech Training) at the university. Anyone want to give us some quick feedback about those five days? Rafaela?

[As many eyes move to Rafaela Nueva, a few minds wander elsewhere.]

MR. POKEE: [with a slight eye roll] *Here we go again. If it's not one fad, it's another. I've been at this for years, and I can't fit one more thing on my plate. I don't have a computer at home, and I don't see why having one here is supposed to matter to me. Sure, if the kids want to use it, in their free time, to type—excuse me!—word process their papers, that's fine. But I am not about to waste another series of Saturdays on workshops that have nothing to do with my teaching style, my courses, and my students. My kids aren't sure which is bigger, our sun or our moon, but I suppose playing computer games will be more fun than learning.*

MS. HOPALONG: *Okay, okay, I've got it. We have all this new equipment and the kids probably know how to use it better than I do. At home my own kids taught me to do overheads for lessons and, now, if I don't get a handle on this Internet stuff, my students will be using the Web for who knows what. My daughters just laughed when I asked, "Where exactly is the Web?" (But I recognize that laugh. I'm not really sure they know.) When they hooked me into that chat room of teachers last night, it was weird but kind of fun. People were talking about tricks to learn students' names at the beginning of school. I got two good ideas that I'll try next week. Glad I learned how to type as a teenager. At least I could keep up with the conversation. Is that what they call it . . . conversation?*

MS. READDI: *This is so amazing. I'm student teaching and I'm totally nervous about the job. But these people are totally nervous about computers! The tech part is so easy! Even my college had what they've just purchased around here. I'll never forget my science methods course. We tested water samples from schools all over the country through a website. Most of my profs were using PowerPoint presentations when I started as an undergrad. Our dorm rooms were online . . . we used to see how much of a paper we could write without going to the library. Taking that Ed Tech course junior year may have been my best move. The faculty here see me as a resource.*

MR. APPLETOSS: *Funny how so many of the teachers are spooked by computers. I've always liked technology. Being the AV guy gave me a step up. From the stage crew in elementary school to the "AV Squad" in middle school, I have always been at home with machines. For the past eight years, teachers have come to me to solve their computer problems. Heck, I had my first computer when they were called by names, not numbers . . .*

MRS. GUDBRAKE: *I suspect it's going to be the same old, same old . . . but my kids lose, because they are the Title I pull-out crowd. Our rich kids, especially the boys, already have better equipment at home than we have in the "new" tech lab. They're using it for reports, term papers, college applications even their own Web pages. They've got access, opportunity, skills, equipment, summer computer camps, and the computer club. Too many of my Title I students have never touched a mouse, except when they try to corner one at home.*

Teachers approach technology with varying levels of confidence. Some are technological pathfinders, taking to computers with skill and excitement. Others adapt slowly, but with support and training they do eventually adapt. Still others suffer from **technophobia,** an anxiety that renders all mechanical things foreign, alien, and frightening. Answering machines and VCRs can intimidate technophobes, who some authors describe as digitally challenged.[16] But tech training for teachers is expanding as school districts, universities, and educational associations offer numerous technology workshops across the nation (see wwwnea.org/technology).[17] Yet sometimes the answers to technology puzzles are not found in workshops; they are right before our eyes. In a Colorado program, fourth- and fifth-grade students serve as technology mentors for teachers.[18] The average American student spends more than twice as much time on the computer at home than at school, and has a home computer of higher quality than the one at school. One out of every five teenagers has a personal Web page, and middle and high school students typically use the Internet for study independently, without teacher guidance or knowledge.[19] (See Figure 13.2.)

The Apple Classrooms of Tomorrow (ACOT) project followed teachers over several years as they learned to use computers and software. The researchers identified five stages of "instructional evolution" as shown in Figure 13.3.[20]

As you sort out which of these stages might best describe your place in the cyber classroom, some perspective might be in order. One reason why so many teachers,

OVERHEAD 146–148
Where Students Learn about Technology

Internet Use: Purpose and Location

Instructional Evolution

FIGURE 13.2

Where students learn about technology.

NOTE: Percentages do not add up to 100 because of rounding.

SOURCE: *Education Week*/MDR/ Harris Interactive Poll of Students and Technology, 2001.

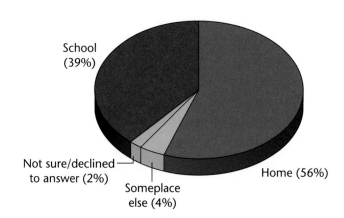

REFLECTION: Where have you learned the most about computers? How might economic class, culture, race, and gender influence student responses?

FIGURE 13.3

Five stages of instructional evolution.

Entry Stage	Filled with all the trepidation and excitement of doing something new, teachers begin to learn to use technology, but wonder if the time and effort will bear fruit.
Adoption Stage	Small technological activities, such as word processing or drill and practice, are blended into the classroom.
Adaption Stage	Thorough integration of technology means that word-processing, presentation tools, and content specific software are a regular and effective part of classroom life.
Appropriation Stage	Teachers use technology effortlessly in and beyond the classroom, and find it hard to imagine teaching without it.
Invention Stage	Teachers experiment with new instructional techniques: interdisciplinary problem-based learning, team teaching and independent study prevail. Collaboration and problem solving with technology become commonplace.

CRITICAL THINKING QUESTION

So, if your class were the jury, what's their vote on the educational effectiveness of computers and the Internet? Poll them and see.

especially older teachers, have been slow to take to the cyber classroom could be the long and unhappy history of hyped educational breakthroughs, breakthroughs that delivered far less than promised. Television, open space classrooms, and teaching machines were all expected to revolutionize teaching in their day. None did. The jury is still out on the educational effectiveness or merit of computers and the Internet. People have invested far more energy and resources in placing computers in classrooms than in figuring out if all these computers will be worth the effort. And some teachers are sitting on the sidelines, waiting to see if this latest innovation will really make a difference.

It's the Teaching, Not the Technology

Perspective is too often lost in the glitz surrounding exciting new technologies. "New" can be exhilarating; "new" can also disappoint. Software developer and educator George Brackett reminds us, "Technologies do not change schools in any sense worth talking about. Thoughtful, caring, capable people change schools, sometimes with the help of technology, sometimes not, and sometimes even despite it. Too often we focus on the technology rather than the reform."[21]

Technology should be seen as a teacher's tool, and not the other way around. The first step is deciding how best to use that tool.[22] Here are some of the typical reasons educators give for using computers in school:

- *Increase basic skills* in math, reading and writing, as well as content areas, through sample quizzes, drill-and-practice, and additional course-related information. This reason becomes particularly attractive in this time of standardized testing.

- *Motivate students* through multimedia materials that capture their interest.

- *Promote higher order thinking* by introducing simulations, problem-based learning, Internet research, collaborative work, and student authoring programs.

- *Increase academic resources* by bringing the unlimited written and visual assets of the Internet into local schools.

- *Increase responsiveness to different learning styles* including special needs children, or students for whom the typical classroom culture means academic and/or social distress.

- *Improve workplace preparation* as students learn keyboarding skills, software applications, and technological operations common to future employment.

- *Save work for teachers* by creating a class Web page. A great deal of administrative time can be saved: Homework assignments, worksheets, notes, and exam dates can be posted on the Web page, and parent communication accomplished through e-mail. In fact, grading software can track attendance, average grades, and chart the results while even more cutting-edge programs use artificial intelligence, such as the Intelligent Essay Assessor (IEA), to grade essays.

- *Strengthen teacher performance* by adding resources, such as a PowerPoint presentation or a video clip, to create more dramatic and effective teacher presentations.

FOCUS QUESTION 4
How can teachers effectively use computers and the Internet?

OVERHEAD 149
How Much Do You Think Computers Have Helped Student Learning?

Typically, computers have been used for drill and practice, simple programming, and educational games.

INTERACTIVE ACTIVITY
Using Technology in
Education. See examples
of how technology is
used in the classroom.

- *Make testing easier for teachers* by having computers create and grade tests, and maintain student records.
- *Modernize the school culture* by reshaping American education for the twenty-first century, moving beyond pencil and paper, chalk and chalkboards, into instant access to the world's digital resources.

Goals for using technology vary, as does the effectiveness of technology as used in schools. The following descriptions offer specific examples of how technology can enhance effective teaching strategies (many effective strategies were discussed in Chapter 3). Since technology can also short-circuit learning, we note potential pitfalls as well.

CLASS ACTIVITY:
SITE SEEING
IM, Activity 13:5

Multiple Intelligences Technologies open a wide door to Howard Gardner's world of multiple intelligences. For instance, authoring tools such as PowerPoint, Netscape Composer, TimeLiner, and Kid Pix Studio, enable students to create presentations and projects that incorporate text, animation, graphics, video, and sound, integrating several intelligence areas. The computer allows students to compose music, even if they are unable to read a note. In science and art classrooms, computer modeling programs teach and enhance spatial learning. A physical education or dance teacher could improve kinesthetic and visual learning through digital video recordings of student motion, enabling careful analysis of movement techniques. Gardner suggests still another use: "If, for example, we want students to be civil to one another, we need to develop their interpersonal skills. This could be done by recording tense interactions on video and having students choose the best human(e) means of reducing the tension; by involving students in chat rooms or discussion forums that include opportunities for helpfulness or deceit; or by creating cartoon simulations or virtual reality scenarios of human dilemmas where the student has options to interact in different ways."[23] While Howard Gardner is impressed with the potential marriage of technology with his multiple intelligences approach, he has also voiced concern about teachers who get enamored with the technological wizardry, and lose sight of the educational goal.

CRITICAL THINKING
QUESTION
Technologies are sometimes
considered *hardware*—that
lacks the soft touch
necessary for interpersonal
learning. What additional
tech examples can students
provide to support
interpersonal intelligence?

Problem-Based Learning David Williamson Schaffer, a lecturer at the Harvard Graduate School of Education, points out that the current information age brings us back to John Dewey. Thanks to technology, teachers can now guide students in real-world problem solving, often through collaborations with government or business.[24] The federally funded Challenge 2000 Multimedia Project has assisted many teachers in creating successful problem-based learning (PBL) experiences. For example, in Belmont, California, elementary school students produced a multimedia presentation that documented the 150-year history of their town. The students used HyperStudio, a student-authoring tool, to create an interactive history with video clips, digital pictures, and animated photographs. The students interviewed and videotaped members of the community, and conferred with the curator of a local museum. The "Belmont Then and Now Project" was not just a skill-building effort, for ultimately it taught the community and visitors about the area's history, and became an exhibit in the Belmont Historical Society.[25] (See also pblmm.k12.ca.us.)

TEACHING TIP
Can students contribute,
from their own experience,
examples of PBL with and
without technology? How
might they redesign those
activities with the expanded
technologies of today?

The U.S. FIRST Robotics competition offers another example of problem-based learning. Nationally, hundreds of schools compete to create robots that perform tasks such as picking up balls and placing them in a trough. Upon entering the contest, each school receives a kit, which contains the control system, motors, and a

A Computer Primer in the Classroom

WHAT IS THE INTERNET?

The **Internet** is the name given to the network of computers all over the world that are linked not only to each other but to a massive amount of information on an endless array of topics contained on many of those computers.

WHAT WILL I NEED TO GET CONNECTED?

For teachers, the key is learning how to access, view, and use this information; to broaden the classroom to include the resources provided by museums, libraries, news sources, and media outlets. The easiest way to access the Internet is through the **World Wide Web** (WWW). In order to see the Web, your computer needs an Internet connection, such as a modem, and Web browser software. Browser software tells the computer how to find and display WWW pages.

E-MAIL

One of the first Internet features was electronic mail (**e-mail** for short). As the name suggests, e-mail is similar to traditional mail service (haughtily called "snail mail" by Internet users) but usually takes just seconds or minutes to be delivered. One of the most significant advantages of e-mail (and many other Internet tools) is that it is basically free. Another benefit is that, unlike your postal address, which is tied to a fixed location, on the Internet your address "follows you." No matter where you are in the world, as long as you can find a client computer and access the Internet, you can receive or send mail.

THE WORLD WIDE WEB

Whenever you see an address that starts with "www" or "http://" (they often are advertised on television or radio and in newspapers or magazines) you are seeing a location on the World Wide Web.

Perhaps the most educationally exciting use for the WWW is the opportunity it affords students to connect with other users around the world. Students can write their own homepages that connect the outside world with their classrooms. Examples of such projects include:

- Students can create surveys for Internet users around the world to answer through a hyperlink connected to a class e-mail address.
- An ESL class might create a homepage celebrating each of their respective cultures, including links to homepages in their own countries.
- A reading and writing class could build a creative writing homepage filled with student work.
- Foreign language students can converse with native speakers on other continents by e-mail or by using advanced Internet tools that allow for the transmission of video and sound through the computers. Conversely, your class can help others touch up on their English.
- Students can participate in an online science fair, presenting science projects using text and graphics.
- Electronic student publications—school yearbooks, newspapers, and literary magazines—can be made accessible to the rest of the world.
- Students interested in science can browse pictures uploaded by NASA, along with resources from almost every major science or health organization.

NOTE: The primer on the Internet was written by Paul Degnan and was updated by Sara Kindler, both graduates of the School of Education at American University.

> **REFLECTION:** To some, this primer is "old news"; to others, it finally brings meaning to mysterious words and letters. Where are you on this continuum? Are there still words and letters that puzzle? Use our text website (www.mcgraw-hill.com/sadker7e) to see if others can answer your question.

number of other components. The students work together on building the robot for a period of six weeks, sacrificing many hours after school and weekends. (Much time is invested beforehand in the classroom preparing for the competition as well.) Students do the bulk of the planning and constructing themselves, but teachers and outside engineers provide guidance. (For a look at one of these projects, check out www.usfirst.org/robotics.)

Teachers need to be concerned about hazards associated with problem-based learning. Whenever students are involved with the real world, inappropriate comments or behaviors can be amplified and cause problems for students, teachers, and the school. Moreover, collaboration with private companies raises the specter of inappropriate commercialism and improper business influence in education. Both dangers call for careful planning and constant monitoring when using problem-based learning.

OVERHEAD 150
Monitoring Strategies

Cooperative Learning and Scaffolding Educators get concerned when technology isolates and alienates students. Several software products are specifically designed to encourage student cooperation. "Knowledge Forum" is a website that promotes cooperative learning and guides individuals to deeper levels of thought. Participants share information on the Internet, consider questions and ideas, and work together to solve problems. For example, students who are trying to develop a theory enter information in appropriate stages of the Theory Building feature: "My Theory, I Need to Understand, New Information, This Theory Cannot Explain, Much Better Theory, Putting Our Knowledge Together." Students are able to comment on each other's findings and connect ideas graphically. (For more information, visit www.knowledgeforum.com.) As in any cooperative or independent learning activities, effective teachers monitor student work and interactions to ensure that they are making progress and working well with one another.

Mastery Learning Many software products and websites take advantage of the good fit between computer technology and the goal of mastery learning. Working at their own pace, students can master concepts about Newtonian mechanics (ThinkerTools software) or develop mathematical skills (see www.renlearn.com/am). When mastery learning software is matched with traditional in-class learning, the result is called an **integrated learning system (ILS).** In Metrotech High School in Phoenix, Arizona, students attend classes to prepare for careers in areas as disparate as auto mechanics and television production, but they use software outside of class to refine their math and reading skills. The software diagnoses their levels of academic proficiency and then offers individualized programs designed to improve students' academic skills—all outside of class time, yet critical for in-class progress and success. Teachers need to carefully monitor all aspects of the ILS to verify that the program meets students' individual needs and that appropriate progress is being made, and to supply additional instruction as needed.

VIDEO SEGMENT 32
Integrating Technology
into Teaching

Wait Time and Teacher Feedback The sometimes hectic pace of classroom interaction can make it difficult for teachers to patiently wait and offer each student specific and helpful suggestions. With technology, patience and precise reactions are easier to come by. The T-I Navigator, for example, enables each student to communicate instantly with the teacher through an individual wireless terminal. The teacher can ask a question and each student takes the time needed to punch in a private response. Students instantly learn whether their answers are correct, and teachers can adjust instruction accordingly. The T-I Navigator ensures that each student has time to respond, and that each student does in fact respond. Classroom interaction becomes both more thoughtful, and more equitable. What are the downsides? For one, a false sense of security may develop as teachers get to know the electronic student at the cost of personal connection. Students also need the opportunity to develop interpersonal skills, such as speaking and listening in public settings, skills that could be lost with an overreliance on this sort of technology.

Deep Teaching Not long ago, the depth of curricular study was measured by the number of books in the school. Today's school library consists of tens of millions of articles, books, and media brought to the student's desk via the Internet. The key to deep teaching is no longer *finding* material; it is *choosing* material. Many professional organizations such as the National Council for the Social Studies (NCSS) list appropriate websites and online publications. TrackStar is a website where groups of teachers not only identify Internet resources by topic, but also include annotations, quizzes, sound bites, film clips, games, activities, and lesson plans (check out scrtec.org/track).

The Internet is an amazing source of wonderful—and awful—material. For the teacher, the major challenge is figuring out which is which, and helping students do the same. The dangers are not only the well-publicized Internet pornography and pedophilia websites, but also a minefield of misinformation, propaganda, and even hate, all parading as objective information. Groups with objective and even distinguished sounding names can be little more than "fronts" promoting a political or social position. Teachers are well-advised to check with librarians, professional associations, established government agencies, and watchdog groups that monitor hate organizations, to assess the quality and objectivity of Internet resources. Vigilance is not only the eternal price of democracy, it is the educator's entrance fee to the Internet.

Direct Teaching Traditional teacher-centered approaches can be enhanced by technology. Direct teaching and lecturing, for example, rely on effective presentations, and one of the more ubiquitous technological products in and beyond schools is the PowerPoint™ presentation. These computer-projected images are clear, organized, and appear like a "published" page for all the class to see. But savvy teachers tap other technology as well. Videotapes, computer graphics, and even digital microscopes can provide effective visuals. Even guest speakers can be transported to class via a Web camera. CUSeeMe can provide a camera for the speaker, and another in the class, facilitating a two-way exchange carried over the Internet. Videoconferencing and teleconferencing with other teachers and with subject matter experts is yet another possibility with CUSeeMe. (To find out more, visit www.globalschoolhouse.org/cu).

Special Populations For students with a variety of special needs or unique learning styles, technology can provide a real boost to teacher effectiveness. Several rich examples of this potential impact are technological devices designed for those with disabilities, called **assistive** or **adaptive technology.** Assistive technologies include wheelchairs, switches that respond to voice commands, and computer programs that read material for blind students. Students with visual motor problems can use voice-activated software or specialized touch screens to direct the computer's actions. Those with learning disabilities report that computers (especially handheld computers) are useful for taking notes in class and keeping their schedules organized. And learning disabled students especially benefit from such tools as Spellcheck. The list of adaptive technology devices promises to grow in the years ahead.[26]

The educational barriers facing poor students can be partially offset when schools offer take-home laptops. Schools provide training to both students and their parents in order to enrich the learning environment at home. The hope is that parental interest will not only

CLASS ACTIVITY:
Your Technology Breakthrough
IM, Activity 13:10

IN THE NEWS

A *Gooru* in the Classroom

Forget about desks and whiteboards; the Gooru is a prototype of what tomorrow's classrooms may look like. The three-part technology system straps on to each student and consists of an interactive PDA (called a GooBall), a backpack with its own power source, and a removable flexible screen. Students stand, sit, or lie on the floor as they learn. Each Gooru includes wireless connection to the Internet, and an alert system that provides students with relevant articles and books. The Gooru even monitors student heart rate and body temperature. The teacher's role is to help individual students who encounter problems.

SOURCE: *WIRED*, April 8, 2002.

 What's new in education? Click on *News Feeds.*

result in helping their children with homework, but might extend to their attaining a General Equivalency Degree for themselves over the Internet, if they never completed high school. One such program is called ESTRELLA, and provides online curriculum in Spanish, aimed at migrant farm workers and their families.[27] (Visit www.estrella.org for more information.)

RAP 4.9
Website of the Month,
p. 571

What are the pitfalls of such efforts, and can such "assistance" become too much? Some critics suggest that use of spelling and grammar tools for special education students (as well as others) can short-circuit learning, and that sending laptops home can lead to inappropriate use, from visiting pornography and hate groups' websites to unsupervised Internet shopping excursions. (The *Frame of Reference* "A Teacher's Toolbox to Avoid E-Pitfalls" provides educators with suggestions on how to avoid some of the more common technological problems.)

The Global Curriculum   Teachers and students exploring the Internet's educational possibilities have been termed **Internauts,** trailblazers on this new educational frontier not limited by distance or national boundaries.[28] What are some of the options open to today's Internauts?

- **Virtual field trips** transport students to the National Zoo in Washington, D.C., where zookeepers share their knowledge of the animals and students can pose questions via a "chat interface." Similar virtual field trips take students to the ocean depths or to outer space on NASA's Shuttle site.

- **Distance learning** provides courses online that instantly cross national borders. Distance learning is today's "e-quivalent" of correspondence courses, providing educational options to home schooling families, those working unusual or unpredictable hours, commuters who would rather travel the Internet than the interstate, and individuals who simply like learning on their own time and in their own place.

- **Simulations** recreate events, such as elections, cross-cultural meetings, and historical events, to enhance realism and promote learning.

FOCUS QUESTION 5
In what ways does global education refocus the curriculum?

CRITICAL THINKING QUESTION
Reflect back on the devastating terrorist attacks on New York and Washington made on September 11, 2001. How has the global village been shaped and reshaped since that day? What contributions have schools, via technology, made?

The "global village" created by the Internet is real, but the content of its curriculum is still being shaped. If you were to design a "Curriculum for the World," what issues, concepts, and skills would you include? Perhaps you might teach conflict-resolution strategies, to avoid a cataclysmic nuclear war. Problem-solving strategies could be useful in tackling ecological issues, such as global warming, deforestation, and toxic waste disposal. Maybe your curriculum would promote cross-cultural knowledge and communication skills to increase tolerance and understanding of the cultural, ethnic, and religious groups that share our planet. Educators investigating a world-based curriculum call their work **global education.**[29]

Author William Kniep suggests four domains for global inquiry:

1. *Human values.* The universal values shared by humanity, as well as the diverse values of various groups

2. *Global systems.* Emphasis on global systems and an interdependent world, including economy, ecology, politics, and technology

3. *Global issues and problems.* Worldwide concerns and challenges, including peace and security, environmental issues, and human rights

4. *Global history.* Including the evolution of universal and diverse human values, the history of global systems, and the roots of global problems.[30]

Unsound Software. Much of the software out there is made for profit, not children, and is not based on sound pedagogy. Seek endorsements and objective evaluations from respected colleagues. Often software developed in a university setting is more likely to be academically sound.

Stereotypes and Violence. The forms of bias discussed in Chapter 7 apply to technology as well. Stereotyping, omission, and unreality, for example, thrive in software and on the Internet. And many computer games, even for the very young, are filled with violence. Evaluating materials for bias and violence is not only recommended, it is pretty much required.

Screen Potato Syndrome. Americans love technology, and have grown up in a media-rich environment, so it is not surprising that computer-generated images can mesmerize teachers and students, and lull them into an apathetic, nonactive learning role. Variety is still important, so get yourself and your students away from the computer screen and into role-plays, manipulatives, and "low-tech" learning options.

Information Overload. The wealth of technological imagery and video possibilities, not to mention overheads, slides, or simulations, can short-circuit learning. Make certain that students have enough time to digest and process what they have learned.

Internet Junk. While journals have editorial boards and libraries carefully evaluate acquisitions based on budgetary and other criteria, the Internet furnishes no such safeguards. Wonderful resources are provided along with propaganda, political advocacy, and hate literature. Most schools use filters to censor student access to inappropriate Internet material. Filters are not perfect, however, and teachers still should monitor what material students are accessing. You would be wise to teach your students how to evaluate Internet material. For example, have them ask: Who is providing this material? Is it an objective source? Does this group have a particular agenda? Is the material fact, or opinion? (Or opinion, disguised as fact?) Is the material current?

Internet Cheating. Nearly one in five students reports knowing someone who has used the Internet to cheat, but there are resources to detect cheating.[1] The Glatt Plagiarism Screening Program tests student's knowledge about information in the essays they have handed in. Check the Plagiarism Resource Center at The University of Virginia for free software and links to related sites at www.plagiarism.phys.virginia.edu. Working with students on their papers, from the draft stage to final product, will minimize plagiarism and the downloading of student papers provided on the Internet. By the way, there are also websites that provide answers to the problems or tests found in your students' textbooks, so you may want to supplement published homework activities and tests with your own.

[1]Joshua Benton, "For Some, Net Puts Library on Shelf," *DallasNews.com*, September 4, 2001.

REFLECTION: Which of these tech-tips do you find particularly helpful—or troubling? Can you add one of your own?

Schools around the country and the world are combining technology and global education. In Massachusetts, middle school students completed a unit on environmental science through a live teleconference with students from Karlsruhe, Germany,[31] while in another Massachusetts school students learned through direct computer discussion about the realities of life in another part of the globe from students in Kindersley, Saskatchewan.[32] Global educators, like technology advocates, emphasize the need to "educate children for the world they are entering rather than the world they are leaving behind."[33] (The U.S. Department of Education provides a useful portal for many of these projects: www.globaled.org/issues/166/.)

- The First People's Project provides a site, in Spanish and English, for students from indigenous cultures. The goal is for students to learn about different cultures; students can also get involved in humanitarian efforts (see www.iearn.org.au/clp).

- Over six thousand schools from Mexico, the United States, and Canada participate in wildlife migration studies in the western hemisphere by recording sightings in their areas. "Journey North: A Global Study of Wildlife

GLOBAL VIEW
Eighty-five percent of European youth agreed with the statement that they "would rather spend a great day outside than a great day online," which indicates that the Internet is not necessarily a way of life, but a useful tool and an interesting diversion. Intelligence Factory, *The Double Click Generation* (2001).

Migration" teaches students how they can protect wildlife by creating or protecting habitats (see www.learner.org/jnorth).

- At the Holocaust/Genocide Project, students produce a magazine called *An End to Intolerance* (see www.iearn.org/hgp/aeti/student-magazine.html).
- World Wise Schools is a Peace Corps project where classrooms can partner with a Peace Corps volunteer and follow them as they do their work during the course of a year (see www.peacecorps.gov/wws).

The rate of technological innovation is so fast that even as today's applications are being disseminated, newer ones are being tested. Will the next generation of computers continue the trend toward less expensive, smaller, yet more powerful machines, yielding pocket computers that outperform today's desktops? Will the next generation of computers converse with us, eliminating the need for keyboard skills and programming? Will we be able to print letters and papers by simply speaking, or will simply thinking our thoughts be enough to create computer commands? Will we still print papers, or will we be able to instruct our computer to transmit information, not only to other computers but also to people's minds? Will the next breakthrough be true artificial intelligence, computers that can counsel us on our professional and personal lives, becoming mechanical mentors? Or are these little more than fanciful illusions, examples of America's overconfidence in all things technological?

The Virtual Teacher

FOCUS QUESTION 6
How is teaching redefined by virtual schools?

TEACHING TIP
Encourage your class to brainstorm circumstances, like those mentioned in the text, when virtual courses would be an addition to curriculum and a benefit to students. What would they want to teach?

INTERACTIVE ACTIVITY
The Virtual High School. Click on the Virtual High School website to observe an online classroom.

Picture this: You are a teacher in a very pleasant, comfortable, but small high school. You would love to offer a course about Native Americans, but your small school has only two students who want to enroll. During the year, you meet other students who express interest in many specialized courses, from marine biology and advanced physics to Latin American literature. Your Lilliputian school does not offer those courses either. Are you and your students out of options? Cheer up! All is not lost. You can join the Virtual High School, where you can teach your course, and your students can enroll in other specialized courses.

Started in 1997 by the Concord Consortium and the Public Schools in Hudson, Massachusetts, the **Virtual High School (VHS)** was the first large-scale project to create Internet-based courses at the high school level and now includes 150 schools serving thousands of students. Many states have followed suit and boast not only their own virtual high schools, but virtual middle and elementary schools as well. Virtual elementary schools have caused concern among those who believe that young children need personal contact with peers, but for many rural families, home schoolers and others, virtual elementary schools are seen as a positive development.[34]

Now a small town in Colorado can offer an anthropology course even after the anthropology teacher has left, and students in Amman, Jordan can be their classmates. Virtual classes are offered over the Internet and are **asynchronous** (that is, people can join classroom activities at any time of the day or night), so students from around the nation or around the world can take the same course. Unique and highly specialized courses are now being offered, thanks to the VHS.

How do virtual schools work? Although virtual schools differ from each other, the original VHS in Concord is basically a barter system, in which participating high schools contribute a teacher's time to develop and deliver one VHS netcourse. In return, the school is allowed to enroll twenty of its students in other netcourses offered by VHS. The courses offered do not compete with the regular offerings at each participating high school but are designed to augment local curricula. Each participating instructor receives training to become a VHS teacher, to learn how to teach on the Internet. Course offerings have included Bioethics Symposium; Earth 2525: A Time Traveler's Guide to Planet Earth; A Model United Nations Simulation Using the Internet; Business in the 21st Century; Folklore and Literature of Myth, Magic and Ritual; and Writing: From Inner Space to Cyberspace.

Some critics worry that the VHS isolates students from teachers, but many report that in fact VHS courses are more personal and individualized than typical classes. Recounts one new recruit to the Virtual High School, "In just two weeks, I feel like I know my Virtual High School teacher better than I ever knew any of my face-to-face teachers."[35]

Virtual high schools are being touted as an effective response to the teacher shortage, and the future may bring a dramatic increase in this new type of instruction. What is it like to teach in a virtual school? While many of the effective teaching practices that we discussed apply to virtual teaching, tasks do differ. As you read the following account of a virtual teacher's day, you may want to consider the differences and similarities between traditional and virtual teaching. (If you want to visit and take a tour of the Virtual High School in cyberspace, visit our online learning center to link to the Virtual High School.)

RELATED READING
Next: The Future Just Happened by Michael Lewis (2001).

A DAY IN THE LIFE OF A TEACHER: ANA'S STORY

Ana teaches in a small, rural school in Massachusetts. She started incorporating Internet research into her classes a couple of years ago but wondered how else she could use the Internet in her instruction. When her school was considering joining VHS, Ana applied to be one of the first VHS teachers. She enrolled in the Concord Consortium's graduate-level Teacher's Learning Conference (TLC), with about thirty other teachers from around the country, and began developing a netcourse, which she has delivered three times, to a total of sixty students in the VHS cooperative.

Part of what Ana loves about VHS is the way it has made her take a fresh look at her instructional methods after fifteen years of teaching. She has found that her evaluation is carrying over into her local classroom as well. She also loves being a "pioneer" and being connected to an intimate network of other teachers around the country.

8:00 A.M. Teachers' Lounge

Before her first local class of the day, Ana uses a phone line in her school's teachers' lounge to check in on her VHS course. She plugs in her laptop, connects to the phone line, and opens her Internet browser. She logs onto the VHS site, goes to the VHS Faculty Lounge to check for any new announcements, and then accesses her class over the Internet. This semester, Ana has students from eight states and fourteen high schools in her class. She wants to see if any new work assignments or discussion comments have come in from students over the weekend. She loves seeing work come in from her students at all hours of the day, sometimes seven days a week. She assigns work on a weekly basis, making it possible for all twenty students to contribute equally to the course, despite their varying schedules and time zones. After checking her course, Ana quickly peruses her e-mail to see if anyone has sent her a private message and then logs out to go teach her onsite classes.

2:15 P.M. Teachers' Lounge

Ana has finished teaching her reduced load of onsite courses for the day and now switches gears to focus on her VHS course. Ana sets up her laptop and opens up Lotus Notes, so she can work on her course. Her students can access the class on any computer with an Internet

PROFILE IN EDUCATION Christa McAuliffe and Sally Ride— Sisters in the Sky

Christa McAuliffe

Christa McAuliffe's name is deeply etched in American history as the teacher who died in the *Challenger* explosion. Honest and direct, she did not hesitate to speak out on behalf of the constituency she represented: American public school teachers and students.

Astronaut Sally Ride had flown the *Challenger* just over a year earlier, but her world also exploded with the *Challenger's* final voyage in 1986. The astronauts who died were more than her friends; they were members of a unique club, tethered to one another for their very survival. Ride served on the Presidential team chosen to investigate the *Challenger* explosion.

In her younger days, Sally Ride was a nationally ranked junior tennis player. She left the tour, however, because: "I couldn't always control the trajectory of the ball and this was unbearably frustrating. I need things to make sense."[1] Ride studied physics at Stanford University, reveling in science's precision and logic. After receiving her doctorate, she was one of more than eight thousand men and women who applied to become an astronaut. Thirty-five were accepted, six were women, and one of those women was Sally Ride. On June 18, 1983, she climbed into the flight engineer's seat of the *Challenger*, the first American woman in space. "The

Sally Ride

thing I'll remember most about the flight is that it was fun. It was the most fun I'll ever have in my life."[2]

Sally Ride's fascination with technology and exploration of the universe remains steadfast. "Science is fun. Science is curiosity. We all have natural curiosity. Science is a process of investigating, solving puzzles."[3] Now a physics professor at UC–San Diego, Ride's primary mission, like that of Christa McAuliffe before her, is to propel the study of science and technology in students of all ages and backgrounds. "Our future lies with today's kids and tomorrow's space exploration."[4] Adviser to two national science education programs, EarthKAM and Imaginary Lines, Ride designs lessons that extend far beyond the traditional classroom walls.

EarthKAM is an international program involving middle school students in the excitement of space exploration. The curriculum begins in classrooms, where students and teachers study a region or landmark on Earth to be photographed. They might elect to learn about deforestation in the Amazon, dust storms in Africa, or volcanoes in Hawaii. After calculating variables such as latitude and longitude, students send their data via the World Wide Web to

EarthKAM at Mission Control in Houston where the coordinates are programmed into digital cameras on the Space Shuttle or International Space Station. Pictures from space are then transmitted back to the classroom. Ride's hope is that the interactive nature of EarthKAM will do "nothing short of revolutionize science education in America."[5]

Sally Ride knows that young women are especially unlikely to take flight in science and technology careers. In elementary school, roughly the same numbers of girls and boys are interested in science and math. But beginning in about sixth grade, more girls than boys disengage from these subjects. Ride created Imaginary Lines to stop this leak in the pipeline. The program targets middle school girls interested in science and technology, and networks them through interactive projects and role modeling. At the heart of the program are Sally Ride and her message: "math and science will take you places." And her students are inspired. "She's a spectacular teacher. Dr. Ride's a hero at bringing the excitement of science into the classroom."[6]

[1]Janet Wiscombe, "Ask Sally Ride about Her Research," *LA Times Magazine* (August 29, 1999). [2]Carolyn Blacknall. *Sally Ride: First American Woman in Space* (Minneapolis: Dillon Press, 1984). [3]Ibid. [4]Ibid. [5]Wiscombe, "Ask Sally Ride about Her Research." [6]Ibid.

REFLECTION: Visit EarthKAM, Imaginary Lines, and McAuliffe/Challenger Center online. How might these resources support learning through technology? Would you use them in your classroom? Why or why not?

www.mhhe.com/ sadker

To learn more about Christa McAuliffe and Sally Ride click on *Profiles in Education.*

browser, but she needs to use Lotus Notes software to make certain additions and changes to the course. Ana didn't know anything about using this software before she joined VHS, but the TLC professional development netcourse trained her to create and manage her course within Notes' LearningSpace environment.

Creating a New Team Profile in the CourseRoom

Ana fine-tunes next week's assignment, which she will unlock soon for students who want to get an early start. She uses the instructor's tools in the CourseRoom to create student teams. Next week, she will ask the students to pair up and start working on a long-term project. The assignment centers around gathering and comparing regional information, so she partners students from different states when she creates the new teams. After she creates teams, the students will be able to create work documents that can be accessed and edited only by the two members of each team and the teacher.

Creating a New Discussion Topic in the CourseRoom

Next, Ana creates a new discussion topic to go along with the team assignments. She creates a link from the Schedule document, which describes the assignment, right to the new discussion thread where she wants students to post comments. Ana reads the new student comments and posts some responses to facilitate a deeper group discussion. A few new work assignments have been posted by students, marked "submitted for grading." Ana marks up the documents and resaves them in the CourseRoom. Her students will be able to open their graded work privately to read Ana's edits and comments. Finally, Ana enters her comments and grades in the student's online portfolios, located in the Profiles database.

The Portfolio View in the Profiles Database

After dinner, Ana sets up the laptop on her desk at home. Ana is one of TLC graduates asked to act as a mentor for the group of teachers currently in TLC training. Ana has been assigned as the "buddy" to a group of three teachers who are developing netcourses in a similar content area. The "newbies" in Ana's group are expected to comment and offer suggestions on each other's work. The latest assignment was to create and post a group activity for the proposed netcourse. Ana reads the three group activities created by her group members, smiling at their creativity. She posts a response to one of the activities, which she thinks is especially strong. (The teacher asks his students to do a hands-on experiment at home with their family and then to share their data with the class by posting their results in the CourseRoom. The students are asked to compare and contrast their findings with the rest of the class.) Ana writes some positive feedback to that assignment and tells the group that, in her experience, assignments are most successful when they balance work both on and off the computer. Ana is having a lot of fun sharing her expertise and experiences with this new group of teachers. It helps her feel connected to the project and keeps her from feeling isolated within her own course. Ana finishes and shuts down her computer for the night, the end of another VHS day.

Did you notice the combination of technology and sound teaching practice? Virtual teaching enabled Ana to take time and thoughtfully respond to each student, to get to know them as individuals (without ever really "meeting" them). She was able to have students from different areas share regional data, and display important issues and findings on the course website, activities she would be unable to do without the technology. Virtual teaching demands organization and good scheduling, and it is clear that this appeals to Ana. Looks like Ana is sold on the VHS process, but of course, being a fictional teacher, that was not much of a challenge. There are downsides to virtual education, and not everybody thrives in this environment. How do you feel about virtual teaching?

CRITICAL THINKING QUESTION
Review the VHS pages and identify sound teaching practices. (We noted that Ana incorporated Internet research; participated in staff development; took a "new look" at instruction; was connected with others; reviewed assignments on her own time; fine-tuned assignments; provided individual feedback; followed-up on outstanding or absent work; acted as a buddy (mentor); encouraged hands-on learning off-line; and Ana was having fun!)

Technology and Equity

FOCUS QUESTION 7
Does technology exacerbate racial, class, geographic, and gender divisions?

**CLASS ACTIVITY:
COMPUTER EDUCATION
EXPERIENCE**
IM, Activity 13:3

OVERHEAD 151
The Digital Divide on Computer Use

RELATED READING
Geeks: How Two Lost Boys Rode the Internet Out of Idaho by J. Katz (2000).

While technology has many cheerleaders, not everyone gets to be a player. Wealth, race, gender, and geography influence computer and Internet access, creating a **digital divide.** Being white, Asian, and wealthy translates into greater access to computers and to the Internet, especially high-speed Internet.[36] Classrooms in wealthier communities are more likely to be connected to the Internet than those in poorer communities.[37] The good news is that the digital divide is shrinking; the bad news is that equal access does not mean equal use.[38] As Professor Henry Jay Becker warns, "Efforts to ensure equal access to computer-related learning opportunities at school must move beyond a concern with the numbers of computers in different schools toward an emphasis on how well those computers are being used to help children develop intellectual competencies and technical skills."[39] The lack of teacher training and the absence of a challenging curriculum can short-circuit even the most advanced technology.[40] Wealthier students use the Internet more frequently, and perhaps more productively, than poorer ones. (See Figure 13.4.)

The digital divide is also a gender divide. In the early years, girls are as interested in computers as boys are, but by upper elementary school, male-oriented video games and software fan the flames of female disaffection. Cyber-athletics, cyber-combat, and even cyber-violence against women send powerful messages that this is a male (and

FIGURE 13.4

Playing or learning? In the summer between kindergarten and 1st grade, 80 percent of children from high-income families used their home computers on a weekly basis, compared with 60 percent of children from low-income families. There were also disparities in how those children used their home computers.

SOURCE: "Young Children's Access to Computers in the Home and at School in 1999 and 2000," U.S. Department of Education, National Center for Education Statistics, March 2003.

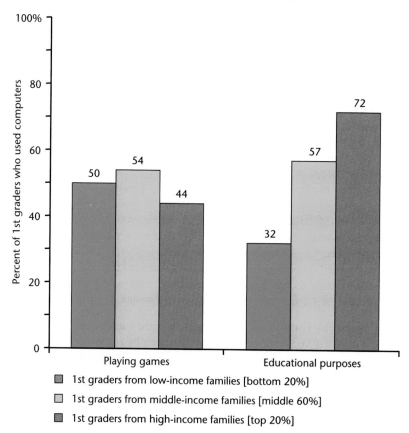

1st graders from low-income families [bottom 20%]
1st graders from middle-income families [middle 60%]
1st graders from high-income families [top 20%]

REFLECTION: Do you believe that teachers would work with poorer families to enhance the productive use of computers and the Internet at home? If so, how might this be done?

potentially dangerous) domain. No wonder boys flock to video arcades, computer summer camps, technology electives, and computer clubs. Schools sex-type computer courses by placing them in the math department where girls often "are not free to roam" because of a strong "male" culture."[41] Males constitute over 80 percent of high school students taking advanced placement tests in computer science, and comprise about the same percentage of computer professionals.[42]

Geography contributes to another digital divide. Running fiber optic cables to rural schools is often an expense that telecommunications companies avoid, a challenge that has been called the **last mile problem.**[43] The connections that are made are often slow, posing difficulties for students participating in online classes. Perhaps Internet connections via satellite or more advanced future technologies will resolve this problem, but for now, rural America is on the wrong side of the digital divide.[44]

Before we leave this topic, we should reflect for a moment on the global divide as well. English dominates the Internet, disenfranchising most people. And where language does not disenfranchise, lack of finances does. The result is that the Internet is largely a tool of western and high-tech nations. (See Figure 13.5.)

CRITICAL THINKING QUESTION
How is technology in rural schools different from and similar to urban and suburban environments?

OVERHEAD 152
Rural America

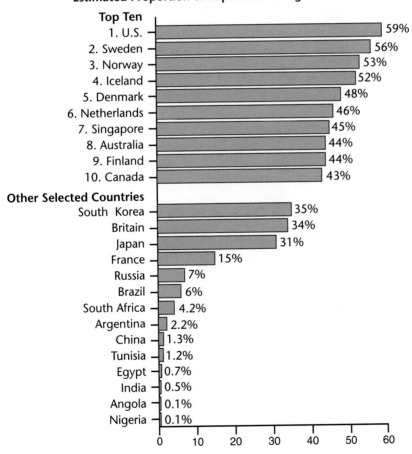

Estimated Proportion of Population Using the Web

FIGURE 13.5
The international digital divide.

SOURCE: U.N. Human Development Report 2001, NUA Internet Surveys, Population Reference Bureau.

REFLECTION: How might wealth, population size, language, and type of government play a role in Web access?

While most American students have computer access at school, there are tremendous differences in how, when, and why they are used. Predict the use and impact of computers in each of these three school settings.

Is Computer Technology Worth the Effort?

"If technology is the answer, what was the question?"[45] We have yet to identify clear goals for technology or to determine how to measure progress toward these goals.

> Traditional theory says that kids need to know discrete skills in computation or reading so that's what teachers teach . . . But most of the people who are excited about technology in schools . . . care more about having kids do sophisticated writing or engage in complex reasoning or learn to figure out things like adults do. And we don't have great ways of measuring such outcomes.[46]

The bottom line is that the monumental investments in computer technology have not been matched by monumental gains in student achievement. In fact, researchers are divided on the academic benefits brought by computers. Evidence suggests that drills and tutorials in science, social science, and math may be effective, but more advanced simulations, like virtual dissections, are not. Perhaps with more sophisticated uses of technology in the future, more effective learning will occur—or perhaps not.[47] Sometimes technology can hamper learning. Students who become too dependent on calculators can see their mathematics test scores tumble.[48] Other

GLOBAL VIEW
"Virtually 100 percent of Finnish young people aged 14 to 21 have mobile phones. What's more, research shows that half of their use is for SMS calls, short messages of up to 160 characters that can be typed on the keypad . . . swapping about a hundred SMS messages monthly." Seppo Kari, "From Ears to Eyes," *Interactions* (1999).

OVERHEAD 153
The International Digital Divide

RAP 4.6
Computers in the Classroom: Bane or Boom? p. 567

503

Here are a few suggestions for creating a more equitable technological society:

- Connect with one of the over 20,000 organizations that are helping to bridge the digital divide (such as PowerUP, www.powerup.org), or start your own.
- Explore partnerships with neighborhood businesses interested in supporting the school technology program.
- Recruit volunteers from the community to share their expertise in technology with the students at school.
- Help make technology available to at-risk groups after school, in public places and in clubs. Request that your school keep computer labs open after hours.

- Create a Student Tech Corps of savvy students to mentor less savvy students (and maybe you!).
- Bring role models to class to speak about women and people of color succeeding in technology careers.
- Encourage students to evaluate the school district's policy and practice on making computers and the Internet available to students in poorer schools in your community.
- Organize a "borrowing" program between wealthier schools with laptops and those with fewer resources.

REFLECTION: Can you add two more ideas to this list? Which are you most likely to implement?

---

studies indicate word processing produces longer, higher-quality writing by students, although many teachers complain about the spelling and grammatical shortcuts that characterize students' e-mail.[49] Technology has created some ethical dilemmas as well. Nearly 40 percent of college students use the cut-and-paste function on their computers to lift text from the Internet. Text-messaging on cell phones has been used to share information during exams. High-tech cheating is rarely reported by students.[50]

Though computers have demonstrated only limited educational effectiveness, support for technology in schools remains high. Most adults believe that computers offer essential workplace skills—an important, if nonacademic goal. The public also believes that computers and the Internet provide a window on the latest information, and that somehow computers make education both more efficient and more enjoyable.

But Stanford University professor Larry Cuban sees problems on the horizon. When academic advances do not follow technological advances, we often blame teachers for not adequately embracing new technology. If teachers are not to blame, we place our criticism on the doorstep of an unresponsive school bureaucracy unable to manage change. If that does not work, then we explain failure in terms of insufficient resources, a public unwilling to fund costly technology. Rarely do Americans question the technology itself. Cuban points out that we know little about using technology to enhance instruction, that the problem may not be teachers, administrators, or funding; it may be America's unbridled faith in technology.[51]

It is helpful for teachers to maintain perspective when it comes to technology. While it is unlikely that education will be redefined completely in the near future, it is also clear that technology's influence is growing. Consider technology mastery as part of your professional development. Attend relevant courses and workshops and observe colleagues applying technology, but do not lose your skepticism. Be wary of "magic bullets," simple solutions to complex educational problems.

MULTIPLE INTELLIGENCE CONNECTION

Metaphors make an implicit comparison, one which calls attention to similarities between two things by speaking of one *as if* it were another. Have students develop metaphors responding to concepts and terms in this chapter. Here are some starters: *Technology is a rotten prune; My computer is a backpack; Educational television is the sky.*

Computers in Education *Enable* Us to . . .

TEACH MORE EFFECTIVELY

With computers we can individualize instruction, grant students autonomy, and empower students to learn at their own pace, rather than wait for the teacher's personal attention. Each learner benefits from having an omnipresent tutor to individually tailor schoolwork.

REACH AND TEACH MORE STUDENTS

Computers and Internet access can expand the educational horizons of children in isolated rural communities, children with limited community resources, or those children who are homebound because of disability or illness.

MAKE THE WORLD OUR CLASSROOM

Students with Internet access can directly tap resources in their communities or venture beyond their neighborhoods to other regions, nations, or cultures. Students can draw from limitless books, articles, pictures, and sound clips; follow links to experts or virtual field trips; and participate in real-time communications across the globe.

TURN LATCHKEY KIDS INTO CONNECTED KIDS

Too many youngsters have no one to talk to and are hesitant to ask questions of adults or teachers. The Internet offers a homework helper, a companion at the end of the school day, or a chat room of friends so that no one needs be home alone.

GET READY FOR THE FUTURE

Technology encourages interdisciplinary and collaborative work, facilitates problem-based learning, and provides an outlet for students to express their creativity. Students at ease with technology will be assets to future employers.

Computers in Education *Disable* Us Because . . .

EFFECTIVE TEACHING ALL BUT DISAPPEARS

Good teaching requires a personal connection. A teacher gazing at a student who is gazing at a computer screen is not teaching effectively. The Internet is unmonitored, filled with erroneous information, political propaganda, and phony research.

THE DIGITAL WORLD REMAINS DIVIDED

Technology amplifies economic disparities, awarding clear advantage to children from wealthy, high-tech homes attending wealthy, high-tech schools. Poor students soon discover technology's unwelcome mat tripping them up at the door of most career options.

STUDENTS RISK BECOMING ANTISOCIAL

Too many of today's youngsters can surf the Internet, but are unable to form personal connections. The Internet is home to countless narrow-interest groups that fragment society instead of unifying it. Technology can magnify antisocial behaviors, as children send destructive e-mails, organize sinister chat rooms, or create computer viruses.

COMPUTERS ARE A HEALTH RISK

Computer use is associated with increased eyestrain, repetitive motion injury, and the obesity that comes from a sedentary life style. Furthermore, how "healthy" is it for students to have easy access (via the Internet) to bombmaking information, or pornographic material?

FUNDAMENTAL SKILLS ARE SIDELINED

As spelling and grammar tools correct student writing, and computer screens replace engagement with books, real learning is compromised. Tomorrow's workers may become powerless automatons.

 ## YOU BE THE JUDGE

Do you believe that computers are an educational asset or a liability? In what ways has your education been enriched— or diminished—by technology? How might you plan to safeguard your students against dangers listed above?

SUMMARY

CHAPTER REVIEW

Go to the Online Learning Center to take a quiz, practice with key terms, and review concepts from the chapter.

CURRENT NEWS FROM POWERWEB

Go to Chapter 13 on the Online Learning Center to read current articles and to access news feeds about:

- Technology and Education
- The World Wide Web

1. Has technology changed schools?

   Technology continues to influence life in school, yet schools have remained remarkably unchanged through the years. Slates were replaced by chalkboards which are being replaced by whiteboards, part of a stream of technological innovations that has made its way into the classroom.

2. How does television affect children?

   While television holds great educational promise, with high-quality programming such as *Sesame Street* and *Blue's Clues,* much of television fare is distorted, unproductive and, at times, damaging. Viewers are treated to a video society that is often violent and replete with stereotypes, populated mostly by males, and few young children. Advertising, often targeted at young viewers, adversely influences children's behavior, including their diets and spending habits. While video libraries and cable channels, such as C-SPAN, A&E, and The History Channel, offer new media learning opportunities, the introduction of *Channel One,* a for-profit enterprise that brings current events and commercials into classrooms, raises questions about the role of commercial television in public schools.

3. Why is computer technology difficult to implement in schools?

   Today, virtually all schools are connected to the Internet, although budgets have been strained connecting classrooms to the Internet access. Schools in poorer communities continue to have fewer classrooms online. While some teachers resist technology, others experience "computer evolution," growing from entry level fear to exploring new and exciting uses.

4. How can teachers effectively use computers and the Internet?

   Hardware, software, and websites can tie into effective teaching strategies such as multiple intelligences, problem-based and cooperative learning, and direct and deep teaching. Virtual field trips take students around the world, online learning activities can create fascinating learning communities, and personal tutors diagnose learning needs. Assistive or adaptive technology helps special needs students succeed in school. Technology raises some serious concerns for teachers, including monitoring the material that comes in on the Internet, avoiding some of the health risks of computers, and teaching students to detect and mediate the stereotypes and violence that are so much a part of software and Internet resources.

5. In what ways does global education refocus the curriculum?

   Global education investigates world topics like conflict reduction and ecology that span national borders. Websites now available to students focus on international issues from child labor and animal migration to confronting intolerance and racism.

6. How is teaching redefined by virtual schools?

   The Virtual High School is an example of how technology alters schooling. Through the use of the Internet, e-mail, and other technological tools, students and teachers in different geographic areas and time zones can work together. Virtual teaching offers tomorrow's teachers another type of instructional career.

7. Does technology exacerbate racial, class, geographic, and gender divisions?

   Technology has not been an equal opportunity educational resource. Inequity continues to be a major problem as race, gender, and economic status influence access to home computers and high-speed Internet. Wealthier Americans, especially Asian and white males, are the most likely to use computers in school, and the most likely to realize salary benefits from that involvement after graduation, while rural America lags in Internet connections. Non-English speaking and poorer nations also trail behind in technological innovations.

EXTENDED LEARNING

CASE STUDIES

- Molly Thomas: A technology staff developer shares her frustrations with the district assistant superintendent for curriculum and instruction after a meeting with school-level technology support people runs amok.

READINGS

- Frederick Bennett. "The Future of Computer Technology in K–12 Education."
- Lindsey S. Hamlin and William T. Ryan. "Probing Plagiarism in the Virtual Classroom."
- Katrina A. Meyer. "The Web's Impact on Student Learning."
- Jana M. Willis and Lauren Cifuentes. "Moving Beyond the Training Environment to a Vision of Technology Integration in the Classroom Curriculum: A Case Study."

Go to Chapter 13 on your *Resources for Exploring Education* CD-ROM to access Case Studies and Readings.

KEY TERMS AND PEOPLE

assistive (adaptive) technology, 493
asynchronous, 496
Channel One, 483
digital divide, 500
distance learning, 494
dot.kids, 485
e-mail, 491
E-rate, 484

educational television programming, 483
global education, 494
integrated learning systems (ILS), 492
Internauts, 494
Internet, 491
last mile problem, 501

Christa McAuliffe, 498
Sally Ride, 498
simulations, 494
technophobia, 487
virtual field trips, 494
Virtual High School (VHS), 496
World Wide Web, 491

DISCUSSION QUESTIONS AND ACTIVITIES

1. Agree or disagree with each of the following:

   "Television viewing leads to misinformation."

   "Television viewing leads to unbridled capitalism, which often injures children."

   "Television viewing is a wasted educational resource."

   "Television viewing . . . " (You complete and support the sentence.)

 WEB-*TIVITIES*

1. Television in Schools: *Channel One*

2. Why has technology not radically altered the way teachers teach and the way students learn? Can you envision a technological breakthrough that will revolutionize schools? Describe it.

3. Suggest six uses of the computer and the Internet in your classroom. Then identify six potential problems associated with computer and Internet use.

4. Do you think it is important to include global education in the curriculum? Why or why not? What are some dangers inherent in a global education curriculum?

5. Describe the advantages and disadvantages of the Virtual High School or a similar program. Would you like to teach a virtual class? Why?

REEL TO REAL TEACHING

PAY IT FORWARD (2000)
Run Time: 123 minutes

Synopsis: Trevor McKinney, a twelve-year-old boy in a small California town, accepts a teacher's challenge: Earn extra credit by creating and putting into action a plan to change the world for the better.

Reflection:

1. What is the connection of *Pay It Forward* with technology? Visit the Pay It Forward Foundation at www.payitforwardfoundation.org to find out! As a teacher, how might you use this site? What knowledge, values, or skills would you want your students to learn from participating in the Pay It Forward project?

2. Video is a common form of technology often used in schools. Discuss the benefits and limitations of using this educational medium. In your answer, apply what you have learned about effective instruction, forces that shape the curriculum, and technology's impact on learning. Consider, too, how this book's *Reel to Real Teaching* feature has contributed to your learning.

3. *Pay It Forward* tackles issues that many of your future students will experience: student-on-student violence, family alcoholism, domestic abuse, and parental separation. Do you think film is a helpful tool to confront these issues? Describe the pros and cons as well as how you might use film in your classroom to confront social injustices.

Follow-up Activity: Take on Mr. Simonet's challenge: Create a project that makes our world a better place. Your project might improve your own local school or community. It may have a national or even international impact. Use technology (for example, television, film, the Internet) to implement your plan. Share your ideas on the Critics Corner, and invite your peers throughout the country to participate.

www.mhhe.com/sadker7e

How do you rate this film? Go to *Reel to Real Teaching* in the Critics Corner to review this film.

FOR FURTHER READING

Bringing the Internet to School, by Janet Ward Schofield and Ann Locke Davidson (2002). The authors examine the challenges of using the Internet in K–12 education, within the existing social organization, classroom structure, and teacher/student behavior norms. They discuss the contrast between the mission of those who shaped the Internet and educators who want to use the Internet as an instrument for change. The authors outline both the pros and cons of using the Internet in schools, and the conditions needed for effective use of this technology in the school setting.

Oversold and Underused: Computers in the Classroom, by Larry Cuban (2003). Combining a historical overview of school technologies with statistical data and direct observation of classroom practices, Cuban contends that when teachers are not given a say in how the technology might reshape schools, computers are merely souped-up typewriters and that technology leads to intellectual, emotional and social disengagement.

Student Cheating and Plagiarism in the Internet Era: A Wake-Up Call for Educators & Parents, by Ann Lathrop and Kathleen Foss (2000). Offers constructive school policies and teaching strategies to promote academic integrity as well as tips on how to identify material copied from the Internet.

Technology and Social Inclusion: Rethinking the Digital Divide, by Mark Marschauer (2003). Drawing on theory from political science, economics, sociology, psychology, communications, education, and linguistics, the book examines the ways in which differing access to technology contributes to social and economic stratification or inclusion. The book takes a global perspective, presenting case studies from developed and developing countries, including Brazil, China, Egypt, India, and the United States.

Using Technology Evaluation to Enhance Student Learning, by Barbara Means and Geneva D. Haertel (2003). This practical volume examines diverse approaches for improving teaching and learning through technology, addressing issues of administration, strategic planning, curricular integration, and staff development. It reviews multiple approaches for implementing technology successfully in the classroom, with an emphasis on curricular and leadership strategies.

Your First Classroom

FOCUS QUESTIONS

1. What are the stages of teacher development?
2. What resources do school districts provide for a teacher's first year in the classroom?
3. How do school districts, states, and the National Board for Professional Teaching Standards recognize and reward teachers?
4. What are the differences between the National Education Association and the American Federation of Teachers?
5. Are America's schools a secret success story, doing better than the press and the public believe?

 WHAT DO YOU THINK? What Teaching Skills Are of Most Value? Check off the teaching skills you believe are most important. See how your criteria compare to those of your colleagues.

CHAPTER PREVIEW

It looks so small: the distance between the students' chairs and the teacher's desk. But traveling from a student's desk to a teacher's desk represents an enormous journey. This chapter is intended to prepare you for that transformation, from student to teacher.

As you enter your first classroom, chances are that you will focus on lesson planning, classroom management, and preparing for those visits by your supervisor. In short, you will be all about classroom survival. With time and experience, you will begin to refine your teaching strategies and focus less on survival skills and more on ways to enhance student learning. While we would love to serve up some ready-to-use answers to help

you meet these first year classroom challenges, truth is, there are many questions that only you will be able to answer. Here are just a few for you to consider: Where should I teach? How can I win that ideal (at least satisfying) teaching position? What will my first year be like? Should I join a teachers' association? Should I stay in teaching long term? If so, what are the routes to advancement? And with all the negative press I read about schools, is this something that I want to do? This chapter provides you with some insights and practical advice about making that first year of teaching a successful one, and perhaps the beginning of many rewarding years.

CHAPTER FOCUS
This chapter prepares the reader for the transformation from a student to teacher. New teachers are confronted with a plethora of issues: Will I be good at teaching? Should I join a teachers' association? How do I juggle the concerns of parents, students, administrators, and my colleagues? Should I stay in teaching long term? If so, what are the routes to advancement? Insights and practical advice are provided about the influential first teaching year. For a chapter outline, see the IM.

510

Stages of Teacher Development

Will I be able to manage this class? Can I get through the curriculum? Do I know my subject well enough? Will the other teachers like me? Will the administrators rehire me? Am I going to be a good teacher? Will I like this life in the classroom?

When you begin teaching, the questions that occupy you are mostly about your ability, about visits by supervisors, and about managing students. By the second year, teachers are more experienced (and confident), and they usually move beyond these questions, shifting the focus of their attention to student performance. For example, experienced teachers might spend time analyzing the needs of individual students, exploring a new curriculum strategy, and asking such questions as How can I help this shy child? and Why is this student encountering learning problems? If a colleague is achieving success using a new teaching strategy, an experienced teacher might observe, then adapt that strategy. As talented and experienced teachers mature, their interests and vision extend beyond their own classrooms. At this more advanced stage, they work to develop programs that could benefit large numbers of students. The chart in Figure 14.1 suggests stages that teachers pass through as they become more skilled in their craft.[1]

Attempts to reform education and improve student achievement are dependent on our ability to move teachers through these developmental stages. Although earlier studies by James Coleman and others seemed to call into question the educational impact of teachers, comprehensive studies in the 1990s found that teacher performance is critical. Every dollar spent to increase teacher qualifications (as measured by teacher test scores, number of graduate degrees, professional training, etc.) improves students' academic performance more than money invested in most other areas. Although teachers applaud efforts to reduce class size or provide schools with up-to-date computer technology, research reveals that teacher expertise is more important. In fact, *teacher qualifications and skills are among the MOST important factors in improving student performance.*[2]

What do we mean by a qualified and skillful teacher? The most effective teachers not only demonstrate mastery of the subjects they teach but also are adept in the methods of teaching and understand student development. Unfortunately, too many teachers receive little support, make little progress in their subject area or their teaching skills, and never grow to the more sophisticated levels of teaching. Some teachers struggle to master the initial survival level: Approximately one-third of all new teachers leave teaching within the first five years.[3]

Will you like teaching, be good at it, and advance through these developmental stages? The answer may be determined by your first impressions, your initial experiences as a teacher, and school districts know it. That is why a growing number of districts are investing resources to ensure that, when you step into your first classroom, you will not be alone.

While some teachers are "naturals," gifted classroom instructors from the first day they step foot in a classroom, most of us benefit from a support system that helps us refine our teaching skills. Ongoing support, in the form of professional development, is provided, not just for new teachers but for all teachers. States and school districts have long required continuous graduate training and credits for teachers in order to maintain their licenses. In recent years, many school districts have gone further, creating and implementing induction programs for beginning teachers.

GRABBER: WHAT'S A TEACHER?
IM

FOCUS QUESTION 1
What are the stages of teacher development?

OVERHEAD 154
Stages of Teacher Development

OVERHEAD 155
School Resources and Student Achievement

OVERHEAD 156
Classroom Applications of Gardner's Theory of Multiple Intelligences

Figure 14.1
Stages of teacher development.

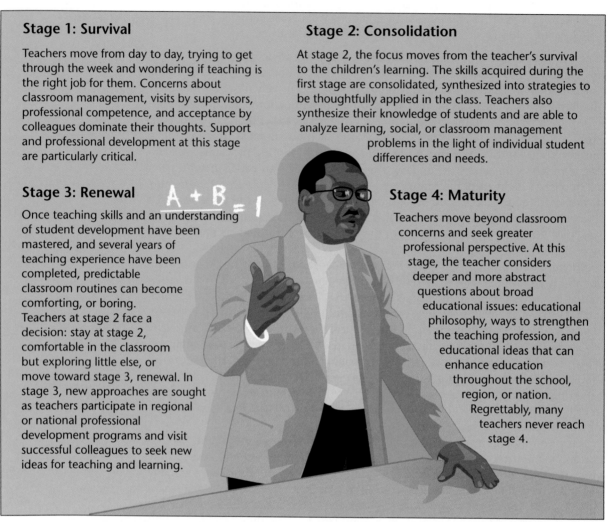

Stage 1: Survival

Teachers move from day to day, trying to get through the week and wondering if teaching is the right job for them. Concerns about classroom management, visits by supervisors, professional competence, and acceptance by colleagues dominate their thoughts. Support and professional development at this stage are particularly critical.

Stage 2: Consolidation

At stage 2, the focus moves from the teacher's survival to the children's learning. The skills acquired during the first stage are consolidated, synthesized into strategies to be thoughtfully applied in the class. Teachers also synthesize their knowledge of students and are able to analyze learning, social, or classroom management problems in the light of individual student differences and needs.

Stage 3: Renewal

Once teaching skills and an understanding of student development have been mastered, and several years of teaching experience have been completed, predictable classroom routines can become comforting, or boring. Teachers at stage 2 face a decision: stay at stage 2, comfortable in the classroom but exploring little else, or move toward stage 3, renewal. In stage 3, new approaches are sought as teachers participate in regional or national professional development programs and visit successful colleagues to seek new ideas for teaching and learning.

Stage 4: Maturity

Teachers move beyond classroom concerns and seek greater professional perspective. At this stage, the teacher considers deeper and more abstract questions about broad educational issues: educational philosophy, ways to strengthen the teaching profession, and educational ideas that can enhance education throughout the school, region, or nation. Regrettably, many teachers never reach stage 4.

SOURCE: Based on the work of Lillian Katz.

REFLECTION: Have you been taught by teachers representing each of these four developmental stages? Describe behaviors at each of the four levels. If you were to build in strategies to take you from Stage 1 to Stage 4, what might they be?

FOCUS QUESTION 2
What resources do school districts provide for a teacher's first year in the classroom?

VIDEO SEGMENT 33
Your First Day

 ## Your First Year: Induction into the Profession

We wish we could relive the excitement and intensity of our first year in the classroom. Okay, it was not always wonderful, and yes, it was often tough, but truth is, it was magical. Your first year could also be a magical time of learning and growing—or it could be quite the opposite. The quality of support you receive once you begin teaching may be the difference. Many schools understand this challenge and have created supportive climates to not only recruit, but retain teachers. A growing number of educators believe that there is no "teacher shortage" in America; rather there is a teacher retention problem. One out of three teachers leave the classroom within three years, and half leave within five years.[4] **Induction programs** "provide some systematic and sustained assistance to beginning teachers for at least one school year," in the hope that such support will create the first of many magical years.[5] Induction programs typically match new teachers, called **intern teachers,** with an experienced instructor, sometimes called a consulting teacher or mentor.

Mentors

Mentors may be assigned by the school administration, or by the local teachers' association, or by a combination of the two. **Mentors** guide intern teachers through the school culture and norms, shedding light on the "official" and "hidden" school governments (which memos need a quick response, which do not; who keeps the key to the supply room; where the best VCRs are hidden). Mentors can offer information about curricular materials, as well as observe a class to offer insights into teaching skills. In the best of circumstances, they help new teachers become skilled professionals. On a personal level, mentors can be valuable confidants, providing a friendly ear and helpful advice through new, and sometimes difficult, times. They may be able to help new teachers work out scheduling problems or smooth out stressful communication with a student, parent, administrator, or colleague (no minor feat during a year filled with new faces). Effective mentoring increases the likelihood that a teacher will remain in teaching. No wonder that even when personal mentors are not available, schools improvise by turning to tele-mentors, also called **e-mentors,** who offer advice and support over the Internet. (Visit teaching.com).[6]

If having a mentor sounds appealing, and you find yourself in a school district that does not provide official mentors, you can certainly try to recruit an unofficial mentor to guide you through that first year. You might want to ask colleagues or administrators about teachers known for creative lessons or effective management or who generally might lend a helpful hand to a rookie such as yourself.

In many programs, mentors provide more than friendly support; they have an official responsibility to assess new teachers and to file reports to school supervisors. A poor performance report from a mentor can result in a recommendation for extra training for an intern teacher, which could be absolutely wonderful in solving a persistent problem. If the problem is not resolved with additional resources and training, continuous negative classroom observations can lead to dismissal. Obviously, a mentor's evaluation responsibilities can inhibit open and effective communication, particularly if a new teacher is struggling and is concerned about being rehired.

Observation

Whether new teachers are assigned a mentor, find a mentor, or are mentorless, they are likely to have their classroom performance observed. It is not unusual for teachers to be observed three or four times in their first year and, in some districts, much more frequently. Observations come in two varieties: *diagnostic,* designed to help the teachers, and *evaluative,* intended to be used for employment decisions. Sometimes the same observation serves both purposes.

Observations may be conducted by your mentor, an administrator, or a veteran teacher. This last option, called **peer review,** has become popular in a number of school districts, including Minneapolis, Cincinnati, and Columbus, Ohio.[7] These

TEACHING TIP
Can students recall any professional or personal mentors that helped them get where they are today?

CLASS ACTIVITY: IT'S A WRAP
IM, Activity 14:1

TEACHING TIP
Several observation strategies are included with the RAPs and there is a more complete observation guide online. Having students act as observers (and at least appreciate the complexities of the task) might help them feel comfortable when they are in the limelight. You may also have professional stories that illuminate both positive and negative observations.

A CLASSROOM CHALLENGE I JUST HAD TO TAKE

By Mathina Carkci

Mathina Carkci, who wrote about education as a reporter for suburban Maryland newspapers for three years, became a fourth-grade teacher at Bailey's Elementary School in Fairfax County.

The most surprising thing about being a teacher is how often I feel like a failure. I knew that teaching fourth grade would be hard, but I expected to be able to keep up with everything and to succeed. So it's disheartening, just two months into my first job, to feel the weight of things left undone, questionable decisions made and professional duties unmet.

My teacher friends say they used to feel the same way. Some admit they still do. My student-teaching supervisor sympathetically cautions that the first two years are so unlike the "real thing" that they don't count. The teacher across the hall reminds me to take baby steps. My mom, a university professor, promises it will get better. I'm too hard on myself, a former professor tells me; it takes time to grow into the teacher I want to be.

I take some comfort from the fact that friends who were in the same one-year master's certification program at the University of Maryland last year have found it hard from the word go. I called Natalie the evening of her first day, a week before I started.

"If you told me I didn't have to go tomorrow," she said, "I wouldn't."

I called Al on his second day. "After the kids left today, I shut the door and cried," he said.

My friends and family told me I'd be a great teacher. They said they imagined a group of children gazing up at me, accompanying me on exciting journeys that would fill their minds with wonder. "You're such a good person," my husband told me. "The kids are going to love you." It gave me the chills, the way good classical music does, to think of myself and my merry band of students, gallivanting through the curriculum.

So it's difficult to admit now how hard it is to be a first-year teacher: how every single day I feel as if I am drowning; how I spend 12 hours at school each day working and four hours at home worrying; how each evening as I leave school, I have to decide which of 100 equally important things I should leave undone; how I feel so far behind that I will never catch up until Christmas, when I have 10 days "off."

When I get to school, anywhere from an hour and a half to two hours before the kids, a list of tasks swims through my head, and, as the minutes tick away until 8:40 arrives, I run through my priorities. With any luck, I'll have put up the day's schedule, written the daily message to the students and created the math warm-up exercise the

night before. I might respond to kids' journals but change my mind when I realize the math lesson I had planned misses an important element. (Half my mind, all this time, is wondering what the best way is to teach kids to determine the volume of solid shapes.) I might walk to the copier, see the line of other teachers and decide instead to swing by the library to schedule a block of time for my students. Or I might run into the guidance counselor and discuss ways to help a student who's been misbehaving.

Then I notice a student's desk that seems to be exploding papers and books, and wonder how best to help the child get organized: Does she need me to go through the pile with her, paper by paper? (And when would I do that?) Or should I write her a note and carve out a chunk of the day for her to organize things herself? Or do I need to have a talk with the whole class about keeping things straight?

It isn't as if I wasn't well prepared or don't have support. My year-long internship, including 12 weeks of student teaching, gave me a taste of the challenges I'd face. A mentor at my school, Bailey's Elementary, meets with me regularly, and Fairfax County bends over backward to provide new teachers with help. Bailey's teems with kind, helpful colleagues. Volunteers, including my mom who comes in every Friday, offer assistance of all sorts. Short of having a personal assistant 12 hours a day, I don't think there's anything more anyone could do to ease my transition.

Idealistic grad school conversations about pedagogy and democracy in the classroom made me surer than ever that I was right to go into teaching, that here was where I would make my impact on a part of the world that mattered to me. The master's program helped me build a solid educational philosophy based on wanting children to discover for themselves how rewarding learning can be.

I never thought my career switch would be easy. I had covered education when I was a newspaper reporter, so I'd seen the kinds of tightropes that many teachers walk. But I wanted to do something more active than writing about them. As a teacher, I could be with students every day and show them in tangible ways that their ideas mattered.

I try to make this happen in the classroom, but as we all know, theory and practice don't always overlap. I spend more time thinking up ways to get students to hand in homework than I do thinking about how to help them to pursue their own questions, or promoting their curiosity. Despite having vowed not to use rewards and punishments as a method of controlling the class, I have found myself giving kids extra recess for walking quietly in line or sending them back to their seats if they seem disruptive. My interactions with kids are less positive than I once hoped they would be, and I say "No," without explanation, far more often than I would like. Instead of designing creative, hands-on lessons in every subject, I sometimes teach straight from the book in science and social studies classes.

But, in the end, I don't think I'm really a failure. We have meetings, where my whole class tries to solve problems anyone puts on the agenda. I play with the kids at recess, which might make me seem more like another kid than like a teacher, but I think it also helps them to see me as someone worth following. I've managed to avoid being ruled by the lesson plan. The other day, two boys invented their own way of conducting a science project that involved analyzing rocks, and, when I realized their way was better, I encouraged the rest of the class to go with it instead of following the instructions.

I may not be on the same social studies textbook chapter as the other fourth-grade teachers, and I'll probably be late returning standardized tests to the assistant principal, but I think my kids know they're important to me. I see it in tiny, fleeting moments. I see it when a student says, "Mrs. Carkci, I wish you could come to my house for the weekend. That would be fun." I see it when a boy writes to me to ask if I will take him to the movies, or when a girl gives me a goofy smile after I've led the class down the hall taking giant, silly steps. I'm proud that a girl believes

it is okay to ask "Why in America do people speak lots of languages, while in Vietnam, they only speak one language?" Or that a boy knows I will encourage him to pursue his question, "Who invented the planets?"

Once or twice, early on, I considered quitting. But no longer. I like helping my 21 students learn about the four regions of Virginia; I enjoy encouraging them to write and to use new paragraphs for new ideas; and I thrive on watching them become mathematical thinkers. Just the other day a student told me, out of the blue, that he'd noticed how the desks in our classroom were like intersecting lines. It was our geometry unit made real.

I can't imagine what it will be like in two years, when I have figured out a good response to tattling and when I have prepared a classroom set of spelling games. I don't love teaching yet, but I am beginning to catch glimpses of what it will be like when I do.

SOURCE: Copyright 1998, Mathina Carkci, published in *The Washington Post* Company, Sunday, November 8, 1998, C3.

REFLECTION: What insights and clues suggest that Mathina will succeed as a teacher? Do you share any of her attributes? Which teaching skills might you need to further refine?

districts, sometimes in cooperation with local teacher associations, identify their strongest teachers to evaluate and assist others, an approach that recognizes the movement toward greater teacher professionalism and autonomy.

What do observers look for during classroom observations of beginning teachers? It is wise for beginning teachers to ask a mentor or colleague about which skills and qualities are particularly valued in these observations. Some teachers find it useful (if a bit disconcerting) to arrange to be videotaped, so they can pinpoint strategies to improve their instruction. An evaluation framework, used by the Toledo Public Schools, offers insight into the typical skills and attributes considered worth evaluating. (See Figure 14.2.)

Observations, whether official or informal, are usually followed by a conference in which the mentor or supervisor shares the high points and "not-as-high-as-we-would-like" points of your teaching. Take notes and carefully consider these comments. You may find the comments to be useful, even insightful, offering you wise counsel on how to improve. Your attitude and openness in these conferences indicates your willingness to analyze your teaching and refine your teaching skills.

Professional Development Programs

School systems sponsor an amazing variety of professional training options, for new and veteran teachers, both during the summer and throughout the school year.

Figure 14.2
Intern assessment form.

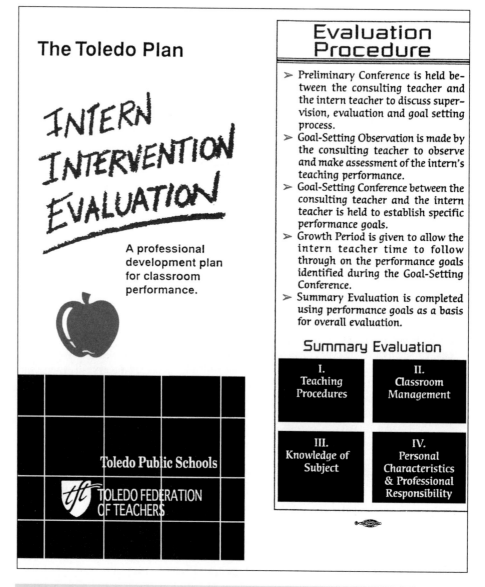

REFLECTION: The four evaluation areas on this form (I. Teaching Procedures, II. Classroom Management, III. Knowledge of Subject, IV. Personal Characteristics and Professional Responsibility) have been discussed in this text. As you glance over the form, which skills do you see as your strengths? Which ones need more study and practice? What specific steps in your teacher education program will prepare you to successfully pass this evaluation?

Through these programs, teachers might satisfy state requirements for renewal of teacher licensure, work toward an endorsement or a license in a second teaching field, attend a summer institute to master new skills, obtain an advanced degree, or earn a higher salary.

Most teacher pay schedules are connected to professional development. Sometimes salaries are linked to the number of hours invested in courses and training programs, so that a teacher who takes thirty graduate credits at a college or thirty

TEACHER SUMMARY EVALUATION REPORT

Name _____

College _____

School _____ Date _____

Grade or   Period of   Period of   Period of
Subject _____ Sept.-Dec. ☐   Jan.-March ☐   Apr.-Dec. ☐

Certification _____

Number of Observations and Time _____ Conference Time _____

Intern semester completed _____

Check on March and Dec Report	Check on March Report Only	Contract Status
☐ Outstanding	☐ Recommended for first one-year contract	☐ First year contract
☐ Satisfactory	☐ Recommended for a second one-year contract	☐ Second year contract
☐ Unsatisfactory		☐ Four-year contract
☐ Written comment only	☐ Recommended for initial four-year contract	☐ One-year contract
☐ Irregular term		☐ Continuing contract
☐ Recommended for 2nd semester intern program	☐ Recommended for third one-year contract	☐ Long-term substitute (60 or more days)
	☐ Not recommended for reappointment	

* OUTSTANDING: Performance shows exceptional professional qualities and growth.
  SATISFACTORY: Performance at expected and desired professional qualities and growth.
* UNSATISFACTORY: Performance shows serious weaknesses or deficiencies.
* For more complete definition refer to page 10 in the Toledo Plan.
* Unsatisfactory and/or outstandings must have a written supportive statement.

	Out-standing	Satis-factory	Unsatis-factory
I. TEACHING PROCEDURES			
A. Skill in planning			
B. Skill in assessment and evaluation			
C. Skill in making assignments			
D. Skill in developing good work-study habits			
E. Resourceful use of instructional material			
F. Skill in using motivating techniques			
G. Skill in questioning techniques			
H. Ability to recognize and provide for individual differences			
I. Oral and written communication skills			
J. Speech, articulation and voice quality			
II. CLASSROOM MANAGEMENT			
A. Effective classroom facilitation and control			
B. Effective interaction with pupils			
C. Efficient classroom routine			
D. Instructional leadership			
E. Is reasonable, fair and impartial in dealing with students			
III. KNOWLEDGE OF SUBJECT–ACADEMIC PREPARATION			
IV. PERSONAL CHARACTERISTICS AND PROFESSIONAL RESPONSIBILITY			
A. Shows a genuine interest in teaching			
B. Personal appearance			
C. Skill in adapting to change			
D. Adheres to accepted policies and procedures of Toledo Public Schools			
E. Accepts responsibility both inside and outside the classroom			
F. Has a cooperative approach toward parents and school personnel			
G. Is punctual and regular in attendance			

Evaluator's Signature _____   Teacher's Signature _____   Principal's Signature _____
(when required)   (when required)

Evaluator's Position _____

                    Date of Conference _____

DIRECTIONS

1. Rate all categories, bold face and subcategories.
2. Attach all supporting documents that have been signed or initialed.

Figure 14.2
(concluded)

TEACHING TIP
The Toledo Plan won a 2001 Innovations in American Government Award from Harvard's Kennedy School of Government and the Council for Excellence in Government. Highly regarded veteran teachers work first with new or struggling teachers and then make the recommendation as to who should stay or leave the field. This unique collaboration between management and the teacher's union is paying off for the students in higher achievement. www.innovations.harvard.edu.

training hours offered by a school district would get a certain salary raise. In other districts, salary increases are tied to evaluations of teacher performance.

School districts vary greatly in their approaches to professional training. Sometimes districts identify a topic (e.g., student portfolio development or emotional intelligence), invite in one or more speakers to make a presentation on that topic, and require the whole faculty to participate. These professional development efforts are scheduled before, during, and at the end of the academic year. Teachers call them **in-service** days, while students are more likely to consider them vacation days. Many have criticized these one-time programs as "dog and pony" shows, charging that brief presentations given to a large group of educators lack long-term impact.

Other staff development strategies require more time and offer greater focus on a specific subject or skill area. Examples of this more in-depth approach include meetings and workshops over the course of a year to improve the science program and weekly sessions on relevant software. Recent research has underscored the value of teacher-designed programs, closely tied to practical classroom skills. Educational reformers suggest that the best **professional development** programs

OVERHEAD 157
Quality Staff Development

- Connect directly to the teacher's work with students
- Link subject content with teaching skills
- Use a problem-solving approach
- Reflect research findings
- Are sustained and supported over time[8]

How can professional development programs incorporate these characteristics? One way is to ask teachers to prepare portfolios for board certification or merit review. Portfolio construction encourages teachers to develop insight and reflection about their instruction by creating tangible examples of their competence. Hopefully, over time, these examples will document their progress and development. Some school districts create a "teaching academy" that offers courses directly linked to particular teacher needs. Over the period of a semester, summer, or year, teachers might enroll in these courses to improve their questioning skills, create more equitable classroom participation, establish effective management strategies, or implement a new curriculum. Many programs tie course assignments to daily instructional activities, providing a useful link between professional development and real-world application.

CRITICAL THINKING
QUESTION
The most significant action research projects are of deep interest to the teacher-researcher. Ask students to project compelling educational issues that might *keep them awake at night.*

Collaborative action research (CAR) also connects daily teaching responsibilities with professional growth, but in this case through the use of research. Typically, a group of teachers identifies a genuine problem in the school or classes, designs ways to address the problem, and then evaluates their success. If the teachers are concerned about the poor performance of girls in high school science courses, for example, they might decide to experiment with new methods to improve that performance. One teacher might try cooperative learning strategies in her science class, while a second teacher develops techniques to involve parents in their daughters' science work. A third teacher might initiate a new science curriculum designed to motivate female students. Each of these approaches would be evaluated and the most effective selected for use by all teachers. CAR encourages thoughtful, objective analysis of real teacher concerns.

Professional development takes many forms: graduate degree programs, collaborative action research projects, and teaching academies or in-service days. A quick glance at Figure 14.3 should convince you of the wide range of professional development programs. These descriptions are adapted from *Education Week,* a weekly news-

Figure 14.3

These announcements provide a taste of the continuous learning opportunities available to educators.

Professional Development
Once a Teacher, Always a Learner

What Works in Schools—Increasing Student Achievement Through Research-Based Practices, Alexandria, VA

The Role of the Arts in the Transformation of School Culture, Cambridge, MA

Learning & the Brain: Using Brain Research as the Pathway to Student Memory, Motivation, and Achievement, Cambridge, MA

No Teacher Left Behind: Technology Across the Curriculum, Smithtown, NY

Making Algebra Child's Play, Buffalo, NY

Hands-on Science workshop by the American Association for the Advancement of Science, K–6, Washington, DC

Teacher Training Sessions: National Foundation for Teaching Entrepreneurship, San Francisco, CA

Annual Conference for Year-Round Education, Waikiki, HI

Educational Theatre Association: Lighting for Musicals, Orlando, FL;

Disciplined-Based Theatre Education, Austin, TX

Teachers' Symposium, American Montessori Society, Albuquerque, NM

Urban Education: Atlanta, GA

Learning Disabilities: Attention Deficit/Hyperactivity Disorder teachers grades 1–6, NYC

Six Traits, Methods of Assessing Student Writing, 2-day immersion, McCook, NE

Rap, Rhythm, and Rhyme, Transforming Teaching, KIPP Academy, Bronx, NY

Reaching all Students: Assessment in a Standards-Based Environment, Worcester, MA

Shape the Future of Technological Literacy by Opening Communication Lines Between Educators and Engineers, by the Institute of Electrical and Electronic Engineers, Baltimore, MD

The Nuts and Bolts of Operating a Local Teacher Organization by the National Association of Catholic School Teachers, Philadelphia, PA

Character Education Training and Information Conference, Baltimore, MD

Success, Standards, and Struggling Secondary Students: K–12 educators who work with at-risk youth, Renton, WA

National 1 Day Conference for Substitute Teachers, Petersburg, VA

Making Sense of Looping: Non-Graded Primary and Multi-age Classrooms, Cleveland, OH

Raising Standards in Rural Education, Fort Collins, CO

International Conference on Computers in Education, Beijing, China

Integrating the Curriculum with Multiple Intelligences: The Balancing Act, Bloomington, IN

Council of School Attorneys' Advocacy Seminar and School Law Retreat, San Antonio, TX

SOURCE: Adapted from *Education Week on the Web;* and *Teacher Magazine,* 2001, 2003.

REFLECTION: Which of these opportunities do you find most interesting? Why? (You might need to consider numerous factors from geography to finances.)

paper and Internet publication that covers national education events, so they reflect realistic opportunities available to teachers.

Personalizing Schools

From a new teacher's perspective, what were once familiar school surroundings soon become strange. Teachers and students see school very differently. As a teacher, you will likely be shocked by the endless stream of paperwork that engulfs you, and you will struggle to learn the names of the students in your classes, as many as 150 students or more at the secondary level. You will work even harder getting to know the people behind the names. Typically, you will have only three to five scheduled hours a week to prepare your lessons or coordinate with your colleagues. You will find little time to meet with individual students, much less their parents. Much of your professional day will be spent trying to manage students in a world of adult isolation.[9] This school organization is at least a century old, and new teachers, as well as experienced ones, often find it both dehumanizing and inadequate.

It is not surprising, therefore, that educators are reconceptualizing schools in order to make them more responsive to the intellectual and emotional needs of both teachers and students. As you contemplate where you want to begin your teaching career, you may want to consider how school organization will affect your life in the classroom.

One major school reorganization effort is intended to nurture learning communities, an effort to create a more intimate and goal-oriented environment. When **learning communities** are established, students and teachers get to know each other both personally and intellectually as they develop shared academic goals and values. Reducing class size and lengthening school periods are two of several organizational changes that can reduce student alienation and build learning communities.

In other nations, teachers assume a greater number of responsibilities; as a result, they work more intensively with each student. In Japan, Germany, Switzerland, and Sweden, for example, teachers serve as counselors as well as instructors and have a greater range of interactions with their students. To meet their expanded responsibilities, teachers are given additional time to confer with their colleagues and plan their lessons. There are fewer support staff and administrators in these countries, and greater emphasis is placed on the teacher-student connection. While teachers constitute 60 to 80 percent of the school staff in European and Asian countries, they represent only 43 percent of the education staff in the United States. In fact, in the United States, the number of administrators and nonteaching staff members has more than doubled over the past three decades. Reformers believe student performance will not improve unless we reverse this trend.[10] (See Figure 14.4 for an international comparison of staffing patterns.)

Finding That First Teaching Position

The U.S. Department of Education projects that two million teachers will be needed over the next decade.[11] (See Figure 14.5 for the projected change in regional K–12 enrollments over the next few years.) With teachers in short supply, and many veteran teachers retiring, new teachers are in the driver's seat—sort of. If you are licensed or have an endorsement in certain fields, such as special education, bilingual education, chemistry, math, and physics, you are indeed in the driver's seat. You may find yourself courted by many school districts. (Isn't that nice!) Several districts now recruit teachers from abroad for these difficult-to-fill positions. As one Houston recruiter

Figure 14.4
International comparisons of teacher staffing patterns.

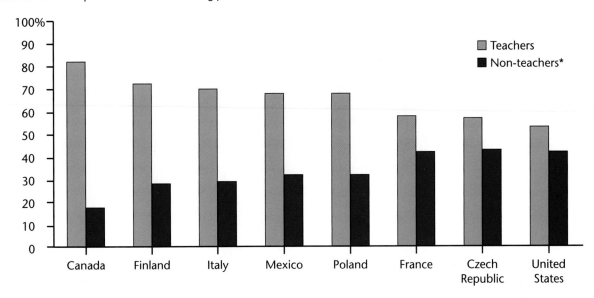

*Non-teachers include administrators, professional support, and maintenance.

SOURCE: Organization for Economic Cooperation Development (OECD), *Education at a Glance,* 2003. Teaching Staff and Non-Teaching Staff Employment in Public and Private Institutions.

REFLECTION: Why do you believe that U.S. schools are staffed so differently from other nations? Do you have a suggestion for an ideal or preferred teacher-staff ratio? In your years of schooling, have you been aware of the non-instructional staff and how they have contributed to your education? Explain.

explained, "We saw more physics teachers in one week in Moscow than we see here in two or three years."[12] Also, if you want to teach in an urban or rural school district, you will most likely have an easy time finding a position.

But the teacher shortage is no guarantee that you will find a teaching position anywhere you want. Districts with high salary schedules and positive teacher morale, often located in popular locations with education-friendly communities, have little need to lure candidates. Since candidates flock to these districts, you will have a tougher time competing for one of these positions. And something else to keep in mind is that while many new teachers are fresh out of college, others are more mature and experienced workers. Termed "career switchers," these new recruits have left other occupations to become teachers, bringing years of skills and experiences to the classroom. They are changing our image of "new" teachers.[13] You can research the ever-changing market for teaching positions online, at websites such as Education Job Openings (www.nationjob.com/education) and Recruiting New Teachers (www.rnt.org).

When pondering where to apply for your first teaching position, the community and your colleagues are just some factors to consider. You may want to make a list of other issues that matter to you:

What subject or grade level do I prefer? What kind of community and students do I want to serve? What part of the country appeals to me? Is there a particular school organization I like? What educational philosophy and school culture am I most comfortable with? How

OVERHEADS 159–160
Where the Students Are by State

Where the Students Are by Region

GLOBAL VIEW
Teaching exchanges go in many international directions. Provide a panel of speakers who have taught outside the United States. (The American Schools, Department of Defense Schools and Peace Corps volunteer teachers would offer diverse perspectives.)

Figure 14.5
Where the students are. As you consider where to teach, you may want to know where enrollments are likely to increase.

SOURCE: U.S. Department of Education, National Center for Education Statistics 2003, Common Core of Data surveys; and State Public Elementary and Secondary Enrollment Model. Figure 7.

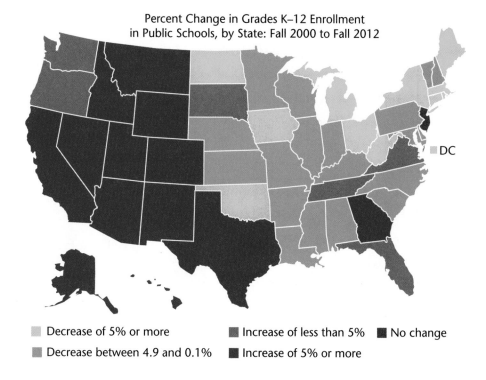

Percent Change in Grades K–12 Enrollment in Public Schools, by State: Fall 2000 to Fall 2012

■ Decrease of 5% or more   ■ Increase of less than 5%   ■ No change
■ Decrease between 4.9 and 0.1%   ■ Increase of 5% or more

SOURCE: U.S. Department of Education, National Center for Education Statistics 2003, Common Core of Data surveys; and State Public Elementary and Secondary Enrollment Model. Figure 8.

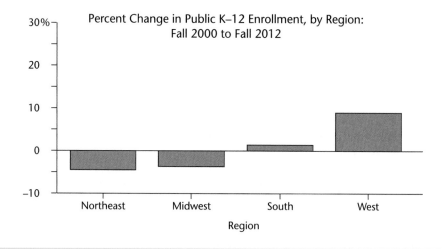

Percent Change in Public K–12 Enrollment, by Region: Fall 2000 to Fall 2012

RELATED READING
Crossing Over to Canaan: The Journey of New Teachers in Diverse Classrooms by Gloria Ladson-Billings (2001).

RAP 4.10
Showtime: Go on an Information Interview, p. 572

REFLECTION: Do national trends like these influence your career decisions? Why or why not?

important to me are incentives for superior teaching? What salary and benefits am I seeking? Am I more interested in a private or public school, or perhaps a charter or magnet school? Am I flexible and open to different options or focused in my preferences?

Many of the activities in this book, including the *You Be the Judge* in the first chapter, the inventory of your educational philosophy in Chapter 9, and the *RAPs*, will help you answer these questions. Once you sort out your priorities and identify the schools that are right for you, the next task is to get that first job.

Education World asked second-year teachers to reflect on their first year in the classroom, their successes and failures, and offer advice for new teachers:

- *Take charge.* Have a clear management plan, with well-defined rewards and consequences. Explain it to the students, send it home to the parents, and ask for signatures on the plan.
- *Keep students busy and engaged.* Have a number of potential class activities available. Bored kids get into trouble; busy kids stay out of trouble.
- *Get peer support.* If you are not assigned an official mentor, find an unofficial one.
- *Get parental support.* From extra supplies to celebration plans, parents are a hidden teacher resource, but only if they are pulled into class activities.
- *Organize yourself.* Develop a system that will keep you organized. There is a lot going on in teaching, grading, and monitoring dozens of children for hours each day.

- *Organize your students.* Teach students how to organize their homework, notebooks, etc.
- *Write and reflect.* Keep a journal to help you reflect on your first year, and become a stronger teacher your second year.
- *Have fun.* Teaching is not only stressful; it is joyful. Get into it and have fun!

SOURCE: *Education World* (www.educationworld.com/help/about.shtml).

REFLECTION: Compare this advice with the more formal areas of teacher effectiveness cited in the research and by the National Board for Professional Teacher Standards. What are the similarities and differences?

Résumés, Portfolios, and Interviews

The most crucial documents in your job search may well be your résumé and your portfolio. A résumé presents a concise description of your strengths and competencies, while a portfolio offers a more comprehensive profile, which might include videotapes of your teaching; sample lesson plans; journals; supervisor's observations; letters from parents, students, and administrators; and examples of student work. The *RAPs* in this text have put you on the road to creating your own portfolio.

If the résumé and portfolio do their job, you will be invited for an interview. Interviews give employers the chance to see if someone who looks good on paper also looks promising in real life. Some portfolio superstars become interview "also-rans." Conversely, some candidates who bring mediocre credentials emerge from an interview with a job offer. Knowing how to diagnose and respond to the interviewer's needs makes the difference. Since résumés, portfolios, and interviews are important steps on your career road, we have pulled together some pointers for you to consider in the next chapter, "Question and Answer Guide to Entering the Teaching Profession."

 ## Teacher Recognition

Project yourself into the future. You have worked hard in your school, and you are widely acclaimed as a terrific teacher (congratulations!). After some wonderful years in the classroom, you begin to think about what lies ahead. Having parents, students, and colleagues sing your praises is wonderful, but is there more than that? How are dedicated and excellent teachers recognized and rewarded? Without formal and meaningful recognition, frustration may well follow, a sentiment captured in all-too-typical teacher comments, such as the following:

CLASS ACTIVITY: SIMULATED INTERVIEWS
IM, Activity 14:3

INTERACTIVE ACTIVITY
Your Portfolio. Visit the Online Portfolio section of the Online Learning Center to learn more about portfolios, and for guidance and resources to create your own portfolio.

TEACHING TIP
Initially, what else would students want to know before they *sign on* to a new teaching position? Now, what creative (legal and productive!) strategies can they propose that will yield that valuable information?

Interview procedures vary by school and district—a meeting with the principal, a formal review by a panel of administrators, faculty and school parents, a roundtable discussion with potential colleagues—any or all could await you. How might you prepare for each of these situations? Would you be more comfortable in one rather than another setting? Why?

How would I describe my teaching? Well, let me put it this way—I work hard. Free time is a thing of the past. My students are really important to me, and I'm willing to go the extra mile to give them feedback, organize field trips and projects, meet with them or their parents, and give them a stimulating classroom. In fact, most Saturdays I'm working on grades or new projects. And I think it pays off—my kids are blossoming! That's a great feeling. But sometimes I wonder if it's all worth it. Is anyone ever going to notice my hard work? Brad down the hall just comes in and does his job without a second thought, and his paycheck looks just like mine. It doesn't seem fair. Teachers who deserve it should be able to earn something more—more money, more respect.

FOCUS QUESTION 3
How do school districts, states, and the National Board for Professional Teaching Standards recognize and reward teachers?

This view is held by thousands of teachers struggling for professional recognition. Working hard in a demanding profession, teachers often do not feel valued or appreciated, and many leave the field each year as a result.

While not a comprehensive solution to the problem, North Carolina has made a grand gesture in response to teacher burnout. The state opened a mountain lodge dedicated to pampering teachers. Over the course of a school year, nearly two thousand teachers, about 2 percent of the state's teachers, are invited to spend five days in the combination spa and mini-university. Sumptuous meals, outdoor walks, and quiet contemplation recharge a teacher's batteries, and are a way of saying thanks for their efforts. Although in-service courses are a part of the week's schedule, they are kept to a minimum and the focus is on relaxation. As one teacher remarked, "This is the closest teachers get to being treated like the corporate world."[14] Perhaps the future will bring more teacher spas, but for now, we will focus on three more common approaches to teacher recognition: board certification, merit pay, and career ladders.

The **National Board for Professional Teaching Standards (NBPTS)** is establishing higher standards for teaching and grants special certification to superior teachers. **Merit pay** is a plan to give additional financial compensation to teachers

OVERHEAD 161
Approaches to Teacher Recognition

who demonstrate excellence, though different plans define excellence differently. **Career ladders** allow teachers to take on additional responsibilities along with their teaching as a way of advancing in the field. Each of these solutions has drawbacks as well as advantages. Nevertheless, all three influence how teachers are recognized.

The National Board for Professional Teaching Standards

In 1987, the National Board for Professional Teaching Standards (NBPTS) was formed to promote teaching excellence through recognition of superior teachers. The NBPTS awards **board certification** to experienced teachers based on superior performance. It is available to all licensed teachers who hold a baccalaureate degree and have taught (in either public or private school) for a minimum of three years. In a few years, you may want to join the growing number of teachers participating in this effort. In January 1995, eighty-six National Board Certified Teachers were recognized; by 2000, almost ten thousand teachers had achieved board status. When the NBPTS was launched, former North Carolina governor James Hunt, Jr., proclaimed,

> For once in this country, we are working out standards for measuring excellence rather than minimum competency. The certification process has the potential to transform the current educational system, leverage current investment in teaching, and build a national consensus for increased support of schools.[15]

Part of the effort to assess, train, and reward qualified teachers involves direct observation of classroom teaching performance.

Deciding who will be board certified is the task of the sixty-three members of the independent, nonpartisan NBPTS. Most board members are classroom teachers, but others are school administrators, state political leaders, university officials, representatives from professional organizations, and business and community leaders.[16] Imagine yourself as a newly appointed board member responsible for determining what skills and behaviors identify truly excellent teachers, teachers who will be known as board certified. How would you begin? The board began by identifying five criteria: mastery of subject area, commitment to students, ability to effectively manage a classroom, continuous analysis of teaching performance, and a commitment to learning and self-improvement (see Chapter 3, "Teacher Effectiveness," for additional information about these five criteria).[17]

To demonstrate expertise to the NBPTS, teachers must complete a series of performance-based assessments, including written exercises that reflect mastery of their subject and understanding of the most effective teaching methods. Board candidates must also submit student work samples, videotapes of their teaching, and participate in simulations and interviews held at special assessment centers.[18]

Perhaps the biggest question is: What does board certification mean? Clearly, being recognized as exceptional is psychologically rewarding. Considering that there are literally millions of teachers in the United States, to be among a selected few is a major boost. Board certification has become a catalyst for rewarding superior teachers with salary increases and new job responsibilities. Several hundred local school districts and forty states provide some incentive for teachers who are board certified. However, such recognition is not universal. When funds are in short supply or a school district's organizational structure is inflexible, board-certified teachers may receive few tangible rewards or new responsibilities, despite their excellence. As you enter the teaching profession, you will want to stay abreast of the activities concerning the national board and determine if you want to work toward board certification. (For a current update of NBPTS activities, visit www.nbpts.org.)

Merit Pay

Merit pay plans attempt to make teaching more accountable, as well as more financially rewarding, by linking teacher performance and teacher salary. It sounds like a pretty good idea, so little surprise that the National Science Board, the National Association of Secondary School Principals, the National Association of Elementary School Principals, the American Association of School Administrators, and the National Commission on Excellence in Education all support merit pay. But on closer inspection, merit pay may not be such a wonderful idea.[19] Why would some oppose merit? Let's listen in on a faculty meeting to see what merit pay really involves for teachers.

Dr. Moore faced her staff and began, "You know the school board gave our district the go-ahead to develop a merit pay proposal. There are several different approaches. Just one example: Rochester, New York, awards merit pay for teachers who receive a second teaching license in reading; work in its professional development academy; accept teaching assignments in more challenging, low-achieving schools; or receive national board certification. To help us understand our options, I'd like to outline some of the different plans and then open the floor for your reactions." You watch intently as she clicks through a PowerPoint presentation to illustrate the different plans. "Basically, there are four different types of merit pay:

"*Merit pay based on student performance.* This rewards teachers whose students make gains on standardized tests. It implies that a good teacher will help students achieve in the content areas.

"*Merit pay based on teacher performance.* Under this program, the district would develop criteria to measure your teaching effectiveness, and you would receive raises based on evaluations by outside observers.

"*Merit pay based on individualized productivity plans.* Do you remember the personal goals each of you wrote for this school year? This plan would ask you to write more detailed goals for what you would like to accomplish this year. Once they are approved, you would receive financial bonuses based on how much you accomplish.

"*Merit pay based on the teaching assignment.* With this plan, you could receive compensation according to how difficult or how much in demand your teaching position is. Our math, science, and special education teachers would probably receive the greatest bonuses if we were to adopt this plan."

IN THE NEWS

Merit Pay

Teachers in Robbinsdale, Minnesota, have an important project due every five years. That's when they assemble their portfolios documenting their teaching skills. Teachers who do well on their portfolio assignments will be paid an additional $15,000 each year for five years. That amounts to $75,000 above their regular salary. The performance pay replaces automatic salary increments.

SOURCE: *Education Week on the Web,* February 1998.

 What's new in education? Click on *News Feeds.*

You think this sounds very interesting. There seem to be mixed feelings among the teachers, however. You overhear a number of different opinions:

"This sounds great! I can finally get that bonus I deserve for all my extra hours."

"I wonder how this can work. After all, does the teacher with all the smart kids really deserve a raise if they do well on tests?"

"I don't think I'd feel comfortable if other people found out I was getting merit pay. Teaching is supposed to mean working as a team, not competing for bonuses."

"Only the people who are in good with the supervisors will get merit pay. How can that be fair?"

"I think we need some sort of merit pay system in teaching that will give all of us something to work for."

TEACHING TIP
Staying with the characters at Dr. Moore's staff meeting, have students generate additional opinions regarding merit pay. What beliefs underlie the various teacher convictions?

Merit pay leads to strained relationships among teachers, serious questions as to how success is measured, fear of "playing politics," and a sense of manipulation by outside forces. While some teachers are excited about the possibility of a higher salary, others see merit pay as a "bribe." Little wonder that educational historians David Tyack and Larry Cuban write that "The history of merit performance-based salary plans has been a merry-go-round" as districts initially embrace such plans, only to drop them after a brief trial. But in spite of these failures, school officials keep "proposing merit pay again and again."[20]

Career Ladder Programs

Career ladder programs offer another teacher recognition strategy. The career ladder is designed to create different levels for teachers by creating a "ladder" that one can climb to receive increased pay through increased work responsibility and status.[21] By the beginning of the 1990s, more than half the states had established a career ladder or an incentive program with state assistance. Some critics argue that career ladders have the same drawbacks as merit pay—a lack of clear standards or appropriate evaluation tools—but others claim that career ladders can be more effective because they are rooted in professionalism. The distinguishing characteristic of the career ladder is the increased responsibility given to the teacher. The Rochester, New York, *Career in Teaching* plan is a good example. Here, an outstanding teacher has the opportunity to become a "master" or "mentor teacher," write curricula, select textbooks, or plan staff development programs while continuing to teach in the classroom.[22] Thus, good teachers are not removed from the classroom, yet they earn increased responsibility and salary.

CRITICAL THINKING QUESTION
This question was not rhetorical. What are additional ways to earn more respect *and* more money for teachers?

All teacher recognition plans share the goal of making the teaching profession more attractive and more rewarding, whether through official certification, financial compensation, or increased professional responsibility. In what other ways might teachers be able to earn more respect or more money? As you enter the teaching profession, you will want to be aware of the kinds of incentives available in different school districts and consider which incentives appeal to you.

FOCUS QUESTION 4
What are the differences between the National Education Association and the American Federation of Teachers?

Educational Associations

In colonial times, teachers typically were meek and quiet public servants. In fact, some of them actually were servants, since they had obtained the money to pay for their passage to America by indenturing themselves. Their pitiful wages were equivalent to those of a farmhand. In order to survive, many teachers were forced to board with a different family each week.[23] (Can you imagine eating dinner with a different student's family every week?) Low salaries were the rule through much of the nation's history. Even by 1874, in Massachusetts, male teachers were paid a monthly salary of $24.51. Women earned less than $8. This lowly status provided one motivation for teachers to organize.

In 1794, the Society of Associated Teachers of New York City became the first teacher association in this country. In 1857, this movement went national when the National Teachers' Association was formed, later to become the **National Education Association (NEA).** Half a century later, in 1916, the **American Federation of Teachers (AFT)** was created as a union of teachers affiliated with the American Federation of Labor. Through **collective bargaining** (that is, all the teachers in a school system bargaining as one group through a chosen representative), through organized actions (including strikes), and through public relations efforts, the NEA and the AFT succeeded in improving both the salaries and the working conditions of teachers, and they continue to influence teachers' professional lives.

In your first few years as a teacher, you will find yourself in a new environment and without the protection of tenure. Teacher associations, such as the NEA and the AFT, can help alleviate that sense of vulnerability by providing you with collegial support, opportunities for professional growth, and the security that one derives from participating in a large and influential group. Today, teaching is one of the most organized occupations in the nation. Nine out of ten teachers belong to either the NEA or AFT. Six out of ten teachers are represented by one or the other in collective bargaining. It is not too early for you to start thinking about which one may best represent you.

Which Educational Association Speaks for You?

You have been a teacher in Mediumtown for all of two weeks, and you know about five faces and three names of other faculty members. You have just learned that your colleagues will be meeting to decide whether Mediumtown teachers should keep their affiliation with the Mediumtown Teachers' Association (a local chapter of the National Education Association), or create a new chapter associated with the American

OVERHEADS 163–164
History of Teacher Associations

Teacher Associations

Often marked by acrimony and bitterness, strikes changed the traditional image of teachers as meek and passive public servants.

"America is on trial," declared Margaret Haley, standing before the National Education Association convention. Poor salaries, overcrowded classrooms, and the lack of teacher voice in school policy and curricular decisions, she argued, all undermine teachers' effectiveness.

Though Haley's charges sound disquietingly current, she was not critiquing today's curricular standards created by nonteachers, or the growing dependence on standardized tests to measure both students and teachers, or even the top-down management style of some current school administrators. In fact, Margaret Haley gave this speech a century ago. In 1904, she became the first woman and the first teacher to speak from the floor of an NEA convention. Her speech, "Why Teachers Should Organize," condemned as undemocratic the practice of treating a teacher as an "automaton, a mere factory hand whose duty it is to carry out mechanically and unquestioningly the ideas and orders of those clothed with the authority."[1]

Haley was born in 1851 in Joliet, Illinois, to Irish immigrant parents who valued education and fairness. Haley learned to read from her mother, who used the Bible and a pictorial history of Ireland to educate her daughter. Her father was an active member of local stone quarry and construction unions, who shared accounts of heated union rallies with young Margaret as bedtime stories. Her father also championed the rights and talents of women, and taught Margaret about suffragette Susan B. Anthony and America's first woman physician, Elizabeth Blackwell. Such lessons planted the seeds for Margaret Haley's later efforts to empower women teachers.

At Cook County Normal School, Haley eagerly studied the progressive ideas set forth by John Dewey, embracing the school as a democratic training ground for students and teachers. But when she entered the classroom in Chicago's poor stockyard district, she encountered a vastly different reality. The curriculum she used was uninspiring and imposed by educational bureaucrats, and she was expected to teach it to fifty or sixty sixth graders. In the warm months, swarms of bugs visited her classroom, and in the winter, Haley shivered along with her students. Working in such deplorable conditions, she increasingly understood that teachers needed to fight the factory mentality of schools.

After twenty years of teaching in Chicago schools, Haley left the classroom to devote herself full-time to educational reform efforts through unions. As vice president and business agent for the Chicago Teachers' Federation (CTF), Haley transformed the fledgling organization into a national voice fighting for, "the right for the teacher to call her soul her own."[2]

Haley's first action for the CTF was to force the Illinois Supreme Court to wrest unpaid taxes from five public utility companies—money that was earmarked for teachers' salaries. For Haley, now known as the "Lady Labor Slugger," the victory was one for both education and democracy: Teachers were given a raise and Chicago businesses were forced to uphold their civic responsibility.

Unlike other teacher associations of the time, Haley deliberately limited the CTF to elementary school teachers. Women consequently dominated the organization, challenging the prevailing wisdom that women should remain quiet, confined to their classrooms. Through the CTF, teachers could become social activists. Under Haley's leadership, Chicago teachers won a tenure law, a pension plan, and were given power over curriculum and discipline. Haley also engineered a successful campaign to affiliate her union with the Chicago Federation of Labor. The status of teachers, in Haley's mind, was little more than that of a white-collar proletariat, strikingly similar to blue-collar manual workers. Although the CTF's alliance with labor shocked many teachers, the union ultimately helped the CTF gain political power. Though women could not yet vote, they worked with male labor workers to support a range of progressive issues: child labor laws, women's suffrage, and equal wages for men and women.

A century ago, Margaret Haley called for teachers "to save the schools for democracy and to save democracy in the schools."[3] Her tireless efforts and astute political skills helped create more humane schools for both teachers and students. Haley died in 1939.

[1] Nancy Hoffman, *Woman's "True" Profession: Voices from the History of Teaching* (Old Westbury, NY: The Feminist Press, 1981), p. 291. [2] David Neiman (Producer), *Only a Teacher*, Part 2: *Those Who Can . . . Teach* (Princeton: Films for the Humanities and Sciences, 2000). [3] Ibid.

REFLECTION: Had you heard of Margaret Haley before reading this profile? If not, you are not alone. Why do we know so few of education's heroes, teachers whose efforts have improved the lives of teachers?

www.mhhe.com/ sadker   To learn more about Margaret Haley, click on *Profiles in Education.*

Federation of Teachers. You are not wild about attending another meeting, but it would be a chance to meet some of your new colleagues and a way to determine which organization speaks for you (and since the text is drawing to a close, this may be the last meeting you can eavesdrop on). So you decide to go.

At the meeting, NEA and AFT brochures are distributed, and speakers begin making their pitch. You flip through a brochure that gives you a bit of the NEA's long history. When the forty-three founders gathered in the mid-nineteenth century, they intended to form a broad organization that would encompass many different educational interests and groups. But school administrators and college professors dominated the NEA, and teachers had a limited role. During the 1960s and 1970s, the NEA became a stronger advocate of teachers' rights, and by the 1980s and 1990s, the association was also advocating various educational reforms.

The brochure describes the NEA as the largest professional and employee organization in the nation. It enrolls 2.6 million members, including elementary and secondary teachers, higher-education faculty, retired educators, and educational support personnel. It also offers many services, from journals such as *NEA Today* to training on issues like women's leadership, child abuse protections, technology and academic freedom, to legal services, if a teacher needs to be represented in court. The NEA members work to elect pro-education candidates and to promote legislation beneficial to teachers and students. (See www.nea.org.)

You are so impressed with the accomplishments and promise of the NEA and the local MEA that you're about ready to pay your membership dues. Just then, a teacher who has been sitting quietly next to you leans over and says, "I belong to the MFT, the Mediumtown Federation of Teachers. We're the local affiliate of the American Federation of Teachers. Don't sign anything until you've heard our side." He introduces himself with "just call me Al" and takes the floor.

"When John Dewey became our first member back in 1916, he recognized that teachers need their own organization. Teachers are the backbone of the educational system, and we must speak for ourselves. That is why the AFT will continue to be exclusively of teachers, by teachers, and for teachers.

"It was the AFT that backed school desegregation years before the 1954 Supreme Court decision that established the principle that separate is not equal. We ran freedom schools for Southern black students, and we have a strong record on academic freedom and civil rights.

"It was the AFT that demanded and fought for the teacher's right to bargain collectively. It was the AFT leaders who went to jail to show the nation their determination that teachers would no longer stand for second-class status. It was the AFT that won New York City teachers their pay increases and other benefits.

"And, as part of the great labor movement, the AFL-CIO, the AFT continues to show the nation that through the power of the union the voice of America's teachers will be heard."

You take a look at the AFT brochure. Even with only a million members, the AFT has significant influence. In 1961, the AFT strike in New York City gave it a national spotlight, and AFT membership began to grow in labor-oriented urban areas. Strikes increased, but so did salaries. In Washington, DC, Boston, Cleveland, Chicago, and other cities, teachers decided to join the AFT. Militancy brought the AFT both members and victories, usually confined in urban centers. The AFT's image as a streetwise, scrappy union has shifted since the 1970s. In fact, through the ideas and activities of

Milestones in the birth and growth of teacher associations.

1794	The Society of Associated Teachers of New York City becomes the country's first teacher association.
1840–1861	Thirty state teacher associations form.
1857	The first National Teachers' Association is formed. In the late 1870s, this group merges with the National Association of School Superintendents and the American Normal School Association to become the National Education Association (NEA).
1902	A group of teachers from San Antonio, Texas, becomes the first to join a labor union, the American Federation of Labor (AFL).
1916	The American Federation of Teachers (AFT) is formed.
1920s	The AFT has more than 10,000 members.
1940s	More than 200,000 teachers belong to the NEA (up from about 7,000 in 1910). More than 30,000 teachers belong to the AFT.
1940s–1950s	More than 100 strike threats are carried out.
1960s–1970s	The AFT and then the NEA take up militant tactics, including even more frequent strikes.
1980s–1990s	Teacher organizations are involved in political action and show growing concern for increased professionalism.
1998	NEA members reject AFT merger plan. Talks for a future merger continue.

REFLECTION: Predict the future of teacher organizations and speculate when and what the next two or three entries might be.

---

its long-time president, Albert Shanker, the AFT took a leadership role in education reform. Shanker supported national exams for students as well as national standards for teachers and was a pioneer in the creation of charter schools. The AFT also supports induction programs that enable new teachers to work with master teachers and the active recruitment of people of color into the teaching profession.[24] The AFT provides services similar to the NEA, although on a smaller scale. (See www.aft.org.)

As you weigh the relative merits of the two organizations, you overhear some teachers muttering that they don't care to join either group and that in their opinion the NEA and AFT put the salaries of teachers above the needs of children. Listening more closely, you hear these teachers claim that teacher associations have pitted administrators against teachers, and teachers against the public, creating needless hostility. Even worse, these critics charge, unions too often protect incompetent teachers who should be removed from the classroom.

Still, you are intrigued by the promise of collective action. In fact, you cannot help but speculate about a merger of these two professional organizations, a merger that has in fact been under discussion for several years. A consolidation of the NEA and AFT would form an incredibly powerful union of over three million teachers.[25] Such an organization could wield enormous national leverage, potentially gaining significant benefits for education in general and teachers in particular. And if they merged, you would not have to choose at all! But for right now, you have a decision to make. Does either the NEA or the AFT speak for you?

CRITICAL THINKING QUESTION

An organization's powers may be very different depending upon locale, leadership, and particular history. How can you distinguish NEA and AFT practices for your students? What unique circumstances impact your local districts?

Professional Associations and Resources

In addition to the NEA and the AFT, you will find many resources that can help you in your professional development. Publications such as *Education Week* keep teachers abreast of educational developments. (The online version is available at www. edweek.org.) Journals, professional training, university courses, and professional associations can help you not only in those critical first few years, but throughout your teaching career as you refine your teaching techniques and adapt curricular resources. The Internet is a great source of classroom ideas and practical advice. Teacher-Zone (www.teacher-zone.com), The New Teacher page (www.geocities.com/Athens/Delphi/ 762), and Beginning Teacher's Tool Box (www.inspiringteachers.com), are typical of the online resources now available. And sometimes, just talking to others and learning about techniques for stress reduction can make all the difference in that first job, which is the idea behind Teachers Helping Teachers (www.pacificnet.net/~mandel).

Here are a few organizations that you may find helpful:

- *The Association for Supervision and Curriculum Development* is an international, nonprofit, nonpartisan association of professional educators whose jobs cross all grade levels and subject areas. (www.ascd.org)

- *National Middle School Association* works to improve the educational experiences afforded young adolescents, ages 10–15 years. (www.nmsa.org)

- *National Association for the Education of Young People* pulls together preschools, child care, primary schools, cooperatives, and kindergarten educators and parents in projects to improve the quality and certification of these schools. (www.naeyc.org)

Reg Weaver, NEA president, was a middle school science teacher from Illinois, and a 30-year classroom veteran. He is a leader in opposing vouchers and fighting for the rights of teachers and students. His persistence is summed up in a quotation he sometimes uses in speeches: "Courage doesn't always roar. Sometimes courage is the voice at the end of the day that says, 'I'll try again tomorrow.'"

Sandra Feldman. After three years of elementary school teaching, she became a field representative for the UFT (United Federation of Teachers), the New York chapter of the AFT. Now, as the first woman leader of the AFT since 1930, Feldman has several items on her agenda, including improving urban schools and reducing class size.

- *National Association for Gifted Children* advances the opportunities and school programs for gifted students. (www.nagc.org)
- *The Council for Exceptional Children* is the largest international professional organization dedicated to improving educational outcomes for individuals with exceptionalities, students with disabilities, and the gifted. (www.cec.sped.org)

If you are interested in subject matter specialties, many organizations, journals, and websites can meet your needs. Here is a brief sample:

- *American Alliance for Health, Physical Education, Recreation and Dance* (www.aahperd.org)
- *National Council for Teachers of English* (www.ncte.org)
- *National Council for the Social Studies* (www.ncss.org)
- *National Science Teachers Association* (www.nsta.org)
- *Teachers of Speakers of Other Languages* (www.tesol.org)
- *National Council for the Teachers of Mathematics* (www.nctm.org)

RAP 4.6
Class Comedy Club, 4:5,
p. 567

As a teacher, you will find yourself in a learning community, not only teaching students, but continually improving your own knowledge and skills. We hope that these resources and others in this text will set you on that path of continuous learning and improvement. You may not have decided on whether teaching is right for you and you may still have a question or two left unanswered. That is what the final chapter is all about. In our last chapter, we share some of the frequent questions that students ask us about teaching. But before we get to that last chapter, there is one central (really irksome) question that we want to address now: Are America's schools failing? It is discouraging for teachers to invest their talent and energy only to be told by politicians and journalists that our schools are doing poorly. We would like to offer a platform to another side of the story, presenting a perspective we rarely hear.

American Schools: Better Than We Think?

School bashing is nothing new; it is as American as apple pie. In fact, some educators believe not only that the current wave of criticism is old hat, but that it is terribly misguided, because today's schools are doing as well as they ever have—maybe, just maybe, they are doing better.

FOCUS QUESTION 5
Are America's schools a secret success story, doing better than the press and the public believe?

GLOBAL VIEW
Juku schools are often called *cram schools* and accompanied Japan's phenomenal economic growth after the mid-1960s.

Critics decry the low performance by U.S. students on international tests. But school advocates point out that test results may reflect cultural and curricular differences, not a failing educational system. Consider that Japanese middle school students score significantly higher than U.S. students on algebra tests, but most Japanese students take algebra a year or two earlier than U.S. students do. Moreover, most Japanese children attend private academies, called *Juku* schools, after school and on weekends. By 16 years of age, the typical Japanese student has attended at least two more years of classes than has a U.S. student. Yet because of the greater comparative effectiveness of U.S. colleges in relation to Japanese colleges, many of these differences evaporate on later tests. (Perhaps there are two lessons here: (1) U.S. students should spend more time in school and (2) the Japanese need to improve the quality of their colleges.)

American Schools Have Failed Society Because . . .

INTERNATIONAL TESTS DOCUMENT POOR STUDENT PERFORMANCE

How embarrassing for the students in the richest, most powerful nation in the world to do so miserably on tests. Our students typically trail students in Korea, Japan, and most of Western Europe.

TOO MANY STUDENTS DROP OUT OR ACT OUT

The lack of discipline, decorum and control in America's schools is a sign that basic values are missing, poor management is commonplace, and school violence and dropouts are rampant.

WORKERS LACK BASIC SKILLS

America does not produce enough scientists, engineers, and mathematicians, and our workers lack not only key technical skills, but basic reading and writing competencies as well. American companies are now forced to provide remedial instruction to our ill-prepared workers.

SCHOOLS HAVE BECOME A MONOPOLY

The power of teacher unions and the inertia of the school bureaucracies have robbed schools of initiative and creativity. Competition through vouchers and charter schools is the answer.

American Schools Have Served Society Well Because . . .

INTERNATIONAL TEST SCORES MISS THE POINT

Americans value individuality and creativity, characteristics absent from these tests. Lower scores are due to the high number of American poor taking these tests, a sign of our society's failure, not school failure.

STUDENT SUCCESS IS REAL

Graduation rates are up for the poor, for non-English speakers, and for special education students. And incidences of violence have actually been reduced.

WORKERS ARE AMONG THE BEST IN THE WORLD

Many Americans are unaware of the fact that our colleges produce a higher percentage of engineers and scientists than any other nation in the world, and our workers are among the most educated and skilled in the world. America is an economic superpower because of our worker productivity.

THEY REPRESENT THE DEMOCRATIC IDEAL

Jefferson and Mann were right: The nation's future rests on public schools. Vouchers and privatization take money from already underfunded public schools and hurt free, democratic education.

 YOU BE THE JUDGE

Why do Americans struggle over such a basic question? Do arguments about school effectiveness influence your decision to teach? Do school critics serve a useful purpose by prodding the public to create more effective schools, or are they more likely to mislead the public and discourage teachers?

Student selection also affects test scores. In other countries, students who do not speak the dominant language are routinely excluded. In some nations, only a small percentage of the most talented students are selected or encouraged to continue their education and go on to high school. As one might imagine, a highly selective population does quite well on international tests. In the United States, the full range of students is tested: strong and weak, English-speaking and non-English-speaking students. A larger number of American test-takers are likely to be poor. Comparing all of America's students with another nation's best is an unfair comparison.

CLASS ACTIVITY:
TRACK MEDIA
REPORTING
IM, Activity 14:2

Americans value a comprehensive education, one in which students are involved in a wide array of activities, from theater to sports to community service. The U.S. public typically values spontaneity, social responsibility, and independence in their children, values that are not assessed in international tests. Consider the way a South Korean teacher identifies the students selected for the International Assessment of Education Progress (IAEP).

> The math teacher . . . calls the names of the 13-year-olds in the room who have been selected as part of the IAEP sample. As each name is called, the student stands at attention at his or her desk until the list is complete. Then, to the supportive and encouraging applause of their colleagues, the chosen ones leave to [take the assessment test.][26]

GLOBAL VIEW
The IAEP is administered by the Center for the Assessment of Educational Progress (CAEP), a division of Educational Testing Service (ETS). It is funded through the National Science Foundation (NSF), the U.S. Department of Education's National Center for Education Statistics (NCES) and Carnegie Corporation.

U.S. students taking international exams do not engender cheers from their classmates and do not view such tests as a matter of national honor, as do the South Korean students. Too often, our culture belittles intellectuals and mocks gifted students.

Despite these obstacles, on several key tests the nation's students are doing quite well. For example, by the mid-1990s, American students had achieved the second-highest average score among thirty-one nations on international comparisons of reading. The proportion of students scoring above 650 on the SAT mathematics tests had reached an all-time high. The number of students taking Advanced Placement (AP) tests soared, a sign that far more students are in the race for advanced college standing. Improvements have been documented on the California Achievement Test, the Iowa Test of Basic Skills, and the Metropolitan Achievement Test, tests used across the nation to measure student learning. One of the most encouraging signs has been the performance of students of color, whose scores have risen dramatically. Among 17-year-old African American students, average reading scores on the NAEP tests rose dramatically.[27] Decades ago, many of these students probably would not have even been in school, much less taking tests. In 1940, the overall high school graduation rate in the United States was only 38 percent; by the 2000s, it approached 90 percent. Other indicators reflect that students are not only staying in school longer but also are enrolling in more advanced math and science classes. U.S. schools are teaching more students, students are staying in school for longer periods of time, and children are studying more challenging courses than ever before.

Then why is there a national upheaval about education—why all the furor about our failing schools and why the demands for radical school reform? Educators have advanced a number of possible explanations:[28]

MULTIPLE INTELLIGENCE CONNECTION
Want to end on a high note? Using a traditional children's tune (i.e. *Row, Row, Row, Your Boat*) have students write a quick song that reveals their positive feelings about American schools. Can they sing it in rounds?

- Journalists and politicians have been critiquing schools since the founding of our nation.

- Adults tend to romanticize what schools were like when they attended as children, for they always studied harder and learned more than their children do (and when they went to school, they had to walk through four feet of snow, uphill, in both directions!).

- Americans hold unrealistic expectations. They want schools to conquer all sorts of social and academic ills, from illiteracy to teenage pregnancy, and to accomplish everything from teaching advanced math to preventing AIDS.

- Schools today work with tremendous numbers of poor students, non-English-speaking children, and special education students who just a few years ago would not be attending school as long or, in some cases, would not be attending school at all.

- In *The Manufactured Crisis,* David Berliner and Bruce Biddle put much of the blame for the current criticism on neoconservative policies of the 1990s supporting private schools, business interests, and vouchers. These policies marked the beginning of a major assault on public education, on federal involvement in schools, and on equal education programs targeting minority groups and women.

- Berliner and Biddle also finger the press, which has been all too willing to publish negative stories about schools—stories based on questionable sources. Sloppy, biased reporting has damaged the public's perception of schools.

It is helpful to remember two points. First, criticism can be fruitful. If additional attention and even criticism help shape stronger schools, then the current furor will have at least some positive impact. Second, there are countless students in all parts of the country who work diligently every day and perform with excellence. The United States continues to produce leaders in fields as diverse as medicine and sports, business and entertainment. To a great extent, these success stories are also the stories of talented and dedicated teachers. Although their quiet daily contributions rarely reach the headlines, teachers do make a difference. You represent the next generation of teachers who will, no doubt, weather difficult times and sometimes adverse circumstances to touch the lives of students and to shape a better America.

INTERACTIVE ACTIVITY
Edspeak. Do you know what these education-related terms mean?

SUMMARY

1. **What are the stages of teacher development?**

   Teachers provided with sufficient support can move through a series of stages: survival, consolidation, renewal, and maturity, growing from personal concerns (such as classroom management) to broader educational issues (school strategies that could enhance student learning). Studies underscore that, dollar for dollar, investments in teacher qualifications and training translate into improved student achievement.

2. **What resources do school districts provide for a teacher's first year in the classroom?**

   Mentors, or consulting teachers, provide both personal and professional support, and sometimes evaluate new teachers. Effective professional development links subject content with teaching skills, uses problem solving, and is research-based and supported over time. Collaborative action research investigates real classroom problems in an effort to improve the quality of student learning.

3. **How do school districts, states, and the National Board for Professional Teaching Standards recognize and reward teachers?**

   Established in 1987, the National Board for Professional Teaching Standards (NBPTS) seeks to identify and assess experienced teachers performing at a superior level. Most states and many school districts offer additional incentives for board certification, including salary bonuses and supplementary responsibilities. Merit pay offers teachers more money based on various criteria, including gains in student performance, typically measured by standardized tests; teacher performance, as measured by outside evaluators; individualized plans, in which teachers have a voice in setting their own goals; and the nature of the teaching assignment. Career ladders allow teachers to increase their responsibilities and salary as they advance. Merit pay and career ladders offer additional money for superior performance, but critics charge that these programs are compromised and do not improve education.

CHAPTER REVIEW

Go to the Online Learning Center to take a quiz, practice with key terms, and review concepts from the chapter.

CURRENT NEWS FROM POWERWEB

Go to Chapter 14 on the Online Learning Center to read current articles and to access news feeds about:

- Education Standards
- Teachers' Attitudes
- The Profession of Teaching

4. What are the differences between the National Education Association (NEA) and the American Federation of Teachers (AFT)?

The NEA is the largest professional and employee association in the nation. Formed during the second half of the 1800s, initially it was slow to work for the needs of its members, but by the 1960s and 1970s, the NEA became a strong teacher rights advocate. While significantly smaller, the AFT has historically taken a more militant position, demonstrated by its early support of teacher strikes. Today both the NEA and the AFT offer a range of services, including magazines, journals, and other professional communications; legal assistance; workshops and conferences; assistance in collective bargaining; and political activism. The NEA and AFT continue to explore a possible merger.

5. Are America's schools a secret success story, doing better than the press and the public believe?

The lower performance of American students on international tests may be attributed to curricular and cultural differences, not necessarily to educational deficiencies. Many indicators, from SAT scores to high school graduation rates, reflect an improvement in American schools. According to Berliner and Biddle, school bashing reflects an old tradition of journalists and a popular activity of today's neoconservative politicians. Despite all this, America's schools may be doing far better than we realize.

Go to Chapter 14 on your *Resources for Exploring Education* CD-ROM to access Case Studies, Readings, and Media Observations.

EXTENDED LEARNING

CASE STUDIES

- Diane News: In a school district beginning a gifted and talented program, a teacher must choose four students to recommend for the program from her class, but she has five potential candidates.

- Christie Raymond: A woman in the first month of her first full-time position teaching music in an elementary school loves the work as long as the children are singing, but dislikes the school's emphasis on and her part in disciplining the students.

- Melissa Reid: An enthusiastic young student teacher struggles to gain the respect and improve the behavior of her senior-level composition class and is devastated by one of her student's papers which is full of vindictiveness and hatred toward her.

READINGS

- Emily Calhoun. "Action Research for School Improvement."

- Susan K. Lynn, "The Winding Path: Understanding the Career Cycle of Teachers."

KEY TERMS AND PEOPLE

American Federation of
    Teachers (AFT), 529
board certification, 526
career ladders, 526

collaborative action research
    (CAR), 518
collective bargaining, 529
e-mentor, 513

Margaret Haley, 530
induction program, 513
in-service, 518
intern teachers, 513

DISCUSSION QUESTIONS AND ACTIVITIES

1. How might you redefine or modify any of the stages of teacher development? Can these stages be applied to other careers? Think of teachers you have observed. What are the specific behaviors and skills that place a teacher at each of these stages?

2. Survey local school districts and analyze their first-year induction programs. What resources do they provide new teachers to assist them in making a successful transition into teaching? Will this affect your decision as to where to teach? You might want to research first-year teacher induction programs in the library or on the Internet to get a sense of the range of resources offered to first-year teachers.

3. What do you look for in a mentor? What strategies can you use to recruit such a mentor in your first teaching job?

4. In order to get a sense of the breadth of professional opportunities available to you, add to the list started in this book. Pull together notices of professional service courses, workshops, and other opportunities available to teachers. To do this, you may want to review professional journals and also contact local school districts, professional associations, state department of education, and colleges.

5. Develop some potential topics for a collaborative action research project. Consider undertaking this project as a research activity during your teaching education program.

 WEB-*TIVITIES*

1. Observation: Peer Review
2. Finding That First Teaching Position
3. The National Board for Professional Teaching Standards
4. Teacher Recognition: Merit Pay
5. Teacher Associations: the NEA and AFT

REEL TO REAL TEACHING: IT'S YOUR TURN

You've been invited to watch films and reflect and respond to *Reel to Reals* throughout this book. It is now time to switch roles! As future teachers, you will be challenged to develop assignments that are clear and promote meaningful learning. It is also common to use media in the classroom to inspire and inform students who are accustomed to *edutainment*. So, we are inviting you to apply your skills and creativity to write this chapter's *Reel to Real Teaching*.

Activity: Choose a film or television show with an educational theme. Here are a few suggestions:

- A new film that has just burst onto the movie scene.
- A film about education that has not been reviewed in earlier chapters. Browse your favorite video stores, educational resource center or online listings for some ideas.
- A film suitable to your subject area and grade level. For example, the *Luzhin Defence* for mathematics, *Gandhi* for social studies, *Amadeus* for music, *Billy Elliot* for character education. Visit Teach with Movies at www.teachwithmovies.org for additional movie titles.
- A film mentioned in this text that you haven't yet seen.
- A television show, such as *Boston Public*.

Now, design an original *Reel to Real Teaching*, using the template presented in previous chapters.

1. Write a brief synopsis of the film.

2. Develop three or four reflection questions that encourage readers to connect the film's story with chapter content and with personal experiences.

3. Create a follow-up activity that applies themes from the film to real first-year classroom experiences, effective teaching, or your teaching interests.

Reflection: Add a brief, special paragraph that examines your development of the Reel to Real. How did it feel to change roles and create an activity? What did you learn from the process? Were you able to integrate content from the textbook? Did you enjoy initiating an activity versus responding to someone else's assignment? Was creativity the toughest part? Did you struggle with clear and concise directions?

Click on *Reel to Real Teaching* to submit your own film activity. Be sure to include a synopsis, reflection questions, and a follow-up activity.

FOR FURTHER READING

A Classroom of Her Own, by Dana Haight Canttani (2002). This book follows six new teachers on the job as they strive to develop confidence and competence in instructional, professional, and cultural realms. Topics explored include authority with colleagues, parents, and students; professional identity; emotional expression including anger, fear, and courage; moral dilemmas and integrity; and effective instruction.

Exploring the Moral Heart of Teaching: Toward a Teacher's Creed, by David Hansen (2001). Drawing on classroom observations, teacher testimony, and philosophical reflection, this book examines why teaching is essential in human life and why the most important factor in teaching is the *person* who teaches.

Handbook for the Beginning Teacher, by Courtney Moffatt and Thomas Moffatt (2003). Filled with teaching ideas, tips, and checklists for classroom success, including instructional techniques for students with different learning styles, with special needs, and from diverse cultural backgrounds. The many charts, outlines, and teacher materials are readily available for teacher use across the curriculum and grade level.

How to Develop a Professional Portfolio: A Manual for Teachers, by Dorothy Campbell (2000). Demonstrates how creating a professional portfolio allows teachers to play an active role in documenting their competence and achievements.

They Led by Teaching, by Sherry L. Field and Michael J. Berson (eds.) (2003). This inspirational collection of essays provides insights into the lives and careers of some influential educators, including Myra Sadker, co-author of this textbook.

Q and A Guide to Entering the Teaching Profession

FOCUS QUESTIONS

1. What does the education job market look like? (or, put another way, will I be able to find a satisfying teaching position?)
2. Can I make a decent salary as a teacher?
3. How can new teachers increase their chances of working in a school of their choice?
4. What do I need in order to teach—a license or certification? (and how do I get one!)
5. What teacher competency tests do I need to take?
6. Why do teachers seek tenure? (and should I?)
7. Are there jobs in education outside of the classroom?

 WHAT DO YOU THINK? What Questions Do You Have? Click on Ask the Author to submit any questions you still have. See what questions others have asked and the author's responses.

CHAPTER PREVIEW

Beyond questions concerning education as a field of study, students often have personal and practical questions about teaching, the kinds of questions that are more likely to be asked after class or during office hours. Students considering an education career want to know everything from where the jobs are to how to land a teaching position, from how teachers are licensed to what kinds of education careers are available beyond the classroom. We trust that this chapter will answer some of the questions you are asking, and even some you never thought to raise.

CHAPTER FOCUS
When students consider a career, they often bring more questions than can be answered during a semester's coursework. This chapter is intended to offer many answers and provide a change of pace in the textbook's structure. For a chapter outline, see the IM.

What Are My Chances of Finding a Teaching Position?

This is a practical and quite natural question for you to be asking right now. After all, you are thinking about investing time, energy, money, and talent in preparing yourself to become a teacher, so it makes sense to ask whether you will be able to land a position when you graduate. Here is a shortcut to sorting out your employment possibilities, the **"four Ws"**: *when, what, where,* and *who.* Let's begin with *when.*

Although you may not have planned when you would enter teaching, the good news is that this is a terrific time to be looking for a position in education. While there are few guarantees when it comes to predicting national labor needs, several factors suggest that there will be a significant number of teaching positions available into the next decade. Perhaps we can appreciate the current situation better if we take a look at "the bad old days."

Historically, the demand for new teachers has resembled a roller coaster ride. In the 1950s and 1960s, a teaching shortage meant virtually anyone would be hired as a teacher, with or without the proper credentials. Back then, new graduates of teacher education programs enjoyed the view from the roller coaster as it soared. By the 1970s, the teacher employment roller coaster had begun to descend. Shrinking school budgets and the end of the baby boom had led to far more teachers than there were positions; as more teachers were licensed than positions existed, **teacher oversupply** became part of the educational lexicon, and teacher unemployment was common. By the 1980s and 1990s, the roller coaster was back on the ascent, as teacher retirements increased and student enrollments began to climb.

Strong demand for new teachers continues into the twenty-first century.[1] An increasing student population, calls for smaller class sizes, ongoing teacher retirements, and the relative attractiveness of a teaching career have increased the demand for teachers.

Let's consider the second *W: what* subject and grade level you plan to teach. Teachers of certain subjects, such as science and math, are in short supply, and many school districts are being forced to hire science and math teachers who have not taken enough courses to qualify for a license in these fields. Science, computer science, and math are "hot" fields; in many districts, so are bilingual and special education.[2] One way to make yourself more marketable is to consider course work and school experiences in subjects and skills that are in demand.

Population shifts and political actions affect teacher demand, and they contribute to the third *w, where.* Recently, teacher shortages were felt in western and southwestern states (Arizona, California, Alaska, and Hawaii), while the need for new teachers was generally lower in the Northeast, Great Lakes, and Middle Atlantic areas.[3] But, despite these general trends, there are notable exceptions; for example, population increases in some communities in New Jersey and New Hampshire created local teacher shortages. Large cities, one of the more challenging classroom environs, also continue to experience a shortage of new teachers. In high-poverty urban and rural districts alone, more than 700,000 new teachers will be needed in the next decade.[4]

As we discussed earlier in the text, local and state governments are experimenting with new methods of school organization, changes that may impact the job market and go beyond the traditional four Ws. **Privatization** (the movement to turn over school management to private companies), voucher systems, and even charter schools challenge traditional employment practices by introducing productivity measures, individual school decision making, and the participation of parents and others in personnel actions. Many schools now monitor teacher competence through tests,

GRABBER: A 5TH "W"

IM

FOCUS QUESTION 1

What does the education job market look like? (or, put another way, will I be able to find a satisfying teaching position?)

and may even link pay increments to student achievement. These changes may affect teacher supply and demand in particular regions and schools in the years ahead.

States and local communities also differ in their resources and priorities. Wealthier districts are more likely to sponsor a greater variety of programs and course offerings and to establish smaller average class sizes, actions that translate into a need for more teachers, while many urban areas struggle to find qualified teachers and adequate resources. School districts from Dallas to Detroit to Washington, DC, offer an ever-increasing array of incentives, including thousands of dollars in signing bonuses. The federal government offers housing assistance and student loan forgiveness to recruit teachers to urban schools.[5]

RELATED READING
The $100,000 Teacher: The Solution to America's Declining Public School System by Brian Crosby (2001).

Who Are My Teaching Colleagues? What Are the Demographics of Today's Teachers?

There are three million teachers in America, and the typical teacher is a 42-year-old white woman who has been teaching for sixteen years. Despite efforts to recruit people of color into teaching, most teachers are white and non-Hispanic. Although 17 percent of students are African American, fewer than 8 percent of all teachers are African American; while 16 percent of students are Hispanic, only 6 percent of teachers are Hispanic. About three out of four teachers are women, and recruiting men and people of color to teaching remains a challenge.[6] (See Figure 15.1.)

You will not be alone as a new teacher: Nearly one in four of your colleagues will have begun teaching within the past five years. Your next few years may also mirror their activities, as more than half of your colleagues have earned a master's degree, and three out of four participate in annual professional development activities.[7]

TEACHER TIP
Following each question and answer section, have students finish the following statement in the margin. "I learned . . . " and "A question I still have is . . . ?"

OVERHEAD 165
New K–12 Teachers by Race/Ethnicity and Gender

What Are My Chances for Earning a Decent Salary?

The truth is that teaching offers incredible rewards, and these rewards go beyond salary. If you love teaching, as we do, it will be a joy to go to work, and a worthy way

Racial/Ethnic Distribution of New K–12 Teachers

- Asian American 1%
- American Indian .5%
- Hispanic 4%
- Black 7%
- White 85%

Percentage of New Male K–12 Teachers by Race/Ethnicity

- White 24%
- Black 27%
- Hispanic 24%
- Asian American 31%
- Pacific Islander 26%
- American Indian 26%
- Alaskan Native 67%

(0 20 40 60 80 100)

FIGURE 15.1

New K–12 teachers by race/ethnicity and by gender.

SOURCE: National Education Association (NEA), *Fact Sheet on Teacher Shortages* (Washington, DC: NEA, 2001).

REFLECTION: How can teacher education programs recruit more students of color? What might attract more men into elementary teaching?

FOCUS QUESTION 2
Can I make a decent salary
as a teacher?

to invest your life. That joy, however, does not appear on your pay stub, and we are not alone in our belief that teachers are not paid what they deserve. The good news is that teachers' salaries have been improving in the last twenty years, although teachers still earn less than other white-collar workers, such as accountants, engineers, and computer systems analysts. But when state budgets are tight, teacher salaries suffer. Starting teachers now average over $30,000 a year, and experienced teachers are paid from $30,000 to the mid-$50,000. But these are only averages. Some school districts pay teachers six figures, while others barely pay $20,000 a year. It would be wise to contact specific school districts of interest for a copy of their salary schedule.[8]

Do Private Schools Pay Less than Public Schools?

Yes. Private or independent schools generally pay teachers lower salaries. Although many extraordinary teachers work in private schools, private school teachers as a group have less schooling, less experience, and participate less in professional development than do public school teachers—differences that are used to explain their lower salaries. But, while the salaries are lower, many private schools offer teachers a different set of benefits—smaller classes, more motivated students, more supportive parents, a greater sense of community, a greater sense of teacher autonomy, a shorter school year, a more challenging curriculum, and sometimes, housing and meals. Private schools, like their public counterparts, vary significantly in their academic standing, salaries, and employment practices. If you are interested in teaching in this arena, remember that each school needs to be evaluated on an individual basis. While some private schools are quite competitive with local public school employment benefits and are academically demanding, others do not compare as well.[9]

How Do I Apply for a Teaching Job? Do I Need a Résumé or a Portfolio?

The first step is to prepare a résumé to submit to prospective employers. When your résumé is strong, school districts will want a closer look, and that's when a portfolio or an interview will be requested. Résumés and portfolios open doors, so let's take a closer look at how best to construct them.

FOCUS QUESTION 3
How can new
teachers increase their
chances of working in a
school of their choice?

CLASS ACTIVITY:
RÉSUMÉ REVIEW
IM, Activity 15:2

At the top of your résumé, list your contact information: name, address, telephone, and e-mail address. But the heart of the **résumé** is your relevant education and experience. Indicate your formal education background—your college and university, your major and your minor (if you have one), and describe your student teaching experience, as well as other educational accomplishments. Summarize relevant work experiences. If you offered private instruction, worked as a camp counselor or at a religious school, or volunteered at a day care center or in a recreation program for the elderly, include these and note dates of employment, salient responsibilities, and accomplishments. Many candidates include professional objectives and a brief educational philosophy at the beginning of a résumé. If you take this approach, you might write an employment objective that details the type of teaching position you are seeking. You could also include some of the reasons that propel you to teach and perhaps a brief statement about your educational philosophy and beliefs. Your résumé should be typed in a clear and readable format; there are software templates available to help you. Check if the school districts you are interested in prefer hard copy or e-mail.

Employers rely on references and recommendations to get a clearer picture of applicants. Remember, as you list professors, supervisors, previous employers and cooperating teachers as references, you need to ask their permission and give them a "heads up" that they may be contacted. This is not only a basic courtesy, but also a way to measure their willingness to recommend you. Consider supplying them with "talking points" to aid them in preparing your recommendation.

Today, many school districts are going beyond résumés and recommendations, and are asking for a more in-depth view of you and your skills. A **portfolio** is a collection of materials that demonstrates your knowledge, competencies, and accomplishments as a teacher candidate. A portfolio does more than document your qualifications for a prospective teaching job (as a résumé does); it is a purposeful and reflective presentation of your professional development as a teacher.

People have different views concerning portfolios. Some see them as elaborate and lengthy presentations, while others consider an enhanced résumé with a few attachments to be a portfolio. Typically, portfolios include:[10]

OVERHEAD 166
General Portfolio Collection

RAP 4.8
Pruning Your Portfolio, p. 569

I. Statement of Teaching Philosophy

II. Teaching Credentials

    A. Résumé

    B. Transcripts

    C. Letters of Reference

    D. Teaching Certificate/License

    E. Endorsement(s)

III. Teaching-Related Experiences

    A. Student Teaching

        1. Evaluations by University Supervisor

        2. Evaluations by Cooperating/Mentor Teacher

        3. Letters from Students and Parents

        4. Sample Lesson Plans

        5. Sample Classroom Floor Plans/Management Plans

        6. Reflective Teaching Journal

        7. Examples of Student Work

        8. Photographs of Students/Classrooms

        9. Videotape of Teaching

    B. Employment in Child-Related Fields

    C. Volunteer Work with Children

This text is designed to start you on the road to building a portfolio. The *RAP* activities guide your portfolio development, differentiating between a working and a presentation portfolio (see page 569). The reflection questions and *You Be the Judge* features infused throughout the text are intended to help you consider relevant issues and form your own educational views and beliefs. In organizing the contents of your portfolio, consider using national standards (such as the INTASC standards identified in the *RAP*s) or the state or local standards of the school district to which you are applying for a job. Many teaching candidates rely on a loose-leaf type notebook to organize their portfolio work, allowing for flexibility incorporating and removing material. More recently, digital formats, such as a CD-ROM or a Web page, have become popular. With a digital or **e-portfolio,** you can simultaneously present your qualifications and demonstrate your technological proficiency. In developing your portfolio, ask for input from university supervisors and cooperating teachers; and it is a good idea to practice presenting your portfolio to them as well.

How Do I Prepare for a Successful Interview?

Interviews may be conducted by one or more administrators, a panel of teachers, or a combination of teachers and parents, and the average interview usually lasts thirty minutes to an hour.[11] So how can these precious minutes work for you?

When you walk in for your interview, the first thing that will strike an interviewer is appearance. Your prospective interviewer (or interview team) will be looking not only for appropriate professional attire, but also for such qualities as poise, enthusiasm, self-confidence, and an ability to think quickly and effectively on your feet. Appropriate grammar, a well-developed vocabulary, and clear speech and diction are important. You should be focused about your teaching philosophy and goals if you want to appear confident and purposeful in the interview. If you have developed a portfolio of teaching materials or other information that you are particularly proud of, you should take it to the interview. It cannot hurt to have it present, and it might help win the day.

It is important to be prepared for likely questions. Common interview topics include your personal philosophy of teaching, your teaching strengths and weaknesses, professional goals, employment history, teaching style, and your approach to classroom management. Interviewers commonly look for: enthusiasm, warmth, caring, leadership skills, willingness to learn new things, and confidence.[12] You may also want to note what questions cannot legally be asked—for example, questions about your religion or marital or parental status. Such questions do not relate to your qualifications as a teacher. The Office for Civil Rights is one of several agencies that you can contact if you are victimized by such queries.

> **TEACHING TIP**
> Initially, what else would students want to know before they *sign on* to a new teaching position? Now, what creative (legal and productive!) strategies can they propose that will yield that valuable information?

Do your homework: Find out as much as possible about both the particular school and the community. Talk to friends involved in the school or community, check local newspapers, try the local library, the Internet, or, better yet, stop by the school to talk with the students and others, scour the bulletin boards, and pick up available literature. Once you obtain information about a school or school system, you can begin matching your particular interests and skills with the school district's programs and needs.

As important as such preparatory work is, the most important way of learning what an interviewer is looking for is to listen. Sometimes interviewers state their needs openly, such as "We're looking for a teacher who is fluent in both Spanish and English." In other cases, interviewers merely imply their needs—for example, "Many of the children who attend our school are Hispanic." In this case, you have first to interpret the interviewer's remark and then to check your interpretation with a statement such as "Are you looking for someone who is fluent in both Spanish and English?" Or "Are you looking for someone who has experience in working with Spanish-speaking children?"

After interviewing, it is wise to send the interviewer a brief follow-up note, reminding her or him of how your qualifications meet the school system's needs. The interviewer may have talked with dozens of candidates, and under such circumstances it is easy to be forgotten in a sea of faces—your job is to make sure you stand out.

One word of caution: When a job offer comes your way, analyze the school system to make sure that you really want to teach there before signing on the dotted line. Try to find out

- If teachers in the district view it as a good place to work
- If there have been personnel problems recently and, if so, for what reasons
- What are the benefits and potential problems in the teachers' contract
- Typical class size
- What kind of support services are available
- If the school is adopting organizational changes to personalize the school climate.

If the answers do not please you, you may want to look elsewhere. It is unwise to accept a position with the notion that you will leave as soon as a better offer is made. That attitude can quickly lead to a job-hopping profile that may stigmatize you as someone who is either irresponsible or unable to work well with others. In short, do not simply jump at the first available job offer. If your credentials are good and you know how to market yourself, you will get other teaching offers.

What Do I Need in Order to Teach—a License or Certification? By the Way, What's the Difference?

Project yourself a few years into the future. You have just completed your teacher preparation program. You stop by your local public school office and make a belated inquiry into teacher openings. The school secretary looks up from a cluttered desk, smiles kindly, and says, "We may have an opening this fall. Are you certified? Do you have a license?"

Oops! Certified? License? Now I remember. It's that paperwork thing. . . . I should have filled out that application back at school. I should have gone to that teacher licensure meeting. And I definitely should have read that Sadker textbook more carefully. I knew I forgot something. Now I'm in trouble. All that work and I will not be allowed to teach. What a nightmare!

And then you wake up.

Many people use the terms *teacher certification* and *teaching license* interchangeably (as in "She has her teacher certification" while really meaning "She has her teaching license"). But it is important for you to be able to distinguish between a professional certification and a legal license, so we make the distinction in this book. **Teacher certification** confers professional standing; a **teacher's license** is a legal document. Teacher certification indicates that a professional group recognizes (certifies) that a teacher is competent and has met certain standards. A teacher's license, issued by the state government, grants the legal right to teach, not unlike a driver's license grants the legal right to drive. Both licenses mean that the "minimum" state requirements have been met. If you have been out on the roads recently, you know that meeting these minimum requirements to drive is not an indication that a person can, in fact, drive very well. It is the same with a teacher's license: Not all holders can teach well, especially if they are teaching a subject without adequate training in that field, a sad but not uncommon practice. Nevertheless, the intent of certification and licensure is to maintain high standards for teachers.

CLASS ACTIVITY:
SIMULATED INTERVIEWS
IM, Activity 15:6

Q

FOCUS QUESTION 4
What do I need in order to teach—a license or certification? (and how do I get one!)

CLASS ACTIVITY:
FLASH CARDS
IM, Activity 15:3

CLASS ACTIVITY:
SOONER VERSUS LATER
IM, Activity 15:4

RAP 4.7
Another Mini-Lesson with
Another Mini-Group,
p. 568

Who Awards Licenses, and How Do I Get One?

Teaching licenses are awarded by each of the fifty states and the District of Columbia. In a similar way, states are involved with the licensure of doctors, lawyers, and other professionals and nonprofessionals. When you meet the state's requirements, you can apply for and receive your teacher's license.

You should not assume that your teacher's license will automatically be issued to you when you graduate from your teacher education program, since state departments of education, not colleges and universities, issue teacher's licenses. Some colleges will apply to a designated state department in your name and request a license; others will not. In most states, filling out an application and passing the required national or state tests are all that is needed if you have graduated from an approved, accredited program. But not all teacher education programs are accredited (see the accreditation section of this chapter for more information). Regardless of your program, remember that you will probably need to apply to the state for a teacher's license. (See Appendix 2 for the contact information for the department of education in every state.)

You should also know that each state has its own requirements for teacher licensure. States have different policies concerning what courses teachers should take, what kinds of teacher's licenses should be offered, and even the length of time for which a teacher's license is valid. You may meet the standards in one state, but, if you decide to teach in another, you may find yourself unqualified for its license. Since the courses and experiences you need vary from state to state, it is useful to understand the major areas of preparation relevant to certification and licensure. Joseph Cronin, writing in the *Handbook of Teaching and Policy,* suggests three categories: knowledge of subject matter, knowledge of pedagogy, and practice teaching.[13] Chances are that your course work will fit within these categories.

When you have questions about obtaining a license, consult immediately with your college instructor, adviser, or teacher education placement office, or contact the appropriate state department of education. Do not depend on friends, whose well-intentioned advice may not be accurate.

What Type of License Do I Need? (You Mean, There's More than One?)

Most states issue more than one kind of license in order to differentiate among the applicants' qualifications and career goals. Although the specific names of these licenses (sometimes called certificates, now how's that for confusing!) vary from state to state, there are four common types:

1. An **initial,** or **provisional, license**—also called a *probationary certificate*—is the type frequently issued to beginning teachers and is generally nonrenewable. If you are awarded a provisional license, it means that you have completed most, but not all, of the state's legal requirements to teach. It may also mean that you need to complete some additional course work or that you need to teach for several years before you qualify for a higher or more permanent license. You may find yourself first getting a provisional license, giving you some breathing room as you work to complete all of the state's requirements for a standard, or professional, license.

2. The **standard,** or **professional, license** is issued by the state after you have completed all the requirements to teach in that state. These requirements may include a specified number of courses beyond the bachelor's degree or one or more years of teaching experience.

3. A **special license** is a nonteaching license designed for specialized educational careers, including those in administration, counseling, library science, school social work, and school psychology. If after teaching for several years you decide that you want a career in school counseling (or administration, library science, and so forth), you will have to meet the requirements for this license.

4. A **conditional,** or **emergency, license** is a substandard license that is issued on a temporary basis to meet the needs of communities that do not have licensed teachers available. For example, a small high school in a rural community may not be able to attract a qualified teacher in physics. Faced with the unattractive prospect of not offering its students physics courses, the community may petition the state to award an emergency license to someone who does not meet current licensure standards.

> **IN THE NEWS**
>
> ### From Vienna to the Bronx
>
> Across the region and country, school districts are grappling with teacher shortages in areas such as math, science, special education, and foreign languages. More and more, school districts are looking abroad to fill the gaps. Houston has recruited 100 teachers from the Philippines and Spain. New York has hired 125 math and science teachers from Austria. Los Angeles now recruits in the Philippines, in addition to Canada, Mexico, and Spain, and Chicago gleaned 46 teachers from 25 countries in the last year.
>
> SOURCE: Susan Snyder, "Philadelphia, Chester Upland Look Abroad for Teachers," *Philadelphia Inquirer,* March 26, 2001.
>
> What's new in education? Click on *News Feeds.*

Conditional licenses become commonplace when a shortage of teachers forces states to hire uncertified teachers. Historically, this has even included people who had never completed college. It is an unfortunate fact of life that, even today, when shortages in certain fields or geographic areas arise, substandard teaching licenses are issued.

What Is an Endorsement?

In some cases, a candidate may be licensed to teach in an additional area through what is termed an **endorsement.** For many teachers, especially those teaching in areas that have a large supply of candidates, endorsements can give you the edge over other applicants. You may want to give some consideration to this option. Carefully planning your courses can help you get a second teaching area. So can practical experience. For instance, a teacher may have a standard or professional license in U.S. history but finds herself teaching biology courses as well. Or perhaps she has taken a number of college courses in biology and decides she wants to be recognized as a biology teacher as well as a history teacher. Since she already has a standard or professional license (in history), she need not apply for a new license. Instead, she applies to the state for an *endorsement* in biology. Although she did not take biology methods or student teach in biology, her teaching experience and background are considered for her endorsement in biology. The endorsement means that the state has approved her teaching both history and biology. Sometimes the subjects are more closely related than these. A teacher licensed in bilingual education, for example, with a number of courses in English as a Second Language (ESL), may seek an endorsement in ESL as well.

If I Want to Teach in Another State, Do I Need Another Teacher's License?

Each state issues its own teaching license. If you have a license in one state but want to teach in another, you must reapply for a license there. Although this sounds like a pain, states have created several procedures for making this process less onerous. Let's begin with your teacher education program. If your college or university has a *state-approved* teacher education program, then it has been evaluated and meets state standards. If you are in such a program (check with your college or with your state department of education to find out), then you will receive a state teacher's license when you graduate and be able to teach in that state.

But what if you are graduating from a program in one state, and want to teach in another state? If your teacher education program has also been approved by the **National Association for the Accreditation of Teacher Education (NCATE)**, then it has met a set of standards widely accepted by educators and most states. If you graduate from such an NCATE-approved program, you will find that when you apply to most other states, you will receive at least a probationary license to begin teaching. You may be given a year or two while you are teaching to take additional courses or exams, but at least you can receive a teacher's license fairly quickly. So the second question you should ask: Is your teacher education program NCATE approved?

Moving beyond teacher preparation, states themselves have entered agreements in which they recognize each other's teaching licenses. State Departments of Education have such agreements with other states, which some call **reciprocity agreements** and others call **compacts.** So, for example, if you have a license in Missouri, then thirty or forty other states might say "show me" your Missouri teacher's license and we will issue you one from our state. Sometimes additional courses or tests may be required, while other times they are not. The **National Association of State Directors of Teacher Education and Certification (NASDTEC)** is working to make such interstate compacts widely accepted.

Interested in teaching in another state? First check to see if your teacher education program is state approved or NCATE approved, and see how your new state recognizes such programs. Once you have a license from one state, you can always check to see if the new state where you want to teach has an agreement whereby it recognizes your teacher license.

What Are "Alternative Routes" to Getting a Teacher's License?

Alternative licensing programs are gaining in popularity. Many of these programs enable college graduates to become teachers with less education training than required in traditional teacher education programs. In part, alternative licensure programs are popular due to teacher shortages, a desire to get candidates into teaching positions quickly, and a concern that traditional education programs too rarely attract teachers of color. Only eight states offered alternative routes to licensure in 1984, a movement that began in New Jersey. By 2001, forty-five states and the District of Columbia had implemented some form of alternative licensure option.[14]

How does alternative licensure work? Some states permit selective alternative licensing only, such as at the secondary but not the elementary level, or only in fields in which there are teacher shortages, such as math or science. Some states only allow alternate routes that are designed by higher education institutions. Most alternative programs require a bachelor's degree, and some education course work, though usually far fewer education courses than are typically required. One of the best known of these alternative approaches is Teach for America.

Teach for America recruits applicants who have little if any education background but who are motivated to make a positive contribution by teaching in areas that suffer a teacher shortage, particularly inner-city and rural areas. This program has attracted individuals whose altruistic response is reminiscent of Peace Corps volunteers, and whose academic background is typically quite strong.[15] Alternative programs like Troops to Teachers and Teach for America have drawn a higher percentage of mathematics and science applicants than have traditional programs, and have an impressive track record in recruiting applicants of color. Studies indicate that alternative programs have produced almost five times the proportion of teachers of color as traditional programs. For example, in Texas, 41 percent of the teachers entering the profession through the alternative teacher licensure program are from non-European ancestry, compared with only 9 percent of all the teachers in the state. Advocates of alternative approaches point to these statistics as proof that there is more than one way to prepare teachers.[16]

Not everyone views alternative routes to teacher preparation as terrific innovations. For one, the attrition rate for these programs is quite high: Many who volunteer to join also volunteer to leave, and no wonder. With limited preparation, these rookies wade into challenging teaching situations in some of the nation's most troubled and impoverished communities.

Studies of alternative licensure preparation have indicated that graduates of alternative programs represent more of an attempt at a "quick fix" for teacher shortages than a permanent solution. In many cases, their not-yet-honed teaching skills are unlikely to be improved, since graduates of alternative programs are less committed to staying in teaching or to pursuing graduate studies than are students from traditional teacher education programs. (In fact, about 2 percent of the alternative teachers report that they did not graduate from college.) Although alternative preparation programs try to attract older, more experienced Americans to a teaching career, more than half of those enrolled are fresh out of college. Many teacher educators are concerned that this approach is a step back to times past, when anyone who wanted to teach was hired. They fear that the alternative preparation of teachers signals a retreat from efforts toward full teacher professionalism. Some also worry about the elementary and secondary students who will be in classrooms with these new and not well-prepared teachers.

Despite the attention that alternative licensure programs have received in the press, alternative programs prepare relatively few teachers; their graduates typically stay in teaching for only a brief period of time; and, when competing for a position, alternative candidates are often at a disadvantage.[17] Because these programs are relatively new, studies of their effectiveness will undoubtedly continue in the years ahead.

What Are Teacher Competency Tests?

Most states require teacher competency tests, and others are experimenting with additional forms of evaluation, such as supervised internships. Why are teachers facing new hurdles and higher standards? One reason is that, during the past few decades, the public became outraged about reports of students' declining standardized test scores and illiterate high school graduates. Between the 1960s and the 1980s, average SAT scores tumbled 42 points on the verbal and 26 points on the mathematical sections of the test. In 1983, the U.S. Department of Education published *A Nation at Risk,* highlighting these depressing test scores and calling for significant school changes, including fewer electives, an increase in core course requirements, more student testing, and better paid and more qualified teachers. In response, many states required elementary and secondary students, as well as teachers, to pass **minimum competency tests.** The movement for state-required competency tests spread—or

FOCUS QUESTION 5
What teacher competency tests do I need to take?

raced—from a few states in the Southeast to the overwhelming majority of states across the nation. Since the early 1990s, most states have been using standardized tests for admission into teaching programs, for certification, and for licensure.[18] (See Appendix 2 for more information about state testing requirements.) Chances are strong that you will be tested, perhaps more than once, if you decide to enter teaching. Some of these tests are sponsored by states, and applicants have been required to write essays on topics related to education, as well as to pass basic skills tests of spelling, grammar, and punctuation. Some states also test mathematical skills. In other cases, states or local districts have developed more complex, competency-based evaluation systems. But many states now use a national exam, most often the Praxis.

Praxis Assessment for Beginning Teachers is a three-part teacher assessment. The *Praxis I: Preprofessional Skills Test* consists of hour-long academic skills tests in reading, writing, and mathematics. These basic tests apply to prospective teachers in all fields and all grades, and are required in most states for admission into teacher education, or to obtain an initial teacher license.[19] *Praxis I* can be taken in the standard paper-and-pencil format on specified dates around the country or by means of a more costly computer version, with far more flexible timing, widespread availability, and immediate scoring.

The *Praxis II* assesses subject area, pedagogy, and professional education knowledge, offering more than 140 exams in subjects ranging from art to social studies. *Praxis III* is a classroom performance assessment of teaching skills, covering classroom management, instructional planning, and assessment of student learning. While *Praxis III* is the most authentic assessment of beginning teachers, it is also the most challenging and costly test to implement, and it has not yet gained the widespread popularity of *Praxis I* and *II*.

Educators differ as to whether the Praxis series or other competency tests are necessary. Those who support competency exams maintain that the exams lend greater credibility and professionalism to the process of becoming a teacher. They claim that such tests identify well-educated applicants who can apply their knowledge in the classroom. They cite examples of teachers who cannot spell, write, or perform basic mathematical computations, and they plead persuasively that students must be protected from such incompetent teachers.

Some critics of the teacher exams argue that they are incredibly easy and not a real measure of competence. Other critics believe that such tests are more a political gesture than a way of improving education.[20] Part of the problem is the lack of evidence supporting the idea that teacher testing predicts teacher performance.[21] Some believe that the current process of state licensure and the period of assessment prior to tenure are sufficient to filter out incompetent teachers. Still others worry that we do not really know what makes good teachers, and we know even less about how to create tests to separate the good from the bad. We don't have tests that can measure enthusiasm, dedication, caring, and sensitivity—qualities that students associate with great teachers. Test makers are constantly working to respond to these charges, and to create more effective tests.

Another provocative and controversial problem is the impact of standardized competency tests on diversity. Historically, when African American teachers were systematically paid less, such tests were used as a vehicle for teachers of color to attain salary equity with whites. More recently, however, test results in states across the nation document the problems African American and Hispanic teacher candidates are having in passing such exams, problems that have been attributed to reasons ranging from test bias to social and educational differences. The continued use of such exams may deter people of color from becoming teachers. And the pipeline of nonwhite teaching candidates, already only a trickle, is in danger of dwindling further.[22] Nevertheless, the courts have ruled that such tests are an acceptable means of screening teacher candidates.[23] And with strong public sentiment favoring such tests, they are likely to be a part of the teacher education landscape for the foreseeable future.

How Do Teaching Contracts Work?

Congratulations! You have been hired by the school system of your choice, and a contract is placed before you. Before you sign it, there are a few things you should know about teacher contracts. This contract represents a binding agreement between you and the school district. It will be signed by you as the teacher being hired and by an agent of the board of education, often the superintendent. The contract usually sets the conditions of your work, perhaps including specific language detailing your instructional duties, and, of course, your salary.

If you do not have tenure, you will receive a new contract each year. Once you earn tenure, you will be working under a continuing contract and will probably be asked to notify the school district each year as to whether you plan to teach for the district the following year.

What Are Some Advantages of Tenure?

A teacher was once asked to leave his teaching position in Kentucky because he was leading an "un-Christian" personal life. He was Jewish.

A second-grade teacher was dismissed from her teaching assignment in Utah because of her dress. She wore miniskirts.

In Massachusetts, a teacher was fired because of his physical appearance. He had grown a beard.

Fortunately, these teachers all had one thing in common: **tenure.** And tenure prevented their school districts from following through on dismissal proceedings.

A vast majority of states currently have tenure laws. A newly hired teacher is considered to be in a probationary period. The **probationary teaching period** can be two, three, or even five years for public school teachers and about six years for college professors. After demonstrating teaching competence for the specific period, the teacher is awarded tenure, which provides a substantial degree of job security. Generally, a tenured teacher can be fired only for gross incompetence, insubordination, or immoral acts or because of budget cuts stemming from declining enrollments. In practice, public schools rarely fire a tenured teacher.

Since teachers have enjoyed the protection of tenure for many years, it is easy to forget how important this protection is. To get a fresh perspective on tenure, consider what life in schools might be like without it.

Without tenure, hundreds, perhaps thousands, of financially pressed school systems could respond to pressure from taxpayers by firing their experienced teachers and replacing them with lower-paid, less experienced teachers. This would significantly reduce school budgets, usually the largest cost item in the local tax structure. After two or three more years, these teachers would also face the financial ax. In short, teachers would once again become an itinerant, poorly paid profession. Would anyone really benefit?

Without tenure, the fear of dismissal would cause thousands of teachers to avoid controversial topics, large and small. Many teachers would simply become a mirror of

FOCUS QUESTION 6
Why do teachers seek tenure? (and should I?)

OVERHEAD 167
Debate on Tenure

their communities, fearing to stir intellectual debate or to teach unsettling ideas be-cause job security had become their prime objective. Classrooms would become quiet and mundane places, devoid of the excitement that comes from open discussion of controversial ideas.

Without tenure, many teachers would have to modify their personal lifestyles. In some communities, they would have to avoid places where liquor is served; in others, their clothing or hairstyles would have to be altered. Any behavior that differed from the norms of the community would be potentially dangerous, for such behavior could provide the spark that would trigger public clamor for dismissal. A conformist philosophy would spread from the classroom to teachers' personal lives.

In short, without some protection such as tenure, teaching would take a giant step backward. Tenure provides teachers with the fundamental security that allows them to develop and practice their profession without fear of undue pressure or intimida-tion. Unfortunately, not all teachers have respected the academic freedom provided by tenure, as we shall see in the next section.

What Are Some Disadvantages of Tenure?

Over the years, it has become apparent that the protection of academic freedom through the tenure process has entailed serious drawbacks. One such drawback is the reality that ineffective teachers are protected from dismissal. Many of these ineffec-tive teachers view tenure as a right to job security without acknowledging a corre-sponding responsibility to continue professional growth. Feeling that they are no longer subject to serious scrutiny, such teachers fail to keep up with new develop-ments in their field, and each year they drag out old lesson plans and fading lecture notes for yet another outdated performance. Who pays the price for such ineffective teaching? The students, of course. Think back a moment. How many ineffective, tenure-protected teachers were you subjected to during your total school experience? How many do you face at present?

During the past few years, attempts to reform or dismantle tenure have gained mo-mentum. Some school districts have extended the amount of time it takes to be awarded tenure. In Florida, a recent law reduced the time that poor-performing teach-ers are given to improve from one year to ninety days. New Hampshire's Republican lawmakers failed in their attempt to require teachers to pass tests and renew their li-censes every three years, while a special Colorado task force has been formed to ex-plore ways to limit tenure. One reason for these attempts is the cost involved in dismissing a tenured teacher. A New York School Boards Association Study showed that, in that state in the mid-1990s, it took an average of 455 days and $177,000 to dismiss a teacher. If the teacher appealed, the average price rose to $317,000.[24]

As you can see, tenure is a double-edged sword. It serves the extremely important function of preserving academic freedom and protecting teachers from arbitrary and unjust dismissal. But it also provides job security for ineffective teachers, bad news for the students of these teachers or for the new and more competent teachers trying to enter the profession.

Are Untenured Teachers Protected?

Many believe that, until tenure is granted, they are extremely vulnerable, virtually without security. This is not true. During the 1970s, in *Goldberg v. Kelly, Board of*

Regents v. Roth, and *Perry v. Sinderman,* the United States Supreme Court outlined several of the rights that are enjoyed by nontenured teachers. In many circumstances, these rights include advance notice of the intention to dismiss a teacher, clearly stated reasons for termination, and a fair and open hearing. In addition, teacher organizations, such as the National Education Association (NEA) and the American Federation of Teachers (AFT), provide legal assistance for teachers who might be subjected to the arbitrary and unjust action of a school system. If the AFT and the NEA ever merge, one result may be even greater legal protection for teachers.

If, during your probationary years, you feel that you have been unfairly victimized by the school administration, you should seek legal advice. Even nontenured teachers possess rights, but these rights are effective only if they are exercised.

Can Principals Be Tenured?

Although about a dozen states still grant tenure or equivalent rights to principals, this protection has all but disappeared. Historically, a satisfactory probationary period of one to five years would result in principals earning tenure, as teachers do. Not anymore. Many of the same arguments used against granting teachers tenure (a shield for mediocrity or even incompetence, a lengthy process to remove poor performers, and so on) have been successfully used to rescind tenure for principals. The crux of the argument seems to be how one views principals. Those who see them as managers believe that, if they are not managing well, they should be fired. Others view principals as master teachers (from the term "principal teacher"), who should be afforded the same protections from arbitrary political pressures and inappropriate personnel decisions as other teachers. The management view is clearly winning out.[25]

What Kinds of Educational Careers Are Available Beyond Classroom Teaching?

FOCUS QUESTION 7
Are there jobs in education outside of the classroom?

CLASS ACTIVITY: MADISON AVENUE
IM, Activity 15:5

The assumption that your education degree has prepared you only for a teaching career is a widespread myth. Actually, there are dozens of education-related careers, although tunnel vision often keeps them from view. (See *Frame of Reference:* Education Want Ads.) Obviously, if you are interested in school administration or a counseling career, starting as a classroom teacher makes a lot of sense and gives you an important perspective that will serve you well in these other school careers. But beyond administration and counseling lie many other options. The following list is intended to give you some idea of the less typical but potentially quite rewarding **nontraditional educational careers** available to you.[26]

Early Childhood Education. If you want to stay in touch with teaching but prefer a climate other than the typical classroom, you may want to explore such options as **day care centers.** Early childhood education is a vital component of the nation's educational system. Working parents seek quality options, not only for child care but for child education and development as well.

Although day care rarely offers much pay or status, a number of talented educators find early childhood education incredibly satisfying. If you are creative and flexible, you might even be able to develop your own facility. For example, some department stores advertise a day care service for shopping parents. You might consider opening a similar early childhood program and marketing your "children's center" to other stores, shopping malls, or businesses. (Check out your state's laws regarding operating standards, building restrictions, number of children permitted, and so on.) If you

You may find your education niche beyond the traditional classroom. Here are some authentic employment opportunities printed in the "want ads" of newspapers.

CAN YOU TEACH?

The largest computer software and network training company in the world is looking for additional full-time instructors to teach classes. Candidates must possess excellent presentation skills. Computer experience is helpful but not necessary; we will train you.

EDUCATIONAL CONSULTANT

We are seeking an experienced Education Consultant with classroom teaching background for per diem contracted and long-term assignments, with expertise in one or more of the following: dimensions of learning, performance assessments, state learning standards, early literacy, cooperative learning, differentiated instruction.

PRIVATE GIRLS' HIGH SCHOOL

seeks Director of Technology/Computer Teacher, Classroom Experience Necessary.

ELEMENTARY ZOO INSTRUCTOR

The Education Department of the Zoo, one of the country's foremost institutions of informal science teaching, is seeking a dynamic instructor for its elementary-level programs. A highly interactive teaching approach, creativity, and a theatrical background will be helpful. This position involves program development for parents and teachers in addition to direct instruction of children ages 4–12. Excellent oral and written communication skills required.

EDITOR/WRITER

Familiar with higher edu. issues needed for Publications Dept. Will work with campus colleagues and assoc. staff to develop a natl. quarterly newsletter for faculty & administrators. Must know curriculum development, have solid editorial and publications mgmt. skills, research aptitude, & good writing skills.

Major nonprofit YOUTH SERVICE AGENCY seeks to fill the following positions (Bilingual, Spanish/English preferred): YOUTH COUNSELOR: B.A. 2 years experience in social service setting, PROGRAM COORDINATOR: B.A. 3–5 years experience, strong supervisory/communication skills necessary.

EDUCATIONAL RESEARCHER

Research and develop abstracts for www-based project about science and math education. Writing skills, attention to detail, ability to synthesize information quickly, and confident phone skills. Background in education helpful.

EDUCATIONAL COORDINATOR

The Historical Society seeks a creative, self-motivated team player to plan, implement, & promote educational programs for schools, families, & adults. Responsibilities incl.: organizing public programs & tours: coordinating National History Day, providing services for schools.

CHILD CARE DIRECTOR

Join our management team! Nonprofit corporate-sponsored child care management co., looking for a talented director to manage our state-of-the-art center. Must have ECE experience and have been through NAEYC accred. process.

LEARNING CENTERS offering individualized diagnostic and prescriptive programs are looking for dynamic PT cert. teachers to instruct students of all ages in reading, writing, math, and algebra.

SUBSTANCE ABUSE PREVENTION INTERVENTION SPECIALISTS

Seeking experienced professionals to provide services to students in substance abuse prevention and intervention. Will provide both group and individual counseling and conduct peer leadership groups for students at risk at various schools.

AMERICAN INTERNATIONAL SCHOOLS

Seeking excellent candidates. June interview in major cities. Two years of experience reqd.

WORKSITE TEACHER

Conduct worksite visits & act as liaison between worksite & classroom instruction, BA plus 2 yrs. teaching experience with adults req'd.

LOVE TO TEACH?

Are you considering a career change where you can continue to use your teaching ability? Call.

PROGRAM ASSISTANT

New vision in schools seeks a program assistant to provide support to a major school reform initiative. Must be meticulous with details & be able to write well, handle multiple projects, & and meet deadlines. Interest in public schools is preferred.

EDITOR

One of the most progressive and respected names in children's publishing is currently seeking an editor for a supplement on early childhood. In addition to a degree, editorial/publishing experience, and early childhood classroom experience, you must be highly creative and possess a strong knowledge of early childhood issues.

COLLEGE GRAD

Prestigious sports program for children sks highly motivated coaches. Sports background & a love for children a must. Education majors a +.

EDUCATIONAL SALES REPS

See our ad in the SALES section under "Education."

VIOLENCE PREVENTION PROGRAM

(Peace Games) seeks F/T director to create curricula & resources for students, parents, & teachers.

TEACH ENGLISH ABROAD

BA/BS required. Interested in education. No exp nec.

SPECIAL EDUCATION

The Learning Center, a place for emotionally disturbed children, has the following possible positions: Resource Counselor, Cert. Teacher, Music Teacher, Level III Secretary, Therapist Assistant.

REFLECTION: Which of these careers do you find most appealing? Which is least appealing? Have you ever explored nonteaching education careers? Why or why not?

enjoy working with young children, you will find opportunities galore in this growing field.

Adult Education. If you prefer to work with a mature population, you might be attracted to **adult (continuing) education** programs. These programs are offered through city and county governments, local school systems, and nearby colleges and universities. In addition, some private businesses now sponsor courses that are related to their products—recreation, crafts, cooking, technical training, and so forth. As the ranks of the retired swell with baby boomers, you can expect this field to grow rapidly. Older Americans often have the time, interest, and income to pursue education in topics, skills, and hobbies that have long eluded them. Elder hostels around the world are responding to the educational demand created by retirees. Researching available programs may take time, but you are apt to discover a variety of adult learning programs that can provide nontraditional teaching opportunities.

Pupil Service Professionals. Service professionals—school social workers, counselors, and psychologists—typically work as a team, assisting teachers in creating more effective learning environments. These professionals receive special training and education to meet the unique needs that frequently emerge in schools. Social workers, for example, work to improve the relationship between home and school. School psychologists, prepared in education and mental health, are responsible for coordinating and evaluating special learning and behavior problems.

Colleges and Universities. You will find many nonteaching, yet education-related, jobs in colleges and universities. To name a few, academic advisers work primarily on a one-to-one basis with students, discussing courses of study; admissions officers respond to the needs of students; alumni relations personnel conduct fund-raising campaigns, organize alumni events, and maintain job placement services; and student services personnel do psychological and vocational counseling, advise international students, and administer residential programs. Most colleges offer their employees tuition benefits, so, if you want to pursue graduate studies, this may be a good way to gain both experience and an advanced degree.

RELATED READING
Chain Reaction: A Call to Compassionate Revolution by Darrell Scott and Steve Rabey (2001).

Community Organizations. Think of a community group. Chances are, that group has an educational mission. Churches, synagogues, and nursing homes can use creative instructors and program planners. For example, a former English teacher, disturbed by the demeaning, artsy-craftsy programs in a local nursing home, inspired the residents to write their life histories, an experience they found very stimulating. Recreation and community centers hire instructors, program planners, and directors for their numerous programs. Hospitals and health clinics need people to plan and deliver training to their professional and administrative staffs. Some of the large municipal zoos conduct programs to protect endangered animal species and to interact with school groups. Libraries and media centers require personnel to maintain and catalog resources and equipment, as well as to train others in their use. Art galleries and museums hire staff to coordinate educational programs for school and civic groups and to conduct tours of their facilities.

The Media. The publishing and broadcasting industries hire people with education backgrounds to help write and promote their educational products. For example, large newspapers, such as *The Washington Post,* maintain staff writers whose job is to cover education, just as other reporters cover crime, politics, and finance. Some newspapers even publish a special edition of their paper for use in schools. Likewise, textbook publishers, educational journals, the Internet service providers, and television talk shows need people familiar with educational principles to help develop their programs.

Private Industry and Public Utilities. Large public and private corporations often rely on education graduates in their programs to train their staffs in areas such as organizational effectiveness, new technology training, civil rights and safety laws, and basic company policies and practices. Sometimes client needs come into play, as many of these firms need people with well-developed instructional skills to demonstrate the use of their sophisticated equipment or products to potential customers. Some education-related companies maintain permanent learning centers and seek persons with education backgrounds to plan and run them. If you like writing, you may want to work on pamphlets, brochures, curricula, and other materials describing a company's services and products, often written by education graduates.

Computer Software Development. With the dramatic increase in the use of educational software in the classroom, many companies are soliciting people with experience in education as consultants to help develop new programs. Creativity, familiarity with child psychology, and knowledge of the principles of learning are important resources for developing software that will appeal to a diverse and competitive market.

Technology. The blossoming of the computer age, with its software, email, websites, and Internet resources, has divided the population into those who are computer literate and those who are computer challenged (sometimes called technophobic). Those who are not yet citizens of cyberworld represent a ready population of potential students. If you enjoy programming, surfing the Net, or designing websites, you may want to become a tech-teacher, teaching these skills in either formal or informal settings. You may consider a position as a technology consultant for schools, helping design websites, create networks, or select software. You may choose to work outside a school organization, as a company representative providing educational services and equipment.

Educational Associations. National, state, and regional educational associations hire writers, editors, research specialists, administrators, lobbyists, and educators for a host of education-related jobs, from research and writing to public relations. There are hundreds of these associations, from the NEA to the American Association of Teachers of French. Check the *National Trade and Professional Associations of the United States and Canada* (Columbia Books, Inc.) for listings and descriptions of positions, or use the *Encyclopedia of Associations* (Gale Research) or the Internet to contact the associations directly.

Government Agencies. A host of local, state, and federal government agencies hire education graduates for training, policy planning, management, research, and so on. Various directories can help you through the maze of the federal bureaucracy. Among these is the *United States Government Manual* (Office of the Federal Register, National Archives and Records Service), which describes the various programs within the federal government, including their purposes and top-level staffs. The Internet is another useful source for exploring career opportunities in government-related education programs.

Global Opportunities. Want an international experience? Consider Department of Defense schools, private international schools, religious and international organizations, military bases offering high school and college courses to armed forces personnel, and the Peace Corps. A number of foreign companies now hire U.S. college graduates to teach English to their workers, positions that are sometimes very well paid. No matter the wages, high or low, the excitement of teaching in another culture (while learning about that culture) is hard to match.

As we indicated (more than once!), we love classroom teaching, but you should know there are many ways that you can serve society with an education background. You may want to explore one or more of these nonclassroom careers, even as an intern or volunteer at first, to see if these career paths appeal to you.

In this chapter—and in this text—we have tried to answer your questions about teaching. (If we missed one, we invite you to submit it to the website using the OLC Ask the Author button.) We hope that you have found this text chock-full of useful and interesting information, and that you have enjoyed reading this book. In fact, we hope that you enjoyed it so much that you choose to keep the book as a useful reference in the future (and do not resell it to the used bookstore!). But more than that, we hope that you are gaining greater clarity on your decision about whether teaching is for you, and whatever that decision turns out to be, we wish you the best of luck!

CLASS ACTIVITY: UNANSWERED QUESTIONS ABOUT THE TEACHING PROFESSION
IM, Activity 15:1

SUMMARY

1. What does the education job market look like? (or, put another way, will I be able to find a satisfying teaching position?)

   Growth in the student population, efforts to reduce class size, and ongoing teacher retirements have increased the demand for teachers, while budget shortfalls have curtailed hiring in some areas. It is predicted that more than two million teachers will be needed in the next decade, and certain areas, such as math, science, bilingual and special education are experiencing a serious teacher shortage. Urban school districts and the federal government are offering signing bonuses, housing assistance, and loan forgiveness to attract teachers, but rural areas also face a teacher shortage. While students of color constitute nearly 40 percent of the school population, only about 15 percent of new teachers are of color.

2. Can I make a decent salary as a teacher?

   Teacher salaries have steadily improved in the last twenty years, although increases have been more modest in the last ten years. Beginning teachers average above $30,000, the average teacher earns in the $40,000, yet some school districts pay considerably more.

3. How can new teachers increase their chances of working in a school of their choice?

   A strong résumé provides prospective employers with critical information. A portfolio goes beyond a résumé by providing actual artifacts of a candidate's qualifications. Some portfolios, called e-portfolios, can be constructed and transferred electronically. Exploring a teaching position takes careful planning, as do interviews. Teaching candidates need to learn about the schools and faculties they are considering joining, and give careful consideration to questions such as: Do other teachers enjoy working in this school? Are benefits satisfactory? What are the children like? What kind of support do teachers receive? Does the community support its school system?

4. What do I need in order to teach—a license or certification? (and how do I get one!)

   Teacher certification indicates that a professional group recognizes or certifies that a teacher is competent and has met certain standards. A teacher's license, issued by the state government, grants the legal right to teach. Teacher certification is a professional designation; a teacher's license is a legal document. Requirements for teacher licensure differ from state to state. A teacher's license in one state may not be valid in another, unless the states have entered into a compact or reciprocity agreement. Accreditation of college-level teacher education programs can facilitate new graduates becoming eligible for multistate teacher licenses.

   States issue various types of teaching licenses, from initial or probationary to special licenses for administration and counseling. Endorsements enable experienced teachers to gain additional licensure in a second subject area.

5. What teacher competency tests do I need to take?

   Teacher competency tests are used for admission into teacher education programs, for certification, and for licensure. Teacher competency tests are required in most states. (See Appendix 1 for more specific details.) *Praxis I* focuses on basic literacy, *Praxis II* on pedagogy and subject area competence, and the less used *Praxis III* on classroom performance. Many states have designed their own competency tests, which they require prospective teachers to take before being licensed. The purpose, use and appropriateness of teacher tests is intensely debated by educators and politicians. Despite these controversies, there is strong support from the public and from politicians for testing teachers and their students.

6. Why do teachers seek tenure? (and should I?)

After demonstrating teaching competence for the specified period (usually 2–5 years), a teacher may be awarded tenure, which provides a substantial degree of job security. While tenure preserves academic freedom and protects teachers from arbitrary and unjust dismissal, it can also provide job security for ineffective teachers.

7. Are there jobs in education outside of the classroom?

An education degree prepares you not only for a teaching career, but for many education-related careers as well, in areas such as early childhood education, adult education, counseling and advising, and distance learning, and in organizations such as nonprofits, educational associations, private corporations, government agencies, and the media.

 WEB-*TIVITIES*

1. Becoming Informed About the Job Market
2. Developing a Portfolio
3. Teacher Tenure
4. The Third W—Where?

KEY TERMS AND PEOPLE

adult (continuing) education, 557

conditional (emergency) license, 549

day care centers, 555

e-portfolio, 545

endorsement, 549

four *Ws*, 542

initial (provisional) license, 548

minimum competency tests, 551

National Association of State Directors of Teacher Education and Certification (NASDTEC), 550

National Council for the Accreditation of Teacher Education (NCATE), 550

nontraditional educational careers, 555

portfolios, 545

Praxis Assessment for Beginning Teachers, 552

privatization, 542

probationary teaching period, 553

reciprocity (compact) agreements, 550

résumé, 544

special license, 549

standard (professional) license, 548

Teach for America, 550

teacher certification, 547

teacher oversupply, 542

teacher's license, 547

tenure, 553

Part IV: Tomorrow

4.1 Nontraditional Hero

Purpose: We know that students need inspiring figures—individuals who serve as role models and motivate students. Although heroes come from all backgrounds, curricular materials do not always reflect diversity. The result is a disconnect between the growing diversity of America's students and the curriculum they study. You can enhance your curriculum by adding to the list of nontraditional champions in your texts. (Consider ethnicity, race, gender, age, class, lifestyle, disability, and circumstances as you select your hero.) You may also want to define different kinds of heroism as you tackle this project. Identifying such heroes has the additional advantage of broadening your own scholarship.

Activity: Select a unique individual or hero who has made a difference. Strive to select someone from a subject area that you will be teaching. Develop a lesson about this person. Make the language, content, and style relevant to the grade level you plan to teach. Develop visuals to enhance your presentation, perhaps a billboard or poster of this person.

Artifact: "Nontraditional Hero Lesson." Save your lesson plan and supporting material for your portfolio, and for use when you begin teaching.

Bonus Artifact: As a way to blend technology with this activity, develop the lesson using PowerPoint software. Include ten or fewer slides in your presentation, and strive to limit text on each slide. Create a powerful presentation. Present the PowerPoint lesson to your college class. Afterward, tweak the presentation so that it is ready to be presented in your first classroom. PowerPoint software is available for both Windows and Macintosh. For more information on PowerPoint go to www.microsoft.com/office/powerpoint/default.asp.

Reflection: What has this activity taught you about nontraditional heroes? Was it easy to select a nontraditional hero? How might you plan to have your students seek out similar heroes? What was the reaction of the class to your presentation and your "hero"? Did you attempt the Bonus Artifact? If so, were you familiar with PowerPoint before this activity? What are your thoughts on using this software? Will it become a staple of your teaching? Include the reflection and artifact in your portfolio.

4.2 Getting to Know Whom?

Purpose: Chapter 12, "The Struggle for Educational Opportunity," exposed some of life's heritage and happenings that influence who we are. Many of us have grown up in relatively homogeneous environments, knowing individuals of similar backgrounds and cultures. Meaningful conversations about how race, nationality, gender, substance abuse, and family crisis impact our own education are rare when diverse backgrounds are missing, yet such conversations could add essence and texture to your understanding of students.

INTASC PRINCIPLE 2:
Human Development and Learning

Activity: Partner with a classmate, campus colleague, or friend who comes from a different background than you. Use the issues mentioned in the chapter to conduct an interview that will uncover information, stories, and perhaps feelings. Strive to interview more than one person. Concentrate on being a good and an active listener. Some opening thoughts might include:

- How do you identify your race or ethnicity?
- How would you describe your family heritage?
- How would you describe your family structure and patterns of daily life?
- Do you have memories of bias and discrimination?
- What are your recollections of your educational experience?
- What are some things you wished your teachers knew about you that perhaps they didn't?
- What are some things teachers could do to help all groups get along better?
- What other concerns have you experienced or witnessed that denied or impeded educational opportunity?
- Do you have recollections about friends who struggled with substance abuse (drinking, drugs, and smoking), depression and suicide, or sexuality and teen pregnancy?
- How has diversity influenced your own education or your commitment to teach?

 FORM:

Getting to Know You

Artifact: "Diversity Insights for My Classroom." From your interview, cull answers that relate directly to the classroom. In about a paragraph, sum up ways that you can apply what you learned during the interview to your teaching.

Reflection: How are you and your interviewee different? How are you similar? How might this anecdotal information add to your understanding of child and human development? What aspects of your partner's cognitive, social, and emotional growth paralleled your own schooling? All in all, what words might describe your conversation: *insightful, laborious, superficial, intimate?* What words do you think your partner might use as a description? Will this paragraph and the information learned during the interview be useful when you enter the classroom? Why or why not? Attach your reflection to your artifact and include in your portfolio.

4.3 A Novel Read

INTASC PRINCIPLE 3:
Diversity in Learning

Purpose: Great teachers have an incredible ability to care, really deeply, about children. Such teachers learn about their students, hold high expectations for them, and fully appreciate their diverse cultural perspectives and learning styles. One marvelous way to understand youngsters is to read literature about the challenges they face. The right books will not only inspire you, but also will expand your awareness of diverse learners.

Activity: Maybe this is a *RAP* activity you will save for summer vacation or a beach-based holiday. Or let this be a change of pace from your textbooks and research papers. Your education faculty will probably have additions to this book list. Pick a book and dig into it:

Teacher, Sylvia Ashton-Warner

Warriors Don't Cry: A Searing Memoir of the Battle to Integrate Little Rock's Central High, Melba Patillo Beals

Mentors, Masters and Mrs. MacGregor: Stories of Teachers Making a Difference, Jane Bluestein (Editor)

Bury My Heart at Wounded Knee, Dee Brown

America Is in the Heart, Carlos Bulosan

Family Values: A Lesbian Mother's Fight for Her Son, Phyllis Burke

Black Ice, Lorene Cary

House on Mango Street, Sandra Cisneros

The Water Is Wide, Patrick Conroy

Reflections of a Rock Lobster: A Story About Growing Up Gay Aaron Fricke

One Child, Torey Hayden

Up the Down Staircase, Bel Kaufman

Among Schoolchildren, Tracy Kidder

Coming of Age in Mississippi, Ann Moody

The Bluest Eye, Toni Morrison

900 Shows a Year, Stuart Palonsky

The Education of a WASP, Lois Stalvey

Native Son, Richard Wright

Artifact: "Lessons from Literature." After reading one of the selections from this list, or a book of your choice with a school/education theme, write a book review that focuses on lessons and themes from the book that can be applied to the classroom. The goal of your review is not only to inform classmates about the strengths and weaknesses, but also to extract lessons about effective teaching practices.

Reflection: What did you learn from reading this book? Did you "unlearn" or abandon any misconceptions after your reading? Can you identify implications for your classroom? Would you assign this book to your students or suggest it for a faculty book club? Include your book report and reflection in your portfolio.

4.4 If the Walls Could Speak

INTASC PRINCIPLE 4:
Variety of
Instructional
Strategies

Purpose: It is human nature to surround oneself with items that represent our unique heritage and experiences. Teachers cannot afford to fall into this pattern. Teachers can work to ensure that their classrooms reflect the rich diversity of both their students and their country. Teachers must work to ensure that their classrooms are nonsexist and nonracist. One way to achieve this goal is through classroom bulletin boards and other displays.

Activity: On a poster board or in your classroom, create a bulletin board representing diverse set of people and cultures. Use magazines, newspaper, the Internet, personal pictures, and so on. Strive to include "regular" people and events as well as famous people and events.

Artifact: "Seeing Diversity." Take a photo of your display, and if appropriate, save it for possible use in your classroom. Then stand back and be an objective judge by rating your bulletin board for diversity and equality using the following chart:

FORM:
Seeing Diversity

Seeing Diversity	Not at All				Very
	1	2	3	4	5
Clarity of Presentation					
Attractiveness					
Variety of Cultures Featured					
Equal Representation of Men and Women					
Mixture of Regular and Famous People					
Inclusion of Other Diversity Issues (Disability, Age, etc.)					
Overall Quality					
Overall Usefulness					

Reflection: What did you learn from this experience? Was it a challenge to create such a display? What part of this activity was easy? Did you learn how to improve this activity on your next try? Include both your photograph of your "Seeing Diversity" chart and the reflection in your portfolio.

4.5 Class Comedy Club

INTASC PRINCIPLE 5:
Motivation and
Management

Purpose: For all the crises in classrooms and children at risk, humor in the educational workplace survives and even thrives. Thank goodness! Healthful humor (as opposed to targeted humor and sarcasm) can motivate students to participate and learn. Student humor, often unintentional, can be a major factor in keeping you happy and in the business of teaching. While you may never aspire to be a comic, sharing a funny teaching story with your students will help you practice setting a positive and welcoming learning climate.

 FORM:

Class Comedy Club

Activity: While there are books about kids who say and do the darnedest things, as well as e-mail and magazine features filled with funny stories, there is nothing like oral history and the stories of your peers to tickle a funny bone. Begin by freewriting answers to the following questions:

- The funniest teacher I recall from school . . .
- The funniest student happening was . . .
- It sure was funny in school when . . . and she/he/they really did (or didn't) get in trouble . . .
- A teacher walks into a staff lounge . . .
- How many teachers does it take to . . .

Practice and dramatically deliver your funny stories. Encourage your peers to help you embroider them with colorful commentary, body language, and well-timed punchlines. Hone your presentation until you have a tight 5- to 10-minute routine.

Artifact: Videotape or record your "Teaching and Humor" in a comfortable environment. If you feel emboldened, present your education comedy sketch to your classmates.

Reflection: How hard was this activity for you? Can you picture yourself using your "material" in the classroom? What did you learn about yourself from this activity? Be sure to save both your notes and taping for use in your first classroom. Include your taping and reflection in your portfolio.

4.6 Computers in the Classroom: Bane or Boon?

Purpose: You certainly have your own experience, as a student, with computer technology. Are you wired into everything or stonewalling yourself away from it all? We want you to take both sides of the technology debate and fully develop two points of view: pro and con. Researching and refining polarized opinions is a communication challenge!

INTASC PRINCIPLE 6: Communication Skills

Activity: Consider what you have read about and explored in educational technology and generate a balance sheet that both supports and refutes the place of technology in education. (For a model, consider any of the *You Be the Judge* features throughout the textbook that take contrasting views on timely educational topics.) Select a very specific theme, especially one that is related to your subject area or grade level. Generate a title that polarizes opinions such as the following suggestions:

- Word Processing—Helping or Hurting Writing Skills
- Computers in Kindergarten—Absolutely Not or For Sure
- Our Technology Dollars—Classes for the Arts or for Computers
- Computers—One per Classroom or One per Child
- The Internet—Amazing Research Tool or Ticket to Plagiarism

For a more challenging activity, cite research studies to support both positions.

Artifact: "You be the Judge: Technology." Develop and present your chosen topic to your classmates in two ways. You may want to share the written "You Be the Judge," or teach about it using an overhead projector or the chalkboard.

Bonus Artifact: Develop and present "You Be the Judge: Technology" through a PowerPoint presentation. Perhaps you could partner with a classmate for this activity. If you want, you can contrast the two approaches, with one of you teaching with a low-tech approach, while the other one presents using higher tech support.

PowerPoint software is available for both Windows and Macintosh. For more information on PowerPoint go to www.microsoft.com/office/powerpoint/default.asp.

Reflection: By constructing both sides of an issue, what did you learn about balance and fairness in communication? What side of the sheet are you on? Could a reader detect that from your end product? Did you find that your views changed as you worked to present each side convincingly? Did you venture into both the low-tech and high-tech presentations? Why or why not? Include your artifact and reflection in your portfolio.

4.7 Another Mini-Lesson with Another Mini-Group

Purpose: At this stage in your development as an educator, you simply cannot get enough experience teaching. Mirroring *RAP* 1.7, this activity will not only provide more teaching experience, it will afford you a chance to put into action what you've learned.

Activity: Develop and teach a mini-lesson (eight to twelve minutes) using content from the text's fourth section (Chapters 12 through 15) as your focus. Again, your challenge will be to choose a concise topic. While you are free to choose, possible subjects from the reading include: Black Americans—The Struggle for a Chance to Learn; Hispanics—Growing Impact on Schools; An Introduction to Virtual High School, and so on. As with *RAP* 1.7 strive to employ techniques that promote variety in process and content.

Dr. Madeline Hunter's research showed that effective teachers have a methodology when planning and presenting a lesson. She found that no matter what the teacher's style, grade level, subject matter, or economic background of the students, a properly taught lesson contained the following elements:

Dr. Madeline Hunter's Seven-Step Lesson Plan

Anticipatory Set (focus)—Focus learners' attention on the instruction that is about to begin. This could be a teacher demonstration, video, story, puzzle, or a handout prior to the actual lesson. This is also known as a "grabber" and it's a way to get your student's attention and interest.

Purpose (objective)—A clear explanation of what learners will understand and be able to do as a result of the lesson. This section should answer the question: "Why is this important to learn?"

Instructional Strategy—What content and skills need to be taught to accomplish this task? And what are the best teaching strategies needed for this instructional task (lecture, activity, video, group work, etc.)?

Modeling (show)—Provide learners with examples or demonstrations of competencies associated with the lesson.

Guided Practice—Monitor learners as they apply new information.

Check for Understanding—Evaluate whether learners have the information needed to master the objective.

Independent Practice—Assign learners to work independently, without direct teacher assistance.

For more information on Dr. Hunter visit
www.foothill.net/~moorek/lessondesign.html

Artifact: Design a "Lesson Plan: Preparing for Tomorrow's Classroom" using the Hunter format. If this is your first lesson plan, you may want to call it that. If not, come up with a title that reflects your topic or the skill you are working on.

	Need to Improve				Did this Well
	1	2	3	4	5
Anticipatory Set					
Purpose					
Instructional Input					
Modeling					
Guided Practice					
Checking for Understanding					
Independent Practice					

Reflection: You did it! You taught another mini-lesson to your peers, something that many experienced faculty find frightening. Use the following rubric to assess your success. Also record your feelings. How well do you think it went? Include both your lesson plan and the rubric in your portfolio.

FORM:
Mini-Lesson Rubric

4.8 Pruning Your Portfolio

Purpose: Earlier *RAP* activities, reflections, and artifacts helped you create a *working* portfolio. Now is the time to assess your portfolio and decide what is worth keeping or upgrading.

INTASC PRINCIPLE 8:
Assessment

Activity: Evaluate your *working* portfolio. Use the following portfolio assessment rubric below to chart the status of your collection. Score your portfolio according to how well it meets the criteria listed, on a scale of 1 to 5. Provide verbal or written evidence to support your position. Select a partner (or two) and set aside ten minutes to discuss and share your *working* portfolios and the assessment charts.

Artifact:

Portfolio Assessment						
	Not at All				Very	Not Applicable
	1	2	3	4	5	
Item						
Purposeful:						
Selective:						
Diverse:						
Ongoing:						
Reflective:						
Collaborative:						
Other: _____						
Overall Appraisal:						

FORM:

Portfolio
Assessment

Reflection: What have you learned about your portfolio, including both its strengths and weaknesses, from this exercise? What did your discussion with your partners teach you? How could your portfolio be improved? How do you see this portfolio helping you become an effective instructor? How do you see this portfolio helping you attain employment? Attach this reflection to the artifact and include in your portfolio.

4.9 Website of the Month

Purpose: Websites and Internet sources may prove to be of extraordinary benefit to your professional growth. However, quality control does not exist on the Internet, so, to be a reflective and responsible practitioner, you must learn to evaluate Internet sources. Plus you will find it extremely helpful to compile a bank of useful educational websites that you can draw on at any time.

INTASC PRINCIPLE 9: Reflection and Responsibility

Activity: Select three educational websites. (Links from our textbook site are certainly a good starting place.) Choose one that is relevant to a subject matter area; another that is interactive, featuring bulletin boards or opportunities to chat with colleagues; and a third that is monitored or sponsored by a professional organization such as the NEA or AFT. Use the rubric below to evaluate each of these sites.

OLC FORM:
Assessing the Internet

Artifact: "Assessing the Internet"

	Need to Improve				Did This Well
	1	2	3	4	5
Frequency of Updates					
Ease of Navigation					
Accuracy					
Clarity of Content					
Value of Content					
_____ (Your criterion)					
_____ (Your criterion)					
Overall Appraisal:					

Reflection: What other criteria can you use to decide which websites and Internet re-sources are reliable? Are there techniques and shortcuts to *surfing* educational sites? What web addresses might offer lesson plans, emotional support for new teachers, factual materials for curriculum planning, and colleagues for an issue-based dialogue? Attach your reflection to the artifact and include in your portfolio.

4.10 Showtime: Go on an Information Interview

INTASC PRINCIPLE 10:
Relationships and
Partnerships

Purpose: Interviewing for employment can be a daunting experience. As with all new and difficult endeavors the more experience you gain the easier the task becomes. You will find it easier to begin the interviewing process by participating in a series of information interviews. This type of interview is pretty low stress and revolves around the interviewee simply learning about the employer, job, and the employer's needs without the pressure to "land" a job.

Activity: Armed with what you have learned in this class and other education courses and experiences, set up at least one information interview with an official from a school or grade level that you could envision yourself teaching at. Use the questions below as a guide for the interview. What other questions might you add? Record both the questions and answers for future interviews.

 FORM:

Information
Interview

Artifact: "Information Interview"

1. What is the school district looking for in a teacher-candidate?
2. Are there any special training or experience beyond state certification that the district looks for or requires?
3. In what subject areas and at what grade levels does the district have the greatest need?
4. What should a teacher-candidate know about the students and families in this district?
5. How are teachers evaluated in this district?
6. What emphasis does this district place on standardized tests?
7. What is the average class in this district?
8. Does the district have a mentor program for new teachers, and if so how does it work?
9. What is the process for applying to this district?
10. Are there any additional suggestions for gaining employment in this district?

Reflection: How did the interview go? Were you nervous? What did you learn? What might you do differently next time? Did anything surprise you? Would you want to work in this district? Do you now feel more comfortable about future interviews? At-tach your reflection to your artifact and include in your portfolio.

Praxis Teacher Competency Exams and Sample Test Questions

Praxis

The Praxis Series is an Educational Testing Service (ETS) program that provides tests and other services for states to use as part of their teacher licensure process. Some colleges and universities use these assessments to qualify individuals for entry into teacher education programs.

The Praxis Series is the choice of most states that include tests as part of their teacher licensure process. You will take The Praxis Series if you want to teach public school in one of these states or if you want to enter a teacher education program at a college or university that uses Praxis I: Academic Skills Assessments. Different states and institutions require different tests in the Praxis Series, so be sure you know which tests you need before you register.

The three categories of assessments in the Praxis Series correspond to the three milestones in teacher development.

Praxis I: Academic Skills Assessment. These assessments are designed to be taken early in the student's college career to measure reading, writing, and mathematics skills vital to all teacher candidates. The assessments are available in two formats, paper-based and computer-based. Both measure similar academic skills, but the computer-based tests (CBTs) are tailored to each candidate's performance. CBTs also offer a wider range of question types, provide an immediate score in reading and math, and are available on demand throughout the year by appointment, eliminating the need to register in advance. The paper-based tests, called the PPST or Pre-Professional Skills Tests, are given six times a year.

Praxis II: Subject Assessments. These assessments measure candidates' knowledge of the subjects they will teach, as well as how much they know about teaching that subject. More than 140 content tests are available. The tests are regularly updated, and several are available in each subject field, so a state can customize its program by selecting the assessments that best match its own licensure requirements. For added flexibility, each state can base its assessments on standard multiple-choice questions or incorporate

new candidate-constructed-response modules. These performance-based items allow test-takers to demonstrate in-depth knowledge and reinforce the importance of writing in the teaching profession.

Praxis III: Classroom Performance Assessments. These assessments are used at the beginning teaching level to evaluate all aspects of a beginning teacher's classroom performance. Designed to assist in making licensure decisions, these comprehensive assessments are conducted in the classroom by trained local assessors who use a set of consistent, reliable, nationally validated criteria.

If you are planning to take one or more of these tests, you need a copy of *The Praxis Series: Professional Assessments for Beginning Teachers, Registration Bulletin.* The bulletin is free and provides complete test information plus test registration instructions. It's available online at www.ets.org/praxis, or you can request one by calling 1-609-771-7395. *Tests at a Glance* and *Praxis Study Guides* are other Praxis "must have" resources. These booklets include detailed descriptions of topics covered, test-taking strategies, sample tests, and scoring guides, and are available online at www.ets.org/praxis or by calling 1-800-537-3161.

The states and territories listed below use the Praxis Series tests as part of their teacher licensure process. You should check with each state to find out which tests are required, passing scores, and other information.

Alaska	Louisiana
Arkansas	Maine
California	Maryland
Connecticut	Minnesota
Delaware	Mississippi
District of Columbia	Missouri
Florida	Montana
Georgia	Nebraska
Guam	Nevada
Hawaii	New Hampshire
Indiana	New Jersey
Kentucky	New Mexico

North Carolina	Tennessee
Ohio	Texas
Oklahoma	U.S. Virgin Islands
Oregon	Vermont
Pennsylvania	Virginia
Rhode Island	West Virginia
South Carolina	Wisconsin

National Evaluation Systems

While the Praxis assessments from ETS have received a great deal of attention, National Evaluation Systems, Inc. assesses almost as many prospective teachers, but is less well-known. The reason is that NES customizes its exams for individual states. The Praxis series is administered to about 500,000 aspiring teachers; NES assesses just under 400,000. Some states use both NES and Praxis exams to assess their teachers. Specific information about NES-created tests is available directly from teacher licensure departments in:

Alaska	Michigan
California	New Mexico
Colorado	New York
Illinois	Oklahoma
Massachusetts	Texas

Sample Test Questions

The following sample test questions are from Praxis II: Subject and Assessment: Principles of Learning and Teaching. For additional items visit the Praxis website at www.ets.org/praxis and download *Tests at a Glance.* Good luck!

Principles of Learning and Teaching: Grades 7–12

The sample questions that follow illustrate the kinds of questions in the test. They are not, however, representative of the entire scope of the test in either content or difficulty. Answers with explanations follow the questions.

CASE HISTORY: 7–12

<u>Directions:</u> The case history is followed by two short-answer questions.

Mr. Payton
Scenario

Mr. Payton teaches world history to a class of thirty heterogeneously grouped students ages fourteen to sixteen. He is working with his supervisor, planning for his self-evaluation to be completed in the spring. At the beginning of the third week of school, he begins gathering material that might be helpful for the self-evaluation. He has selected one class and three students from this class to focus on.

Mr. Payton's first impression of the three students

Jimmy has attended school in the district for ten years. He repeated fifth and seventh grades. Two years older than most of the other students in class and having failed twice, Jimmy is neither dejected nor hostile. He is an outgoing boy who, on the first day of class, offered to help me with "the young kids" in the class. He said, "Don't worry about me remembering a lot of dates and stuff. I know it's going to be hard, and I'll probably flunk again anyway, so don't spend your time thinking about me."

Burns is a highly motivated student who comes from a family of world travelers. He has been to Europe and Asia. These experiences have influenced his career choice, international law. He appears quiet and serious. He has done extremely well on written assignments and appears to prefer to work alone or with one or two equally bright, motivated students. He has a childhood friend, one of the slowest students in the class.

Pauline is a withdrawn student whose grades for the previous two years have been mostly C's and D's. Although Pauline displays no behavior problems when left alone, she appears not to be popular with the other students. She often stares out the window when she should be working. When I speak to Pauline about completing assignments, she becomes hostile. She has completed few of the assignments so far with any success. When I spoke to her counselor, Pauline yelled at me, "Now I'm in trouble with my counselor too, all because you couldn't keep your mouth shut!"

Mr. Payton's initial self-analysis, written for his supervisor

I attend workshops whenever I can and consider myself a creative teacher. I often divide the students into groups for cooperative projects, but they fall apart and are far from "cooperative." The better-performing students, like Burns, complain about the groups, claiming that small-group work is boring and that they learn more working alone or with students like themselves. I try to stimulate all the students' interest through class discussions. In these discussions, the high-achieving students seem more interested in impressing me than in listening and responding to what other students have to say. The low-achieving students seem content to be silent. Although I try most of the strategies I learn in workshops, I usually find myself returning to a modified lecture and the textbook as my instructional mainstays.

Background information on lesson to be observed by supervisor

Goals:

- To introduce students to important facts and theories about Catherine the Great
- To link students' textbook reading to other sources of information
- To give students practice in combining information from written and oral material
- To give students experience in note taking

I assigned a chapter on Catherine the Great in the textbook as homework on Tuesday. Students are to take notes on their reading. I gave Jimmy a book on Catherine the Great with a narrative treatment rather than the factual approach taken by the textbook. I told him the only important date is the date Catherine began her reign. The book has more pictures and somewhat larger print than the textbook.

I made no adaptation for Burns, since he's doing fine. I offered to create a study guide for Pauline, but she angrily said not to bother. I hope that Wednesday's lecture will make up for any difficulties she might experience in reading the textbook.

Supervisor's notes on Wednesday's lesson

Mr. Payton gives a lecture on Catherine the Great. First he says, "It is important that you take careful notes because I will be including information that is not contained in the chapter you read as homework last night. The test I will give on Friday will include both the lecture and the textbook information."

He tape records the lecture to supplement Pauline's notes but does not tell Pauline about the tape until the period is over because he wants her to do the best note taking she can manage. During the lecture, he speaks slowly, watching the class as they take notes. In addition, he walks about the classroom and glances at the students' notes.

Mr. Payton's follow-up and reflection

Tomorrow the students will use the class period to study for the test. I will offer Pauline earphones to listen to the tape-recorded lecture. On Friday, we will have a short-answer and essay test covering the week's work.

Class notes seem incomplete and inaccurate, and I'm not satisfied with this test as an assessment of student performance. Is that a fair measure of all they do?

SAMPLE QUESTIONS

This section presents two short-answer questions and sample responses along with the standards used in scoring these responses. When you read these sample responses, keep in mind that they are less polished than if they had been developed at home, edited, and carefully presented. Examinees do not know what questions will be asked and must decide, on the spot, how to respond. Readers assign scores based on the following scoring guide.

GENERAL SCORING GUIDE
A response that receives a score of 2:

- Demonstrates a thorough understanding of the aspects of the case that are relevant to the question
- Responds appropriately to all parts of the question
- If an explanation is required, provides a strong explanation that is well supported by relevant evidence
- Demonstrates a strong knowledge of pedagogical concepts, theories, facts, procedures, or methodologies relevant to the question

A response that receives a score of 1:

- Demonstrates a basic understanding of the aspects of the case that are relevant to the question
- Responds appropriately to one portion of the question
- If an explanation is required, provides a weak explanation that is supported by relevant evidence

- Demonstrates some knowledge of pedagogical concepts, theories, facts, procedures, or methodologies relevant to the question

A response that receives a score of 0:

- Demonstrates misunderstanding of the aspects of the case that are relevant to the question
- Fails to respond appropriately to the question
- Is not supported by relevant evidence
- Demonstrates little knowledge of pedagogical concepts, theories, facts, procedures, or methodologies relevant to the question

No credit is given for a blank or off-topic response.

Directions: Questions 1 and 2 require you to write short answers. You are not expected to cite specific theories or texts in your answers; however, your responses to the questions will be evaluated with respect to professionally accepted principles and practices in teaching and learning. Be sure to answer all parts of the questions. Write your answers in the spaces indicated in the response book.

Question 1

In his self-analysis, Mr. Payton says that the better-performing students say small-group work is boring and that they learn more working alone or only with students like themselves. Assume that Mr. Payton wants to continue using cooperative learning groups because he believes they have value for all students.

- Describe TWO strategies he could use to address the concerns of the students who have complained.
- Explain how each strategy suggested could provide an opportunity to improve the functioning of cooperative learning groups. Base your response on principles of effective instructional strategies.

Sample Response that Received a Score of 2

Mr. Payton has to be creative to find strategies that will address the concerns of the students who have complained and still support the strengths of cooperative learning. One way he can do that is to assign these students a variety of roles in which they can share their insights and knowledge with others in a way that will provide them recognition and will help other students. He can also build specific requirements that provide

for individual work into the cooperative work, either before the groups meet or as the groups are working. This individual work provides the more able or motivated students with an opportunity to demonstrate their insights and knowledge and be given appropriate credit for them. The individual work can also serve as a basis for the group work.

Sample Response that Received a Score of 1

I understand why these students are concerned. But Mr. Payton shouldn't just give up on cooperative learning groups. I had a situation like this, when four really bright and eager kids just didn't want to work with students who were less able or less motivated. One thing he could do would be to assign his groups very carefully, so that one of the complaining kids is in each group. He could then use a system where he begins the cooperative work by regrouping, numbering the kids in each group 1, 2, 3, 4. First, all the "1's" work together, all the "2's" work together, and so forth. All the kids who complained would have the same number. After they have had the opportunity to work together on an advanced level, the groups would reform. The "1's" could go back to their own groups and share with them what the "1" group came up with. In this way, they have the intellectual stimulation of working together first, and then the status of sharing with other kids.

Sample Response that Received a Score of 0

Probably the best thing he can do is to let the complaining kids work individually. They are only going to resent the less able kids and will probably end up insulting them. The kids who are complaining will learn more if they work individually and can push themselves to their limits. The other kids can work at a level more appropriate to their ability.

Question 2

In the introduction to the lesson to be observed, Mr. Payton briefly mentions the modification he has or has not made for some students. Review his comments about modifications for Jimmy and Burns.

- For each of these two students, describe ONE different way Mr. Payton might have provided a modification to offer a better learning situation for each.
- Explain how each modification could offer a better learning situation. Base your explanation

on principles of varied instruction for different kinds of learners.

Sample Response that Received a Score of 2

For Burns who is a bright, independent learner, providing him the opportunity to take extra responsibility for mastering challenging material and figuring out how to help his classmates understand it might help him to be more open and positive in his classroom behavior. For example, he might use more complex materials to access information, or might create a program using technology to share his knowledge and insights with others. For Jimmy, Mr. Payton might have a conference with him to find out how he was expected to learn social studies in the past and why he is so accepting of failing social studies. This conference may lead to a strategy such as the use of information presented visually or orally, or the use of graphic organizers to access information, or an alternate means of demonstrating his understanding if written assessments are part of the problem.

Sample Response that Received a Score of 1

Jimmy is a very interesting student to consider. He has a history of failure, and seems to accept the fact that he may fail again. However, he seems quite outgoing so he might be willing to try if approached right. I think the first thing Mr. Payton could do would be to sit down and talk with him. He needs to try to figure out why Jimmy failed in the past. He might ask him if he has any ideas about how he learns best—and things teachers have had him do that don't help him. Then, with this information, Mr. Payton might be able to come up with some approaches based on Jimmy's learning style. If Jimmy says he hates to read, Mr. Payton needs to find a way for him to access the information other than reading! Another thing Mr. Payton might do is adjust what he expects Jimmy to learn. Jimmy says he has problems with "a lot of dates and stuff." But he may be interested in other aspects of history—why people did the things they did, for example. By tailoring the study of history to aspects that might be more appropriate for Jimmy, Mr. Payton might have a better chance of helping Jimmy succeed.

Sample Response that Received a Score of 0

I think the modification he should make for both students is to be much clearer about what the expectations of the course are. Sometimes students are tuned out or bored because they just don't know what is expected of them. Maybe Mr. Payton needs to post his expectations prominently in the room so that both of these students can see what is expected. The expectations also need to indicate what is required for passing, so that Jimmy and Burns will know what the limits are.

Discrete Multiple–Choice Questions

Directions: Questions 3–5 are not related to the previous case. For each question, select the best answer and mark the corresponding space on your answer sheet.

3. A teacher gives his students a list of terms to use in an essay and intends the list to serve as a kind of learning support called a scaffold. If the students use the list effectively, which of the following would be an appropriate next step for the teacher to take when assigning the students their next essay?

    (A) Asking the students to come up with their own list of terms to use in the new assignment

    (B) Giving the students a longer list of terms to use in the new assignment

    (C) Giving the students a list of terms and asking them to write down a definition of each before beginning the new assignment

    (D) Asking the students to use the same terms in the new assignment

4. The concept of the placement of students in the "least restrictive" educational environment developed as a result of efforts to

    (A) equalize educational opportunities for females and minorities

    (B) normalize the lives of those children with disabilities who were being educated in isolation from their peers

    (C) obtain increased federal funding for the noneducational support of children living in poverty

    (D) reduce the overall costs of educating students with special needs

5. A teacher would get better information from a criterion-referenced test than from a norm-referenced test about which of the following?

    (A) How much each individual student has learned about a particular aspect of the curriculum

    (B) How each individual student's knowledge of a particular aspect of the curriculum compares to that of students across the school district and state

(C) How each individual student's knowledge of a particular aspect of the curriculum compares to that of a national sample of students at the same age level

(D) How much of what each student knows about a particular aspect of the curriculum is based on prior knowledge

Questions 6–7 are based on the following passages. *The following passages are taken from a debate about the advantages and disadvantages of a constructivist approach to teaching.*

Why constructivist approaches are effective

The point of constructivist instruction is to have students reflect on their questions about new concepts in order to uncover their misconceptions. If a student cannot reason out the answer, this indicates a conceptual problem that the teacher needs to address. It takes more than content-related professional expertise to be a "guide on the side" in this process. Constructivist teaching focuses not on what the teacher knows, but on what and how the student learns. Expertise is focused on teaching students how to derive answers, not on giving them the answers. This means that a constructivist approach to teaching must respond to multiple different learning methods and use multiple approaches to content. It is a myth that constructivist teaching never requires students to memorize, to drill, to listen to a teacher explain, or to watch a teacher model problem-solving of various kinds. What constructivist approaches take advantage of is a basic truth about human cognition: we all make sense of new information in terms of what we already know or think we know. And each of us must process new information in our own context and experience to make it part of what we really know.

Why constructivist approaches are misguided

The theory of constructivism is appealing for a variety of reasons—especially for its emphasis on direct student engagement in learning. However, as they are implemented, constructivist approaches to teaching often treat memorization, direct instruction, or even open expression of teacher expertise as forbidden. This demotion of the teacher to some sort of friendly facilitator is dangerous, especially in an era in which there is an unprecedented number of teachers teaching out of their fields of expertise. The focus of attention needs to be on how much teachers know about the content being taught.

Students need someone to lead them through the quagmire of propaganda and misinformation that they confront daily. Students need a teacher who loves the subject and has enough knowledge to act as an intellectual authority when a little direction is needed. Students need a teacher who does not settle for minimal effort but encourages original thinking and provides substantive intellectual challenge.

6. The first passage suggests that reflection on which of the following after a lesson is an essential element in constructivist teaching?

(A) The extent to which the teacher's knowledge of the content of the lesson was adequate to meet students' curiosity about the topic

(B) The differences between what actually took place and what the teacher planned

(C) The variety of misconceptions and barriers to understanding revealed by students' responses to the lesson

(D) The range of cognitive processes activated by the activities included in the lesson design and implementation

7. The author of the second passage would regard which of the following teacher behaviors as essential for supporting student learning?

(A) Avoiding lecture and memorization

(B) Allowing students to figure out complex problems without the teacher's intervention

(C) Emphasizing process rather than content knowledge

(D) Directly guiding students' thinking on particular topics

ANSWERS

1. See sample responses on page A–4.

2. See sample responses on page A–4.

3. The best answer is A. A scaffold is a temporary learning aid, designed to help the student to grow in independence as a learner; thus, once the skill the scaffold is intended to help teach has been mastered, the scaffold should be withdrawn. Asking the students to come up with their own list of terms to use in the new assignment in effect withdraws the scaffold and

encourages independence. None of the actions described in the other answer choices does these things.

4. The best answer is B. The concept of "least restrictive" stems from P.L. 94-142 and subsequent legislation regarding the education of students with disabilities and implies that special students are not to be classified by disability and given permanent special placement on the basis of these classifications. Rather, they are to be moved to special settings only if necessary and only for as long as necessary.

5. The best answer is A. Criterion-referenced tests are developed to assess knowledge and understanding of specified standards for learning particular content. They are designed to enable individual students or groups of students who have studied the same material to assess how much they have learned as compared to the criterion, or standard. A norm-group performance is not required for a criterion-referenced test, since the goal is to measure knowledge against a predefined knowledge standard. Whether a person passes a criterion-referenced test is not judged in relation to how other applicants performed (which would be norm-referenced) but in relation to an established standard for minimum number correct.

6. The best answer is C. Constructivist teaching depends on the connection of new information to already learned information or understandings, whether or not they are accurate. The passage says, "The point of constructivist instruction is to have students reflect on their questions about new concepts in order to uncover their misconceptions. If a student cannot reason out the answer, this indicates a conceptual problem that the teacher needs to address." Thus, a consideration of barriers and/or misconceptions in response to the presentation of new material is an essential follow-up to a constructivist lesson.

7. The best answer is D. The second author maintains that students require teacher guidance and a direct expression of the teacher's expert content knowledge in order to learn most effectively. Choices A (avoiding lecturing), B (learning without teacher intervention), and C (de-emphasis on content knowledge) are not consistent with this approach to teaching. Direct guidance of students' thinking is consistent with the second author's approach.

State Offices for Teacher Certification and Licensure

ALABAMA
Teacher Education and Certification
Alabama Department of Education
50 North Ripley Street
P.O. Box 302101
Montgomery, AL 36104
Phone: 334-242-9977
www.alsde.edu

ALASKA
Teacher Education and Certification
Alaska Department of Education
801 West 10th Street, Suite 200
Juneau, AK 99801-1894
Phone: 907-465-2831
www.educ.state.ak.us

ARIZONA
Teacher Certification
Arizona Department of Education
P.O. Box 6490
Phoenix, AZ 85005
Phone: 602-542-4367
www.ade.state.az.us

ARKANSAS
Office of Professional Licensure
Arkansas Department of Education
4 State Capitol Mall,
Rooms 106B/107B
Little Rock, AR 72201
Phone: 501-682-4342
www.arkedu.state.ar.us

CALIFORNIA
California Commission on Teacher
Credentialing (CTC)
Information Services Unit
P.O. Box 944270
1900 Capitol Avenue
Sacramento, CA 94233-2700
Phone: 916-445-7254 or
888-921-2682
www.ctc.ca.gov

COLORADO
Educator Licensing
Colorado Department of Education
201 East Colfax Avenue, Room 105
Denver, CO 80203
Phone: 303-866-6628
www.cde.state.co.us

CONNECTICUT
Bureau of Certification and Teacher
Preparation

Connecticut State Department of
Education
P.O. Box 150471, Room 243
Hartford, CT 06115-0471
Phone: 860-713-6969
www.state.ct.us/sde

DELAWARE
Delaware Department of Education
John G. Townsend Building
401 Federal Street
P.O. Box 1402
Dover, DE 19903-1402
Phone: 302-739-4601
www.doe.state.de.us

DISTRICT OF COLUMBIA
Educational Credentialing and
Standards Branch
District of Columbia Public Schools
825 North Capitol Street, N.E.
6th Floor
Washington, DC 20002
Phone: 202-442-5377
www.k12.dc.us

FLORIDA
Bureau of Educator Certification
Florida Department of Education
Suite 201, Turlington Building
325 West Gaines Street
Tallahassee, FL 32399-0400
Phone: (in-state toll-free number)
800-445-6739 or (out-of-state
number) 850-488-2317
www.firn.edu/doe

GEORGIA
The Georgia Professional Standards
Commission
1454 Twin Towers East
Atlanta, GA 30334
Phone: 404-657-9000 or
800-869-7775 (in Georgia)
www.gapsc.com

HAWAII
Division of Administrative Services,
Personnel Services Branch
ATTN: Personnel Development and
Certification Section
Hawaii Department of Education
P.O. Box 2360
Honolulu, HI 96804

Phone: 808-586-3276
www.doe.k12.hi.us

IDAHO
Bureau of Certification and
Professional Standards
Idaho State Department of
Education
650 West State Street
P.O. Box 83720
Boise, ID 83720-0027
Phone: 208-332-6880
www.sde.state.id.us

ILLINOIS
Division of Professional Certification
Illinois State Board of Education
100 North First Street
Springfield, IL 62777
Phone: 800-845-8749
www.isbe.state.il.us

INDIANA
Indiana Professional Standards
Board
251 East Ohio Street, Suite 201
Indianapolis, IN 46204-2133
Phone: 317-232-9010
www.in.gov/psb

IOWA
Iowa Board of Educational Examiners
Iowa Department of Education
Grimes State Office Building
Des Moines, IA 50319-0146
Phone: 515-281-3245
www.state.ia.useducate/

KANSAS
Certification and Teacher Education
Kansas State Department of
Education
120 S.E. 10th Avenue
Topeka, KS 66612-1182
Phone: 785-291-3678
www.ksbe.state.ks.us

KENTUCKY
Education Professional Standards
Board
Division of Certification
Kentucky Department of Education
1024 Capital Center Drive,
Suite 225

Frankfort, KY 40601
Phone: 502-573-4606
www.kde.state.ky.us

LOUISIANA
Teacher Certification and Higher
Education
Office of Quality Educators
Louisiana Department of
Education
P.O. Box 94064
Baton Rouge, LA 70804-9064
Phone: 877-453-2721 or
225-342-3490
www.doe.state.la.us

MAINE
Maine Department of Education
23 State House Station
Augusta, ME 04333
Phone: 207-624-6600
www.state.me.us/education

MARYLAND
Division of Certification &
Accreditation
Maryland State Department of
Education
200 W. Baltimore Street
Baltimore, MD 21201
Phone: 410-767-0412
www.msde.state.md.us

MASSACHUSETTS
Teacher Certification and
Credentialing Office
Massachusetts Department of
Education
350 Main Street, P.O. Box 9140
Malden, MA 02148-9140
Phone: 781-338-6600
www.doe.mass.edu

MICHIGAN
Office of Professional Preparation
Services
Michigan Department of
Education
P.O. Box 30008
Lansing, MI 48909
Phone: 517-373-1925
www.state.mi.us

MINNESOTA
Personnel Licensing Team
Minnesota Department of Children,
Families and Learning
1500 Highway 36 West
Roseville, MN 55113-4266
Phone: 651-582-8691
www.educ.state.mn.us

MISSISSIPPI
Educator Licensure/Certification
Mississippi Department of Education
359 North West Street
Jackson, MS 39205
Phone: 601-359-3483
www.mde.k12.ms.us

MISSOURI
Teacher Certification
Division of Teacher Quality and
Urban Education
P.O. Box 480
Jefferson City, MO 65102-0480
Phone: 573-751-0051 or
573-751-3847
www.dese.state.mo.us

MONTANA
Certification and Licensure
Montana Office of Public
Instruction
P.O. Box 202501
Helena, MT 59620-2501
Phone: 406-444-3150
www.metnet.state.mt.us

NEBRASKA
Teacher Education and Certification
Nebraska Department of Education
301 Centennial Mall South
P.O. Box 94987
Lincoln, NE 68509
Phone: 402-471-2496
www.nde.state.ne.us

NEVADA
Teacher Licensure Office
Nevada Department of Education
1820 East Sahara, Suite 205
Las Vegas, NV 89104-3746
Phone: 775-486-6458
www.nde.state.ne.us

NEW HAMPSHIRE
Bureau of Credentialing
New Hampshire Department of
Education
101 Pleasant Street
Concord, NH 03301-3860
Phone: 603-271-2408
www.ed.state.nh.us

NEW JERSEY
Office of Licensing and Credentials
New Jersey Department of
Education
CN 500
Trenton, NJ 08625-0500
Phone: 609-292-2070
Homepage: www.state.nj.us/education

NEW MEXICO
Professional Licensure Unit
New Mexico State Department of
Education
Education Building
Santa Fe, NM 87501-2786
Phone: 505-827-6587
www.sde.state.nm.us

NEW YORK
Office of Teaching
New York State Education
Department
89 Washington Avenue
Albany, NY 12234
Phone: 518-474-3852
www.highered.nysed.gov/tcert

NORTH CAROLINA
Licensure Section
Department of Public Instruction
301 North Wilmington Street
Raleigh, NC 27601-2825
Phone: 919-807-3310
www.dpi.state.nc.us

NORTH DAKOTA
North Dakota Education Standards
and Practices Board
North Dakota Capitol Building
600 East Boulevard Avenue,
Department 202, 9th Floor
Bismarck, ND 58505-0080
Phone: 701-328-2264
www.state.nd.us/espb

OHIO
Office of Certification/Licensure
Ohio Department of Education
25 South Front Street
Columbus, OH 43215-4183
Phone: 877-644-6338
www.ode.state.oh.us

OKLAHOMA
Professional Standards Section
Oklahoma Department of Education
Hodge Education Building,
Room 211
2500 North Lincoln Boulevard
Oklahoma City, OK 73105
Phone: 405-521-3337
www.sde.state.ok.us

OREGON
Teachers Standards and Practices
Commission
255 Capitol Street NE, Suite 105
Salem, OR 97310-1332
Phone: 503-378-3586
www.ode.state.or.us

PENNSYLVANIA
Bureau of Teacher Certification and
Preparation
Pennsylvania Department of
Education
333 Market Street
Harrisburg, PA 17126-0333
Phone: 717-787-3356
www.pde.state.pa.us

RHODE ISLAND
Rhode Island Department of
Education
Shepard Building
255 Westminster Street
Providence, RI 02903
Phone: 401-222-4600
www.ridoe.net

SOUTH CAROLINA
Division of Teacher Quality
South Carolina Department of
Education
1600 Gervais Street
Columbia, SC 29201
Phone: 877-885-5280 (in-state toll
free) or 803-734-8466 (out-of-state
and local callers)
www.sde.state.sc.us

SOUTH DAKOTA
Office of Policy and Accountability
Department of Education and
Cultural Affairs
700 Governors Drive
Pierre, SD 57501
Phone: 605-773-3553
www.state.sd.us/deca

TENNESSEE
State Department of Education
Office of Teacher Licensing

5th Floor, Andrew Johnson Tower
710 James Robertson Parkway
Nashville, TN 37243-0377
Phone: 615-532-4880
www.state.tn.us/
education/lic_home.htm

TEXAS
State Board for Educator
Certification
1001 Trinity Street
Austin, TX 78701-2603
Phone: 512-469-3000
www.sbec.state.tx.us

UTAH
Educator Licensing
Utah State Office of Education
250 East 500 South
Salt Lake City, UT 84111
Phone: 801-538-7740
www.usoe.k12.ut.us/
cert

VERMONT
Licensing Office
Vermont Department of Education
120 State Street
Montpelier, VT 05620-2501
Phone: 802-828-2445
www.state.vt.us/educ/
license/index.htm

VIRGINIA
Division of Teacher Education and
Licensure
Virginia Department of Education
P.O. Box 2120
Richmond, VA 23218
Phone: 804-371-2522
www.pen.k12.va.us

WASHINGTON
Professional Certification
Office of Superintendent of Public
Instruction
Old Capitol Building
P.O. Box 47200
Olympia, WA 98504-7200
Phone: 360-753-6773
www.access.wa.gov

WEST VIRGINIA
Office of Professional Preparation
West Virginia Department of
Education
1900 Kanawha Boulevard
East Building 6, Room 252
Charleston, WV 25305-0330
Phone: 304-558-7826
www.wv.us

WISCONSIN
Bureau for Education, Licensing,
and Placement
Wisconsin Department of Public
Instruction
125 South Webster Street
P.O. Box 7841
Madison, WI 53707-7841
Phone: 608-266-1788
www.dpi.state.wi.us

WYOMING
Professional Teaching Standards
Board
Wyoming State Department of
Education
2300 Capitol Avenue
Hathaway Building, 2nd Floor
Cheyenne, WY 82002-0050
Phone: 307-777-7675
www.k12.wy.us

A Summary of Selected Reports on Education Reform

Title	Source	Data
The Paideia Proposal (1982)	Mortimer Adler for the Paideia Group	Twenty-two members contributed to a philosophical analysis of educational needs.
A Nation at Risk: The Imperative for Educational Reform (1983)	The National Commission on Excellence in Education—U.S. Department of Education	Eighteen political and educational leaders commissioned papers and reviewed available materials, including national and international test scores.
American's Competitive Challenge: The Need for a Response (1983)	Business—Higher Education Forum	Sixteen representatives of business and higher education reviewed expert opinions and past surveys.
Action for Excellence: A Comprehensive Plan to Improve Our Nation's Schools (1983)	Task Force of the Education Commission of the States, chaired by Governor James Hunt	Forty-one governors, legislators, labor leaders, business leaders, and school board members collected data and interpreted results.
Academic Preparation for College: What Students Need to Know and Be Able to Do (1983)	Education Equality Project—The College Board	Two hundred high school and college teachers and college board members collected and interpreted test results.
Making the Grade (1983)	Twentieth-Century Fund Task Force on Federal Elementary and Secondary Education Policy	Eleven members of state, local, and higher education organizations reviewed research studies.
Educating Americans for the 21st Century: A Report to the American People and the National Science Board (1983)	National Science Board Commission on Pre-College Education in Mathematics, Science and Technology	Commission members and others reviewed a number of professional association, business, and other education programs.
The Good High School: Portraits of Character and Culture (1983)	Sara Lawrence Lightfoot	Field study of six private and public schools.
High School: A Report on Secondary Education in America (1983)	The Carnegie Foundation for the Advancement of Teaching	Ernest Boyer chaired a national panel of educators and citizens, which reviewed past research and undertook field studies in public high schools.
A Place Called School (1983)	John Goodlad	Presents observations of and responses to questionnaires administered in schools over an eight-year period.

Recommendations

The book urges a radical reorganization to focus on three areas: (1) the development of personal, mental, moral, and spiritual growth; (2) citizenship; and (3) basic skills. Teaching methods and subject areas would be revised, and there would be a core curriculum for all students from elementary through secondary education.

The report's powerful rhetoric, such as the "rising tide of mediocrity" and "a nation at risk," galvanized public attention regarding school reform. The report suggests that poor school performance threatens our nation's economic health. It emphasizes rigorous courses, a core curriculum, the recruiting of talented teachers, and a thorough assessment of student and teacher competence.

The report indicates that a major reason for U.S. economic problems and falling productivity is the inadequate education of the nation's workers, who need more schooling in mathematics, science, critical-thinking skills, and verbal expression.

The report urges state leadership to develop action plans for improving education, including more community involvement, additional funds, better preparation and pay for teachers, stronger curricular offerings, greater accountability, more effective principals, and better programs for poorly achieving students.

More rigorous preparation for college is called for, including better-trained teachers, more demanding elementary and secondary curricula, and higher expectations of students. Colleges should also provide remedial help for ill-prepared students and should work more closely with high schools in preparing students for college.

The report states that the criticism of U.S. schools is exaggerated and that schools are fundamentally doing their job. Suggestions for improvement include federal aid for schools, a clearer focus on educational quality, a continued commitment to educational equity, and support for local decision making.

Emphasizing a strong mathematics and science curriculum, the report highlights the need to attract individuals with these skills into teaching.

Although this is not technically a reform report, the author's observations of four public and two private high schools provide valuable insights into effective and ineffective school practices.

The report recommends a heavy emphasis on English (particularly writing) and a strong academic core for all students. It suggests elimination of the vocational track and advocates a five-year teacher education program.

This report recommends making the principal a manager and creating a "head teacher" to focus on instructional improvement. Goodlad also calls for grouping students in clusters rather than by grade level. The book highlights the need for a greater variety of teaching methods to deal with student diversity.

GLOSSARY

A

ability grouping The assignment of pupils to homogeneous groups according to intellectual ability or level for instructional purposes.

academic freedom The opportunity for teachers and students to learn, teach, study, research, and question without censorship, coercion, or external political and other restrictive influences.

academic learning time The time a student is actively engaged with the subject matter and experiencing a high success rate.

academies The private or semipublic secondary schools in the United States from 1830 through 1870 that stressed practical subjects.

accelerated program The more rapid promotion of gifted students through school.

accountability Holding schools and teachers responsible for student performance.

accreditation Certification of an education program or a school that has met professional standards of an outside agency.

achievement tests Examinations of the knowledge and skills acquired, usually as a result of specific instruction.

adequate education Provides a legal approach for ensuring educational opportunities for poorer students based on state constitution guarantees for an efficient, thorough, or uniform education. Calls for adequate education have replaced previous calls for equal educational expenditures.

adequate yearly progress (AYP) Under the *No Child Left Behind Act,* each state establishes annual criteria to determine school district and school achievement. Schools that fail to meet the AYP criteria (often determined by standardized tests) are held accountable and may be closed.

adult education Courses and programs offered to high school graduates by colleges, business, industry, and governmental and private organizations that lead to academic degrees, occupational preparation, and the like.

advanced placement Courses and programs in which younger students can earn college credit.

aesthetics The branch of philosophy that examines the nature of beauty and judgments about it.

affective domain The area of learning that involves attitudes, values, and emotions.

affirmative action A plan by which personnel policies and hiring practices reflect positive steps in the recruiting and hiring of women and people of color.

allocated time The amount of time a school or an individual teacher schedules for a subject.

alternative families Family units that differ from the traditional image; examples include foster care children, single parents, central role of grandparents, and gay couples.

alternative licensure A procedure for acquiring a teacher's license for those who have not graduated from a traditional state approved teacher education program.

alternative school A private or public school that provides religious, academic, or other alternatives to the regular public school.

American Federation of Teachers (AFT) A national organization of teachers that is primarily concerned with improving educational conditions and protecting teachers' rights.

assertive discipline A behavior modification program developed by Lee and Marlene Canter designed to "catch" and reward students being good, while discouraging off-task and inappropriate behavior.

assistive (adaptive) technology Devices that help the disabled to perform and learn more effectively, from voice-activated keyboards and mechanical wheelchairs to laptops for class note taking and personal scheduling.

asynchronous Nonsimultaneous. Students enrolled in an Internet course need not participate at the same time, and may take the course although they live in different time zones.

authentic assessment A type of evaluation that represents actual performance, encourages students to reflect on their own work, and is integrated into the student's whole learning process. Such tests usually require that students synthesize knowledge from different areas and use that knowledge actively.

B

back to basics During the 1980s, a revival of the back-to-basics movement evolved out of concern for declining test scores in math, science, reading, and other areas. Although there is not a precise definition of back to basics, many consider it to include increased emphasis on reading, writing, and arithmetic, fewer electives, and more rigorous grading.

behavioral objective A specific statement of what a learner must accomplish in order to demonstrate mastery.

behaviorism A psychological theory that interprets human behavior in terms of stimuli-response.

behavior modification A strategy to alter behavior in a desired direction through the use of rewards.

bilingual education Educational programs in which students of limited or no English-speaking ability attend classes taught in English, as well as in their native language. There is great variability in these programs in terms of goals, instructional opportunity, and balance between English and a student's native language.

block grants Federal dollars provided to the states, with limited federal restrictions, for educational aid and program funding.

block scheduling Using longer "blocks" of time to schedule classes results in fewer but longer periods given to each subject. It is designed to promote greater in-depth study.

board certification Recognition of advanced teaching competence, awarded to teachers who demonstrate high levels of knowledge, commitment, and professionalism through a competitive review process administered by the National Board for Professional Teaching Standards.

board of education Constituted at the state and local levels, this agency is responsible for formulating educational policy. Members are sometimes appointed but, more frequently, are elected at the local level.

bond A certificate of debt issued by a government guaranteeing payment of the original investment plus interest by a specified future date. Bonds are used by local communities to raise the funds they need to build or repair schools.

Buckley Amendment The 1974 Family Educational Rights and Privacy Act granting parents of students under 18, and students 18 or over the right to examine their school records.

busing A method for remedying segregation by transporting students to create more ethnically or racially balanced schools. Before busing and desegregation were linked, busing was not a controversial issue, and, in fact, the vast majority of students riding school buses are not involved in desegregation programs.

C

canon The collection of literature and other works that typically reflects a white, Euro-centered view of the world.

career technical education A program to teach elementary and secondary students about the world of work by integrating career awareness and exploration across the school curriculum.

career ladder A system designed to create different status levels for teachers by developing steps one can climb to receive increased pay through increased responsibility or experience.

Carnegie unit A credit awarded to a student for successfully completing a high school course. It is used in determining graduation requirements and college admissions.

categorical grant Financial aid to local school districts from state or federal agencies for specific purposes.

certification State government or professional association's evaluation and approval of an applicant's competencies.

character education A model comprised of various strategies that promote a defined set of core values to students.

charter school A group of teachers, parents, and even businesses may petition a local school board, or state government, to form a charter school which is exempt from many state and local regulations. Designed to promote creative new schools, the charter represents legal permission to try new approaches to educate students. First charter legislation was passed in Minnesota in 1991.

chief state school officer The executive head of a state department of education. The chief state school officer is responsible for carrying out the mandates of the state board of education and enforcing educational laws and regulations. This position is also referred to as *state superintendent*.

child abuse Physical, sexual, or emotional violation of a child's health and well-being.

child advocacy movement A movement dedicated to defining and protecting the rights of children. Child advocates recognize that children are not yet ready to assume all the rights and privileges of adults, but they are firmly committed to expanding the rights currently enjoyed by children and to no longer treating children as objects or of the property of others.

child-centered instruction (individual instruction) Teaching that is designed to meet the interests and needs of individual students.

classroom climate The physical, emotional, and aesthetic characteristics, as well as the learning resources, of a school classroom.

cognitive domain The area of learning that involves knowledge, information, and intellectual skills.

Coleman report A study commissioned by President Johnson (1964) to analyze the factors that influence the academic achievement of students. One of the major findings of James Coleman's report was that schools in general have relatively little impact on learning. Family and peers were found to have more impact on a child's education than the school itself did.

collaborative action research Connects teaching and professional growth through the use of research relevant to classroom responsibilities.

collective bargaining A negotiating procedure between employer and employees for resolving disagreements on salaries, work schedules, and other conditions of employment. In collective bargaining, all teachers in a school system bargain as one group through chosen representatives.

Comer model James Comer of Yale has created and disseminated a program that incorporates a team of educational and mental health professionals to assist children at risk by working with their parents and attending to social, educational, and psychological needs.

Committee of Ten In 1892, the National Education Association formed the committee, influenced by college presidents, to reform the nation's high schools. The result was an academically oriented curriculum geared for colleges, and the creation of the Carnegie unit as a measure of progress through the high school curriculum.

common school A public, tax-supported school. First established in Massachusetts, the school's purpose was to create a common basis of knowledge for children. It usually refers to a public elementary school.

community schools Schools connected with a local community to provide for the educational needs of that community.

compensatory education Educational experiences and opportunities designed to overcome or compensate for difficulties associated with a student's disadvantaged background.

competency The ability to perform a particular skill or to demonstrate a specified level of knowledge.

comprehensive high school A public secondary school that offers a variety of curricula, including vocational, academic, and general education programs.

compulsory attendance A state law requiring that children and adolescents attend school until reaching a specified age.

computer-assisted instruction (CAI) Individualized instruction between a student and programmed instructional material stored in a computer.

computer-managed instruction (CMI) A recordkeeping procedure for tracking student performance using a computer.

conditional teacher's license Sometimes called an emergency license, a substandard license that is issued on a temporary basis to meet a pressing need.

consolidation The trend toward combining small or rural school districts into larger ones.

constructivism With roots in cognitive psychology, this educational approach is built on the idea that people construct their understanding of the world. Constructivist teachers gauge a student's prior knowledge, then carefully orchestrate cues, classroom activities, and penetrating questions to push students to higher levels of understanding.

content standards The knowledge, skills, and dispositions that students should master in each subject. These standards are often linked to broader themes and sometimes to testing programs.

cooperative learning In classrooms using cooperative learning, students work on activities in small groups, and they receive rewards based on the overall group performance.

core curriculum A central body of knowledge that schools require all students to study.

corporal punishment Disciplining students through physical punishment by a school employee.

critical pedagogy An education philosophy that unites the theory of critical thinking with actual practice in real-world settings. The purpose is to eliminate the cultural and educational control of the dominant group, to have students apply critical thinking skills to the real world and become agents for social change.

cultural difference theory This theory asserts that academic problems can be overcome if educators study and mediate the cultural gap separating school and home.

cultural literacy Knowledge of the people, places, events, and concepts central to the standard literate culture.

cultural pluralism Acceptance and encouragement of cultural diversity.

curriculum (formal, explicit) Planned content of instruction that enables the school to meet its aims.

curriculum development The processes of assessing needs, formulating objectives, and developing instructional opportunities and evaluation.

D

dame schools Primary schools in colonial and other early periods in which students were taught by untrained women in the women's own homes.

day care centers Facilities charged with caring for children. The quality of care varies dramatically and may range from well-planned educational programs to little more than custodial supervision.

decentralization The trend of dividing large school districts into smaller and, it is hoped, more responsive units.

deductive reasoning Working from a general rule to identify particular examples and applications to that rule.

de facto segregation The segregation of racial or other groups resulting from circumstances, such as housing patterns, rather than from official policy or law.

deficit theory A theory that asserts that the values, language patterns, and behaviors that children from certain racial and ethnic groups bring to school put them at an educational disadvantage.

de jure segregation The segregation of racial or other groups on the basis of law, policy, or a practice designed to accomplish such separation.

delegate representative Form of representative government in which the interests of a particular geographic region are represented through an individual or "delegate." Some school boards are organized so that members act as delegates of a neighborhood or region.

Department of Education U.S. cabinet-level department in charge of federal educational policy and the promotion of programs to carry out policies.

descriptive data Information that provides an objective depiction of various aspects of school or classroom life.

desegregation The process of correcting past practices of racial or other illegal segregation.

detrack The movement to eliminate school tracking practices, which often have racial, ethnic, and class implications.

differentiated instruction Instructional activities are organized in response to individual differences rather than content standards. Teachers are asked to carefully consider each student's needs, learning style, life experience, and readiness to learn.

digital divide A term used to describe the technological gap between the "haves" and "have nots." Race, gender, class, and geography are some of the demographic factors influencing technological access and achievement.

direct teaching A model of instruction in which the teacher is a strong leader who structures the classroom and sequences subject matter to reflect a clear academic focus. This model emphasizes the importance of a structured lesson in which presentation of new information is followed by student practice and teacher feedback.

disability A learning or physical condition, a behavior, or an emotional problem that impedes education. Educators now prefer to speak of "students with disabilities," not "handicapped students," emphasizing the person, not the disability.

distance learning Courses, programs, and training provided to students over long distances through television, the Internet, and other technologies.

dot.kids An adult-supervised Internet domain designed to protect children from inappropriate Internet content.

dual-track system The European traditional practice of separate primary schools for most children and secondary schools for the upper class.

due process The procedural requirements that must be followed in such areas as student and teacher discipline and placement in special education programs. Due process exists to safeguard individuals from arbitrary, capricious, or unreasonable policies, practices, or actions. The essential elements of due process are (1) a notice of the charge or actions to be taken, (2) the opportunity to be heard, (3) and the right to a defense that reflects the particular circumstances and nature of the case.

E

e-mentor Mentors who work over the Internet to advise, counsel, and support others. Some schools use e-mentors for beginning teachers.

early childhood education Learning undertaken by young children in the home, in nursery schools, preschools, and in kindergartens.

eclecticism In this text, the drawing on of elements from several educational philosophies or methods.

Edison Schools (Edison Project) An educational company that contracts with local school districts, promising to improve student achievement while making a profit in the process.

educable child A mentally retarded child who is capable of achieving only a limited basic learning and usually must be instructed in a special class.

educational malpractice A new experimental line of litigation similar to the concept of medical malpractice. Educational malpractice is concerned with assessing liability for students who graduate from school without fundamental skills. Unlike medical malpractice, many courts have rejected the notion that schools or educators be held liable for this problem.

educational park A large, campuslike facility often including many grade levels and several schools and often surrounded by a variety of cultural resources.

educational television programming Television programs that promote learning.

educational vouchers Flat grants or payments representing the cost of educating a student at a school. Awarded to the parent or child to enable free choice of a school—public or private—the voucher payment is made to the school that accepts the child.

Eight-Year Study Educator Ralph Tyler's study in the 1930s that indicated the effectiveness of progressive education.

elementary school An educational institution for children in grades 1 through 5, 6, or 8, often including kindergarten.

emergency license A substandard license that recognizes teachers who have not met all the requirements for licensure. It is issued on a temporary basis to meet the needs of communities that do not have licensed teachers available.

EMO (Educational Maintenance Organization) The term is borrowed from Health Maintenance Organizations (HMOs) and refers to the growing number of profit-driven companies in the business of public education.

emotional intelligence (EQ) Personality characteristics, such as persistence, can be measured as part of a new human dimension referred to as EQ. Some believe that EQ scores may be better predictors of future success than IQ scores.

empiricism The philosophy that maintains that sensory experiences, such as seeing, hearing, and touching, are the ultimate sources of all human knowledge. Empiricists believe that we experience the external world by sensory perception; then, through reflection, we conceptualize ideas that help us interpret the world.

enculturation The process of acquiring a culture; a child's acquisition of the cultural heritage through both formal and informal educational means.

endorsement Having a license extended through additional work to include a second teaching field.

engaged time The part of time that a teacher schedules for a subject in which the students are actively involved with academic subject matter. Listening to a lecture, participating in a class discussion, and working on math problems all constitute engaged time.

English grammar school The demand for a more practical education in eighteenth-century America led to the creation of these private schools that taught commerce, navigation, engineering, and other vocational skills.

environmental education The study and analysis of the conditions and causes of pollution, overpopulation, and waste of natural resources, and of the ways to preserve Earth's intricate ecology.

epistemology The branch of philosophy that examines the nature of knowledge and learning.

e-portfolio A digital version of the teacher's professional portfolio.

equal educational opportunity Refers to giving every student the educational opportunity to develop fully whatever talents, interests, and abilities he or she may have, without regard to race, color, national origin, sex, disability, or economic status.

equity Educational policy and practice that are just, fair, and free from bias and discrimination.

essentialism An educational philosophy that emphasizes basic skills of reading, writing, mathematics, science, history, geography, and language.

establishment clause A section of the First Amendment of the U.S. Constitution that says that Congress shall make no law respecting the establishment of religion. This clause prohibits nonparochial schools from teaching religion.

ethics The branch of philosophy that examines questions of right and wrong, good and bad.

ethnic group A group of people with a distinctive culture and history.

ethnocentrism The tendency to view one's own culture as superior to others, or to fail to consider other cultures in a fair or equitable manner.

evaluation Assessment of learning and instruction.

exceptional learners Students who require special education and related services in order to realize their full potential. Categories of exceptionality include retarded, gifted, learning disabled, emotionally disturbed, and physically disabled.

existentialism A philosophy that emphasizes the ability of an individual to determine the course and nature of his or her life and the importance of personal decision making.

expectation theory First made popular by Rosenthal and Jacobson, this theory holds that a student's academic performance can be improved if a teacher's attitudes and beliefs about that student's academic potential are modified.

expulsion Dismissal of a student from school for a lengthy period, ranging from one semester to permanently.

extracurriculum The part of school life that comprises activities, such as sports, academic and social clubs, band, chorus, orchestra, and theater. Many educators think that the extracurriculum develops important skills and values, including leadership, teamwork, creativity, and diligence.

F

failing school The term given to a school when a large proportion of its students do not do well on standardized tests or other academic measures. Critics charge that students attending such schools are not receiving their constitutionally guaranteed adequate education.

fair use A legal principle allowing limited use of copyrighted materials. Teachers must observe three criteria: brevity, spontaneity, and cumulative effect.

five factor theory School effectiveness research emphasizes five factors, including effective leadership, monitoring student progress, safety, a clear vision, and high expectations.

Flanders Interaction Analysis An instrument developed by Ned Flanders for categorizing student and teacher verbal behavior. It is used to interpret the nature of classroom verbal interaction.

flexible scheduling A technique for organizing time more effectively in order to meet the needs of instruction by dividing the school day into smaller time modules that can be combined to fit a task.

foundation program Program for distribution of state funds designed to guarantee a specified minimum level of educational support for each child.

Franklin Academy A colonial high school founded by Benjamin Franklin that accepted females as students and promoted a less classical, more practical curriculum.

full service school These schools provide a network of social services from nutrition and health care to parental education and transportation, all designed to support the comprehensive educational needs of children.

future shock Term coined by Alvin Toffler. It refers to the extraordinarily accelerated rate of change and the disorientation of those unable to adapt to rapidly altered norms, institutions, and values.

futurism The activity of forecasting and planning for future developments.

G

gender bias (see sex discrimination) The degree to which an individual's beliefs and behavior are unduly influenced on the basis of gender.

gendered career A term applied to the gender stereotyping of career and occupational fields. Teaching, for example, was initially gendered male, and today is gendered female, particularly at the elementary school level.

gifted learner There is great variance in definitions and categorizations of the "gifted." The term is most frequently applied to those with exceptional intellectual ability, but it may also refer to learners with outstanding ability in athletics, leadership, music, creativity, and so forth.

global education Because economics, politics, scientific innovation, and societal developments in different countries have an enormous impact on children in the United States, the goals of global education include increased knowledge about the peoples of the world, resolution of global problems, increased fluency in foreign languages, and the development of more tolerant attitudes toward other cultures and peoples.

guaranteed tax base program Adds state funds to local tax revenues, especially in poorer communities in order to enhance local educational expenditures.

Gun-free Schools Act Enacted in Congress in 1994, schools can lose federal funds if they do not have a zero-tolerance policy mandating one-year expulsions for students bringing firearms to schools. The vast majority of schools report zero-tolerance policies for firearms.

H

Head Start Federally funded pre-elementary school program to provide learning opportunities for disadvantaged students.

heterogeneous grouping A group or class consisting of students who show normal variation in ability or performance. It differs from homogeneous grouping, in which criteria, such as grades or scores on standardized tests, are used to group students similar in ability or achievement.

hidden (implicit) curriculum What students learn, other than academic content, from what they do or are expected to do in school; incidental learnings.

hidden government The unofficial power structure within a school. It cannot be identified by the official title, position, or functions of individuals. For example, it reflects the potential influence of a school secretary or custodian.

higher-order questions Questions that require students to go beyond memory in formulating a response. These questions require students to analyze, synthesize, evaluate, and so on.

home schooling A growing trend (but a longtime practice) of parents educating their children at home, for religious or philosophical reasons.

homogeneous grouping The classification of pupils for the purpose of forming instructional groups having a relatively high degree of intellectual similarity.

hornbook A single sheet of parchment containing the Lord's Prayer and letters of the alphabet. It was protected by a thin sheath from the flattened horn of a cow and fastened to a wooden board—hence, the name. It was used during the colonial era in primary schools.

humanistic education A curriculum that stresses personal student growth; self-actualizing, moral, and aesthetic issues are explored.

I

idealism A doctrine holding that knowledge is derived from ideas and emphasizing moral and spiritual reality as a preeminent source of explanation.

ideologues Home school advocates focused on avoiding public schools in order to impart their own set of values.

inclusion The practice of educating and integrating children with disabilities into regular classroom settings.

independent school A nonpublic school unaffiliated with any church or other agency.

individualized education program (IEP) The mechanism through which a disabled child's special needs are identified, objectives and services are described, and evaluation is designed.

individualized instruction Curriculum content and instructional materials, media, and activities designed for individual learning. The pace, interests, and abilities of the learner determine the curriculum.

Individuals with Disabilities Education Act (IDEA) Federal law passed in 1990, which extends full education services and provisions to people identified with disabilities.

induction A formal program assisting new teachers to successfully adjust to their role in the classroom.

inductive reasoning Drawing generalizations based on the observation of specific examples.

informal education In many cultures, augments or takes the place of formal schooling as children learn adult roles through observation, conversation, assisting, and imitating.

infrastructure The basic installations and facilities on which the continuance and growth of a community depend.

in loco parentis Latin term meaning "in place of the parents"; that is, a teacher or school administrator assumes the duties and responsibilities of the parents during the hours the child attends school.

instruction The process of implementing a curriculum.

integrated curriculum (interdisciplinary curriculum) Subject matter from two or more areas combined into thematic units (i.e., literature and history resources to study civil rights laws).

integration The process of educating different racial and ethnic groups together, and developing positive interracial contacts.

interest centers Usually associated with an open classroom, such centers provide independent student activities related to a specific subject.

Internet The worldwide computer network that rapidly facilitates information dissemination.

J

junior high school A two- or three-year school between elementary and high school for students in their early adolescent years, commonly grades 7 and 8 or 7 through 9.

K

kindergarten A preschool, early childhood educational environment first designed by Froebel in the mid-nineteenth century.

L

labeling Categorizing or classifying students for the purposes of educational placement. One unfortunate consequence may be that of stigmatizing students and inhibiting them from reaching their full potential.

laboratory schools Schools often associated with a teacher preparation institution for practice teaching, demonstration, research, or innovation.

land grant colleges State colleges or universities offering agricultural and mechanical curricula, funded originally by the Morrill Act of 1862.

last mile problem Geography contributes to a digital divide, in part because running fiber optic cables to rural schools is often an expense that telecommunications companies avoid.

latchkey (self-care) kids A term used to describe children who go home after school to an empty house; their parents or guardians are usually working and not home.

Latin grammar school A classical secondary school with a Latin and Greek curriculum preparing students for college.

learning communities The creation of more personal collaboration between teachers and students to promote similar academic goals and values.

learning disability An educationally significant language and/or learning deficit.

least restrictive environment The program best suited to meeting a disabled student's special needs without segregating the student from the regular educational program.

license Official approval of a government agency for an individual to perform certain work, such as a teacher's license granted by a state.

limited English proficiency (LEP) A student who has a limited ability to understand, speak, or read English and who has a native language other than English.

logic The branch of philosophy that deals with reasoning. Logic defines the rules of reasoning, focuses on how to move from one set of assumptions to valid conclusions, and examines the rules of inference that enable us to frame our propositions and arguments.

looping The practice of teaching the same class for several years, over two or even more grades. The purpose is to build stronger teacher-student connections.

lower-order questions Questions that require the retrieval of memorized information and do not require more complex intellectual processes.

M

magnet school A specialized school open to all students in a district on a competitive or lottery basis. It provides a method of drawing children away from segregated neighborhood schools while affording unique educational specialties, such as science, math, and the performing arts.

mainstreaming The inclusion of special education students in the regular education program. The nature and extent of this inclusion should be based on meeting the special needs of the child.

malfeasance Deliberately acting improperly and causing harm to someone.

mastery learning An educational practice in which an individual demonstrates mastery of one task before moving on to the next.

McGuffey Reader For almost 100 years, this reading series promoted moral and patriotic messages and set the practice of reading levels leading toward graded elementary schools.

mentor A guide or an adviser, and a component of some first-year school induction programs designed to assist new teachers.

merit pay A salary system that periodically evaluates teacher performance and uses these evaluations in determining salary.

metacognition Self-awareness of our thinking process as we perform various tasks and operations. For example, when students articulate how they think about academic tasks, it enhances their thinking and enables teachers to target assistance and remediation.

metaphysics The area of philosophy that examines the nature of reality.

microteaching A clinical approach to teacher training in which the teacher candidate teaches a small group of students for a brief time while concentrating on a specific teaching skill.

middle schools Two- to four-year schools of the middle grades, often grades 6 through 8, between elementary school and high school.

minimum competency tests Exit-level tests designed to ascertain whether students have achieved basic levels of performance in such areas as reading, writing, and computation. Some states require that a secondary student pass a minimum competency test in order to receive a high school diploma.

misfeasance Failure to act in a proper manner to prevent harm.

moral stages Promoted by Lawrence Kohlberg as a model of moral development in which individuals progress from simple moral concerns, such as avoiding punishment, to more sophisticated ethical beliefs and actions.

Morrill Act Federal legislation (1862) granting federal lands to states to establish colleges to promote more effective and efficient agriculture and industry. A second Morrill Act, passed in 1890, provided federal support for "separate but equal" colleges for African Americans.

multicultural education Educational policies and practices that not only recognize but also affirm human differences and similarities associated with gender, race, ethnicity, nationality, disability, and class.

multiple intelligences A theory developed by Howard Gardner to expand the concept of human intelligence to include such areas as logical-mathematical, linguistic, bodily-kinesthetic, musical, spatial, interpersonal, intrapersonal, and naturalist.

N

National Assessment of Educational Progress (NAEP) Program to ascertain the effectiveness of U.S. schools and student achievement.

National Association of State Directors of Teacher Education and Certification (NASDTEC) An organization, comprising participating state departments of education, that evaluates teacher education programs in higher education.

National Board for Professional Teaching Standards (NBPTS) A professional organization charged with establishing voluntary standards for recognizing superior teachers as board certified.

National Council for the Accreditation of Teacher Education (NCATE) An organization that evaluates teacher education programs in many colleges and universities. Graduates of programs approved by the NCATE receive licenses in over half the states, pending the successful completion of required state exams.

national curricular standards Nationally prescribed or recommended standards, content skills, and testing.

National Defense Education Act Federally sponsored programs (1958) to improve science, math, and foreign language instruction in schools.

National Education Association (NEA) The largest organization of educators, the NEA is concerned with the overall improvement of education and of the conditions of educators. It is organized at the national, state, and local levels.

networking The term used to describe the intentional effort to develop personal connections with individuals who could be helpful in finding positions or gaining professional advancement.

New England Primer One of the first textbooks in colonial America, teaching reading and moral messages.

nonfeasance Failure to exercise appropriate responsibility that results in someone's being harmed.

nongraded school A school organization in which grade levels are eliminated for two or more years.

nonverbal communication The act of transmitting and/or receiving messages through means not having to do with oral or written language, such as eye contact, facial expressions, and body language.

normal school A two-year teacher education institution popular in the nineteenth century, many of which were expanded to become today's state colleges and universities.

norm-referenced tests Tests that compare individual students with others in a designated norm group.

Northwest Ordinance (1785, 1787) Provided for the sale of federal lands in the Northwest territory to support public schools.

null curriculum The curriculum that is not taught in schools.

O

objective The purpose of a lesson expressed in a statement.

objective-referenced tests Tests that measure whether students have mastered a designated body of knowledge rather than how they compare with other students in a norm group.

observation techniques Structured methods for observing various aspects of school or classroom activities.

Old Deluder Satan Law (1647) Massachusetts colony law requiring teachers in towns of fifty families or more and that schools be built in towns of one hundred families or more. Communities must teach children to read so that they can read the Bible and thwart Satan.

open classroom Based on the British model, it refers not only to an informal classroom environment but also to a philosophy of education. Students pursue individual interests with the guidance and support of the teacher; interest centers are created to promote this individualized instruction. Students may also have a significant influence in determining the nature and sequence of the curriculum. It is sometimes referred to as *open education.*

open enrollment The practice of permitting students to attend the school of their choice within their school system. It is sometimes associated with magnet schools and desegregation efforts.

open-space school A school building without interior walls. Although it may be designed to promote the concept of the open classroom, the open-space school is an architectural concept rather than an educational one.

opportunity to learn standards (also called delivery standards) These standards attempt to recognize and respond to individual differences and circumstances. Poorer students learning in schools with fewer resources should receive more appropriate and adequate learning opportunities, and if some students need more time to take tests, additional time should be provided.

oral tradition Spoken language is the primary method for instruction in several cultures around the world. Word problems are used to teach reasoning, proverbs to instill wisdom, and stories to teach lessons about nature, history, religion, and social customs.

outcome based education (OBE) An educational approach that emphasizes setting learning outcomes and assessing student progress toward attaining those goals, rather than focusing on curricular topics.

P

paraprofessional A lay person who serves as an aide, assisting the teacher in the classroom.

parochial school An institution operated and controlled by a religious denomination.

peace studies The study and analysis of the conditions of and need for peace, the causes of war, and the mechanisms for the nonviolent resolution of conflict. It is also referred to as *peace education.*

pedagogical cycle A system of teacher-student interaction that includes four steps: structure—teacher introduces the topic; question—teacher asks questions; respond—student answers or tries to answer questions; and react—teacher reacts to student's answers and provides feedback.

pedagogues Term given to home school advocates motivated by humanistic rather than religious goals.

pedagogy The science of teaching.

peer review The practice of having colleagues observe and assess teaching, as opposed to administrators.

perennialism The philosophy that emphasizes rationality as the major purpose of education. It asserts that the essential truths are recurring and universally true; it stresses Great Books.

performance standards Statements that describe what teachers or students should be able to do, and how well they should do it.

permanent license Although there is some variation from state to state, a permanent license is issued after a candidate has completed all the requirements for full recognition as a teacher. Requirements may include a specified number of courses beyond the bachelor's degree or a specified number of years of teaching.

philosophy The love of or search for wisdom; the quest to understand the meaning of life.

phonics An approach to reading instruction that emphasizes decoding words by sounding out letters and combinations of letters (as contrasted with the whole language approach).

political philosophy An approach to analyzing how past and present societies are arranged and governed and how better societies may be created in the future.

portfolio Compilations of work (such as papers, projects, videotapes) assembled to demonstrate growth, creativity, and competence. Often advocated as a more comprehensive assessment than test scores.

Praxis series of tests Developed by ETS to assess teachers' competence in various areas: reading, writing, math, professional and subject area knowledge. Praxis test requirements differ among states. (see Appendix 1)

primary school A separately organized and administered elementary school for students in the lower elementary grades, usually grades 1 through 3, and sometimes including preprimary years.

private school A school controlled by an individual or agency other than the government, usually supported by other than public funds. Most private schools are parochial.

privatization The movement toward increased private sector, for-profit involvement in the management of public agencies, including schools.

probationary teaching period A specified period of time in which a newly hired teacher must demonstrate teaching competence. This period is usually three years for public school teachers and six years for college professors. Generally, on satisfactory completion of the probationary period, a teacher is granted tenure.

problem-based learning An approach that builds a curriculum around intriguing real-life problems and asks students to work cooperatively to develop and demonstrate their solutions.

professional development School district efforts to improve knowledge, skills and performance of its professional staff.

progressive education An educational philosophy emphasizing democracy, student needs, practical activities, and school-community relationships.

property tax Local real estate taxes (also cars and personal property) historically used to fund local schools.

provisional license Also referred to as a *probationary license,* a provisional license is frequently issued to beginning teachers. It may mean that a person has completed most, but not all, of the state requirements for permanent licensure. Or it may mean that the state requires several years of teaching experience before it will qualify the teacher for permanent licensure.

R

racial discrimination Actions that limit or deny a person or group any privileges, roles, or rewards on the basis of race.

racism Attitudes, beliefs, and behavior based on the notion that one race is superior to other races.

rationalism The philosophy that emphasizes the power of reason and the principles of logic to derive statements about the world. Rationalists encourage schools to emphasize teaching mathematics, because mathematics involves reason and logic.

readability formulas Formulas that use objective, quantitative measures to determine the reading level of textbooks.

reciprocity States recognize and honor another state's actions, such as recognizing a teacher's license in one state as valid in another.

reconstructionism (reconstructionist) Also called social reconstructionism, this is a view of education as a way to improve the quality of life, to reduce the chances of conflict, and to create a more humane world.

reflective teaching Predicated on a broad and in-depth understanding of what is happening in the classroom, reflective teaching promotes thoughtful consideration and dialogue about classroom events.

résumé A summary of a person's education and experiences, often used for application to school or employment.

revenue sharing The distribution of federal money to state and local governments to use as they decide.

Robin Hood Laws As a result of court actions, many states are redistributing revenue from wealthier to poorer communities to equalize educational funding, a process not unlike the efforts of the hero of Sherwood Forest.

romantic critics Critics such as Paul Goodman, Herbert Kohl, and John Holt who believed that schools were stifling the cognitive and affective development of children. Individual critics stressed different problems or solutions, but they all agreed that schools were producing alienated, uncreative, and unfulfilled students.

rubric A scoring guide that describes what must be done, and often describes performance levels ranging from novice to expert, or from a failing grade to excellence.

S

sabbatical A leave usually granted with full or partial pay after a teacher has taught for a specified period of time (for example, six years). Typically, it is to encourage research and professional development. While common at the university level, it is rare for K–12 teachers.

scaffolding Taking from the construction field, scaffolding provides support to help a student build understanding. The teacher might use cues or encouragement or well-formulated questions to assist a student in solving a problem or mastering a concept.

school-based management The recent trend in education reform that stresses decision making on the school level. In the past, school policies were set by the state and the districts. Now the trend is for individual schools to make their own decisions and policies.

school choice The name given to several programs in which parents choose what school their child will attend.

school financing Refers to the ways in which monies are raised and allocated to schools. The methods differ widely from state to state, and many challenges are being made in courts today because of the unequal distribution of funds within a state or among states.

school infrastructure The basic facilities and structures that underpin a school plant, such as plumbing, sewage, heat, electricity, roof, masonry, and carpentry.

school superintendent The chief administrator of a school system, responsible for implementing and enforcing the school board's policies, rules, and regulations, as well as state and federal requirements. The superintendent is directly responsible to the school board and is the formal representative of the school community to outside individuals and agencies.

School to Work Opportunities Act Programs that link school learning to job settings, often developed in partnerships between school and industry.

schools without walls An alternative education program that involves the total community as a learning resource.

second-generation segregation When a school's multiracial populations are separated through tracking, extracurricular activities, and even in informal social events, the school is considered to be in second-generation segregation.

secular humanism The belief that people can live ethically without faith in a supernatural or supreme being. Some critics have alleged that secular humanism is a form of religion and that publishers are promoting secular humanism in their books.

self-censorship (also called stealth censorship) In order to avoid possible problems and parental complaints, some educators quietly remove a book from a library shelf or a course of study. Teachers practice the same sort of self-censorship when they choose not to teach a topic or not to discuss a difficult issue.

separate but equal A legal doctrine that holds that equality of treatment is accorded when the races are provided substantially equal facilities, even though those facilities are separate. This doctrine was ruled unconstitutional in regard to race.

service credit By volunteering in a variety of community settings, from nursing homes to child care facilities, students are encouraged to develop a sense of community and meet what is now a high school graduation requirement in some states.

sex discrimination Any action that limits or denies a person or group of persons opportunities, privileges, roles, or rewards on the basis of sex.

sexism The collection of attitudes, beliefs, and behavior that results from the assumption that one sex is superior to the other.

sex-role stereotyping Attributing behavior, abilities, interests, values, and roles to a person or group of persons on the basis of sex. This process ignores individual differences.

sexual harassment Unwanted, repeated, and unreturned sexual words, behaviors, or gestures prohibited by federal and some state laws.

simulation A role-playing technique in which students take part in re-created, life-like situations.

social reconstructionism (See Reconstructionism.)

sociogram A diagram that is constructed to record social interactions, such as which children interact frequently and which are isolates.

Socratic method An educational strategy attributed to Socrates in which a teacher encourages a student's discovery of truth by questions.

special education Programs and instruction for children with physical, mental, emotional, or learning disabilities or gifted students who need special educational services in order to achieve at their ability level.

special license A nonteaching license that is designed for specialized educational careers, such as counseling, library science, and administration.

state adoption The process by which members of a textbook adoption committee review and select the books used throughout a state. Advocates of this process say that it results in a common statewide curriculum that unites educators on similar issues and makes school life easier for students who move within the state. Critics charge that it gives too much influence to large states and results in a "dumbed down" curriculum.

state board of education The state education agency that regulates policies necessary to implement legislative acts related to education.

state department of education An agency that operates under the direction of the state board of education, accrediting schools, certifying teachers, appropriating state school funds, and so on.

stepfamilies These relationships are created when divorced or widowed parents remarry, creating a whole set of new relationships, including stepchildren, stepgrandparents, and stepparents.

street academies Alternative schools designed to bring dropouts and potential dropouts, often inner-city youths, back into the educational mainstream.

student-initiated questions These are content-related questions originating from the student, yet comprising only a small percentage of the questions asked in class.

superintendent of schools The executive officer of the local school district.

T

taxonomy A classification system of organizing information and translating aims into instructional objectives.

teacher centers Sites to provide training to improve teaching skills, inform teachers of current educational research, and develop new curricular programs.

teacher flexibility Adapting a variety of skills, abilities, characteristics, and approaches, according to the demands of each situation and the needs of each student.

Teach for America A program that places unlicensed college graduates in districts with critical teacher shortages as they work toward attaining a teacher license.

tenure A system of employment in which teachers, having served a probationary period, acquire an expectancy of continued employment. The majority of states have tenure laws.

Tesseract Formerly Educational Alternatives, this private company works in the public school sector, attempting to improve school efficiency and student achievement, while making a profit.

textbook adoption states States, most often those in the South and West, that have a formal process for assessing, choosing, and approving textbooks for school use.

Title I Section of the Elementary and Secondary Education Act that provides federal funds to supplement local education resources for students from low-income families.

tracking The method of placing students according to their ability level in homogeneous classes or learning experiences. Once a student is placed, it may be very difficult to move up from one track to another. The placements may reflect racism, classism, or sexism.

transitional bilingual education Teaching students in their primary language until they can learn in English.

trustee representatives This conception of a school board member's role differs from the delegate approach, as members are viewed as representatives of the entire community, rather than representing the narrower interests of a particular group or neighborhood.

tuition tax credits Tax reductions for parents or guardians of children attending public or private schools.

U

unobtrusive measurement A method of observing a situation without altering it.

unremarked revolution The unheralded but persistent move of schools away from formal tracking programs.

V

values clarification A model, comprising various strategies, that encourages students to express and clarify their values on different topics.

virtual field trip Visiting distant sites and events via the computer and the Internet.

vouchers A voucher is like a coupon, and it represents money targeted for schools. In a voucher system, parents use educational vouchers to "shop" for a school. Schools receive part or all of their per-pupil funding from these vouchers. In theory, good schools would thrive and poor ones would close for lack of students.

W

wait time The amount of time a teacher waits for a student's response after a question is asked and the amount of time following a student's response before the teacher reacts.

whole language approach Teaching reading through an integration of language arts skills and knowledge, with a heavy emphasis on literature (as contrasted with a phonics approach).

women's studies Originally created during the 1970s to study the history, literature, psychology, and experiences of women, topics typically missing from the traditional curriculum.

World Wide Web Most common connection to the Internet; contains numerous sites which can be accessed by a Web browser.

Z

zero reject The principle that no child with disabilities may be denied a free and appropriate public education.

zero-tolerance policies Such rigorous rules offer schools little or no flexibility in responding to student infractions related to alcohol, drugs, tobacco, violence, and weapons. These policies have been developed by both local school districts and a number of state legislatures, and in most cases, students who violate such policies must be expelled.

zone of proximal development The area where students can move from what they know to new learning, a zone where real learning is possible.

CHAPTER 1 BECOMING A TEACHER

1. Anne Meek, "America's Teachers: Much to Celebrate," *Educational Leadership* 55, no. 5 (February 1998), pp. 12–16; National Education Association, *Status of the American Public School Teacher,* 1995–96 (Washington, DC: NEA, 1997).

2. Amy DePaul, *What to Expect Your First Year of Teaching* (Washington, DC: U.S. Department of Education, September 1998), p. 28.

3. Quoted in Ann Lieberman and Lynn Miller, *Teachers, Their World and Their Work* (Alexandria, VA: Association for Supervision and Curriculum Development, 1984), p. 22.

4. Louis Harris and Associates, *The Metropolitan Life Survey of the American Teacher 2001* (New York: Metropolitan Life Insurance Company, 2001).

5. Lieberman and Miller, *Teachers, Their World and Their Work,* p. 47.

6. William Lyon Phelps, quoted in Oliver Ikenberry, *American Education Foundations* (Columbus, OH: Merrill, 1974), p. 389.

7. Quoted in Myron Brenton, *What's Happened to Teacher?* (New York: Coward, McCann & Geoghegan, 1970), p. 164.

8. Stephen Gordon quoted in "What Keeps Teachers Going?," *Educational Leadership* 60, no. 8 (May 2003), p. 18.

9. Steve Twomey and Richard Morin, "Teachers: Besieged, Delighted," *The Washington Post,* July 4, 1999, pp. A1, A12.

10. "Quality Counts, 2000, Who Should Teach," *Education Week* (Bethesda, MD: Editorial Projects) 19(18) pp. 8–9.

11. Quoted in Brenton, *What's Happened to Teacher?* p. 97.

12. Ibid., p. 94.

13. Ellen Hogan Steele, "Reflections on a School Strike II," *Phi Delta Kappan* 57, no. 9 (May 1976), pp. 590–92; Carol Davis quote from "Are You Treated Like a Professional? Or a Tall Child?" *NEA Today,* December 1988, p. 4.

14. Jillian N. Lederhouse, "Show Me the Power" Education Week, June 13, 2001; *Teachers' Working Conditions: Findings from The Condition of Education 1996* (Washington, DC: National Center for Educational Research and Improvement, 1996), p. 12; see also NEA surveys, such as *The Conditions and Resources of Teaching.*

15. Ron Brandt, "On Teacher Empowerment: A Conversation with Ann Lieberman," *Educational Leadership* 46, no. 8 (May 1989), pp. 23–24.

16. Adopted from Robert Howsam et al., *Educating a Profession, Report on the Bicentennial Commission of Education for Profession of Teaching* (Washington, DC: American Association of Colleges for Teacher Education, 1976), pp. 6–7.

17. Ibid., pp. 8–9.

18. *Tomorrow's Teachers: A Report of the Holmes Group* (East Lansing, MI: Holmes Group, 1986).

19. Carnegie Forum on Education and the Economy, Task Force on Teaching as a Profession, *A Nation Prepared: Teachers for the Twenty-First Century* (New York: Forum, 1986).

20. John Goodlad, "A Study of the Education of Educators: One Year Later," *Phi Delta Kappan* 73, no. 4 (December 1991), pp. 311–16.

21. "America's Classrooms Gain More Than 7,800 National Board Certified Teachers® in 2002" (Arlington, VA: NBPTS News Release), November 26, 2002.

22. Michael Podgursky, "Should States Subsidize National Certification?" *Education Week on the Web,* April 11, 2001.

23. Linda Darling-Hammond, "Who Will Speak for the Children?: How 'Teach for America' Hurts Urban Schools and Students," *Phi Delta Kappan* 76, no. 1 (September 1994), pp. 21–34; for the other side of this debate, see Wendy Kopp, "Ten Years of Teach for America" in *Education Week on the Web,* June 21, 2000.

24. Linda Darling-Hammond, "The Futures of Teaching," *Educational Leadership* 46, no. 3 (November 1988), p. 6.

25. Idiko Laczko-Kerr and David Berliner, "In Harm's Way: How Uncertified Teachers Hurt Their Students," *Educational Leadership* 60, no. 8 (May 2003), pp. 34–39.

26. Linda Darling-Hammond, "Keeping Good Teachers: Why It Matters What Leaders Can Do," *Educational Leadership* 60, no. 8 (May 2003), pp. 7–13.

27. "Research-Based Characteristics of High-Quality Teacher Preparation," *ASCD SmartBrief 1,* no. 4 (February 19, 2003).

28. *Different Drummers: How Teachers of Teachers View Public Education* (New York: Public Agenda, 1997).

29. David C. Berliner, "A Personal Response to Those Who Bash Teacher Education," *Journal of Teacher Education* 51, no. 5 (November/December 2000), pp. 358–71; Suzanne M. Wilson, Robert E. Floden, and Joan Ferrini-Mundy, "Teacher Preparation Research: An Insider's View from the Outside," *Journal of Teacher Education 53,* no. 3 (May/June 2002), pp. 190–204.

30. Ibid., p. 363. See also D. Gitomer, A. Latham, and R. Ziomek, *The Academic Quality of Prospective Teachers: The Impact of Admissions and Licensure Testing* (Princeton, NJ: Educational Testing Service, 1999); "Attracting the Best and the Brightest?" *Quality Counts 2000: Who Should Teach, Education Week on the Web.*

31. Carol Langdon, "The Fourth Phi Delta Kappa Poll of Teachers' Attitudes Toward the Public Schools," *Phi Delta Kappan* 79, no. 3 (November 1997), pp. 212–20; for other public reaction to education issues, follow the annual Kappan report on the Gallup Poll, such as Lowell C. Rose, Alee M. Gallup, and Stanley M. Elam, "The 29th Annual Phi Delta Kappa/Gallup Poll of the Public's Attitudes Toward Schools," *Phi Delta Kappan* 79, no. 1 (September 1997): pp. 41–56.

32. Arthur E. Wise, "What's Wrong with Teacher Certification?" *Education Week 22,* no. 30 (April 9, 2003), pp. 56, 42.

33. Andy Baumgartner, "A Teacher Speaks Out: Insights from the National Teacher of the Year," *The Washington Post,* March 26, 2000, p. B4.

34. Robert Gates, " Questions Every Teacher Should Answer," *Classroom Leadership* (August 1999), pp. 1–3; Kevin and Jackie Freiberg, *Nuts!* (New York: Broadway Books, 1996), pp. 320–27.

CHAPTER 2   STUDENT DIVERSITY

1. *Do We Still Need Public Schools?* (Washington, DC: Center on National Educational Policy and Phi Delta Kappa, 1996), p. 14; Maxine Schwartz Seller, "Immigrants in the Schools—Again: Historical and Contemporary Perspectives on the Education of Post 1965 Immigrants in the United States," *Educational Foundations* 3, no. 1 (Spring 1989), pp. 53–75.

2. Kenneth Dunn and Rita Dunn, "Dispelling Outmoded Beliefs About Student Learning," *Educational Leadership* 45, no. 7 (March 1987), pp. 55–63.

3. James Keefe, *Learning Style Theory and Practice* (Reston, VA: National Association of Secondary School Principals, 1987); Paul Zielbauer, "Considering a Later Bell for Connecticut's Sleepy Children," *The New York Times,* February 20, 2001 (www.nytimes.com); Tamara Henry, "Open Up Schools, Let Sun Shine In: Creature Comforts Can Aid Learning," *USA Today,* 22 March 2001, p. 8D.

4. Dunn and Dunn, "Dispelling Outmoded Beliefs About Student Learning"; see also G. Price, "Which Learning Style Elements Are Stable and Which Tend to Change?" *Learning Styles Network Newsletter* 4, no. 2 (1980), pp. 38–40; J. Vitrostko, *An Analysis of the Relationship Among Academic Achievement in Mathematics and Reading, Assigned Instructional Schedules and the Learning Style Time Preferences of Third-, Fourth-, Fifth-, and Sixth-Grade Students,* unpublished doctoral dissertation, St. John's University, Jamaica, New York, 1983.

5. Howard Gardner and Thomas Hatch, "Multiple Intelligences Go to School: Educational Implications of the Theory of Multiple Intelligences," *Educational Researcher* 18, no. 8 (November 1989), p. 5.

6. Kathy Checkley, "The First Seven . . . and the Eighth: A Conversation with Howard Gardner," *Educational Leadership* 55, no. 1 (September 1997), pp. 8–13; Howard Gardner, "Beyond the I.Q.: Education and Human Development," *Harvard Educational Review* 57, no. 2 (spring 1987), pp. 187–93.

7. Thomas Armstrong, "Multiple Intelligences: Seven Ways to Approach Curriculum," *Educational Leadership* 52 (November 1994), pp. 26–28; see also Howard Gardner, *Intelligence Reframed: Multiple Intelligences for the 21st Century* (New York: Basic Books, 1999).

8. Howard Gardner, "Reflections on Multiple Intelligences: Myths and Messages," *Phi Delta Kappan* 77, no. 3

(November 1995), pp. 200–9; Veronica Borruso Emig, "A Multiple Intelligence Inventory," *Educational Leadership* 55, no. 1 (September 1997), pp. 47–50.

9. Thomas R. Hoerr, "How the New City School Applies the Multiple Intelligences," *Educational Leadership* 52 (November 1994), pp. 29–33.

10. Nancy Gibbs, "The E.Q. Factor," *Time* 146, no. 14 (October 2, 1995), pp. 60–68.

11. Ibid. See also Kevin R. Kelly and Sidney M. Moon, "Personal and Social Talents," *Phi Delta Kappan* 79, no. 10 (June 1998), pp. 743–46.

12. Daniel Goleman, "Emotional Intelligence: Why It Can Matter More Than IQ," *Learning* (May/June 1996), pp. 49–50; see a sample application of EQ in Emily Wax, "Educating More Than the Mind," *The Washington Post,* October 4, 2000, p. B3.

13. The demographic information in the following section is based on the following: "Overview of Race and Hispanic Origin," *Census 2000 Brief* (Washington, DC: U.S. Census Bureau, March 2001); "Projections of the Resident Population by Race, Hispanic Origin, and Nativity: 2025 to 2045," *Census 2000 Brief* (Washington, DC: U.S. Census Bureau, March 2001); "Profiles of General Demographic Characteristics," *Census 2000* (Washington, DC: U.S. Census Bureau, March 2001). William Branigin, "Nearly 1 in 10 in U.S. Is Foreign Born, Census Says," *The Washington Post,* April 9, 1997, p. A18; Jessica I. Sandham, "Graduates Growing More Diverse, Study Finds," *Education Week on the Web,* April 1, 1998; *Statistical Abstract of the United States, 1997* (Washington, DC: U.S. Department of Commerce, Bureau of the Census, 1996); *Youth Indicators* (Washington, DC: National Center for Education Statistics, Department of Education, 1996).

14. S. D. McLemore and H. D. Romo, *Racial and Ethnic Relations in America* (Boston: Allyn & Bacon, 1998): John O'Neil, "Why Are the Black Kids Sitting Together?" *Educational Leadership* 55, no. 5 (December 1997/January 1998), pp. 12–17; Robert Slavin, "Research on Cooperative Learning: Consensus and Controversy," *Educational Leadership* 47, no. 4 (December 1989/ January 1990), pp. 52–54.

15. Slavin, "Research on Cooperative Learning"; McLemore and Romo, *Racial and Ethnic Relations in America;* see also James C. Hendrix, "Cooperative Learning: Building a Democratic Community," *Clearinghouse* 69, no. 6 (July–August 1996), pp. 333–36.

16. James Banks, "Multicultural Education: Characteristics and Goals," in James A. Banks and Cherry A. McGee Banks (eds.), *Multicultural Education: Issues and Perspectives* 4th ed. (Boston: Allyn & Bacon, 2001), pp. 3–30.

17. Carol Gilligan, *In a Different Voice: Psychological Theory and Women's Development* (Cambridge, MA: Harvard University Press, 1982). See also Mary Field Belenky, Blythe McVicker Clinchy, Nancy Rule Goldberger, and Jill Mattuck Tarule, *Women's Ways of Knowing: The Development of Self, Voice, and Mind* (New York: Basic Books, 1986).

18. Geneva Gay, "Achieving Educational Equality Through Curriculum Desegregation," *Phi Delta Kappan* 72, no. 1 (September 1990), pp. 56–62.

19. Peter Schmidt, "New Survey Discerns Deep Divisions Among U.S. Youths on Race Relations," *Education Week*, March 25, 1992, p. 5.

20. James Banks, "Approaches to Multicultural Curriculum Reform," in Banks and Banks, *Multicultural Education*, pp. 225–46.

21. James Crawford, ed., *Language Loyalties: A Source Book on the Official English Controversy* (Chicago: University of Chicago Press, 1992); see also Jonathon Zimmerman, "A Babel of Tongues," *U.S. News & World Report*, 24 November 1997, p. 39.

22. Diane Ravitch, "Politicization and the Schools: The Case of Bilingual Education," in *Taking Sides,* James W. Noll (ed.) (Guilford, CT: Dushkin, 1997), pp. 232–40.

23. Harold Hodgkinson, quoted in *Education Week,* May 14, 1986, pp. 14–40.

24. D. Hugo Lopez and Merle T. Mora, "Bilingual Education and the Labor Market Earnings Among Hispanics: Evidence Using High School and Beyond," *READ Perspectives* (Amherst, MA: Institute for Research in English Acquisition and Development), 1998.

25. Jorge Amselle, "Adios, Bilingual Ed," *Policy Review* no. 86, November 1997 (Washington, DC: Heritage Foundation), pp. 52–55.

26. Rene Sanchez and William Booth, "California Rejection: A Big Blow to Bilingualism: Decisive Vote Could Set Pace for Rest of Nation," *The Washington Post,* June 4, 1998, p. A16; Peter Baker, "Education Dept Faults Anti-Bilingual Measure," *The Washington Post,* April 28, 1998, p. A3; Lisa Anderson, "Bilingual Debate Reaches Boiling Point: Battle Wages with Ballots, Initiatives, Studies, Placards," *Tribune on the Web,* May 29, 2001.

27. Yilu Zhao, "Wave of Pupils Lacking English Strains Schools," *The New York Times,* 5 August 2002, online.

28. James Crawford, *Hold Your Tongue: Bilingualism and the Politics of "English Only"* (New York: Addison-Wesley, 1992), pp. 111–12.

29. Pat Kossan, "School's Chief Getting Tough on English Fluency, Horne Wants Loopholes Closed in Arizona Law," *The Arizona Republic,* May 28, 2003, online.

30. Gary A. Cziko, "The Evaluation of Bilingual Education: From Necessity and Probability to Possibility," *Educational Researcher* 21, no. 2 (March 1992), p. 24; J. David Ramirez, "Executive Summary," *Bilingual Research Journal* 16 (Winter/Spring, 1992), pp. 1–245.

31. Rosalie Pedalino Porter, New York City Study. *READ Perspectives* 12 (2), 1995, quoted in Robert F. McNergney and Joanne M. Herbert, *Foundations of Education* (Needham Heights, MA: Allyn & Bacon, 1998), p. 311.

32. Peter Schmidt, "Three Types of Bilingual Education Effective, E.D. Study Concludes," *Education Week* February 20, 1991, pp. 1, 23.

33. Wayne Thomas and Virginia Collier, "Two Languages Are Better Than One," *Educational Leadership* 55, no. 4

(December 1997/ January 1998), pp. 23–26; Kenneth J. Cooper, "Riley Endorses Two-Way Bilingual Education," *The Washington Post,* March 26, 2000, p. A2; Cara Simmon, "School Puts New Accent on Learning Two Languages," *Seattle Times,* April 1, 2003, online.

34. These categories build on the ones described by William Heward and Rodney A. Cavanaugh, "Educational Equality for Students with Disabilities," in James Banks and Cherry Banks (eds.), *Multicultural Education* (Boston: Allyn & Bacon, 1997), pp. 301–33; as well as William Heward and Michael Orlansky, "Educational Equality for Exceptional Students," in James Banks and Cherry Banks (eds.), *Multicultural Education* (Boston: Allyn & Bacon, 1989), pp. 231–50.

35. United States Department of Education, Office of Special Education Programs. Twenty-third Annual Report to Congress on the Implementation of the Individuals with Disabilities Education Act, Washington, DC (2001).

36. Susan DeFord, "Inclusive Classrooms," *Washington Post Magazine,* February 8, 1998, p. 8.

37. Marie Killilea, *Karen* (New York: Dell, 1952), p. 171.

38. Ed Martin, quoted in "PL 94-142," *Instructor* 87, no. 9 (1978), p. 63.

39. Michael D. Simpson, "Rights Watch: Who's Paying for Special Ed?" *NEA Today* 15, no. 9 (May 1997), p. 20.

40. Sandra Blakeslee, "Study Shows Increase in Autism," *The New York Times,* January 1, 2003, online.

41. "Disproportionate Identification of Students with Learning Disabilities," *ASCD SmartBrief 1,* no. 3 (February 5, 2003); Shari Rudavsky, "Report Targets Special Needs: Limits Urged on Enrollment," *Boston Globe,* December 29, 2002, p. A27.

42. "Special Report/ Racial Inequities in Special Education," *Education Leadership 60,* no. 4 (December 2002/January 2003), p. 91; Jay Mathews, "Study Finds Racial Bias in Special Ed," *Washington Post,* 3 March 2001, p. A1.

43. Katherine Seligman, "Hyperactive Girls Escape Detection," *San Francisco Chronicle,* 1 October 2002, p. A-1; Anand Vaishnav and Bill Dedman, "Special Ed Gender Gap Stirs Worry," *Boston Globe,* July 8, 2002, p. A1.

44. Suzy Ruder, "We Teach All," *Educational Leadership 58,* no. 1 (September 2000), pp. 49–51; Mary Beth Doyle, "Transition Plans for Students with Disabilities," *Educational Leadership 58,* no. 1 (September 2000), pp. 46–48.

45. United States Department of Education, Office of Special Education Programs. Twenty-third Annual Report to Congress on the Implementation of the Individuals with Disabilities Education Act, Washington, DC (2001).

46. Quoted in David Milofsky, "Schooling the Kid No One Wants," *The New York Times Magazine,* January 2, 1977, pp. 24–29.

47. Solomon Moore, "Special Ed Joins the Mainstream," *Los Angeles Times*, October 2002, online.

48. The anecdotes and many of the quotations in this section were cited in Gene I. Maeroff, "The Unfavored Gifted Few," *New York Times Magazine,* August 21,

1977, reprinted in Celeste Toriero (ed.), *Readings in Education 78/79* (Guilford, CT: Dushkin, 1978).

49. Valerie Strauss, "Looking for a Few Wise Children, *The Washington Post*, September 17, 2002, p. A11.

50. John F. Feldhusen, "Programs for the Gifted Few or Talent Development for the Many?" *Phi Delta Kappan* 79, no. 10 (June 1998), pp. 735–38.

51. Judy Galbraith, "Gifted Youth and Self-Concept," *Gifted Education* 15, no. 2 (May 1989), pp. 15–17.

52. Ibid., p. 16.

53. Robert Morris, "Educating Gifted for the 1990s," *Gifted Education* 15, no. 2 (May 1989), pp. 50–52; for more information about gender bias, see *Gender Gaps: Where Schools Still Fail Our Children* (Washington, DC: American Association of University Women Educational Foundation, 1998).

54. Susan Winebrenner, "Gifted Students Need an Education, Too," *Educational Leadership* 58, no. 1 (September 2000), pp. 52–56.

55. John Feldhusen, "Synthesis of Research on Gifted Youth," *Educational Leadership* 46, no. 6 (March 1989), pp. 6–11.

56. Lisa Leff, "Gifted, Talented, and Under Siege," *Washington Post Educational Review,* April 5, 1992, p. 14.

57. Quoted in Galbraith, "Gifted Youth and Self-Concept," p. 17.

CHAPTER 3   TEACHER EFFECTIVENESS

1. Among the resources on teacher effectiveness that you may want to consult are the *Journal of Teacher Education, Handbook of Research on Teaching,* and *The Review of Research in Education.*

2. N. Filby Fisher, E. Marleave, L. Cahen, M. Dishaw, M. Moore, and D. Berliner, *Teaching Behaviors, Academic Learning Time, and Student Achievement: Final Report of Beginning Teacher Evaluation Study* (San Francisco: Far West Laboratory, 1978).

3. John Goodlad, *A Place Called School* (New York: McGraw-Hill, 1984).

4. Barbara M. Taylor, David P. Pearson, Kathleen F. Clark, and Sharon Walpole, "Effective Schools/Accomplished Teachers," *Reading Teacher* 53 (1999), pp. 156–59.

5. Herbert Walberg, Richard Niemiec, and Wayne Frederick, "Productive Curriculum Time," *The Peabody Journal of Education* 69, no. 3 (1994), pp. 86–100; Steve Nelson, *Instructional Time as a Factor in Increasing Student Achievement* (Portland, OR: Northwest Regional Lab, 1990); David Berliner, "The Half-Full Glass: A Review of Research on Teaching," in Philip Hosferd (ed.), *Using What We Know About Teaching* (Alexandria, VA: Association for Supervision and Curriculum Development, 1984).

6. C. M. Evertson, E. T. Emmer, B. S. Clements, J. P. Sanford, and M. E. Worsham, *Classroom Management for Elementary Teachers* (Englewood Cliffs, NJ: Prentice Hall, 1984). See also Carolyn Evertson and Alene Harris,

7. Robert Slavin, "Classroom Management and Discipline," in *Educational Psychology: Theory into Practice* (Englewood Cliffs, NJ: Prentice Hall, 1986); Vernon F. Jones and Louise S. Jones, *Comprehensive Classroom Management: Creating Communities of Support and Solving Problems* (Needham Heights, MA: Allyn & Bacon, 2001), pp. 251–55.

8. E. T. Emmer, C. M. Evertson, J. P. Sanford, B. S. Clements, and M. E. Worsham, *Classroom Management for Secondary Teachers* (Englewood Cliffs, NJ: Prentice Hall, 1984); B. Malone, D. Bonitz, and M. Rickett, "Teacher Perceptions of Disruptive Behavior: Maintaining Instructional Focus," *Educational Horizons* 76, no. 4 (1998), pp. 189–94.

9. Jacob Kounin, *Discipline and Group Management in Classrooms* (New York: Holt, Rinehart & Winston, 1970).

10. Jere E. Brophy, "Classroom Organization and Management," *The Elementary School Journal* 83, no. 4 (1983), pp. 265–85.

11. Thomas L. Good and Jere E. Brophy, *Looking in Classrooms* (New York: Longman, 2000), pp. 219–20.

12. Marilyn E. Gootman, *The Caring Teacher's Guide to Discipline: Helping Young Students Learn Self-Control, Responsibility, and Respect* (Thousand Oaks, CA: Corwin Press, 1997).

13. Kathleen Cushman, *Fires in the Bathroom: Advice for Teachers from High School Students* (New York: The New Press, 2003).

14. Majorie Coeyman, "It's 8 A.M., and Everything Is Not Under Control," *The Christian Science Monitor*, October 8, 2002, online.

15. David Berliner, "What Do We Know About Well-Managed Classrooms? Putting Research to Work," *Instructor* 94, no. 6 (February 1985), p. 15; Carol Cummings, *Winning Strategies for Classroom Management* (Alexandria, VA: Association for Supervision and Curriculum Development, 2000).

16. Arno Bellack, *The Language of the Classroom* (New York: Teachers College Press, 1966).

17. Several of the sections on the pedagogical cycle are adopted from Myra and David Sadker, *Principal Effectiveness—Pupil Achievement (PEPA) Training Manual* (Washington, DC: American University, 1986).

18. Donald Cruickshank, "Applying Research on Teacher Clarity," *Journal of Teacher Education* 36 (1985), pp. 44–48.

19. Myra Sadker and David Sadker, "Questioning Skills" in James M. Cooper (ed.), *Classroom Teaching Skills,* 7th ed. (Boston: Houghton Mifflin, 2003); P. Smagoinsky, "The Social Construction of Data: Methodological Problems of Investigation Learning in the Zone of Proximal Development," *Review of Educational Research* 65, no. 3 (1995), pp. 191–212.

20. Robert Slavin, "The Lesson," in *Educational Psychology: Theory into Practice.*

21. John Dewey, *How We Think,* rev. ed. (Boston: D. C. Heath, 1933), p. 266.

22. Myra Sadker and David Sadker, "Sexism in the Schoolroom of the 80s," *Psychology Today* 19 (March 1985), pp. 54–57.

23. Benjamin Bloom (ed.), *Taxonomy of Educational Objectives, Handbook I: Cognitive Domain* (New York: David McKay, 1956).

24. Myra Sadker and David Sadker, "Questioning Skills" in James Cooper (ed.), *Classroom Teaching Skills;* Trevor Kerry, "Classroom Questions in England," *Questioning Exchange* 1, no. 1, (1987), p. 33; Arthur C. Grassier and Natalie K Person, "Question Asking During Tutoring," *American Educational Research Journal* 31 (1994), pp. 104–37; William S. Carlsen, "Questioning in Classrooms: A Sociolinguistic Perspective," *Review of Educational Research* 61 (1991), pp. 157–78; Meredith D. Gall, "Synthesis of Research on Teacher's Questioning," *Educational Leadership* 42 (1984), pp. 40–47; David Berliner, "The Half-Full Glass: A Review of Research on Teaching," in Philip L. Hosford (ed.), *Using What We Know About Teaching*, pp. 51–84; L. M. Barden, "Effective Questions and the Ever-Elusive Higher-Order Question," *American Biology Teacher* 57, no. 7 (1995), pp. 423–26; Meredith D. Gall and T. Rhody, "Review of Research on Questioning Techniques," in William W. Wilen (ed.), *Questions, Questioning Techniques, and Effective Teaching* (Washington, DC: National Education Association, 1987), pp. 23–48; G. Brown and R. Edmondson, "Asking Questions," in E. C. Wragg (ed.), *Classroom Teaching Skills* (New York: Nichols, 1984), pp. 97–119; William W. Wilen and Ambrose A. Clegg, "Effective Questions and Questioning: A Research Review," *Theory and Research in Social Education,* 14, (1986), pp. 153–61.

25. Adapted from Myra Sadker and David Sadker, "Questioning Skills" in James M. Cooper (ed.), *Classroom Teaching Skills.*

26. Mary Budd Rowe, "Wait Time: Slowing Down May Be a Way of Speeding Up!" *Journal of Teacher Education* 37 (January/February 1986), pp. 43–50; Mary Budd Rowe, "Science, Silence, and Sanctions," *Science and Children* 34 (September 1996), pp. 35–37; Jim B. Mansfield, "The Effects of Wait-time on Issues of Gender Equity, Academic Achievement, and Attitude Toward a Course," *Teacher Education and Practice* 12, no. 1 (Spring/Summer 1996), pp. 86–93.

27. D. Bridges, "A Philosophical Analysis of Discussion" in J. Dillion (ed.), *Questioning and Discussion: A Multidisciplinary Study* (Norwood, NJ: Alblex, 1988), p. 26; A. E. Edwards and D. G. P. Westgate, *Investigating Classroom Talk,* Social Research and Educational Studies Series: 4 (London and Philadelphia: Falmer, 1987), p. 170.

28. Myra Sadker, David Sadker, and Susan Klein, "The Issue of Gender in Elementary and Secondary Education," *Review of Research in Education* 17 (1991), pp. 269–334.

29. Goodlad, *A Place Called School.*

30. Jere E. Brophy, "Teacher Praise: A Functional Analysis," *Review of Educational Research* 51 (1981), pp. 5–32.

31. Gary Davis and Margaret Thomas, *Effective Schools and Effective Teachers* (Boston: Allyn & Bacon, 1989); Charles A. Dana Center, University of Texas at Austin, *Hope for Urban Education: A Study of Nine High-Performing, High-Poverty, Urban Elementary Schools* (Washington, DC: U.S. Department of Education, Planning and Evaluation Service, 1999). www.ed.gov./pubs/urbanhope/execsumm.html.

32. Susan Black, "Stretching Students Minds: Effective Teaching Is about What Students Will Learn, Not Just What They Will Do," *American School Board Journal* (June 2001). www.asbj.com/current/research.html; Metropolitan Life Inc, *The American Teacher* (New York: Metropolitan Life Company, 2001), pp. 13–15.

33. Bruce R. Joyce and Emily F. Calhoun, *Learning Experiences: The Role of Instructional Theory and Research* (Alexandria, VA: Association for Curriculum and Supervision, 1996); Barak Rosenshine, "Synthesis of Research on Explicit Teaching," *Educational Leadership* 43, no. 4 (May 1986), pp. 60–69. See also Davis and Thomas, *Effective Schools and Effective Teachers.*

34. David Johnson, Roger Johnson, Edythe Johnson Holubee, and Patricia Roy, *Circles of Learning: Cooperation in the Classroom* (Alexandria, VA: Association of Supervision and Curriculum Development, 1984); Robert Slavin, "Research on Cooperative Learning: Consensus and Controversy," *Educational Leadership* 47, no. 4 (December 1989/January 1990), pp. 52–54.

35. Robert E. Slavin, "Cooperative Learning in Middle and Secondary Schools," *Clearinghouse* 69, no. 4 (March–April 1996), pp. 200–4; Robert E. Slavin, "Cooperative Learning," *Review of Educational Research* 50 (summer 1980), pp. 315–42. See also Robert Slavin, *Cooperative Learning: Student Teams* (Washington, DC: National Education Association, 1987).

36. Robert E. Slavin, *Cooperative Learning: Theory, Research, and Practice* (Boston: Allyn & Bacon, 1995); Roger Johnson and David Johnson, "Student Interaction: Ignored but Powerful." *Journal of Teacher Education* 36 (July–August 1985), p. 24. See also Robert Slavin, "Synthesis of Research on Cooperative Learning," *Educational Leadership* 48, no. 5 (February 1991), pp. 71–82; Susan Ellis and Susan Whalen, "Keys to Cooperative Learning, " *Instructor* 101, no. 6 (February 1992), pp. 34–37.

37. David Meichenbaum and Andrew Biemiller, *Nurturing Independent Learners: Helping Students Take Charge of Their Learning* (Cambridge, MA: Brookline Books, 1998); Joan S. Hyman and S. Alan Cohen, "Learning for Mastery: Ten Conclusions After 15 Years and 3000 Schools," *Educational Leadership* 36 (November 1979), pp. 104–9.

38. Glenn Hymel, "Harnessing the Mastery Learning Literature: Past Efforts, Current Status, and Future Directions," Paper presented at the annual meeting of the American Educational Research Association, Boston, MA, 1990; Thomas Guskey and Sally Gates, "Synthesis of Research on the Effects of Mastery Learning in

Elementary and Secondary Classrooms," *Educational Leadership* 43 (May 1986), pp. 73–80.

39. Diane Curtis, "The Power of Projects," *Educational Leadership* 60, no. 1 (September 2002), pp. 50–53; Linda Torp and Sara Sage, *Problems as Possibilities: Problem-Based Learning for K–12 Education* (Alexandria, VA: Association for Supervision and Curriculum Development, 1998); Robert Delisle, *How to Use Problem-Based Learning in the Classroom* (Alexandria, VA: Association for Supervision and Curriculum Development, 1997).

40. Jere Brophy, "Probing the Subtleties of Subject-Matter Teaching," *Educational Leadership* 49, no. 7 (April 1992), pp. 4–8.

41. Carol Ann Tomlinson, "Reconcilable Differences? Standards-Based Teaching and Differentiation," *Educational Leadership* 58, no. 1 (September 2000), pp. 6–11.

42. Richard Prawat, "From Individual Differences to Learning Communities—Our Changing Focus," *Educational Leadership* 49, no. 7 (April 1992), pp. 9–13.

43. Joellen Killion and Guy Todnem, "A Process for Personal Theory Building," *Educational Leadership* 48, no. 6 (March 1991), pp. 14–16.

44. Bud Wellington, "The Promise of Reflective Practice," *Educational Leadership* 48, no. 6 (March 1991), pp. 4–5.

CHAPTER 4   SCHOOLS: CHOICES AND CHALLENGES

1. James Shaver and William Strong, *Facing Value Decisions: Rationale Building for Teachers* (Belmont, CA: Wadsworth, 1976).

2. Ernest L. Boyer, *High School: A Report on Secondary Education in America* (New York: Harper & Row, 1983), pp. 209–10.

3. Linda Perlstein, "'Serving' the Community Without Leaving School," *The Washington Post,* June 28, 1999, pp. A1, A6.

4. *The Condition of Education 2001,* U.S. Department of Education, NCES, Indicator 16: Social and Cultural Outcomes, Community Service Participation in Grades 6–12, p. 142. nces.ed.gov/pubs2001/2001072_2.pdf.

5. Bill Bigelow, "The Human Lives Behind the Labels: The Global Sweatshop, Nike, and the Race to the Bottom," *Phi Delta Kappan* 79, no. 2 (October 1997), pp. 112–19.

6. Paulo Freire, *The Pedagogy of the Oppressed* (New York: Herder & Herder, 1970).

7. John Goodlad, *A Place Called School* (New York: McGraw-Hill, 1984), pp. 35–39.

8. Arthur Eugene Bestor, *Educational Wastelands: The Retreat from Learning in Our Public Schools* (Urbana: University of Illinois Press, 1953), p. 75.

9. Boyer, *High School,* p. 5.

10. National Commission on Excellence in Education, *A Nation at Risk: The Imperative for Educational Reform* (Washington, DC: U.S. Government Printing Office, 1983), p. 1.

11. David Hill, "Fixing the System from the Top Down," *Teacher Magazine* (September/October 1989), pp. 50–55.

12. David L. Clark and Terry A. Astuto, "Reconstructing Reform: Challenges to Popular Perceptions About Teachers and Students," *Phi Delta Kappan* 75, no. 7 (March 1994), pp. 512–20.

13. Donald C. Ohlrich, "Education Reforms: Mistakes, Misconceptions, Miscues," *Phi Delta Kappan* 170, no. 7 (March 1989), pp. 512–17.

14. Valerie Strauss, "When Success Doesn't Add Up," *The Washington Post on the Web,* December 2000.

15. Clinton Boutwell, "People Without People," *Phi Delta Kappan* 79, no. 2 (October 1997), pp. 104–11.

16. Joy Dryfoos, "Full Service Schools," *Educational Leadership* 53, no. 7 (April 1996), pp. 18–23.

17. Henry J. Perkinson, *The Imperfect Panacea: American Faith in Education* (New York: McGraw-Hill, 1995), p. 191.

18. Debra Viadero, "Students Learn More in Magnets Than Other, Study Finds," *Education Week,* March 6, 1996, p. 6; Caroline Hendrie, "Magnets Value in Desegregating Schools Is Found to Be Limited," *Education Week on the Web,* November 13, 1996; "Research Notes," *Education Week on the Web,* September 16, 1998.

19. A. S. Byrk, Valerie Lee, and P. B. Holland, *Catholic Schools and the Common Good* (London: Harvard University Press, 1993).

20. "Another Round on Vouchers," *The Washington Post,* December 18, 2000, p. A26; Terry Moe, "The Public Revolution Private Money Might Bring," *The Washington Post,* May 9, 1999, p. B3. For more on the legal dispute, see *Jackson v. Benson* (1998), which held that vouchers used for religious school tuition did not violate the Wisconsin State Constitution. A Cleveland Scholarship and Tutoring Program, which uses vouchers for religious schools, was found to violate the First Amendment of Ohio's State Constitution, and is being appealed to the U.S. Supreme Court.

21. David Stout, "Public Money Can Pay Religious-School Tuition, Court Rules," *The New York Times,* June 27, 2002, online.

22. Timothy McDonald, "The False Promise of Voucher," *Education Leadership* 59, no. 7 (April 2002), pp. 33–37; Kaleem M. S. Caire, "The Truth about Vouchers," *Education Leadership* 59, no. 7 (April 2002), pp. 33–37; Joseph P. Viteritti, "Coming Around on School Choice," *Education Leadership* 59, no. 7 (April 2002), pp. 44–48; Mark Walsh, "Voucher Advocates Plan Multistate Battle," *Education Week,* October 16, 2002, online; "Poll: Most Oppose Vouchers," *The Washington Post,* August 21, 2002, p. A4; Majorie Coeyman, "Vouchers Get a Boost from Black Alliance," *The Christian Science Monitor on the Web,* July 10, 2001; Scott Stephens, "Support for School Vouchers a Struggle in Many States," *Plain Deal Reporter on the Web,* April 1, 2001.

23. Alex Molnar, "Charter Schools: The Smiling Face of Disinvestment," *Educational Leadership* 54, no. 2 (October 1996), pp. 9–15; Jean Casey, Kathleen Andreson, Barbara Yelverton, and Linda Wedeen, "A Status Report on Charter Schools in New Mexico," *Phi*

Delta Kappan 83, no. 7 (March 2002), pp. 518–24; Jessica Sandman, "Challenges to Charter Laws Mount," *Education Week,* May 2, 2001, pp. 1, 24, 25.

24. Bruno V. Manno, Chester E. Finn, Louann A. Bierlein, and Gregg Vanurek, "How Charter Schools Are Different: Lessons and Implications from a National Study," *Phi Delta Kappan* 79, no. 7 (March 1998), pp. 489–98.

25. Thomas L. Good and Jennifer Braden, "Charter Schools: Another Reform Failure or a Worthwhile Investment?" *Phi Delta Kappan* 81, no. 10, June 2000, pp. 745–50.

26. Michael Winerip, "When It Goes Wrong at a Charter," *The New York Times,* March 5, 2003, online.

27. Meredith May, "Report Critical of Charter Schools: Uncredentialed Teachers, Funding Shortage, Racial Isolation Cited," *San Francisco Chronicle,* April 8, 2003.

28. Molnar, "Charter Schools," p. 10.

29. Joel Spring, *American Education* (New York: McGraw-Hill, 1996), pp. 184–85.

28. Chuck Sudetic, "Reading, Writing and Revenue," *Mother Jones,* May–June 2001, pp. 84–95.

30. Diana B. Henriques, "Edison Schools' Founder to Take It Private," *New York Times,* July 15, 2003, nytimes.com; Gerald Bracey, "The 12th Bracey Report on the Condition of Public Education," *Phi Delta Kappan* 84, no. 2 (October 2002), pp. 135–50; Chris Brennan, "Ex-Edison Official: Company Lacks Integrity," *Phillynews.com,* July 24, 2002; Michael Fletcher, "Private Enterprise, Public Woes in Phila School," *The Washington Post*, September 17, 2002, p. A1; Susan Snyder and Martha Woodall, "42 Schools to Be Privatized," *Philadelphia Inquirer,* April 18, 2002, online; Chuck Sudetic, "Reading, Writing and Revenue," *Mother Jones,* May–June 2001, pp. 84–95.

31. Mike Hoffman, "Upstarts: Staking Out a Share of Public-School Gold," *Inc* (June 1998), pp. 25–27.

32. Mark Walsh, "Question[s?] About Finances Put Edison Project at Crossroad," *Education Week,* August 3, 1994, pp. 18–19; Walter Farrell, Jr., James Johnson, Cloyzelle Jones, and Marty Sapp, "Will Privatizing Schools Really Help Inner-City Students of Color?" *Educational Leadership* 52, no. 1 (September 1994), pp. 72–75.

33. Michael Winerip, "Schools for Sale," *New York Times Magazine,* June 14, 1998, pp. 42–49, 80, 86, 88–89; Mark Walsh, "Business," *Education Week on the Web,* March 4, 1998; Lynn Schnaiberg, "Seeking a Competitive Advantage," *Education Week on the Web,* December 8, 1999; Mark Walsh, "Report Card on For-Profit Industry Still Incomplete," *Education Week on the Web,* December 15, 1999.

34. Pedro Noguerar, "More Democracy Not Less: Confronting the Challenge of Privatization in Public Education," *Journal of Negro Education* 623, no. 2 (1994), p. 238.

35. Justin Blum and Jay Mathews, "Quality Uneven, Despite Popularity," *The Washington Post,* June 19, 2003, pp. A1, A12.

36. Jane H. Holloway, "Research Link," *Educational Leadership* 39, no. 7 (April 2002), pp. 84–85.

37. Alex Molnar interviewed in "Giving Kids the Business, an Interview with Alex Molnar," *The Education Industry:*

The Corporate Takeover of Public Schools, www.corpwatch.org/feature/education/; see also Alex Molnar, *Giving Kids the Business: The Commercialization of America's Schools* (Boulder, CO: Westview Press, 1996); see also Majorie Coeyman, "Vouchers Get a Boost from Black Alliance."

38. Kenneth Howe, Margaret Eisenhart, and Damian Betebenner, "The Price of Public School Choice," *Educational Leadership* 39, no. 7 (April 2002), pp. 20–24.

39. Bruce Fuller, "Is School Choice Working?" *Educational Leadership* 54, no. 2 (October 1996), pp. 37–40; Lorna Jimerson, "Hidden Consequences of School Choice: Impact on Programs, Finances, and Accountability," paper presented at the American Educational Research Association annual meeting, San Diego, CA (1998); Steven Glazerman, "School Quality and Social Stratification: The Determinants and Consequences of Parental Choice," paper presented at the American Educational Research Association annual meeting, San Diego, CA (1998); Edd Doerr, "The Empty Promise of School Vouchers," *USA Today Magazine* 125, no. 2622 (New York: Society for the Advancement of Education), March 1997, pp. 89–90.

40. Caroline Mayer, "Today's Lesson, Sponsored by . . . " *Washington Post,* June 15, 2003, pp. A1, A8.

41. Neil Buckley, "Obesity Campaign Eyes School Drinks," *Financial Times.com,* MSNBC News Online (June 2003); Alex Molnar, "The Corporate Branding of Our Schools," *Educational Leadership* 60, no. 2 (October 2002), pp. 74–78.

42. Alfie Kohn, "The 500-Pound Gorilla," *Phi Delta Kappan* 84, no. 2 (October 2002), p. 117.

43. Molnar, "The Corporate Branding of Our Schools," p. 76.

44. "Live and Learn," *Harper's Bazaar* (September 1994), pp. 268–70.

45. Patricia Lines, "Educating a Minority: How Families, Policymakers, and Public Educators View Home Schooling," *Journal of Early Education and Family Review* 5, no. 3 (January/February 1998), pp. 25–28; Patricia Lines, "Home Schooling," *Eric Digest* 95 (1995), pp. 1–3; Brian Ray, "Customization through Homeschooling," *Education Leadership* 59, no. 7 (April 2002), pp. 50–54.

46. M. Mayberry, "Characteristics and Attitudes of Families Who Home School," *Education and Urban Society* 21 (1988), pp. 32–41; M. Mayberry, "Home-based Education in the United States: Demographics, Motivations, and Educational Implications," *Educational Review* 41, no. 2 (1989), pp. 171–80.

47. J. A. Van Galen, "Schooling in Private: A Study of Home Education," doctoral dissertation, University of North Carolina, Chapel Hill, 1986.

48. Brian Ray, "Customization through Homeschooling," *Education Leadership* 59, no. 7 (April 2002), p. 50.

49. Rob Reich, "The Civic Perils of Home Schooling" *Education Leadership* 59, no. 7 (April 2002), pp. 56–59.

50. "Home-Taught Students Miss School Activities," *The Washington Post,* November 26, 1995, pp. B-1, B-5;

Chris Jeub, "Why Parents Choose Home Schooling," *Educational Leadership* 52, no. 1 (September 1994), pp. 50–52.

51. Darwin L. Webb, "Homeschools and Interscholastic Sports: Denying Participation Violates United States Constitutional Due Process and Equal Protection Rights," *Journal of Law and Education* 26, no. 3 (July 1997), pp. 123–32; Gary Knowles, James A. Muchmore, and Holly W. Spaulding, "Home Education as an Alternative, to Institutionalized Education," *The Education Forum* 58 (spring 1994), pp. 238–43.

52. Barbara Kantrowitz and Pat Wingert, "Learning at Home: Does It Pass the Test?" *Newsweek,* October 5, 1998, pp. 64–71; "Charter 'Profit': Will Michigan Heap Money on an Electronic Charter School?" *The American School Board Journal* 181, no. 9 (September 1994), pp. 27–28; "The Dawn of Home Schooling," *Newsweek,* October 10, 1994, p. 67; see also, Nancy Trejos, "Home Schooling's Net Effect," *The Washington Post,* July 16, 2000, pp. C1, C9.

CHAPTER 5   LIFE IN SCHOOLS

1. Philip W. Jackson, *Life in Classrooms* (New York: Holt, Rinehart & Winston, 1968).

2. Ibid.

3. Manuel Justiz, "It's Time to Make Every Minute Count," *Phi Delta Kappan* 65, no. 7 (March 1984), pp. 483–85; see also Herbert Walberg, "Families as Partners in Educational Productivity," *Phi Delta Kappan* 65, no. 6 (February 1984), pp. 397–400.

4. John Goodlad, A *Place Called School* (New York: McGraw-Hill, 1984).

5. Quoted in Ernest L. Boyer, *High School* (New York: Harper & Row, 1983); C. Fisher, N. Filby, E. Marliave, L. Cohen, M. Dishaw, J. Moore, and D. Berliner, *Teacher Behaviors, Academic Learning Time, and Student Achievement,* Final Report of Phase III-B, Beginning Teacher Evaluation Study (San Francisco: Far West Laboratory for Educational Research and Development, 1978).

6. G. Madaus et al., *School Effectiveness: A Reassessment of the Evidence* (New York: McGraw-Hill, 1980).

7. Jackson, *Life in Classrooms.*

8. Ned Flanders, "Intent, Action, and Feedback: A Preparation for Teaching," *Journal of Teacher Education* 14, no. 3 (September 1963), pp. 251–60.

9. Arno Bellack, *The Language of the Classroom* (New York: Teachers College Press, 1965).

10. Romiett Stevens, "The Question as a Measure of Classroom Practice," in *Teachers College Contributions to Education* (New York: Teachers College Press, 1912).

11. W. D. Floyd, *An Analysis of the Oral Questioning Activity in Selected Colorado Primary Classrooms.* Unpublished doctoral dissertation, Colorado State College, 1960.

12. Myra Sadker and David Sadker, "Questioning Skills," in James Cooper (ed.), *Classroom Teaching Skills,* 7th ed. (Boston: Houghton Mifflin, 2003).

13. Mary Budd Rowe, "Wait Time: Slowing Down May Be a Way of Speeding Up!" *Journal of Teacher Education* 37 (1986), pp. 43–50.

14. Goodlad, A *Place Called School.*

15. Talcott Parsons, "The School as a Social System: Some of Its Functions in Society," in Robert Havinghurst and Bernice Neugarten, (eds.), *Society and Education* (Boston: Allyn & Bacon, 1967), pp. 191–214.

16. Robert Lynd and Helen Lynd, *Middletown: A Study in American Culture* (New York: Harcourt Brace Jovanovich, 1929).

17. W. Lloyd Warner, Robert Havinghurst, and Martin Loeb, *Who Shall Be Educated?* (New York: Harper & Row, 1944).

18. August Hollingshead, *Elmtown's Youth* (New York: Wiley, 1949).

19. Robert Havighurst et al., *Growing Up in River City* (New York: Wiley, 1962).

20. Ernest L. Boyer, *High Schools: A Report on Secondary Education in America* (New York: Harper & Row, 1983).

21. Shirl Gilbert and Geneva Gay, "Improving the Success in School of Poor Black Children," *Phi Delta Kappan* 67, no. 2 (October 1985), pp. 133–38.

22. Ray Rist, "Student Social Class and Teacher Expectations. The Self-Fulfilling Prophecy of Ghetto Education," *Harvard Education Review* 40, no. 3 (1970), pp. 411–51.

23. Jeannie Oakes, "Two Cities' Tracking and Within-School Segregation," *Teachers College Record* 96, no. 4 (summer 1995), pp. 681–90.

24. Jeannie Oakes and Martin Lipton, "Detracking Schools: Early Lessons from the Field," *Phi Delta Kappan* 73, no. 6 (February 1992), pp. 448–54.

25. James Rosenbaum, "If Tracking Is Bad, Is Detracking Better?", *American Educator.* Washington, DC: American Federation of Teachers (Winter 1999–2000), pp. 24–29, 47.

26. Samuel Lucas, *Tracking Inequality: Stratification and Mobility in American High Schools* (New York: Teachers College Press, 1999).

27. Rebecca Gordon and Libero Della Piana, *Testing, Tracking, and Students of Color in U.S. Public Schools* (Oakland, CA: Applied Research Center, 1999).

28. Jeannie Oakes, *Multiplying Inequalities: The Effects of Race, Social Class, and Tracking on Opportunities to Learn Mathematics and Sciences* (Santa Monica, CA: RAND, 1990), (ED329615).

29. Carol Ascher, "Successful Detracking in Middle and Senior High Schools," *ERIC/CUE Digest* 82 (New York: ERIC Clearinghouse on Urban Education, October 10, 1992). (ED351426); Gary Burnett, "Alternatives to Ability Grouping: Still Unanswered Questions," *ERIC/CUE Digest* 111 (New York: ERIC Clearinghouse on Urban Education, December 1995), (ED390947).

30. Quoted in "Tracking," *Education Week on the Web,* October 14, 1998; see also Susan Allan, "Ability Grouping Research Reviews: What Do They Say About Grouping and the Gifted?" *Educational Leadership* 48,

no. 6 (March 1991), pp. 60–65; Adam Gamoran, "Alternative Use of Ability Grouping in Secondary Schools: Can We Bring High-Quality Instruction to Low-Ability Classes?" *American Journal of Education* 102 (1993), pp. 1–22; Robert E. Slavin, "Achievement Effects of Ability Grouping in Secondary Schools: A Best-Evidence Synthesis," *Review of Educational Research* 60 (1990), pp. 471–99.

31. Quoted in Raphaela Best, *We've All Got Scars* (Bloomington: Indiana University Press, 1983), p. 9.

32. Ibid., p. 10.

33. Ibid., p. 162.

34. Susan Snyder, "The Philadelphia Experiment: Inside the Schools Targeted for Change, Separating Boys and Girls," *The Philadelphia Inquirer,* September 6, 2002, online at www.philly.com.

35. Steven Sher, "Some Kids Are Nobody's Best Friend," *Today's Education,* 71 no. 1. (February/March 1982), pp. 23–29.

36. "Unpopular Children," *The Harvard Education Letter,* Harvard Graduate School of Education in association with Harvard University Press, January/February 1989, pp. 1–3. See also Lisa Wolcott, "Relationships: The Fourth 'R,'" *Teacher* (April 1991), pp. 26–27.

37. Quoted from a student letter in the *Arlingtonian,* May 13, 1993.

38. Zappa, Coleman, Friedenberg, Vonnegut, and Ford are quoted in Ralph Keyes, *Is There Life After High School?* (Boston: Little, Brown, 1976).

39. James Coleman, *The Adolescent Society* (New York: Free Press, 1961).

40. Goodlad, *A Place Called School.*

41. Quoted in Boyer, *High School,* p. 202.

42. Ibid., p. 206.

43. Sara Lawrence Lightfoot, *The Good High School* (New York: Basic Books, 1983).

44. David Owen, *High School* (New York: Viking Press, 1981).

45. Keyes, *Is There Life After High School?*

46. Lloyd Temme, quoted in Keyes, *Is There Life After High School?*

47. Mel Brooks and Dustin Hoffman are quoted in Keyes, *Is There Life After High School?*

48. Quoted in Boyer, *High School.*

49. Patricia Hersch, *A Tribe Apart: A Journey Into the Heart of American Adolescence* (New York: Random House, 1999).

50. The Metropolitan Life Survey of the American Teacher 2000. *Are We Preparing Students for the 21st Century?* (New York: Harris Interactive, Inc., 2000).

51. *The Metropolitan Life Survey of the American Teacher, 1984–1995: Old Problems, New Challenges* (New York: Louis Harris and Associates, 1995).

52. Quoted in Ernest L. Boyer, "What Teachers Say About Children in America," *Educational Leadership* 46, no. 8 (May 1989), p. 73.

53. Ibid.

54. Ibid., p. 74.

55. Frances Ianni, "Providing a Structure for Adolescent Development," *Phi Delta Kappan* 70, no. 9 (May 1989), p. 677.

56. Patrick Welsh, *Tales Out of School* (New York: Viking, 1986), pp. 41–42.

57. Urie Bronfenbrenner, "Alienation and the Four Worlds of Childhood," *Phi Delta Kappan* 67, no. 6 (February 1986), pp. 430–35.

58. Lightfoot, *The Good High School.*

59. Quoted in Ianni, "Providing a Structure for Adolescent Development," p. 680.

60. Grace Pung Guthrie and Larry Guthrie, "Streamlining Interagency Collaboration for Youth At Risk," *Educational Leadership* 49, no. 1 (September 1991), pp. 17–22.

61. Alfie Kohn, "Caring Kids: The Role of Schools," *Phi Delta Kappan* 72, no. 7 (March 1991), pp. 496–506.

62. Carnegie Council on Adolescent Development, *Turning Points: Preparing American Youth for the 21st Century,* excerpted in "The American Adolescent: Facing a Vortex of New Risks," *Education Week,* June 21, 1989, p. 22.

63. Ibid.

64. Edward A. Wynne, "Looking at Schools," *Phi Delta Kappan* 62, no. 5 (January 1981), pp. 377–81.

65. George Weber, *Inner-City Children Can Be Taught to Read: Four Successful Schools* (Washington, DC: D.C. Council for Basic Books, 1971).

66. Ronald Edmonds, "Some Schools Work and More Can," *Social Policy* 9 (1979), pp. 28–32.

67. Barbara Taylor and Daniel Levine, "Effective Schools Projects and School-Based Management," *Phi Delta Kappan* 72, no. 5 (January 1991), pp. 394–97. See also Herman Meyers, "Roots, Trees, and the Forest: An Effective Schools Development Sequence." Paper delivered at the American Educational Research Association, San Francisco, April 1992.

68. Lightfoot, *The Good High School.*

69. Ibid., p. 67.

70. David Clark, Linda Lotto, and Mary McCarthy, "Factors Associated with Success in Urban Elementary Schools," *Phi Delta Kappan* 61, no. 7 (March 1980), pp. 467–70. See also David Gordon, "The Symbolic Dimension of Administration for Effective Schools." Paper delivered at the American Educational Research Association, San Francisco, April 1992.

71. William Rutherford, "School Principals as Effective Leaders," *Phi Delta Kappan* 67, no. 1 (September 1985), pp. 31–34. See also R. McClure, "Stages and Phases of School-Based Renewal Efforts." Paper presented at the annual meeting of the American Educational Research Association, New Orleans, 1988.

72. Steven C. Schlozman, "The Shrink in the Classroom: Fighting School Violence," *Ed Leadership* 60, no. 2 (October 2002). pp. 89–90.

73. *The Metropolitan Life Survey of the American Teacher 1999* (New York: Harris Interactive, Inc., 2001), pp. 39, 42.

74. Lowell C. Rose and Alec M. Gallup, "The 30th Annual Gallup Poll of the Public's Attitudes Toward the Public Schools," *Phi Delta Kappan* 80, no. 1 (September 2002), p. 49.

75. Lightfoot, *The Good High School;* Kevin Dwyer and D. Osher, *Safeguarding Our Children: An Action Guide* (Washington, DC: U.S. Department of Education, August 2000).

76. Wilbur Brookover, Laurence Beamer, Helen Efthim, Douglas Hathaway, Lawrence Lezotte, Stephen Miller, Joseph Passalacqua, and Louis Tornatzky, *Creating Effective Schools* (Holmes Beach, FL: Learning Publications, 1982).

77. Herbert Walberg, Rosanne Paschal, and Thomas Weinstein, "Homework's Powerful Effects on Learning," *Educational Leadership* 42 (1985), pp. 76–79.

78. Robert Rosenthal and Lenore Jacobson, *Pygmalion in the Classroom* (New York: Holt, Rinehart & Winston, 1968).

79. Patrick Proctor, "Teacher Expectations: A Model for School Improvement," *Elementary School Journal* (March 1984), pp. 469–81; William Wayson, "The Politics of Violence in Schools: Double Speak and Disruptions in Public Confidence," *Phi Delta Kappan* 67, no. 2 (October 1985), pp. 127–32.

80. *Metropolitan Life Survey of the American Teacher 2001* (New York: Harris Interactive, Inc., 2001), p. 61.

81. Larry Cuban, "Effective Schools: A Friendly but Cautionary Note," *Phi Delta Kappan* 64, no. 10 (June 1983), pp. 695–96; Daniel Levine, "Creating Effective Schools: Findings and Implications from Research and Practice," *Phi Delta Kappan* 72, no. 5 (January 1991), pp. 389–93.

82. Rebecca Jones, "What Works: Researchers Tell What Schools Must Do to Improve Student Achievement," *The American School Board Journal* 185, no. 4 (April 1998), pp. 28–32, 33; Mary Anne Raywid, "Synthesis of Research: Small Schools: A Reform That Works," *Educational Leadership* (December 1997/January 1998), pp. 34–39; Kenneth J. Cooper, "9 Schools Show How to Make the Grade," *The Washington Post,* January 13, 2000, p. A17; Ann Marie Moriarity, "Just Right: School Size Matters," *The Washington Post* (August 7, 2002), p. H9; Alan B. Kruger, "Smaller Classes Help Many," *USA Today* (August 2, 2002), p. 8A; "The Effect of Classroom Practice on Student Achievement," *ASCD SmartBrief* 1, no. 11 (May 27, 2003), online; Catherine Gewertz, "Trusting' School Community Linked to Student Gains," *Education Week,* October 16, 2002, online.

CHAPTER 6   WHAT STUDENTS ARE TAUGHT IN SCHOOL

1. Hilda Taba, *Curriculum Development: Theory and Practice* (New York: Harcourt Brace Jovanovich, 1962).

2. John Goodlad, *A Place Called School* (New York: McGraw-Hill, 1984).

3. National Center for Education Statistics, *The Condition of Education 1995.* Indicator 43, Extracurricular Activities (Washington, DC: U.S. Department of Education); Feminist Majority Foundation, *Empowering Women in Sports,* Washington, DC, 1995.

4. Allyce Holland and Thomas Andre, "Participation in Extracurricular Activities in Secondary School: What Is Known, What Needs to Be Known," *Review of Educational Research* 57, no. 4 (Winter 1987), pp. 437–66; John Holloway. "Extracurricular Activities: The Path to Academic Success? *Educational Leadership* 57, no. 4 (December 1999/January 2000); T. Coladarci and C. Cobb, "Extracurricular Participation, School Size, and Achievement and Self-Esteem among High School Students: A National Look." *Journal of Research in Rural Education* 12, 1996, pp. 92–103; J. Mahoney and R. Cairns. "Do Extracurricular Activities Protect against Early School Dropout?" *Developmental Psychology* 33, no. 2, 1997, pp. 241–53; National Center for Education Statistics, *The Condition of Education 1995.* Indicator 43, Extracurricular Activities. Washington, DC, July 1995.

5. National Center for Education Statistics, *Trends Among High School Seniors, 1972–1992* (Washington, DC: U.S. Department of Education, 1995); American Association of University Women, *Gender Gaps: Where Schools Still Fail Our Children,* (Washington, DC: AAUW, 1998); National Center for Educational Statistics. *Trends in Educational Equity for Girls and Women.* Indicator 20, Washington DC, 2000.

6. B. Bradford Brown, "The Vital Agenda for Research on Extracurricular Influences: A Reply to Holland and Andre," *Review of Educational Research* 58, no. 1 (spring 1988), pp. 107–11; T. Coladarci and C. Cobb, "Extracurricular Participation, School Size, and Achievement and Self-Esteem among High School Students," pp. 92–103; W. Jordan and S. Nettles. *How Students Invest Their Time Out of School: Effects on School Engagement, Perceptions of Life Chances, and Achievement.* Baltimore: Center for Research on the Education of Students Placed at Risk, 1999; National Center for Education Statistics, *The Condition of Education, 1995.* Indicator 43, Extracurricular Activities. Washington, DC, July 1995.

7. National Association of Secondary School Principals, *The Mood of American Youth* (Reston, VA: National Association of Secondary School Principals, 1984); John Holloway, "Extracurricular Activities"; Karen Rasmussen. The Changing Sports Scene. *Educational Leadership, 57,* no. 4 December 1999/January 2000, pp. 26–29; U.S. Department of Education. "The Role of School in United States Adolescents' Lives: Time Use in Adolescents' Lives." *The Educational System in the United States: Case Study Findings,* Washington DC, March 1999.

8. Data from *High School and Beyond* reported in "Extracurricular Activity Participants Outperform Other Students," *OERI Bulletin* (September 1986), p. 2.

9. Stephen Hamilton, "Synthesis of Research on the Social Side of Schooling," *Educational Leadership* 40, no. 5 (February 1983), pp. 65–72.

10. Jerome Bruner, *The Process of Education* (Cambridge, MA: Harvard University Press, 1960).

11. Donald Irish, "Death Education: Preparation for Living," in Betty Green and Donald Irish (eds.), *Death Education: Preparation for Living* (Cambridge, MA: Schenkman, 1971), pp. 45–68.

12. Ben Brodinsky, "Back to the Basics: The Movement and Its Meaning," *Phi Delta Kappan* 58, no. 7 (March 1977), pp. 522–27.

13. George Gallup, "Gallup Poll of the Public's Attitudes Toward the Public Schools," *Phi Delta Kappan* 64, no. 1 (September 1982), p. 39.

14. Philip Cusick, *The Egalitarian Ideal and the American High School* (New York: Longman, 1983).

15. Sara Lawrence Lightfoot, *The Good High School* (New York: Basic Books, 1983).

16. Ernest L. Boyer, *High School: A Report on Secondary Education in America,* The Carnegie Foundation for the Advancement of Teaching (New York: Harper & Row, 1983).

17. Goodlad, *A Place Called School,* p. 298.

18. Theodore Sizer, *Horace's Compromise: The Dilemma of the American High School* (Boston: Houghton Mifflin, 1984), p. 89.

19. Mortimer Adler, "The Paideia Proposal," *The Rotation,* September 1982.

20. E. D. Hirsch, Jr., *Cultural Literacy* (Boston: Houghton Mifflin, 1987).

21. E. D. Hirsch, Jr., "Cultural Literacy: Let's Get Specific," *NEA Today,* (January 1988), p. 18.

22. Carla Haymesfeld, "Filling the Hole in Whole Language," *Educational Leadership* 46, no. 6 (March 1989), pp. 65–68. James Collins, "How Johnny Should Read," *Time,* October 27, 1997, pp. 78–81; Karin Chenoweth, "Reading Wars, Take 2," *The Washington Post,* May 16, 1999, p. 17.

23. Sandra Stotsky, "Whose Literature? America's!" *Educational Leadership* 49, no. 4 (December 1991/January 1992), pp. 53–56.

24. California Department of Education, *Recommended Literature: Kindergarten Through Grade Twelve* (July 15, 2001). www.cde.ca.gov/ci/literature.

25. David Barton, "Classic Debate!" *Sacramento Bee,* April 3, 1998, p. SC-1.

26. Erika Hayasaki, "2 Rs Left in School," *Los Angeles Times,* May 19, 2003, online.

27. Philip Cohen, "Challenging History: The Past Remains a Battleground for Schools," *Association for Supervision and Curriculum Development Curriculum Update* (Winter 1995), p. 2; Mike Bowler, "Teachers Fear Social Studies Is Becoming History," *The Baltimore Sun,* May 6, 2003, online.

28. "Kids Flunk Geography, Survey Finds," Associated Press, November 20, 2002.

29. National Center for Educational Statistics, *National Center for Educational Progress: Civics,* 1998 National Test Questions and Performance Results. (Washington, DC: U.S. Department of Education). nces.ed.gov/nationsreportcard/itmrls/ITMRLS.HTM.

30. Jacqueline Trescott, "Two for the History Books," *Washington Post,* September 18, 2002; p. C2; Michele Kurtz, "History Studies Pose a Hot Topic," *Boston Globe,* October 22, 2002; p. B1.

31. David J. Hoff, "Math Council Again Mulling Its Standards," *Education Week on the Web,* November 4, 1998; National Council of Teachers of Mathematics, *Principles and Standards for School Mathematics: An Overview (2000).* www.nctm.org/standards/ principles.htm; National Center for Education Statistics, NAEP Achievement Scores (2000).

32. Ethan Bronner, "U.S. Trails the World in Math and Science," *The New York Times,* February 25, 1998, p. 10.

33. Steve Olson, "Science FRICTION." *Education Week on the Web,* September 30, 1998.

34. Jay Mathews, "Teaching Physics First Ignites Debate," *The Washington Post,* January 29, 2003, p. A8.

35. Hugh McIntosh, "What Should Students Know? How Should Teachers Teach?" *National Research Council News Report* 43, no. 1 (Winter 1993), pp. 2–6; Project 2061 (American Association for the Advancement of Science), *Benchmarks for Science Literacy* (New York: Oxford University Press, 1993).

36. Valerie Strauss, "Language Classes Leave Students Tongue-Tied," *The Washington Post,* June 3, 2003, p. A9.

37. American Council on the Teaching of Foreign Languages, *Standards for Foreign Language Learning: Preparing for the 21st Century* (Lawrence Kansas: American Council on the Teaching of Foreign Language, 1996).

38. National Center for Educational Statistics, NAEP Facts, *Frequency of Arts Instruction for Students,* 4, no 3 (Washington, DC: U.S. Department of Education, December 1999). http://nces.ed.gov/pubs2000/ 2000510.pdf

39. Tamara Henry, "Study: Arts Education Has Academic Effect," *USA TODAY,* May 20, 2002, p. 6D.

40. Debra Viadero, "38-Member Panel Adopts 81 Standards for the Arts," *Education Week,* February 9, 1994, p. 5; Jane Bonbright, "Special Report: National Assessment of Educational Progress in the Arts," *JOPERD* 69, no. 8 (October 1998).

41. National Center for Health Statistics, National Health and Nutrition Examination Survey, *Prevalence of Overweight among Children and Adolescents: United States* (1999–2000). www.cdc.gov/nchs/products/ pubs/pubd/hestats/overwght99.htm.

42. National Association for Sport and Physical Education, *Shape of the Nation Report* (Reston, VA: National Association for Sport and Physical Education, 1997); Scott McCredie, "As Kids Get Wider, Schools Struggle to Squeeze in Enough Fitness Time," *Seattle Times,* September 4, 2002, online; President's Council on Physical Fitness and Sports, *Research Digest* 3, no. 13 (March 2001), p. 9 www.fitness.gov/digest301.pdf.

43. "Issues: Should physical education classes return to teaching males and females separately?" *JOPERD* 70, no. 1 (January 1999), pp. 11–13; Linda Jean Carpenter and R. Vivian Costa, "Courtside: Coed Physical Education and the Law," *Strategies* 14, no. 6 (July/August 2001), pp. 5–8.

44. *Gender Gaps: Where Schools Still Fail Our Children* (Washington, DC: Commissioned by the American Association of University Women, 1998); President's Council on Physical Fitness and Sports, *Research Digest* 3, no. 13 (March 2001). www.fitness.gov/digest301.pdf.

45. National Center for Chronic Disease Prevention and Health Promotion, Comprehensive School Health Education, *School Health Policies and Program Study: Project Summary* (2000). www.cdc.gov/nccdphp/dash/cshedef.htm; Timothy Egan, "Body-Conscious Boys Adopt Athletes' Taste for Steroids," *The New York Times,* November 22, 2002, online.

46. U.S. Newswire, *Highest-Ever Support for Sex Education* (June 2, 1999), www.feminist.org.

47. Steve Sternberg, "Sex Education Stirs Controversy," *USA TODAY,* July, 7, 2002, online.

48. John G. Wirt, "A New Federal Law on Vocational Education: Will Reform Follow?" *Phi Delta Kappan* 72, no. 6 (February 1991), pp. 425–33.

49. National Center for Educational Statistics, *The Condition of Education 2001.* Indicator 35, Section 4, Quality of Elementary and Secondary School Environments (Washington, DC: U.S. Department of Education), p. 62.

50. Marjorie Coeyman, "Practical skills vs. three R's: A Debate Revives," *Christian Science Monitor,* July 8, 2003, online.

51. National Coalition for Women and Girls in Education, *Invisible Again: The Impact of Changes in Federal Funding on Vocational Programs for Women and Girls* (A Report from National Coalition for Women and Girls in Education, Washington, DC: October 2001).

52. Louis Raths, Selma Wasserman, Arthur Jones, and Arnold Rothstein, *Teaching for Thinking: Theory and Application* (Columbus, OH: Merrill, 1966.) See also Selma Wasserman, "Teaching for Thinking: Louis E. Raths Revisited," *Phi Delta Kappan* 68, no. 6 (February 1987), pp. 460–66.

53. Summaries of these approaches are found in Barbara Presseisen, *Thinking Skills: Research and Practice* (Washington, DC: National Education Association, 1986). See also R. Feuerstein, *Instrumental Enrichment An Intervention Program for Cognitive Modifiability* (Baltimore: University Park Press, 1980); A. H. Schoenfeld, "Measures of Problem-Solving Instruction," *Journal for Research in Mathematics Education* 13 (1962); E. de Bono, "The Cognitive Research Trust (CORT) Thinking Program," in W. Maxwell (ed.), *Thinking: The Expanding Frontier* (Hillsdale, NJ: Erlbaum, 1983); Joseph Hester, *Teaching for Thinking: A Program for School Improvement Through Teaching Critical Thinking Across the Curriculum* (Durham, NC: Carolina Academic Press, 1994), pp. 1–23.

54. J. Wink, *Critical Pedagogy: Notes from the Real World* (New York: Addison Wesley Longman, 1999), pp. 28–45.

55. Robert Slavin, "PET and the Pendulum: Faddism in Education and How to Stop It," *Phi Delta Kappan* 70, no. 6 (June 1989), p. 752.

56. Michael Apple, "Curriculum in the Year 2000: Tensions and Possibilities," *Phi Delta Kappan* 64, no. 5 (January 1983), p. 323.

57. Abner Peddiwell (Harold Benjamin), *The Saber-Tooth Curriculum* (New York: McGraw-Hill, 1939).

CHAPTER 7   STANDARDS, TESTING, AND CONTROVERSY OVER WHO CONTROLS THE CURRICULUM

1. Paul Barry, "Interview: A Talk with A. Bartlett Giamatti," *College Review Board* (Spring 1982), p. 48.

2. Michael Fletcher, "States Worry New Law Sets Up Schools to Fail," *The Washington Post,* January 2, 2003, p. A1.

3. Rod Paige, "An Overview of America's Education Agenda," *Phi Delta Kappan,* May 2002, pp. 708–713.

4. Diana Jean Schemo, "New Federal Rule Tightens Demands on Schools," *The New York Times,* November 27, 2002, online; Michael A. Fletcher, "States Worry New Law Sets Schools Up to Fail," *The Washington Post,* January 2, 2003, p. A1.

5. Sam Dillon, "States Cut Test Standards to Avoid Sanctions," *The New York Times,* May 22, 2003, nytimes.com; David Hoff, "States Revise the Meaning of 'Proficient,'" *Education Week* 22, no. 6, October 9, 2002, pp. 1, 24, 25; Duke Helfand, "State Keeps Education Standards," *Los Angeles Times,* January 9, 2003, LATimes.com.

6. Diana Jean Schemo, "Poor Rural Schools Try to Meet New Federal Rules," *The New York Times,* December 2, 2002, online; Don Joling, "Rural Schools in Alaska Lag Behind Federal Plan," *Seattle Times,* May 14, 2003, seattletimes.com; Diana Jean Schemo, "New Federal Rule Tightens Demands on Schools," *The New York Times,* November 27, 2002, nytimes.com; Rick Karlin, "Federal School Act a Possible Litigation Magnet," *Albany Times Union,* February 13, 2003, online; Jay Mathews, "Inside the No Child Left Behind Law," *The Washington Post,* January 28, 2003, washingtonpost.com.

7. Sam Dillon, "New Law May Leave Rural Teachers Behind," *The New York Times,* June 23, 2003, nytimes.com; "Report: Nation Has Climb to Meet Teacher-Quality Requirement, *CNN Student News,* July 16, 2003, cnn.com; Gerald W. Bracey, "The 12th Bracey Report on the Condition of Public Education," *Phi Delta Kappan* 84, no. 2, October 2002, pp. 113–50; Leslie S. Kaplan and William A. Owings, "The Politics of Teacher Quality," *Phi Delta Kappan* 84, no. 9, May 2003, pp. 687–92.

8. O. L. Davis, "New Policies and New Directions: Be Aware of the Foolprints! Notice to Nightmares!" *Journal of Curriculum and Supervision* 18, no. 2, (Winter 2003), pp. 103–109; Gerald W. Bracey, "The 12th Bracey Report on the Condition of Public Education," *Phi Delta Kappan* 84, no. 2, October 2002, pp. 113–50; David Goodman, "No Child Left Unrecruited," *Mother Jones,* November/December 2002, MotherJones.com; Jay Mathews, "Inside the No Child Left Behind Law," *The Washington Post,* January 28, 2003, washingtonpost.com.

9. John Merrow, "Undermining Standards," *Phi Delta Kappan* 82, no. 9 (May 2001), pp. 653–59.

10. John Elson, "History, the Sequel," *Time,* 7 November 1994, p. 53; see also Von Wiener, "History Lesson," *The New Republic,* January 2, 1995, pp. 9–11.

11. Joel Spring, *American Education* (New York: McGraw-Hill, 1996), pp. 237–41.

12. Lyn Nell Hancock with Nina Archer Biddle, "Red, White—and Blue," *Newsweek,* November 7, 1994, p. 54.

13. Christopher T. Cross, "The Standards Wars: Some Lessons Learned," *Education Week on the Web,* October 21, 1998, pp. 1–4.

14. "Seeking Stability for Standards Based Education," *Education Week on the Web,* Quality Counts 2001 Survey in 2001 Editorial Projects in Education 20, no. 17 (January 11, 2001), pp. 8, 9.

15. Merrow, "Undermining Standards," p. 655.

16. Kate Zernike, "Scarsdale Mothers Succeed in First Boycott of 8th-Grade Test," *New York Times on the Web,* May 4, 2001.

17. Michael A. Fletcher, "High Stakes Rise, School Group Put Exam to Test," *The Washington Post,* July 9, 2001, p. A1; "Seeking Stability for Standards Based Education," *Education Week on the Web;* Mathew Pinzur, "Fear of Failure Leads to FCAT Rebellion," *Miami Herald,* May 13, 2003, www.miami.com; Michele Kurtz, "Berkshire District to Flout MCAS Rule," *Boston Globe,* February 21, 2003, p. B5; Rosalind Rossi," Chicago Refuses to Give Bad Exam," *Chicago Sun Times,* October 16, 2002, online; David Hoff, "Teacher Probed for Role in Anti-Testing Activity," *Education Week* 21, no. 36, May 15, 2002, p. 3.

18. Monty Neill, "The Dangers of Testing." *Educational Leadership* 60, no. 5, February 2003, pp. 43–46; Michael A. Fletcher, "Exit Exam Hurt At-Risk Students," *The Washington Post,* August 14, 2002, p. A7; Dan DePasquale and Frank Adams, "Midland Voices: Beware the Risks of Statewide Testing," Snowbizz.com; Jennifer Medina, "Top-Performing School Teaches Art of Test-Taking," *The New York Times,* March 28, 2003, nytimes.com; Audrey L. Amrein and David C. Berliner "High-Stakes Testing, Uncertainty, and Student Learning" *Education Policy Analysis Archives* 10, no. 18, March 2002, http://epaa.asu.edu/epaa/v10n18.

19. Diana Jean Schemo, "Education Secretary Defends School System He Once Led," *The New York Times,* July 26, 2003, nytimes.com; Jay Heubert and Robert Hauser, eds., *High Stakes: Testing for Tracking, Promotion, and Graduation* (Washington, DC: National Research Council, 1998); Dan DePasquale and Frank Adams, "Midland Voices: Beware the Risks of Statewide Testing," Snowbizz.com; Alfie Kohn, *The Case Against Standardized Testing: Raising Scores and Ruining Schools* (Portsmouth, NH: Heinemann, 2000); Linda McNeil, "Contradictions of School Reform: Educational Costs of Standardized Testing" *Phi Delta Kappan* 81, no. 10, (June 2000), pp. 729–34.

20. Linda McNeil, "Creating New Inequities: Contradictions of Reform," *Phi Delta Kappan* 81, no. 10, (June 2000), pp. 729–34.

21. John Merrow, "Undermining Standards," *Phi Delta Kappan* 82, no. 9 (May 2001), pp. 653–59; James W. Popham, "Why Standardized Tests Don't Measure Quality Education," *Educational Leadership* 56, no 6, 1999; pp. 8–15; Alfie Kohn, *The Case Against Standardized Testing: Raising Scores and Ruining Schools,* (Portsmouth, NH: Heinemann, 2000); James Hoffman, Assaf Czop, Lori Paris, and Scott Paris, "High-Stakes Testing in Reading: Today in Texas, Tomorrow?" *The Reading Teacher* 54, no. 5 (February 2001), pp. 482–92; "Quality Counts 2001: A Better Balance." *Education Week* 20, no. 16 (Bethesda, MD: Editorial Projects); Audrey L. Amrein and David C. Berliner, "High-Stakes Testing, Uncertainty, and Student Learning" *Education Policy Analysis Archives* 10, no. 18 (March 2002), epaa.asu.edu/epaa/v10n18.

22. Connie Langland, "Tests No Help to Learning," *Philadelphia Inquirer,* May 29, 2003, www.phillly.com.

23. James Hoffman, Assaf Czop, Lori Paris, and Scott Paris, "High-Stakes Testing in Reading: Today in Texas, Tomorrow?" *The Reading Teacher* 54, no. 5 (February 2001), pp. 482–92.

24. James Traub, "The Test Mess," *The New York Times,* April 7, 2002, nytimes.com.

25. Nancy Kober, "Teaching to the Test: The Good, the Bad, and Who's Responsible," *TestTalk for Leaders,* Issue 1 (June 2002); Michele Kurtz and Anand Vaishnav, "Student's MCAS Answer Means 449 Others Pass." *Boston Globe,* December 5, 2002, p. A1.

26. Sam Dillon, "Before the Answer, the Question Must Be Correct," *The New York Times,* July 16, 2003, nytimes.com.

27. Diana B. Henriques and Jacques Steinberg, "Right Answer, Wrong Score: Test Flaws Take Toll," *New York Times on the Web,* May 20, 2001; Norman Draper, "Testing Firm to Pay Students $7 Million for Grading Goof," *Minneapolis-St. Paul Star Tribune,* November 26, 2002, startribune.com; Tamara Henry, "Results Are in for States' Student Tests," *USA Today,* June 19, 2002, p. 7D.

28. Kevin Rothstein, "Instructors: Testing Hurts Teaching," *Boston Herald,* March 5, 2003, online; Michele Kurtz, "Teachers' Views Mixed on Testing," *Boston Globe,* March 5, 2003, p. B5.

29. Kathleen Kennedy Manzo, "Protests Over State Testing Widespread," *Education Week on the Web,* May 16, 2001.

30. Abby Goodnough, "Strains of Fourth-Grade Tests Drive Off Veteran Teachers," *New York Times on the Web,* June 14, 2001; Liz Seymour, "SOL Tests Create New Dropouts," *The Washington Post,* July 17, 2001, pp. A1, A8.

31. Tana Thomson, "105-year-old Saline County Test in Nation's Spotlight." *The Salina Journal,* July 9, 2000.

32. Richard Elmore, "Testing Trap," adapted from *Education Next* 105, September–October 2002, p. 35.

33. Grant Wiggins, "Teaching to the (Authentic) Test," *Educational Leadership* 46, no. 7 (April 1989), pp. 41–47. See also Rieneke Zessoules and Howard Gardner, "Authentic Assessment: Beyond the Buzzword and into

the Classroom," in Vito Perrone (ed.) *Expanding Student Assessment* (Alexandria, VA: Association for Supervision and Curriculum Development, 1991).

34. Gene I. Maeroff, "Assessing Alternative Assessment," *Phi Delta Kappan* 73, no. 4 (December 1991), pp. 272–81.

35. Theodore Sizer, *Horace's School: Redesigning the American High School* (New York: Houghton Mifflin, 1992).

36. Rebecca Jones, "Textbook Troubles," *American School Board Journal,* December 2000, pp. 18–21.

37. Harriet Tyson Bernstein, *A Conspiracy of Good Intentions: America's Textbook Fiasco* (Washington, DC: The Council for Basic Education, 1988), p. 2.

38. Ibid., p. 20.

39. Rodger Farr and Michael Tulley, "Do Adoption Committees Perpetuate Mediocre Textbooks?" *Phi Delta Kappan* 66, no. 7 (March 1985), pp. 467–71.

40. Bonnie Ambruster, Jean Osborn, and Alice Davison, "Readability Formulas May Be Dangerous to Your Textbooks," *Educational Leadership* 42, no. 7 (April 1985), pp. 18–20.

41. Susan Ohanian, "Ruffles and Flourishes," *Atlantic Monthly,* September 1987, pp. 20–22.

42. Quoted in Bernstein, *A Conspiracy of Good Intentions,* p. 19.

43. Quoted in David Elliott, Kathleen Carter Nagel, and Arthur Woodward, "Do Textbooks Belong in Elementary School Studies?" *Educational Leadership* 42, no. 7 (April 1985), pp. 21–25; see also Rebecca Jones, "Textbook Troubles," *American School Board Journal,* V187 (December 2000).

44. Jean Osborn, Beau Fly Jones, and Marcy Stein, "The Case for Improving Textbooks," *Educational Leadership* 42, no. 7 (April 1985), pp. 9–16; see also Michael Apple, "Regulating the Text: The Social Historical Roots of State Control." Paper delivered at the American Educational Research Association, San Francisco, April 1992.

45. Howard Lyon, "Buyer Beware: Why We Must Hold Publishers Accountable for Textbook Mistakes," *American School Board Journal,* December 2000, pp. 22–24.

46. "Not Crystal Clear: Mistakes in Science Texts," *The Washington Post,* January 30, 2001, p. 11.

47. Rebecca Jones, "What Works: Researchers Tell What Schools Must Do to Improve Student Achievement," *American School Board Journal* 185, no. 4 (April 1998), pp. 32–33.

48. The forms of bias were developed by Myra Sadker and David Sadker for Title IX equity workshops.

49. Bernstein, *A Conspiracy of Good Intentions,* pp. 35–36.

50. Quoted in Edward B. Jenkinson, "The Significance of the Decision in 'Scopes II,'" *Phi Delta Kappan* 68, no. 6 (February 1987), p. 446.

51. Frances Goodrich and Albert Hackett, *The Diary of Anne Frank, In Great Waves Breaking,* Bernard J. Weiss (ed.) (New York: Holt, Rinehart & Winston, 1983), p. 387.

52. Transcripts of proceedings in *Mozert,* July 14, 1986, p. 24, as quoted in Jenkinson, *Scopes II.*

53. Robert Marzano and David Arredondo, *Tactics for Thinking—Teacher's Manual* (Alexandria, VA: Association for Supervision and Curriculum Development, 1986), p. 11; quoted in Edward Jenkinson, "The New Age of Schoolbook Protest," *Phi Delta Kappan* 10, no. 1 (September 1988), p. 66.

54. Thomas McDaniel, "On Trial: The Right to Think," *Educational Leadership* 49, no. 4 (December 1991/January 1992), p. 85.

55. Perry Glanzer, "Religion in Public Schools," *Phi Delta Kappan* 80, no. 3 (October 1998), p. 220.

56. Craig Timberg, "Bible's Second Coming," *The Washington Post,* June 4, 2000, p. A1.

57. "Public School Drops Christian Textbooks," *The Washington Post,* September 17, 1999, p. 2.

58. Anthony Podesta, "For Full Discussion of Religion in the Schools," *The Wall Street Journal,* November 12, 1986, p. 32. See also Perry Glanzer, "Religion in Public Schools: In Search of Fairness," *Phi Delta Kappan* 80, no. 3 (November 1998), pp. 219–22.

59. "Religion in Class: More Needed, Report Says," *The Washington Post,* December 5, 2000, p. A-22.

60. Debra Viadero, "Christian Movement Seen Trying to Influence Schools," *Education Week,* April 15, 1992, p. 8.

61. Liz Leyden, "Story Hour Didn't Have a Happy Ending," *The Washington Post,* December 3, 1998, A3.

62. L. Adler, *Curriculum Challenges in California: Third statewide survey of challenges to curriculum materials and services* (Fullerton: California State University, ERIC Document Reproduction Service, 1993), (No. 375 475).

63. Myra Sadker and David Sadker, *Now upon a Time: A Contemporary View of Children's Literature* (New York: Harper & Row, 1977).

64. "Ten Most Challenged Books in 2002," Office for Intellectual Freedom, American Library Association on the Web, 2003.

65. Suzanne Fisher Staples, "Why Johnny Can't Read: Censorship in American Libraries," *Digital Library and Archives,* Virginia Tech University on the Web (Winter 1996).

66. *Attacks on the Freedom to Learn,* People for the American Way, 1995–1996 report.

67. "Ten Most Challenged Books in 2002," Office for Intellectual Freedom, American Library Association on the Web, 2003.

68. Kathleen Kennedy Manzo, "Despite Flap, Seattle to Keep Grant for Books About Homosexuality," *Education Week on the Web,* May 28, 1997.

69. Quoted in Lynne Cheney, *Humanities in America: A Report to the President, Congress and the American People* (Washington, DC: National Endowment for the Humanities, 1988), p. 17.

70. Quoted in William Bennett, *American Education: Making It Work* (Washington, DC: U.S. Department of Education, 1988).

71. Allan Bloom, *The Closing of the American Mind* (New York: Simon & Schuster, 1987), p. 63.

72. E. D. Hirsch, Jr., *What Your First Grader Needs to Know, and What Your Second Grader Needs to Know* (New York: Doubleday, 1991).

73. James Banks, "Multicultural Education: For Freedom's Sake," *Educational Leadership* 49, no. 4 (December 1991/January 1992), pp. 32–36.

CHAPTER 8 THE HISTORY OF AMERICAN EDUCATION

1. Sheldon Cohen, *A History of Colonial Education, 1607–1776* (New York: Wiley, 1974).

2. Nathaniel Shurtlett, ed., *Records of the Governor and Company of the Massachusetts Bay in New England, II* (Boston: Order of the Legislature, 1853); see also H. Warren Button and Eugene F. Provenzo, Jr., *History of Education and Culture in America* (Englewood Cliffs, NJ: Prentice Hall, 1983).

3. James Hendricks, "Be Still and Know! Quaker Silence and Dissenting Educational Ideals, 1740–1812," *Journal of the Midwest History of Education Society,* Annual Proceedings, 1975; R. Freeman Butts and Lawrence A. Cremin, *A History of Education in American Culture* (New York: Holt, 1953).

4. Lawrence A. Cremin, *American Education: The Colonial Experience, 1607–1783* (New York: Harper & Row, 1970); see also Button and Provenzo, *History of Education and Culture in America.*

5. James C. Klotter, "The Black South and White Appalachia," *Journal of American History* (March 1980), pp. 832–49.

6. John H. Best, *Benjamin Franklin on Education* (New York: Teachers College Press, 1962).

7. Jonathon Messerli, *Horace Mann: A Biography* (New York: Alfred A. Knopf, 1972); Steven Tozer, Paul Violas, and Guy Senese, *School and Society* (Boston: McGraw-Hill, 1998).

8. Lawrence Cremin, *The Transformation of the School: Progressivism in American Education, 1876–1957* (New York: Alfred A. Knopf, 1961).

9. Jackie M. Blount, "Spinsters, Bachelors and Other Gender Transgressors in School Employment, 1850–1990," *Review of Educational Research* 70, no. 1, (spring 2000), pp. 83–101.

10. E. Marcus, *Making History: The Struggle for Gay and Lesbian Equal Rights, 1945–1990, An Oral History* (New York: Harper Collins Publishers, 1992).

11. Blount, "Spinsters, Bachelors and Other Gender Transgressors in School Employment, 1850–1990," p. 94.

12. Edward A. Krug, *The Shaping of the American High School, 1880–1920,* I (New York: Harper & Row, 1964); see also John D. Pulliam, *History of Education in America,* 4th ed. (Columbus, OH: Merrill, 1987); Joel Spring, *The American School, 1642–1985* (New York: Longman, 1986).

13. M. Lee Manning, "A Brief History of the Middle School," *The Clearing House* 73, no. 4, March–April 2000, p. 192.

14. National Education Association, *Report of the Committee on Secondary School Studies* (Washington, DC: U.S. Government Printing Office, 1893).

15. Gerald Grant, *The World We Created at Hamilton High* (Cambridge, MA: Harvard University Press, 1988).

16. Special thanks to Kate Volker for developing the Crandall and Ashton-Warner biographies.

CHAPTER 9 PHILOSOPHY OF EDUCATION

1. William Bagley, "The Case for Essentialism in Education," *National Education Association Journal 30,* no. 7 (1941), pp. 202–20.

2. Robert M. Hutchins, *The Higher Learning in America* (New Haven, CT: Yale University Press, 1962), p. 78.

3. Mortimer Adler, *Reforming Education* (Boulder, CO: Westview Press, 1977), pp. 84–85.

4. John Dewey, *Experience and Education* (New York: Macmillan, 1963).

5. Larry Cuban, *How Teachers Taught,* 2nd edition (New York: Teachers College Press, 1993).

6. Paulo Freire, *Pedagogy of the Oppressed* (New York: Continuum Press, 1989).

7. Maxine Greene, *Landscapes of Learning* (New York: Teachers College Press, 1978); See also Maxine Greene, "Reflections on Teacher as Stranger" in C. Kridel (ed.) *Books of the Century Catalog* (Columbia, SC: University of South Carolina, Museum of Education, 2000).

8. Lee Canter, "Assertive Discipline: More Than Names on a Board and Marbles in a Jar," *Phi Delta Kappan,* 71, 1989, pp. 57–61.

9. Timothy Reagan, *Non-Western Educational Traditions: Alternative Approaches to Educational Thought and Practice* (Mahwah, NJ: Lawrence Earlbaum Associates, 1996).

10. *Aristotle, Politics,* trans. and intro. by T. A. Sinclair (Middlesex, England: Penguin, 1978).

CHAPTER 10 FINANCING AND GOVERNING AMERICA'S SCHOOLS

1. Mark G. Yudof, David L. Kip, Betsy Levin, *Educational Policy and the Law,* 3rd ed. (St. Paul: West, 1992), p. 658; Betsy Levin, Thomas Muller, and Corazon Sandoval, *The High Cost of Education in Cities* (Washington, DC: The Urban Institute, 1973).

2. Barry Siegel, "Parents Get a Lesson in Equality," *Los Angeles Times* (Washington edition), April 13, 1992, pp. A-1, A-18–A-19.

3. *Robinson v. Cahill,* 69 N.J. 133 (1973); *Abbott v. Burke,* 119 N.J. 287 (1990) (known as *Abbott I*); *Abbott v. Burke,* 153 N. J. 480 (1998) (known *as Abbott V*).

4. Peter Enrich, "Leaving Equality Behind: New Directions in School Finance Reform," *Vanderbilt Law Review* 48(1995), pp. 101–194; for a description of this movement to adequacy arguments, visit nces.ed.gov/edfin/litigation/Contents.asp. For a discussion of the impact in Wisconsin, see Daniel W. Hildebrand, "2000 Significant Court Decisions,"

Wisconsin Lawyer 74, no. 6 (June 2001). Similar analyses are available in other such law updates.

5. Joshua Benton, "One District Reaps the Benefit of Another's Belt-tightening," *The Dallas Morning News,* December 12, 2002, www.dallasnews.com; David Mace, "Act 60 Reform Likely," *Rutland Herald,* January 6, 2003, online; "Tennessee's School Funding Declared Unconstitutional Again," *Associated Press,* October 9, 2002, CNN.COM.

6. Richard Rothstein, "Equalizing Education Resources on Behalf of Disadvantaged Children," *A Nation at Risk: Preserving Public Education as an Engine for Social Mobility,* Richard D. Kahlenberg, editor (New York: The Century Foundation Press, 2000), p. 74.

7. W. E. Thro, "The Third Wave: The Impact of the Montana, Kentucky and Texas Decisions on the Future of Public School Finance Reform Litigation," *Journal of Law and Education* 199, no. 2 (spring 1990), pp. 219–50; Robert F. McNergney and Joanne M. Herbert, *Foundations of Education: The Challenge of Professional Practice* (Boston: Allyn & Bacon, 1995), pp. 475–78; Chris Pipho, "Stateline: The Scent of the Future," *Phi Delta Kappan* 76 (September 1994), pp. 10–11; Greg Kocher, "Group Says Education Not Getting Enough Money Due It by Law," *Lexington Herald-Leader,* June 25, 2003, www.kentucky.com.

8. Cited in *Campaign for Fiscal Equality v. New York,* 86 N.Y. 2d 307 (1995); see also Bess Keller, "School Finance Case Draws to Close in N.Y.," *Education Week,* August 2, 2000.

9. Lori Montgomery, "Maryland Seeks 'Adequacy,' Recasting School Debate," *The Washington Post,* April 22, 2002, p. A1.

10. Robert Slavin, "How Can Funding Equity Ensure Enhanced Achievement?" *Journal of Educational Finance* 24, no. 4 (Spring 1999), pp. 519–28.

11. Bruce J. Biddle and David C. Berliner, "Unequal School Funding in the United States," *Education Leadership* 59, no. 8, May 2002, pp. 48–59; Diana Jean Schemo, "Neediest Schools Receive Less Money, Report Finds," *The New York Times,* August 9, 2002, www.nytimes.com.

12. Thomas Toch, "Separate but Not Equal," *Agenda* 1 (spring 1991), pp. 15–17.

13. Peter Keating, "How to Keep Your State and Local Taxes Down," *Money* 24, no. 1 (January 1995), pp. 86–92.

14. Bill Norris, "Losing Ticket in Lotteries," *Times Educational Supplement,* March 19, 1993, p. 17.

15. Joetta L. Sack, "Priorities Emerging for ESEA Reauthorization," *Education Week on the Web,* September 30, 1998; Anne C. Lewis, "Washington Report: House Democrats Criticize (in Unison) the Education Block Grant: Republicans Sing a Different Tune," *Phi Delta Kappan* 65, no. 6 (February 1984), pp. 379–80.

16. Kris Axtman, "Schools Bend under Tight Budgets," *The Christian Science Monitor,* November 20, 2002, online; "Schools Cut Costs With 4-Day Weeks," September 11, 2002, CNN.COM; Richard Rothstein, "Raising School Standards and Cutting Budget: Huh?" *The New York Times,* July 10, 2002, nytimes.com.

17. Jay Matthews, "More Public Schools Using Private Dollars," *The Washington Post,* August 28, 1995, pp. A-1, A-8; Justin Blum, "PTAs Give Some D.C. Schools an Edge," *The Washington Post,* April 17, 2000, p. B1; Nancy Trejos, "Schools Turning to No-Fuss Fundraising Online," *The Washington Post,* May 23, 2000, p. A1.

18. Anne Lewis, "Washington Seen: Buildings in Disrepair," *Education Digest* 60, no. 8 (April 1995); p. 71; Jacques Steinberg and John Sullivan, "In Disrepair for Years, Many Schools Pose a Risk," *New York Times,* February 2, 1998, p. A-21; "Educator's Wish List: Infrastructure Tops High-Tech," *The Washington Post,* October 24, 2000, p. A-13; "Fast Response Survey System, Survey on the Conditions of Public School Facilities," U.S. Department of Education, National Center for Education Statistics, Washington, DC, 1999.

19. For an insightful discussion of school boards, see Joel Spring, *American Education* (New York: McGraw-Hill, 2002), pp. 178–82.

20. Chester Finn, "Reinventing Local Control," in Patricia First and Herbert Walberg (eds.), *School Boards: Changing Local Control* (Berkeley: McCutchan, 1992); Emily Feistritzer, "A Profile of School Board Presidents," in *School Boards: Changing Local Control;* Neal Pierce, "School Boards Get Failing Grades, in Both the Cities and the Suburbs," *Philadelphia Inquirer,* April 27, 1992, p. 11; Mary Jordan, "School Boards Need Overhaul, Educators Say," *The Washington Post,* April 5, 1992, p. A-51.

21. Jay Mathews, "Playing Politics in Urban City Schools," *The Washington Post,* September 11, 2002, washingtonpost.com.

22. Cited in Joel Spring, *American Education* (New York: McGraw-Hill, 2002), pp. 180–81.

23. Jay Mathews, "Nontraditional Thinking in Central Office," The School Administrator Web Edition, *The Washington Post,* June 2001; Tamar Lewin, "Leaders from Other Professions Reshape America's Schools, from Top to Bottom," *The New York Times,* June 8, 2000; Nancy Mitchell, "Nontraditional School Bosses," *Denver Rocky Mountain News,* April 16, 2001; Abby Goodnough, "Retired General Takes on New Mission: Schools," *New York Times,* November 6, 2002, nytimes.com; Jennifer Steinhauer, "Bloomberg Picks a Lawyer to Run New York Schools," *The New York Times,* July 30, 2002, nytimes.com.

24. Joanna Richardson, "Contracts Put Superintendents to Performance Test," *Education Week,* September 14, 1994, pp. 1, 12.

25. Emily Wax, "A Tough Time at the Head of the Classes," *The Washington Post,* June 18, 2002, p. A9.

26. Vincent L. Ferrandino, "Challenges for 21st-Century Elementary School Principals," *Phi Delta Kappan* 82, no. 6 (February 2001), pp. 440–42; Linda Borg, "The Principal Dilemma Facing Schools in R.I.," *The Providence Journal,* projo.com/education (August 26, 2001); Jacques Steinberg, "One Principal's World (The Unscripted Version)," *The New York Times,* January 1, 2003, nytimes.com.

27. "Seeing the Big Picture" in Education Vital Signs, *American School Board Journal,* December 1999.

28. Ferrandino, "Challenges for 21st-Century Elementary School Principals."

29. James G. Cibula, "Two Eras of Urban Schooling: The Decline of Law and Order and the Emergence of New Organizational Forms," *Education and Urban Society,* 29, no. 3 (May 1997), pp. 317–41.

30. Quoted in "Building Better Business Alliances," *Instructor* (winter 1986); (special issue), p. 21; see also Brian Dumaine, "Making Education Work," *Fortune,* spring 1990 (special issue), pp. 12–22.

31. For a good overview of school consolidation, see Karen Irmsher, "School Size." *ERIC Digest,* no. 113 (Eugene, OR: ERIC Clearinghouse on Educational Management, July 1997) (ED414615).

32. Catherine Gewertz, "The Breakup: Suburbs Try Smaller High Schools," *Education Week on the Web,* May 2, 2001; Craig Howley and Marty Strange and Robert Bickel, "Research about School Size and School Performance in Impoverished Communities," (Charleston, WV: ERIC Clearinghouse on Rural Education and Small Schools, December 2000); William Ayers, Gerald Bracey, and Greg Smith, "The Ultimate Education Reform? Make Schools Smaller," (Milwaukee: Center for Education Research, Analysis, and Innovation, University of Wisconsin–Milwaukee, December 14, 2000).

33. See Marianne Perle and David Baker, *Job Satisfaction Among America's Teachers: Effects of Workplace Conditions, Background Characteristics, and Teacher Compensation* (Washington, DC: National Center for Education Statistics, U.S. Department of Health, Education and Welfare, August 1997), pp. 41–42; See also John Lane and Edgar Epps (eds.), *Restructuring the Schools: Problems and Prospects* (Berkeley: McCutchan, 1992); Jeff Archer, "New Roles Tap Expertise of Teachers," *Education Week,* May 30, 2001.

34. Fern Shen, "New Strategy for School Management," *The Washington Post,* February 17, 1998, pp. B-1, B-7.

35. Ann Bradley and Lynn Olson, "The Balance of Power: Shifting the Lines of Authority in an Effort to Improve Schools," *Education Week,* February 24, 1993, p. 10.

CHAPTER 11 SCHOOL LAW AND ETHICS

1. Julius Menacker and Ernest Pascarella, "How Aware Are Educators of Supreme Court Decisions That Affect Them?" *Phi Delta Kappan* 64, no. 6 (February 1983), pp. 424–26; Louis Fischer, David Schimmel, and Cynthia Kelly, *Teachers and the Law* (New York: Longman, 2002).

2. Louis Fischer and David Schimmel, *The Civil Rights of Teachers* (New York: Harper & Row, 1973).

3. The legal situations and interpretations included in this text are adapted from a variety of sources, including Myra Sadker and David Sadker, *Sex Equity Handbook for Schools* (New York: Longman, 1982); Fischer and Schimmel, *The Civil Rights of Teachers,* and *Your Legal Rights and Responsibilities: A Guide for Public School Students* (Washington, DC: U.S. Department of Health, Education and Welfare, n.d.); Fischer, Schimmel, and Kelly, *Teachers and the Law;* Michael LaMorte, *School Law: Cases and Concepts* (Needham Heights, MA: Allyn & Bacon, 2002).

4. Sadker and Sadker, *Sex Equity Handbook for Schools.*

5. *Gebser v. Lago Vista Independent School District* (96 U.S. 1866 (1998); Greg Henderson, "Court Says Compensatory Damages Available Under Title IX," UPI, February 26, 1992; *North Haven Board of Education v. Bell,* 456 U.S. 512 (1982); *Franklin v. Gwinnett County Schools,* 503 U.S. 60 (1992).

6. *Thompson v. Southwest School District,* 483 F. Supp. 1170 (W.D.M.W. 1980). See also *Board of Trustees v. Stubblefield,* 94 Cal. Rptr. 318, 321 [1971]; *Morrison v. State Board of Education,* 461 P. 2d 375 [1969]; *Pettit v. State Board of Education,* 513 P. 2nd 889 [Cal. 1973]; *Blodgett v. Board of Trustees, Tamalpais Union High School District,* 97 Cal. Rptr. 406 (1970); Fischer, Schimmel, and Kelly, *Teachers and the Law;* Human Rights Campaign Foundation, "Discrimination in the Workplace" (August 7, 2003). Available online at www.hrc.org/worknet/nd/nd_facts.asp#2.

7. *Kingsville Independent School District v. Cooper,* 611 F. 2d 1109 (5th Cir. 1980); *Parducci v. Rutland,* 316 F. Supp. 352 (M.D. Ala. 1979); *Brubaker v. Board of Education, School District 149, Cook County, Illinois,* 502 F. 2d 973 (7th Cir. 1974). See also Martha McCarthy and Nelda Cambron, *Public School Law: Teachers' and Students' Rights* (Boston: Allyn & Bacon, 1997).

8. *Pickering v. Board of Education of Township High School District 205, Will County,* 391 U.S. 563 (1968); *Givhan v. Western Line Consolidated School District,* 439 U.S. 410 (1979); Nathan L. Essex, *School Law and the Public Schools: A Practical Guide for School Leaders* (Boston: Allyn & Bacon, 2001).

9. *Basic Books v. Kinko's Graphics Corp.,* 758 F. Supp. 1522 (S.D.N.Y.1991); Miriam R. Krasno, "Copyright and You," *Update,* winter 1983; Thomas J. Flygare, "Photocopying and Videotaping for Educational Purposes: The Doctrine of Fair Use," *Phi Delta Kappan* 65, no. 8 (April 1984), pp. 568–69; Gary Becker, "Copyright in a Digital Age: How to Comply with the Law and Set a Good Example for Students," *American School Board Journal* 187, no. 6 (June 2000), pp. 26–27; Constance S. Hawke, *Computer and Internet Use on Campus: A Legal Guide to Issues of Intellectual Property, Free Speech, and Privacy* (San Francisco: Jossey-Bass, 2001); Hall Davidson, "The Educators' Guide to Copyright and Fair Use," *Technology & Learning* 23, no. 3 (October 2002), pp. 26–32.

10. 115 ILCS 5/13 (1993 State Bar Edition); Ind. Code Ann 20-7.5-1-14 (West 1995); Nev. Rev. State 288.260 (1995); see also Michael La Morte, *School Law: Cases and Concepts* (Needham Heights, MA: Allyn & Bacon, 2002); *Hortonville Joint School District No. 1 v. Hortonville Education Association,* 426 U.S. 482 (1976).

11. Fisher, Schimmel, and Kelly, *Teachers and the Law,* p. 473; for privacy issues on the Internet, see Jeffrey T. Sultanik, "Legal Rights in Cyberspace," *School Business Affairs* 63, no. 5 (May 1997), pp. 25–33.

12. See Louis Fischer, David Schimmel, and Cynthia Kelly, *Teachers and the Law* (New York: Longman, 2002); *Owasso Independent School District v. Falvo* 534 U.S. 426 (2002).

13. Sadker and Sadker, *Sex Equity Handbook for Schools;* Fischer, Schimmel, and Kelly, *Teachers and the Law.*

14. *Goss v. Lopez,* 419 U.S. 565 (1975); *Wood v. Strickland,* 420 U.S. 308 (1975); *Ingraham v. Wright,* 430 U.S. 651 (1977); Martha McCarthy and Dean Webb, "Balancing Duties and Rights," *Principal Leadership* 1, no. 1 (September 2000), pp. 16–21; Michael Martin, "Does Zero Mean Zero? Balancing Policy with Procedure in the Fight Against Weapons at School," *American School Board Journal* 187, no. 3 (March 2000), pp. 39–41; National Center for Educational Statistics, *Indicators of School Crime and Safety, 2000* (Washington, DC, 2001); *James v. Unified School District No. 512,* 899 F. Supp. 530 (1995).

15. *Tinker v. Des Moines Independent Community School District,* 393 U.S. 503 (1969); *Beussink v. Woodland R-IV School District,* 30 F. Supp. 2d 1175 (1998); Jamin Raskin, *We the Students: Supreme Court Cases for and about Students* (Washington, DC: CQ Press, 2000).

16. *Bethel School District No. 403 v. Fraser,* 478 U.S. 675 (1986); *J. S. v. Bethlehem Area School District,* 757A. 2d 412 (2000); Kathleen Conn, "Offensive Student Web Sites: What Should Schools Do?" *Educational Leadership* 50, no. 5 (February 2001), pp. 74–77.

17. Benjamin Sendor, "Guidance on Graduation Prayer," *The American School Board Journal* (April 1997), pp. 17–18; Benjamin Sendor, "When May School Clubs Meet?" *The American School Board Journal* (August 1997), pp. 14–15; Ralph D. Mawdsley, "Religion in the Schools: Walking a Fine Legal Line," *School Business Affairs* 63, no. 5 (May 1997), pp. 5–10; *Engel v. Vitale,* 370 U.S. 421 (1962); *School District of Abington Township v. Schempp* and *Murray v. Curlett,* 373 U.S. 203 (1963); *Lee v. Weisman,* 112 U.S. 2649, (1992); *Good News Club v. Milford Central Schools,* 99 U.S. 2036 (2001); *Santa Fe Independent School District v. Doe,* 99 U.S. 62 (2000); John Sank, "Patriotism Push: New Laws Require Kids to Say the Pledge, Pass Civics Course." *Rocky Mountain News* (August 4, 2003). Available online at www.rockymountainnews.com; United States Department of Education, *No Child Left Behind Guidance on Constitutionally Protected Prayer in Public Elementary and Secondary Schools* (February 7, 2003). Available online at www.ed.gov/inits/religionandschools/ prayer_guidance.html.

18. *Bellnier v. Lund,* 438 F. Supp. 47 (N.Y. 1977); *Doe v. Renfrou,* 635 F. 2d 582 (7th Cir. 1980), *cert. denied,* 101 S. Ct. 3015 (1981); *Veronia School District v. Acton,* 115 U.S. 2386 (1995); *New Jersey v. T.L.O.,* 105 U.S. 733 (1985); *Board of Education of Independent School District No. 92 of Pottawatomie County v. Earls,* no 01-3332 (2002).

19. *Hazelwood School District v. Kuhlmeier,* 108 S. Ct. 562 (1988); *Shanley v. Northeast Independent School District,* 462 F. 2d 960 (5th Cir. 1972); *Gambino v. Fairfax County School Board,* 564 F. 2d 157 (4th Cir. 1977).

20. Fischer, Schimmel, and Kelly, *Teachers and the Law.*

21. "U.S. Supreme Court Decision on Teacher-Student Sexual Harassment Changing Legal Landscape," *Educator's Guide to Controlling Sexual Harassment* 5, no. 12 (September 1998), pp. 1, 3, 4–5; Joel Spring, *American Education* (New York: McGraw-Hill, 1996), p. 276; *Davis v. Monroe County Board of Education,* 97 U.S. 843 (1999).

22. Harris Interactive Poll, *Hostile Hallways: Bullying, Teasing, and Sexual Harassment in School* (Washington, DC: American Association of University Women, 2001); Raskin, *We the Students: Supreme Court Cases for and about Students;* Gay, Lesbian and Straight Education Network, "State of the States" (August 26, 2002). Available online at www.glsen.org; National Center for Lesbian Rights, "Victory in School Discrimination Case" (April 4, 2003). Available online at www.nclrights.org/releases/massey040303.htm; United States Department of Education, Office of Civil Rights (1997). *Sexual Harassment: It's Not Academic.* Available online at www.ed.gov/offices/OCR/docs/ocrshpam.html.

23. Millicent Lawson, "False Accusations Turn Dream into Nightmare in Chicago," *Education Week,* August 2, 1994, p. 16; Harris Interactive Poll, *Hostile Hallways: Bullying, Teasing, and Sexual Harassment in School;* Mark Walsh, "High Court Addresses Harassment," *Education Week,* July 8, 1999, pp. 1, 30–31.

24. Fred Hechinger, *Fateful Choices: Healthy Youth for the 21st Century* (New York: Carnegie Council on Adolescent Development, 1992); Administration on Children, Youth, and Families U.S. Department of Health and Human Services. Child Maltreatment (October 23, 2002). Available online at www.acf.hhs.gov/programs/cb/ publications/cm00/outcover.htm.

25. Louis Harris and Associates, *The Metropolitan Life Survey of the American Teacher, Part III Students Voice Their Opinions on: Learning About Values and Principles in School* (New York: Louis Harris and Associates, 1996); Stephen Bates, "A Textbook of Virtues," *The New York Times,* January 8, 1995, education supplement, p. EL-161.

26. Character Education Partnership Online, "Public Support for Character Education," www.character.org (August 7, 2003).

27. Bates, "A Textbook of Virtures": Irene McHenry, "Conflict in Schools: Fertile Ground for Moral Growth," *Phi Delta Kappan* 82, no. 3 (November 2000), pp. 223–27; Meg Lundstrom, "Character Makes a Comeback," *Instructor* 109, no. 3 (October 1999), pp. 25–28.

28. David Carr, "Moral Formation, Cultural Attachment or Social Control: What's the Point of Values Education?" *Educational Theory* 50, no. 1 (Winter 2000), pp. 49–62; Susan Gilbert, "Scientists Explore the Molding of Children's Morals." *The New York Times* (March 18, 2003), section F, p. 5.

29. Joan F. Goodman, "Objections (and Responses) to Moral Education," *Education Week* 20, no. 38 (May 30, 2001), pp. 32, 35; Debra Viadero, "Nice Work." *Education Week* 22, no. 33 (April 30, 2003), pp. 38–41.

30. Alfie Kohn, "How Not to Teach Values," *Phi Delta Kappan* 78, no. 8 (April 1997), pp. 428–37; Goodman, "Objections (and Responses) to Moral Education."

31. Howard Kirschenbaum, "A Comprehensive Model for Values Education and Moral Education," *Phi Delta Kappan* 73, no. 10 (June 1992), pp. 771–76.

32. Diane Berreth and Sheldon Berman, "The Moral Dimensions of Schools," *Educational Leadership* 54, no. 8 (May 1997), pp. 24–27; Karl Hostetler, *Ethical Judgment in Teaching* (Boston: Allyn & Bacon, 1997); Katherine Simon, "Making Room for Moral Questions in the Classroom," *Education Week* 21, no. 10 (November 7, 2001), pp. 51, 68.

CHAPTER 12   THE STRUGGLE FOR EDUCATIONAL OPPORTUNITY

1. Andrew Hacker, *Two Nations: Black, White, Separate, Hostile, Unequal* (New York: Charles Scribner's, 1992), pp. 31–32.

2. Lowell C. Rose and Alec M. Gallup, "The 33rd Annual Phi Delta Kappa/Gallup Poll of the Public's Attitude Toward the Public Schools," *Phi Delta Kappan* 83, no. 1 (September 2001), pp. 41–58; Lowell C. Rose and Alec M. Gallup, "The 35th Annual Phi Delta Kappan/Gallup Poll of the Public's Attitude Toward the Public Schools," *Phi Delta Kappan* 85, no. 1 (September 2003), pp. 41–56.

3. Ana Maria Villegas, "Culturally Responsive Pedagogy for the 1990s and Beyond," Washington, DC: ERIC Clearinghouse on Teacher Education, American Association of Colleges for Teacher Education, 1991.

4. Adapted from *The State of America's Children Yearbook 2001*. Children's Defense Fund (www.childrensdefense.org/keyfacts.htm); *America's Children: Key National Indicators of Well-Being, 2001* (www.childstats.gov/ac2001/ac01.asp).

5. Much of the earlier educational history discussion of Native Americans, African Americans, and Latinos is based on Meyer Weinberg, *A Chance to Learn: A History of Race and Education in the United States* (New York: Cambridge University Press, 1977).

6. Robert S. Catterill, *The Southern Indians: The Story of the Civilized Tribes Before Removal* (1954; reprinted, Norman: University of Oklahoma Press, 1966).

7. William Denmert, "Indian Education: Where and Whither?" *Education Digest* 42 (December 1976). See also Ron Holt, "Fighting for Equality: Breaking with the Past," *NEA Today*, March 1989, pp. 10–11; NEA Ethnic Report, *Focus on American Indian/Alaska Natives*, October 1991; Mary Ann Zehr, "Indian Tribes Decry Plan to Privatize BIA-Run Schools," *Education Week* 21, no. 30, April 10, 2002, pp. 20, 23.

8. Lee Little Soldier, "Is There an 'Indian' in Your Classroom?" *Phi Delta Kappan* 78, no. 8 (April 1997), pp. 650–53.

9. Susie King Taylor, *Reminiscences of My Life in Camp with the 33rd U.S. Colored Troop Late First S.C. Volunteers* (1902; reprinted, New York: Amo Press, 1968).

10. W. E. B. Du Bois, "The United States and the Negro," *Freedomways* (1971), quoted in Weinberg, *A Chance to Learn.*

11. Joel Spring, *American Education* (Boston: McGraw-Hill, 2002), p. 110.

12. National Advisory Commission on Civil Disorders, *Report of the National Advisory Commission on Civil Disorders* (Washington, DC: U.S. Government Printing Office, 1968), p. 369. See also Andrew Hacker, *Two Nations Black and White, Separate, Hostile, Unequal* (New York: Charles Scribner's, 1992).

13. Louis Fischer, David Schimmel, and Cynthia Kelly, *Teachers and the Law* (New York: Addison Wesley Longman, 1999), p. 352; "Narrow Use of Affirmative Action Preserved in College Admissions," CNN.COM, June 25, 2003; Greg Winter, "Schools Resegregate, Study Finds," *The New York Times*, January 21, 2003, nytimes.com.

14. Gary Orfield, Erica D. Franenberg, and Chungmei Lee, "The Resurgence of School Segregation," *Educational Leadership* 60, no. 4 (December 2002/January 2003), pp. 16–20; Darryl Fears, "Schools Racial Isolation Growing," *The Washington Post*, July 18, 2001, p. A3; Richard Morin and Claudia Deane, "Defending Desegregation," *The Washington Post*, July 24, 2001, p. A19.

15. James Comer, "All Our Children," *School Safety*, Winter 1989, p. 19.

16. Genaro C. Arms, "Hispanics Outnumber Blacks in U.S.," Associated Press, January 21, 2003, chicagotribune.com.

17. Census, Population Project of the United States 1993–2050, CPS Report No. P25-1105, 1993; *Overview of Race and Hispanic Origins* (Washington, DC: U.S. Department of Commerce, Bureau of the Census, March 2001).

18. President's Advisory Commission on Educational Excellence for Hispanic Americans, *Our Nation on the Fault Line: Hispanic American Education* (Washington, DC, 1996).

19. Daniel Aragón Ulibarrì, "Hispanics Choose to Drop Out of School?" *Santa Fe New Mexican*, March 2000 (www.ushispanic.net/USHisp/articles/HispDropouts.html); Anne Turnbaugh Lockwood and Patricia Anne DiCerbo, eds. "Transforming Education for Hispanic Youth: Broad Recommendations for Policy and Practice," *Issues Brief*, National Clearinghouse for Bilingual Education, no. 1 (January 2000); Sara Olkon, "Hispanic Dropout Rate Rises," *The Miami Herald*, June 13, 2003, herald.com.

20. The Handbook of Texas Online. *Crystal City Revolts* (The Texas State Historical Association, July 23, 2001). www.tsha.utexas.edu/handbook/online/articles/view/CC/wmc1.html

21. Quoted in Weinberg, *A Chance to Learn.*

22. National Center for Education Statistics, *Condition of Excellence 2003* (Washington, DC: U.S. Department of Education, 2003).

23. *Puerto Rico Herald,* May 10, 2001. www.puertorico-herald.org/issues/2001/vol5n19/Media1-en.shtml.

24. President's Advisory Commission on Educational Excellence for Hispanic Americans, *Our Nation on the Fault Line: Hispanic American Education.*

25. Federal Interagency Forum on Child and Family Statistics, *America's Children: Key National Indicators of Well-Being* (Washington, DC, 1997).

26. Much of the information on the history of Asian Americans is adapted from James Banks, *Teaching Ethnic Studies* (Boston: Allyn & Bacon 1996).

27. National Center for Education Statistics, *Early Child Longitudinal Study, Kindergarten Class of 1998–99* (Washington, DC: U.S. Department of Education, 1999).

28. U.S. Department of Education, National Center for Education Statistics, Recent College Graduates Surveys (1977) and 1993 Baccalaureate and Beyond Longitudinal Study, First Follow-up (B&B: 93/94); *The Condition of Education 1996*, Supplemental Table 35–90; U.S. Bureau of the Census, Statistical Abstract of the United States (1998); findings from *Statistical Abstract of the United States,* (Washington, DC: U.S. Census Bureau, 2000).

29. Carlos Ovando, "Interrogating Stereotypes: The Case of the Asian 'Model Minority,' " *Newsletter of the Asian Culture Center* (Indiana University, Fall 2001). www.modelminority.com/academia/interrogating.htm.

30. Fred Cordova, *Filipinos: Forgotten Asian-Americans* (Dubuque, IA: Kendall/Hunt, 1983), pp. 9–57; Brian Ascalon Roley, "Filipinos—The Hidden Majority," *San Francisco Chronicles*, August 20, 2001, p. A-17.

31. Arthur W. Helweg and Usha M. Helweg, *Immigrant Success Story—East Indians in America* (Philadelphia, PA: University of Pennsylvania Press, 1990). See also Srirajasekhar Bobby Koritala, "A Historical Perspective of Americans of Asian India Origin, 1790–1997," www.tiac.net/users/koritala/india/history.htm.

32. Laurie Olsen, "Crossing the Schoolhouse Border: Immigrant Children in California," *Phi Delta Kappan* 70, no. 3 (November 1988), p. 213.

33. J. Shaheen, *The TV Arab* (Bowling Green, Ohio: Bowling Green State University, 1984).

34. For more information about Arab Americans, visit the website of the American-Arab Anti-Discrimination Committee at www.adc.org.

35. Patty Adeed and G. Pritchy Smith, "Arab Americans: Concepts and Materials," in James Banks (ed), *Teaching Ethnic Studies* (Boston: Allyn and Bacon, 1997), pp. 489–510.

36. Myra Sadker and David Sadker, "Sexism in the Classroom of the 80s," *Psychology Today* (March 1986). See also Myra Sadker, David Sadker, and Susan Klein, "The Issue of Gender in Elementary and Secondary Education," in Gerald Grant, ed., *Review of Research in Education* (Washington, DC: American Educational Research Association, 1991), pp. 269–334; American Association of University Women, *How Schools Shortchange Girls* (Washington, DC: American Association of University Women, 1992). See also Myra Sadker and David Sadker, *Failing at Fairness: How Our Schools Cheat Girls* (New York: Touchstone Press, 1995).

37. M. Carey Thomas, "Present Tendencies in Women's Education," *Education Review* 25 (1908), pp. 64–85. Quoted in David Tyack and Elisabeth Hansot, *Learning Together: A History of Coeducation in American Schools* (New Haven: Yale University Press, 1990), p. 68.

38. Adapted from "Through the Back Door: The History of Women's Education" and "Higher Education: Colder by Degrees," Myra Sadker and David Sadker, *Failing at Fairness: How Our Schools Cheat Girls*; Michael Kimmel, *The Gendered Society* (New York: Oxford University Press, 2000); Susan Faludi, *Stiffed: The Betrayal of American Men* (New York: William Morrow & Company, 2000); William Pollack, *Real Boys: Rescuing Our Sons from the Myths of Boyhood* (New York: Random House, 1998).

39. Quoted in John O'Neil, "A Generation Adrift?" *Educational Leadership* 49, no. 2 (September 1991), pp. 4–10.

40. Fred Hechinger, *Fateful Choices: Healthy Youth for the 21st Century* (New York: Carnegie Council on Adolescent Development, 1992), p. 2; Children's Defense Fund, *Key Facts: Children's Health Coverage in 1999* (www.childrensdefense.org/healthy-start-chip-keyfacts.htm).

41. U.S. Census Bureau, Statistical Abstracts of the United States, *Current Population Survey 2002: Household by Size* (Washington, DC: U.S. Census Bureau, 2002).

42. Pat Wingert, "I do, I do—Maybe," *Newsweek*, November 2, 1998; Karen S. Peterson, "Cohabitation Is Increasing, Census Data Confirm," *USA Today*, August 13, 2001 (www.usatoday.com/news/census/2001-05-15-cohabitate.htm).

43. "Divorce Detrimental to Kids' Academics," *USA Today*, June 4, 2002, p. A2.

44. U.S. Department of Labor, Bureau of Labor Statistics, "Employment Status of Population by Sex, Marital Status, and Presence and Age of Own Children, 2001–2002," Table 5 (Washington, DC: U.S. Department of Labor, 2003).

45. Phyllis Moen, "Couples and Careers Study," *Cornell Employment and Family Institute* (Cornell University Ithaca, NY: 1999). www.blcc.cornell.edu/cci/current.html.

46. Jerry Adler, "Tomorrow's Child," *Newsweek*, November 2, 1998.

47. The Annie E. Casey Foundation, *Kids Count Data Book* (Washington, DC: Center for the Study of Social Policy, 1992).

48. Candy Carlile, "Children of Divorce," *Childhood Education* 64, no. 4 (1991), pp. 232–34.

49. Beverly Bliss, *Step Families*, Parenthood in America Proceedings of the conference held in Madison, Wisconsin (1998). http://parenthood.library.wisc.edu/Bliss/Bliss.html.

50. Michael A. Fletcher, "Interracial Marriages Eroding Barriers," *The Washington Post*, December 29, 1998, p. A-1; Michael A. Fletcher, "The Myth of the Melting Pot, America's Racial and Ethnic Divide," *The*

Washington Post, December 28, 1998, p. A1. www.washingtonpost.com/wpsrv/national/daily/dec98/melt29.htm.

51. Eitzen, "Problem Students"; Lizette Peterson-Homer, "Latchkey Children," *Gale Encyclopedia of Childhood & Adolescence*. Gale Research, 1998; Sandra L. Hofferth and Zita Januniene, "Life After School," *Educational Leadership* 58, no. 7 (April 2001), pp. 10–23; Sue Shellenbarger, "Home Alone After School Is OK for Some Children," *The Wall Street Journal,* November 14, 2002, www.wsj.com.

52. This anecdote is based on information in Children's Defense Fund, *A Vision for America's Future*, pp. 27–36. Washington, DC, 1989.

53. John Holloway, "Research Link: Addressing the Needs of Homeless Students," *Educational Leadership* 60, no. 4 (December 2002/January 2003), pp. 89–90; Linda Jacobson, "ESEA Includes New Requirements on Educating Homeless Students," *Education Week*, August 7, 2002, www.edweek.com.

54. "Schools Dropouts: Home and School Effects," ASCD *RESEARCH BRIEFS 1*, no. 9, April 29, 2003, www.ascd.org.

55. U.S. Department of Education, *Youth Indicators 1996: Trends in the Well-Being of American Youth* (Washington, DC: National Center for Education Statistics, 1996; National Center for Educational Statistics, *High School Completion Rates Dropout Rates in the United States* (Washington, DC: U.S. Department of Education, 1999). http://nces.ed.gov/pubs2002/dropout/figures3.asp; National Center for Educational Statistics, *Dropout Rates in the United States* (Washington, DC: U.S. Department of Education, 2000). http://nces.ed.gov/pubs2002/droppub_2001.

56. National Dropout Prevention Center Network, *Effective Strategies* (Clemson University, South Carolina, 2001). www.dropoutprevention.org/2levelpages/strategies.html.

57. Rebecca Vesely, "Some States Rejecting Abstinence-Only Sex Ed," *Women's E News,* March 11, 2002, www.womensenews.org; Ceci Connolly, "Texas Teaches Abstinence, with Mixed Grades," *The Washington Post,* January 21, 2003, p. A1.

58. House Select Committee on Children, Youth, and Families, *A Decade of Denial: Teens and AIDS in America* (Washington, DC: U.S. Government Printing Office, 1992).

59. Centers for Disease Control and Prevention, *HIV Surveillance Report* 13, no. 2 (Atlanta, GA, 2002).

60. Center on Addiction and Substance Abuse, *Malignant Neglect: Substance Abuse and America's Schools* (Columbia University: New York, 2001). www.casacolumbia.org/newsletter1457/newsletter_show.htm?doc_id=80623.

61. Roberto Suro, "Study Finds Decline in Teen Substance Abuse," *The Washington Post*, December 19, 1998, p. A-3. Addiction Science Research and Education Center, *Alcohol Facts* (Austin, TX. 2000). www.utexas.edu/reserch/asrec/alcoholfacts.html.

62. Paul Taylor, "Surgeon General Links Teen Drinking to Crime, Injuries, Unsafe Sex," *The Washington Post*, April 14, 1992, p. A-1.

63. *Education Update* 9, no. 4 (fall 1986).

64. DeNeen Brown, "Fairfax Teenagers' LSD Arrests Send Parents a 'Wake-up Call,' " *The Washington Post*, April 27, 1992, p. B-1.

65. National Institute on Drug Abuse, *Fact Sheet on Teenage Smoking and Substance Abuse* (Bethesda, MD, 2003).

66. National Mental Health Association, *Fact Sheet: Teen Suicide* (Alexandria, VA, 2003). Available online at www.nmha.org/infoctr/factsheets/82.cfm; American Psychiatric Association, *Let's Talk About the Facts: Teen Suicide* (Washington, DC, 2003). Available online at www.psych.org/public_info/teen.cfm.

67. Jeanne Wright, "Treating the Depressed Child" *The Washington Post*, December 2, 1996, p. C-5.

68. Quoted in Paul Gibson, "Gay Male and Lesbian Youth Suicide," in Marcia Feinleib, ed., *Report of the Secretary's Task Force on Youth Suicide* (Washington, DC: U.S. Department of Health and Human Services, January 1989), pp. 3-110–3-142. See also James Sears, "Helping Students Understand and Accept Sexual Diversity," *Educational Leadership* 49, no. 1 (September 1991), pp. 54–56.

69. Jesse Green, "This School Is Out," *New York Times Magazine*, October 14, 1991, pp. 32–36, 59, 68.

70. Jessica Portner, "Districts Adopting Policies to Protect Gay Students' Rights," *Education Week*, October 5, 1994, p. 8; "More Inclusive Anti-Intimidation Policy Approved," *Cincinnati Enquirer*, August 28, 2001; Alan Horowitz, "Addressing Homophobic Behavior in the Classroom," *Online Resource Center* (Gay Lesbian and Straight Network: Washington, DC), June 5, 2001 (www.glsen.org/templates/resources/record.html?section=14&record=820); Katherine Zoepf, "Trying to Make His Special Students Feel Ordinary," *The New York Times,* September 12, 2003, nytimes.com.

71. Katherine Corcoran, "Bullying, Slurs Are Rampant, Nationwide Survey Finds," *San Jose Mercury News,* December 13, 2002, www.bayarea.com; Brooke Donald, "Students Still Afraid Despite Fewer Weapons, Crime," *Detroit News,* December 10, 2002, detroitnews.net.

72. Doug Cooper and Jennie L. Snell, "Bullying—Not Just a Kid Thing," *Educational Leadership* 60, no. 6 (March 2003), pp. 22–25; Dan Olweis, "A Profile of Bullying at School," *Educational Leadership* 60, no. 6 (March 2003), pp. 12–17.

CHAPTER 13 TECHNOLOGY IN EDUCATION

1. Jeffrey Mortimer, "How TV Violence Hits Kids," *Education Digest* 60, no. 2 (October 1994), pp. 16–19.

2. *Balancing Acts: Work/Family Issues on Primetime TV Shows* (Washington, DC: The National Partnership for Women and Families, 1998); Jack Levin, "Mapping Social Geography," *Bostonia* (March/April 1989), pp. 64–65.

3. "Study Links TV, Music to Teen Drinking," *USA Today on the Web,* November 2, 1998; Annette Licitra, "Psychologists Spell Out Dangers of Unregulated TV Watching," *Education Daily,* February 26, 1992.

4. Richard P. Adler, "Children's Television Advertising: History of the Issue," in Edward Palmer and Aimee Dorr, eds., *Children and the Faces of Television* (New York: Academic Press, 1980), pp. 46–47.

5. Daniel Anderson and Patricia Collins, *The Impact on Children's Education: Television's Influence on Cognitive Development* (Washington, DC: U.S. Department of Education, April 1988).

6. Licitra, "Psychologists Spell Out Dangers."

7. Bruce Watkins, Althea Huston-Stein, and John Wright, "Effects of Planned Television Programming," in Edward Palmer and Aimee Dorr, eds., *Children and the Faces of Television* (New York: Academic Press, 1980), pp. 46–49.

8. Julie Salamon, "Children's TV Catches Up with How Kids Watch," *The New York Times,* June 9, 2002, nytimes.com.

9. Susan Herzog, "Selling Out Kids: Commercialism in Public Schools," *Our Children* 23, no. 3 (November 1997); pp. 6–10; Jason Vaughn, "Big Business and the Blackboard: A Winning Combination for the Classroom," *Journal of Law and Education* 26, no. 2 (April 1997), pp. 35–46; David Streitfeld, "Low Marks for Channel One," *The Washington Post,* May 2, 1992, p. C-5; Drew Tiene, "Channel One," *International Journal of Instructional Media* 21, no. 3 (1994): pp. 181–89; Drew Tiene, "Teens React to Channel One," *Tech Trends* 39 (April/May 1994), pp. 17–20.

10. For more information about Channel One and critics of commercialism in school, visit The Center for Commercial Free Public Education website at www.commercial free.org/index.html.

11. Todd Oppenheimer, "The Computer Delusion," *The Atlantic Monthly* (July 1997), pp. 45–48, 50–56, 61–62.

12. Rhea Borja, "Digital Whiteboards Outsell Traditional Chalkboards," *Education Week* 22, no. 13 (November 27, 2002), p. 8; "Chalkboards Replaced by Marker Board, Computers," *Houston Chronicle,* May 29, 2002, www.chron.com.

13. David McGuire, "President Signs 'Dot-Kids' Legislation," *The Washington Post,* December 4, 2002, washingtonpost.com.

14. Sara Dexter and Ron Anderson, "Teachers' Views of the Influence of Computers on Changes in Their Instructional Practice." Paper presented at the American Educational Research Association, April 1998; Bob Hoffman, "Integrating Technology into Schools," *NAASP Bulletin* (January 1997), pp. 51–55.

15. Emily Wax, "Teachers Confront Computer Fears," *The Washington Post,* June 29, 2000; p. B3; see also "Technology Counts, 2001: The New Divides," *Education Week* 20, no. 35, May 10, 2001.

16. Lyn Nell Hancock, Patricia Wingert, D. Rosenberg, and A. Samuels, "The Haves and the Have-Nots," *Newsweek,* February 27, 1995, p. 53.

17. Susan E. Ansell and Jennifer Park, "Tracking Tech Trends," *Education Week,* May 8, 2003, www.edweek.org.

18. Clorinda Valenti, "Preparing Teachers for the High-Tech Classroom," in David T. Gordon, ed., *The Digital Classroom* (Cambridge: Harvard College, 2000), pp. 78–87.

19. Kathryn M. Doherty and Greg Orlofsky, "Student Survey Says," *Education Week on the Web,* May 10, 2001; Ariana Eunjung Cha, "Dear Web Diary, SO Much to Tell!", *The Washington Post,* September 2, 2001, p. A1; Ellen McCarthy, "Wanted: Web-Savvy Schooling," *The Washington Post,* August 15, 2002, p. 5.

20. Glenn Kleiman, "Myth and Realities about Technology in K–12 Schools," in David T. Gordon, ed., *The Digital Classroom* (Cambridge: Harvard College, 2000), pp. 7–15.

21. George Brackett, Technologies Don't Change Schools—Caring, Capable People Do," in David T. Gordon, ed., *The Digital Classroom* (Cambridge: Harvard College, 2000), pp. 29–30.

22. Peter W. Foltz, Darrel Laham, Thomas K. Landauer, "Automated Essay Scoring: Applications to Educational Technology." Paper presented at the ED-Media/ED-Telecom '99, World Conference on Educational Multimedia/Hypermedia & Educational Telecommunications, Seattle, WA, 19–24 June 1999; "Tech's Answer to Testing," *Education Week,* May 8, 2003, www.edweek.org; Michelle Galley, "The Teacher's New Test," *Education Week,* May 8, 2003, www.edweek.org.

23. Howard Gardner, "Can Technology Exploit the Many Ways of Knowing?", in David T. Gordon, ed., *The Digital Classroom* (Cambridge: Harvard College, 2000), pp. 32–35.

24. David Williamson Schaffer, "This Is Dewey's Vision Revisited," in David T. Gordon, ed., *The Digital Classroom,* (Cambridge: Harvard College 2000), pp. 176–178.

25. William R. Penuel, Barbara Means, and Michael Simkins, "The Multimedia Challenge," *Educational Leadership* 58, no. 2 (October 2000), p. 34.

26. Charles A. MacArthur, "Using Technology to Enhance the Writing Processes of Students with Learning Disabilities," *Journal of Learning Disabilities* 29, no. 4 (1996), pp. 344–54; Debra K. Bauder, "Assistive Technology: Learning Devices for Special Needs Students," *Media & Methods* 32, no. 3 (1996), pp. 16, 18; Nancy Trejos, "Handheld PCs Put to the Test," *The Washington Post,* September 4, 2001, pp. B1, B2; Jennifer Medina, "Technology Eases the Way for the Visually Impaired," *The New York Times,* July 3, 2002, nytimes.com; Michael P. Bruno, "High-Tech Help for Disabled Children," Washtech.com, May 10, 2002, p. 5.

27. Jeri Kinser, Brenda Pessin, and Pat Meyertholen, "From the Fields to the Laptop," *Learning and Leading with Technology,* ISTE, February.

28. Carla Schutte, "Going Global," *Electronic School,* February 1995, pp. A39–A40; Elaine K. Bailey and Morton Cotlar, "Teaching via the Internet," *Communication Education* 43 (April 1994), pp. 184–93; Carol S. Holzberg, "Technology in Special Education," *Technology and Learning* 14 (April 7, 1994), pp. 18–21.

29. Barbara Benham Tye and Kenneth Tye, *Global Education: A Study of School Change* (Albany: State University of New York Press, 1992), pp. 1–13.

30. Andrew F. Smith, "A Brief History of Pre-collegiate Global and International Studies Education," in John Fonte and Andre Ryerson, eds. *Education for America's role in World Affairs* (New York: University Press of America, 1994), p. 15.

31. John LeBaron and Rebecca Warshawsky, "Satellite Teleconferencing Between Massachusetts and Germany," *Educational Leadership* 48, no. 7 (April 1991), pp. 61–64.

32. Bruce Watson, "The Wired Classroom: American Education Goes On-Line," *Phi Delta Kappan* 72, no. 2 (October 1990), pp. 109–12.

33. William Kniep, "Global Education as School Reform," *Educational Leadership* 47, no. 1 (September 1989), p. 45.

34. Rhea R. Borja, "Virtual High Schools Gain a Following," *Richmond Times Dispatch*, August 7, 2001; Rodney Thrash, "Virtual School Looks to Expand Base of Students," *Detroit Free Press on the Web*, September 5, 2001; Michelle Galley, "Despite Concerns, Online Elementary Schools Grow," *Education Week* 22, no. 16 (January 8, 2003), pp. 1, 12.

35. Mary Anne Mather, "Virtual Schooling: Going the Distance—Any Distance—to School," *Technology and Learning*, 1 April 1998; Mary Lord, "On Line Students E-mail Music to a Teacher's Ears," *U.S. News on Line*, December 28, 1998; Sandy Kleffman, Internet Creates a National Classroom," *The Atlanta Jounal-The Atlanta Constitution*, July 27, 1997.

36. Andrew Trotter, "Closing the Digital Divide," *Education Week* 20, no. 35 (2001), pp. 37–38, 40; Maisie McAdoo, "The Real Digital Divide: Quality Not Quantity," in David T. Gordon, ed., *The Digital Classroom* (Cambridge: Harvard College, 2000), pp. 143–51; American Association of University Women, *Gender Gaps: Where School Still Fails Our Children* (Washington, DC: American Association of University Women, 1998); "Dividing Lines," *Education Week* 20, no. 35 (2001), p. 12.

37. Robert C. Johnson, "Money Matters," *Education Week* 20, no. 35 (2001), p. 14; "Internet Access in U.S. Public Schools and Classrooms: 1994–2000," National Center for Education Statistics, U.S. Department of Education, 2002.

38. Ansell and Park, "Tracking Tech Trends;" Andy Sullivan, "'Digital Divide' Shrinks Among Children—Study," Reuters, March 19, 2003.

39. Tamar Lewin, "Children's Computer Use Grows, but Gaps Persist, Study Says," *The New York Times*, January 22, 2001, p. A11.

40. Karla Scoon Reid, "Racial Disparities," *Education Week* 20, no. 35 (2001), p. 16.

41. A. Game and R. Pringle, *Gender at Work* (Boston: Allen & Unwin, 1983), p. 83.

42. American Association of University Women, *Gender Gaps: Where Schools Still Fail Our Children*; John Gehring, "Not Enough Girls," *Education Week* 10, no. 35 (2001), pp. 18–19; www.electronic-school.com, e-wire (June 1999); Margaret Riel, "A Title IX for the Technology Divide?" in David T. Gordon, ed., *The Digital Classroom* (Cambridge: Harvard College, 2000), pp. 161–170; Ellen McCarthy, "Where Girls and Tech Make a Match," *The Washington Post*, March 20, 2003, p. E1; Jane Margolis, "The Computer World Could Use More IT Girls," *The Los Angeles Times*, May 21, 2003, latimes.com.

43. Mary Ann Zehr, "Rural Connections," *Education Week* 10, no. 35 (2001), pp. 24–25.

44. Ibid.

45. V. Robinson, "Methodology and Research-Practice Gap," *Educational Researcher* 27, no. 1 (1998): pp. 17–26.

46. J. Salpeter, "Taking Stock: What's the Research Saying?" *Technology and Learning* 18, no. 9 (1998); Mark Windschitl, "The WWW and Classroom Research: What Path Should We Take?" *Educational Researcher* 27, no. 1 (January/February 1998), pp. 28–32.

47. Cara Branigan, "Study Probes Technology's Effect on Math and Science," *eSchool News*, January 8, 2003, eschoolnews.com.

48. Kevin Bushweller, "Beyond Machines," *Education Week* 20, no. 35 (2001), p. 34.

49. "The Effects of Computers on Student Writing: What the Research Tells Us," *ASCD SmartBrief* 1, no. 7 (April 1, 2003), www.ascd.org; Jennifer Lee, "Nu Shortcuts in School R 2 Much 4 Teachers," *The New York Times*, September 19, 2002, nytimes.com; Victoria Irwin, "Hop, Skip . . . and Software?" *The Christian Science Monitor*, March 11, 2003, www.csmonitor.com.

50. Kelly Heyboer, "Cut-and-Paste Turn It In—You Call That Cheating?" *New Jersey Star Ledger*, August 28, 2003, www.NJ.com.

51. Andrew Trotter, "A Question of Effectiveness," *Education Week on the Web*, October 1, 1998; Larry Cuban, *Teachers and Machines: The Classroom Use of Technology since 1920* (New York: Teachers College Press, 1986).

CHAPTER 14   YOUR FIRST CLASSROOM

1. Lilian Katz, "The Development of Preschool Teachers," *The Elementary School Journal* 73, no. 1 (October 1972), pp. 50–54.

2. Linda Darling-Hammond, "Teachers and Teaching: Testing Policy Hypothesis from a National Commission Report," *Educational Researcher* 27, no. 1 (January/February 1998), pp. 5–15; "Teachers Are the Key," *Reading Today* 14, no. 4 (February/March 1997), pp. 3–4; Debra Viadero, "Studies Say Students Learn More from Licensed Teachers," *Education Week* 22, no. 3 (September 18, 2002), p. 7; Michelle Krupa, "Class Size Is Not So Important, Study Says," *The Times-Picayune*, February 10, 2003, www.timespicayune.com.

3. National Center for Educational Statistics, *Characteristics of Stayers, Movers, and Leavers: Results from the Teacher Followup Survey, 1994–1995* (Washington, DC: U.S. Department of Education, 1997).

4. Susan Moore Johnson, Susan Kardos, and Edward Liu, "New Teachers' Experiences of Hiring and Professional Culture: A Four State Survey Study," The Project on the

Next Generation of Teachers, Harvard Graduate School of Education (Cambridge, MA, 2003); Ben Feller, "Teacher Shortage Misdiagnosed, Group Says," *Minneapolis Star Tribune,* January 29, 2003, startribune.com; Association of Curriculum and Supervision, "Teaching Out of the Field: An Overlooked Factor in Unqualified Teaching," *ASCD SmartBriefs* 1, no. 5, March 5, 2003.

5. L. Huling-Austin, "Research on Learning to Teach: Implications for Teacher Induction and Mentoring," *Journal of Teacher Education* 43, no. 3 (May/June 1992), pp. 173–78.

6. Rhea Borja, "E-Mentors' Offer Online Support, Information for Novice Instructors," *Education Week* 21, no. 29 (April 3, 2002), p. 12; "Induction and Teacher Turnover," *Teaching Quality RESEARCH MATTERS,* The Southeast Center for Teaching Quality, Issue 5, May 2003, p. 1.

7. Ellen Nakashima, "Montgomery Teachers May Face Peer Review," *The Washington Post,* January 2, 1999, pp. B-1, B-6.

8. Judith W. Little, "Teachers' Professional Development in a Climate of Educational Reform," *Educational Evaluation and Policy Analysis* 15 (1993), pp. 129–51; Linda Darling-Hammond and Milbrey W. McLaughlin, "Policies That Support Professional Development in an Era of Reform," in Milbrey W. McLaughlin and Ida Oberman, eds., *Teaching and Learning: New Policies, New Practices* (New York: Teachers College Press, 1996), pp. 208–18.

9. National Education Association, *Status of the American Public School Teacher, 1995–1996* (Washington, DC: National Education Association, 1997).

10. Organization for Economic Cooperation and Development (OECD), *Education at a Glance, OECD Indicators* (Paris: OECD, 1995), pp. 176–77.

11. Julie Blair, "Lawmakers Plunge into Teacher Pay," *Education Week* 20, no. 23 (February 21, 2001), pp. 1, 16.

12. Jeff Archer, "Recruitment Pinch Fuels Global Trade in K–12 Teachers," *Education Week* 20, no. 22 (February 14, 2001), p. 8; Lynette Holloway, "Foreign Teachers Receive a Short Course on the City," *The New York Times on the Web,* August 14, 2001.

13. Susan Moore Johnson, Susan Kardos, and Christine Sanni, "Research on New Teaching Shows a Changing Profession: 43% of New Teachers in New Jersey Plan to Leave Classroom Teaching; Nearly Half Are Mid-Career Entrants," *Harvard Graduate School of Education on the Web,* August 27, 2001; Lee Foster, "New Teachers Relish Mid-Life Career Change," *The Hartford Courant on the Web,* October 23, 2000.

14. Jacques Steinberg, "Giving the Teacher Balm for Burnout," *The New York Times on the Web,* January 7, 2001.

15. Quoted in "Forging a Profession," *Teacher* (September/October 1989), pp. 12, 16.

16. National Board for Professional Teaching Standards website (www.nbpts.org).

17. "National Certification Picks Up Steam," *American Teacher* 76, no. 6 (May/June 1992), p. 3.

18. National Board for Professional Teaching Standards website (www.nbpts.org).

19. Briant Farnsworth, Jerry Debenham, and Gerald Smith, "Designing and Implementing a Successful Merit Pay Program for Teachers," *Phi Delta Kappan* 73, no. 4 (December 1991), pp. 320–25.

20. Kenneth J. Cooper, "Performance Pay for Teachers Catches On," *The Washington Post,* February 26, 2000, p. A4; Alfie Kohn, "The Folly of Merit Pay," *Education Week* 23, no. 3 (September 17, 2003), pp. 44, 31.

21. *Is "Paying for Performance" Changing Schools?* The SREB Career Ladder Clearinghouse Report 1988 (Atlanta: Southern Regional Education Board), p. 8.

22. Adam Urbanski, "The Rochester Contract: A Status Report," *Educational Leadership* 46, no. 3 (November 1988), pp. 48–52.

23. Much of the information in this section was drawn from Marshall O. Donley, Jr.'s excellent article, "The American School Teacher: From Obedient Servant to Militant Professional," *Phi Delta Kappan* 58, no. 1 (September 1976), pp. 112–17.

24. Albert Shanker, "Where We Stand: Is It Time for National Standards and Exams?" *American Teacher* 76, no. 6 (May/June 1992), p. 5.

25. Jeff Archer, "NEA Board Approves AFT 'Partnership' Pact," *Education Week on the Web,* February 21, 2001.

26. Lapointe quoted in Gerald W. Bracey, "The Second Bracey Report on the Condition of Public Education," *Phi Delta Kappan* (October 1992), pp. 104–17, cited in David C. Berliner and Bruce J. Biddle, *The Manufactured Crisis,* (Reading, MA: Addison Wesley, 1995), p. 54.

27. Gerald W. Bracey, "U.S. Students: Better Than Ever," *The Washington Post,* December 22, 1995, p. A-9; and Robert J. Samuelson, "Three Cheers for Schools," *Newsweek,* December 4, 1995, p. 61. See also Berliner and Biddle, *The Manufactured Crisis,* pp. 13–64.

28. Berliner and Biddle, *The Manufactured Crisis,* p. 146; see also Richard Rothstein, *The Way We Were? The Myths and Realities of America's Student Achievement* (Washington, DC: Century Fund, 1998).

CHAPTER 15   Q AND A GUIDE TO ENTERING THE TEACHING PROFESSION

1. National Center for Education Statistics (NCES), *Projections of Education Statistics to 2011.* Washington, DC: U.S. Department of Education, 2001; National Center for Education Statistics (NCES), *Predicting the Need for Newly Hired Teachers in the United States to 2008–2009* (Washington, DC: U.S. Department of Education, 1999).

2. Ibid.

3. American Association for Employment in Education, *Educator Supply and Demand in the United States, 1999* (Columbus, OH: AAEE, 2001).

4. National Education Association (NEA), *Fact Sheet on Teacher Shortages* (Washington, DC: NEA, 2001).

5. Barbara Kantrowitz and Pat Wingert, "Teachers Wanted," *Newsweek,* October 2000, pp. 37–42; Julie Blair, "Districts Wooing Teachers with Bonuses, Incentives" in *Education Week on the Web,* August 2, 2000.

6. National Center for Education Statistics (NCES), *Digest of Education Statistics, 2002* (Washington, DC: U.S. Department of Education, 2002).

7. NEA, *Status of the American Public School Teacher,* Washington, DC, 2003.

8. American Federation of Teachers (AFT), *Survey and Analysis of Teacher Salary Trends, 2002* (Washington, DC: AFT, 2002).

9. National Center for Education Statistics (NCES), *Job Satisfaction among America's Teachers: Effects of Workplace Conditions, Background Characteristics, and Teacher Compensation* (Washington, DC: U.S. Department of Education, 1997); National Center for Education Statistics (NCES), *Public and Private Schools: How Do They Differ? Findings from the Condition of Education, 1997* (Washington, DC: U.S. Department of Education, 1997).

10. Patricia L. Rieman, *Teaching Portfolios: Presenting Your Professional Best* (New York: McGraw-Hill Companies, 2000).

11. Maria Mihalik, "Thirty Minutes to Sell Yourself," *Teacher,* April 1991, p. 32d.

12. Ibid., p. 32e.

13. Joseph Cronin, "State Regulations of Teacher Preparation," in Lee Shulman and Gary Sykes (eds.), *Handbook of Teaching and Policy* (New York: Longman, 1983), p. 174.

14. C. Emily Feistrizter and David T. Chester, *Alternative Teacher Certification: A State by State Analysis, 2001* (Washington, DC: National Center for Educational Information, 2001).

15. NEA, *Status of the American Public School Teacher.*

16. Feistrizter and Chester, *Alternative Teacher Certification.*

17. Jessica Sandman, "Study Finds Alternative Teachers Less Qualified, But Meeting Needs," *Education Week on the Web,* September 10, 1997.

18. Brenda Freeman and Ann Schopen, "Quality Reform in Teacher Education: A Brief Look at the Admissions Testing Movement," *Contemporary Education,* 62(4), p. 279; Educational Testing Service (ETS), *The Praxis Exam: State by State Requirements.*

19. Educational Testing Service (ETS), *The Praxis Exam: State by State Requirements* (Princeton, NJ: ETS, 2001).

20. Thomas Toch, *In the Name of Excellence* (New York: Oxford University Press, 1991), p. 164.

21. National Research Council, *Testing Teacher Candidates: The Role of Licensure Tests in Improving Teacher Quality* (Washington, DC: National Academy Press, 2001).

22. National Center for Education Statistics (NCES), *Condition of Education, 2001* (Washington, DC: U.S. Department of Education, 2001); National Center for Education Statistics (NCES), *America's Teachers: Profile of a Profession, 1993–1994* (Washington, DC: U.S. Department of Education, 1997).

23. Freeman and Schopen, "Quality Reform in Teacher Education: A Brief Look at the Admissions Testing Movement"; National Research Council, *Testing Teacher Candidates: The Role of Licensure Tests in Improving Teacher Quality* (Washington, DC: National Academy Press, 2001).

24. Kerry White, "In a Push for Accountability, Tenure Becomes a Target," *Education Week on the Web,* June 25, 1997.

25. Caroline Hendrie, "Principals Losing Tenure," *Teacher Magazine on the Web,* April 1998.

26. Special thanks to Diana Coleman, Kevin Dwyer, Phyllis Lerner, and Kathryn McNerney for their assistance in preparing this section.

CREDITS

PHOTO CREDITS

PART I

p. 2: © Bob Daemmrich/The Image Works.

CHAPTER 1

p. 11: © Bonnie Kamin Photography; p. 18: Butch Martin Inc./Image Bank/Getty; p. 27: © AP/Wide World Photos.

CHAPTER 2

p. 39: © Bonnie Kamin/PhotoEdit; p. 40: © Lori Adamski Peek/Getty; p. 45 (top): © Bettmann/Corbis; p. 45 (bottom): © Rhonda Sidney/PhotoEdit; p. 47: © Ellen Sinisi/The Image Works; p 51: © Bill Bachmann/PhotoEdit; p. 52: © Woodfin Camp/Woodfin Camp & Associates; p. 58: © Florida State Archive; p. 61: AP Photo/Joe Raymond; p. 65: © David Young-Wolf/PhotoEdit.

CHAPTER 3

p. 76: © Jeff Greenberg/Unicorn Stock Photos; p. 80: © Bob Daemmrich Photography; p. 81: © MacDonald Photography/Index Stock Imagery; p. 85 (top left): © Bob Daemmrich/The Image Works; p. 85 (bottom left): © Mark Richards/PhotoEdit; p. 85 (right): © Richard Hutchings/Photo Researchers; p. 90: © Mary Kate Denny/PhotoEdit; p. 95: © Bill Cramer; p. 97: © Gabe Palmer; p. 98: © Gabe Palmer; p. 100: © Stanford University; p. 102: © Gabe Palmer.

PART II

p. 124: © Will & Deni McIntyre/Photo Researchers.

CHAPTER 4

p. 127: © Dana White/PhotoEdit; p. 131: © Spencer Grant/Photo Researchers; p. 142: George Zimbel; p. 147: © James Wilson/Woodfin Camp & Associates; p. 148: © AP/Wide World Photos; p. 154 (top): © Joseph Sohm; ChromoSohm Inc/Corbis; p. 154 (bottom): © N.R. Rowan/Stock Boston; p. 155 (left): © Macduff Everton/Corbis; p. 155 (right): © Michael Newman/Photo Edit.

CHAPTER 5

p. 165: © Jeff Greenberg/Unicorn Stock Photos; p. 169: © Frank Siteman/Stock Boston; p. 171: © Grant Leduc; p. 175: © UCLA/GSE; p. 177: © Jeff Greenberg/Photo Researchers; p. 183: © Tom Pollack; p. 189: © Jim Pickerell/Stock Connection; p. 191: © Ulrike Welsch Photography; p. 194 (top): © Mary Kate Denny/PhotoEdit; p. 194 (bottom): © David Young-Wolf/PhotoEdit; p. 195 (top): © Ian Shaw/Tony Stone/Getty; p. 195 (bottom): © Reuters.

CHAPTER 6

p. 205: © Tony Freeman/PhotoEdit; p. 213: © Culver Pictures; p. 214: © Bob Daemmrich Photography; p. 219: Courtesy of Lisa Delpit, Adam Taylor Photographer; p. 220: © David Young-Wolf/PhotoEdit; p. 224 (top): © Bob Daemmrich/Stock Boston; p. 224 (bottom): © Michael Pole/Corbis; p. 225 (top): © Aneal Vohra/index Stock Imagery; p. 225 (bottom): © Owen Franken/Corbis.

CHAPTER 7

p. 246 (left): Republished with permission of Globe Newspaper Company Inc./The Boston Globe; p. 246 (right): © AP/Wide World Photos; p. 253: © Alfie Kohn; p. 261: © Michael Newman/Photo Edit; p. 263: © Jim Pozarik; p. 266: © AP/Wide World Photos; p. 267: © Jeffrey W. Meyers/Stock Market/Corbis.

PART III

P. 282: © John Welzenbach.

CHAPTER 8

p. 286: © Culver Pictures; p. 288: © North Wind Picture Archives; p. 289: © Bettmann/Corbis; p. 292: © Bettmann/Corbis; p. 295: © Bettmann/Corbis; p. 299: © Peter Chartrand; p. 301: © Bob Daemmrich/The Image Works; p. 304 (top): © H. Schmeiser/Unicorn Stock Photos; p. 304 (bottom): © Rick Stiller

Photoworks; p. 305: © J. Shive/H. Armstrong Roberts; p. 309 (top): © Stock Montage; p. 309 (bottom): © Culver Pictures; p. 310 (top): Johann Heinrich Pestalozzi © New York Public Library Picture Collection; p. 310 (bottom): © New York Public Library Picture Collection; p. 311 (top): © New York Public Library Picture Collection; p. 311 (bottom): © Culver Pictures; p. 312: © Culver Pictures; p. 313: © AP/Wide World Photos; p. 314 (top): © Syndicated Features Limited/The Image Works; p. 314 (bottom): © Bettmann/Corbis; p. 315: © Bettmann/Corbis; p. 316 (top): © Bettmann/Corbis; p. 316 (bottom): © Katherine Bendo, NYC; p. 317: © Wallace Britton/Black Star; p. 318 (top): © Raimondo Borea & Associates; p. 318 (bottom): © New School for Social Research; p. 319: © Jeremy Bigwood.

CHAPTER 9

p. 342 (left; top to bottom): © Columbia University Teacher's College; © University of Chicago-News & Information Office; © Special Collections, Morris Library, Southern Illinois University, Carbondale, IL/Morris Library Special Collections; © AP/Wide World Photos; p. 342 (right; top to bottom): © The Core Knowledge Foundation; © Bettmann/Corbis; © Nel Noddings; © John Pinderhughes; © Special Collections, Milbank Memorial Library, Teachers College, Columbia University; p. 344 (top): © Andy Sacks/Tony Stone/Getty; p. 344 (bottom left): © Michelle Bridwell/PhotoEdit; p. 344 (bottom right): © Bill Aron/PhotoEdit; p. 345 (left): © David Young-Wolf/PhotoEdit; p. 345 (right): © Dennis McDonald/PhotoEdit.

CHAPTER 10

p. 360: © Bob Daemmrich/The Image Works; p. 365: © AP/Wide World Photos; p. 370 (top): © Yvonne Hemsey/Liaison/Getty; p. 370 (bottom): © Robert Frerck/Woodfin Camp & Associates; p. 377: © Kolvoord/The Image Works; p. 379: © National School Boards Association; p. 382: © Tony Freeman/PhotoEdit; p. 383: © AP/Wide World Photos; p. 385: © Lori Grinker/Woodfin Camp & Associates.

CHAPTER 11

p. 397: © James Wilson/Woodfin Camp & Associates; p. 401: © Renato Rotolo; p. 403: © Acey Harper/TimePix/Getty; p. 407: © AP/Wide World Photos; p. 409: © Michael Newman/PhotoEdit.

PART IV

p. 438: © Justin Sullivan/Getty Images.

CHAPTER 12

p. 444: © Bettmann/Corbis; p. 446: © Library of Congress; p 447: © Ellis Herwig/Stock Boston; p. 448: © A. Ramey/PhotoEdit; p. 450: © Jonathon Nourok/PhotoEdit; p. 450: © Bettmann/Corbis; p. 454: © Bonnie Kamin/PhotoEdit; p. 459: © Brown Brothers; p. 461 (top): © Grant Leduc; p. 461 (bottom): © Leif Skoogfors/Woodfin Camp & Associates; p. 462 (top): © Lambert/Hulton Archives/Getty; p. 462 (bottom): © American Stock/Hulton Archives/Getty; p. 463 (left): © William R. Sallaz/Duomo Photography, Inc.; p. 463 (right): © William R. Sallaz/Duomo Photography, Inc.; p. 464: © Hulton Archives/Getty; p. 466: © Tony Freeman/PhotoEdit; p. 468: © AP/Wide World Photos; p. 469: © Will & Deni McIntyre/Photo Researchers; p. 471 (top): © UPI/Corbis.

CHAPTER 13

p. 485: © Contact Press Images/Woodfin/Alon Reininger/Woodfin Camp & Associates; p. 489: © Lawrence Migdale/www.migdale.com; p. 498 (left): © TimePix/Getty; p. 498 (right): © TimePix/Getty; p. 502 (top): © Paul Conklin/PhotoEdit; p. 502 (bottom): © Jonathon Nourok/PhotoEdit.

CHAPTER 14

p. 524 (top): © Michael Newman/Photo Edit; p. 524 (bottom): © Michael Newman/Photo Edit; p. 525: © Michael Newman/Photo Edit; p. 529: © AP/Wide World Photos; p. 530: © Chicago Historical Society; p. 533 (left): © AP/Wide World Photos; p. 533 (right): © American Federation of Teachers.

INDEX